FINANCIAL ACCOUNTING

Strayer University

8th Edition/2012

WEYGANDT • KIMMEL • KIESO

FINANCIAL ACCOUNTING
8TH EDITION/2012

Strip Image 1 © Radius Images/Getty Images
Strip Image 2 © Compassionate Eye Foundation/Andrew Olney/OJO Images Ltd
Strip Image 3 © Purestock/Getty Images
Strip Image 4 © Les and Dave Jacobs/Getty Images
Strip Image 5 © Patrick Lane/Getty Images
Strip Image 6 © Tanya Constantine/Getty Images
Strip Image 7 © Robert Nicholas/Getty Images
Strip Image 8 © Blend Images/Hill Street Studios/Getty Images
Strip Image 9 © Mark Edward Atkinson/Getty Images
Strip Image 10 © Patrick Lane/Getty Images
Strip Image 11 © momentimages/Getty Images
Strip Image 12 © David Lees/Getty Images
Strip Image 13 © Tim Kitchen/Getty Images
Strip Image 14 © PhotoAlto/Frederic Cirou/Getty Images

Cover Image © jocic /Shutterstock

To order books or for customer service, please call 1(800)-CALL-WILEY (225-5945).

Printed in the United States of America.

ISBN 978-1-118-48432-6
Printed and bound by Courier Kendallville.

10 9 8 7 6 5 4 3

ACCOUNT CLASSIFICATION AND PRESENTATION

Account Title	Classification	Financial Statement	Normal Balance
	A		
Accounts Payable	Current Liability	Balance Sheet	Credit
Accounts Receivable	Current Asset	Balance Sheet	Debit
Accumulated Depreciation—Buildings	Plant Asset—Contra	Balance Sheet	Credit
Accumulated Depreciation—Equipment	Plant Asset—Contra	Balance Sheet	Credit
Administrative Expenses	Operating Expense	Income Statement	Debit
Advertising Expense	Operating Expense	Income Statement	Debit
Allowance for Doubtful Accounts	Current Asset—Contra	Balance Sheet	Credit
Amortization Expense	Operating Expense	Income Statement	Debit
	B		
Bad Debt Expense	Operating Expense	Income Statement	Debit
Bonds Payable	Long-Term Liability	Balance Sheet	Credit
Buildings	Plant Asset	Balance Sheet	Debit
	C		
Cash	Current Asset	Balance Sheet	Debit
Common Stock	Stockholders' Equity	Balance Sheet	Credit
Copyrights	Intangible Asset	Balance Sheet	Debit
Cost of Goods Sold	Cost of Goods Sold	Income Statement	Debit
	D		
Debt Investments	Current Asset/Long-Term Investment	Balance Sheet	Debit
Depreciation Expense	Operating Expense	Income Statement	Debit
Discount on Bonds Payable	Long-Term Liability—Contra	Balance Sheet	Debit
Dividend Revenue	Other Income	Income Statement	Credit
Dividends	Temporary account closed to Retained Earnings	Retained Earnings Statement	Debit
Dividends Payable	Current Liability	Balance Sheet	Credit
	E		
Equipment	Plant Asset	Balance Sheet	Debit
	F		
Freight-Out	Operating Expense	Income Statement	Debit
	G		
Gain on Disposal of Plant Assets	Other Income	Income Statement	Credit
Goodwill	Intangible Asset	Balance Sheet	Debit
	I		
Income Summary	Temporary account closed to Retained Earnings	Not Applicable	(1)
Income Tax Expense	Income Tax Expense	Income Statement	Debit
Income Taxes Payable	Current Liability	Balance Sheet	Credit
Insurance Expense	Operating Expense	Income Statement	Debit
Interest Expense	Other Expense	Income Statement	Debit
Interest Payable	Current Liability	Balance Sheet	Credit
Interest Receivable	Current Asset	Balance Sheet	Debit
Interest Revenue	Other Income	Income Statement	Credit
Inventory	Current Asset	Balance Sheet (2)	Debit

Account Title	Classification	Financial Statement	Normal Balance
L			
Land	Plant Asset	Balance Sheet	Debit
Loss on Disposal of Plant Assets	Other Expense	Income Statement	Debit
M			
Maintenance and Repairs Expense	Operating Expense	Income Statement	Debit
Mortgage Payable	Long-Term Liability	Balance Sheet	Credit
N			
Notes Payable	Current Liability/ Long-Term Liability	Balance Sheet	Credit
P			
Patents	Intangible Asset	Balance Sheet	Debit
Paid-in Capital in Excess of Par—Common Stock	Stockholders' Equity	Balance Sheet	Credit
Paid-in Capital in Excess of Par—Preferred Stock	Stockholders' Equity	Balance Sheet	Credit
Preferred Stock	Stockholders' Equity	Balance Sheet	Credit
Premium on Bonds Payable	Long-Term Liability—Adjunct	Balance Sheet	Credit
Prepaid Insurance	Current Asset	Balance Sheet	Debit
R			
Rent Expense	Operating Expense	Income Statement	Debit
Retained Earnings	Stockholders' Equity	Balance Sheet and Retained Earnings Statement	Credit
S			
Salaries and Wages Expense	Operating Expense	Income Statement	Debit
Salaries and Wages Payable	Current Liability	Balance Sheet	Credit
Sales Discounts	Revenue—Contra	Income Statement	Debit
Sales Returns and Allowances	Revenue—Contra	Income Statement	Debit
Sales Revenue	Revenue	Income Statement	Credit
Selling Expenses	Operating Expense	Income Statement	Debit
Service Revenue	Revenue	Income Statement	Credit
Short-Term Investments	Current Asset	Balance Sheet	Debit
Stock Investments	Current Asset/Long-Term Investment	Balance Sheet	Debit
Supplies	Current Asset	Balance Sheet	Debit
Supplies Expense	Operating Expense	Income Statement	Debit
T			
Treasury Stock	Stockholders' Equity	Balance Sheet	Debit
U			
Unearned Service Revenue	Current Liability	Balance Sheet	Credit
Utilities Expense	Operating Expense	Income Statement	Debit

(1) The normal balance for Income Summary will be credit when there is a net income, debit when there is a net loss. The Income Summary account does not appear on any financial statement.

(2) If a periodic system is used, Inventory also appears on the income statement in the calculation of cost of goods sold.

The following is a sample chart of accounts. It does not represent a comprehensive chart of all the accounts used in this textbook but rather those accounts that are commonly used. This sample chart of accounts is for a company that generates both service revenue as well as sales revenue. It uses the perpetual approach to inventory. If a periodic system was used, the following temporary accounts would be needed to record inventory purchases: Purchases; Freight-In; Purchase Returns and Allowances; and Purchase Discounts.

CHART OF ACCOUNTS

Assets	Liabilities	Stockholders' Equity	Revenues	Expenses
Cash	Notes Payable	Common Stock	Service Revenue	Administrative Expenses
Accounts Receivable	Accounts Payable	Paid-in Capital in Excess of Par—Common Stock	Sales Revenue	Amortization Expense
Allowance for Doubtful Accounts	Unearned Service Revenue	Preferred Stock	Sales Discounts	Bad Debt Expense
Interest Receivable	Salaries and Wages Payable	Paid-in Capital in Excess of Par—Preferred Stock	Sales Returns and Allowances	Cost of Goods Sold
Inventory	Interest Payable	Treasury Stock	Interest Revenue	Depreciation Expense
Supplies	Dividends Payable	Retained Earnings	Gain on Disposal of Plant Assets	Freight-Out
Prepaid Insurance	Income Taxes Payable	Dividends		Income Tax Expense
Land	Bonds Payable	Income Summary		Insurance Expense
Equipment	Discount on Bonds Payable			Interest Expense
Accumulated Depreciation—Equipment	Premium on Bonds Payable			Loss on Disposal of Plant Assets
Buildings	Mortgage Payable			Maintenance and Repairs Expense
Accumulated Depreciation—Buildings				Rent Expense
Copyrights				Salaries and Wages Expense
Goodwill				Selling Expenses
Patents				Supplies Expense
				Utilities Expense

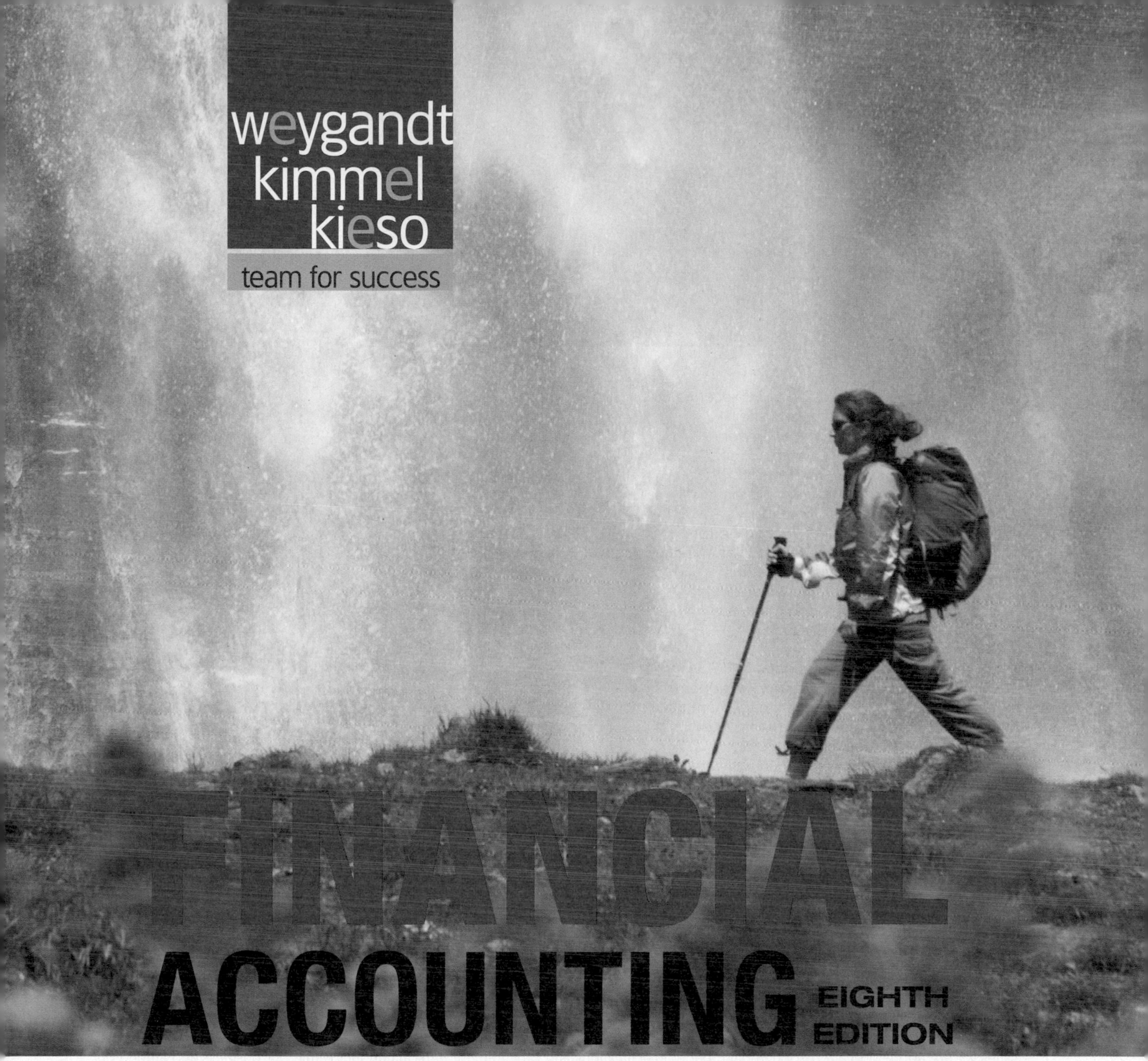

weygandt
kimmel
kieso

team for success

FINANCIAL ACCOUNTING

EIGHTH EDITION

Jerry J. Weygandt PhD, CPA

University of Wisconsin—Madison
Madison, Wisconsin

Paul D. Kimmel PhD, CPA
University of Wisconsin—Milwaukee
Milwaukee, Wisconsin

Donald E. Kieso PhD, CPA
Northern Illinois University
DeKalb, Illinois

John Wiley & Sons, Inc.

Dedicated to
*the **Wiley sales representatives***
who sell our books and service
our adopters in a professional
and ethical manner, and to
Enid, Merlynn, and Donna

Vice President & Executive Publisher	George Hoffman
Associate Publisher	Christopher DeJohn
Operations Manager	Yana Mermel
Senior Content Editor	Ed Brislin
Development Editor	Terry Ann Tatro
Development Editor	Margaret Thompson
Content Manager	Dorothy Sinclair
Senior Production Editor	Valerie Vargas
Associate Director of Marketing	Amy Scholz
Marketing Manager	Karolina Zarychta Honsa
Lead Product Designer	Allison Morris
Product Designer	Greg Chaput
Media Specialist	Daniela DiMaggio
Design Director	Harry Nolan
Senior Designer	Maureen Eide
Cover & Interior Designer	Kristine Carney
Production Management Services	Ingrao Associates
Senior Illustration Editor	Anna Melhorn
Senior Photo Editor	Mary Ann Price
Senior Editorial Assistant	Jacqueline Kepping
Senior Marketing Assistant	Courtney Luzzi
Cover Design	Kristine Carney
Cover Photo	© Bill Stevenson/Aurora Photos, Inc.

This book was set in New Aster by Aptara®, Inc. and printed and bound by Courier-Kendallville.
The cover was printed by Courier-Kendallville.

Founded in 1807, John Wiley & Sons, Inc. has been a valued source of knowledge and understanding for more than 200 years, helping people around the world meet their needs and fulfill their aspirations. Our company is built on a foundation of principles that include responsibility to the communities we serve and where we live and work. In 2008, we launched a Corporate Citizenship Initiative, a global effort to address the environmental, social, economic, and ethical challenges we face in our business. Among the issues we are addressing are carbon impact, paper specifications and procurement, ethical conduct within our business and among our vendors, and community and charitable support. For more information, please visit our website: www.wiley.com/go/citizenship.

ISBN-13 978-0-470-92938-4

Printed in the United States of America

10 9 8 7 6 5 4 3 2 1

Dear Student,

Why This Course? *Remember your biology course in high school? Did you have one of those "invisible man" models (or maybe something more high-tech than that) that gave you the opportunity to look "inside" the human body? This accounting course offers something similar: To understand a business, you have to understand the financial insides of a business organization. An accounting course will help you understand the essential financial components of businesses. Whether you are looking at a large multinational company like Microsoft or Starbucks or a single-owner software consulting business or coffee shop, knowing the fundamentals of accounting will help you understand what is happening. As an employee, a manager, an investor, a business owner, or a director of your own personal finances—any of which roles you will have at some point in your life—you will make better decisions for having taken this course.*

"Whether you are looking at a large multinational company like Microsoft or Starbucks or a single-owner software consulting business or coffee shop, knowing the fundamentals of accounting will help you understand what is happening."

Why This Book? *Hundreds of thousands of students have used this textbook. Your instructor has chosen it for you because of its trusted reputation. The authors have worked hard to keep the book fresh, timely, and accurate.*

This textbook contains features to help you learn best, whatever your learning style. To understand what your learning style is, spend about 10 minutes to take the learning style quiz at the book's companion website. Then, look at page xiii for how you can apply an understanding of your learning style to this course. When you know more about your own learning style, browse through pages xiv–xvi. These pages describe the main features you will find in this textbook and explain their purpose.

How To Succeed? *We've asked many students and many instructors whether there is a secret for success in this course. The nearly unanimous answer turns out to be not much of a secret: "Do the homework." This is one course where doing is learning. The more time you spend on the homework assignments—using the various tools that this textbook provides—the more likely you are to learn the essential concepts, techniques, and methods of accounting. Besides the textbook itself, the book's companion website also offers various support resources.*

Good luck in this course. We hope you enjoy the experience and that you put to good use throughout a lifetime of success the knowledge you obtain in this course. We are sure you will not be disappointed.

Jerry J. Weygandt
Paul D. Kimmel
Donald E. Kieso

Your Team for Success in Accounting

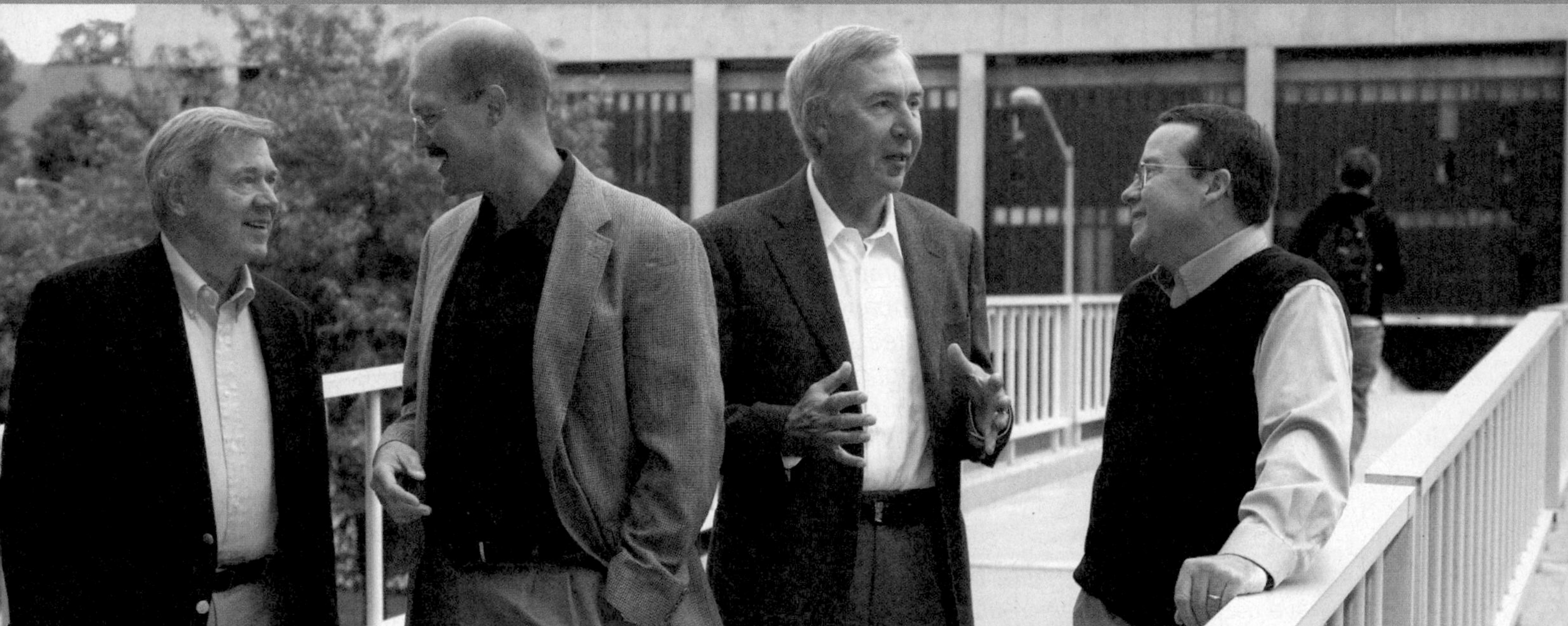

Wiley Accounting is your partner in accounting education. We want to be the first publisher you think of when it comes to quality content, reliable technology, innovative resources, professional training, and unparalleled support for your accounting classroom.

Your Wiley Accounting Team for Success is comprised of three distinctive advantages that you won't find with any other publisher:

- Author Commitment
- Wiley Faculty Network
- WileyPLUS

Author Commitment:

A Proven Author Team of Inspired Teachers

The Team for Success authors bring years of industry and academic experience to the development of each textbook that relates accounting concepts to real-world experiences. This cohesive team brings continuity of writing style, pedagogy, and problem material to each course from Principles to Intermediate so you and your students can seamlessly progress from introductory through advanced courses in accounting.

The authors understand the mindset and time limitations of today's students. They demonstrate an intangible ability to effectively deliver complex information so it is clear and understandable while staying one step ahead of emerging global trends in business.

Wiley Faculty Network:

A Team of Educators Dedicated to Your Professional Development

The Wiley Faculty Network (WFN) is a global group of seasoned accounting professionals who share best practices in teaching with their peers. Our Virtual Guest Lecture Series provides the opportunity you need for professional development in an online environment that is relevant, convenient, and collaborative. The quality of these seminars and workshops meets the strictest standards, so we are proud to be able to offer valuable CPE credits to attendees.

With 24 faculty mentors in accounting, it's easy to find help with your most challenging curriculum questions—just ask our experts!

WileyPLUS:

An Experienced Team of Support Professionals

The *WileyPLUS* Account Managers understand the time constraints of busy instructors who want to provide the best resources available to their students with minimal headaches and planning time. They know how intimidating new software can be, so they are sure to make the transition easy and painless.

Account Managers act as your personal contact and expert resource for training, course set-up, and shortcuts throughout the *WileyPLUS* experience.

Your success as an educator directly correlates to student success, and that's our goal. The Wiley Accounting Team for Success truly strives for YOUR success! Partner with us today!

www.wileyteamforsuccess.com

Author Commitment

Collaboration. Innovation. Experience.

After decades of success as authors of textbooks like this one, Jerry Weygandt, Paul Kimmel, and Don Kieso understand that teaching accounting goes beyond simply presenting data. The authors are truly effective because they know that teaching is about telling compelling stories in ways that make each concept come to life.

Teacher / Author / Professional

Through their textbooks, supplements, online learning tools, and classrooms, these authors have developed a comprehensive pedagogy that engages students in learning and faculty with teaching.

These authors collaborate throughout the entire process. The end result is a true collaboration where each author brings his individual experience and talent to the development of every paragraph, page, and chapter, thus creating a truly well-rounded, thorough view on any given accounting topic.

Many Ways in One Direction

Our **Team for Success** has developed a teaching system that addresses every learning style. Each year brings new insights, feedback, ideas, and improvements on how to deliver the material to every student with a passion for the subject in a format that gives them the best chance to succeed.

The key to the team's approach is in understanding that, just as there are many different ways to learn, there are also many different ways to teach.

In Their Own Words

Visit the Wiley **Team for Success** website to hear from the authors first-hand as they discuss their teaching styles, collaboration, and the future of accounting.

www.wileyteamforsuccess.com

Author Commitment

Jerry Weygandt

Jerry J. Weygandt, PhD, CPA, is Arthur Andersen Alumni Emeritus Professor of Accounting at the University of Wisconsin—Madison. He holds a Ph.D. in accounting from the University of Illinois. Articles by Professor Weygandt have appeared in the *Accounting Review, Journal of Accounting Research, Accounting Horizons, Journal of Accountancy*, and other academic and professional journals. These articles have examined such financial reporting issues as accounting for price-level adjustments, pensions, convertible securities, stock option contracts, and interim reports. Professor Weygandt is author of other accounting and financial reporting books and is a member of the American Accounting Association, the American Institute of Certified Public Accountants, and the Wisconsin Society of Certified Public Accountants. He has served on numerous committees of the American Accounting Association and as a member of the editorial board of the Accounting Review; he also has served as President and Secretary-Treasurer of the American Accounting Association. In addition, he has been actively involved with the American Institute of Certified Public Accountants and has been a member of the Accounting Standards Executive Committee (AcSEC) of that organization. He has served on the FASB task force that examined the reporting issues related to accounting for income taxes and served as a trustee of the Financial Accounting Foundation. Professor Weygandt has received the Chancellor's Award for Excellence in Teaching and the Beta Gamma Sigma Dean's Teaching Award. He is on the board of directors of M & I Bank of Southern Wisconsin. He is the recipient of the Wisconsin Institute of CPA's Outstanding Educator's Award and the Lifetime Achievement Award. In 2001 he received the American Accounting Association's Outstanding Educator Award.

Paul Kimmel

Paul D. Kimmel, PhD, CPA, received his bachelor's degree from the University of Minnesota and his doctorate in accounting from the University of Wisconsin. He is an Associate Professor at the University of Wisconsin—Milwaukee, and has public accounting experience with Deloitte & Touche (Minneapolis). He was the recipient of the UWM School of Business Advisory Council Teaching Award, the Reggie Taite Excellence in Teaching Award and a three-time winner of the Outstanding Teaching Assistant Award at the University of Wisconsin. He is also a recipient of the Elijah Watts Sells Award for Honorary Distinction for his results on the CPA exam. He is a member of the American Accounting Association and the Institute of Management Accountants and has published articles in *Accounting Review, Accounting Horizons, Advances in Management Accounting, Managerial Finance, Issues in Accounting Education, Journal of Accounting Education*, as well as other journals. His research interests include accounting for financial instruments and innovation in accounting education. He has published papers and given numerous talks on incorporating critical thinking into accounting education, and helped prepare a catalog of critical thinking resources for the Federated Schools of Accountancy.

Don Kieso

Donald E. Kieso, PhD, CPA, received his bachelor's degree from Aurora University and his doctorate in accounting from the University of Illinois. He has served as chairman of the Department of Accountancy and is currently the KPMG Emeritus Professor of Accountancy at Northern Illinois University. He has public accounting experience with Price Waterhouse & Co. (San Francisco and Chicago) and Arthur Andersen & Co. (Chicago) and research experience with the Research Division of the American Institute of Certified Public Accountants (New York). He has done post doctorate work as a Visiting Scholar at the University of California at Berkeley and is a recipient of NIU's Teaching Excellence Award and four Golden Apple Teaching Awards. Professor Kieso is the author of other accounting and business books and is a member of the American Accounting Association, the American Institute of Certified Public Accountants, and the Illinois CPA Society. He has served as a member of the Board of Directors of the Illinois CPA Society, then AACSB's Accounting Accreditation Committees, the State of Illinois Comptroller's Commission, as Secretary-Treasurer of the Federation of Schools of Accountancy, and as Secretary-Treasurer of the American Accounting Association. Professor Kieso is currently serving on the Board of Trustees and Executive Committee of Aurora University, as a member of the Board of Directors of Kishwaukee Community Hospital, and as Treasurer and Director of Valley West Community Hospital. From 1989 to 1993 he served as a charter member of the national Accounting Education Change Commission. He is the recipient of the Outstanding Accounting Educator Award from the Illinois CPA Society, the FSA's Joseph A. Silvoso Award of Merit, the NIU Foundation's Humanitarian Award for Service to Higher Education, a Distinguished Service Award from the Illinois CPA Society, and in 2003 an honorary doctorate from Aurora University.

IFRS
TOKYO
BEIJING
PARIS
LONDON
NEW YORK
Ready When You Are
The emerging importance of
International Financial Reporting Standards
presents challenges in how you teach
and how your students learn Accounting.

IFRS Review and Assessment Content

Integrated Content The Eighth Edition provides many new IFRS review and assessment tools that both instructors and students can easily incorporate into an introduction to financial accounting course. In the margin of the textbook narrative, International Notes highlight key differences between U.S. and international accounting standards as well as important IFRS updates.

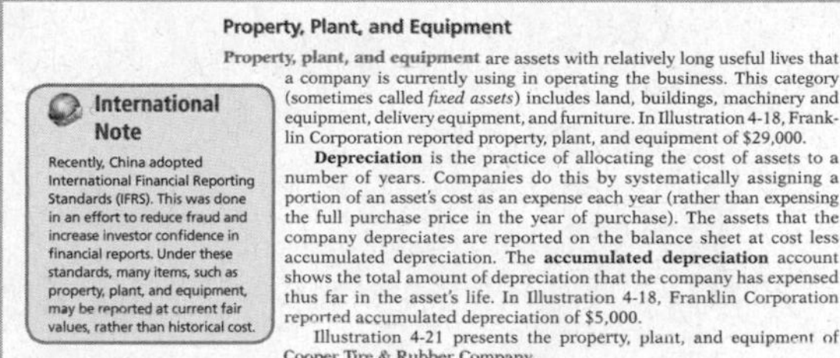

Property, Plant, and Equipment

Property, plant, and equipment are assets with relatively long useful lives that a company is currently using in operating the business. This category (sometimes called *fixed assets*) includes land, buildings, machinery and equipment, delivery equipment, and furniture. In Illustration 4-18, Franklin Corporation reported property, plant, and equipment of $29,000.

Depreciation is the practice of allocating the cost of assets to a number of years. Companies do this by systematically assigning a portion of an asset's cost as an expense each year (rather than expensing the full purchase price in the year of purchase). The assets that the company depreciates are reported on the balance sheet at cost less accumulated depreciation. The **accumulated depreciation** account shows the total amount of depreciation that the company has expensed thus far in the asset's life. In Illustration 4-18, Franklin Corporation reported accumulated depreciation of $5,000.

Illustration 4-21 presents the property, plant, and equipment of Cooper Tire & Rubber Company.

International Note

Recently, China adopted International Financial Reporting Standards (IFRS). This was done in an effort to reduce fraud and increase investor confidence in financial reports. Under these standards, many items, such as property, plant, and equipment, may be reported at current fair values, rather than historical cost.

A Look at IFRS: Review and Practice Each chapter also closes with an IFRS module that includes:

- **Key Points** that provide visual and textual highlights of IFRS topics that relate to concepts in a particular chapter. Students are presented with IFRS transactions, illustrations, and representations of IFRS financial statements.

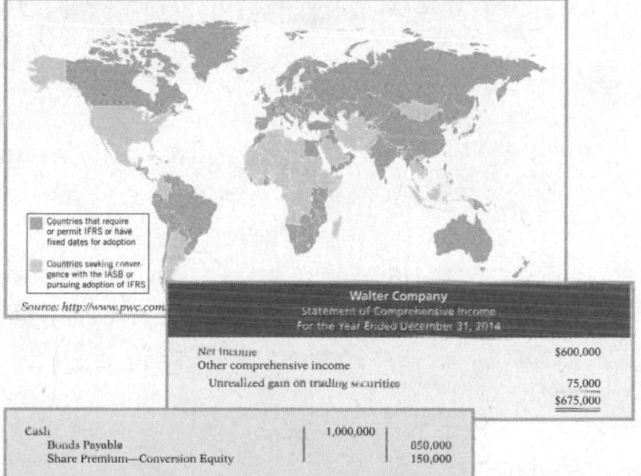

Walter Company
Statement of Comprehensive Income
For the Year Ended December 31, 2014

Net Income	$600,000
Other comprehensive income	
Unrealized gain on trading securities	75,000
	$675,000

Cash	1,000,000	
Bonds Payable		850,000
Share Premium—Conversion Equity		150,000

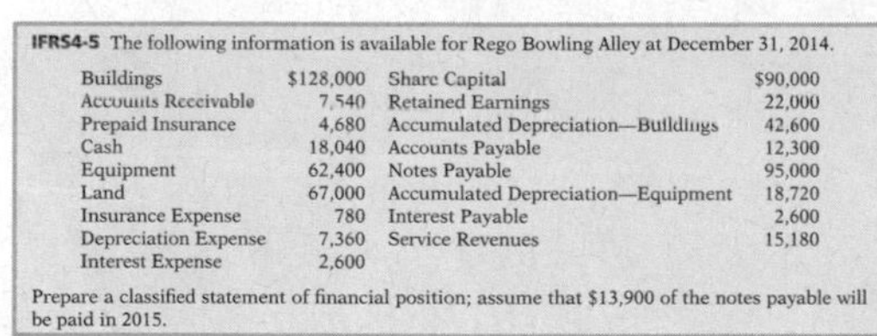

IFRS4-5 The following information is available for Rego Bowling Alley at December 31, 2014.

Buildings	$128,000	Share Capital	$90,000
Accounts Receivable	7,540	Retained Earnings	22,000
Prepaid Insurance	4,680	Accumulated Depreciation—Buildings	42,600
Cash	18,040	Accounts Payable	12,300
Equipment	62,400	Notes Payable	95,000
Land	67,000	Accumulated Depreciation—Equipment	18,720
Insurance Expense	780	Interest Payable	2,600
Depreciation Expense	7,360	Service Revenues	15,180
Interest Expense	2,600		

Prepare a classified statement of financial position; assume that $13,900 of the notes payable will be paid in 2015.

- **Looking to the Future** discussions of upcoming IFRS challenges and issues.
- **IFRS Practice** that includes both multiple-choice self-test questions and exercises.

- **International Financial Reporting Problems** that address Zetar plc's (a U.K. manufacturer of confectionary and natural snacks) financial statements, which are found in Appendix C.

Comprehensive Teaching Materials IFRS review and assessment content is also incorporated into instructor resources such as the test bank, computerized test bank, PowerPoint lecture slides, and instructor's manual.

WileyPLUS

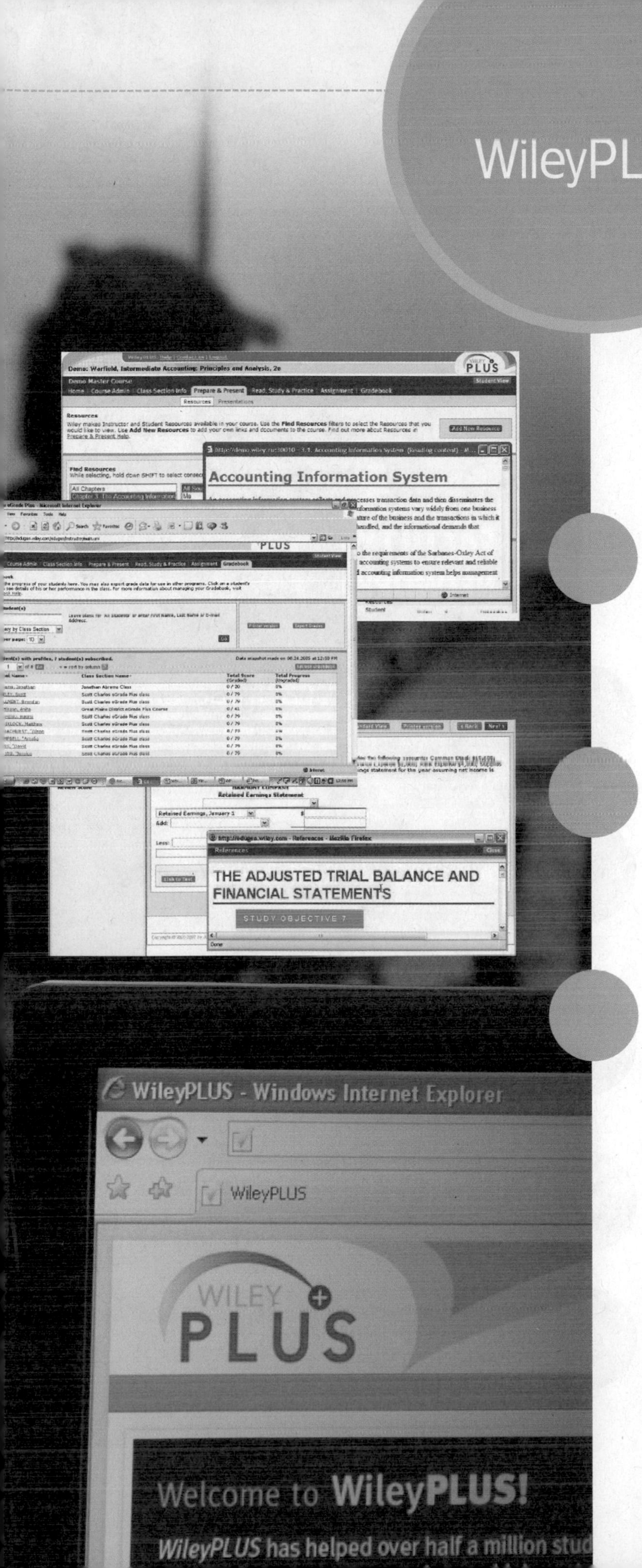

Prepare and Present

Create outstanding class presentations using a wealth of resources, such as PowerPoint™ slides, interactive simulations, and more. Plus you can easily upload any materials you have created into your course and combine them with the resources contained in *WileyPLUS*.

Track Your Progress

Keep track of your students' progress via an instructor's gradebook, which allows you to analyze individual and overall class results. This gives you an accurate and realistic assessment of your students' progress and level of understanding.

Create Assignments

Automate the assigning and grading of homework or quizzes by using the provided question banks or by writing your own. Student results will be automatically graded and recorded in your gradebook. *WileyPLUS* also links homework problems to relevant sections of the online text, hints, or solutions—context-sensitive help where students need it most!

What TYPE of learner are you?

Understanding each of these basic learning styles enables the authors to engage students' minds and motivate them to do their best work, ultimately improving the experience for both students and faculty.

	Intake: To take in the information	To make a study package	Text features that may help you the most	Output: To do well on exams
VISUAL	• Pay close attention to charts, drawings, and handouts your instructors use. • Underline. • Use different colors. • Use symbols, flow charts, graphs, different arrangements on the page, white spaces.	Convert your lecture notes into "page pictures." To do this: • Use the "Intake" strategies. • Reconstruct images in different ways. • Redraw pages from memory. • Replace words with symbols and initials. • Look at your pages.	The Navigator/Feature Story/Preview Infographics/Illustrations Accounting equation analyses Highlighted words Comprehensive DO IT! Problem/Action Plan Questions/Exercises/Problems Financial Reporting Problem Comparative Analysis Problem Real-World Focus	• Recall your "page pictures." • Draw diagrams where appropriate. • Practice turning your visuals back into words.
AURAL	• Attend lectures and tutorials. • Discuss topics with students and instructors. • Explain new ideas to other people. • Use a tape recorder. • Leave spaces in your lecture notes for later recall. • Describe overheads, pictures, and visuals to somebody who was not in class.	You may take poor notes because you prefer to listen. Therefore: • Expand your notes by talking with others and with information from your textbook. • Tape-record summarized notes and listen. • Read summarized notes out loud. • Explain your notes to another "aural" person.	Preview Insight Boxes DO IT! Action Plan Summary of Learning Objectives Glossary Comprehensive DO IT! Problem/Action Plan Self-Test Questions Questions/Exercises/Problems Financial Reporting Problem Comparative Analysis Problem Real-World Focus Decision-Making Across the Organization Communication Activity Ethics Case	• Talk with the instructor. • Spend time in quiet places recalling the ideas. • Practice writing answers to old exam questions. • Say your answers out loud.
READING/ WRITING	• Use lists and headings. • Use dictionaries, glossaries, and definitions. • Read handouts, textbooks, and supplementary library readings. • Use lecture notes.	• Write out words again and again. • Reread notes silently. • Rewrite ideas and principles into other words. • Turn charts, diagrams, and other illustrations into statements.	The Navigator/Feature Story/Study Objectives/Preview DO IT! Action Plan Summary of Learning Objectives Glossary/Self-Test Questions Questions/Exercises/Problems Writing Problems Financial Reporting Problem Comparative Analysis Problem Real-World Focus Decision-Making Across the Organization Communication Activity All About You	• Write exam answers. • Practice with multiple-choice questions. • Write paragraphs, beginnings and endings. • Write your lists in outline form. • Arrange your words into hierarchies and points.
KINESTHETIC	• Use all your senses. • Go to labs, take field trips. • Listen to real-life examples. • Pay attention to applications. • Use hands-on approaches. • Use trial-and-error methods.	You may take poor notes because topics do not seem concrete or relevant. Therefore: • Put examples in your summaries. • Use case studies and applications to help with principles and abstract concepts. • Talk about your notes with another "kinesthetic" person. • Use pictures and photographs that illustrate an idea.	The Navigator/Feature Story/Preview Infographics/Illustrations DO IT! Action Plan Summary of Learning Objectives Comprehensive DO IT! Problem/Action Plan Self-Test Questions Questions/Exercises/Problems Financial Reporting Problem Comparative Analysis Problem Real-World Focus Decision-Making Across the Organization Communication Activity All About You	• Write practice answers. • Role-play the exam situation.

Features of the Eighth Edition

The Eighth Edition expands our emphasis on student learning and improves upon a teaching and learning package that instructors and students have rated the highest in customer satisfaction.

What's New?

International Financial Reporting Standards

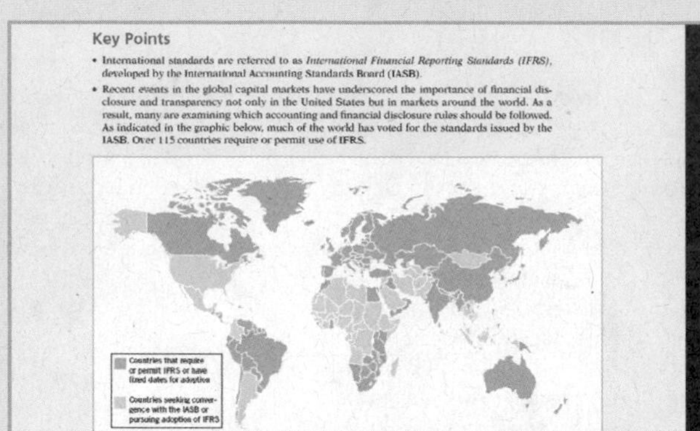

Key Points

- International standards are referred to as *International Financial Reporting Standards (IFRS)*, developed by the International Accounting Standards Board (IASB).
- Recent events in the global capital markets have underscored the importance of financial disclosure and transparency not only in the United States but in markets around the world. As a result, many are examining which accounting and financial disclosure rules should be followed. As indicated in the graphic below, much of the world has voted for the standards issued by the IASB. Over 115 countries require or permit use of IFRS.

As we continue to strive to reflect the constant changes in the accounting environment, we have added new material on International Financial Reporting Standards (IFRS). We have added a comprehensive new section at the end of each chapter, *A Look at IFRS*, which includes an overview section, addresses differences between GAAP and IFRS (*Key Points*), describes convergence efforts (*Looking to the Future*), and provides students with the opportunity to test their understanding through self-test questions and exercises (*IFRS Practice*). An international financial reporting problem is also included, based on Zetar plc's (a U.K. candy company) financial statements, provided in a new Appendix C of the textbook.

International Insights (and *International Notes* in the margin) also provide a global perspective of the accounting topics discussed in the textbook.

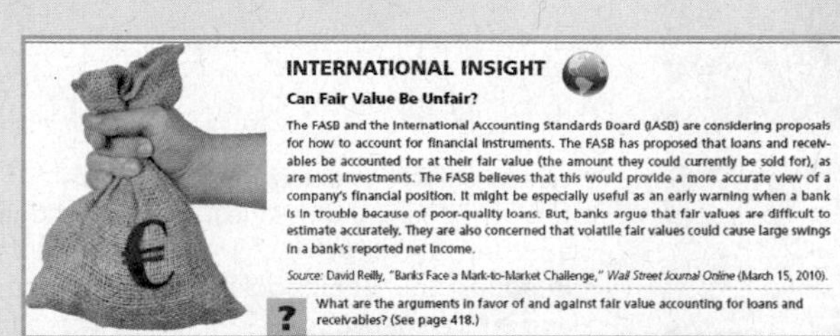

INTERNATIONAL INSIGHT

Can Fair Value Be Unfair?

The FASB and the International Accounting Standards Board (IASB) are considering proposals for how to account for financial instruments. The FASB has proposed that loans and receivables be accounted for at their fair value (the amount they could currently be sold for), as are most investments. The FASB believes that this would provide a more accurate view of a company's financial position. It might be especially useful as an early warning when a bank is in trouble because of poor-quality loans. But, banks argue that fair values are difficult to estimate accurately. They are also concerned that volatile fair values could cause large swings in a bank's reported net income.

Source: David Reilly, "Banks Face a Mark-to-Market Challenge," *Wall Street Journal Online* (March 15, 2010).

? What are the arguments in favor of and against fair value accounting for loans and receivables? (See page 418.)

PEOPLE, PLANET, AND PROFIT INSIGHT

Selling Green

Here is a question an executive of PepsiCo was asked: Should PepsiCo market green? The executive indicated that the company should, as he believes it's the No. 1 thing consumers all over the world care about. Here are some thoughts on this issue:

If you are going to market green, what are some things we've learned? I'll share with you one thing we've learned at PepsiCo.

Sun Chips are part of the food business I run. It's a "healthy snack." We decided that Sun Chips, if it's a healthy snack, should be made in facilities that have a net-zero footprint. In other words, I want off the electric grid everywhere we make Sun Chips. We did that. Sun Chips should be made in a facility that puts back more water than it uses. It does that. And we partnered with our suppliers and came out with the world's first compostable chip package.

Now, there was an issue with this package: It was louder than the New York subway, louder than jet engines taking off. What would a company that's committed to green do: walk away or stay committed? If your people are passionate, they're going to fix it for you as long as you stay committed. Six months later, the compostable bag has half the noise of our current package.

So the view today is: we should market green, we should be proud to do it . . . it has to be a 360 process, both internal and external. And if you do that, you can monetize environmental sustainability for the shareholders.

Source: "Four Problems—and Solutions," *Wall Street Journal* (March 7, 2011), p. R2.

? What is meant by "monetize environmental sustainability" for shareholders? (See page 267.)

People, Planet, and Profit

Today's companies are evaluating not just their profitability but also their corporate social responsibility. In this edition, we have profiled some of these companies, such as PepsiCo, to highlight their sustainable business practices.

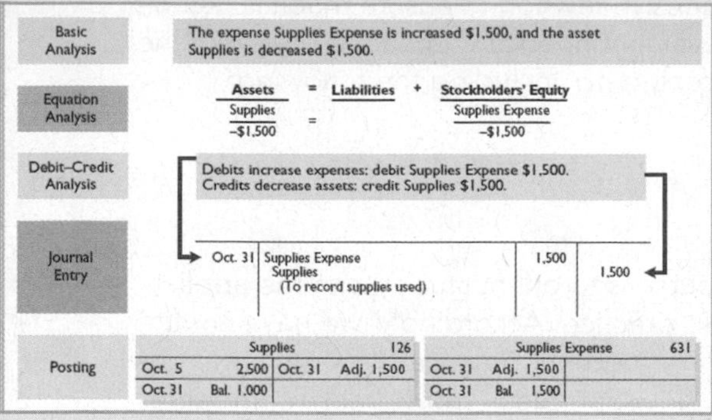

Basic Analysis
The expense Supplies Expense is increased $1,500, and the asset Supplies is decreased $1,500.
Equation Analysis
Assets = Liabilities + Stockholders' Equity
Supplies = Supplies Expense
−$1,500 −$1,500
Debit–Credit Analysis
Debits increase expenses: debit Supplies Expense $1,500.
Credits decrease assets: credit Supplies $1,500.
Journal Entry
Oct. 31 Supplies Expense 1,500
Supplies 1,500
(To record supplies used)
Posting
Supplies 126
Oct. 5 2,500 Oct. 31 Adj. 1,500
Oct. 31 Bal. 1,000
Supplies Expense 631
Oct. 31 Adj. 1,500
Oct. 31 Bal. 1,500

The Accounting Cycle

For many students, success in an introductory accounting course hinges on developing a sound conceptual understanding of the accounting cycle. In the past, we have received positive feedback regarding the framework that we have employed to introduce the recording process in Chapter 2. In this edition, we have expanded our use of this framework to cover the entire accounting cycle in Chapters 1–4.

Accounting Principles

For many students, learning about the conceptual framework can be somewhat tedious. Yet, at the same time, we believe that students need a good understanding of the accounting assumptions, principles, and constraints that accountants use as a basis for recording and reporting financial information. As a result, we decided to integrate our discussion of accounting principles throughout the textbook as they relate to the topic at hand. However, we also realize that students might find it helpful to have a summary of all the concepts, which we provide in a **new Chapter 3 Appendix**, *Concepts in Action.*

Chart of Accounts

It is important to always try to eliminate unnecessary barriers to student understanding. Sometimes, the accounting course can seem unnecessarily complicated to students because so many account titles are used. In order to reduce possible confusion and to keep students focused on those concepts that really matter, we undertook to streamline the number of accounts used in the textbook, supplements, and *WileyPLUS*. See inside the front cover of the textbook for a sample chart of accounts, which represent the majority of the account titles used.

Anatomy of a Fraud

Many users of our textbook have responded favorably to our *Anatomy of a Fraud* feature, previously only included in Chapter 7 (Fraud, Internal Control, and Cash). They have requested that we expand it throughout the textbook to demonstrate the importance of internal controls to all assets and liabilities. Accordingly, in this edition, we have expanded the *Anatomy of a Fraud* feature to all appropriate chapters.

ANATOMY OF A FRAUD

Bobbi Jean Donnelly, the office manager for Mod Fashions Corporations design center, was responsible for preparing the design center budget and reviewing expense reports submitted by design center employees. Her desire to upgrade her wardrobe got the better of her, and she enacted a fraud that involved filing expense-reimbursement requests for her own personal clothing purchases. She was able to conceal the fraud because she was responsible for reviewing all expense reports, including her own. In addition, she sometimes was given ultimate responsibility for signing off on the expense reports when her boss was "too busy." Also, because she controlled the budget, when she submitted her expenses, she coded them to budget items that she knew were running under budget, so that they would not catch anyone's attention.

Total take: $275,000

The Missing Control

Independent internal verification. Bobbi Jean's boss should have verified her expense reports. When asked what he thought her expenses for a year were, the boss said about $10,000. At $115,000 per year, her actual expenses were more than 10 times what would have been expected. However, because he was "too busy" to verify her expense reports or to review the budget, he never noticed.

Source: Adapted from Wells, *Fraud Casebook* (2007), pp. 79–90.

Hallmark Features of the Eighth Edition

This edition was subject to an overall, comprehensive revision to ensure that it is technically accurate, relevant, and up-to-date. We have continued and enhanced many of the features of the Seventh Edition of *Financial Accounting,* including the following:

Real-World Emphasis

One of the goals of the financial accounting course is to orient students to the application of accounting principles and techniques in practice. Accordingly, we have continued our practice of using numerous examples from real companies throughout the textbook. The names of these real companies are highlighted in red.

ACCOUNTING ACROSS THE ORGANIZATION

Wall Street No Friend of Facebook

In the 1990s, it was the dream of every young technology entrepreneur to start a company and do an initial public offering (IPO), that is, list company shares on a stock exchange. It seemed like there was a never-ending supply of 20-something-year-old technology entrepreneurs that made millions doing IPOs of companies that never made a profit and eventually failed. In sharp contrast to this is Mark Zuckerberg, the 27-year-old founder and CEO of Facebook. If Facebook did an IPO, he would make billions of dollars. But, he is in no hurry to go public. Because his company doesn't need to invest in factories, distribution systems, or even marketing, it doesn't need to raise a lot of cash. Also, by not going public, Zuckerberg has more control over the direction of the company. Right now, he and the other founders don't have to answer to outside shareholders, who might be more concerned about short-term investment horizons rather than long-term goals. In addition, publicly traded companies face many more financial reporting disclosure requirements.

Source: Jessica E. Vascellaro, "Facebook CEO in No Rush to 'Friend' Wall Street," *Wall Street Journal Online* (March 4, 2010).

? Why has Mark Zuckerberg, the CEO and founder of Facebook, delayed taking his company's shares public through an initial public offering (IPO)? (See page 596.)

Also, throughout the chapters, **Insight** and **Accounting Across the Organization** boxes show how people, often in non-accounting functions, in actual companies make decisions using accounting information. These high-interest boxes focus on various themes—ethics, international, investor, and corporate social responsibility concerns. *Guideline Answers* to the critical thinking questions are provided near the end of each chapter.

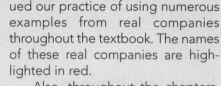

DO IT! Exercises

Brief **DO IT!** exercises ask students to apply their newly acquired knowledge. The **DO IT!** exercises include an *Action Plan,* which reviews the necessary steps to complete the exercise, as well as a *Solution* so students can have immediate feedback. A **Comprehensive DO IT!** problem at the end of each chapter allows students a final check of their understanding before they do their homework. **DO IT! Review** problems are part of the end-of-chapter homework material.

Accounting Equation Analyses

We include **accounting equation analyses** in the margin next to key journal entries. They will help students understand the impact of an accounting transaction on the components of the accounting equation, on the stockholders' equity accounts, and on the company's cash flows.

ISSUING BONDS AT A PREMIUM

To illustrate the issuance of bonds at a premium, we now assume the Candlestick, Inc. bonds described above sell for $108,111 (108.111% of face value) rather than for $92,639. The entry to record the sale is:

Jan. 1	Cash	108,111	
	Bonds Payable		100,000
	Premium on Bonds Payable		8,111
	(To record sale of bonds at a premium)		

A	=	L	+	SE
+108,111				
		+100,000		
		+8,111		

Cash Flows
+108,111

Candlestick adds the premium on bonds payable **to the bonds payable amount** on the balance sheet, as shown in Illustration 10-16.

Financial Statements

Students will be more willing to commit time and energy to a topic when they believe it is relevant to their future careers. There is no better way to demonstrate relevance than to ground discussions in the real world. To that end, we include financial statements from actual companies regularly throughout the textbook.

Kellogg Company
Balance Sheet (partial)
($ in millions)

Stockholders' equity	
Common stock, $0.25 par value, 1,000,000,000 shares authorized	
Issued: 418,669,193 shares	$ 105
Capital in excess of par value	388
Retained earnings	4,217
Treasury stock, at cost 28,618,052 shares	(1,357)
Accumulated other comprehensive income (loss)	(827)
Total stockholders' equity	$ 2,526

Marginal Notes

Helpful Hints in the margin further clarify concepts being discussed. **Ethics Notes** point out ethical points related to the nearby text discussion. **Alternative Terminology** lets students know about interchangeable words and phrases. **International Notes** provide a global perspective of the accounting topics being discussed.

Comprehensive Homework Material

Each chapter concludes with revised Self-Test Questions, Questions, Brief Exercises, **DO IT!** Review, Exercises, and Problems. An icon identifies Exercises and Problems that can be solved using **Excel templates** at the book's companion website. The **Continuing Cookie Chronicle** uses the business activities of a fictional company to help students apply accounting topics to a realistic entrepreneurial situation.

Broadening Your Perspective Section

We have revised and updated the **Broadening Your Perspective** section at the end of each chapter. Elements in this section include the following:

- Financial Reporting Problem: PepsiCo, Inc.
- Comparative Analysis Problem: PepsiCo, Inc. vs. The Coca-Cola Company
- Real-World Focus
- Decision-Making Across the Organization
- Communication Activity
- Ethics Case
- All About You
- FASB Codification Activity

These assignments are designed to help develop students' decision-making and critical-thinking skills.

Content Changes by Chapter

Chapter 1 Accounting in Action

- New format of transaction analyses, so students see Basic Analysis and Equation Analysis together, for a better understanding of the dual effect on the accounting equation.
- New Accounting Across the Organization box, about how Rhino Foods uses accounting to recruit new employees.
- Updated Ethics Insight, to include recent relief efforts in Haiti.
- New International Insight, about why South Korean companies must comply with international accounting standards.
- New People, Planet, and Profit Insight, about whether corporations should take into account environmental and social performance as part of their financial results.
- New International Note, about the format differences that exist between GAAP and IFRS financial statements.

Chapter 2 The Recording Process

- Rewrote Debits and Credit section, to provide additional instruction/explanation to students.
- New Investor Insights, about Chicago Cubs' major revenue and expense accounts and why SOX is important.

Chapter 3 Adjusting the Accounts

- Updated revenue recognition discussion to reflect the proposed new accounting standard, whereby revenue should be recognized in the accounting period in which services are performed (formerly when revenue was earned).
- New Ethics Insight, about real-world companies' abuse of the revenue recognition principle.
- New International Insight, about the Chinese government's inconsistent use of cash accounting.
- New People, Planet and Profit Insight, about how companies' disposal of waste materials might lead to accounting issues.
- Updated discussion of The Basics of Adjusting Entries section, including new transaction analysis format (Basic Analysis, Equation Analysis, Debit-Credit Analysis, Journal Entry, and Posting) for adjusting entries examples, providing continuity from Chapters 1 and 2.
- New Appendix 3B, Concepts in Action, about the accounting assumptions, principles, and constraints that accountants use as a basis for recording and reporting financial information.

Chapter 4 Completing the Accounting Cycle

- New People, Planet, and Profit Insight, about the dimensions that influence a company's reputation and consumer behavior.
- New Accounting Across the Organization box, about managing working capital efficiently.

Chapter 5 Accounting for Merchandising Operations

- Updated Feature Story, to include more recent Wal-Mart sales information.
- Added additional explanation to Sales Returns and Allowances section, to increase student understanding.
- New *Anatomy of a Fraud*, about cashier-related fraud.
- Revised Accounting Across the Organization box, to reflect recent information on Costco.
- Added new illustration in Sales Discounts section, so students could better visualize how net sales are composed of sales revenue, sales returns and allowances, and sales discounts.
- New People, Planet, and Profit Insight, about how companies can market their green efforts.
- New Ethics Insight, about disclosing other gains and losses in a separate line item.
- Rewrote Appendix 5A, Determining Cost of Goods Sold Under a Periodic System, to improve student understanding.

Chapter 6 Inventories

- New Accounting Across the Organization boxes, about JIT risks and rewards and Wal-Mart's experience with using RFID to improve inventory control.
- New Ethics Insight, about manipulating inventory records.

- New *Anatomy of a Fraud*, about altering inventory figures.
- Expanded discussion in Cost Flow Assumptions section, to ensure student understanding of accounting requirements for cost flow assumption chosen.

Chapter 7 Fraud, Internal Control, and Cash

- New People, Planet, and Profit Insight, about the need for internal controls for sustainability accounting.
- New Ethics Insight boxes, "Big Theft at Small Companies" and "How Employees Steal."
- New Helpful Hint about how petty cash receipts satisfy internal control procedures.
- New Investor Insight, about Madoff's Ponzi scheme.

Chapter 8 Accounting for Receivables

- Rewrote Types of Receivables section, to include more general discussion of receivables.
- New *Anatomy of a Fraud*, about an accounts receivable clerk who committed fraud at a large not-for-profit foundation.
- Added new material on recent home foreclosures in section on Valuing Accounts Receivable.
- New International Insight, about the IASB's push for fair value and the FASB's response to it.
- Expanded discussion of Disposing of Notes Receivable section, to include a timeline illustration to increase student understanding.
- New Accounting Across the Organization box, about Countrywide's "Fast and Easy" loan program.

Chapter 9 Plant Assets, Natural Resources, and Intangible Assets

- New DO IT! on revised depreciation.
- New *Anatomy of a Fraud*, about WorldCom.
- New People, Planet, and Profit Insight, about BHP Billiton's sustainability report and how it measures the success or failure of its environmental policies.
- New International Insight, about Japan's Internet company Softbank Corp.

Chapter 10 Liabilities

- New Accounting Across the Organization boxes, about the amount of payroll deductions and taxes, and the trend of companies to borrow more from bond investors than banks.
- New *Anatomy of a Fraud*, about using fake employees to collect paychecks.
- In Accounting for Bond Issues section, added more general discussion to ensure student understanding.

Chapter 11 Corporations: Organization, Stock Transactions, Dividends, and Retained Earnings

- Added more real-company detail to Characteristics of a Corporation section, to increase student engagement/interest.
- New Accounting Across the Organization boxes, about Facebook's status as a privately held company.
- New People, Planet, and Profit Insight, about how most investors believe environmental and social factors impact shareholder value.
- New *Anatomy of a Fraud*, about SafeNet's employees abusing company stock option plan.
- New Investor Insight, about Warren Buffett's company Berkshire Hathaway.

Chapter 12 Investments

- Updated Categories of Securities section, to reflect proposed new FASB classifications for debt and stock investments.

Chapter 13 Statement of Cash Flows

- New *Anatomy of a Fraud*, about Parmalat's multiple frauds.
- New Appendix 13C, Statement of Cash Flows—T-Account Approach.

Chapter 14 Financial Statement Analysis

- New *Anatomy of a Fraud*, about using Benford's Law (statistics) to detect fraud.
- New Investor Insight, about the limitations of the current ratio in financial statement analysis.

End-of-Textbook

- New Appendix C, financial statements of Zetar plc (U.K. candy company).

Teaching and Learning Supplementary Material

For Instructors

In addition to the support instructors receive from *WileyPLUS* and the Wiley Faculty Network, we offer the following useful supplements.

Book's Companion Website. On this website, *www.wiley.com/college/weygandt*, instructors will find the Solutions Manual, Test Bank, Instructor's Manual, Computerized Test Bank, and other resources.

Instructor's Resource CD. The Instructor's Resource CD (IRCD) contains all the instructor supplements. The IRCD gives instructors the flexibility to access and prepare instructional materials based on their individual needs.

Solutions Manual. The Solutions Manual contains detailed solutions to all questions, brief exercises, exercises, and problems in the textbook, as well as suggested answers to the questions and cases. The estimated time to complete exercises, problems, and cases is provided.

Solution Transparencies. The solution transparencies feature detailed solutions to brief exercises, exercises, problems, and *Broadening Your Perspective* activities. Transparencies can be easily ordered from the book's companion website.

Instructor's Manual. Included in each chapter are lecture outlines with teaching tips, chapter reviews, illustrations, and review quizzes.

Teaching Transparencies. The teaching transparencies are 4-color acetate images of the illustrations found in the Instructor's Manual. Transparencies can be easily ordered from the book's companion website.

Test Bank and Computerized Test Bank. The test bank and computerized test bank allow instructors to tailor examinations according to study objectives and learning outcomes, including AACSB, AICPA, and IMA professional standards. Achievement tests, comprehensive examinations, and a final exam are included.

PowerPoint™. The PowerPoint™ presentations contain a combination of key concepts, images, and problems from the textbook.

Blackboard. Blackboard offers an integrated set of course management tools that enable instructors to easily design, develop, and manage Web-based and Web-enhanced courses.

For Students

Book's Companion Website. On this website, students will find:

- *Exercises: Set B* and *Challenge Exercises*
- *Problems: Set C*
- *Self-Tests and Additional Self-Tests*

Student Study Guide. Each chapter of the Study Guide contains a chapter review, chapter outline, and a glossary of key terms. Demonstration problems, multiple-choice, true/false, matching, and other exercises are also included.

Working Papers. The working papers are printed templates that can help students correctly format their textbook accounting solutions. Working paper templates are available for all end-of-chapter brief exercises, exercises, problems, and cases.

Excel Working Papers. The *Excel Working Papers* are Excel templates that students can use to correctly format their textbook accounting solutions.

Excel Primer: Using Excel in Accounting. The online Excel primer and accompanying Excel templates allow students to complete select end-of-chapter exercises and problems identified by a spreadsheet icon in the margin of the textbook.

Problem-Solving Survival Guide. This tutorial is designed to improve students' success rates in solving homework assignments and exam questions. Each chapter includes an overview of key topics; a purpose statement and link to study objectives for each homework assignment; numerous review tips to alert students to common pitfalls and misconceptions; and reminders to concepts and principles. Multiple-choice exercises and cases similar to common homework assignments or exam questions enhance students' problem-solving proficiency. Solutions not only explain answers but also discuss an approach to similar types of accounting problems.

Mobile Applications. Quizzing and reviewing content is available for download on iTunes.

Acknowledgments

Financial Accounting has benefited greatly from the input of focus group participants, manuscript reviewers, those who have sent comments by letter or e-mail, ancillary authors, and proofers. We greatly appreciate the constructive suggestions and innovative ideas of reviewers and the creativity and accuracy of the ancillary authors and checkers.

Eighth Edition

Dawn Addington
Central New Mexico Community College

Audrey Agnello
Niagara County Community College

Matt Anderson
Michigan State University

Joe Anthony
Michigan State University

Art Baja
Ohlone College

Felicia Baldwin
City College of Chicago—Richard J. Daley

John Blahnik
Lorain County Community College

Brian Bratten
University of Kentucky—Lexington

Jerry Braun
Daytona State College

Erin Burrell
University of Central Florida

Lisa Capozzoli
College of DuPage

Bruce Cassel
SUNY Dutchess Community College

Milton Chavez-Arias
Ohlone College

Kung Chen
University of Nebraska—Lincoln

Suzanne Counte
St. Louis Community College—Meramec

Robin D'Agati
Palm Beach State College

Karl Dahlberg
Rutgers University—Newark

Dori Danko
Grand Valley State University

Alan Davis
Community College of Philadelphia

Andrew DeJoseph
College of Mount Saint Vincent

Naman Desai
University of Central Florida

Martin Epstein
Central New Mexico Community College

Ann Esarco
McHenry County College

Caroline Falconetti
Nassau Community College

Roger Gee
San Diego Mesa College

Severin Grabski
Michigan State University

Hassan Hefzi
California State Polytechnic University—Pomona

Janice Holmes
Louisiana State University—Baton Rouge

John Hoskins
University of Alabama—Huntsville

Leslie Hubbard
Solano Community College

Daniel Hunt
Ivy Tech Community College

John Illig
State College of Florida

Nancy Kelly
Middlesex Community College

Ridgway Knight
Santa Monica College

Linda Marquis
Northern Kentucky University

Maureen McBeth
College of DuPage

Jeanette Milius
Iowa Western Community College

Mary Beth Nelson
North Shore Community College

Oluwakemi Onwuchekwa
University of Central Florida

Hong Pak
California State Polytechnic University—Pomona

Richard Pettit
Mountain View College

Raymond Reisig
Pace University—Pleasantville

Chuck Smith
Iowa Western Community College

Ashley Soliz
Delta State University

Jalal Soroosh
Loyola University Maryland

Grace Stuart-Tuggle
Palm Beach State College

Richard Van Ness
Schenectady County Community College

Cynthia Vanoosterum
Ivy Tech Community College

Robert Walsh
University of Dallas

Barbara Warschawski
Schenectady County Community College

Bob Willis
Rogers State University

Jeffrey Wong
Bellevue College

Marj Yuschak
Rutgers University—New Brunswick

Prior Edition

John Ahmad
Northern Virginia Community College—Annandale

Colin Battle
Broward College

Beverly Beatty
Anne Arundel Community College

Jaswinder Bhangal
Chabot College

Leroy Bugger
Edison State College

Anne Cardozo
Broward College

Kimberly Charland
Kansas State University

Lisa Cole
Johnson County State College

Kathy Crusto-Way
Tarrant County College

Robin D'Agati
Palm Beach State College

Karl E. Dahlberg
Rutgers University

Tony Dellarte
Luzerne County Community College

Pam Donahue
Northern Essex Community College

Kathy Dunne
Rider University

Dora Estes
Volunteer State Community College

Mary Falkey
Prince George's Community College

Lori Grady
Bucks County Community College

Joyce Griffin
Kansas City Kansas Community College

Lester Hall
Danville Community College

Becky Hancock
El Paso Community College

Audrey Hunter
Broward College

Donna Johnston-Blair
Santa Clara University

Naomi Karolinski
Monroe Community College

Kenneth Koerber
Bucks County Community College

Sandra Lang
McKendree University

Cathy Xanthaky Larson
Middlesex Community College

David Laurel
South Texas College

Michael Lawrence
Portland Community College

Pamela Legner
College of DuPage

Suneel Maheshwari
Marshall University

Lori Major
Luzerne County Community College

Jim Martin
University of Montevallo

Evelyn McDowell
Rider University

Glenn Pate
Palm Beach State College

Yvonne Phang
Borough of Manhattan Community College

Mike Prockton
Finger Lakes Community College

Jessica Rakow
Louisiana State University

Richard Sarkisian
Camden County College

Mark Savitskie
Wayne State University

Beth Secrest
Walsh University

William Serafin
Community College of Allegheny County

Walter Silva
Massachusetts Bay Community College

Lois Slutsky
Broward College

Frank Stangota
Rutgers University

Dennis Stovall
Grand Valley State University

Shafi Ullah
Broward College

WileyPLUS Developers and Reviewers

Carole Brandt-Fink
Laura McNally
Melanie Yon

Ancillary Authors, Contributors, Proofers, and Accuracy Checkers

LuAnn Bean
Florida Institute of Technology

Jack Borke
University of Wisconsin—Platteville

Sandra Cohen
Columbia College Chicago

Larry Falcetto
Emporia State University

Mark Gleason
Metropolitan State University

Coby Harmon
University of California—Santa Barbara

Douglas Kieso
Aurora University

Kirk Lynch
Sandhills Community College

Kevin McNelis
New Mexico State University

Jill Misuraca
Central Connecticut State University

Barbara Muller
Arizona State University

Yvonne Phang
Borough of Manhattan Community College

John Plouffe
California State University—Los Angeles

Rex Schildhouse
San Diego Community College—Miramar

Lynn Stallworth
Appalachian State University

Diane Tanner
University of North Florida

Dick Wasson
San Diego State University

Andrea Weickgenannt
Xavier University

Bernie Weinrich
Lindenwood University

We appreciate the exemplary support and commitment given to us by associate publisher Chris DeJohn, marketing manager Karolina Zarychta Honsa, operations manager Yana Mermel, senior content editor Ed Brislin, development editors Terry Ann Tatro and Margaret Thompson, lead product designer Allie Morris, product designer Greg Chaput, vice president of higher education production and manufacturing Ann Berlin, designers Maureen Eide and Kristine Carney, illustration editor Anna Melhorn, photo editor Mary Ann Price, project editor Suzanne Ingrao of Ingrao Associates, indexer Steve Ingle, Denise Showers at Aptara, Cyndy Taylor, and project manager Angel Chavez at Integra. All of these professionals provided innumerable services that helped the textbook take shape.

Finally, our thanks to Amy Scholz, Susan Elbe, George Hoffman, Tim Stookesberry, Joe Heider, and Steve Smith for their support and leadership in Wiley's College Division. We will appreciate suggestions and comments from users—instructors and students alike. You can send your thoughts and ideas about the textbook to us via email at: *wileyauthorfeedback@gmail.com.*

Jerry J. Weygandt
Madison, Wisconsin

Paul D. Kimmel
Milwaukee, Wisconsin

Donald E. Kieso
DeKalb, Illinois

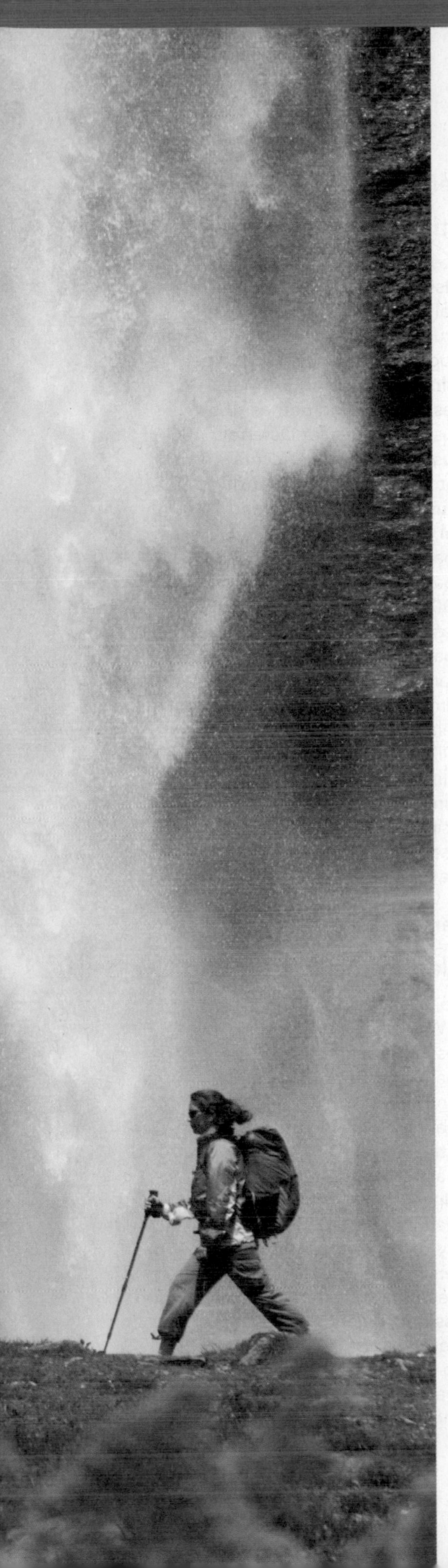

Brief Contents

Contents

Chapter 9

Plant Assets, Natural Resources, and Intangible Assets 422

Chapter 10

Liabilities 474

Chapter 11

Corporations: Organization, Stock Transactions, Dividends, and Retained Earnings 536

Chapter 12

Investments 600

Chapter 13

Statement of Cash Flows 644

Chapter 14

Financial Statement Analysis 710

Appendix A

Specimen Financial Statements: PepsiCo, Inc. A-1

Appendix B

Specimen Financial Statements: The Coca-Cola Company B-1

Appendix C

Specimen Financial Statements: Zetar plc C-1

Appendix D

Time Value of Money D-1

Appendix E

Payroll Accounting E-1

Appendix F

Subsidiary Ledgers and Special Journals F-1

Appendix G

Other Significant Liabilities G-1

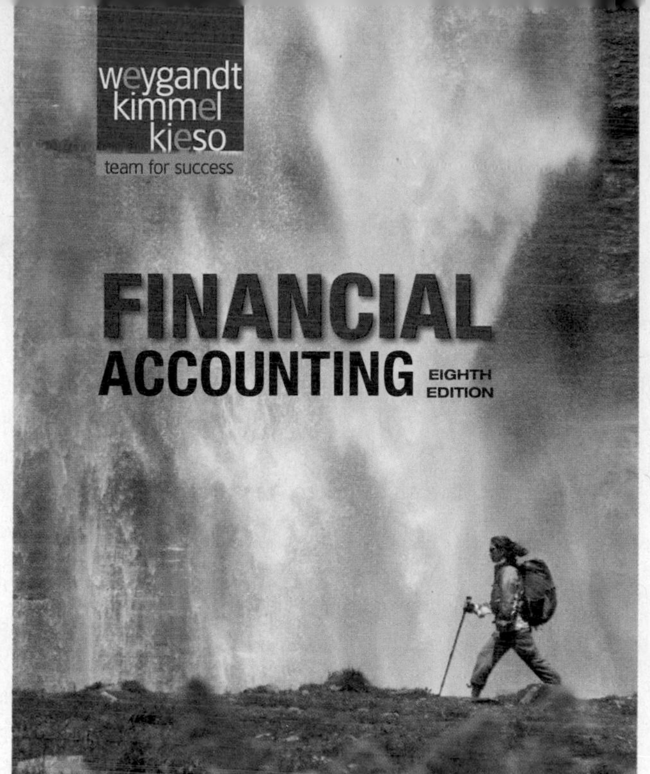
weygandt
kimmel
kieso
team for success
FINANCIAL
ACCOUNTING
EIGHTH
EDITION

Chapter 1 Accounting in Action

Feature Story

Knowing the Numbers

Many students who take this course do not plan to be accountants. If you are in that group, you might be thinking, "If I'm not going to be an accountant, why do I need to know accounting?" In response, consider the quote from Harold Geneen, the former chairman of IT&T: "To be good at your business, you have to know the numbers—cold."

Success in any business comes back to the numbers. You will rely on them to make decisions, and managers will use them to evaluate your performance. That is true whether your job involves marketing, production, management, or information systems.

In business, accounting and financial statements are the means for communicating the numbers. If you don't know how to read financial statements, you can't really know your business.

Many companies spend significant resources teaching their employees basic accounting so that they can read financial statements and understand how their actions affect the company's financial results. One such company is Springfield ReManufacturing Corporation (SRC). When Jack Stack and 11 other managers purchased SRC for 10 cents a share, it was a failing division of International Harvester. Jack's 119 employees, however, were counting on him for their livelihood. He decided that for the company to

The Navigator is a learning system designed to prompt you to use the learning aids in the chapter and set priorities as you study.

Learning Objectives give you a framework for learning the specific concepts covered in the chapter.

✔ The Navigator

- Scan Learning Objectives
- Read Feature Story
- Read Preview
- Read text and answer **DO IT!** p. 11 ▢ p. 14 ▢ p. 21 ▢ p. 25
- Work Comprehensive **DO IT!** p. 26
- Review Summary of Learning Objectives
- Answer Self-Test Questions
- Complete Assignments
- Go to **WileyPLUS** for practice and tutorials
-  Read A Look at IFRS p. 49

Learning Objectives

After studying this chapter, you should be able to:

1. Explain what accounting is.
2. Identify the users and uses of accounting.
3. Understand why ethics is a fundamental business concept.
4. Explain generally accepted accounting principles.
5. Explain the monetary unit assumption and the economic entity assumption.
6. State the accounting equation, and define its components.
7. Analyze the effects of business transactions on the accounting equation.
8. Understand the four financial statements and how they are prepared.

 **The Navigator**

survive, every employee needed to think like a businessperson and to act like an owner. To accomplish this, all employees at SRC took basic accounting courses and participated in weekly reviews of the company's financial statements. SRC survived, and eventually thrived. To this day, every employee (now numbering more than 1,000) undergoes this same training.

Many other companies have adopted this approach, which is called "open-book management." Even in companies that do not practice open-book management, employers generally assume that managers in all areas of the company are "financially literate."

Taking this course will go a long way to making you financially literate. In this book, you will learn how to read and prepare financial statements, and how to use basic tools to evaluate financial results. Appendices A and B provide real financial statements of two well-known U.S. companies, PepsiCo, Inc. and The Coca-Cola Company. Appendix C includes the financial statements of Zetar plc, a U.K. candy company. Throughout this textbook, we attempt to increase your familiarity with financial reporting by providing numerous references, questions, and exercises that encourage you to explore these financial statements.

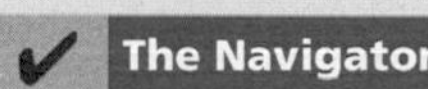

*The **Feature Story** helps you picture how the chapter topic relates to the real world of accounting and business. You will find references to the story throughout the chapter.*

Preview of Chapter 1

The opening story about Springfield ReManufacturing Corporation highlights the importance of having good financial information and knowing how to use it to make effective business decisions. Whatever your pursuits or occupation, the need for financial information is inescapable. You cannot earn a living, spend money, buy on credit, make an investment, or pay taxes without receiving, using, or dispensing financial information. Good decision-making depends on good information.

The purpose of this chapter is to show you that accounting is the system used to provide useful financial information. The content and organization of Chapter 1 are as follows.

*The **Preview** describes and outlines the major topics and subtopics you will see in the chapter.*

ACCOUNTING IN ACTION

What Is Accounting?	The Building Blocks of Accounting	The Basic Accounting Equation	Using the Accounting Equation	Financial Statements
• Three activities • Who uses accounting data	• Ethics in financial reporting • Generally accepted accounting principles • Measurement principles • Assumptions	• Assets • Liabilities • Stockholders' equity	• Transaction analysis • Summary of transactions	• Income statement • Retained earnings statement • Balance sheet • Statement of cash flows

✔ The Navigator

What Is Accounting?

LEARNING OBJECTIVE 1

Explain what accounting is.

Essential terms are printed in blue when they first appear, and are defined in the end-of-chapter glossary.

What consistently ranks as one of the top career opportunities in business? What frequently rates among the most popular majors on campus? What was the undergraduate degree chosen by Nike founder Phil Knight, Home Depot co-founder Arthur Blank, former acting director of the Federal Bureau of Investigation (FBI) Thomas Pickard, and numerous members of Congress? Accounting.[1] Why did these people choose accounting? They wanted to understand what was happening financially to their organizations. Accounting is the financial information system that provides these insights. In short, to understand your organization, you have to know the numbers.

Accounting consists of three basic activities—it **identifies**, **records**, and **communicates** the economic events of an organization to interested users. Let's take a closer look at these three activities.

Three Activities

As a starting point to the accounting process, a company identifies the **economic events relevant to its business**. Examples of economic events are the sale of snack chips by PepsiCo, the providing of telephone services by AT&T, and the payment of wages by Ford Motor Company.

Once a company like PepsiCo identifies economic events, it **records** those events in order to provide a history of its financial activities. Recording consists of keeping a **systematic**, **chronological diary of events**, measured in dollars and cents. In recording, PepsiCo also classifies and summarizes economic events.

Finally, PepsiCo **communicates** the collected information to interested users by means of **accounting reports**. The most common of these reports are called **financial statements**. To make the reported financial information meaningful, PepsiCo reports the recorded data in a standardized way. It accumulates information resulting from similar transactions. For example, PepsiCo accumulates all sales transactions over a certain period of time and reports the data as one amount in the company's financial statements. Such data are said to be reported **in the aggregate**. By presenting the recorded data in the aggregate, the accounting process simplifies a multitude of transactions and makes a series of activities understandable and meaningful.

A vital element in communicating economic events is the accountant's ability to **analyze and interpret** the reported information. Analysis involves use of ratios, percentages, graphs, and charts to highlight significant financial trends and relationships. Interpretation involves **explaining the uses**, **meaning**, **and limitations of reported data**. Appendix A of this textbook shows the financial statements of PepsiCo, Inc. Appendix B illustrates the financial statements of The Coca-Cola Company. We refer to these statements at various places throughout the textbook. (In addition, in the *A Look at IFRS* section at the end of each chapter, the U.K. company Zetar plc is analyzed.) At this point, these financial statements probably strike you as complex and confusing. By the end of this course, you'll be surprised at your ability to understand, analyze, and interpret them.

Illustration 1-1 summarizes the activities of the accounting process.

---

[1]The appendix to this chapter describes job opportunities for accounting majors and explains why accounting is such a popular major.

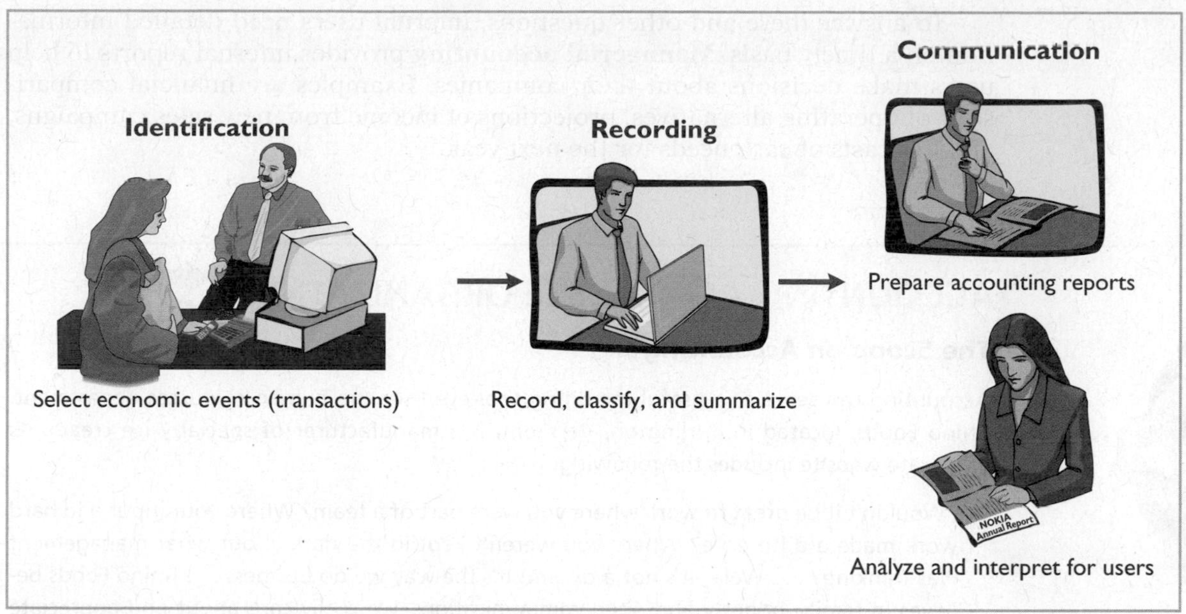

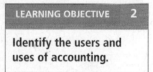

Illustration 1-1
The activities of the accounting process

You should understand that the accounting process **includes** the bookkeeping function. **Bookkeeping** usually involves **only** the recording of economic events. It is therefore just one part of the accounting process. In total, accounting involves **the entire process of identifying, recording, and communicating economic events.**[2]

Who Uses Accounting Data

LEARNING OBJECTIVE 2

Identify the users and uses of accounting.

The specific financial information that a user needs depends upon the kinds of decisions the user makes. There are two broad groups of users of financial information: internal users and external users.

INTERNAL USERS

Internal users of accounting information are managers who plan, organize, and run the business. These include marketing managers, production supervisors, finance directors, and company officers. In running a business, internal users must answer many important questions, as shown in Illustration 1-2.

Illustration 1-2
Questions that internal users ask

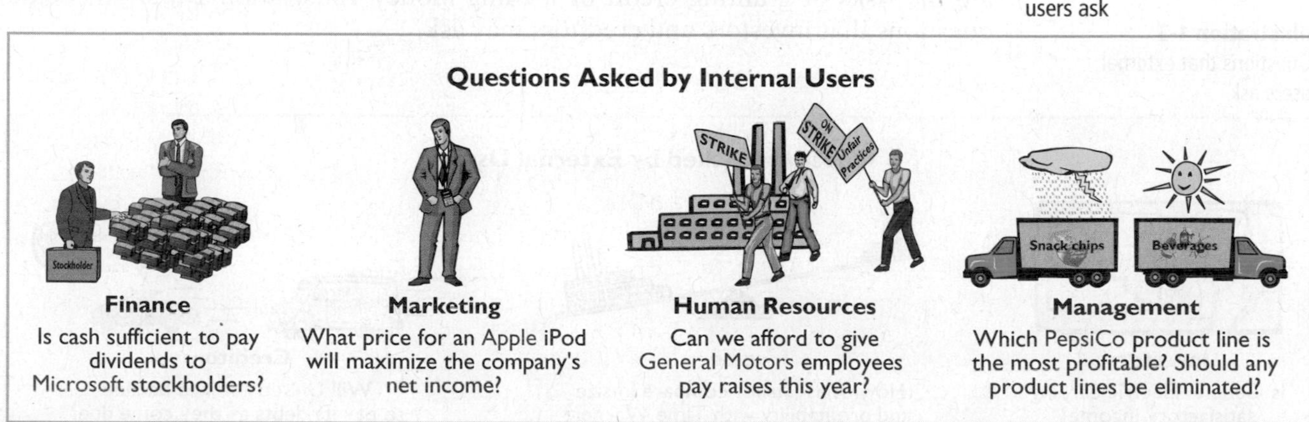

Questions Asked by Internal Users
Stockholder
STRIKE
ON STRIKE
Unfair Practices
Snack chips
Beverages
Finance
Is cash sufficient to pay dividends to Microsoft stockholders?
Marketing
What price for an Apple iPod will maximize the company's net income?
Human Resources
Can we afford to give General Motors employees pay raises this year?
Management
Which PepsiCo product line is the most profitable? Should any product lines be eliminated?

[2]The origins of accounting are generally attributed to the work of Luca Pacioli, an Italian Renaissance mathematician. Pacioli was a close friend and tutor to Leonardo da Vinci and a contemporary of Christopher Columbus. In his 1494 text *Summa de Arithmetica, Geometria, Proportione et Proportionalite,* Pacioli described a system to ensure that financial information was recorded efficiently and accurately.

To answer these and other questions, internal users need detailed information on a timely basis. **Managerial accounting** provides internal reports to help users make decisions about their companies. Examples are financial comparisons of operating alternatives, projections of income from new sales campaigns, and forecasts of cash needs for the next year.

ACCOUNTING ACROSS THE ORGANIZATION

The Scoop on Accounting

Accounting can serve as a useful recruiting tool even for the human resources department. Rhino Foods, located in Burlington, Vermont, is a manufacturer of specialty ice cream. Its corporate website includes the following:

> "Wouldn't it be great to work where you were part of a team? Where your input and hard work made a difference? Where you weren't kept in the dark about what management was thinking? . . . Well—it's not a dream! It's the way we do business . . . Rhino Foods believes in family, honesty and open communication—we really care about and appreciate our employees—and it shows. Operating results are posted and monthly group meetings inform all employees about what's happening in the Company. Employees also share in the Company's profits, in addition to having an excellent comprehensive benefits package."

Source: *www.rhinofoods.com/workforus/workforus.html.*

Accounting Across the Organization boxes demonstrate applications of accounting information in various business functions.

? What are the benefits to the company and to the employees of making the financial statements available to all employees? (See page 48.)

EXTERNAL USERS

External users are individuals and organizations outside a company who want financial information about the company. The two most common types of external users are investors and creditors. **Investors** (owners) use accounting information to make decisions to buy, hold, or sell ownership shares of a company. **Creditors** (such as suppliers and bankers) use accounting information to evaluate the risks of granting credit or lending money. Illustration 1-3 shows some questions that investors and creditors may ask.

Illustration 1-3
Questions that external users ask

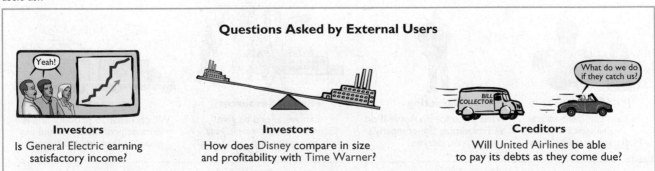

Questions Asked by External Users

Yeah!

Investors
Is General Electric earning satisfactory income?

Investors
How does Disney compare in size and profitability with Time Warner?

BILL COLLECTOR

What do we do if they catch us?

Creditors
Will United Airlines be able to pay its debts as they come due?

Financial accounting answers these questions. It provides economic and financial information for investors, creditors, and other external users. The information needs of external users vary considerably. **Taxing authorities**, such as the Internal Revenue Service, want to know whether the company complies with tax laws. **Regulatory agencies**, such as the Securities and Exchange Commission or the Federal Trade Commission, want to know whether the company is operating within prescribed rules. **Customers** are interested in whether a company like General Motors will continue to honor product warranties and support its product lines. **Labor unions**, such as the Major League Baseball Players Association, want to know whether the owners have the ability to pay increased wages and benefits.

The Building Blocks of Accounting

A doctor follows certain standards in treating a patient's illness. An architect follows certain standards in designing a building. An accountant follows certain standards in reporting financial information. For these standards to work, a fundamental business concept must be at work—ethical behavior.

Ethics in Financial Reporting

LEARNING OBJECTIVE 3

Understand why ethics is a fundamental business concept.

People won't gamble in a casino if they think it is "rigged." Similarly, people won't play the stock market if they think stock prices are rigged. In recent years, the financial press has been full of articles about financial scandals at Enron, WorldCom, HealthSouth, AIG, and others. As the scandals came to light, mistrust of financial reporting in general grew. One article in the *Wall Street Journal* noted that "repeated disclosures about questionable accounting practices have bruised investors' faith in the reliability of earnings reports, which in turn has sent stock prices tumbling." Imagine trying to carry on a business or invest money if you could not depend on the financial statements to be honestly prepared. Information would have no credibility. There is no doubt that a sound, well-functioning economy depends on accurate and dependable financial reporting.

United States regulators and lawmakers were very concerned that the economy would suffer if investors lost confidence in corporate accounting because of unethical financial reporting. In response, Congress passed the **Sarbanes-Oxley Act** (SOX, or Sarbox). Its intent is to reduce unethical corporate behavior and decrease the likelihood of future corporate scandals. As a result of SOX, top management must now certify the accuracy of financial information. In addition, penalties for fraudulent financial activity are much more severe. Also, SOX increased the independence of the outside auditors who review the accuracy of corporate financial statements and increased the oversight role of boards of directors.

Ethics Note 

Circus-founder P.T. Barnum is alleged to have said, "Trust everyone, but cut the deck." What Sarbanes-Oxley does is to provide measures that (like cutting the deck of playing cards) help ensure that fraud will not occur.

The standards of conduct by which one's actions are judged as right or wrong, honest or dishonest, fair or not fair, are **ethics**. Effective financial reporting depends on sound ethical behavior. To sensitize you to ethical situations in business and to give you practice at solving ethical dilemmas, we address ethics in a number of ways in this book:

Ethics Notes help sensitize you to some of the ethical issues in accounting.

1. A number of the *Feature Stories* and other parts of the textbook discuss the central importance of ethical behavior to financial reporting.
2. *Ethics Insight* boxes and marginal *Ethics Notes* highlight ethics situations and issues in actual business settings.

3. Many of the *People, Planet, and Profit Insight* boxes focus on ethical issues that companies face in measuring and reporting social and environmental issues.
4. At the end of the chapter, an *Ethics Case* simulates a business situation and asks you to put yourself in the position of a decision-maker in that case.

When analyzing these various ethics cases, as well as experiences in your own life, it is useful to apply the three steps outlined in Illustration 1-4.

Illustration 1-4
Steps in analyzing ethics cases and situations

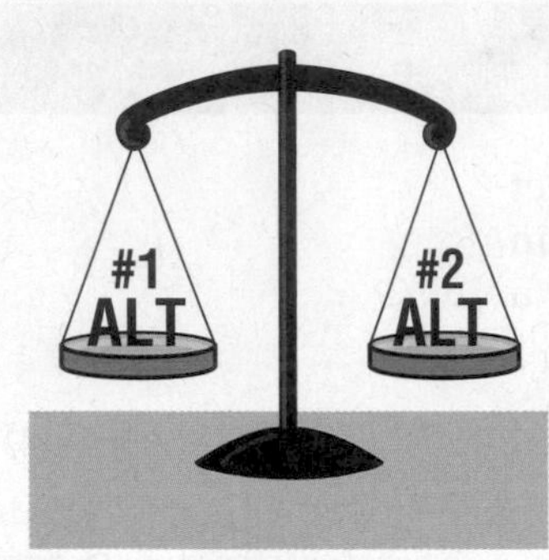

I. Recognize an ethical situation and the ethical issues involved.
Use your personal ethics to identify ethical situations and issues. Some businesses and professional organizations provide written codes of ethics for guidance in some business situations.

2. Identify and analyze the principal elements in the situation.
Identify the *stakeholders*—persons or groups who may be harmed or benefited. Ask the question: What are the responsibilities and obligations of the parties involved?

3. Identify the alternatives, and weigh the impact of each alternative on various stakeholders.
Select the most ethical alternative, considering all the consequences. Sometimes there will be one right answer. Other situations involve more than one right solution; these situations require an evaluation of each and a selection of the best alternative.

Insights *provide examples of business situations from various perspectives—ethics, investor, international, and corporate social responsibility.*

ETHICS INSIGHT

The Numbers Behind Not-for-Profit Organizations

Accounting plays an important role for a wide range of business organizations worldwide. Just as the integrity of the numbers matters for business, it matters at least as much for not-for-profit organizations. Proper control and reporting help ensure that money is used the way donors intended. Donors are less inclined to give to an organization if they think the organization is subject to waste or theft. The accounting challenges of some large international not-for-profits rival those of the world's largest businesses. For example, after the Haitian earthquake, the Haitian-born musician Wyclef Jean was criticized for the poor accounting controls in a relief fund that he founded. Since then, he has hired a new accountant and improved the transparency regarding funds raised and spent.

What benefits does a sound accounting system provide to a not-for-profit organization? (See page 48.)

LEARNING OBJECTIVE 4

Explain generally accepted accounting principles.

Generally Accepted Accounting Principles

The accounting profession has developed standards that are generally accepted and universally practiced. This common set of standards is called **generally accepted accounting principles (GAAP)**. These standards indicate how to report economic events.

The primary accounting standard-setting body in the United States is the **Financial Accounting Standards Board (FASB)**. The **Securities and Exchange Commission (SEC)** is the agency of the U.S. government that oversees U.S. financial markets and accounting standard-setting bodies. The SEC relies on the FASB to develop accounting standards, which public companies must follow. Many countries outside of the United States have adopted the accounting standards issued by the **International Accounting Standards Board (IASB)**. These standards are called **International Financial Reporting Standards (IFRS)**.

As markets become more global, it is often desirable to compare the result of companies from different countries that report using different accounting standards. In order to increase comparability, in recent years the two standard-setting bodies have made efforts to reduce the differences between U.S. GAAP and IFRS. This process is referred to as **convergence**. As a result of these convergence efforts, it is likely that someday there will be a single set of high-quality accounting standards that are used by companies around the world. Because convergence is such an important issue, we highlight any major differences between GAAP and IFRS in *International Notes* (as shown in the margin here) and provide a more in-depth discussion in the *A Look at IRFS* section at the end of each chapter.

International Note

Over 100 countries use International Financial Reporting Standards (called IFRS). For example, all companies in the European Union follow international standards. The differences between U.S. and international standards are not generally significant.

International Notes highlight differences between U.S. and international accounting standards.

Measurement Principles

GAAP generally uses one of two measurement principles, the cost principle or the fair value principle. Selection of which principle to follow generally relates to trade-offs between relevance and faithful representation. **Relevance** means that financial information is capable of making a difference in a decision. **Faithful representation** means that the numbers and descriptions match what really existed or happened—it is factual.

Helpful Hint
Relevance and *faithful representation* are two primary qualities that make accounting information useful for decision-making.

Helpful Hints further clarify concepts being discussed.

COST PRINCIPLE

The **cost principle** (or historical cost principle) dictates that companies record assets at their cost. This is true not only at the time the asset is purchased, but also over the time the asset is held. For example, if Best Buy purchases land for $300,000, the company initially reports it in its accounting records at $300,000. But what does Best Buy do if, by the end of the next year, the fair value of the land has increased to $400,000? Under the cost principle, it continues to report the land at $300,000.

FAIR VALUE PRINCIPLE

The **fair value principle** states that assets and liabilities should be reported at fair value (the price received to sell an asset or settle a liability). Fair value information may be more useful than historical cost for certain types of assets and liabilities. For example, certain investment securities are reported at fair value because market value information is usually readily available for these types of assets. In determining which measurement principle to use, companies weigh the factual nature of cost figures versus the relevance of fair value. In general, most companies choose to use cost. Only in situations where assets are actively traded, such as investment securities, do companies apply the fair value principle extensively.

INTERNATIONAL INSIGHT

The Korean Discount

If you think that accounting standards don't matter, consider recent events in South Korea. For many years, international investors complained that the financial reports of South Korean companies were inadequate and inaccurate. Accounting practices there often resulted in huge differences between stated revenues and actual revenues. Because investors did not have faith in the accuracy of the numbers, they were unwilling to pay as much for the shares of these companies relative to shares of comparable companies in different countries. This difference in stock price was often referred to as the "Korean discount."

In response, Korean regulators decided that, beginning in 2011, companies will have to comply with international accounting standards. This change was motivated by a desire to "make the country's businesses more transparent" in order to build investor confidence and spur economic growth. Many other Asian countries, including China, India, Japan, and Hong Kong, have also decided either to adopt international standards or to create standards that are based on the international standards.

Source: Evan Ramstad, "End to 'Korea Discount'?" *Wall Street Journal* (March 16, 2007).

What is meant by the phrase "make the country's businesses more transparent"? Why would increasing transparency spur economic growth? (See page 48.)

Assumptions

LEARNING OBJECTIVE 5

Explain the monetary unit assumption and the economic entity assumption.

Assumptions provide a foundation for the accounting process. Two main assumptions are the **monetary unit assumption** and the **economic entity assumption**.

MONETARY UNIT ASSUMPTION

The **monetary unit assumption** requires that companies include in the accounting records only transaction data that can be expressed in money terms. This assumption enables accounting to quantify (measure) economic events. The monetary unit assumption is vital to applying the cost principle.

This assumption prevents the inclusion of some relevant information in the accounting records. For example, the health of a company's owner, the quality of service, and the morale of employees are not included. The reason: Companies cannot quantify this information in money terms. Though this information is important, companies record only events that can be measured in money.

ECONOMIC ENTITY ASSUMPTION

An economic entity can be any organization or unit in society. It may be a company (such as Crocs, Inc.), a governmental unit (the state of Ohio), a municipality (Seattle), a school district (St. Louis District 48), or a church (Southern Baptist). The **economic entity assumption** requires that the activities of the entity be kept separate and distinct from the activities of its owner and all other economic entities. To illustrate, Sally Rider, owner of Sally's Boutique, must keep her personal living costs separate from the expenses of the boutique. Similarly, McDonald's, Coca-Cola, and Cadbury-Schweppes are segregated into separate economic entities for accounting purposes.

Ethics Note

The importance of the economic entity assumption is illustrated by scandals involving Adelphia. In this case, senior company employees entered into transactions that blurred the line between the employees' financial interests and those of the company. For example, Aldephia guaranteed over $2 billion of loans to the founding family.

PROPRIETORSHIP A business owned by one person is generally a **proprietorship**. The owner is often the manager/operator of the business. Small service-type businesses (plumbing companies, beauty salons, and auto repair shops), farms, and small retail stores (antique shops, clothing stores, and used-book stores) are often proprietorships. **Usually only a relatively small amount of money (capital) is necessary to start in business as a proprietorship. The owner (proprietor) receives any profits, suffers any losses, and is personally liable for all debts of the business.** There is no legal distinction between the business as an economic unit and the owner, but the accounting records of the business activities are kept separate from the personal records and activities of the owner.

PARTNERSHIP A business owned by two or more persons associated as partners is a **partnership**. In most respects a partnership is like a proprietorship except that more than one owner is involved. Typically a partnership agreement (written or oral) sets forth such terms as initial investment, duties of each partner, division of net income (or net loss), and settlement to be made upon death or withdrawal of a partner. Each partner generally has unlimited personal liability for the debts of the partnership. **Like a proprietorship, for accounting purposes the partnership transactions must be kept separate from the personal activities of the partners.** Partnerships are often used to organize retail and service-type businesses, including professional practices (lawyers, doctors, architects, and certified public accountants).

CORPORATION A business organized as a separate legal entity under state corporation law and having ownership divided into transferable shares of stock is a **corporation**. The holders of the shares (stockholders) **enjoy limited liability**; that is, they are not personally liable for the debts of the corporate entity. Stockholders **may transfer all or part of their ownership shares to other investors at any time** (i.e., sell their shares). The ease with which ownership can change adds to the attractiveness of investing in a corporation. Because ownership can be transferred without dissolving the corporation, the corporation **enjoys an unlimited life**.

Although the combined number of proprietorships and partnerships in the United States is more than five times the number of corporations, the revenue produced by corporations is eight times greater. Most of the largest companies in the United States—for example, ExxonMobil, Ford, Wal-Mart Stores Inc., Citigroup, and Apple—are corporations.

> DO IT!

Basic Concepts

*The **DO IT!** exercises ask you to put newly acquired knowledge to work. They outline the Action Plan necessary to complete the exercise, and they show a Solution.*

Indicate whether each of the five statements presented below is true or false.

1. The three steps in the accounting process are identification, recording, and communication.
2. The two most common types of external users are investors and company officers.
3. Congress passed the Sarbanes-Oxley Act to reduce unethical behavior and decrease the likelihood of future corporate scandals.
4. The primary accounting standard-setting body in the United States is the Financial Accounting Standards Board (FASB).
5. The cost principle dictates that companies record assets at their cost. In later periods, however, the fair value of the asset must be used if fair value is higher than its cost.

Action Plan

✔ Review the basic concepts learned to date.

✔ Develop an understanding of the key terms used.

Solution

1. True 2. False. The two most common types of external users are investors and creditors. 3. True. 4. True. 5. False. The cost principle dictates that companies record assets at their cost. Under the cost principle, the company must also use cost in later periods.

Related exercise material: **E1-1, E1-2, E1-3, E1-4, and DO IT! 1-1.**

 **The Navigator**

ACCOUNTING ACROSS THE ORGANIZATION

Spinning the Career Wheel

One question that students frequently ask is, "How will the study of accounting help me?" It should help you a great deal, because a working knowledge of accounting is desirable for virtually *every field* of endeavor. Some examples of how accounting is used in other careers include:

General management: Imagine running Ford Motors, Massachusetts General Hospital, Northern Virginia Community College, a Subway franchise, a Trek bike shop. All general managers need to understand accounting data in order to make wise business decisions.

Marketing: A marketing specialist at a company like Procter & Gamble develops strategies to help the sales force be successful. But making a sale is meaningless unless it is a profitable sale. Marketing people must be sensitive to costs and benefits, which accounting helps them quantify and understand.

Finance: Do you want to be a banker for Bank of America, an investment analyst for Goldman Sachs, a stock broker for Merrill Lynch? These fields rely heavily on accounting. In all of them you will regularly examine and analyze financial statements. In fact, it is difficult to get a good finance job without two or three courses in accounting.

Real estate: Are you interested in being a real estate broker for Prudential Real Estate? Because a third party—the bank—is almost always involved in financing a real estate transaction, brokers must understand the numbers involved: Can the buyer afford to make the payments to the bank? Does the cash flow from an industrial property justify the purchase price? What are the tax benefits of the purchase?

? How might accounting help you? (See page 48.)

The Basic Accounting Equation

LEARNING OBJECTIVE 6

State the accounting equation, and define its components.

The two basic elements of a business are what it owns and what it owes. **Assets** are the resources a business owns. For example, Google has total assets of approximately $40.5 billion. Liabilities and owner's equity are the rights or claims against these resources. Thus, Google has $40.5 billion of claims against its $40.5 billion of assets. Claims of those to whom the company owes money (creditors) are called **liabilities**. Claims of owners are called **stockholders' equity**. Google has liabilities of $4.5 billion and stockholders' equity of $36 billion.

We can express the relationship of assets, liabilities, and stockholders' equity as an equation, as shown in Illustration 1-5.

Illustration 1-5
The basic accounting equation

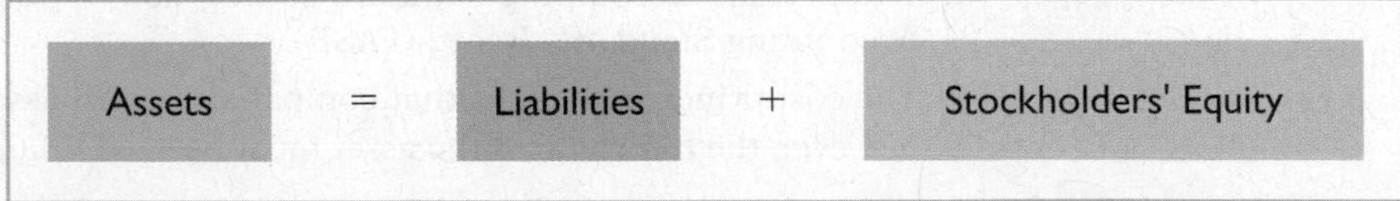

This relationship is the **basic accounting equation**. Assets must equal the sum of liabilities and stockholders' equity. Liabilities appear before stockholders' equity in the basic accounting equation because they are paid first if a business is liquidated.

The accounting equation applies to all **economic entities** regardless of size, nature of business, or form of business organization. It applies to a small proprietorship such as a corner grocery store as well as to a giant corporation such as PepsiCo. The equation provides the **underlying framework** for recording and summarizing economic events.

Let's look in more detail at the categories in the basic accounting equation.

Assets

As noted above, **assets** are resources a business owns. The business uses its assets in carrying out such activities as production and sales. The common characteristic possessed by all assets is **the capacity to provide future services or benefits**. In a business, that service potential or future economic benefit eventually results in cash inflows (receipts). For example, consider Campus Pizza, a local restaurant. It owns a delivery truck that provides economic benefits from delivering pizzas. Other assets of Campus Pizza are tables, chairs, jukebox, cash register, oven, tableware, and, of course, cash.

Liabilities

Liabilities are claims against assets—that is, existing debts and obligations. Businesses of all sizes usually borrow money and purchase merchandise on credit. These economic activities result in payables of various sorts:

- Campus Pizza, for instance, purchases cheese, sausage, flour, and beverages on credit from suppliers. These obligations are called **accounts payable**.
- Campus Pizza also has a **note payable** to First National Bank for the money borrowed to purchase the delivery truck.
- Campus Pizza may also have **salaries and wages payable** to employees and **sales and real estate taxes payable** to the local government.

All of these persons or entities to whom Campus Pizza owes money are its **creditors**.

Creditors may legally force the liquidation of a business that does not pay its debts. In that case, the law requires that creditor claims be paid **before** ownership claims.

Stockholders' Equity

The ownership claim on total assets is **stockholders' equity**. It is equal to total assets minus total liabilities. Here is why: The assets of a business are claimed by either creditors or stockholders. To find out what belongs to stockholders, we subtract creditors' claims (the liabilities) from the assets. The remainder is the stockholders' claim on the assets—stockholders' equity. It is often referred to as **residual equity**—that is, the equity "left over" after creditors' claims are satisfied.

Helpful Hint
In some situations, accountants use the term *owner's equity* and in others *owners' equity*. *Owner's* refers to one owner (the case with a sole proprietorship), and *owners'* refers to multiple owners (the case with partnerships). The term *stockholders' equity* refers to ownership in corporations.

The stockholders' equity section of a corporation's balance sheet generally consists of (1) common stock and (2) retained earnings.

COMMON STOCK

A corporation may obtain funds by selling shares of stock to investors. **Common stock** is the term used to describe the total amount paid in by stockholders for the shares they purchase.

RETAINED EARNINGS

The **retained earnings** section of the balance sheet is determined by three items: revenues, expenses, and dividends.

REVENUES **Revenues are the gross increases in stockholders' equity resulting from business activities entered into for the purpose of earning income.** Generally, revenues result from selling merchandise, performing services, renting property, and lending money.

Helpful Hint
The effect of revenues is positive—an increase in stockholders' equity coupled with an increase in assets or a decrease in liabilities.

Revenues usually result in an increase in an asset. They may arise from different sources and are called various names depending on the nature of the business. Campus Pizza, for instance, has two categories of sales revenues—pizza sales and beverage sales. Other titles for and sources of revenue common to many businesses are sales, fees, services, commissions, interest, dividends, royalties, and rent.

Helpful Hint
The effect of expenses is negative—a decrease in stockholders' equity coupled with a decrease in assets or an increase in liabilities.

EXPENSES Expenses are the cost of assets consumed or services used in the process of earning revenue. **They are decreases in stockholders' equity that result from operating the business.** Like revenues, expenses take many forms and are called various names depending on the type of asset consumed or service used. For example, Campus Pizza recognizes the following types of expenses: cost of ingredients (flour, cheese, tomato paste, meat, mushrooms, etc.); cost of beverages; wages expense; utilities expense (electric, gas, and water expense); telephone expense; delivery expense (gasoline, repairs, licenses, etc.); supplies expense (napkins, detergents, aprons, etc.); rent expense; interest expense; and property tax expense.

DIVIDENDS Net income represents an increase in net assets which are then available to distribute to stockholders. The distribution of cash or other assets to stockholders is called a **dividend**. Dividends reduce retained earnings. However, dividends are **not an expense**. A corporation first determines its revenues and expenses and then computes net income or net loss. If it has net income, and decides it has no better use for that income, a corporation may decide to distribute a dividend to its owners (the stockholders).

In summary, the principal sources (increases) of stockholders' equity are investments by stockholders and revenues from business operations. In contrast, reductions (decreases) in stockholders' equity result from expenses and dividends. These relationships are shown in Illustration 1-6.

Illustration 1-6
Increases and decreases in stockholders' equity

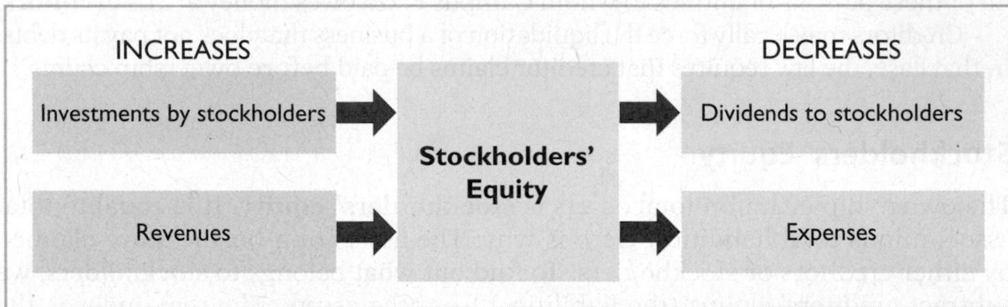

> DO IT!

Stockholders' Equity Effects

Action Plan
- ✔ Understand the sources of revenue.
- ✔ Understand what causes expenses.
- ✔ Review the rules for changes in stockholders' equity: Investments and revenues increase stockholders' equity. Expenses and dividends decrease stockholders' equity.
- ✔ Recognize that dividends are distributions of cash or other assets to stockholders.

Classify the following items as issuance of stock (I), dividends (D), revenues (R), or expenses (E). Then indicate whether each item increases or decreases stockholders' equity.

(1) Rent Expense
(2) Service Revenue
(3) Dividends
(4) Salaries and Wages Expense

Solution

1. Rent Expense is an expense (E); it decreases stockholders' equity. 2. Service Revenue is a revenue (R); it increases stockholders' equity. 3. Dividends is a distribution to stockholders (D); it decreases stockholders' equity. 4. Salaries and Wages Expense is an expense (E); it decreases stockholders' equity.

Related exercise material: **BE1-1, BE1-2, BE1-3, BE1-4, BE1-5, E1-5, E1-6, E1-7, and DO IT! 1-2.**

Using the Accounting Equation

LEARNING OBJECTIVE 7

Analyze the effects of business transactions on the accounting equation.

Transactions (**business transactions**) are a business's economic events recorded by accountants. Transactions may be external or internal. **External transactions** involve economic events between the company and some outside enterprise. For example, Campus Pizza's purchase of cooking equipment from a supplier, payment of monthly rent to the landlord, and sale of pizzas to customers are external transactions. **Internal transactions** are economic events that occur entirely within one company. The use of cooking and cleaning supplies are internal transactions for Campus Pizza.

Companies carry on many activities that do not represent business transactions. Examples are hiring employees, answering the telephone, talking with customers, and placing merchandise orders. Some of these activities may lead to business transactions: Employees will earn wages, and suppliers will deliver ordered merchandise. The company must analyze each event to find out if it affects the components of the accounting equation. If it does, the company will record the transaction. Illustration 1-7 demonstrates the transaction-identification process.

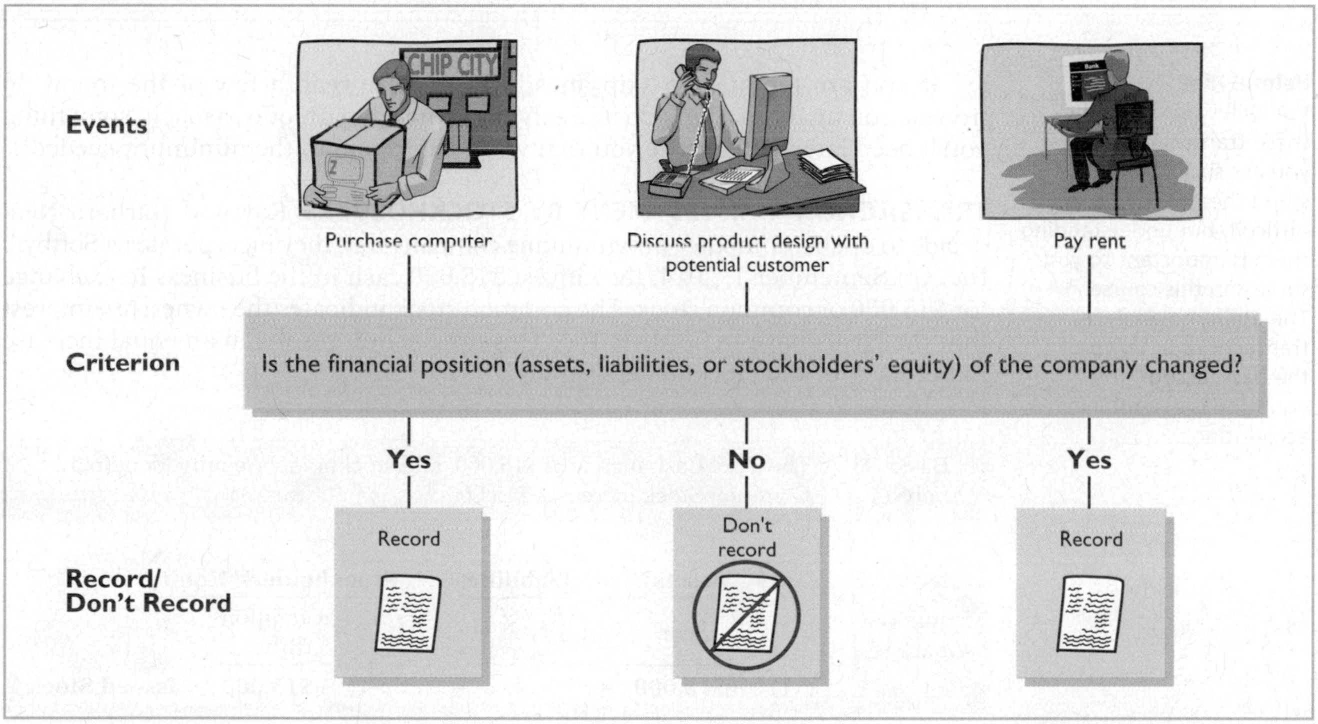

Illustration 1-7
Transaction-identification process

Each transaction must have a dual effect on the accounting equation. For example, if an asset is increased, there must be a corresponding (1) decrease in another asset, (2) increase in a specific liability, or (3) increase in stockholders' equity.

Two or more items could be affected. For example, as one asset is increased $10,000, another asset could decrease $6,000 and a liability could increase $4,000. Any change in a liability or ownership claim is subject to similar analysis.

Transaction Analysis

In order to analyze transactions, we will examine a computer programming business (Softbyte Inc.) during its first month of operations. As part of this analysis, we will expand the basic accounting equation. This will allow us to better illustrate the impact of transactions on stockholders' equity. Recall that stockholders' equity is comprised of two parts: common stock and retained earnings. Common stock is affected when the company issues new shares of stock in exchange for cash. Retained earnings is affected when the company earns revenue, incurs expenses, or pays dividends. Illustration 1-8 shows the **expanded accounting equation.**

Illustration 1-8
Expanded accounting equation

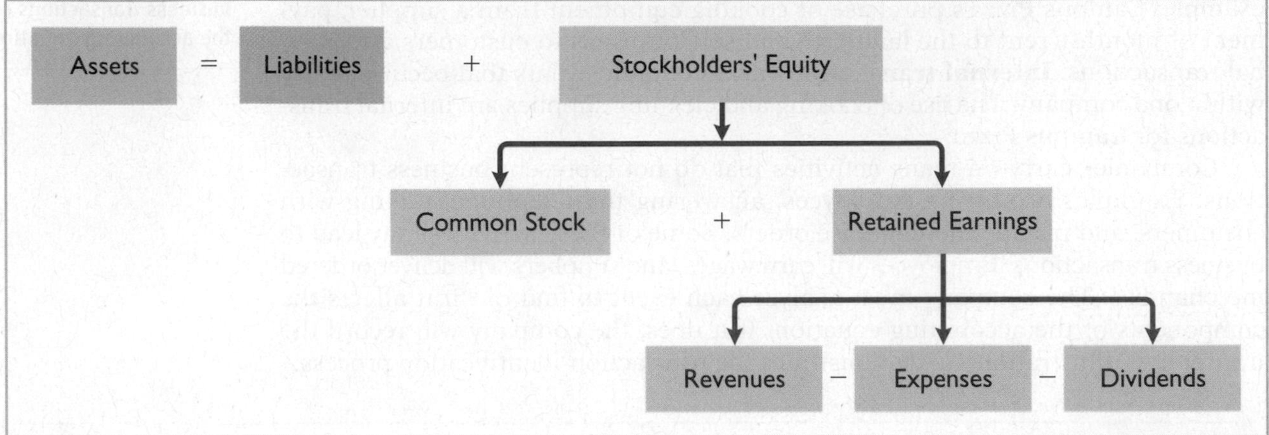

Helpful Hint
You will want to study these transactions until you are sure you understand them. They are not difficult, but understanding them is important to your success in this course. The ability to analyze transactions in terms of the basic accounting equation is essential in accounting.

If you are tempted to skip ahead after you've read a few of the following transaction analyses, don't do it. Each has something unique to teach, something you'll need later. (We assure you that we've kept them to the minimum needed!)

TRANSACTION 1. INVESTMENT BY STOCKHOLDERS Ray and Barbara Neal decide to open a computer programming company that they incorporate as Softbyte Inc. On September 1, 2014, they invest $15,000 cash in the business in exchange for $15,000 of common stock. The common stock indicates the ownership interest that the Neals have in Softbyte Inc. This transaction results in an equal increase in both assets and stockholders' equity.

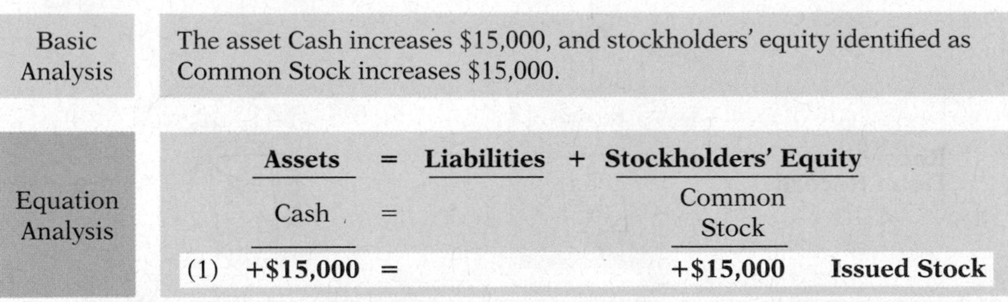

Basic Analysis: The asset Cash increases $15,000, and stockholders' equity identified as Common Stock increases $15,000.

Equation Analysis:

	Assets	=	Liabilities	+	Stockholders' Equity	
	Cash	=			Common Stock	
(1)	+$15,000	=			+$15,000	Issued Stock

Observe that the equality of the basic equation has been maintained. Note also that the source of the increase in stockholders' equity (in this case, issued stock) is indicated. Why does this matter? Because investments by stockholders do not represent revenues, and they are excluded in determining net income. Therefore, it is necessary to make clear that the increase is an investment rather than revenue from operations. Additional investments (i.e., investments made by stockholders after the corporation has been initially formed) have the same effect on stockholders' equity as the initial investment.

TRANSACTION 2. PURCHASE OF EQUIPMENT FOR CASH Softbyte Inc. purchases computer equipment for $7,000 cash. This transaction results in an equal increase and decrease in total assets, though the composition of assets changes.

Basic Analysis	Cash decreases $7,000, and the asset Equipment increases $7,000.

Equation Analysis

	Assets			=	Liabilities	+	Stockholders' Equity
	Cash	+	Equipment	=			Common Stock
	$15,000						$15,000
(2)	**−7,000**		**+$7,000**				
	$ 8,000	+	$ 7,000	=			$15,000
	$15,000						

Observe that total assets are still $15,000. Common stock also remains at $15,000, the amount of the original investment.

TRANSACTION 3. PURCHASE OF SUPPLIES ON CREDIT Softbyte Inc. purchases for $1,600 from Acme Supply Company computer paper and other supplies expected to last several months. Acme agrees to allow Softbyte to pay this bill in October. This transaction is a purchase on account (a credit purchase). Assets increase because of the expected future benefits of using the paper and supplies, and liabilities increase by the amount due Acme Company.

Basic Analysis	The asset Supplies increases $1,600, and the liability Accounts Payable increases by $1,600.

Equation Analysis

	Assets					=	Liabilities	+	Stockholders' Equity
	Cash	+	Supplies	+	Equipment	=	Accounts Payable	+	Common Stock
	$8,000				$7,000				$15,000
(3)			**+$1,600**				**+$1,600**		
	$8,000	+	$ 1,600	+	$7,000	=	$ 1,600	+	$15,000
			$16,600				$16,600		

Total assets are now $16,600. This total is matched by a $1,600 creditor's claim and a $15,000 ownership claim.

TRANSACTION 4. SERVICES PROVIDED FOR CASH Softbyte Inc. receives $1,200 cash from customers for programming services it has provided. This transaction represents Softbyte's principal revenue-producing activity. Recall that **revenue increases stockholders' equity**.

Basic Analysis	Cash increases $1,200, and revenues (specifically, Service Revenue) increase $1,200.

Equation Analysis

	Assets					=	Liabilities	+	Stockholders' Equity							
											Retained Earnings					
	Cash	+	Supplies	+	Equipment	=	Accounts Payable	+	Common Stock	+	Rev.	−	Exp.	−	Div.	
	$8,000		$1,600		$7,000		$1,600		$15,000							
(4)	**+1,200**										**+$1,200**					**Service Revenue**
	$9,200	+	$1,600	+	$7,000	=	$1,600	+	$15,000	+	$ 1,200					
			$17,800						$17,800							

The two sides of the equation balance at $17,800. Service Revenue is included in determining Softbyte's net income.

Note that we do not have room to give details for each individual revenue and expense account in this illustration. Thus, revenues (and expenses when we get to them) are summarized under one column heading for Revenues and one for Expenses. However, it is important to keep track of the category (account) titles affected (e.g., Service Revenue) as they will be needed when we prepare financial statements later in the chapter.

TRANSACTION 5. PURCHASE OF ADVERTISING ON CREDIT Softbyte receives a bill for $250 from the *Daily News* for advertising but postpones payment until a later date. This transaction results in an increase in liabilities and a decrease in stockholders' equity.

Basic Analysis Accounts Payable increases $250, and stockholders' equity decreases $250 due to Advertising Expense.

Equation Analysis

	Assets			= Liabilities +	Stockholders' Equity				
	Cash	+ Supplies	+ Equipment	= Accounts Payable	+ Common Stock	+ Retained Earnings Rev.	− Exp.	− Div.	
	$9,200	$1,600	$7,000	$1,600	$15,000	$1,200			
(5)				**+250**			**−$250**		**Advertising Expense**
	$9,200 +	$1,600 +	$7,000	= $1,850	+ $15,000	+ $1,200	− $250		
	$17,800			$17,800					

The two sides of the equation still balance at $17,800. Retained Earnings decreases when Softbyte incurs the expense. Expenses do not have to be paid in cash at the time they are incurred. When Softbyte pays at a later date, the liability Accounts Payable will decrease and the asset Cash will decrease (see Transaction 8). The cost of advertising is an expense (rather than an asset) because Softbyte has used the benefits. Advertising Expense is included in determining net income.

TRANSACTION 6. SERVICES RENDERED FOR CASH AND CREDIT Softbyte Inc. provides $3,500 of programming services for customers. The company receives cash of $1,500 from customers, and it bills the balance of $2,000 on account. This transaction results in an equal increase in assets and stockholders' equity.

Basic Analysis Three specific items are affected: Cash increases $1,500, Accounts Receivable increases $2,000, and Service Revenue increases $3,500.

Equation Analysis

	Assets				= Liabilities +	Stockholders' Equity				
	Cash	+ Accounts Receivable	+ Supplies	+ Equipment	= Accounts Payable	+ Common Stock	+ Retained Earnings Rev.	− Exp.	− Div.	
	$ 9,200		$1,600	$7,000	$1,850	$15,000	$1,200	$250		
(6)	**+1,500**	**+$2,000**					**+3,500**			**Service Revenue**
	$10,700 +	$ 2,000 +	$1,600 +	$7,000	= $1,850	+ $15,000	+ $4,700	− $250		
	$21,300				$21,300					

Softbyte earns revenues when it provides the service, and therefore it recognizes $3,500 in revenue. In exchange for this service, it received $1,500 in Cash and Accounts Receivable of $2,000. This Accounts Receivable represents customers' promise to pay $2,000 to Softbyte in the future. When it later receives collections on account, Softbyte will increase Cash and will decrease Accounts Receivable (see Transaction 9).

TRANSACTION 7. PAYMENT OF EXPENSES Softbyte pays the following expenses in cash for September: store rent $600, salaries and wages of employees $900, and utilities $200. These payments result in an equal decrease in assets and expenses.

Basic Analysis	Cash decreases $1,700, and the specific expense categories (Rent Expense, Salaries and Wages Expense, and Utilities Expense) decrease stockholders' equity by the same amount.

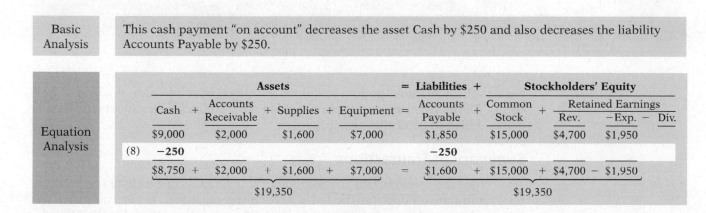

Equation Analysis

	Assets				= Liabilities +	Stockholders' Equity				
	Cash +	Accounts Receivable +	Supplies +	Equipment =	Accounts Payable +	Common Stock +	Retained Earnings Rev. −	Exp. −	Div.	
	$10,700	$2,000	$1,600	$7,000	$1,850	$15,000	$4,700	$ 250		
(7)	−1,700							−600		Rent Exp.
								−900		Sal./Wages Exp.
								−200		Utilities Exp.
	$ 9,000 +	$2,000 +	$1,600 +	$7,000 =	$1,850 +	$15,000 +	$4,700 −	$1,950		
	$19,600				$19,600					

The two sides of the equation now balance at $19,600. Three lines are required in the analysis to indicate the different types of expenses that have been incurred.

TRANSACTION 8. PAYMENT OF ACCOUNTS PAYABLE Softbyte pays its $250 *Daily News* bill in cash. The company previously (in Transaction 5) recorded the bill as an increase in Accounts Payable and a decrease in stockholders' equity.

Basic Analysis	This cash payment "on account" decreases the asset Cash by $250 and also decreases the liability Accounts Payable by $250.

Equation Analysis

	Assets				= Liabilities +	Stockholders' Equity			
	Cash +	Accounts Receivable +	Supplies +	Equipment =	Accounts Payable +	Common Stock +	Retained Earnings Rev.	− Exp. −	Div.
	$9,000	$2,000	$1,600	$7,000	$1,850	$15,000	$4,700	$1,950	
(8)	−250				−250				
	$8,750 +	$2,000 +	$1,600 +	$7,000 =	$1,600 +	$15,000 +	$4,700 −	$1,950	
	$19,350				$19,350				

Observe that the payment of a liability related to an expense that has previously been recorded does not affect stockholders' equity. Softbyte recorded the expense (in Transaction 5) and should not record it again.

TRANSACTION 9. RECEIPT OF CASH ON ACCOUNT Softbyte receives $600 in cash from customers who had been billed for services (in Transaction 6). This transaction does not change total assets, but it changes the composition of those assets.

Basic Analysis Cash increases $600, and Accounts Receivable decreases $600.

Equation Analysis

	Assets							=	Liabilities	+	Stockholders' Equity						
	Cash	+	Accounts Receivable	+	Supplies	+	Equipment	=	Accounts Payable	+	Common Stock	+	Retained Earnings Rev.	−	Exp.	−	Div.
	$8,750		$2,000		$1,600		$7,000		$1,600		$15,000		$4,700		$1,950		
(9)	+600		−600														
	$9,350	+	$1,400	+	$1,600	+	$7,000	=	$1,600	+	$15,000	+	$4,700	−	$1,950		
	$19,350								$19,350								

Note that the collection of an account receivable for services previously billed and recorded does not affect stockholders' equity. Softbyte already recorded this revenue (in Transaction 6) and should not record it again.

TRANSACTION 10. DIVIDENDS The corporation pays a dividend of $1,300 in cash to Ray and Barbara Neal, the stockholders of Softbyte Inc. This transaction results in an equal decrease in assets and stockholders' equity.

Basic Analysis Cash decreases $1,300, and stockholders' equity decreases $1,300 due to dividends.

Equation Analysis

	Assets							=	Liabilities	+	Stockholders' Equity							
	Cash	+	Accounts Receivable	+	Supplies	+	Equipment	=	Accounts Payable	+	Common Stock	+	Retained Earnings Rev.	−	Exp.	−	Div.	
	$ 9,350		$1,400		$1,600		$7,000		$1,600		$15,000		$4,700		$1,950			
(10)	−1,300																−$1,300	Dividends
	$ 8,050	+	$1,400	+	$1,600	+	$7,000	=	$1,600	+	$15,000	+	$4,700	−	$1,950	−	$ 1,300	
	$18,050								$18,050									

Note that the dividend reduces retained earnings, which is part of stockholders' equity. **Dividends are not expenses.** Like stockholders' investments, dividends are excluded in determining net income.

Summary of Transactions

Illustration 1-9 summarizes the September transactions of Softbyte Inc. to show their cumulative effect on the basic accounting equation. It also indicates the transaction number and the specific effects of each transaction. Finally, Illustration 1-9 demonstrates a number of significant facts:

1. Each transaction must be analyzed in terms of its effect on:
   (a) The three components of the basic accounting equation.
   (b) Specific types (kinds) of items within each component.
2. The two sides of the equation must always be equal.
3. The Common Stock and Retained Earnings columns indicate the causes of each change in the stockholders' claim on assets.

Transaction	Cash	+ Accounts Receivable	+ Supplies	+ Equipment	= Accounts Payable	+ Common Stock	+ Rev.	− Exp.	− Div.	
	Assets				**= Liabilities +**	**Stockholders' Equity**	Retained Earnings			
(1)	+$15,000					+ $15,000				**Issued Stock**
(2)	−7,000			+$7,000						
(3)			+$1,600		+$1,600					
(4)	+1,200						+$1,200			**Service Revenue**
(5)					+250			−$250		**Advert. Expense**
(6)	+1,500	+$2,000					+3,500			**Service Revenue**
(7)	−1,700							−600		**Rent Expense**
								−900		**Sal./Wages Exp.**
								−200		**Utilities Expense**
(8)	−250				−250					
(9)	+600	−600								
(10)	−1,300								−$1,300	**Dividends**
	$ 8,050 +	$1,400 +	$1,600 +	$7,000 =	$1,600 +	$15,000 +	$4,700 −	$1,950 −	$1,300	
	$18,050				**$18,050**					

Illustration 1-9
Tabular summary of Softbyte Inc. transactions

There! You made it through transaction analysis. If you feel a bit shaky on any of the transactions, it might be a good idea at this point to get up, take a short break, and come back again for a brief (10- to 15-minute) review of the transactions, to make sure you understand them before you go on to the next section.

> DO IT!

Tabular Analysis

Action Plan

✔ Analyze the effects of each transaction on the accounting equation.

✔ Use appropriate category names (not descriptions).

✔ Keep the accounting equation in balance.

Transactions made by Virmari & Co., a public accounting firm, for the month of August are shown below. Prepare a tabular analysis which shows the effects of these transactions on the expanded accounting equation, similar to that shown in Illustration 1-9.

1. Stockholders purchased shares of stock for $25,000 cash.
2. The company purchased $7,000 of office equipment on credit.
3. The company received $8,000 cash in exchange for services performed.
4. The company paid $850 for this month's rent.
5. The company paid a dividend of $1,000 in cash to stockholders.

Solution

Transaction	Cash	+ Equipment	= Accounts Payable	+ Common Stock	+ Rev.	− Exp.	− Div.	
	Assets		**= Liabilities +**	**Stockholders' Equity**	Retained Earnings			
(1)	+$25,000			+$25,000				
(2)		+$7,000	+$7,000					
(3)	+8,000				+$8,000			**Service Revenue**
(4)	−850					−$850		**Rent Expense**
(5)	−1,000						− $1,000	**Dividends**
	$31,150 +	$7,000 =	$7,000 +	$25,000 +	$8,000 −	$850 −	$1,000	
	$38,150		$38,150					

Related exercise material: **BE1-6, BE1-7, BE1-8, BE1-9, E1-6, E1-7, E1-8, E1-9, E1-10,** and **DO IT! 1-3.**

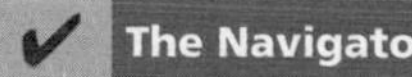

Financial Statements

LEARNING OBJECTIVE 8

Understand the four financial statements and how they are prepared.

Companies prepare four financial statements from the summarized accounting data:

1. An **income statement** presents the revenues and expenses and resulting net income or net loss for a specific period of time.
2. A **retained earnings statement** summarizes the changes in retained earnings for a specific period of time.
3. A **balance sheet** reports the assets, liabilities, and stockholders' equity of a company at a specific date.
4. A **statement of cash flows** summarizes information about the cash inflows (receipts) and outflows (payments) for a specific period of time.

International Note

The primary types of financial statements required by GAAP and IFRS are the same. In practice, some format differences do exist in presentations employed by GAAP companies compared to IFRS companies.

These statements provide relevant financial data for internal and external users. Illustration 1-10 shows the financial statements of Softbyte Inc. Note that the statements shown in Illustration 1-10 are interrelated:

1. Net income of $2,750 on the **income statement** is added to the beginning balance of retained earnings in the **retained earnings statement**.
2. Retained earnings of $1,450 at the end of the reporting period shown in the **retained earnings statement** is reported on the **balance sheet**.
3. Cash of $8,050 on the **balance sheet** is reported on the **statement of cash flows**.

Helpful Hint
The income statement, retained earnings statement, and statement of cash flows are all for a *period* of time, whereas the balance sheet is for a *point* in time.

Also, explanatory notes and supporting schedules are an integral part of every set of financial statements. We illustrate these notes and schedules in later chapters of this textbook.

Be sure to carefully examine the format and content of each statement in Illustration 1-10. We describe the essential features of each in the following sections.

Income Statement

The income statement reports the success or profitability of the company's operations over a specific period of time. For example, Softbyte Inc.'s income statement is dated "For the Month Ended September 30, 2014." It is prepared from the data appearing in the revenue and expense columns of Illustration 1-9 (page 21). The heading of the statement identifies the company, the type of statement, and the time period covered by the statement.

Alternative Terminology
The income statement is sometimes referred to as the *statement of operations, earnings statement,* or *profit and loss statement.*

Alternative Terminology notes present synonymous terms that you may come across in practice.

The income statement lists revenues first, followed by expenses. Finally, the statement shows net income (or net loss). When revenues exceed expenses, **net income** results. When expenses exceed revenues, a **net loss** results.

Although practice varies, we have chosen in our illustrations and homework solutions to list expenses in order of magnitude. (We will consider alternative formats for the income statement in later chapters.)

Note that the income statement does not include investment and dividend transactions between the stockholders and the business in measuring net income. For example, as explained earlier, the cash dividend from Softbyte Inc. was not regarded as a business expense. This type of transaction is considered a reduction of retained earnings, which causes a decrease in stockholders' equity.

Retained Earnings Statement

Softbyte Inc.'s retained earnings statement reports the changes in retained earnings for a specific period of time. The time period is the same as that covered by

Illustration 1-10
Financial statements and their interrelationships

Softbyte Inc.
Income Statement
For the Month Ended September 30, 2014

Revenues		
Service revenue		$ 4,700
Expenses		
Salaries and wages expense	$900	
Rent expense	600	
Advertising expense	250	
Utilities expense	200	
Total expenses		1,950
Net income		**$2,750**

Softbyte Inc.
Retained Earnings Statement
For the Month Ended September 30, 2014

Retained earnings, September 1	$ 0
Add: Net income	**2,750**
	2,750
Less: Dividends	1,300
Retained earnings, September 30	**$1,450**

Softbyte Inc.
Balance Sheet
September 30, 2014

Assets		
Cash		**$ 8,050**
Accounts receivable		1,400
Supplies		1,600
Equipment		7,000
Total assets		$18,050
Liabilities and Stockholders' Equity		
Liabilities		
Accounts payable		$ 1,600
Stockholders' equity		
Common stock	**$15,000**	
Retained earnings	**1,450**	**16,450**
Total liabilities and stockholder's equity		$18,050

Softbyte Inc.
Statement of Cash Flows
For the Month Ended September 30, 2014

Cash flows from operating activities		
Cash receipts from revenues		$ 3,300
Cash payments for expenses		(1,950)
Net cash provided by operating activities		1,350
Cash flows from investing activities		
Purchase of equipment		(7,000)
Cash flows from financing activities		
Sale of common stock	$15,000)	
Payment of cash dividends	(1,300)	13,700
Net increase in cash		8,050
Cash at the beginning of the period		0
Cash at the end of the period		**$8,050**

Helpful Hint The heading of each statement identifies the company, the type of statement, and the specific date or time period covered by the statement.

Helpful Hint Note that final sums are double-underlined, and negative amounts (in the statement of cash flows) are presented in parentheses.

Helpful Hint The arrows in this illustration show the interrelationships of the four financial statements.
1. Net income is computed first and is needed to determine the ending balance in retained earnings.
2. The ending balance in retained earnings is needed in preparing the balance sheet.
3. The cash shown on the balance sheet is needed in preparing the statement of cash flows.

the income statement ("For the Month Ended September 30, 2014"). Data for the preparation of the retained earnings statement come from the retained earnings columns of the tabular summary (Illustration 1-9) and from the income statement (Illustration 1-10, page 23).

The first line of the statement shows the beginning retained earnings amount. Then come net income and dividends. The retained earnings ending balance is the final amount on the statement. The information provided by this statement indicates the reasons why retained earnings increased or decreased during the period. If there is a net loss, it is deducted with dividends in the retained earnings statement.

Balance Sheet

Softbyte Inc.'s balance sheet reports the assets, liabilities, and stockholders' equity at a specific date (September 30, 2014). The company prepares the balance sheet from the column headings and the month-end data shown in the last line of the tabular summary (Illustration 1-9).

Observe that the balance sheet lists assets at the top, followed by liabilities and stockholders' equity. Total assets must equal total liabilities and stockholders' equity. Softbyte Inc. reports only one liability, Accounts Payable, on its balance sheet. In most cases, there will be more than one liability. When two or more liabilities are involved, a customary way of listing is as shown in Illustration 1-11.

Illustration 1-11
Presentation of liabilities

Liabilities	
Notes payable	$ 10,000
Accounts payable	63,000
Salaries and wages payable	18,000
Total liabilities	**$91,000**

The balance sheet is like a snapshot of the company's financial condition at a specific moment in time (usually the month-end or year-end).

Statement of Cash Flows

Helpful Hint
Investing activities pertain to investments made by the company, not investments made by the owners.

The statement of cash flows provides information on the cash receipts and payments for a specific period of time. The statement of cash flows reports (1) the cash effects of a company's operations during a period, (2) its investing transactions, (3) its financing transactions, (4) the net increase or decrease in cash during the period, and (5) the cash amount at the end of the period.

Reporting the sources, uses, and change in cash is useful because investors, creditors, and others want to know what is happening to a company's most liquid resource. The statement of cash flows provides answers to the following simple but important questions.

1. Where did cash come from during the period?
2. What was cash used for during the period?
3. What was the change in the cash balance during the period?

As shown in Softbyte Inc.'s statement of cash flows in Illustration 1-10, cash increased $8,050 during the period. Net cash flow provided from operating activities increased cash $1,350. Cash flow from investing transactions decreased cash $7,000. And cash flow from financing transactions increased cash $13,700. At this time, you need not be concerned with how these amounts are determined. Chapter 13 will examine in detail how the statement is prepared.

PEOPLE, PLANET, AND PROFIT INSIGHT

Beyond Financial Statements

Should we expand our financial statements beyond the income statement, retained earnings statement, balance sheet, and statement of cash flows? Some believe we should take into account ecological and social performance, in addition to financial results, in evaluating a company. The argument is that a company's responsibility lies with anyone who is influenced by its actions. In other words, a company should be interested in benefiting many different parties, instead of only maximizing stockholder's interests.

A socially responsible business does not exploit or endanger any group of individuals. It follows fair trade practices, provides safe environments for workers, and bears responsibility for environmental damage. Granted, measurement of these factors is difficult. How to report this information is also controversial. But, many interesting and useful efforts are underway. Throughout this textbook, we provide additional insights into how companies are attempting to meet the challenge of measuring and reporting their contributions to society, as well as their financial results, to stockholders.

? Why might a company's stockholders be interested in its environmental and social performance? (See page 48.)

> DO IT!

Financial Statement Items

Presented below is selected information related to Flanagan Corporation at December 31, 2014. Flanagan reports financial information monthly.

Equipment	$10,000	Utilities Expense	$ 4,000
Cash	8,000	Accounts Receivable	9,000
Service Revenue	36,000	Salaries and Wages Expense	7,000
Rent Expense	11,000	Notes Payable	16,500
Accounts Payable	2,000	Dividends	5,000

(a) Determine the total assets of Flanagan at December 31, 2014.

(b) Determine the net income that Flanagan reported for December 2014.

(c) Determine the stockholders' equity of Flanagan at December 31, 2014.

Action Plan

✔ Remember the basic accounting equation: assets must equal liabilities plus stockholders' equity.

✔ Review previous financial statements to determine how total assets, net income, and stockholders' equity are computed.

Solution

(a) The total assets are $27,000, comprised of Cash $8,000, Accounts Receivable $9,000, and Equipment $10,000.

(b) Net income is $14,000, computed as follows.

Revenues		
Service revenue		$36,000
Expenses		
Rent expense	$11,000	
Salaries and wages expense	7,000	
Utilities expense	4,000	
Total expenses		22,000
Net income		$14,000

(c) The ending stockholders' equity of Flanagan Corporation is $8,500. By rewriting the accounting equation, we can compute stockholders' equity as assets minus liabilities, as follows.

Total assets [as computed in (a)]		$27,000
Less: Liabilities		
Notes payable	$16,500	
Accounts payable	2,000	18,500
Stockholders' equity		$ 8,500

Note that it is not possible to determine the corporation's stockholders' equity in any other way, because the beginning total for stockholders' equity is not provided.

Related exercise material: **BE1-10, BE1-11, E1-9, E1-12, E1-13, E1-14, E1-15, E1-16, and DO IT! 1-4.**

Comprehensive DO IT!

The ***Comprehensive DO IT!*** *is a final review of the chapter. The* ***Action Plan*** *gives tips about how to approach the problem, and the* ***Solution*** *demonstrates both the form and content of complete answers.*

Legal Services Inc. was incorporated on July 1, 2014. During the first month of operations, the following transactions occurred.

1. Stockholders invested $10,000 in cash in exchange for common stock of Legal Services Inc.
2. Paid $800 for July rent on office space.
3. Purchased office equipment on account $3,000.
4. Provided legal services to clients for cash $1,500.
5. Borrowed $700 cash from a bank on a note payable.
6. Performed legal services for client on account $2,000.
7. Paid monthly expenses: salaries $500, utilities $300, and advertising $100.

Instructions

(a) Prepare a tabular summary of the transactions.

(b) Prepare the income statement, retained earnings statement, and balance sheet at July 31 for Legal Services Inc.

Solution to Comprehensive DO IT!

(a)

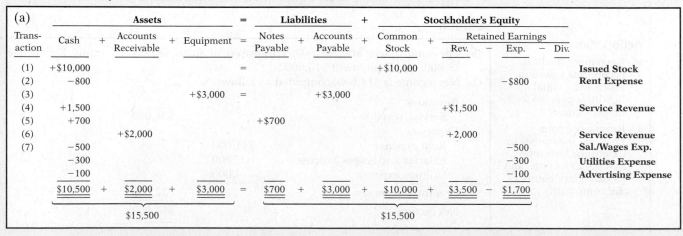

	Assets				=	Liabilities			+	Stockholder's Equity									
												Retained Earnings							
Transaction	Cash	+	Accounts Receivable	+	Equipment	=	Notes Payable	+	Accounts Payable	+	Common Stock	+	Rev.	−	Exp.	−	Div.	
(1)	+$10,000					=					+$10,000							**Issued Stock**
(2)	−800														−$800			**Rent Expense**
(3)					+$3,000	=			+$3,000									
(4)	+1,500												+$1,500					**Service Revenue**
(5)	+700						+$700											
(6)			+$2,000										+2,000					**Service Revenue**
(7)	−500														−500			**Sal./Wages Exp.**
	−300														−300			**Utilities Expense**
	−100														−100			**Advertising Expense**
	$10,500	+	$2,000	+	$3,000	=	$700	+	$3,000	+	$10,000	+	$3,500	−	$1,700			
	$15,500						$15,500											

Action Plan

- ✔ Make sure that assets equal liabilities plus stockholders' equity after each transaction.
- ✔ Investments and revenues increase stockholders' equity. Dividends and expenses decrease stockholders' equity.
- ✔ Prepare the financial statements in the order listed.
- ✔ The income statement shows revenues and expenses for a period of time.
- ✔ The retained earnings statement shows the changes in retained earnings for the same period of time as the income statement.
- ✔ The balance sheet reports assets, liabilities, and stockholders' equity at a specific date.

(b)

Legal Services Inc.
Income Statement
For the Month Ended July 31, 2014

Revenues		
Service revenue		$3,500
Expenses		
Rent expense	$800	
Salaries and wages expense	500	
Utilities expense	300	
Advertising expense	100	
Total expenses		1,700
Net income		$1,800

Legal Services Inc.
Retained Earnings Statement
For the Month Ended July 31, 2014

Retained earnings, July 1	$ –0–
Add: Net income	1,800
Retained earnings, July 31	$1,800

Legal Services Inc.
Balance Sheet
July 31, 2014

Assets		
Cash		$10,500
Accounts receivable		2,000
Equipment		3,000
Total assets		$15,500
Liabilities and Stockholder's Equity		
Liabilities		
Notes payable	$ 700	
Accounts payable	3,000	
Total liabilities		$ 3,700
Stockholder's equity		
Common stock	10,000	
Retained earnings	1,800	11,800
Total liabilities and stockholder's equity		$15,500

 The Navigator

SUMMARY OF LEARNING OBJECTIVES

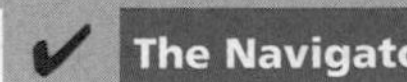

1 **Explain what accounting is.** Accounting is an information system that identifies, records, and communicates the economic events of an organization to interested users.

2 **Identify the users and uses of accounting.** The major users and uses of accounting are as follows. (a) Management uses accounting information to plan, organize, and run the business. (b) Investors (owners) decide whether to buy, hold, or sell their financial interests on the basis of accounting data. (c) Creditors (suppliers and bankers) evaluate the risks of granting credit or lending money on the basis of accounting information. Other groups that use accounting information are taxing authorities, regulatory agencies, customers, and labor unions.

3 **Understand why ethics is a fundamental business concept.** Ethics are the standards of conduct by which actions are judged as right or wrong. Effective financial reporting depends on sound ethical behavior.

4 **Explain generally accepted accounting principles.** Generally accepted accounting principles are a common set of standards used by accountants.

5 **Explain the monetary unit assumption and the economic entity assumption.** The monetary unit assumption requires that companies include in the accounting records only transaction data that can be expressed in terms of money. The economic entity assumption requires that the activities of each economic entity be kept separate from the activities of its owner(s) and other economic entities.

6 **State the accounting equation, and define its components.** The basic accounting equation is:

Assets = Liabilities + Stockholders' Equity

Assets are resources a business owns. Liabilities are creditorship claims on total assets. Stockholders' equity is the ownership claim on total assets.

The expanded accounting equation is:

Assets = Liabilities + Common Stock + Revenues − Expenses − Dividends

Common stock is affected when the company issues new shares of stock in exchange for cash. Revenues are increases in assets resulting from income-earning activities. Expenses are the costs of assets consumed or services used in the process of earning revenue. Dividends are payments the company makes to its stockholders.

7 **Analyze the effects of business transactions on the accounting equation.** Each business transaction must have a dual effect on the accounting equation. For example, if an individual asset increases, there must be a corresponding (1) decrease in another asset, or (2) increase in a specific liability, or (3) increase in stockholders' equity.

8 **Understand the four financial statements and how they are prepared.** An income statement presents the revenues and expenses, and resulting net income or net loss, for a specific period of time. A retained earnings statement summarizes the changes in retained earnings for a specific period of time. A balance sheet reports the assets, liabilities, and stockholders' equity at a specific date. A statement of cash flows summarizes information about the cash inflows (receipts) and outflows (payments) for a specific period of time.

GLOSSARY

Accounting The information system that identifies, records, and communicates the economic events of an organization to interested users. (p. 4).

Assets Resources a business owns. (p. 13).

Balance sheet A financial statement that reports the assets, liabilities, and stockholders' equity of a company at a specific date. (p. 22).

Basic accounting equation Assets = Liabilities + Stockholders' Equity. (p. 12).

Bookkeeping A part of accounting that involves only the recording of economic events. (p. 5).

Common stock Term used to describe the total amount paid in by stockholders for the shares they purchase. (p. 13).

Convergence Effort to reduce differences between U.S. GAAP and IFRS to enhance comparability. (p. 9).

Corporation A business organized as a separate legal entity under state corporation law, having ownership divided into transferable shares of stock. (p. 11).

Cost principle An accounting principle that states that companies should record assets at their cost. (p. 9).

Dividend A distribution by a corporation to its stockholders. (p. 14).

Economic entity assumption An assumption that requires that the activities of the entity be kept separate and distinct from the activities of its owner and all other economic entities. (p. 10).

Ethics The standards of conduct by which one's actions are judged as right or wrong, honest or dishonest, fair or not fair. (p. 7).

Expanded accounting equation Assets = Liabilities + Common Stock + Revenues − Expenses − Dividends. (p. 16).

Expenses The cost of assets consumed or services used in the process of earning revenue. (p. 14).

Fair value principle An accounting principle stating that assets and liabilities should be reported at fair value (the price received to sell an asset or settle a liability). (p. 9).

Faithful representation Numbers and descriptions match what really existed or happened—it is factual. (p. 9).

Financial accounting The field of accounting that provides economic and financial information for investors, creditors, and other external users. (p. 6).

Financial Accounting Standards Board (FASB) A private organization that establishes generally accepted accounting principles in the United States (GAAP). (p. 9).

Generally accepted accounting principles (GAAP) Common standards that indicate how to report economic events. (p. 8).

Income statement A financial statement that presents the revenues and expenses and resulting net income or net loss of a company for a specific period of time. (p. 22).

International Accounting Standards Board (IASB) An accounting standard-setting body that issues standards adopted by many countries outside of the United States. (p. 9).

International Financial Reporting Standards (IFRS) International accounting standards set by the International Accounting Standards Board (IASB). (p. 9).

Liabilities Creditor claims on total assets. (p. 13).

Managerial accounting The field of accounting that provides internal reports to help users make decisions about their companies. (p. 6).

Monetary unit assumption An assumption stating that companies include in the accounting records only transaction data that can be expressed in terms of money. (p. 10).

Net income The amount by which revenues exceed expenses. (p. 22).

Net loss The amount by which expenses exceed revenues. (p. 22).

Partnership A business owned by two or more persons associated as partners. (p. 11).

Proprietorship A business owned by one person. (p. 10).

Relevance Financial information that is capable of making a difference in a decision. (p. 9).

Retained earnings statement A financial statement that summarizes the changes in retained earnings for a specific period of time. (p. 22).

Revenues The gross increase in stockholders' equity resulting from business activities entered into for the purpose of earning income. (p. 13).

Sarbanes-Oxley Act (SOX) Law passed by Congress in 2002 intended to reduce unethical corporate behavior. (p. 7).

Securities and Exchange Commission (SEC) A governmental agency that oversees U.S. financial markets and accounting standard-setting bodies. (p. 9).

Statement of cash flows A financial statement that summarizes information about the cash inflows (receipts) and cash outflows (payments) for a specific period of time. (p. 22).

Stockholders' equity The ownership claim on a corporation's total assets. (p. 13).

Transactions The economic events of a business that are recorded by accountants. (p. 15).

APPENDIX 1A ACCOUNTING CAREER OPPORTUNITIES

LEARNING OBJECTIVE 9

Explain the career opportunities in accounting.

Why is accounting such a popular major and career choice? First, there are a lot of jobs. In many cities in recent years, the demand for accountants exceeded the supply. Not only are there a lot of jobs, but there are a wide array of opportunities. As one accounting organization observed, "accounting is one degree with 360 degrees of opportunity."

Accounting is also hot because it is obvious that accounting matters. Interest in accounting has increased, ironically, because of the attention caused by the accounting failures of companies such as Enron and WorldCom. These widely publicized scandals revealed the important role that accounting plays in society. Most people want to make a difference, and an accounting career provides many opportunities to contribute to society. Finally, the Sarbanes-Oxley Act (SOX) (see page 7) significantly increased the accounting and internal control requirements for corporations. This dramatically increased demand for professionals with accounting training.

Accountants are in such demand that it is not uncommon for accounting students to have accepted a job offer a year before graduation. As the following discussion reveals, the job options of people with accounting degrees are virtually unlimited.

Public Accounting

Individuals in **public accounting** offer expert service to the general public, in much the same way that doctors serve patients and lawyers serve clients. A major portion of public accounting involves **auditing**. In auditing, a certified public accountant (CPA) examines company financial statements and provides an opinion as to how accurately the financial statements present the company's results and financial position. Analysts, investors, and creditors rely heavily on these "audit opinions," which CPAs have the exclusive authority to issue.

Taxation is another major area of public accounting. The work that tax specialists perform includes tax advice and planning, preparing tax returns, and representing clients before governmental agencies such as the Internal Revenue Service.

A third area in public accounting is **management consulting**. It ranges from installing basic accounting software or highly complex enterprise resource planning systems, to providing support services for major marketing projects and merger and acquisition activities.

Many CPAs are entrepreneurs. They form small- or medium-sized practices that frequently specialize in tax or consulting services.

Private Accounting

Instead of working in public accounting, you might choose to be an employee of a for-profit company such as Starbucks, Google, or PepsiCo. In **private** (or **managerial) accounting**, you would be involved in activities such as cost accounting (finding the cost of producing specific products), budgeting, accounting information system design and support, and tax planning and preparation. You might also be a member of your company's internal audit team. In response to SOX, the internal auditors' job of reviewing the company's operations to ensure compliance with company policies and to increase efficiency has taken on increased importance.

Alternatively, many accountants work for not-for-profit organizations such as the Red Cross or the Bill and Melinda Gates Foundation, or for museums, libraries, or performing arts organizations.

Governmental Accounting

Another option is to pursue one of the many accounting opportunities in governmental agencies. For example, the Internal Revenue Service (IRS), Federal Bureau of Investigation (FBI), and the Securities and Exchange Commission (SEC) all employ accountants. The FBI has a stated goal that at least 15 percent of its new agents should be CPAs. There is also a very high demand for accounting educators at public colleges and universities and in state and local governments.

Forensic Accounting

Forensic accounting uses accounting, auditing, and investigative skills to conduct investigations into theft and fraud. It is listed among the top 20 career paths of the future. The job of forensic accountants is to catch the perpetrators of the estimated $600 billion per year of theft and fraud occurring at U.S. companies. This includes tracing money-laundering and identity-theft activities as well as tax evasion. Insurance companies hire forensic accountants to detect insurance frauds such as arson, and law offices employ forensic accountants to identify marital assets in divorces. Forensic accountants often have FBI, IRS, or similar government experience.

"Show Me the Money"

How much can a new accountant make? Take a look at the average salaries for college graduates in public and private accounting.[3] Keep in mind if you also have a CPA license, you'll make 10–15% more when you start out.

Employer	Jr. Level (0–3 yrs.)	Sr. Level (4–6 yrs.)
Public accounting (large firm)	$48,750–$69,250	$66,750–$86,000
Public accounting (small firm)	$41,000–$56,000	$54,000–$69,750
Corporate accounting (large company)	$38,000–$57,250	$55,750–$73,500
Corporate accounting (small company)	$33,500–$49,000	$46,500–$58,750

Illustration 1A-1
Salary estimates for jobs in public and corporate accounting

Serious earning potential over time gives CPAs great job security. Here are some examples of upper-level salaries for managers in corporate accounting. Note that geographic region, experience, education, CPA certification, and company size each play a role in determining salary.

Position	Large Company	Small to Medium Company
Chief financial officer	$183,250–$384,000	$94,250–$175,750
Corporate controller	$122,000–$180,000	$80,500–$134,750
Tax manager	$ 92,250–$130,250	$74,250–$100,250

Illustration 1A-2
Upper-level management salaries in corporate accounting

For up-to-date salary estimates, as well as a wealth of additional information regarding accounting as a career, check out *www.startheregoplaces.com*.

SUMMARY OF LEARNING OBJECTIVE FOR APPENDIX 1A

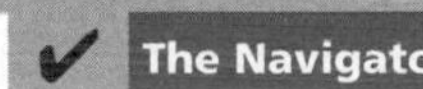

9 **Explain the career opportunities in accounting.** Accounting offers many different jobs in fields such as public and private accounting, government, and forensic accounting. Accounting is a popular major because there are many different types of jobs, with unlimited potential for career advancement.

GLOSSARY FOR APPENDIX 1A

Auditing The examination of financial statements by a certified public accountant in order to express an opinion as to the fairness of presentation. (p. 30).

Forensic accounting An area of accounting that uses accounting, auditing, and investigative skills to conduct investigations into theft and fraud. (p. 30).

Management consulting An area of public accounting ranging from development of accounting and computer systems to support services for marketing projects and merger and acquisition activities. (p. 30).

Private (or managerial) accounting An area of accounting within a company that involves such activities as cost accounting, budgeting, design and support of accounting information systems, and tax planning and preparation. (p. 30).

Public accounting An area of accounting in which the accountant offers expert service to the general public. (p. 30).

Taxation An area of public accounting involving tax advice, tax planning, preparing tax returns, and representing clients before governmental agencies. (p. 30).

[3] "*http://www.startheregoplaces.com/why-accounting/salary-and-demand/* (accessed April 24, 2011).

Self-Test, Brief Exercises, Exercises, Problem Set A, and many more components are available for practice in WileyPLUS.

**Note:* All asterisked Questions, Exercises, and Problems relate to material in the appendix to the chapter.

SELF-TEST QUESTIONS

Answers are on page 48.

(LO 1) **1.** Which of the following is *not* a step in the accounting process?
(a) Identification. (c) Recording.
(b) Verification. (d) Communication.

(LO 2) **2.** Which of the following statements about users of accounting information is *incorrect*?
(a) Management is an internal user.
(b) Taxing authorities are external users.
(c) Present creditors are external users.
(d) Regulatory authorities are internal users.

(LO 4) **3.** The cost principle states that:
(a) assets should be initially recorded at cost and adjusted when the fair value changes.
(b) activities of an entity are to be kept separate and distinct from its owner.
(c) assets should be recorded at their cost.
(d) only transaction data capable of being expressed in terms of money be included in the accounting records.

(LO 5) **4.** Which of the following statements about basic assumptions is *correct*?
(a) Basic assumptions are the same as accounting principles.
(b) The economic entity assumption states that there should be a particular unit of accountability.
(c) The monetary unit assumption enables accounting to measure employee morale.
(d) Partnerships are not economic entities.

(LO 5) **5.** The three types of business entities are:
(a) proprietorships, small businesses, and partnerships.
(b) proprietorships, partnerships, and corporations.
(c) proprietorships, partnerships, and large businesses.
(d) financial, manufacturing, and service companies.

(LO 6) **6.** Net income will result during a time period when:
(a) assets exceed liabilities.
(b) assets exceed revenues.
(c) expenses exceed revenues.
(d) revenues exceed expenses.

(LO 7) **7.** Performing services on account will have the following effects on the components of the basic accounting equation:
(a) increase assets and decrease stockholders' equity.
(b) increase assets and increase stockholders' equity.
(c) increase assets and increase liabilities.
(d) increase liabilities and increase stockholders' equity.

(LO 7) **8.** As of December 31, 2014, Stoneland Company has assets of $3,500 and stockholders' equity of $2,000. What are the liabilities for Stoneland Company as of December 31, 2014?
(a) $1,500. (b) $1,000. (c) $2,500. (d) $2,000.

9. Which of the following events is *not* recorded in the accounting records? (LO 7)
(a) Equipment is purchased on account.
(b) An employee is terminated.
(c) A cash investment is made into the business.
(d) The company pays a cash dividend.

10. During 2014, Gibson Company's assets decreased $50,000 and its liabilities decreased $90,000. Its stockholders' equity therefore: (LO 7)
(a) increased $40,000. (c) decreased $40,000.
(b) decreased $140,000. (d) increased $140,000.

11. Payment of an account payable affects the components of the accounting equation in the following way: (LO 7)
(a) decreases stockholders' equity and decreases liabilities.
(b) increases assets and decreases liabilities.
(c) decreases assets and increases stockholders' equity.
(d) decreases assets and decreases liabilities.

12. Which of the following statements is *false*? (LO 8)
(a) A statement of cash flows summarizes information about the cash inflows (receipts) and outflows (payments) for a specific period of time.
(b) A balance sheet reports the assets, liabilities, and stockholders' equity at a specific date.
(c) An income statement presents the revenues, expenses, changes in stockholders' equity, and resulting net income or net loss for a specific period of time.
(d) A retained earnings statement summarizes the changes in retained earnings for a specific period of time.

13. On the last day of the period, Jim Otto Company buys a $900 machine on credit. This transaction will affect the: (LO 8)
(a) income statement only.
(b) balance sheet only.
(c) income statement and retained earnings statement only.
(d) income statement, retained earnings statement, and balance sheet.

14. The financial statement that reports assets, liabilities, and stockholders' equity is the: (LO 8)
(a) income statement.
(b) retained earnings statement.
(c) balance sheet.
(d) statement of cash flows.

***15.** Services provided by a public accountant include: (LO 9)
(a) auditing, taxation, and management consulting.
(b) auditing, budgeting, and management consulting.
(c) auditing, budgeting, and cost accounting.
(d) internal auditing, budgeting, and management consulting.

Go to the book's companion website, www.wiley.com/college/weygandt, for additional Self-Test Questions.

✔ **The Navigator**

QUESTIONS

1. "Accounting is ingrained in our society and it is vital to our economic system." Do you agree? Explain.
2. Identify and describe the steps in the accounting process.
3. (a) Who are internal users of accounting data? (b) How does accounting provide relevant data to these users?
4. What uses of financial accounting information are made by (a) investors and (b) creditors?
5. "Bookkeeping and accounting are the same." Do you agree? Explain.
6. Jackie Remmers Travel Agency purchased land for $85,000 cash on December 10, 2014. At December 31, 2014, the land's value has increased to $93,000. What amount should be reported for land on Jackie Remmers' balance sheet at December 31, 2014? Explain.
7. What is the monetary unit assumption?
8. What is the economic entity assumption?
9. What are the three basic forms of profit-oriented business organizations?
10. Teresa Alvarez is the owner of a successful printing shop. Recently, her business has been increasing, and Teresa has been thinking about changing the organization of her business from a proprietorship to a corporation. Discuss some of the advantages Teresa would enjoy if she were to incorporate her business.
11. What is the basic accounting equation?
12. (a) Define the terms assets, liabilities, and stockholders' equity.
    (b) What items affect stockholders' equity?
13. Which of the following items are liabilities of Designer Jewelry Stores?
    (a) Cash.
    (b) Accounts payable.
    (c) Dividends.
    (d) Accounts receivable.
    (e) Supplies.
    (f) Equipment.
    (h) Service revenue.
    (g) Salaries and wages payable.
    (i) Rent expense.
14. Can a business enter into a transaction in which only the left side of the basic accounting equation is affected? If so, give an example.
15. Are the following events recorded in the accounting records? Explain your answer in each case.
    (a) The president of the company dies.
    (b) Supplies are purchased on account.
    (c) An employee is fired.
16. Indicate how the following business transactions affect the basic accounting equation.
    (a) Paid cash for janitorial services.
    (b) Purchased equipment for cash.
    (c) Invested cash in the business for stock.
    (d) Paid accounts payable in full.
17. Listed below are some items found in the financial statements of Alex Greenway Co. Indicate in which financial statement(s) the following items would appear.
    (a) Service revenue.
    (b) Equipment.
    (c) Advertising expense.
    (d) Accounts receivable.
    (e) Retained earnings.
    (f) Salaries and wages payable.
18. In February 2014, Paula Klink invested an additional $10,000 in Midtown Company. Midtown's accountant, Jon Shin, recorded this receipt as an increase in cash and revenues. Is this treatment appropriate? Why or why not?
19. "A company's net income appears directly on the income statement and the retained earnings statement, and it is included indirectly in the company's balance sheet." Do you agree? Explain.
20. Jardine Enterprises had a stockholders' equity balance of $158,000 at the beginning of the period. At the end of the accounting period, the stockholders' equity balance was $198,000.
    (a) Assuming no additional investment or distributions during the period, what is the net income for the period?
    (b) Assuming an additional investment of $13,000 but no distributions during the period, what is the net income for the period?
21. Summarized operations for H. J. Oslo Co. for the month of July are as follows.
    Revenues earned: for cash $30,000; on account $70,000.
    Expenses incurred: for cash $26,000; on account $40,000.
    Indicate for H. J. Oslo Co. (a) the total revenues, (b) the total expenses, and (c) net income for the month of July.
22. The basic accounting equation is: Assets = Liabilities + Stockholders' Equity. Replacing the words in that equation with dollar amounts, what is The Coca-Cola Company's accounting equation at December 31, 2010?

BRIEF EXERCISES

Use basic accounting equation.

(LO 6)

BE1-1 Presented below is the basic accounting equation. Determine the missing amounts.

	Assets	=	Liabilities	+	Stockholders' Equity
(a)	$90,000		$50,000		?
(b)	?		$45,000		$70,000
(c)	$94,000		?		$60,000

Use basic accounting equation.
(LO 6)

BE1-2 Given the accounting equation, answer each of the following questions.
(a) The liabilities of Shumway Company are $120,000 and the stockholders' equity is $232,000. What is the amount of Shumway Company's total assets?
(b) The total assets of Shumway Company are $190,000 and its stockholders' equity is $80,000. What is the amount of its total liabilities?
(c) The total assets of Shumway Company are $600,000 and its liabilities are equal to one half of its total assets. What is the amount of Shumway Company's stockholders' equity?

Use basic accounting equation.
(LO 6)

BE1-3 At the beginning of the year, Gonzales Company had total assets of $870,000 and total liabilities of $500,000. Answer the following questions.
(a) If total assets increased $150,000 during the year and total liabilities decreased $80,000, what is the amount of stockholders' equity at the end of the year?
(b) During the year, total liabilities increased $100,000 and stockholders' equity decreased $70,000. What is the amount of total assets at the end of the year?
(c) If total assets decreased $80,000 and stockholders' equity increased $120,000 during the year, what is the amount of total liabilities at the end of the year?

Solve accounting equation.
(LO 6)

BE1-4 Use the accounting equation to answer each of the following questions.
(a) The liabilities of Alli Company are $90,000. Common stock account is $150,000; dividends are $40,000; revenues, $450,000; and expenses, $320,000. What is the amount of Alli Company's total assets?
(b) The total assets of Planke Company are $57,000. Common stock account is $23,000; dividends are $7,000; revenues, $50,000; and expenses, $35,000. What is the amount of the company's total liabilities?
(c) The total assets of Thao Co. are $600,000 and its liabilities are equal to two-thirds of its total assets. What is the amount of Thao Co.'s stockholders' equity?

Identify assets, liabilities, and stockholders' equity.
(LO 6)

BE1-5 Indicate whether each of the following items is an asset (A), liability (L), or part of stockholders' equity (SE).

_____ (a) Accounts receivable	_____ (d) Supplies
_____ (b) Salaries and wages payable	_____ (e) Owner's investment
_____ (c) Equipment	_____ (f) Notes payable

Determine effect of transactions on basic accounting equation.
(LO 7)

BE1-6 Presented below are three business transactions. On a sheet of paper, list the letters (a), (b), and (c) with columns for assets, liabilities, and stockholders' equity. For each column, indicate whether the transactions increased (+), decreased (−), or had no effect (NE) on assets, liabilities, and stockholders' equity.
(a) Purchased supplies on account.
(b) Received cash for providing a service.
(c) Paid expenses in cash.

Determine effect of transactions on accounting equation.
(LO 7)

BE1-7 Follow the same format as BE1-6 above. Determine the effect on assets, liabilities, and stockholders' equity of the following three transactions.
(a) Stockholders invested cash in the business for common stock.
(b) Paid a cash dividend.
(c) Received cash from a customer who had previously been billed for services provided.

Classify items affecting stockholders' equity.
(LO 6)

BE1-8 Classify each of the following items as dividends (D), revenue (R), or expense (E).

_____ (a) Advertising expense	_____ (e) Dividends
_____ (b) Service revenue	_____ (f) Rent revenue
_____ (c) Insurance expense	_____ (g) Utilities expense
_____ (d) Salaries and wages expense	

Determine effect of transactions on stockholders' equity.
(LO 6)

BE1-9 Presented below are three transactions. Mark each transaction as affecting common stock (C), dividends (D), revenue (R), expense (E), or not affecting stockholders' equity (NSE).
_____ (a) Received cash for services performed
_____ (b) Paid cash to purchase equipment
_____ (c) Paid employee salaries.

Prepare a balance sheet.
(LO 8)

BE1-10 In alphabetical order below are balance sheet items for Grande Company at December 31, 2014. Kit Grande is the owner of Grande Company. Prepare a balance sheet, following the format of Illustration 1-10.

Accounts payable	$85,000
Accounts receivable	$72,500
Cash	$44,000
Common stock	$31,500

BE1-11 Indicate whether the following items would appear on the income statement (IS), balance sheet (BS), or retained earnings statement (RE).

Determine where items appear on financial statements. (LO 8)

_______ (a) Notes payable
_______ (b) Advertising expense
_______ (c) Common stock
_______ (d) Cash
_______ (e) Service revenue
_______ (f) Dividends

> DO IT! REVIEW

DO IT! 1-1 Indicate whether each of the five statements presented below is true or false.

Review basic concepts. (LO 1, 2, 4)

1. The three steps in the accounting process are identification, recording, and examination.
2. The two most common types of external users are investors and creditors.
3. Congress passed the Sarbanes-Oxley Act to ensure that investors invest only in companies that will be profitable.
4. The primary accounting standard-setting body in the United States is the Securities and Exchange Commission (SEC).
5. The cost principle dictates that companies record assets at their cost and continue to report them at their cost over the time the asset is held.

DO IT! 1-2 Classify the following items as issuance of stock (I), dividends (D), revenues (R), or expenses (E). Then indicate whether each item increases or decreases stockholders' equity.

Evaluate effects of transactions on stockholders' equity. (LO 6)

1. Dividends
2. Rent revenue
3. Advertising expense
4. Stockholders invest cash in the business

DO IT! 1-3 Transactions made by Callahan and Co., a law firm, for the month of March are shown below. Prepare a tabular analysis which shows the effects of these transactions on the accounting equation, similar to that shown in Illustration 1-9.

Prepare tabular analysis. (LO 7)

1. The company provided $23,000 of services for customers, on credit.
2. The company received $23,000 in cash from customers who had been billed for services (in transaction 1).
3. The company received a bill for $2,000 of advertising, but will not pay it until a later date.
4. The company paid a dividend of $5,000 in cash to stockholders.

DO IT! 1-4 Presented below is selected information related to Narrow Gage Company at December 31, 2014. Narrow Gage reports financial information monthly.

Calculate effects of transactions on financial statement items. (LO 8)

Accounts Payable	$ 3,000	Salaries and Wages Expense	$16,500
Cash	9,000	Notes Payable	25,000
Advertising Expense	6,000	Rent Expense	9,800
Service Revenue	54,000	Accounts Receivable	13,500
Equipment	29,000	Dividends	7,500

(a) Determine the total assets of Narrow Gage Company at December 31, 2014.
(b) Determine the net income that Narrow Gage Company reported for December 2014.
(c) Determine the stockholders' equity of Narrow Gage Company at December 31, 2014.

✔ The Navigator

EXERCISES

E1-1 Sondgeroth Company performs the following accounting tasks during the year.

Classify the three activities of accounting. (LO 1)

______ Analyzing and interpreting information.
______ Classifying economic events.
______ Explaining uses, meaning, and limitations of data.
______ Keeping a systematic chronological diary of events.

______Measuring events in dollars and cents.
______Preparing accounting reports.
______Reporting information in a standard format.
______Selecting economic activities relevant to the company.
______Summarizing economic events.

Accounting is "an information system that **identifies**, **records**, and **communicates** the economic events of an organization to interested users."

Instructions

Categorize the accounting tasks performed by Sondgeroth as relating to either the identification (I), recording (R), or communication (C) aspects of accounting.

Identify users of accounting information.
(LO 2)

E1-2 (a) The following are users of financial statements.

______Customers	______Securities and Exchange Commission
______Internal Revenue Service	______Store manager
______Labor unions	______Suppliers
______Marketing manager	______Vice president of finance
______Production supervisor	

Instructions

Identify the users as being either **external users** or **internal users**.

(b) The following questions could be asked by an internal user or an external user.

______Can we afford to give our employees a pay raise?
______Did the company earn a satisfactory income?
______Do we need to borrow in the near future?
______How does the company's profitability compare to other companies?
______What does it cost us to manufacture each unit produced?
______Which product should we emphasize?
______Will the company be able to pay its short-term debts?

Instructions

Identify each of the questions as being more likely asked by an **internal user** or an **external user**.

Discuss ethics and the cost principle.
(LO 3)

E1-3 Leon Manternach, president of Manternach Company, has instructed Carla Ruden, the head of the accounting department for Manternach Company, to report the company's land in the company's accounting reports at its fair value of $170,000 instead of its cost of $100,000. Manternach says, "Showing the land at $170,000 will make our company look like a better investment when we try to attract new investors next month."

Instructions

Explain the ethical situation involved for Carla Ruden, identifying the stakeholders and the alternatives.

Use accounting concepts.
(LO 4, 5)

E1-4 The following situations involve accounting principles and assumptions.

1. Julia Company owns buildings that are worth substantially more than they originally cost. In an effort to provide more relevant information, Julia reports the buildings at fair value in its accounting reports.
2. Dekalb Company includes in its accounting records only transaction data that can be expressed in terms of money.
3. Omar Shariff, president of Omar's Oasis, records his personal living costs as expenses of the Oasis.

Instructions

For each of the three situations, state if the accounting method used is correct or incorrect. If correct, identify which principle or assumption supports the method used. If incorrect, identify which principle or assumption has been violated.

Classify accounts as assets, liabilities, and stockholders' equity.
(LO 6)

E1-5 Robinson Cleaners has the following balance sheet items.

Accounts payable	Accounts receivable
Cash	Notes payable
Equipment	Salaries and wages payable
Supplies	Common stock

Instructions

Classify each item as an asset, liability, or stockholders' equity.

E1-6 Selected transactions for Spring Green Lawn Care Company are listed below.

Analyze the effect of transactions.

(LO 6, 7)

1. Sold common stock for cash to start business.
2. Paid monthly rent.
3. Purchased equipment on account.
4. Billed customers for services performed.
5. Paid dividends.
6. Received cash from customers billed in (4).
7. Incurred advertising expense on account.
8. Purchased additional equipment for cash.
9. Received cash from customers when service was performed.

Instructions

List the numbers of the above transactions and describe the effect of each transaction on assets, liabilities, and stockholders' equity. For example, the first answer is (1) Increase in assets and increase in stockholders' equity.

E1-7 Collins Computer Timeshare Company entered into the following transactions during May 2014.

Analyze the effect of transactions on assets, liabilities, and stockholders' equity.

(LO 6, 7)

1. Purchased computer terminals for $20,000 from Digital Equipment on account.
2. Paid $3,000 cash for May rent on storage space.
3. Received $15,000 cash from customers for contracts billed in April.
4. Provided computer services to Schmidt Construction Company for $2,400 cash.
5. Paid Central States Power Co. $11,000 cash for energy usage in May.
6. Stockholders invested an additional $32,000 in the business.
7. Paid Digital Equipment for the terminals purchased in (1) above.
8. Incurred advertising expense for May of $900 on account.

Instructions

Indicate with the appropriate letter whether each of the transactions above results in:

(a) An increase in assets and a decrease in assets.
(b) An increase in assets and an increase in stockholders' equity.
(c) An increase in assets and an increase in liabilities.
(d) A decrease in assets and a decrease in stockholders' equity.
(e) A decrease in assets and a decrease in liabilities.
(f) An increase in liabilities and a decrease in stockholders' equity.
(g) An increase in stockholders' equity and a decrease in liabilities.

E1-8 An analysis of the transactions made by J. L. Kang & Co., a certified public accounting firm, for the month of August is shown below. Each increase and decrease in stockholders' equity is explained.

Analyze transactions and compute net income.

(LO 7, 8)

	Assets				= Liabilities +	Stockholders' Equity				
							Retained Earnings			
	Cash +	Accounts Receivable +	Supplies +	Equipment =	Accounts Payable +	Common Stock +	Rev. −	Exp. −	Div.	
1.	+$15,000					+$15,000				
2.	−2,000			+$5,000	+$3,000					
3.	−750		+$750							
4.	+4,600	+$4,500					+$9,100			**Service Revenue**
5.	−1,500				−1,500					
6.	−2,000								−$2,000	
7.	−650							−$650		**Rent Expense**
8.	+450	−450								
9.	−3,900							−3,900		**Sal./Wages Expense**
10.					+500			−500		**Utilities Expense**

Instructions

(a) Describe each transaction that occurred for the month.
(b) Determine how much stockholders' equity increased for the month.
(c) Compute the amount of net income for the month.

Prepare financial statements.
(LO 8)

E1-9 An analysis of transactions for J. L. Kang & Co. was presented in E1–8.

Instructions

Prepare an income statement and a retained earnings statement for August and a balance sheet at August 31, 2014.

Determine net income (or loss).
(LO 7)

E1-10 Kimmy Company had the following assets and liabilities on the dates indicated.

December 31	Total Assets	Total Liabilities
2013	$400,000	$260,000
2014	$480,000	$300,000
2015	$590,000	$400,000

Kimmy began business on January 1, 2013, with an investment of $100,000 from stockholders.

Instructions

From an analysis of the change in stockholders' equity during the year, compute the net income (or loss) for:

(a) 2013, assuming Kimmy paid $15,000 in dividends for the year.
(b) 2014, assuming stockholders made an additional investment of $50,000 and Kimmy paid no dividends in 2014.
(c) 2015, assuming stockholders made an additional investment of $15,000 and Kimmy paid dividends of $30,000 in 2015.

Analyze financial statements items.
(LO 6, 7)

E1-11 Two items are omitted from each of the following summaries of balance sheet and income statement data for two corporations for the year 2014, Steven Craig and Georgia Enterprises.

	Steven Craig	Georgia Enterprises
Beginning of year:		
Total assets	$ 97,000	$129,000
Total liabilities	85,000	(c)
Total stockholders' equity	(a)	75,000
End of year:		
Total assets	160,000	180,000
Total liabilities	120,000	50,000
Total stockholders' equity	40,000	130,000
Changes during year in stockholders' equity:		
Additional investment	(b)	25,000
Dividends	24,000	(d)
Total revenues	215,000	100,000
Total expenses	175,000	55,000

Instructions

Determine the missing amounts.

Prepare income statement and retained earnings statement.
(LO 8)

E1-12 The following information relates to Karen Weigel Co. for the year 2014.

Retained earnings, January 1, 2014	$48,000	Advertising expense	$ 1,800
Dividends during 2014	5,000	Rent expense	10,400
Service revenue	62,500	Utilities expense	3,100
Salaries and wages expense	28,000		

Instructions

After analyzing the data, prepare an income statement and a retained earnings statement for the year ending December 31, 2014.

Correct an incorrectly prepared balance sheet.
(LO 8)

E1-13 Lynn Dreise is the bookkeeper for Sanculi Company. Lynn has been trying to get the balance sheet of Sanculi Company to balance. Sanculi's balance sheet is shown on the next page.

Sanculi Company
Balance Sheet
December 31, 2014

Assets		Liabilities	
Cash	$14,000	Accounts payable	$20,000
Supplies	8,000	Accounts receivable	(8,500)
Equipment	48,000	Common stock	50,000
Dividends	9,000	Retained earnings	17,500
Total assets	$79,000	Total liabilities and stockholders' equity	$79,000

Instructions

Prepare a correct balance sheet.

E1-14 Bear Park, a public camping ground near the Lake Mead National Recreation Area, has compiled the following financial information as of December 31, 2014.

Compute net income and prepare a balance sheet.

(LO 8)

Revenues during 2014—camping fees	$140,000	Notes payable	$ 60,000
Revenues during 2014—general store	47,000	Expenses during 2014	150,000
Accounts payable	11,000	Supplies on hand	2,500
Cash on hand	20,000	Common stock	20,000
Original cost of equipment	105,500	Retained earnings	?
Fair value of equipment	140,000		

Instructions

(a) Determine Bear Park's net income for 2014.
(b) Prepare a balance sheet for Bear Park as of December 31, 2014.

E1-15 Presented below is financial information related to the 2014 operations of Donna Marie Cruise Company.

Prepare an income statement.

(LO 8)

Maintenance and repairs expense	$ 97,000
Utilities expense	10,000
Salaries and wages expense	142,000
Advertising expense	3,500
Ticket revenue	335,000

Instructions

Prepare the 2014 income statement for Donna Marie Cruise Company.

E1-16 Presented below is information related to Williams and Douglas, Attorneys at Law.

Prepare a retained earnings statement.

(LO 8)

Retained earnings, January 1, 2014	$ 23,000
Legal service revenue—2014	340,000
Total expenses—2014	211,000
Assets, January 1, 2014	85,000
Liabilities, January 1, 2014	62,000
Assets, December 31, 2014	168,000
Liabilities, December 31, 2014	80,000
Dividends—2014	64,000

Instructions

Prepare the 2014 retained earnings statement for Williams and Douglas, Attorneys at Law.

E1-17 This information is for Belleview Company for the year ended December 31, 2014.

Prepare a cash flow statement.

(LO 8)

Cash received from revenues from customers	$600,000
Cash received for issuance of common stock	280,000
Cash paid for new equipment	100,000
Cash dividends paid	20,000
Cash paid for expenses	430,000
Cash balance 1/1/14	30,000

Instructions

Prepare the 2014 statement of cash flows for Belleview Company.

EXERCISES: SET B AND CHALLENGE EXERCISES

Visit the book's companion website, at **www.wiley.com/college/weygandt,** and choose the Student Companion site to access Exercise Set B and Challenge Exercises.

PROBLEMS: SET A

Analyze transactions and compute net income.
(LO 6, 7)

P1-1A Kinney's Repair Inc. was started on May 1. A summary of May transactions is presented below.

1. Stockholders invested $10,000 cash in the business in exchange for common stock.
2. Purchased equipment for $5,000 cash.
3. Paid $400 cash for May office rent.
4. Paid $500 cash for supplies.
5. Incurred $250 of advertising costs in the *Beacon News* on account.
6. Received $4,700 in cash from customers for repair service.
7. Declared and paid a $1,000 cash dividend.
8. Paid part-time employee salaries $1,000.
9. Paid utility bills $140.
10. Provided repair service on account to customers $980.
11. Collected cash of $120 for services billed in transaction (10).

Check figures next to some Problems give you a key number, to let you know if you are on the right track with your solution.

Instructions

(a) Total assets $13,140

(a) Prepare a tabular analysis of the transactions, using the following column headings: Cash, Accounts Receivable, Supplies, Equipment, Accounts Payable, Common Stock, and Retained Earnings (with separate columns for Revenues, Expenses, and Dividends). Include margin explanations for any changes in Retained Earnings. Revenue is called Service Revenue.

(b) Net income $3,890

(b) From an analysis of the Retained Earnings columns, compute the net income or net loss for May.

Analyze transactions and prepare income statement, retained earnings statement, and balance sheet.
(LO 6, 7, 8)

P1-2A On August 31, the balance sheet of Donahue Veterinary Clinic showed Cash $9,000, Accounts Receivable $1,700, Supplies $600, Equipment $6,000, Accounts Payable $3,600, Common Stock $13,000, and Retained Earnings $700. During September, the following transactions occurred.

1. Paid $2,900 cash for accounts payable due.
2. Collected $1,300 of accounts receivable.
3. Purchased additional office equipment for $2,100, paying $800 in cash and the balance on account.
4. Earned revenue of $7,300, of which $2,500 is collected in cash and the balance is due in October.
5. Declared and paid a $400 cash dividend.
6. Paid salaries $1,700, rent for September $900, and advertising expense $200.
7. Incurred utilities expense for month on account $170.
8. Received $10,000 from Capital Bank on a 6-month note payable.

Instructions

(a) Ending cash $15,900

(a) Prepare a tabular analysis of the September transactions beginning with August 31 balances. The column headings should be as follows: Cash + Accounts Receivable + Supplies + Equipment = Notes Payable + Accounts Payable + Common Stock + Retained Earnings + Revenues − Expenses − Dividends.

(b) Net income $4,330
Total assets $29,800

(b) Prepare an income statement for September, a retained earnings statement for September, and a balance sheet at September 30.

Prepare income statement, retained earnings statement, and balance sheet.
(LO 8)

P1-3A On May 1, Blue Sky Flying School, a company that provides flying lessons, was started with an investment of $45,000 cash in the business. Following are the assets and liabilities of the company on May 31, 2014, and the revenues and expenses for the month of May.

Cash	$ 4,500	Notes Payable	$28,000
Accounts Receivable	7,200	Rent Expense	1,200
Equipment	64,000	Maintenance and	
Service Revenue	6,800	Repairs Expense	400
Advertising Expense	500	Gasoline Expense	2,500
Accounts Payable	1,400	Utilities Expense	400

No additional investments were made in May, but the company paid dividends of $500 during the month.

Instructions

(a) Prepare an income statement and a retained earnings statement for the month of May and a balance sheet at May 31.

(a) Net income $1,800
Total assets $75,700

(b) Prepare an income statement and a retained earnings statement for May assuming the following data are not included above: (1) $900 of revenue was earned and billed but not collected at May 31, and (2) $1,500 of gasoline expense was incurred but not paid.

(b) Net income $1,200

P1-4A Matt Stiner started a delivery service, Stiner Deliveries, on June 1, 2014. The following transactions occurred during the month of June.

Analyze transactions and prepare financial statements.

(LO 6, 7, 8)

June 1 Stockholders invested $10,000 cash in the business in exchange for common stock.
2 Purchased a used van for deliveries for $14,000. Matt paid $2,000 cash and signed a note payable for the remaining balance.
3 Paid $500 for office rent for the month.
5 Performed $4,800 of services on account.
9 Declared and paid $300 in cash dividends.
12 Purchased supplies for $150 on account.
15 Received a cash payment of $1,250 for services provided on June 5.
17 Purchased gasoline for $100 on account.
20 Received a cash payment of $1,500 for services provided.
23 Made a cash payment of $500 on the note payable.
26 Paid $250 for utilities.
29 Paid for the gasoline purchased on account on June 17.
30 Paid $1,000 for employee salaries.

Instructions

(a) Show the effects of the previous transactions on the accounting equation using the following format.

(a) Total assets $25,800

		Assets				=	Liabilities		+	Stockholders' Equity						
												Retained Earnings				
Date	Cash +	Accounts Receivable	+ Supplies	+ Equipment		=	Notes Payable	+ Accounts Payable	+	Common Stock	+	Rev.	−	Exp.	−	Div.

Include margin explanations for any changes in the Retained Earnings account in your analysis.

(b) Prepare an income statement for the month of June.
(c) Prepare a balance sheet at June 30, 2014.

(b) Net income $4,450
(c) Cash $8,100

P1-5A Financial statement information about four different companies is as follows.

Determine financial statement amounts and prepare retained earnings statement.

(LO 7, 8)

	Crosby Company	Stills Company	Nash Company	Young Company
January 1, 2014				
Assets	$ 75,000	$110,000	(g)	$150,000
Liabilities	50,000	(d)	$ 75,000	(j)
Stockholders' equity	(a)	60,000	45,000	100,000
December 31, 2014				
Assets	(b)	137,000	200,000	(k)
Liabilities	55,000	75,000	(h)	80,000
Stockholders' equity	40,000	(e)	130,000	140,000
Stockholders' equity changes in year				
Additional investment	(c)	15,000	10,000	15,000
Dividends	10,000	(f)	14,000	10,000
Total revenues	350,000	420,000	(i)	500,000
Total expenses	330,000	385,000	342,000	(l)

Instructions

(a) Determine the missing amounts. (*Hint:* For example, to solve for (a), Assets − Liabilities = Stockholders' Equity = $25,000.)

(b) Prepare the retained earnings statement for Stills Company. Assume beginning retained earnings was $20,000.

(c) Write a memorandum explaining the sequence for preparing financial statements and the interrelationship of the retained earnings statement to the income statement and balance sheet.

PROBLEMS: SET B

Analyze transactions and compute net income.
(LO 6, 7)

P1-1B On April 1, Holly Dahl established Holiday Travel Agency. The following transactions were completed during the month.

1. Stockholders invested $10,000 cash in the business in exchange for common stock.
2. Paid $400 cash for April office rent.
3. Purchased office equipment for $2,500 cash.
4. Incurred $300 of advertising costs in the *Chicago Tribune*, on account.
5. Paid $600 cash for office supplies.
6. Earned $8,500 for services provided: $2,000 cash is received from customers, and the balance of $6,500 is billed to customers on account.
7. Declared and paid a $200 cash dividend.
8. Paid *Chicago Tribune* amount due in transaction (4).
9. Paid employees' salaries $2,200.
10. Received $5,700 in cash from customers billed previously in transaction (6).

Instructions

(a) Ending cash $11,500

(a) Prepare a tabular analysis of the transactions using the following column headings: Cash, Accounts Receivable, Supplies, Equipment, Accounts Payable, Common Stock, and Retained Earnings (with separate columns for Revenues, Expenses, and Dividends). Include margin explanation for any changes in Retained Earnings.

(b) Net income $5,600

(b) From an analysis of the Retained Earnings columns, compute the net income or net loss for April.

Analyze transactions and prepare income statement, retained earnings statement, and balance sheet.
(LO 6, 7, 8)

P1-2B Mandy Arnold opened a law office, Mandy Arnold, Attorney at Law, on July 1, 2014. On July 31, the balance sheet showed Cash $4,000, Accounts Receivable $1,500, Supplies $500, Equipment $5,000, Accounts Payable $4,200, and Common Stock $6,000, and Retained Earnings $800. During August, the following transactions occurred.

1. Collected $1,400 of accounts receivable due from clients.
2. Paid $2,700 cash for accounts payable due.
3. Earned revenue of $7,900 of which $3,000 is collected in cash and the balance is due in September.
4. Purchased additional office equipment for $1,000, paying $400 in cash and the balance on account.
5. Paid salaries $3,000, rent for August $900, and advertising expenses $350.
6. Declared and paid a $450 cash dividend.
7. Received $2,000 from Standard Federal Bank; the money was borrowed on a 4-month note payable.
8. Incurred utility expenses for month on account $210.

Instructions

(a) Ending expenses $4,460

(a) Prepare a tabular analysis of the August transactions beginning with July 31 balances. The column headings should be as follows: Cash + Accounts Receivable + Supplies + Equipment = Notes Payable + Accounts Payable + Common Stock + Retained Earnings + Revenues − Expenses − Dividends.

(b) Net income $3,440
Total assets $14,100

(b) Prepare an income statement for August, a retained earnings statement for August, and a balance sheet at August 31.

P1-3B Angelic Cosmetics Co., a company that provides individual skin care treatment, was started on June 1 with an investment of $25,000 cash. Following are the assets and liabilities of the company at June 30 and the revenues and expenses for the month of June.

Prepare income statement, retained earnings statement, and balance sheet.

(LO 8)

Cash	$10,000	Notes Payable	$13,000
Accounts Receivable	4,000	Accounts Payable	1,400
Service Revenue	5,500	Rent Expense	1,600
Supplies	2,000	Gasoline Expense	600
Advertising Expense	500	Utilities Expense	300
Equipment	25,000		

Stockholders made no additional investments in June. The company paid a cash dividend of $900 during the month.

Instructions

(a) Prepare an income statement and a retained earnings statement for the month of June and a balance sheet at June 30, 2014.

(a) Net income $2,500
Total assets $41,000

(b) Prepare an income statement and a retained earnings statement for June assuming the following data are not included above: (1) $800 of revenue was earned and billed but not collected at June 30, and (2) $100 of gasoline expense was incurred but not paid.

(b) Net income $3,200

P1-4B Jessi Paulis started a consulting firm, Paulis Consulting, on May 1, 2014. The following transactions occurred during the month of May.

Analyze transactions and prepare financial statements.

(LO 6, 7, 8)

May 1 Paulis invested $8,000 cash in the business in exchange for stock.
2 Paid $800 for office rent for the month.
3 Purchased $500 of supplies on account.
5 Paid $50 to advertise in the *County News*.
9 Received $3,000 cash for services provided.
12 Declared and paid a $700 cash dividend.
15 Performed $3,300 of services on account.
17 Paid $2,100 for employee salaries.
20 Paid for the supplies purchased on account on May 3.
23 Received a cash payment of $2,000 for services provided on account on May 15.
26 Borrowed $5,000 from the bank on a note payable.
29 Purchased office equipment for $2,300 on account.
30 Paid $150 for utilities.

Instructions

(a) Show the effects of the previous transactions on the accounting equation using the following format.

(a) Total assets $17,800

		Assets			=	Liabilities	+		Stockholders' Equity		
									Retained Earnings		
Date	Cash +	Accounts Receivable	+ Supplies +	Equipment	=	Notes Payable +	Accounts Payable	+ Common Stock +	Rev. −	Exp. −	Div.

Include margin explanations for any changes in the Retained Earnings account in your analysis.

(b) Prepare an income statement for the month of May.

(b) Net income $3,200

(c) Prepare a balance sheet at May 31, 2014.

(c) Cash $13,700

P1-5B Financial statement information about four different companies is shown on the next page.

Determine financial statement amounts and prepare retained earnings statement.

(LO 7, 8)

Instructions

(a) Determine the missing amounts. (*Hint:* For example, to solve for (a), Assets − Liabilities = Stockholders' Equity = $28,000.)

(b) Prepare the retained earnings statement for John Company. Assume beginning retained earnings was $0.

(c) Write a memorandum explaining the sequence for preparing financial statements and the interrelationship of the retained earnings statement to the income statement and balance sheet.

	John Company	Paul Company	George Company	Ringo Company
January 1, 2014				
Assets	$ 78,000	$ 90,000	(g)	$150,000
Liabilities	50,000	(d)	$ 75,000	(j)
Stockholders' equity	(a)	50,000	54,000	100,000
December 31, 2014				
Assets	(b)	117,000	180,000	(k)
Liabilities	55,000	79,000	(h)	80,000
Stockholders' equity	40,000	(e)	100,000	145,000
Stockholders' equity changes in year				
Additional investment	(c)	8,000	10,000	15,000
Dividends	10,000	(f)	12,000	10,000
Total revenues	350,000	390,000	(i)	500,000
Total expenses	335,000	400,000	360,000	(l)

PROBLEMS: SET C

Visit the book's website, at **www.wiley.com/college/weygandt**, and choose the Student Companion site to access Problem Set C.

CONTINUING COOKIE CHRONICLE

*The **Continuing Cookie Chronicle** starts in this chapter and continues in every chapter. You also can find this problem at the book's companion website.*

CCC1 Natalie Koebel spent much of her childhood learning the art of cookie-making from her grandmother. They passed many happy hours mastering every type of cookie imaginable and later creating new recipes that were both healthy and delicious. Now at the start of her second year in college, Natalie is investigating various possibilities for starting her own business as part of the requirements of the entrepreneurship program in which she is enrolled.

A long-time friend insists that Natalie has to somehow include cookies in her business plan. After a series of brainstorming sessions, Natalie settles on the idea of operating a cookie-making school. She will start on a part-time basis and offer her services in people's homes. Now that she has started thinking about it, the possibilities seem endless. During the fall, she will concentrate on holiday cookies. She will offer individual lessons and group sessions (which will probably be more entertainment than education for the participants). Natalie also decides to include children in her target market.

The first difficult decision is coming up with the perfect name for her business. In the end, she settles on "Cookie Creations" and then moves on to more important issues.

Instructions

(a) What form of business organization—proprietorship, partnership, or corporation—do you recommend that Natalie use for her business? Discuss the benefits and weaknesses of each form and give the reasons for your choice.

(b) Will Natalie need accounting information? If yes, what information will she need and why? How often will she need this information?

(c) Identify specific asset, liability, and owner's/stockholders' equity accounts that Cookie Creations will likely use to record its business transactions.

(d) Should Natalie open a separate bank account for the business? Why or why not?

Broadening Your PERSPECTIVE

Financial Reporting and Analysis

Financial Reporting Problem: PepsiCo, Inc.

PEPSICO

BYP1-1 The actual financial statements of PepsiCo, Inc., as presented in the company's 2010 Annual Report, are contained in Appendix A (at the back of the textbook).

Instructions
Refer to PepsiCo's financial statements and answer the following questions.

(a) What were PepsiCo's total assets at December 25, 2010? At December 26, 2009?
(b) How much cash (and cash equivalents) did PepsiCo have on December 25, 2010?
(c) What amount of accounts payable did PepsiCo report on December 25, 2010? On December 26, 2009?
(d) What were PepsiCo's net sales in 2008? In 2009? In 2010?
(e) What is the amount of the change in PepsiCo's net income from 2009 to 2010?

Comparative Analysis Problem: PepsiCo, Inc. vs. The Coca-Cola Company

BYP1-2 PepsiCo's financial statements are presented in Appendix A. The Coca-Cola Company's financial statements are presented in Appendix B.

Instructions
Refer to the financial statements and answer the following questions.

(a) Based on the information contained in these financial statements, determine the following for each company.
  (1) Total assets at December 25, 2010, for PepsiCo, and for Coca-Cola at December 31, 2010.
  (2) Accounts (notes) receivable, net at December 25, 2010, for PepsiCo and at December 31, 2010, for Coca-Cola.
  (3) Net sales for year ended in 2010.
  (4) Net income for year ended in 2010.
(b) What conclusions concerning the two companies can be drawn from these data?

Real-World Focus

BYP1-3 This exercise will familiarize you with skill requirements, job descriptions, and salaries for accounting careers.

Address: **www.careers-in-accounting.com,** or go to **www.wiley.com/college/weygandt**

Instructions
Go to the site shown above. Answer the following questions.

(a) What are the three broad areas of accounting (from "Skills and Talents Required")?
(b) List eight skills required in accounting.
(c) How do the three accounting areas differ in terms of these eight required skills?
(d) Explain one of the key job functions in accounting.
(e) What is the salary range for a junior staff accountant to a Big 4 firm?

Critical Thinking

Decision-Making Across the Organization

BYP1-4 Lucy and Nick Lars, local golf stars, opened the Chip-Shot Driving Range Company on March 1, 2014. They invested $20,000 cash and received common stock in exchange for their investment. A caddy shack was constructed for cash at a cost of $6,000, and $800 was spent on golf

balls and golf clubs. The Lars leased five acres of land at a cost of $1,000 per month and paid the first month's rent. During the first month, advertising costs totaled $750, of which $150 was unpaid at March 31, and $400 was paid to members of the high school golf team for retrieving golf balls. All revenues from customers were deposited in the company's bank account. On March 15, Lucy and Nick received a dividend of $800. A $100 utility bill was received on March 31 but was not paid. On March 31, the balance in the company's bank account was $15,100.

Lucy and Nick thought they had a pretty good first month of operations. But, their estimates of profitability ranged from a loss of $4,900 to net income of $1,650.

Instructions

With the class divided into groups, answer the following.

(a) How could the Lars have concluded that the business operated at a loss of $4,900? Was this a valid basis on which to determine net income?

(b) How could the Lars have concluded that the business operated at a net income of $1,650? (*Hint:* Prepare a balance sheet at March 31.) Was this a valid basis on which to determine net income?

(c) Without preparing an income statement, determine the actual net income for March.

(d) What was the revenue earned in March?

Communication Activity

BYP1-5 Erin Danielle, the bookkeeper for New York Company, has been trying to get the balance sheet to balance. The company's balance sheet is shown below.

New York Company
Balance Sheet
For the Month Ended December 31, 2014

Assets		Liabilities	
Equipment	$22,500	Common stock	$23,000
Cash	9,000	Accounts receivable	(6,000)
Supplies	2,000	Retained earnings	(2,000)
Accounts payable	(8,000)	Notes payable	10,500
	$25,500		$25,500

Instructions

Explain to Erin Danielle in a memo why the original balance sheet is incorrect, and what should be done to correct it.

Ethics Case

BYP1-6 After numerous campus interviews, Jeff Hunter, a senior at Great Northern College, received two office interview invitations from the Baltimore offices of two large firms. Both firms offered to cover his out-of-pocket expenses (travel, hotel, and meals). He scheduled the interviews for both firms on the same day, one in the morning and one in the afternoon. At the conclusion of each interview, he submitted to both firms his total out-of-pocket expenses for the trip to Baltimore: mileage $112 (280 miles at $0.40), hotel $130, meals $36, parking and tolls $18, for a total of $296. He believes this approach is appropriate. If he had made two trips, his cost would have been two times $296. He is also certain that neither firm knew he had visited the other on that same trip. Within 10 days, Jeff received two checks in the mail, each in the amount of $296.

Instructions

(a) Who are the stakeholders (affected parties) in this situation?

(b) What are the ethical issues in this case?

(c) What would you do in this situation?

All About You

BYP1-7 Some people are tempted to make their finances look worse to get financial aid. Companies sometimes also manage their financial numbers in order to accomplish certain goals. Earnings management is the planned timing of revenues, expenses, gains, and losses to smooth out bumps in net income. In managing earnings, companies' actions vary from being within the range of ethical activity, to being both unethical and illegal attempts to mislead investors and creditors.

Instructions

Provide responses for each of the following questions.

(a) Discuss whether you think each of the following actions (adapted from *www.finaid.org/fafsa/*) to increase the chances of receiving financial aid is ethical.
   (1) Spend down the student's assets and income first, before spending parents' assets and income.
   (2) Accelerate necessary expenses to reduce available cash. For example, if you need a new car, buy it before applying for financial aid.
   (3) State that a truly financially dependent child is independent.
   (4) Have a parent take an unpaid leave of absence for long enough to get below the "threshold" level of income.

(b) What are some reasons why a *company* might want to overstate its earnings?

(c) What are some reasons why a *company* might want to understate its earnings?

(d) Under what circumstances might an otherwise ethical person decide to illegally overstate or understate earnings?

BYP1-8 When companies need money, they go to investors or creditors. Before investors or creditors will give a company cash, they want to know the company's financial position and performance. They want to see the company's financial statements—the balance sheet and the income statement. When students need money for school, they often apply for financial aid. When you apply for financial aid, you must submit your own version of a financial statement—the Free Application for Federal Student Aid (FAFSA) form.

Suppose you have $4,000 in cash and $4,000 in credit card bills. The more cash and other assets that you have, the less likely you are to get financial aid. Also, if you have a lot of consumer debt (credit card bills), schools are not more likely to loan you money. To increase your chances of receiving aid, should you use the cash to pay off your credit card bills, and therefore make yourself look "worse off" to the financial aid decision-makers?

YES: You are playing within the rules. You are not hiding assets. You are simply restructuring your assets and liabilities to best conform with the preferences that are built into the federal aid formulas.

NO: You are engaging in a transaction solely to take advantage of a loophole in the federal aid rules. In doing so, you are potentially depriving someone who is actually worse off than you from receiving aid.

Instructions

Write a response indicating your position regarding this situation. Provide support for your view.

FASB Codification Activity

BYP1-9 The FASB has developed the Financial Accounting Standards Board Accounting Standards Codification (or more simply "the Codification"). The FASB's primary goal in developing the Codification is to provide in one place all the authoritative literature related to a particular topic. To provide easy access to the Codification, the FASB also developed the Financial Accounting Standards Board Codification Research System (CRS). CRS is an online, real-time database that provides easy access to the Codification. The Codification and the related CRS provide a topically organized structure, subdivided into topic, subtopics, sections, and paragraphs, using a numerical index system.

You may find this system useful in your present and future studies, and so we have provided an opportunity to use this online system as part of the *Broadening Your Perspective* section.

Instructions

Academic access to the FASB Codification is available through university subscriptions, obtained from the American Accounting Association (at *http://aaahq.org/FASB/Access.cfm*), for an annual fee of $150. This subscription covers an unlimited number of students within a single institution. Once this access has been obtained by your school, you should log in (at *http://aaahq.org/ascLogin.cfm*) and familiarize yourself with the resources that are accessible at the FASB Codification site.

Answers to Chapter Questions

Answers to Insight and Accounting Across the Organization Questions

p. 6 The Scoop on Accounting Q: What are the benefits to the company and to the employees of making the financial statements available to all employees? **A:** If employees can read and use financial reports, a company will benefit in the following ways. The *marketing department* will make better decisions about products to offer and prices to charge. The *finance department* will make better decisions about debt and equity financing and how much to distribute in dividends. The *production department* will make better decisions about when to buy new equipment and how much inventory to produce. The *human resources department* will be better able to determine whether employees can be given raises. Finally, *all employees* will be better informed about the basis on which they are evaluated, which will increase employee morale.

p. 8 The Numbers Behind Not-for-Profit Organizations Q: What benefits does a sound accounting system provide to a not-for-profit organization? **A:** Accounting provides at least two benefits to not-for-profit organizations. First, it helps to ensure that money is used in the way that donors intended. Second, it assures donors that their money is not going to waste and thus increases the likelihood of future donations.

p. 10 The Korean Discount Q: What is meant by the phrase "make the country's businesses more transparent"? Why would increasing transparency spur economic growth? **A:** Transparency refers to the extent to which outsiders have knowledge regarding a company's financial performance and financial position. If a company lacks transparency, its financial reports do not adequately inform investors of critical information that is needed to make investment decisions. If corporate transparency is increased, investors will be more willing to supply the financial capital that businesses need in order to grow, which would spur the country's economic growth.

p. 12 Spinning the Career Wheel Q: How might accounting help you? **A:** You will need to understand financial reports in any enterprise with which you are associated. Whether you become a manager, a doctor, a lawyer, a social worker, a teacher, an engineer, an architect, or an entrepreneur, a working knowledge of accounting is relevant.

p. 25 Beyond Financial Statements Q: Why might a company's stockholders be interested in its environmental and social performance? **A:** Many companies now recognize that being a socially responsible organization is not only the right thing to do, but it also is good for business. Many investment professionals understand, for example, that environmental, social, and proper corporate governance of companies affects the performance of their investment portfolios. For example, British Petroleum's oil leak disaster is a classic example of the problems that can occur for a company and its stockholders. BP's stock price was slashed, its dividend reduced, its executives replaced, and its reputation badly damaged. It is interesting that socially responsible investment funds are now gaining momentum in the marketplace such that companies now recognize this segment as an important investment group.

Answers to Self-Test Questions

1. b **2.** d **3.** c **4.** b **5.** b **6.** d **7.** b **8.** a ($3,500 − $2,000) **9.** b **10.** a ($90,000 − $50,000) **11.** d **12.** c **13.** b **14.** c ***15.** a

A Look at IFRS

Most agree that there is a need for one set of international accounting standards. Here is why:

Multinational corporations. Today's companies view the entire world as their market. For example, Coca-Cola, Intel, and McDonald's generate more than 50% of their sales outside the United States, and many foreign companies, such as Toyota, Nestlé, and Sony, find their largest market to be the United States.

Mergers and acquisitions. The mergers between Fiat/Chrysler and Vodafone/Mannesmann suggest that we will see even more such business combinations in the future.

Information technology. As communication barriers continue to topple through advances in technology, companies and individuals in different countries and markets are becoming more comfortable buying and selling goods and services from one another.

Financial markets. Financial markets are of international significance today. Whether it is currency, equity securities (stocks), bonds, or derivatives, there are active markets throughout the world trading these types of instruments.

Key Points

- International standards are referred to as *International Financial Reporting Standards (IFRS)*, developed by the International Accounting Standards Board (IASB).
- Recent events in the global capital markets have underscored the importance of financial disclosure and transparency not only in the United States but in markets around the world. As a result, many are examining which accounting and financial disclosure rules should be followed. As indicated in the graphic below, much of the world has voted for the standards issued by the IASB. Over 115 countries require or permit use of IFRS.

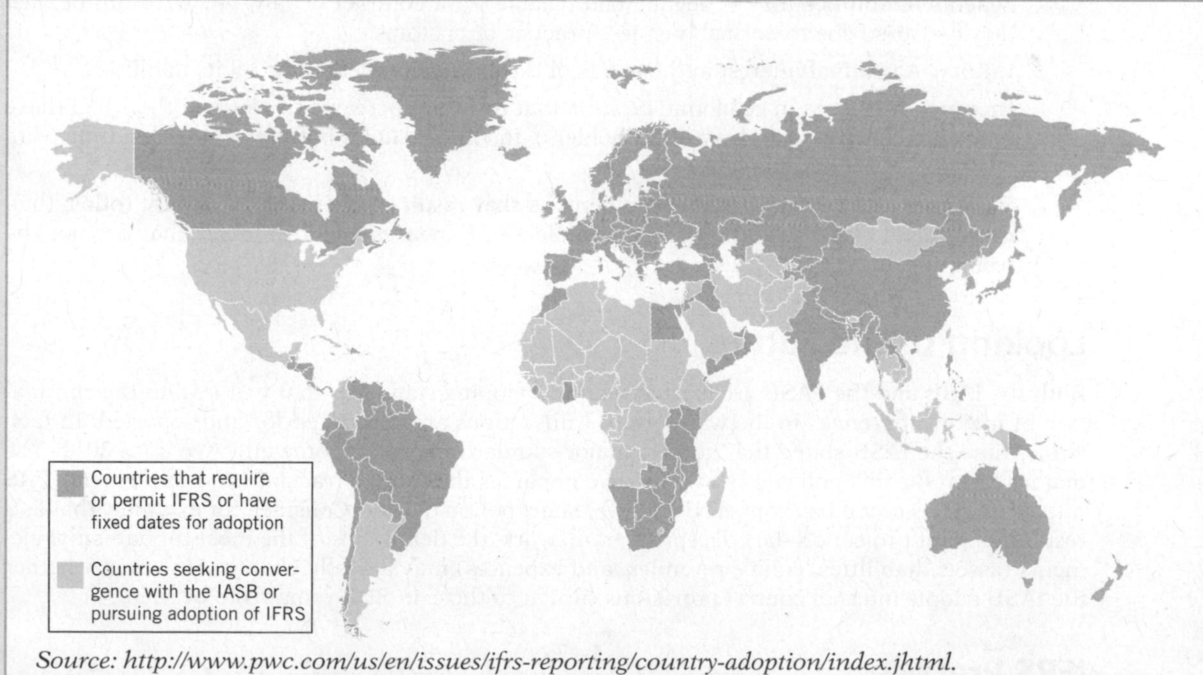

Source: http://www.pwc.com/us/en/issues/ifrs-reporting/country-adoption/index.jhtml.

- U.S standards, referred to as generally accepted accounting principles (GAAP), are developed by the Financial Accounting Standards Board (FASB). The fact that there are differences between what is in this textbook (which is based on U.S. standards) and IFRS should not be surprising because the FASB and IASB have responded to different user needs. In some countries, the primary users of financial statements are private investors. In others, the primary users are tax authorities or central government planners. It appears that the United States and the international standard-setting environment are primarily driven by meeting the needs of investors and creditors.

- The internal control standards applicable to Sarbanes-Oxley (SOX) apply only to large public companies listed on U.S. exchanges. There is a continuing debate as to whether non-U.S. companies should have to comply with this extra layer of regulation. Debate about international companies (non-U.S.) adopting SOX-type standards centers on whether the benefits exceed the costs. The concern is that the higher costs of SOX compliance are making the U.S. securities markets less competitive.
- The textbook mentions a number of ethics violations, such as Enron, WorldCom, and AIG. These problems have also occurred internationally, for example, at Satyam Computer Services (India), Parmalat (Italy), and Royal Ahold (the Netherlands).
- IFRS tends to be simpler in its accounting and disclosure requirements; some people say more "principles-based." GAAP is more detailed; some people say it is more "rules-based." This difference in approach has resulted in a debate about the merits of "principles-based" versus "rules-based" standards.
- U.S. regulators have recently eliminated the need for foreign companies that trade shares in U.S. markets to reconcile their accounting with GAAP.
- The three most common forms of business organization, proprietorships, partnerships, and corporations, are also found in countries that use IFRS. Because the choice of business organization is influenced by factors such as legal environment, tax rates and regulations, and degree of entrepreneurism, the relative use of each form will vary across countries.
- The conceptual framework that underlies IFRS is very similar to that used to develop GAAP. The basic definitions provided in this textbook for the key elements of financial statements, that is, assets, liabilities, equity, revenues (**referred to as income**), and expenses, are simplified versions of the official definitions provided by the FASB. The more substantive definitions, using the IASB definitional structure, are as follows.

  Assets. A resource controlled by the entity as a result of past events and from which future economic benefits are expected to flow to the entity.

  Liabilities. A present obligation of the entity arising from past events, the settlement of which is expected to result in an outflow from the entity of resources embodying economic benefits. Liabilities may be legally enforceable via a contract or law, but need not be, i.e., they can arise due to normal business practice or customs.

  Equity. A residual interest in the assets of the entity after deducting all its liabilities.

  Income. Increases in economic benefits that result in increases in equity (other than those related to contributions from shareholders). Income includes both revenues (resulting from ordinary activities) and gains.

  Expenses. Decreases in economic benefits that result in decreases in equity (other than those related to distributions to shareholders). Expenses includes losses that are not the result of ordinary activities.

Looking to the Future

Both the IASB and the FASB are hard at work developing standards that will lead to the elimination of major differences in the way certain transactions are accounted for and reported. In fact, at one time the IASB stated that no new major standards would become effective until 2011. The major reason for this policy was to provide companies the time to translate and implement IFRS into practice, as much has happened in a very short period of time. Consider, for example, that as a result of a joint project on the conceptual framework, the definitions of the most fundamental elements (assets, liabilities, equity, revenues, and expenses) may actually change. However, whether the IASB adopts internal control provisions similar to those in SOX remains to be seen.

IFRS Practice

IFRS Self-Test Questions

1. Which of the following is *not* a reason why a single set of high-quality international accounting standards would be beneficial?
   (a) Mergers and acquisition activity.
   (b) Financial markets.

(c) Multinational corporations.
(d) GAAP is widely considered to be a superior reporting system.

2. The Sarbanes-Oxley Act determines:
(a) international tax regulations.
(b) internal control standards as enforced by the IASB.
(c) internal control standards of U.S. publicly traded companies.
(d) U.S. tax regulations.

3. IFRS is considered to be more:
(a) principles-based and less rules-based than GAAP.
(b) rules-based and less principles-based than GAAP.
(c) detailed than GAAP.
(d) None of the above.

4. Which of the following statements is *false*?
(a) IFRS is based on a conceptual framework that is similar to that used to develop GAAP.
(b) Assets are defined by the IASB as resources controlled by the entity as a result of past events and from which future economic benefits are expected to flow to the entity.
(c) Non-U.S. companies that trade shares in U.S. markets must reconcile their accounting with GAAP.
(d) Proprietorships, partnerships, and corporations are also found in countries that use IFRS.

5. Which of the following statements is *true*?
(a) Under IFRS, the term income refers to what would be called revenues and gains under GAAP.
(b) The term income is not used under IFRS.
(c) The term income refers only to gains on investments.
(d) Under IFRS, expenses include distributions to owners.

IFRS Exercises

IFRS1-1 Who are the two key international players in the development of international accounting standards? Explain their role.

IFRS1-2 What might explain the fact that different accounting standard-setters have developed accounting standards that are sometimes quite different in nature?

IFRS1-3 What is the benefit of a single set of high-quality accounting standards?

IFRS1-4 Discuss the potential advantages and disadvantages that countries outside the United States should consider before adopting regulations, such as those in the Sarbanes-Oxley Act, that increase corporate internal control requirements.

International Financial Reporting Problem: Zetar plc

IFRS1-5 The financial statements of Zetar plc are presented in Appendix C. The company's complete annual report, including the notes to its financial statements, is available at *www.zetarplc.com*.

Instructions

Visit Zetar's corporate website and answer the following questions from Zetar's 2010 annual report.

(a) What accounting firm performed the audit of Zetar's financial statements?
(b) What is the address of the company's corporate headquarters?
(c) What is the company's reporting currency?
(d) What two segments does the company operate in, and what were the sales for each segment in the year ended April 30, 2010?

Answers to IFRS Self-Test Questions

1. d **2.** c **3.** a **4.** c **5.** a

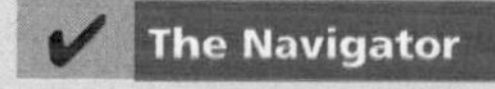

Remember to go back to The Navigator box on the chapter opening page and check off your completed work.

Chapter 2 The Recording Process

Feature Story

Accidents Happen

How organized are you financially? Take a short quiz. Answer *yes* or *no* to each question:

- Does your wallet contain so many debit card receipts that you've been declared a walking fire hazard?
- Was Dwight Howard playing high school basketball the last time you balanced your checkbook?
- Have you ever been tempted to burn down your house so you don't have to try to find all of the receipts and records that you need to fill out your tax return?

If you think it is hard to keep track of the many transactions that make up *your* life, imagine what it is like for a major corporation like Fidelity Investments. Fidelity is one of the largest mutual fund management firms in the world. If you had your life savings invested at Fidelity Investments, you might be just slightly displeased if, when you checked your balance online, a message appeared on the screen indicating that your account information was lost.

To ensure the accuracy of your balance and the security of your funds, Fidelity Investments, like all other companies large and small, relies on a sophisticated accounting information system. That's not to say that Fidelity or any other

✓ The Navigator

- Scan Learning Objectives
- Read Feature Story
- Read Preview
- Read text and answer **DO IT!** p. 59 p. 62 p. 71 p. 76
- Work Comprehensive **DO IT!** p. 76
- Review Summary of Learning Objectives
- Answer Self-Test Questions
- Complete Assignments
- Go to **WileyPLUS** for practice and tutorials

Read A Look at IFRS p. 97

Learning Objectives

After studying this chapter, you should be able to:

1. Explain what an account is and how it helps in the recording process.
2. Define debits and credits and explain their use in recording business transactions.
3. Identify the basic steps in the recording process.
4. Explain what a journal is and how it helps in the recording process.
5. Explain what a ledger is and how it helps in the recording process.
6. Explain what posting is and how it helps in the recording process.
7. Prepare a trial balance and explain its purposes.

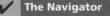

 **The Navigator**

company is error-free. In fact, if you've ever overdrawn your bank account because you failed to track your debit card purchases properly, you may take some comfort from one accountant's mistake at Fidelity Investments. The accountant failed to include a minus sign while doing a calculation, making what was actually a $1.3 billion loss look like a $1.3 billion—yes, *billion*—gain! Fortunately, like most accounting errors, it was detected before any real harm was done.

No one expects that kind of mistake at a company like Fidelity, which has sophisticated computer systems and top investment managers. In explaining the mistake to shareholders, a spokesperson wrote, "Some people have asked how, in this age of technology, such a mistake could be made. While many of our processes are computerized, accounting systems are complex and dictate that some steps must be handled manually by our managers and accountants, and people can make mistakes."

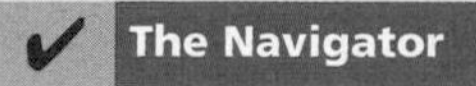

Preview of Chapter 2

In Chapter 1, we analyzed business transactions in terms of the accounting equation. We then presented the cumulative effects of these transactions in tabular form. Imagine a company like Fidelity Investments (as in the Feature Story) using the same tabular format as Softbyte Inc. to keep track of its transactions. In a single day, Fidelity engages in thousands of business transactions. To record each transaction this way would be impractical, expensive, and unnecessary. Instead, companies use a set of procedures and records to keep track of transaction data more easily. This chapter introduces and illustrates these basic procedures and records.

The content and organization of Chapter 2 are as follows.

THE RECORDING PROCESS

The Account	Steps in the Recording Process	The Recording Process Illustrated	The Trial Balance
• Debits and credits • Stockholders' equity relationships • Summary of debit/credit rules	• Journal • Ledger • Posting	• Summary illustration of journalizing and posting	• Limitations of a trial balance • Locating errors • Use of dollar signs

✔ The Navigator

The Account

LEARNING OBJECTIVE 1

Explain what an account is and how it helps in the recording process.

An **account** is an individual accounting record of increases and decreases in a specific asset, liability, or owner's equity item. For example, Softbyte Inc. (the company discussed in Chapter 1) would have separate accounts for Cash, Accounts Receivable, Accounts Payable, Service Revenue, Salaries and Wages Expense, and so on. (Note that whenever we are referring to a specific account, we capitalize the name.)

In its simplest form, an account consists of three parts: (1) a title, (2) a left or debit side, and (3) a right or credit side. Because the format of an account resembles the letter T, we refer to it as a **T-account**. Illustration 2-1 shows the basic form of an account.

Illustration 2-1
Basic form of account

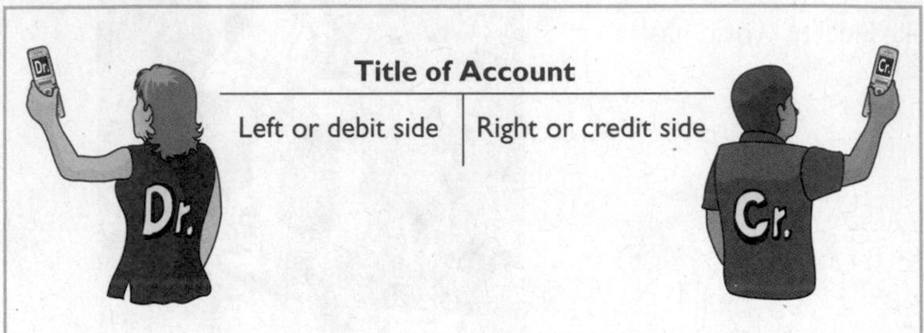

We use this form often throughout this book to explain basic accounting relationships.

Debits and Credits

LEARNING OBJECTIVE 2

Define debits and credits and explain their use in recording business transactions.

The term **debit** indicates the left side of an account, and **credit** indicates the right side. They are commonly abbreviated as **Dr.** for debit and **Cr.** for credit. They **do not** mean increase or decrease, as is commonly thought. We use the terms *debit* and *credit* repeatedly in the recording process to describe **where** entries are made in accounts. For example, the act of entering an amount on the left side of an account is called **debiting** the account. Making an entry on the right side is **crediting** the account.

When comparing the totals of the two sides, an account shows a **debit balance** if the total of the debit amounts exceeds the credits. An account shows a **credit balance** if the credit amounts exceed the debits. Note the position of the debit side and credit side in Illustration 2-1.

The procedure of recording debits and credits in an account is shown in Illustration 2-2 for the transactions affecting the Cash account of Softbyte Inc. The data are taken from the Cash column of the tabular summary in Illustration 1-9 (page 21).

Illustration 2-2
Tabular summary and account form for Softbyte's Cash account

Tabular Summary

Cash
$15,000
−7,000
1,200
1,500
−1,700
−250
600
−1,300
$ 8,050

Account Form

Cash			
(Debits)	15,000	(Credits)	7,000
	1,200		1,700
	1,500		250
	600		1,300
Balance (Debit)	8,050		

Every positive item in the tabular summary represents a receipt of cash; every negative amount represents a payment of cash. **Notice that in the account form we record the increases in cash as debits, and the decreases in cash as credits.** For example, the $15,000 receipt of cash (in red) is debited to Cash, and the −$7,000 payment of cash (in blue) is credited to Cash.

Having increases on one side and decreases on the other reduces recording errors and helps in determining the totals of each side of the account as well as the account balance. The balance is determined by netting the two sides (subtracting one amount from the other). The account balance, a debit of $8,050, indicates that Softbyte had $8,050 more increases than decreases in cash. That is, since it started with a balance of zero, it has $8,050 in its Cash account.

DEBIT AND CREDIT PROCEDURE

In Chapter 1, you learned the effect of a transaction on the basic accounting equation. Remember that each transaction must affect two or more accounts to keep the basic accounting equation in balance. In other words, for each transaction, debits must equal credits. The equality of debits and credits provides the basis for the **double-entry system** of recording transactions.

Under the double-entry system, the dual (two-sided) effect of each transaction is recorded in appropriate accounts. This system provides a logical method for recording transactions. The double-entry system also helps ensure the accuracy of the recorded amounts and helps to detect errors such as those at Fidelity Investments as discussed in the Feature Story. If every transaction is recorded with equal debits and credits, the sum of all the debits to the accounts must equal the sum of all the credits.

International Note

Rules for accounting for specific events sometimes differ across countries. For example, European companies rely less on historical cost and more on fair value than U.S. companies. Despite the differences, the double-entry accounting system is the basis of accounting systems worldwide.

The double-entry system for determining the equality of the accounting equation is much more efficient than the plus/minus procedure used in Chapter 1. On the following pages, we will illustrate debit and credit procedures in the double-entry system.

DR./CR. PROCEDURES FOR ASSETS AND LIABILITIES

In Illustration 2-2 for Softbyte Inc. increases in Cash—an asset—were entered on the left side, and decreases in Cash were entered on the right side. We know that both sides of the basic equation (Assets = Liabilities + Stockholders' Equity) must be equal. It therefore follows that increases and decreases in liabilities will have to be recorded *opposite from* increases and decreases in assets. Thus, increases in liabilities must be entered on the right or credit side, and decreases in liabilities must be entered on the left or debit side. The effects that debits and credits have on assets and liabilities are summarized in Illustration 2-3.

Debits	Credits
Increase assets	Decrease assets
Decrease liabilities	Increase liabilities

Illustration 2-3
Debit and credit effects—assets and liabilities

Asset accounts normally show debit balances. That is, debits to a specific asset account should exceed credits to that account. Likewise, **liability accounts normally show credit balances**. That is, credits to a liability account should exceed debits to that account. The **normal balance** of an account is on the side where an increase in the account is recorded. Illustration 2-4 (page 56) shows the normal balances for assets and liabilities.

Illustration 2-4
Normal balances—assets and liabilities

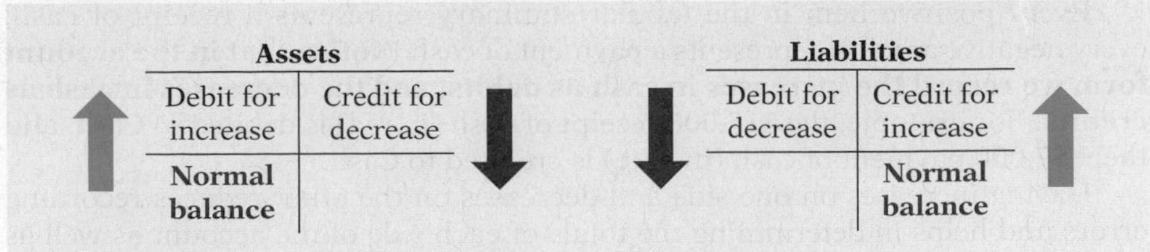

Knowing the normal balance in an account may help you trace errors. For example, a credit balance in an asset account such as Land or a debit balance in a liability account such as Salaries and Wages Payable usually indicates an error. Occasionally, though, an abnormal balance may be correct. The Cash account, for example, will have a credit balance when a company has overdrawn its bank balance (i.e., written a check that "bounced").

STOCKHOLDERS' EQUITY

As Chapter 1 indicated, there are five subdivisions of stockholders' equity: common stock, retained earnings, dividends, revenues, and expenses. In a double-entry system, companies keep accounts for each of these subdivisions, as explained below.

COMMON STOCK Companies issue **common stock** in exchange for the owners' investment paid in to the corporation. Credits increase the Common Stock account, and debits decrease it. For example, when an owner invests cash in the business in exchange for shares of the corporation's stock, the company debits (increases) Cash and credits (increases) Common Stock.

Illustration 2-5 shows the rules of debit and credit for the Common Stock account.

Illustration 2-5
Debit and credit effects—common stock

Debits	**Credits**
Decrease Common Stock	Increase Common Stock

We can diagram the normal balance in Common Stock as follows.

Illustration 2-6
Normal balance—common stock

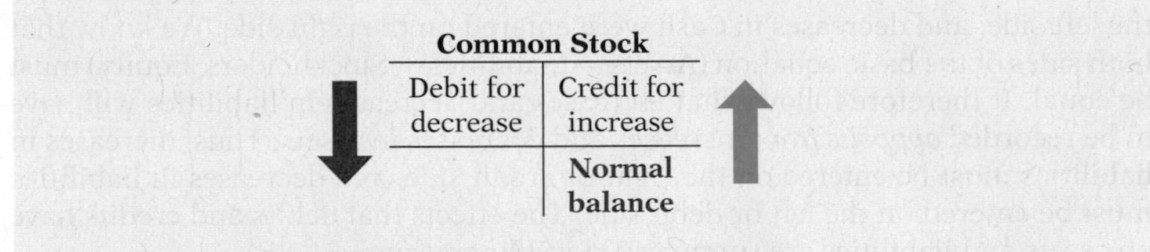

Helpful Hint
The rules for debit and credit and the normal balances of common stock and retained earnings are the same as for liabilities.

RETAINED EARNINGS **Retained earnings** is net income that is kept (retained) in the business. It represents the portion of stockholders' equity that the company has accumulated through the profitable operation of the business. Credits (net income) increase the Retained Earnings account, and debits (dividends or net losses) decrease it, as Illustration 2-7 shows.

Illustration 2-7
Debit and credit effects and normal balance—retained earnings

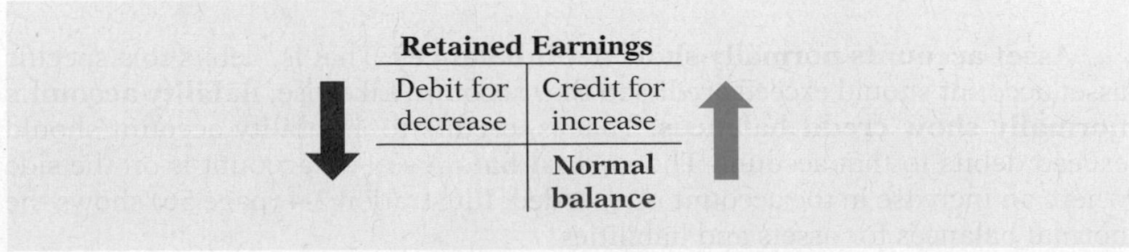

DIVIDENDS A **dividend** is a company's distribution to its stockholders on a pro rata (equal) basis. The most common form of a distribution is a **cash dividend**. Dividends reduce the stockholders' claims on retained earnings. Debits increase the Dividends account, and credits decrease it. Illustration 2-8 shows that this account normally has a debit balance.

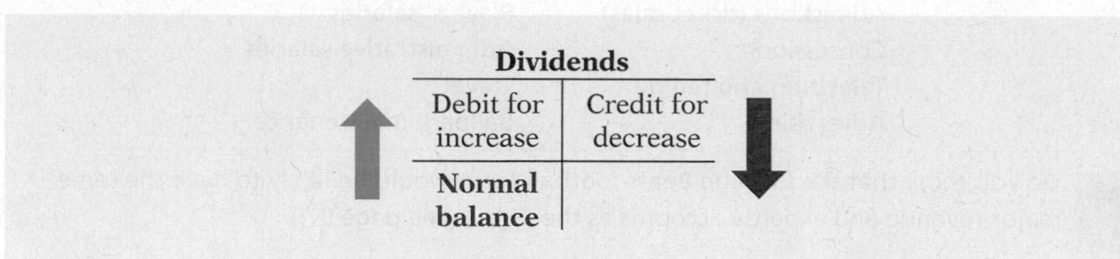

Illustration 2-8
Debit and credit effect and normal balance—dividends

REVENUES AND EXPENSES

The purpose of earning revenues is to benefit the stockholders of the business. When a company earns revenues, stockholders' equity increases. Revenues are a subdivision of stockholders' equity that provides information as to **why** stockholders' equity increased. Credits increase revenue accounts and debits decrease them. Therefore, **the effect of debits and credits on revenue accounts is the same as their effect on stockholders' equity**.

Expenses have the opposite effect: expenses decrease stockholders' equity. Since expenses decrease net income, and revenues increase it, it is logical that the increase and decrease sides of expense accounts should be the reverse of revenue accounts. Thus, debits increase expense accounts, and credits decrease them.

Illustration 2-9 shows the effect of debits and credits on revenues and expenses.

Helpful Hint
Because revenues increase stockholders' equity, a revenue account has the same debit/credit rules as the Common Stock account. Expenses have the opposite effect.

Debits	Credits
Decrease revenues	Increase revenues
Increase expenses	Decrease expenses

Illustration 2-9
Debit and credit effects—revenues and expenses

Credits to revenue accounts should exceed debits. Debits to expense accounts should exceed credits. Thus, revenue accounts normally show credit balances, and expense accounts normally show debit balances. We can diagram the normal balance as follows.

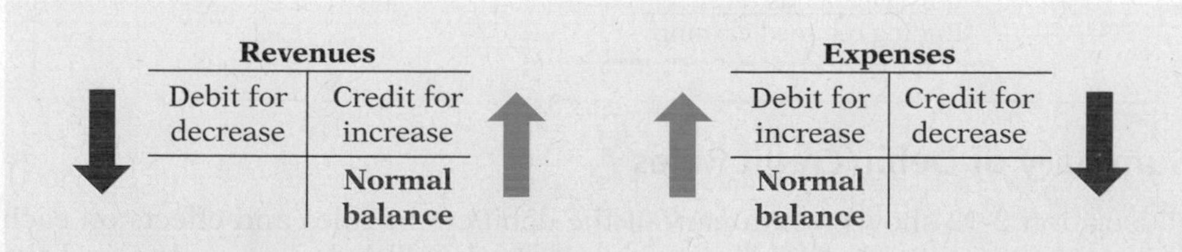

Illustration 2-10
Normal balances—revenues and expenses

INVESTOR INSIGHT

Keeping Score

The Chicago Cubs baseball team has these major revenue and expense accounts:

Revenues	Expenses
Admissions (ticket sales)	Players' salaries
Concessions	Administrative salaries
Television and radio	Travel
Advertising	Ballpark maintenance

? Do you think that the Chicago Bears football team would be likely to have the same major revenue and expense accounts as the Cubs? (See page 97.)

Stockholders' Equity Relationships

As Chapter 1 indicated, companies report common stock and retained earnings in the stockholders' equity section of the balance sheet. They report dividends on the retained earnings statement. And they report revenues and expenses on the income statement. Dividends, revenues, and expenses are eventually transferred to retained earnings at the end of the period. As a result, a change in any one of these three items affects stockholders' equity. Illustration 2-11 shows the relationships related to stockholders' equity.

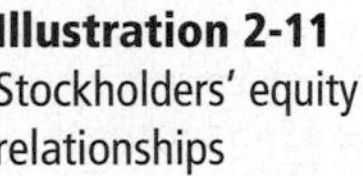

Illustration 2-11
Stockholders' equity relationships

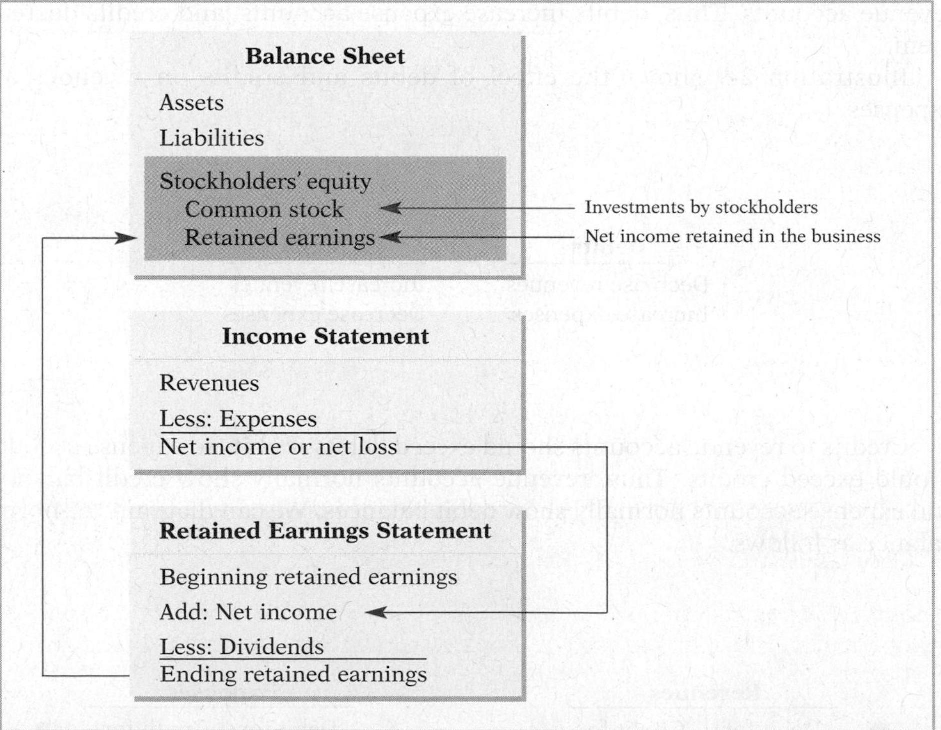

Summary of Debit/Credit Rules

Illustration 2-12 shows a summary of the debit/credit rules and effects on each type of account. Study this diagram carefully. It will help you understand the fundamentals of the double-entry system.

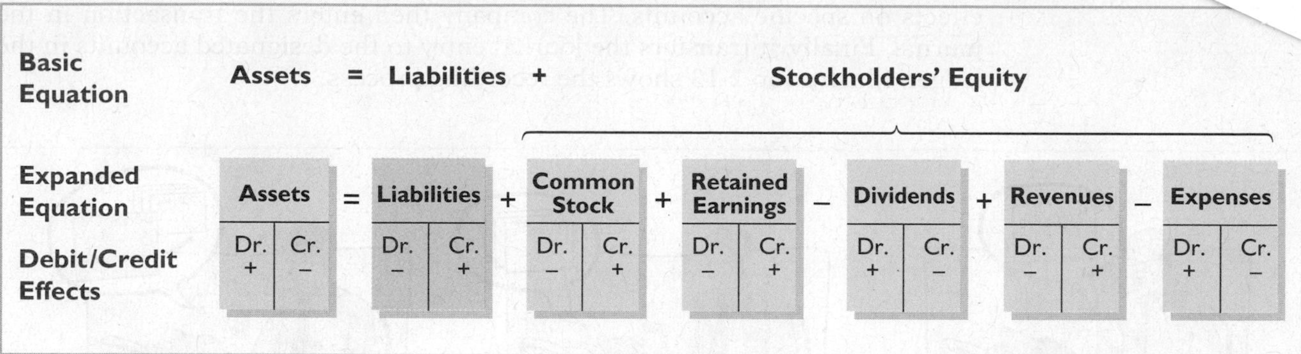

Illustration 2-12
Summary of debit/credit rules

> DO IT!

Normal Balances

Action Plan

✔ Determine the types of accounts needed. Kate will need asset accounts for each different type of asset she invests in the business, and liability accounts for any debts she incurs.

✔ Understand the types of stockholders' equity accounts. When Kate begins the business, she will need only Common Stock. Later, she will need other stockholders' equity accounts.

Kate Browne, president of Hair It Is, Inc., has just rented space in a shopping mall in which she will open and operate a beauty salon. A friend has advised Kate to set up a double-entry set of accounting records in which to record all of her business transactions.

Identify the balance sheet accounts that Hair It Is, Inc., will likely need to record the transactions needed to establish and open the business. Also, indicate whether the normal balance of each account is a debit or a credit.

Solution

Hair It Is, Inc., would likely need the following accounts to record the transactions needed to ready the beauty salon for opening day:

Cash (debit balance)	Equipment (debit balance)
Supplies (debit balance)	Accounts Payable (credit balance)
Notes Payable (credit balance), if the business borrows money	Common Stock (credit balance)

Related exercise material: **BE2-1, BE2-2, BE2-5, E2-1, E2-2, E2-4, and DO IT! 2-1.**

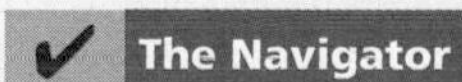
✔ The Navigator

Steps in the Recording Process

LEARNING OBJECTIVE 3
Identify the basic steps in the recording process.

Although it is possible to enter transaction information directly into the accounts without using a journal, few businesses do so. Practically every business uses three basic steps in the recording process:

1. Analyze each transaction for its effects on the accounts.
2. Enter the transaction information in a *journal*.
3. Transfer the journal information to the appropriate accounts in the *ledger*.

The recording process begins with the transaction. **Business documents**, such as a sales slip, a check, a bill, or a cash register tape, provide evidence of the transaction. The company analyzes this evidence to determine the transaction's effects on specific accounts. The company then enters the transaction in the journal. Finally, it transfers the journal entry to the designated accounts in the ledger. Illustration 2-13 shows the recording process.

Illustration 2-13
The recording process

The steps in the recording process occur repeatedly. In Chapter 1, we illustrated the first step, the analysis of transactions, and will give further examples in this and later chapters. The other two steps in the recording process are explained in the next sections.

The Journal

LEARNING OBJECTIVE 4

Explain what a journal is and how it helps in the recording process.

Companies initially record transactions in chronological order (the order in which they occur). Thus, the **journal** is referred to as the book of original entry. For each transaction, the journal shows the debit and credit effects on specific accounts.

Companies may use various kinds of journals, but every company has the most basic form of journal, a **general journal**. Typically, a general journal has spaces for dates, account titles and explanations, references, and two amount columns. (See the format of the journal in Illustration 2-14, page 61.) *Whenever we use the term "journal" in this textbook, we mean the general journal, unless we specify otherwise.*

The journal makes several significant contributions to the recording process:

1. It discloses in one place the **complete effects of a transaction**.
2. It provides a **chronological record** of transactions.
3. It helps **to prevent or locate errors** because the debit and credit amounts for each entry can be easily compared.

JOURNALIZING

Entering transaction data in the journal is known as **journalizing**. Companies make separate journal entries for each transaction. A complete entry consists of: (1) the date of the transaction, (2) the accounts and amounts to be debited and credited, and (3) a brief explanation of the transaction.

Illustration 2-14 shows the technique of journalizing, using the first two transactions of Softbyte Inc. On September 1, stockholders invested $15,000 cash in the corporation in exchange for shares of stock, and Softbyte purchased computer equipment for $7,000 cash. The number J1 indicates that the company records these two entries on the first page of the general journal. (The boxed numbers correspond to explanations in the list below the illustration.)

Illustration 2-14
Technique of journalizing

General Journal				J1
Date	**Account Titles and Explanation**	**Ref.**	**Debit**	**Credit**
2014		[5]		
Sept. 1	[2] Cash		15,000	
[1]	[3] Common Stock			15,000
	[4] (Issued shares of stock for cash)			
1	Equipment		7,000	
	Cash			7,000
	(Purchase equipment for cash)			

[1] The date of the transaction is entered in the Date column.

[2] The debit account title (that is, the account to be debited) is entered first at the extreme left margin of the column headed "Account Titles and Explanation," and the amount of the debit is recorded in the Debit column.

[3] The credit account title (that is, the account to be credited) is indented and entered on the next line in the column headed "Account Titles and Explanation," and the amount of the credit is recorded in the Credit column.

[4] A brief explanation of the transaction appears on the line below the credit account title. A space is left between journal entries. The blank space separates individual journal entries and makes the entire journal easier to read.

[5] The column titled Ref. (which stands for Reference) is left blank when the journal entry is made. This column is used later when the journal entries are transferred to the ledger accounts.

It is important to use correct and specific account titles in journalizing. Erroneous account titles lead to incorrect financial statements. However, some flexibility exists initially in selecting account titles. The main criterion is that each title must appropriately describe the content of the account. Once a company chooses the specific title to use, it should record under that account title all later transactions involving the account.[1]

SIMPLE AND COMPOUND ENTRIES

Some entries involve only two accounts, one debit and one credit. (See, for example, the entries in Illustration 2-14.) An entry like these is considered a **simple entry**. Some transactions, however, require more than two accounts in journalizing. An entry that requires three or more accounts is a **compound entry**. To illustrate, assume that on July 1, Butler Company purchases a delivery truck costing $14,000. It pays $8,000 cash now and agrees to pay the remaining $6,000 on account (to be paid later). The compound entry is as follows.

Illustration 2-15
Compound journal entry

General Journal				J1
Date	**Account Titles and Explanation**	**Ref.**	**Debit**	**Credit**
2014				
July 1	Equipment		14,000	
	Cash			8,000
	Accounts Payable			6,000
	(Purchased truck for cash with balance on account)			

[1] *In homework problems, you should use specific account titles when they are given.* When account titles are not given, you may select account titles that identify the nature and content of each account. The account titles used in journalizing should not contain explanations such as Cash Paid or Cash Received.

In a compound entry, the standard format requires that all debits be listed before the credits.

DO IT!

Recording Business Activities

As president and sole stockholder, Kate Browne engaged in the following activities in establishing her beauty salon, Hair It Is, Inc.

1. Opened a bank account in the name of Hair It Is, Inc. and deposited $20,000 of her own money in this account in exchange for shares of common stock.
2. Purchased equipment on account (to be paid in 30 days) for a total cost of $4,800.
3. Interviewed three applicants for the position of beautician.

In what form (type of record) should Hair It Is, Inc., record these three activities? Prepare the entries to record the transactions.

Action Plan

✔ Understand which activities need to be recorded and which do not. Any that have economic effects should be recorded in a journal.

✔ Analyze the effects of transactions on asset, liability, and stockholders' equity accounts.

Solution

Each transaction that is recorded is entered in the general journal. The three activities would be recorded as follows.

	Debit	Credit
1. Cash	20,000	
Common Stock		20,000
(Issued shares of stock for cash)		
2. Equipment	4,800	
Accounts Payable		4,800
(Purchase of equipment on account)		

3. No entry because no transaction has occurred.

Related exercise material: **BE2-3, BE2-6, E2-3, E2-5, E2-6, E2-7, and DO IT! 2-2.**

The Ledger

LEARNING OBJECTIVE 5

Explain what a ledger is and how it helps in the recording process.

The entire group of accounts maintained by a company is the **ledger**. The ledger keeps in one place all the information about changes in specific account balances.

Companies may use various kinds of ledgers, but every company has a general ledger. A **general ledger** contains all the asset, liability, and stockholders' equity accounts, as shown in Illustration 2-16. *Whenever we use the term "ledger" in this textbook, we mean the general ledger, unless we specify otherwise.*

Illustration 2-16
The general ledger

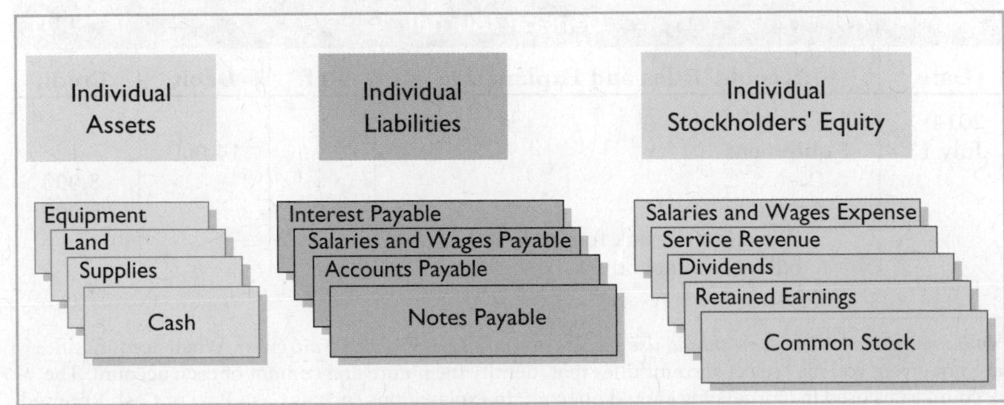

Companies arrange the ledger in the sequence in which they present the accounts in the financial statements, beginning with the balance sheet accounts. First in order are the asset accounts, followed by liability accounts, stockholders' equity accounts, revenues, and expenses. Each account is numbered for easier identification.

The ledger provides the balance in each of the accounts and keeps track of changes in these balances. For example, the Cash account shows the amount of cash available to meet current obligations. The Accounts Receivable account shows amounts due from customers. The Accounts Payable account shows amounts owned to creditors.

ACCOUNTING ACROSS THE ORGANIZATION

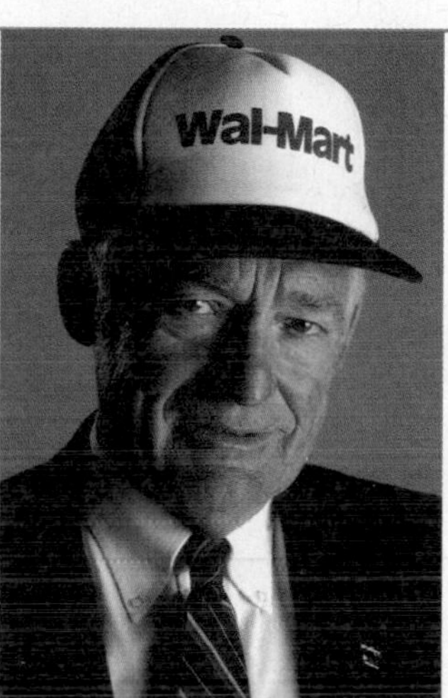

What Would Sam Do?

In his autobiography Sam Walton described the double-entry accounting system he used when Wal-Mart was just getting started: "We kept a little pigeonhole on the wall for the cash receipts and paperwork of each [Wal-Mart] store. I had a blue binder ledger book for each store. When we added a store, we added a pigeonhole. We did this at least up to twenty stores. Then once a month, the bookkeeper and I would enter the merchandise, enter the sales, enter the cash, and balance it."

Source: Sam Walton, *Made in America* (New York: Doubleday, 1992), p. 53.

Why did Sam Walton keep separate pigeonholes and blue binders? Why bother to keep separate records for each store? (See page 97.)

STANDARD FORM OF ACCOUNT

The simple T-account form used in accounting textbooks is often very useful for illustration purposes. However, in practice, the account forms used in ledgers are much more structured. Illustration 2-17 shows a typical form, using assumed data from a cash account.

Illustration 2-17
Three-column form of account

Cash					No. 101
Date	**Explanation**	**Ref.**	**Debit**	**Credit**	**Balance**
2014					
June 1			25,000		25,000
2				8,000	17,000
3			4,200		21,200
9			7,500		28,700
17				11,700	17,000
20				250	16,750
30				7,300	9,450

This is called the **three-column form of account**. It has three money columns—debit, credit, and balance. The balance in the account is determined after each transaction. Companies use the explanation space and reference columns to provide special information about the transaction.

Posting

LEARNING OBJECTIVE 6

Explain what posting is and how it helps in the recording process.

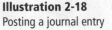

Transferring journal entries to the ledger accounts is called **posting**. This phase of the recording process accumulates the effects of journalized transactions into the individual accounts. Posting involves the following steps.

1. In the **ledger**, enter, in the appropriate columns of the account(s) debited, the date, journal page, and debit amount shown in the journal.
2. In the reference column of the **journal**, write the account number to which the debit amount was posted.
3. In the **ledger**, enter, in the appropriate columns of the account(s) credited, the date, journal page, and credit amount shown in the journal.
4. In the reference column of the **journal**, write the account number to which the credit amount was posted.

Illustration 2-18 shows these four steps using Softbyte Inc.'s first journal entry, the issuance of common stock for $15,000 cash. The boxed numbers indicate the sequence of the steps.

Illustration 2-18
Posting a journal entry

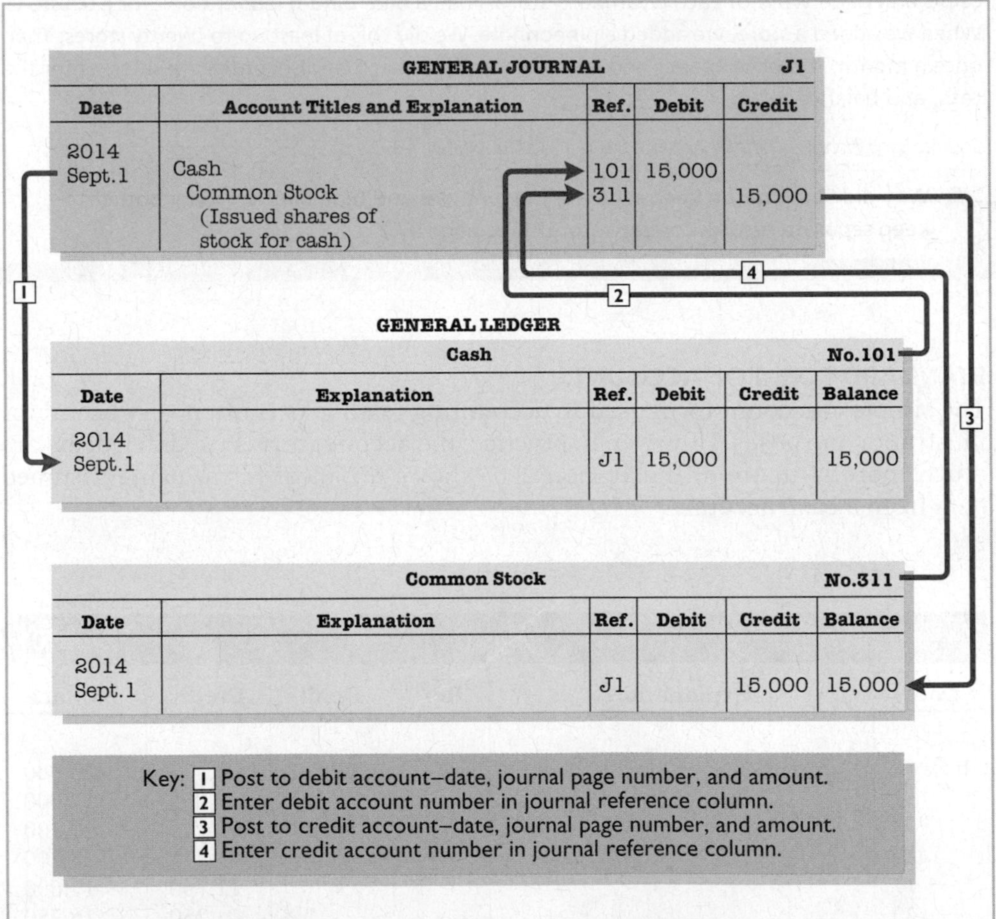

GENERAL JOURNAL J1

Date	Account Titles and Explanation	Ref.	Debit	Credit
2014 Sept. 1	Cash	101	15,000	
	Common Stock	311		15,000
	(Issued shares of stock for cash)			

GENERAL LEDGER

Cash No. 101

Date	Explanation	Ref.	Debit	Credit	Balance
2014 Sept. 1		J1	15,000		15,000

Common Stock No. 311

Date	Explanation	Ref.	Debit	Credit	Balance
2014 Sept. 1		J1		15,000	15,000

Posting should be performed in chronological order. That is, the company should post all the debits and credits of one journal entry before proceeding to the next journal entry. Postings should be made on a timely basis to ensure that the ledger is up to date.[2]

[2] *In homework problems, you can journalize all transactions before posting any of the journal entries.*

The reference column **of a ledger** account indicates the journal page from which the transaction was posted.[3] The explanation space of the ledger account is used infrequently because an explanation already appears in the journal.

CHART OF ACCOUNTS

The number and type of accounts differ for each company. The number of accounts depends on the amount of detail management desires. For example, the management of one company may want a single account for all types of utility expense. Another may keep separate expense accounts for each type of utility, such as gas, electricity, and water. Similarly, a small company like Softbyte Inc. will have fewer accounts than a corporate giant like Dell. Softbyte may be able to manage and report its activities in 20 to 30 accounts, while Dell may require thousands of accounts to keep track of its worldwide activities.

Most companies have a **chart of accounts**. This chart lists the accounts and the account numbers that identify their location in the ledger. The numbering system that identifies the accounts usually starts with the balance sheet accounts and follows with the income statement accounts.

Helpful Hint
On the textbook's endpapers, you will also find an expanded chart of accounts.

In this and the next two chapters, we will be explaining the accounting for Pioneer Advertising Agency Inc. (a service company). The ranges of the account numbers are as follows.

- Accounts 101–199 indicate asset accounts
- 200–299 indicate liabilities
- 300–399 indicate stockholders' equity accounts
- 400–499, revenues
- 500–799, expenses
- 800–899, other revenues
- 900–999, other expenses.

Illustration 2-19 shows the chart of accounts for Pioneer Advertising Agency Inc. Accounts shown in red are used in this chapter. Accounts shown in black are explained in later chapters.

Illustration 2-19
Chart of accounts for Pioneer Advertising Agency Inc.

Pioneer Advertising Agency Inc. Chart of Accounts	
Assets	**Stockholders' Equity**
101 Cash	**311 Common Stock**
112 Accounts Receivable	320 Retained Earnings
126 Supplies	**332 Dividends**
130 Prepaid Insurance	350 Income Summary
157 Equipment	
158 Accumulated Depreciation—Equipment	**Revenues**
	400 Service Revenue
Liabilities	**Expenses**
200 Notes Payable	631 Supplies Expense
201 Accounts Payable	711 Depreciation Expense
209 Unearned Service Revenue	722 Insurance Expense
212 Salaries and Wages Payable	**726 Salaries and Wages Expense**
230 Interest Payable	**729 Rent Expense**
	905 Interest Expense

[3]After the last entry has been posted, the accountant should scan the reference column **in the journal**, to confirm that all postings have been made.

You will notice that there are gaps in the numbering system of the chart of accounts for Pioneer Advertising. Gaps are left to permit the insertion of new accounts as needed during the life of the business.

The Recording Process Illustrated

Illustrations 2-20 through 2-29 show the basic steps in the recording process, using the October transactions of Pioneer Advertising Agency Inc. Pioneer's accounting period is a month. A basic analysis and a debit-credit analysis precede the journalizing and posting of each transaction. For simplicity, we use the T-account form in the illustrations instead of the standard account form.

Study these transaction analyses carefully. **The purpose of transaction analysis is first to identify the type of account involved, and then to determine whether to make a debit or a credit to the account.** You should always perform this type of analysis before preparing a journal entry. Doing so will help you understand the journal entries discussed in this chapter as well as more complex journal entries in later chapters.

In addition, an Accounting Cycle Tutorial is available in *WileyPLUS*. It provides an interactive presentation of the steps in the accounting cycle, using the examples in the illustrations on the following pages.

Illustration 2-20
Investment of cash by stockholders

Helpful Hint
Follow these steps:
1. Determine what type of account is involved.
2. Determine what items increased or decreased and by how much.
3. Translate the increases and decreases into debits and credits.

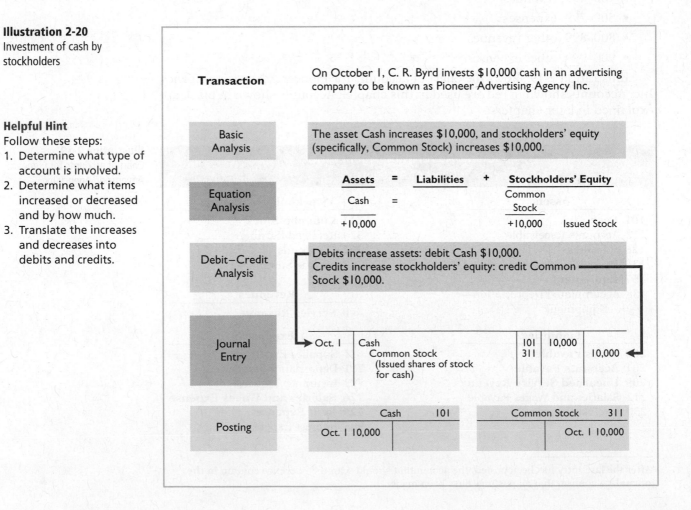

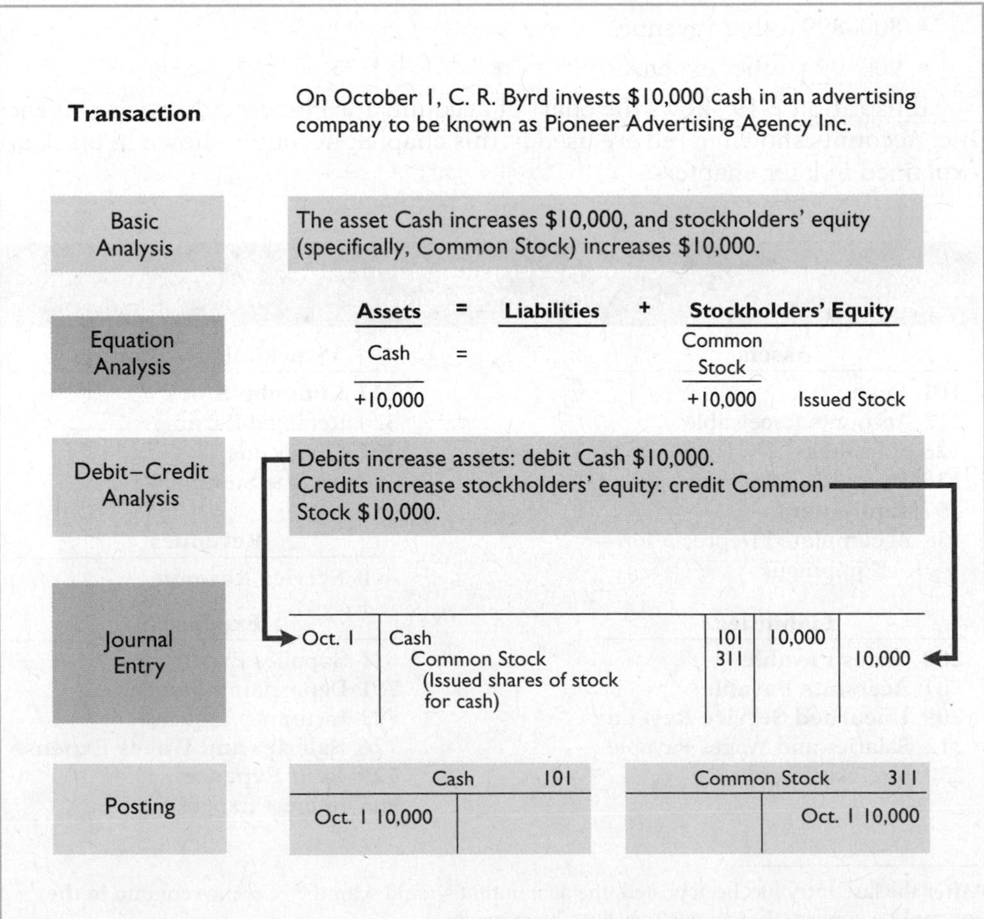

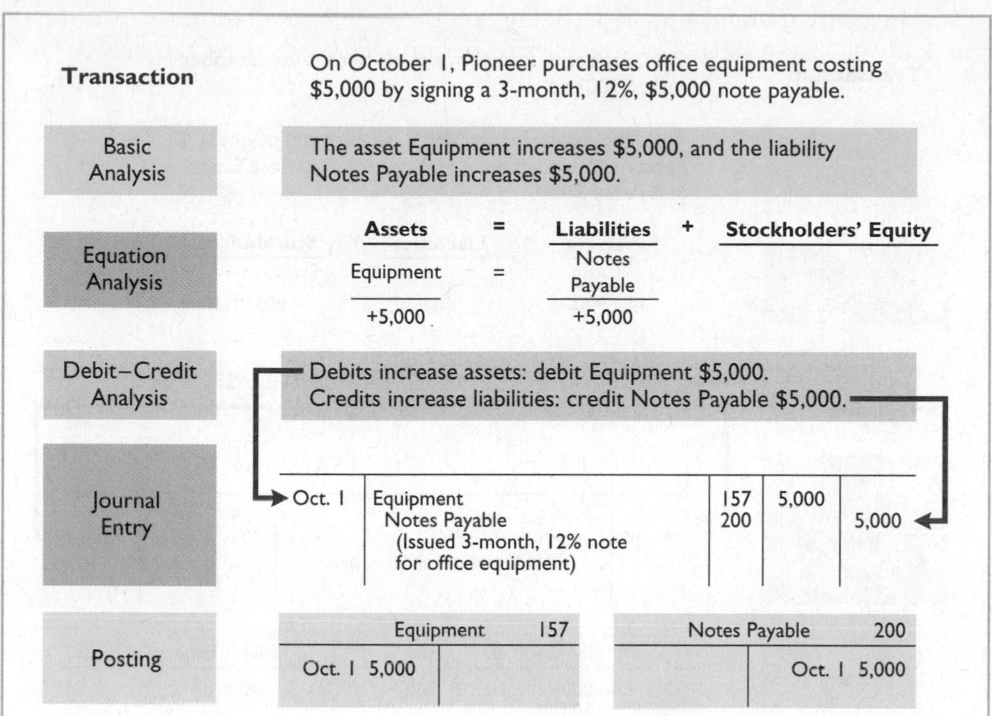

Transaction
On October 1, Pioneer purchases office equipment costing $5,000 by signing a 3-month, 12%, $5,000 note payable.
Basic Analysis
The asset Equipment increases $5,000, and the liability Notes Payable increases $5,000.
Equation Analysis
Assets = Liabilities + Stockholders' Equity
Equipment = Notes Payable
+5,000 +5,000
Debit–Credit Analysis
Debits increase assets: debit Equipment $5,000.
Credits increase liabilities: credit Notes Payable $5,000.
Journal Entry
Oct. 1 Equipment 157 5,000
Notes Payable 200 5,000
(Issued 3-month, 12% note for office equipment)
Posting
Equipment 157
Oct. 1 5,000
Notes Payable 200
Oct. 1 5,000

Illustration 2-21
Purchase of office equipment

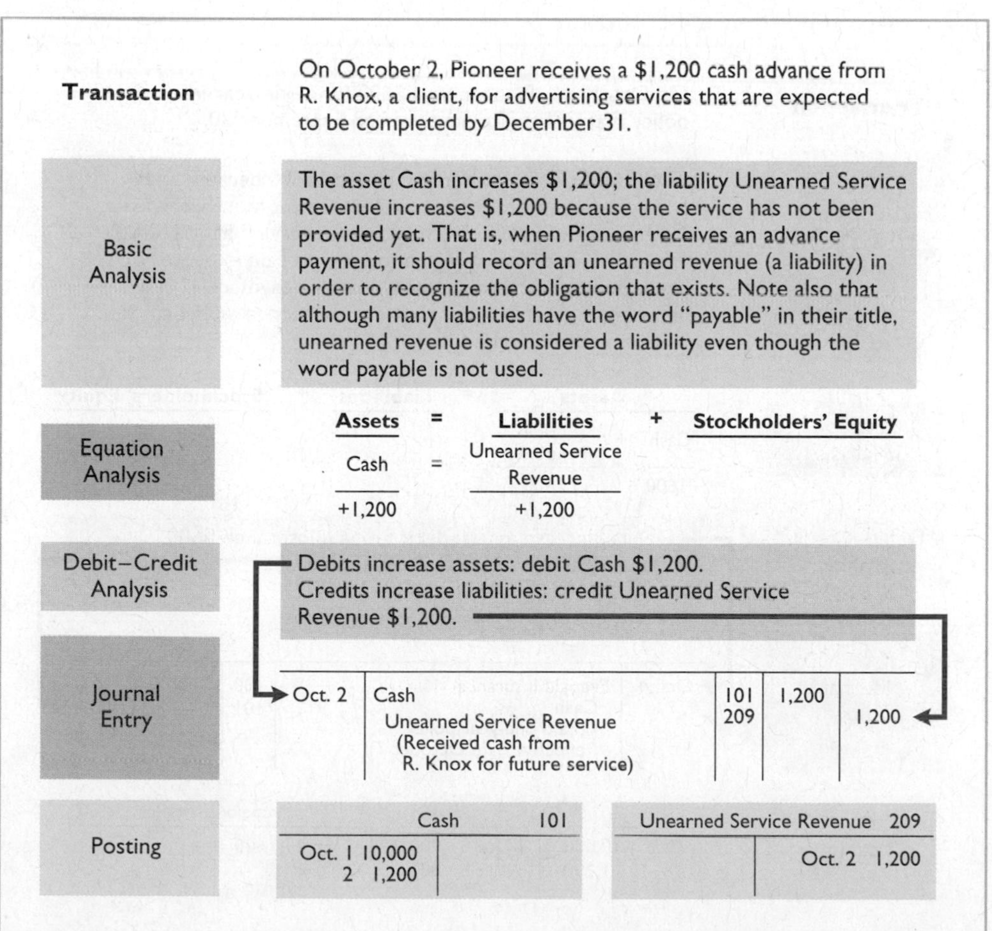

Transaction
On October 2, Pioneer receives a $1,200 cash advance from R. Knox, a client, for advertising services that are expected to be completed by December 31.
Basic Analysis
The asset Cash increases $1,200; the liability Unearned Service Revenue increases $1,200 because the service has not been provided yet. That is, when Pioneer receives an advance payment, it should record an unearned revenue (a liability) in order to recognize the obligation that exists. Note also that although many liabilities have the word "payable" in their title, unearned revenue is considered a liability even though the word payable is not used.
Equation Analysis
Assets = Liabilities + Stockholders' Equity
Cash = Unearned Service Revenue
+1,200 +1,200
Debit–Credit Analysis
Debits increase assets: debit Cash $1,200.
Credits increase liabilities: credit Unearned Service Revenue $1,200.
Journal Entry
Oct. 2 Cash 101 1,200
Unearned Service Revenue 209 1,200
(Received cash from R. Knox for future service)
Posting
Cash 101
Oct. 1 10,000
2 1,200
Unearned Service Revenue 209
Oct. 2 1,200

Illustration 2-22
Receipt of cash for future service

Illustration 2-23
Payment of monthly rent

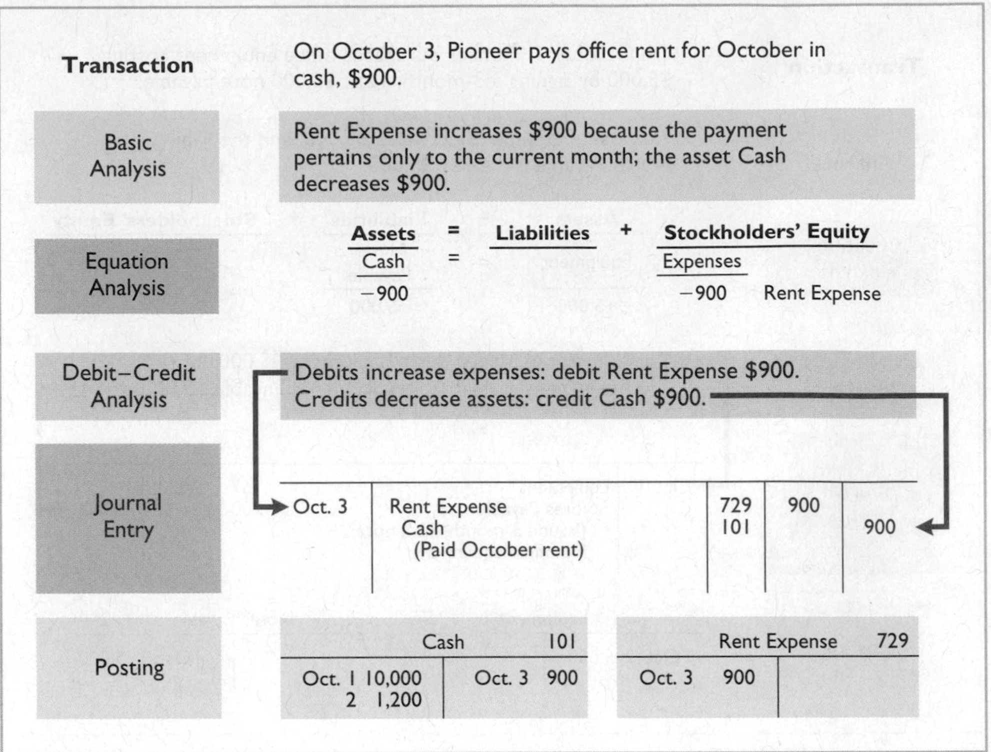

Transaction
On October 3, Pioneer pays office rent for October in cash, $900.
Basic Analysis
Rent Expense increases $900 because the payment pertains only to the current month; the asset Cash decreases $900.
Equation Analysis
Assets = Liabilities + Stockholders' Equity
Cash = Expenses
−900 −900 Rent Expense
Debit–Credit Analysis
Debits increase expenses: debit Rent Expense $900.
Credits decrease assets: credit Cash $900.
Journal Entry
Oct. 3 Rent Expense 729 900
Cash 101 900
(Paid October rent)
Posting
Cash 101
Oct. 1 10,000 Oct. 3 900
2 1,200
Rent Expense 729
Oct. 3 900

Illustration 2-24
Payment for insurance

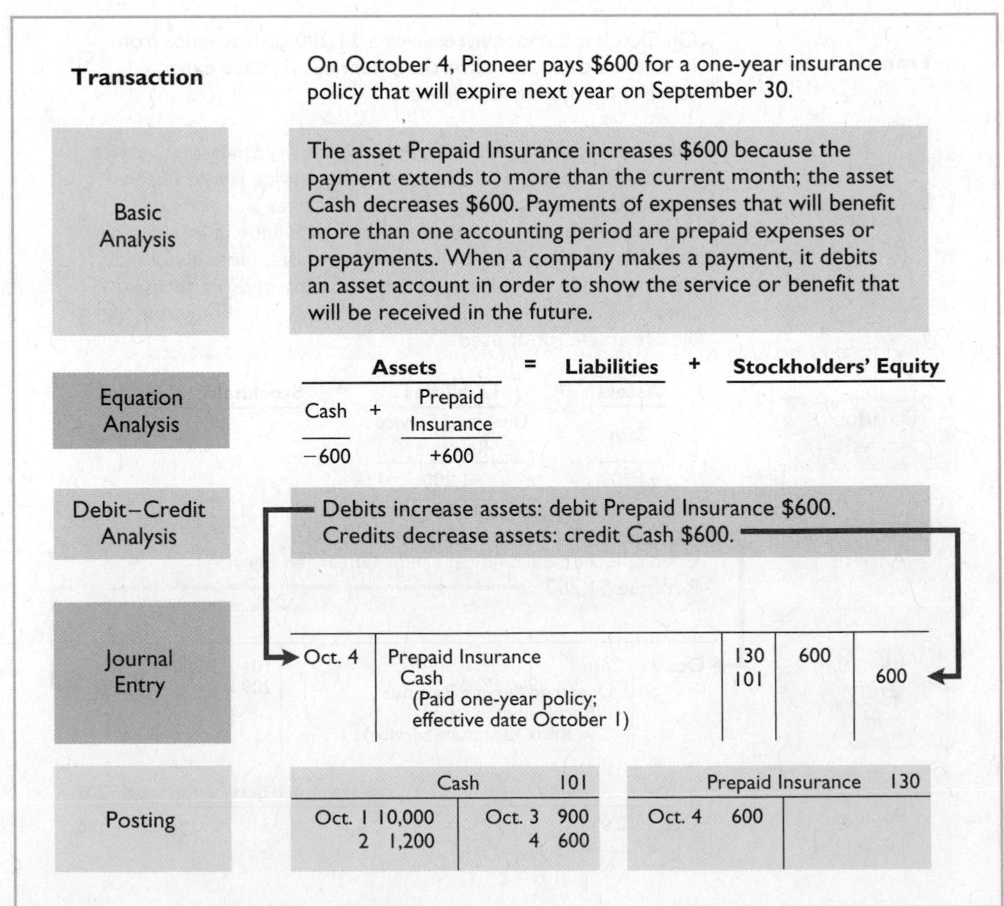

Transaction
On October 4, Pioneer pays $600 for a one-year insurance policy that will expire next year on September 30.
Basic Analysis
The asset Prepaid Insurance increases $600 because the payment extends to more than the current month; the asset Cash decreases $600. Payments of expenses that will benefit more than one accounting period are prepaid expenses or prepayments. When a company makes a payment, it debits an asset account in order to show the service or benefit that will be received in the future.
Equation Analysis
Assets = Liabilities + Stockholders' Equity
Cash + Prepaid Insurance
−600 +600
Debit–Credit Analysis
Debits increase assets: debit Prepaid Insurance $600.
Credits decrease assets: credit Cash $600.
Journal Entry
Oct. 4 Prepaid Insurance 130 600
Cash 101 600
(Paid one-year policy; effective date October 1)
Posting
Cash 101
Oct. 1 10,000 Oct. 3 900
2 1,200 4 600
Prepaid Insurance 130
Oct. 4 600

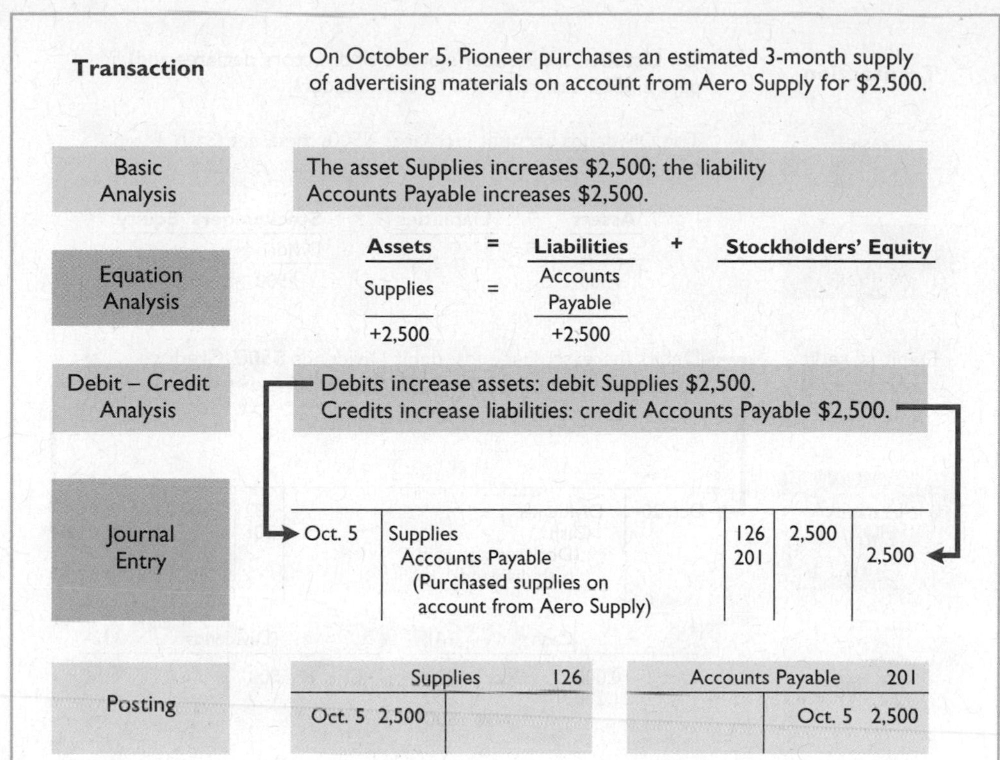

Transaction
On October 5, Pioneer purchases an estimated 3-month supply of advertising materials on account from Aero Supply for $2,500.
Basic Analysis
The asset Supplies increases $2,500; the liability Accounts Payable increases $2,500.
Equation Analysis
Assets = Liabilities + Stockholders' Equity
Supplies = Accounts Payable
+2,500 +2,500
Debit – Credit Analysis
Debits increase assets: debit Supplies $2,500.
Credits increase liabilities: credit Accounts Payable $2,500.
Journal Entry
Oct. 5 Supplies 126 2,500
Accounts Payable 201 2,500
(Purchased supplies on account from Aero Supply)
Posting
Supplies 126
Oct. 5 2,500
Accounts Payable 201
Oct. 5 2,500

Illustration 2-25
Purchase of supplies on credit

Illustration 2-26
Hiring of employees

Event	On October 9, Pioneer hires four employees to begin work on October 15. Each employee is to receive a weekly salary of $500 for a 5-day work week, payable every 2 weeks—first payment made on October 26.
Basic Analysis	A business transaction has not occurred. There is only an agreement between the employer and the employees to enter into a business transaction beginning on October 15. Thus, a debit–credit analysis is not needed because there is no accounting entry. (See transaction of October 26 for first entry.)

Illustration 2-27
Declaration and payment of dividend

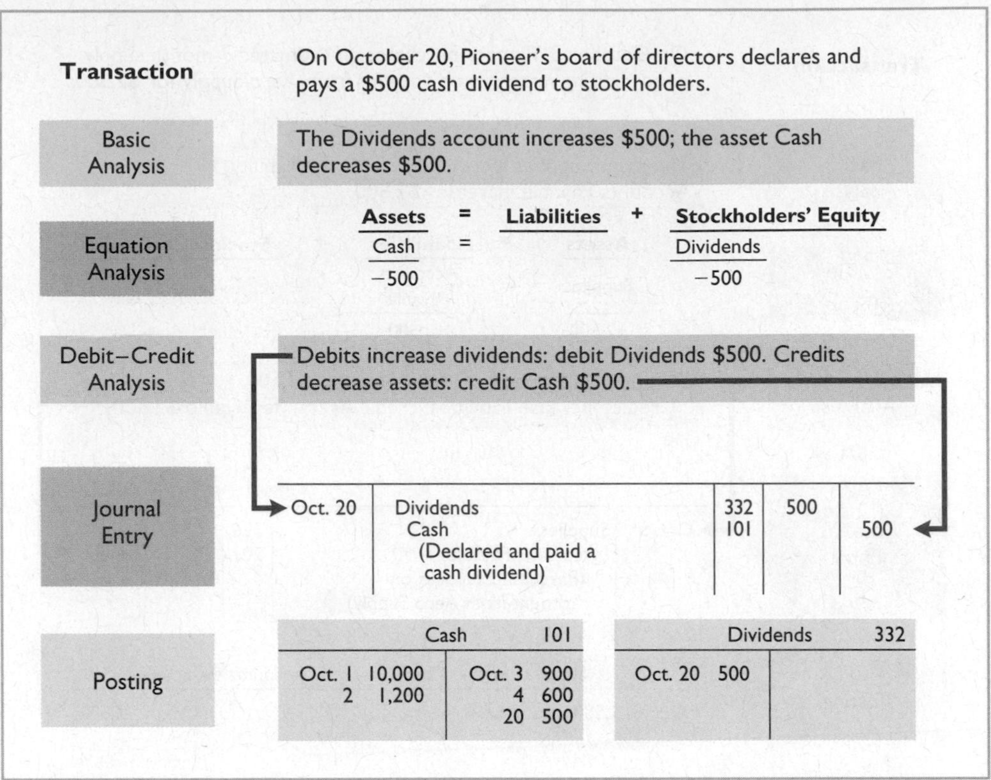

Transaction
On October 20, Pioneer's board of directors declares and pays a $500 cash dividend to stockholders.
Basic Analysis
The Dividends account increases $500; the asset Cash decreases $500.
Equation Analysis
Assets = Liabilities + Stockholders' Equity
Cash = Dividends
−500 −500
Debit–Credit Analysis
Debits increase dividends: debit Dividends $500. Credits decrease assets: credit Cash $500.
Journal Entry
Oct. 20 Dividends 332 500
Cash 101 500
(Declared and paid a cash dividend)
Posting
Cash 101
Oct. 1 10,000 Oct. 3 900
2 1,200 4 600
20 500
Dividends 332
Oct. 20 500

Illustration 2-28
Payment of salaries

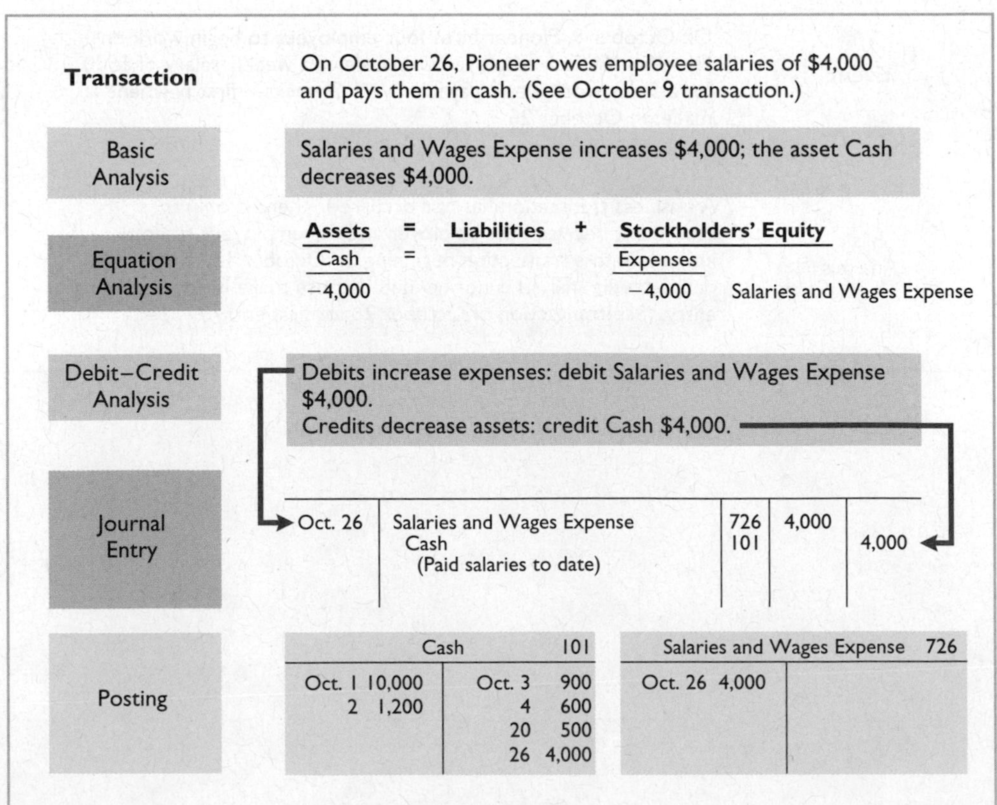

Transaction
On October 26, Pioneer owes employee salaries of $4,000 and pays them in cash. (See October 9 transaction.)
Basic Analysis
Salaries and Wages Expense increases $4,000; the asset Cash decreases $4,000.
Equation Analysis
Assets = Liabilities + Stockholders' Equity
Cash = Expenses
−4,000 −4,000 Salaries and Wages Expense
Debit–Credit Analysis
Debits increase expenses: debit Salaries and Wages Expense $4,000.
Credits decrease assets: credit Cash $4,000.
Journal Entry
Oct. 26 Salaries and Wages Expense 726 4,000
Cash 101 4,000
(Paid salaries to date)
Posting
Cash 101
Oct. 1 10,000 Oct. 3 900
2 1,200 4 600
20 500
26 4,000
Salaries and Wages Expense 726
Oct. 26 4,000

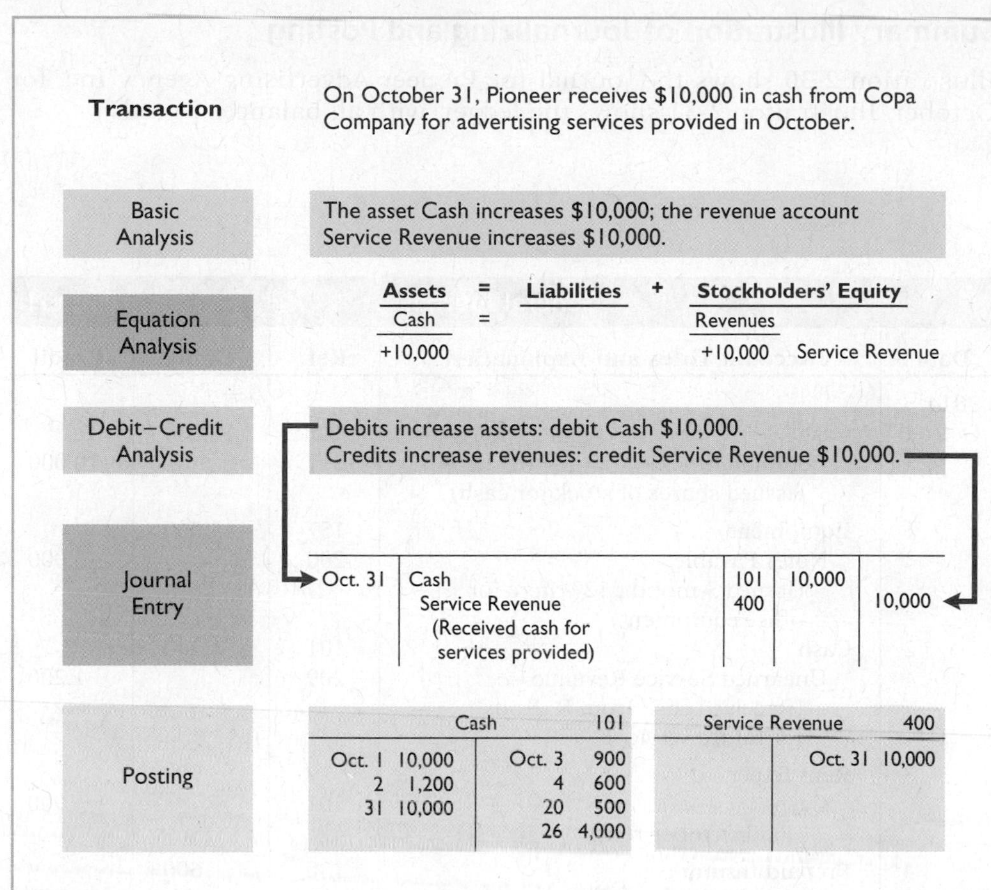

Transaction
On October 31, Pioneer receives $10,000 in cash from Copa Company for advertising services provided in October.
Basic Analysis
The asset Cash increases $10,000; the revenue account Service Revenue increases $10,000.
Equation Analysis
Assets = Liabilities + Stockholders' Equity
Cash = Revenues
+10,000 +10,000 Service Revenue
Debit–Credit Analysis
Debits increase assets: debit Cash $10,000.
Credits increase revenues: credit Service Revenue $10,000.
Journal Entry
Oct. 31 Cash 101 10,000
Service Revenue 400 10,000
(Received cash for services provided)
Posting
Cash 101
Oct. 1 10,000 Oct. 3 900
2 1,200 4 600
31 10,000 20 500
26 4,000
Service Revenue 400
Oct. 31 10,000

Illustration 2-29
Receipt of cash for services provided

> DO IT!

Posting

Kate Browne recorded the following transactions in a general journal during the month of March.

Mar. 4	Cash	2,280	
	Service Revenue		2,280
Mar. 15	Salaries and Wages Expense	400	
	Cash		400
Mar. 19	Utilities Expense	92	
	Cash		92

Post these entries to the Cash account of the general ledger to determine the ending balance in cash. The beginning balance in Cash on March 1 was $600.

Action Plan

✔ Recall that posting involves transferring the journalized debits and credits to specific accounts in the ledger.

✔ Determine the ending balance by netting the total debits and credits.

Solution

Cash			
3/1	600	3/15	400
3/4	2,280	3/19	92
3/31 Bal.	2,388		

Related exercise material: **BE2-7, BE2-8, E2-8, E2-12, and DO IT! 2-3.**

The Navigator

Summary Illustration of Journalizing and Posting

Illustration 2-30 shows the journal for Pioneer Advertising Agency Inc. for October. Illustration 2-31 shows the ledger, with all balances in red.

Illustration 2-30
General journal entries

General Journal — Page J1

Date	Account Titles and Explanation	Ref.	Debit	Credit
2014				
Oct. 1	Cash	101	10,000	
	Common Stock	311		10,000
	(Issued shares of stock for cash)			
1	Equipment	157	5,000	
	Notes Payable	200		5,000
	(Issued 3-month, 12% note for office equipment)			
2	Cash	101	1,200	
	Unearned Service Revenue	209		1,200
	(Received cash from R. Knox for future service)			
3	Rent Expense	729	900	
	Cash	101		900
	(Paid October rent)			
4	Prepaid Insurance	130	600	
	Cash	101		600
	(Paid one-year policy; effective date October 1)			
5	Supplies	126	2,500	
	Accounts Payable	201		2,500
	(Purchased supplies on account from Aero Supply)			
20	Dividends	332	500	
	Cash	101		500
	(Declared and paid a cash dividend)			
26	Salaries and Wages Expense	726	4,000	
	Cash	101		4,000
	(Paid salaries to date)			
31	Cash	101	10,000	
	Service Revenue	400		10,000
	(Received cash for services provided)			

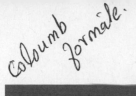

General Ledger

Cash — No. 101

Date	Explanation	Ref.	Debit	Credit	Balance
2014					
Oct. 1		J1	10,000		10,000
2		J1	1,200		11,200
3		J1		900	10,300
4		J1		600	9,700
20		J1		500	9,200
26		J1		4,000	5,200
31		J1	10,000		**15,200**

Supplies — No. 126

Date	Explanation	Ref.	Debit	Credit	Balance
2014					
Oct. 5		J1	2,500		**2,500**

Prepaid Insurance — No. 130

Date	Explanation	Ref.	Debit	Credit	Balance
2014					
Oct. 4		J1	600		**600**

Equipment — No. 157

Date	Explanation	Ref.	Debit	Credit	Balance
2014					
Oct. 1		J1	5,000		**5,000**

Notes Payable — No. 200

Date	Explanation	Ref.	Debit	Credit	Balance
2014					
Oct. 1		J1		5,000	**5,000**

Accounts Payable — No. 201

Date	Explanation	Ref.	Debit	Credit	Balance
2014					
Oct. 5		J1		2,500	**2,500**

Unearned Service Revenue — No. 209

Date	Explanation	Ref.	Debit	Credit	Balance
2014					
Oct. 2		J1		1,200	**1,200**

Common Stock — No. 311

Date	Explanation	Ref.	Debit	Credit	Balance
2014					
Oct. 1		J1		10,000	**10,000**

Dividends — No. 332

Date	Explanation	Ref.	Debit	Credit	Balance
2014					
Oct. 20		J1	500		**500**

Service Revenue — No. 400

Date	Explanation	Ref.	Debit	Credit	Balance
2014					
Oct. 31		J1		10,000	**10,000**

Salaries and Wages Expense — No. 726

Date	Explanation	Ref.	Debit	Credit	Balance
2014					
Oct. 26		J1	4,000		**4,000**

Rent Expense — No. 729

Date	Explanation	Ref.	Debit	Credit	Balance
2014					
Oct. 3		J1	900		**900**

Illustration 2-31
General ledger

The Trial Balance

LEARNING OBJECTIVE 7
Prepare a trial balance and explain its purposes.

A **trial balance** is a list of accounts and their balances at a given time. Customarily, companies prepare a trial balance at the end of an accounting period. They list accounts in the order in which they appear in the ledger. Debit balances appear in the left column and credit balances in the right column.

The trial balance proves the mathematical equality of debits and credits after posting. Under the double-entry system, this equality occurs when the sum of the debit account balances equals the sum of the credit account balances. **A trial balance may also uncover errors in journalizing and posting.** For example, a trial balance may well have detected the error at Fidelity Investments discussed in the Feature Story. **In addition, a trial balance is useful in the preparation of financial statements**, as we will explain in the next two chapters.

The steps for preparing a trial balance are:

1. List the account titles and their balances.
2. Total the debit and credit columns.
3. Prove the equality of the two columns.

Illustration 2-32 shows the trial balance prepared from Pioneer Advertising's ledger. Note that the total debits ($28,700) equal the total credits ($28,700).

Illustration 2-32
A trial balance

Helpful Hint
To sum a column of figures is sometimes referred to as to *foot* the column. The column is then said to be *footed.*

Pioneer Advertising Agency Inc.
Trial Balance
October 31, 2014

	Debit	Credit
Cash	$ 15,200	
Supplies	2,500	
Prepaid Insurance	600	
Equipment	5,000	
Notes Payable		$ 5,000
Accounts Payable		2,500
Unearned Service Revenue		1,200
Common Stock		10,000
Dividends	500	
Service Revenue		10,000
Salaries and Wages Expense	4,000	
Rent Expense	900	
	$28,700	**$28,700**

Helpful Hint
A trial balance is so named because it is a test to see if the sum of the debit balances equals the sum of the credit balances.

A trial balance is a necessary checkpoint for uncovering certain types of errors. For example, if only the debit portion of a journal entry has been posted, the trial balance would bring this error to light.

Limitations of a Trial Balance

A trial balance does not guarantee freedom from recording errors, however. Numerous errors may exist even though the totals of the trial balance columns agree. For example, the trial balance may balance even when (1) a transaction is not journalized, (2) a correct journal entry is not posted, (3) a journal entry is posted twice, (4) incorrect accounts are used in journalizing or posting, or (5) offsetting errors are made in recording the amount of a transaction. As long as equal debits and credits are posted, even to the wrong account or in the wrong amount, the total debits will equal the total credits. **The trial balance does not prove that the company has recorded all transactions or that the ledger is correct.**

Ethics Note

An *error* is the result of an unintentional mistake; it is neither ethical nor unethical. An *irregularity* is an intentional misstatement, which is viewed as unethical.

Locating Errors

Errors in a trial balance generally result from mathematical mistakes, incorrect postings, or simply transcribing data incorrectly. What do you do if you are faced with a trial balance that does not balance? First, determine the amount of the difference between the two columns of the trial balance. After this amount is known, the following steps are often helpful:

1. If the error is $1, $10, $100, or $1,000, re-add the trial balance columns and recompute the account balances.
2. If the error is divisible by 2, scan the trial balance to see whether a balance equal to half the error has been entered in the wrong column.
3. If the error is divisible by 9, retrace the account balances on the trial balance to see whether they are incorrectly copied from the ledger. For example, if a balance was $12 and it was listed as $21, a $9 error has been made. Reversing the order of numbers is called a **transposition error**.
4. If the error is not divisible by 2 or 9, scan the ledger to see whether an account balance in the amount of the error has been omitted from the trial balance, and scan the journal to see whether a posting of that amount has been omitted.

Use of Dollar Signs

Note that dollar signs do not appear in journals or ledgers. Dollar signs are typically used only in the trial balance and the financial statements. Generally, a dollar sign is shown only for the first item in the column and for the total of that column. A single line (a totaling rule) is placed under the column of figures to be added or subtracted. Total amounts are double-underlined to indicate they are final sums. Negative signs or parentheses do not appear in journals or ledgers.

INVESTOR INSIGHT

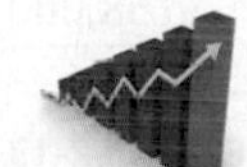

Why Accuracy Matters

While most companies record transactions very carefully, the reality is that mistakes still happen. For example, bank regulators fined Bank One Corporation (now Chase) $1.8 million because they felt that the unreliability of the bank's accounting system caused it to violate regulatory requirements.

Also, in recent years Fannie Mae, the government-chartered mortgage association, announced a series of large accounting errors. These announcements caused alarm among investors, regulators, and politicians because they fear that the errors may suggest larger, undetected problems. This is important because the home-mortgage market depends on Fannie Mae to buy hundreds of billions of dollars of mortgages each year from banks, thus enabling the banks to issue new mortgages.

Finally, before a major overhaul of its accounting system, the financial records of Waste Management, Inc. were in such disarray that 10,000 of the company's 57,000 employees were receiving pay slips that were in error.

The Sarbanes-Oxley Act was created to minimize the occurrence of errors like these by increasing every employee's responsibility for accurate financial reporting.

In order for these companies to prepare and issue financial statements, their accounting equations (debits and credits) must have been in balance at year-end. How could these errors or misstatements have occurred? (See page 97.)

> DO IT!

Trial Balance

The following accounts come from the ledger of SnowGo Corporation at December 31, 2014.

157	Equipment	$88,000	311	Common Stock	$20,000
332	Dividends	8,000	212	Salaries and Wages Payable	2,000
201	Accounts Payable	22,000	200	Notes Payable	19,000
726	Salaries and Wages Expense	42,000	722	Utilities Expense	3,000
112	Accounts Receivable	4,000	130	Prepaid Insurance	6,000
400	Service Revenue	95,000	101	Cash	7,000

Prepare a trial balance in good form.

Action Plan

- ✔ Determine normal balances and list accounts in the order they appear in the ledger.
- ✔ Accounts with debit balances appear in the left column, and those with credit balances in the right column.
- ✔ Total the debit and credit columns to prove equality.

Solution

SnowGo Corporation
Trial Balance
December 31, 2014

	Debit	Credit
Cash	$ 7,000	
Accounts Receivable	4,000	
Prepaid Insurance	6,000	
Equipment	88,000	
Notes Payable		$ 19,000
Accounts Payable		22,000
Salaries and Wages Payable		2,000
Common Stock		20,000
Dividends	8,000	
Service Revenue		95,000
Utilities Expense	3,000	
Salaries and Wages Expense	42,000	
	$158,000	$158,000

Related exercise material: **BE2-9, BE2-10, E2-9, E2-10, E2-11, E2-13, E2-14, and DO IT! 2-4.**

The Navigator

> Comprehensive DO IT!

Transactions

Bob Sample and other student investors opened Campus Laundromat Inc. on September 1, 2014. During the first month of operations, the following transactions occurred.

Sept. 1 Stockholders invested $20,000 cash in the business.
2 Paid $1,000 cash for store rent for the month of September.
3 Purchased washers and dryers for $25,000, paying $10,000 in cash and signing a $15,000, 6-month, 12% note payable.
4 Paid $1,200 for a one-year accident insurance policy.
10 Received a bill from the *Daily News* for advertising the opening of the laundromat $200.
20 Declared and paid a cash dividend to stockholders $700.
30 Determined that cash receipts for laundry fees for the month were $6,200.

The chart of accounts for the company is the same as for Pioneer Advertising Agency Inc. except for the following: No. 610 Advertising Expense.

Instructions

(a) Journalize the September transactions. (Use J1 for the journal page number.)

(b) Open ledger accounts and post the September transactions.

(c) Prepare a trial balance at September 30, 2014.

Solution to Comprehensive DO IT!

(a) **GENERAL JOURNAL** J1

Date	Account Titles and Explanation	Ref.	Debit	Credit
2014				
Sept. 1	Cash	101	20,000	
	Common Stock	311		20,000
	(Stockholders' investment of cash in business)			
2	Rent Expense	729	1,000	
	Cash	101		1,000
	(Paid September rent)			
3	Equipment	157	25,000	
	Cash	101		10,000
	Notes Payable	200		15,000
	(Purchased laundry equipment for cash and 6-month, 12% note payable)			
4	Prepaid Insurance	130	1,200	
	Cash	101		1,200
	(Paid one-year insurance policy)			
10	Advertising Expense	610	200	
	Accounts Payable	201		200
	(Received bill from *Daily News* for advertising)			
20	Dividends	332	700	
	Cash	101		700
	(Declared and paid a cash dividend)			
30	Cash	101	6,200	
	Service Revenue	400		6,200
	(Received cash for services provided)			

Action Plan

- ✔ Make separate journal entries for each transaction.
- ✔ In journalizing, make sure debits equal credits.
- ✔ In journalizing, use specific account titles taken from the chart of accounts.
- ✔ Provide appropriate description of each journal entry.
- ✔ Arrange ledger in statement order, beginning with the balance sheet accounts.
- ✔ Post in chronological order.
- ✔ Use numbers in the reference column to indicate the amount has been posted.
- ✔ In the trial balance, list accounts in the order in which they appear in the ledger.
- ✔ List debit balances in the left column, and credit balances in the right column.

(b) **GENERAL LEDGER**

Cash No. 101

Date	Explanation	Ref.	Debit	Credit	Balance
2014					
Oct. 1		J1	20,000		20,000
2		J1		1,000	19,000
3		J1		10,000	9,000
4		J1		1,200	7,800
20		J1		700	7,100
30		J1	6,200		13,300

Prepaid Insurance No. 130

Date	Explanation	Ref.	Debit	Credit	Balance
2014					
Sept. 4		J1	1,200		1,200

Notes Payable No. 200

Date	Explanation	Ref.	Debit	Credit	Balance
2014					
Sept. 3		J1		15,000	15,000

Accounts Payable No. 201

Date	Explanation	Ref.	Debit	Credit	Balance
2014					
Sept. 10		J1		200	200

Common Stock No. 311

Date	Explanation	Ref.	Debit	Credit	Balance
2014					
Sept. 1		J1		20,000	20,000

Equipment — No. 157

Date	Explanation	Ref.	Debit	Credit	Balance
2014					
Sept. 3		J1	25,000		25,000

Dividends — No. 332

Date	Explanation	Ref.	Debit	Credit	Balance
2014					
Sept. 20		J1	700		700

Service Revenue — No. 400

Date	Explanation	Ref.	Debit	Credit	Balance
2014					
Sept. 30		J1		6,200	6,200

Advertising Expense — No. 610

Date	Explanation	Ref.	Debit	Credit	Balance
2014					
Sept. 10		J1	200		200

Rent Expense — No. 729

Date	Explanation	Ref.	Debit	Credit	Balance
2014					
Sept. 2		J1	1,000		1,000

(c)

Campus Laundromat Inc.
Trial Balance
September 30, 2014

	Debit	Credit
Cash	$13,300	
Prepaid Insurance	1,200	
Equipment	25,000	
Notes Payable		$15,000
Accounts Payable		200
Common Stock		20,000
Dividends	700	
Service Revenue		6,200
Advertising Expense	200	
Rent Expense	1,000	
	$41,400	$41,400

✔ The Navigator

SUMMARY OF LEARNING OBJECTIVES

The Navigator

1 **Explain what an account is and how it helps in the recording process.** An account is a record of increases and decreases in specific asset, liability, or stockholders' equity items.

2 **Define debits and credits and explain their use in recording business transactions.** The terms debit and credit are synonymous with left and right. Assets, dividends, and expenses are increased by debits and decreased by credits. Liabilities, common stock, retained earnings, and revenues are increased by credits and decreased by debits.

3 **Identify the basic steps in the recording process.** The basic steps in the recording process are (a) analyze each transaction for its effects on the accounts, (b) enter the transaction information in a journal, and (c) transfer the journal information to the appropriate accounts in the ledger.

4 **Explain what a journal is and how it helps in the recording process.** The initial accounting record of a transaction is entered in a journal before the data are entered in the accounts. A journal (a) discloses in one place the complete effects of a transaction, (b) provides a chronological record of transactions, and (c) prevents or locates errors because the debit and credit amounts for each entry can be easily compared.

5 **Explain what a ledger is and how it helps in the recording process.** The ledger is the entire group of accounts maintained by a company. The ledger keeps in one place all the information about changes in specific account balances.

6 **Explain what posting is and how it helps in the recording process.** Posting is the transfer of journal entries to the ledger accounts. This phase of the recording process accumulates the effects of journalized transactions in the individual accounts.

7 **Prepare a trial balance and explain its purposes.** A trial balance is a list of accounts and their balances at a given time. Its primary purpose is to prove the equality of debits and credits after posting. A trial balance also uncovers errors in journalizing and posting and is useful in preparing financial statements.

GLOSSARY

Account A record of increases and decreases in specific asset, liability, or stockholders' equity items. (p. 54).

Chart of accounts A list of accounts and the account numbers that identify their location in the ledger. (p. 65).

Common stock Issued in exchange for the owners' investment paid in to the corporation. (p. 56).

Compound entry A journal entry that involves three or more accounts. (p. 61).

Credit The right side of an account. (p. 54).

Debit The left side of an account. (p. 54).

Dividend A distribution by a corporation to its stockholders on a pro rata (equal) basis. (p. 57).

Double-entry system A system that records in appropriate accounts the dual effect of each transaction. (p. 55).

General journal The most basic form of journal. (p. 60).

General ledger A ledger that contains all asset, liability, and stockholders' equity accounts. (p. 62).

Journal An accounting record in which transactions are initially recorded in chronological order. (p. 60).

Journalizing The entering of transaction data in the journal. (p. 60).

Ledger The entire group of accounts maintained by a company. (p. 62).

Normal balance An account balance on the side where an increase in the account is recorded. (p. 55).

Posting The procedure of transferring journal entries to the ledger accounts. (p. 64).

Retained earnings Net income that is kept (retained) in the business. (p. 56).

Simple entry A journal entry that involves only two accounts. (p. 61).

T-account The basic form of an account. (p. 54).

Three-column form of account A form with columns for debit, credit, and balance amounts in an account. (p. 63).

Trial balance A list of accounts and their balances at a given time. (p. 73).

Self-Test, Brief Exercises, Exercises, Problem Set A, and many more resources are available for practice in WileyPLUS.

SELF-TEST QUESTIONS

Answers are on page 97.

(LO 1) **1.** Which of the following statements about an account is *true*?
- (a) In its simplest form, an account consists of two parts.
- (b) An account is an individual accounting record of increases and decreases in specific asset, liability, and stockholders' equity items.
- (c) There are separate accounts for specific assets and liabilities but only one account for stockholders' equity items.
- (d) The left side of an account is the credit or decrease side.

(LO 2) **2.** Debits:
- (a) increase both assets and liabilities.
- (b) decrease both assets and liabilities.
- (c) increase assets and decrease liabilities.
- (d) decrease assets and increase liabilities.

(LO 2) **3.** A revenue account:
- (a) is increased by debits.
- (b) is decreased by credits.
- (c) has a normal balance of a debit.
- (d) is increased by credits.

(LO 2) **4.** Accounts that normally have debit balances are:
- (a) assets, expenses, and revenues.
- (b) assets, expenses, and common stock.
- (c) assets, liabilities, and dividends.
- (d) assets, dividends, and expenses.

5. The expanded accounting equation is: (LO 3)
- (a) Assets + Liabilities = Common Stock + Retained Earnings + Dividends + Revenues + Expenses
- (b) Assets = Liabilities + Common Stock + Retained Earnings + Dividends + Revenues − Expenses
- (c) Assets = Liabilities − Common Stock − Retained Earnings − Dividends − Revenues − Expenses
- (d) Assets = Liabilities + Common Stock + Retained Earnings − Dividends + Revenues − Expenses

6. Which of the following is *not* part of the recording process? (LO 2)
- (a) Analyzing transactions.
- (b) Preparing a trial balance.
- (c) Entering transactions in a journal.
- (d) Posting transactions.

7. Which of the following statements about a journal is *false*? (LO 4)
- (a) It is not a book of original entry.
- (b) It provides a chronological record of transactions.
- (c) It helps to locate errors because the debit and credit amounts for each entry can be readily compared.
- (d) It discloses in one place the complete effect of a transaction.

8. The purchase of supplies on account should result in: (LO 4)
- (a) a debit to Supplies Expense and a credit to Cash.
- (b) a debit to Supplies Expense and a credit to Supplies.

(c) a debit to Supplies and a credit to Accounts Payable.
(d) a debit to Supplies and a credit to Accounts Receivable.

(LO 5) **9.** The order of the accounts in the ledger is:
(a) assets, revenues, expenses, liabilities, common stock, dividends.
(b) assets, liabilities, common stock, dividends, revenues, expenses.
(c) common stock, assets, revenues, expenses, liabilities, dividends.
(d) revenues, assets, expenses, liabilities, common stock, dividends.

(LO 5) **10.** A ledger:
(a) contains only asset and liability accounts.
(b) should show accounts in alphabetical order.
(c) is a collection of the entire group of accounts maintained by a company.
(d) is a book of original entry.

(LO 6) **11.** Posting:
(a) normally occurs before journalizing.
(b) transfers ledger transaction data to the journal.
(c) is an optional step in the recording process.
(d) transfers journal entries to ledger accounts.

(LO 6) **12.** Before posting a payment of $5,000, the Accounts Payable of Senator Corporation had a normal balance of $16,000. The balance after posting this transaction was:
(a) $21,000. (b) $5,000.
(c) $11,000. (d) Cannot be determined.

13. A trial balance: (LO 7)
(a) is a list of accounts with their balances at a given time.
(b) proves the mathematical accuracy of journalized transactions.
(c) will not balance if a correct journal entry is posted twice.
(d) proves that all transactions have been recorded.

14. A trial balance will not balance if: (LO 7)
(a) a correct journal entry is posted twice.
(b) the purchase of supplies on account is debited to Supplies and credited to Cash.
(c) a $100 cash dividend is debited to Dividends for $1,000 and credited to Cash for $100.
(d) a $450 payment on account is debited to Accounts Payable for $45 and credited to Cash for $45.

15. The trial balance of Clooney Corporation had accounts with the following normal balances: Cash $5,000, Service Revenue $85,000, Salaries and Wages Payable $4,000, Salaries and Wages Expense $40,000, Rent Expense $10,000, Common Stock $42,000, Dividends $15,000, and Equipment $61,000. In preparing a trial balance, the total in the debit column is: (LO 7)
(a) $131,000.
(b) $216,000.
(c) $91,000.
(d) $116,000.

Go to the book's companion website, www.wiley.com/college/weygandt, for additional Self-Test Questions.

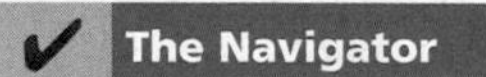

QUESTIONS

1. Describe the parts of a T-account.
2. "The terms *debit* and *credit* mean increase and decrease, respectively." Do you agree? Explain.
3. Jason Hilbert, a fellow student, contends that the double-entry system means each transaction must be recorded twice. Is Jason correct? Explain.
4. Sandra Browne, a beginning accounting student, believes debit balances are favorable and credit balances are unfavorable. Is Sandra correct? Discuss.
5. State the rules of debit and credit as applied to (a) asset accounts, (b) liability accounts, and (c) the stockholders' equity accounts (revenue, expenses, dividends, common stock, and retained earnings).
6. What is the normal balance for each of the following accounts? (a) Accounts Receivable. (b) Cash. (c) Dividends. (d) Accounts Payable. (e) Service Revenue. (f) Salaries and Wages Expense. (g) Common Stock.
7. Indicate whether each of the following accounts is an asset, a liability, or a stockholders' equity account and whether it has a normal debit or credit balance: (a) Accounts Receivable, (b) Accounts Payable, (c) Equipment, (d) Dividends, (e) Supplies.
8. For the following transactions, indicate the account debited and the account credited.
   (a) Supplies are purchased on account.
   (b) Cash is received on signing a note payable.
   (c) Employees are paid salaries in cash.
9. Indicate whether the following accounts generally will have (a) debit entries only, (b) credit entries only, or (c) both debit and credit entries.
   (1) Cash.
   (2) Accounts Receivable.
   (3) Dividends.
   (4) Accounts Payable.
   (5) Salaries and Wages Expense.
   (6) Service Revenue.
10. What are the basic steps in the recording process?
11. What are the advantages of using a journal in the recording process?
12. (a) When entering a transaction in the journal, should the debit or credit be written first?
    (b) Which should be indented, the debit or credit?
13. Describe a compound entry, and provide an example.

14. (a) Should business transaction debits and credits be recorded directly in the ledger accounts?
    (b) What are the advantages of first recording transactions in the journal and then posting to the ledger?
15. The account number is entered as the last step in posting the amounts from the journal to the ledger. What is the advantage of this step?
16. Journalize the following business transactions.
    (a) Alberto Rivera invests $9,000 cash in the business in exchange for shares of common stock.
    (b) Insurance of $800 is paid for the year.
    (c) Supplies of $2,000 are purchased on account.
    (d) Cash of $7,500 is received for services rendered.
17. (a) What is a ledger?
    (b) What is a chart of accounts and why is it important?
18. What is a trial balance and what are its purposes?
19. Joe Kirby is confused about how accounting information flows through the accounting system. He believes the flow of information is as follows.
    (a) Debits and credits posted to the ledger.
    (b) Business transaction occurs.
    (c) Information entered in the journal.
    (d) Financial statements are prepared.
    (e) Trial balance is prepared.

    Is Joe correct? If not, indicate to Joe the proper flow of the information.
20. Two students are discussing the use of a trial balance. They wonder whether the following errors, each considered separately, would prevent the trial balance from balancing. What would you tell them?
    (a) The bookkeeper debited Cash for $600 and credited Salaries and Wages Expense for $600 for payment of wages.
    (b) Cash collected on account was debited to Cash for $900 and Service Revenue was credited for $90.
21. **PEPSICO** What are the normal balances for PepsiCo's Cash, Accounts Payable, and Interest Expense accounts?

BRIEF EXERCISES

BE2-1 For each of the following accounts indicate the effects of (a) a debit and (b) a credit on the accounts and (c) the normal balance of the account.

Indicate debit and credit effects and normal balance. (LO 2)

1. Accounts Payable.
2. Advertising Expense.
3. Service Revenue.
4. Accounts Receivable.
5. Common Stock.
6. Dividends.

BE2-2 Transactions for the Kaustav Sen Company, which provides welding services, for the month of June are presented below. Identify the accounts to be debited and credited for each transaction.

Identify accounts to be debited and credited. (LO 2)

June 1 Kaustav Sen invests $4,000 cash in exchange for shares of common stock in a small welding business.
2 Purchases equipment on account for $900.
3 $800 cash is paid to landlord for June rent.
12 Bills L. Nigh $300 for welding work done on account.

BE2-3 Using the data in BE2-2, journalize the transactions. (You may omit explanations.)

Journalize transactions. (LO 4)

BE2-4 Tim Weber, a fellow student, is unclear about the basic steps in the recording process. Identify and briefly explain the steps in the order in which they occur.

Identify and explain steps in recording process. (LO 3)

BE2-5 J.A. Motzek Inc. has the following transactions during August of the current year. Indicate (a) the effect on the accounting equation and (b) the debit-credit analysis illustrated on pages 66–71 of the text.

Indicate basic and debit-credit analysis. (LO 2)

Aug. 1 Opens an office as a financial advisor, investing $5,000 in cash in exchange for common stock.
4 Pays insurance in advance for 6 months, $1,800 cash.
16 Receives $1,100 from clients for services provided.
27 Pays secretary $1,000 salary.

BE2-6 Using the data in BE2-5, journalize the transactions. (You may omit explanations.)

Journalize transactions. (LO 4)

Post journal entries to T-accounts.
(LO 6)

BE2-7 Selected transactions for the Gilles Company are presented in journal form below. Post the transactions to T-accounts. Make one T-account for each item and determine each account's ending balance.

J1

Date	Account Titles and Explanation	Ref.	Debit	Credit
May 5	Accounts Receivable		5,000	
	Service Revenue			5,000
	(Billed for services provided)			
12	Cash		2,100	
	Accounts Receivable			2,100
	(Received cash in payment of account)			
15	Cash		3,000	
	Service Revenue			3,000
	(Received cash for services provided)			

Post journal entries to standard form of account.
(LO 6)

BE2-8 Selected journal entries for the Gilles Company are presented in BE2-7. Post the transactions using the standard form of account.

Prepare a trial balance.
(LO 7)

BE2-9 From the ledger balances given below, prepare a trial balance for the Starr Company at June 30, 2014. List the accounts in the order shown on page 74 of the text. All account balances are normal.

Accounts Payable $9,000, Cash $6,800, Common Stock $20,000, Dividends $1,200, Equipment $17,000, Service Revenue $6,000, Accounts Receivable $3,000, Salaries and Wages Expense $6,000, and Rent Expense $1,000.

Prepare a correct trial balance.
(LO 7)

BE2-10 An inexperienced bookkeeper prepared the following trial balance. Prepare a correct trial balance, assuming all account balances are normal.

Cheng Company
Trial Balance
December 31, 2014

	Debit	Credit
Cash	$16,800	
Prepaid Insurance		$ 3,500
Accounts Payable		3,000
Unearned Service Revenue	4,200	
Common Stock		13,000
Dividends		4,500
Service Revenue		25,600
Salaries and Wages Expense	18,600	
Rent Expense		2,400
	$39,600	$52,000

> DO IT! REVIEW

Identify normal balances.
(LO 2)

DO IT! 2-1 Graham Kahl has just rented space in a strip mall. In this space, he will open a photography studio, to be called "Picture This!" A friend has advised Graham to set up a double-entry set of accounting records in which to record all of his business transactions.

Identify the balance sheet accounts that Graham will likely need to record the transactions needed to open his business (a corporation). Indicate whether the normal balance of each account is a debit or credit.

DO IT! 2-2 Graham Kahl engaged in the following activities in establishing his photography studio, Picture This!:

Record business activities.

(LO 4)

1. Opened a bank account in the name of Picture This! and deposited $8,000 of his own money into this account in exchange for common stock.
2. Purchased photography supplies at a total cost of $1,600. The business paid $400 in cash and the balance is on account.
3. Obtained estimates on the cost of photography equipment from three different manufacturers.

In what form (type of record) should Graham record these three activities? Prepare the entries to record the transactions.

DO IT! 2-3 Graham Kahl recorded the following transactions during the month of April.

Post transactions.

(LO 6)

April 3	Cash	3,700	
	Service Revenue		3,700
April 16	Rent Expense	600	
	Cash		600
April 20	Salaries and Wages Expense	500	
	Cash		500

Post these entries to the Cash T-account of the general ledger to determine the ending balance in cash. The beginning balance in cash on April 1 was $1,600.

DO IT! 2-4 The following accounts are taken from the ledger of Chillin' Company at December 31, 2014.

Prepare a trial balance.

(LO 7)

200	Notes Payable	$20,000	101	Cash	$6,000
311	Common Stock	25,000	120	Supplies	5,000
157	Equipment	76,000	522	Rent Expense	2,000
332	Dividends	8,000	220	Salaries and Wages Payable	3,000
726	Salaries and Wages Expense	38,000	201	Accounts Payable	9,000
400	Service Revenue	86,000	112	Accounts Receivable	8,000

Prepare a trial balance in good form.

✔ The Navigator

EXERCISES

E2-1 Larry Burns has prepared the following list of statements about accounts.

Analyze statements about accounting and the recording process.

(LO 1)

1. An account is an accounting record of either a specific asset or a specific liability.
2. An account shows only increases, not decreases, in the item it relates to.
3. Some items, such as cash and accounts receivable, are combined into one account.
4. An account has a left, or credit side, and a right, or debit side.
5. A simple form of an account consisting of just the account title, the left side, and the right side, is called a T-account.

Instructions

Identify each statement as true or false. If false, indicate how to correct the statement.

E2-2 Selected transactions for B. Madar, an interior decorating firm, in its first month of business, are shown below and on page 84.

Identify debits, credits, and normal balances.

(LO 2)

Jan.	2	Invested $15,000 cash in the business in exchange for common stock.
	3	Purchased used car for $7,000 cash for use in the business.
	9	Purchased supplies on account for $500.
	11	Billed customers $1,800 for services performed.

16 Paid $200 cash for advertising.
20 Received $700 cash from customers billed on January 11.
23 Paid creditor $300 cash on balance owed.
28 Declared and paid a $1,000 cash dividend.

Instructions
For each transaction indicate the following.

(a) The basic type of account debited and credited (asset, liability, stockholders' equity).
(b) The specific account debited and credited (cash, rent expense, service revenue, etc.).
(c) Whether the specific account is increased or decreased.
(d) The normal balance of the specific account.

Use the following format, in which the January 2 transaction is given as an example.

	Account Debited				Account Credited			
Date	**(a) Basic Type**	**(b) Specific Account**	**(c) Effect**	**(d) Normal Balance**	**(a) Basic Type**	**(b) Specific Account**	**(c) Effect**	**(d) Normal Balance**
Jan. 2	Asset	Cash	Increase	Debit	Stockholders' Equity	Common Stock	Increase	Credit

Journalize transactions.
(LO 4)

E2-3 Data for B. Madar, interior decorating, are presented in E2-2.

Instructions
Journalize the transactions using journal page J1. (You may omit explanations.)

Analyze transactions and determine their effect on accounts.
(LO 2)

E2-4 Presented below is information related to Robbins Real Estate Agency.

Oct. 1 Lynn Robbins begins business as a real estate agent with a cash investment of $20,000 in exchange for common stock.
2 Hires an administrative assistant.
3 Purchases office furniture for $1,900, on account.
6 Sells a house and lot for N. Fennig; bills N. Fennig $3,200 for realty services provided.
27 Pays $850 on the balance related to the transaction of October 3.
30 Pays the administrative assistant $2,500 in salary for October.

Instructions
Prepare the debit-credit analysis for each transaction as illustrated on pages 66–71.

Journalize transactions.
(LO 4)

E2-5 Transaction data for Robbins Real Estate Agency are presented in E2-4.

Instructions
Journalize the transactions. (You may omit explanations.)

Analyze transactions and journalize.
(LO 2, 3, 4)

E2-6 Elvira Industries had the following transactions.

1. Borrowed $5,000 from the bank by signing a note.
2. Paid $2,500 cash for a computer.
3. Purchased $450 of supplies on account.

Instructions
(a) Indicate what accounts are increased and decreased by each transaction.
(b) Journalize each transaction. (Omit explanations.)

Analyze transactions and journalize.
(LO 2, 3, 4)

E2-7 Rockford Enterprises had the following selected transactions.

1. Kris Rockford invested $5,000 cash in the business in exchange for common stock.
2. Paid office rent of $1,100.
3. Performed consulting services and billed a client $4,700.
4. Declared and paid a $700 cash dividend.

Instructions
(a) Indicate the effect each transaction has on the accounting equation (Assets = Liabilities + Stockholders' Equity), using plus and minus signs.
(b) Journalize each transaction. (Omit explanations.)

Analyze statements about the ledger.

(LO 5)

E2-8 Rachel Manny has prepared the following list of statements about the general ledger.

1. The general ledger contains all the asset and liability accounts, but no stockholders' equity accounts.
2. The general ledger is sometimes referred to as simply the ledger.
3. The accounts in the general ledger are arranged in alphabetical order.
4. Each account in the general ledger is numbered for easier identification.
5. The general ledger is a book of original entry.

Instructions

Identify each statement as true or false. If false, indicate how to correct the statement.

Post journal entries and prepare a trial balance.

(LO 6, 7)

E2-9 Selected transactions from the journal of Roberta Mendez, investment broker, are presented below.

Date	Account Titles and Explanation	Ref.	Debit	Credit
Aug. 1	Cash		5,000	
	Common Stock			5,000
	(Investment of cash for stock)			
10	Cash		2,700	
	Service Revenue			2,700
	(Received cash for services provided)			
12	Equipment		5,000	
	Cash			1,000
	Notes Payable			4,000
	(Purchased office equipment for cash and notes payable)			
25	Accounts Receivable		1,600	
	Service Revenue			1,600
	(Billed clients for services provided)			
31	Cash		850	
	Accounts Receivable			850
	(Receipt of cash on account)			

Instructions

(a) Post the transactions to T-accounts.
(b) Prepare a trial balance at August 31, 2014.

Journalize transactions from account data and prepare a trial balance.

(LO 4, 7)

E2-10 The T-accounts below summarize the ledger of Padre Landscaping Company at the end of the first month of operations.

Cash — No. 101

4/1	10,000	4/15	720
4/12	900	4/25	1,500
4/29	400		
4/30	1,000		

Accounts Receivable — No. 112

4/7	3,200	4/29	400

Supplies — No. 126

4/4	1,800		

Accounts Payable — No. 201

4/25	1,500	4/4	1,800

Unearned Service Revenue — No. 209

		4/30	1,000

Common Stock — No. 311

		4/1	10,000

Service Revenue — No. 400

		4/7	3,200
		4/12	900

Salaries and Wages Expense — No. 726

4/15	720		

Instructions

(a) Prepare the complete general journal (including explanations) from which the postings to Cash were made.

(b) Prepare a trial balance at April 30, 2014.

Journalize transactions from account data and prepare a trial balance.

(LO 4, 7)

E2-11 Presented below is the ledger for Sparks Co.

Cash			No. 101
10/1	5,000	10/4	400
10/10	650	10/12	1,500
10/10	3,000	10/15	280
10/20	500	10/30	300
10/25	2,000	10/31	500

Accounts Receivable			No. 112
10/6	800	10/20	500
10/20	940		

Supplies			No. 126
10/4	400		

Equipment			No. 157
10/3	2,000		

Notes Payable			No. 200
		10/10	3,000

Accounts Payable			No. 201
10/12	1,500	10/3	2,000

Common Stock			No. 311
		10/1	5,000
		10/25	2,000

Dividends			No. 332
10/30	300		

Service Revenue			No. 400
		10/6	800
		10/10	650
		10/20	940

Salaries and Wages Expense			No. 726
10/31	500		

Rent Expense			No. 729
10/15	280		

Instructions

(a) Reproduce the journal entries for the transactions that occurred on October 1, 10, and 20, and provide explanations for each.

(b) Determine the October 31 balance for each of the accounts above, and prepare a trial balance at October 31, 2014.

Prepare journal entries and post using standard account form.

(LO 4, 6)

E2-12 Selected transactions for Neve Campbell Company during its first month in business are presented below.

Sept. 1 Invested $10,000 cash in the business in exchange for common stock.
5 Purchased equipment for $12,000 paying $4,000 in cash and the balance on account.
25 Paid $2,400 cash on balance owed for equipment.
30 Declared and paid a $500 cash dividend.

Campbell's chart of accounts shows No. 101 Cash, No. 157 Equipment, No. 201 Accounts Payable, No. 311 Common Stock; No. 332 Dividends.

Instructions

(a) Journalize the transactions on page J1 of the journal. (Omit explanations.)

(b) Post the transactions using the standard account form.

Analyze errors and their effects on trial balance.

(LO 7)

E2-13 The bookkeeper for Stan Tucci Equipment Repair made a number of errors in journalizing and posting, as described below.

1. A credit posting of $400 to Accounts Receivable was omitted.
2. A debit posting of $750 for Prepaid Insurance was debited to Insurance Expense.
3. A collection from a customer of $100 in payment of its account owed was journalized and posted as a debit to Cash $100 and a credit to Service Revenue $100.
4. A credit posting of $300 to Property Taxes Payable was made twice.
5. A cash purchase of supplies for $250 was journalized and posted as a debit to Supplies $25 and a credit to Cash $25.
6. A debit of $495 to Advertising Expense was posted as $459.

Instructions

For each error:

(a) Indicate whether the trial balance will balance.
(b) If the trial balance will not balance, indicate the amount of the difference.
(c) Indicate the trial balance column that will have the larger total.

Consider each error separately. Use the following form, in which error (1) is given as an example.

Error	(a) In Balance	(b) Difference	(c) Larger Column
(1)	No	$400	debit

E2-14 The accounts in the ledger of Tempus Fugit Delivery Service contain the following balances on July 31, 2014.

Prepare a trial balance.
(LO 2, 7)

Accounts Receivable	$10,642	Prepaid Insurance	$ 1,968
Accounts Payable	8,396	Maintenance and Repairs Expense	961
Cash	?	Service Revenue	10,610
Equipment	49,360	Dividends	700
Gasoline Expense	758	Common Stock	40,000
Utilities Expense	523	Salaries and Wages Expense	4,428
Notes Payable	26,450	Salaries and Wages Payable	815
		Retained Earnings	4,636

Instructions

Prepare a trial balance with the accounts arranged as illustrated in the chapter and fill in the missing amount for Cash.

E2-15 The statement of cash flows classifies each transaction as an operating activity, an investing activity, or a financing activity. Operating activities are the types of activities the company performs to generate profits. Investing activities include the purchase of long-lived assets such as equipment or the purchase of investment securities. Financing activities are borrowing money, issuing shares of stock, and paying dividends.

Identify cash flow activities.
(LO 7)

Presented below are the following transactions.

1. Issued stock for $20,000 cash.
2. Issued note payable for $10,000 cash.
3. Purchased office equipment for $11,000 cash.
4. Received $15,000 cash for services provided.
5. Paid $1,000 cash for rent.
6. Paid $600 cash dividend to stockholders.
7. Paid $6,500 cash for salaries.

Instructions

Classify each of these transactions as operating, investing, or financing activities.

EXERCISES: SET B AND CHALLENGE EXERCISES

Visit the book's companion website, at **www.wiley.com/college/weygandt**, and choose the Student Companion site to access Exercise Set B and Challenge Exercises.

PROBLEMS: SET A

P2-1A Prairie Park was started on April 1 by C. J. Amaro and associates. The following selected events and transactions occurred during April.

Journalize a series of transactions.
(LO 2, 4)

Apr. 1 Stockholders invested $50,000 cash in the business in exchange for common stock.
4 Purchased land costing $30,000 for cash.
8 Incurred advertising expense of $1,800 on account.
11 Paid salaries to employees $1,500.

12 Hired park manager at a salary of $4,000 per month, effective May 1.
13 Paid $1,500 cash for a one-year insurance policy.
17 Declared and paid a $1,400 cash dividend.
20 Received $5,700 in cash for admission fees.
25 Sold 100 coupon books for $30 each. Each book contains 10 coupons that entitle the holder to one admission to the park.
30 Received $8,900 in cash admission fees.
30 Paid $900 on balance owed for advertising incurred on April 8.

Amaro uses the following accounts: Cash, Prepaid Insurance, Land, Accounts Payable, Unearned Service Revenue, Common Stock; Dividends; Service Revenue, Advertising Expense, and Salaries and Wages Expense.

Instructions

Journalize the April transactions.

Journalize transactions, post, and prepare a trial balance.

(LO 2, 4, 6, 7)

P2-2A Kara Shin is a licensed CPA. During the first month of operations of her business, Kara Shin, Inc., the following events and transactions occurred.

May 1 Stockholders invested $20,000 cash in exchange for common stock.
2 Hired a secretary-receptionist at a salary of $2,000 per month.
3 Purchased $1,500 of supplies on account from Hartig Supply Company.
7 Paid office rent of $900 cash for the month.
11 Completed a tax assignment and billed client $2,800 for services provided.
12 Received $3,500 advance on a management consulting engagement.
17 Received cash of $1,200 for services completed for Lucille Co.
31 Paid secretary-receptionist $2,000 salary for the month.
31 Paid 40% of balance due Hartig Supply Company.

Kara uses the following chart of accounts: No. 101 Cash, No. 112 Accounts Receivable, No. 126 Supplies, No. 201 Accounts Payable, No. 209 Unearned Service Revenue, No. 311 Common Stock, No. 400 Service Revenue, No. 726 Salaries and Wages Expense, and No. 729 Rent Expense.

Instructions

Trial balance totals $28,400

(a) Journalize the transactions.
(b) Post to the ledger accounts.
(c) Prepare a trial balance on May 31, 2014.

Journalize and post transactions and prepare a trial balance.

(LO 2, 4, 6, 7)

P2-3A Mark Hockenberry owns and manages a computer repair service, which had the following trial balance on December 31, 2013 (the end of its fiscal year).

Byte Repair Service, Inc.
Trial Balance
December 31, 2013

Cash	$ 8,000	
Accounts Receivable	15,000	
Supplies	13,000	
Prepaid Rent	3,000	
Equipment	21,000	
Accounts Payable		$19,000
Common Stock		30,000
Retained Earnings		11,000
	$60,000	$60,000

Summarized transactions for January 2014 were as follows.

1. Advertising costs, paid in cash, $1,000.
2. Additional supplies acquired on account $4,000.
3. Miscellaneous expenses, paid in cash, $1,700.
4. Cash collected from customers in payment of accounts receivable $13,000.
5. Cash paid to creditors for accounts payable due $15,000.
6. Repair services performed during January: for cash $5,000; on account $9,000.
7. Wages for January, paid in cash, $3,000.
8. Dividends during January were $2,000.

Instructions

(a) Open T-accounts for each of the accounts listed in the trial balance, and enter the opening balances for 2014.
(b) Prepare journal entries to record each of the January transactions. (Omit explanations.)
(c) Post the journal entries to the accounts in the ledger. (Add accounts as needed.)
(d) Prepare a trial balance as of January 31, 2014.

Trial balance totals $63,000

P2-4A The trial balance of the Garland Company shown below does not balance.

Prepare a correct trial balance.

(LO 7)

Garland Company
Trial Balance
May 31, 2014

	Debit	Credit
Cash	$ 3,850	
Accounts Receivable		$ 2,750
Prepaid Insurance	700	
Equipment	12,000	
Accounts Payable		4,500
Unearned Service Revenue	560	
Common Stock		11,700
Service Revenue	8,690	
Salaries and Wages Expense	4,200	
Advertising Expense		1,100
Utilities Expense	800	
	$30,800	$20,050

Your review of the ledger reveals that each account has a normal balance. You also discover the following errors.

1. The totals of the debit sides of Prepaid Insurance, Accounts Payable, and Utilities Expense were each understated $100.
2. Transposition errors were made in Accounts Receivable and Service Revenue. Based on postings made, the correct balances were $2,570 and $8,960, respectively.
3. A debit posting to Salaries and Wages Expense of $200 was omitted.
4. A $1,000 cash dividend was debited to Common Stock for $1,000 and credited to Cash for $1,000.
5. A $520 purchase of supplies on account was debited to Equipment for $520 and credited to Cash for $520.
6. A cash payment of $450 for advertising was debited to Advertising Expense for $45 and credited to Cash for $45.
7. A collection from a customer for $420 was debited to Cash for $420 and credited to Accounts Payable for $420.

Instructions

Prepare a correct trial balance. Note that the chart of accounts includes the following: Dividends and Supplies. (*Hint:* It helps to prepare the correct journal entry for the transaction described and compare it to the mistake made.)

Trial balance totals $26,720

P2-5A The Classic Theater opened on April 1. All facilities were completed on March 31. At this time, the ledger showed No. 101 Cash $6,000, No. 140 Land $10,000, No. 145 Buildings (concession stand, projection room, ticket booth, and screen) $8,000, No. 157 Equipment $6,000, No. 201 Accounts Payable $2,000, No. 275 Mortgage Payable $8,000, and No. 311 Common Stock $20,000. During April, the following events and transactions occurred.

Journalize transactions, post, and prepare a trial balance.

(LO 2, 4, 6, 7)

Apr. 2 Paid film rental of $800 on first movie.
3 Ordered two additional films at $1,000 each.
9 Received $1,800 cash from admissions.
10 Made $2,000 payment on mortgage and $1,000 for accounts payable due.
11 Classic Theater contracted with D. Zarle Company to operate the concession stand. Zarle is to pay 18% of gross concession receipts (payable monthly) for the rental of the concession stand.
12 Paid advertising expenses $300.

20 Received one of the films ordered on April 3 and was billed $1,000. The film will be shown in April.
25 Received $5,200 cash from admissions.
29 Paid salaries $1,600.
30 Received statement from D. Zarle showing gross concession receipts of $1,000 and the balance due to The Classic Theater of $180 ($1,000 × 18%) for April. Zarle paid one-half of the balance due and will remit the remainder on May 5.
30 Prepaid $900 rental on special film to be run in May.

In addition to the accounts identified above, the chart of accounts shows No. 112 Accounts Receivable, No. 136 Prepaid Rent, No. 400 Service Revenue, No. 429 Rent Revenue, No. 610 Advertising Expense, No. 726 Salaries and Wages Expense, and No. 729 Rent Expense.

Instructions

Trial balance totals $35,180

(a) Enter the beginning balances in the ledger as of April 1. Insert a check mark (✓) in the reference column of the ledger for the beginning balance.
(b) Journalize the April transactions.
(c) Post the April journal entries to the ledger. Assume that all entries are posted from page 1 of the journal.
(d) Prepare a trial balance on April 30, 2014.

PROBLEMS: SET B

Journalize a series of transactions.

(LO 2, 4)

P2-1B Surepar Disc Golf Course was opened on March 1 by Bill Arnsdorf. The following selected events and transactions occurred during March:

Mar. 1 Invested $60,000 cash in the business in exchange for common stock.
3 Purchased Lee's Golf Land for $38,000 cash. The price consists of land $23,000, shed $9,000, and equipment $6,000. (Make one compound entry.)
5 Advertised the opening of the driving range and miniature golf course, paying advertising expenses of $1,600.
6 Paid cash $2,400 for a one-year insurance policy.
10 Purchased golf discs and other equipment for $1,050 from Parton Company payable in 30 days.
18 Received $340 in cash for golf fees earned.
19 Sold 100 coupon books for $18 each. Each book contains 4 coupons that enable the holder to play one round of disc golf.
25 Declared and paid an $800 cash dividend.
30 Paid salaries of $250.
30 Paid Parton Company in full.
31 Received $200 cash for fees earned.

Bill Arnsdorf uses the following accounts: Cash, Prepaid Insurance, Land, Buildings, Equipment, Accounts Payable, Unearned Service Revenue, Common Stock, Dividends, Service Revenue, Advertising Expense, and Salaries and Wages Expense.

Instructions

Journalize the March transactions.

Journalize transactions, post, and prepare a trial balance.

(LO 2, 4, 6, 7)

P2-2B Judi Dench is a licensed dentist. During the first month of the operation of her business, the following events and transactions occurred.

April 1 Stockholders invested $40,000 cash in exchange for common stock.
1 Hired a secretary-receptionist at a salary of $600 per week payable monthly.
2 Paid office rent for the month $1,400.
3 Purchased dental supplies on account from Halo Company $5,200.
10 Provided dental services and billed insurance companies $6,600.
11 Received $1,000 cash advance from Rich Welk for an implant.
20 Received $2,100 cash for services completed and delivered to Phil Stueben.
30 Paid secretary-receptionist for the month $2,400.
30 Paid $1,900 to Halo Company for accounts payable due.

Judi uses the following chart of accounts: No. 101 Cash, No. 112 Accounts Receivable, No. 126 Supplies, No. 201 Accounts Payable, No. 209 Unearned Service Revenue, No. 311 Common Stock, No. 400 Service Revenue, No. 726 Salaries and Wages Expense, and No. 729 Rent Expense.

Instructions

(a) Journalize the transactions.

(b) Post to the ledger accounts.

(c) Prepare a trial balance on April 30, 2014.

Trial balance totals $53,000

P2-3B Chamberlain Services was formed on May 1, 2014. The following transactions took place during the first month.

Journalize transactions, post, and prepare a trial balance.

(LO 2, 4, 6, 7)

Transactions on May 1:

1. Stockholders invested $50,000 cash in exchange for common stock.
2. Hired two employees to work in the warehouse. They will each be paid a salary of $2,800 per month.
3. Signed a 2-year rental agreement on a warehouse; paid $24,000 cash in advance for the first year.
4. Purchased furniture and equipment costing $30,000. A cash payment of $8,000 was made immediately; the remainder will be paid in 6 months.
5. Paid $1,800 cash for a one-year insurance policy on the furniture and equipment.

Transactions during the remainder of the month:

6. Purchased basic office supplies for $750 cash.
7. Purchased more office supplies for $1,300 on account.
8. Total revenues earned were $20,000—$8,000 cash and $12,000 on account.
9. Paid $400 to suppliers for accounts payable due.
10. Received $3,000 from customers in payment of accounts receivable.
11. Received utility bills in the amount of $260, to be paid next month.
12. Paid the monthly salaries of the two employees, totalling $5,600.

Instructions

(a) Prepare journal entries to record each of the events listed. (Omit explanations.)

(b) Post the journal entries to T-accounts.

(c) Prepare a trial balance as of May 31, 2014.

Trial balance totals $93,160

P2-4B The trial balance of Ron Salem Co. shown below does not balance.

Prepare a correct trial balance.

(LO 7)

Ron Salem Co.
Trial Balance
June 30, 2014

	Debit	Credit
Cash		$ 3,840
Accounts Receivable	$ 2,898	
Supplies	800	
Equipment	3,000	
Accounts Payable		2,666
Unearned Service Revenue	2,200	
Common Stock		9,000
Dividends	800	
Service Revenue		2,380
Salaries and Wages Expense	3,400	
Utilities Expense	910	
	$14,008	$17,886

Each of the listed accounts has a normal balance per the general ledger. An examination of the ledger and journal reveals the following errors.

1. Cash received from a customer in payment of its account was debited for $570, and Accounts Receivable was credited for the same amount. The actual collection was for $750.
2. The purchase of a computer on account for $620 was recorded as a debit to Supplies for $620 and a credit to Accounts Payable for $620.
3. Services were performed on account for a client for $890. Accounts Receivable was debited for $890, and Service Revenue was credited for $89.
4. A debit posting to Salaries and Wages Expense of $700 was omitted.
5. A payment of a balance due for $309 was credited to Cash for $309 and credited to Accounts Payable for $390.
6. The payment of a $600 cash dividend was debited to Salaries and Wages Expense for $600 and credited to Cash for $600.

Trial balance totals $16,348

Instructions

Prepare a correct trial balance. (*Hint:* It helps to prepare the correct journal entry for the transaction described and compare it to the mistake made.)

Journalize transactions, post, and prepare a trial balance.

(LO 2, 4, 6, 7)

GLS

P2-5B The Russo Theater, owned by Alan Russo, will begin operations in March. The Russo will be unique in that it will show only triple features of sequential theme movies. As of March 1, the ledger of Russo showed No. 101 Cash $8,000, No. 140 Land $21,000, No. 145 Buildings (concession stand, projection room, ticket booth, and screen) $10,000, No. 157 Equipment $8,000, No. 201 Accounts Payable $7,000, and No. 311 Common Stock $40,000. During the month of March, the following events and transactions occurred.

Mar. 2 Rented the three *Indiana Jones* movies to be shown for the first 3 weeks of March. The film rental was $3,500; $1,000 was paid in cash and $2,500 will be paid on March 10.

3 Ordered the *Lord of the Rings* movies to be shown the last 10 days of March. It will cost $240 per night.

9 Received $4,000 cash from admissions.

10 Paid balance due on *Indiana Jones* movies rental and $1,600 on March 1 accounts payable.

11 Russo Theater contracted with M. Brewer to operate the concession stand. Brewer is to pay 15% of gross concession receipts (payable monthly) for the right to operate the concession stand.

12 Paid advertising expenses $450.

20 Received $5,000 cash from customers for admissions.

20 Received the *Lord of Rings* movies and paid the rental fee of $2,400.

31 Paid salaries of $2,500.

31 Received statement from M. Brewer showing gross receipts from concessions of $5,000 and the balance due to Russo Theater of $750 ($5,000 × 15%) for March. Brewer paid one-half the balance due and will remit the remainder on April 5.

31 Received $9,000 cash from customers for admissions.

In addition to the accounts identified above, the chart of accounts includes No. 112 Accounts Receivable, No. 400 Service Revenue, No. 429 Rent Revenue, No. 610 Advertising Expense, No. 729 Rent Expense, and No. 726 Salaries and Wages Expense.

Instructions

(a) Enter the beginning balances in the ledger. Insert a check mark (✓) in the reference column of the ledger for the beginning balance.

(b) Journalize the March transactions.

(c) Post the March journal entries to the ledger. Assume that all entries are posted from page 1 of the journal.

Trial balance totals $64,150

(d) Prepare a trial balance on March 31, 2014.

PROBLEMS: SET C

Visit the book's companion website, at **www.wiley.com/college/weygandt**, and choose the Student Companion site to access Problem Set C.

CONTINUING COOKIE CHRONICLE

(*Note:* This is a continuation of the Cookie Chronicle from Chapter 1.)

CCC2 After researching the different forms of business organization, Natalie Koebel decides to operate "Cookie Creations" as a corporation. She then starts the process of getting the business running. In November 2014, the following activities take place.

Nov. 8 Natalie cashes her U.S. Savings Bonds and receives $520, which she deposits in her personal bank account.

8 She opens a bank account under the name "Cookie Creations" and transfers $500 from her personal account to the new account in exchange for common stock.

11 Natalie pays $65 to have advertising brochures and posters printed. She plans to distribute these as opportunities arise. (*Hint:* Use Advertising Expense.)
13 She buys baking supplies, such as flour, sugar, butter, and chocolate chips, for $125 cash.
14 Natalie starts to gather some baking equipment to take with her when teaching the cookie classes. She has an excellent top-of-the-line food processor and mixer that originally cost her $750. Natalie decides to start using it only in her new business. She estimates that the equipment is currently worth $300. She invests the equipment in the business in exchange for common stock.
16 Natalie realizes that her initial cash investment is not enough. Her grandmother lends her $2,000 cash, for which Natalie signs a note payable in the name of the business. Natalie deposits the money in the business bank account. (*Hint:* The note does not have to be repaid for 24 months. As a result, the notes payable should be reported in the accounts as the last liability and also on the balance sheet as the last liability.)
17 She buys more baking equipment for $900 cash.
20 She teaches her first class and collects $125 cash.
25 Natalie books a second class for December 4 for $150. She receives $30 cash in advance as a down payment.
30 Natalie pays $1,320 for a one-year insurance policy that will expire on December 1, 2015.

Instructions

(a) Prepare journal entries to record the November transactions.
(b) Post the journal entries to general ledger accounts.
(c) Prepare a trial balance at November 30.

Broadening Your PERSPECTIVE

Financial Reporting and Analysis

Financial Reporting Problem: PepsiCo, Inc.

BYP2-1 The financial statements of PepsiCo, Inc. are presented in Appendix A. The notes accompanying the statements contain the following selected accounts, stated in millions of dollars.

Accounts Payable	Income Taxes Payable
Accounts Receivable	Interest Expense
Property, Plant, and Equipment	Inventory

Instructions

(a) Answer the following questions.
  (1) What is the increase and decrease side for each account?
  (2) What is the normal balance for each account?
(b) Identify the probable other account in the transaction and the effect on that account when:
  (1) Accounts Receivable is decreased.
  (2) Accounts Payable is decreased.
  (3) Inventory is increased.
(c) Identify the other account(s) that ordinarily would be involved when:
  (1) Interest Expense is increased.
  (2) Property, Plant, and Equipment is increased.

Comparative Analysis Problem: PepsiCo, Inc. vs. The Coca-Cola Company

BYP2-2 PepsiCo's financial statements are presented in Appendix A. Financial statements of The Coca-Cola Company are presented in Appendix B.

Instructions

(a) Based on the information contained in the financial statements, determine the normal balance of the listed accounts for each company.

Pepsi	Coca-Cola
1. Inventory	1. Accounts Receivable
2. Property, Plant, and Equipment	2. Cash and Cash Equivalents
3. Accounts Payable	3. Cost of Goods Sold (expense)
4. Interest Expense	4. Sales (revenue)

(b) Identify the other account ordinarily involved when:
  (1) Accounts Receivable is increased.
  (2) Salaries and Wages Payable is decreased.
  (3) Property, Plant, and Equipment is increased.
  (4) Interest Expense is increased.

Real-World Focus

BYP2-3 Much information about specific companies is available on the Internet. Such information includes basic descriptions of the company's location, activities, industry, financial health, and financial performance.

Address: **biz.yahoo.com/i,** or go to **www.wiley.com/college/weygandt**

Steps

1. Type in a company name, or use index to find company name.
2. Choose **Profile**. Perform instructions (a)–(c) below.
3. Click on the company's specific industry to identify competitors. Perform instructions (d)–(g) below.

Instructions

Answer the following questions.

(a) What is the company's industry?
(b) What was the company's total sales?
(c) What was the company's net income?
(d) What are the names of four of the company's competitors?
(e) Choose one of these competitors.
(f) What is this competitor's name? What were its sales? What was its net income?
(g) Which of these two companies is larger by size of sales? Which one reported higher net income?

Critical Thinking

Decision-Making Across the Organization

BYP2-4 Amy Torbert operates Hollins Riding Academy. The academy's primary sources of revenue are riding fees and lesson fees, which are paid on a cash basis. Amy also boards horses for owners, who are billed monthly for boarding fees. In a few cases, boarders pay in advance of expected use. For its revenue transactions, the academy maintains the following accounts: No. 1 Cash, No. 5 Boarding Accounts Receivable, No. 27 Unearned Boarding Revenue, No. 51 Riding Revenue, No. 52 Lesson Revenue, and No. 53 Boarding Revenue.

The academy owns 10 horses, a stable, a riding corral, riding equipment, and office equipment. These assets are accounted for in accounts No. 11 Horses, No. 12 Building, No. 13 Riding Corral, No. 14 Riding Equipment, and No. 15 Office Equipment.

For its expenses, the academy maintains the following accounts: No. 6 Hay and Feed Supplies, No. 7 Prepaid Insurance, No. 21 Accounts Payable, No. 60 Salaries Expense, No. 61 Advertising Expense, No. 62 Utilities Expense, No. 63 Veterinary Expense, No. 64 Hay and Feed Expense, and No. 65 Insurance Expense.

Amy makes periodic payments of cash dividends to stockholders. To record stockholders' equity in the business and dividends, Torbert maintains three accounts: No. 50 Common Stock, No. 51 Retained Earnings, and No. 52 Dividends.

During the first month of operations, an inexperienced bookkeeper was employed. Amy Torbert asks you to review the following eight entries of the 50 entries made during the month. In each case, the explanation for the entry is correct.

Date	Account	Debit	Credit
May 1	Cash	18,000	
	Common Stock		18,000
	(Invested $18,000 cash in exchange for stock)		
5	Cash	250	
	Riding Revenue		250
	(Received $250 cash for lessons provided)		
7	Cash	500	
	Boarding Revenue		500
	(Received $500 for boarding of horses beginning June 1)		
14	Riding Equipment	80	
	Cash		800
	(Purchased desk and other office equipment for $800 cash)		
15	Salaries Expense	440	
	Cash		440
	(Issued dividend checks to stockholders)		
20	Cash	148	
	Riding Revenue		184
	(Received $184 cash for riding fees)		
30	Veterinary Expense	75	
	Accounts Payable		75
	(Received bill of $75 from veterinarian for services rendered)		
31	Hay and Feed Expense	1,500	
	Cash		1,500
	(Purchased an estimated 2 months' supply of feed and hay for $1,700 on account)		

Instructions

With the class divided into groups, answer the following.

(a) Identify each journal entry that is correct. For each journal entry that is incorrect, prepare the entry that should have been made by the bookkeeper.

(b) Which of the incorrect entries would prevent the trial balance from balancing?

(c) What was the correct net income for May, assuming the bookkeeper reported net income of $4,600 after posting all 50 entries?

(d) What was the correct cash balance at May 31, assuming the bookkeeper reported a balance of $12,475 after posting all 50 entries (and the only errors occurred in the items listed above)?

Communication Activity

BYP2-5 Shandler's Maid Company offers home cleaning service. Two recurring transactions for the company are billing customers for services rendered and paying employee salaries. For example, on March 15, bills totaling $6,000 were sent to customers and $2,000 was paid in salaries to employees.

Instructions

Write a memo to your instructor that explains and illustrates the steps in the recording process for each of the March 15 transactions. Use the format illustrated in the text under the heading, "The Recording Process Illustrated" (page 66).

Ethics Case

BYP2-6 Sara Rankin is the assistant chief accountant at Hokey Company, a manufacturer of computer chips and cellular phones. The company presently has total sales of $20 million. It is the end of the first quarter. Sara is hurriedly trying to prepare a general ledger trial balance so that quarterly financial statements can be prepared and released to management and the regulatory agencies. The total credits on the trial balance exceed the debits by $1,000. In order to meet the 4 p.m. deadline, Sara decides to force the debits and credits into balance by adding the amount of the difference to the Equipment account. She chose Equipment because it is one of the larger account balances; percentage-wise, it will be the least misstated. Sara "plugs" the difference! She believes that the difference will not affect anyone's decisions. She wishes that she had another few days to find the error but realizes that the financial statements are already late.

Instructions

(a) Who are the stakeholders in this situation?
(b) What are the ethical issues involved in this case?
(c) What are Sara's alternatives?

All About You

BYP2-7 Every company needs to plan in order to move forward. Its top management must consider where it wants the company to be in three to five years. Like a company, you need to think about where you want to be three to five years from now, and you need to start taking steps now in order to get there.

Instructions

Provide responses to each of the following items.

(a) Where would you like to be working in three to five years? Describe your plan for getting there by identifying between five and 10 specific steps that you need to take in order to get there.
(b) In order to get the job you want, you will need a résumé. Your résumé is the equivalent of a company's annual report. It needs to provide relevant and reliable information about your past accomplishments so that employers can decide whether to "invest" in you. Do a search on the Internet to find a good résumé format. What are the basic elements of a résumé?
(c) A company's annual report provides information about a company's accomplishments. In order for investors to use the annual report, the information must be reliable; that is, users must have faith that the information is accurate and believable. How can you provide assurance that the information on your résumé is reliable?
(d) Prepare a résumé assuming that you have accomplished the five to 10 specific steps you identified in part (a). Also, provide evidence that would give assurance that the information is reliable.

BYP2-8 If you haven't already done so, in the not-too-distant future you will prepare a résumé. In some ways, your résumé is like a company's annual report. Its purpose is to enable others to evaluate your past, in an effort to predict your future.

A résumé is your opportunity to create a positive first impression. It is important that it be impressive—but it should also be accurate. In order to increase their job prospects, some people are tempted to "inflate" their résumés by overstating the importance of some past accomplishments or positions. In fact, you might even think that "everybody does it" and that if you don't do it, you will be at a disadvantage.

David Edmondson, the president and CEO of well-known electronics retailer Radio Shack, overstated his accomplishments by claiming that he had earned a bachelor's of science degree, when in fact he had not. Apparently, his employer had not done a background check to ensure the accuracy of his résumé. Should Radio Shack have fired him?

YES: Radio Shack is a publicly traded company. Investors, creditors, employees, and others doing business with the company will not trust it if its leader is known to have poor integrity. The "tone at the top" is vital to creating an ethical organization.

NO: Mr. Edmondson had been a Radio Shack employee for 11 years. He had served the company in a wide variety of positions, and had earned the position of CEO through exceptional performance. While the fact that he lied 11 years earlier on his résumé was unfortunate, his service since then made this past transgression irrelevant. In addition, the company was in the midst of a massive restructuring, which included closing 700 of its 7,000 stores. It could not afford additional upheaval at this time.

Instructions

Write a response indicating your position regarding this situation. Provide support for your view.

Answers to Chapter Questions

Answers to Insight and Accounting Across the Organization Questions

p. 58 Keeping Score Q: Do you think that the Chicago Bears football team would be likely to have the same major revenue and expense accounts as the Cubs? **A:** Because their businesses are similar—professional sports—many of the revenue and expense accounts for the baseball and football teams might be similar.

p. 63 What Would Sam Do? Q: Why did Sam Walton keep separate pigeonholes and blue binders? **A:** Using separate pigeonholes and blue binders for each store enabled Walton to accumulate and track the performance of each individual store easily. **Q:** Why bother to keep separate records for each store? **A:** Keeping separate records for each store provided Walton with more information about performance of individual stores and managers, and greater control. Walton would want and need the same advantages if he were starting his business today. The difference is that he might now use a computerized system for small businesses.

p. 75 Why Accuracy Matters Q: In order for these companies to prepare and issue financial statements, their accounting equations (debits and credits) must have been in balance at year-end. How could these errors or misstatements have occurred? **A:** A company's accounting equation (its books) can be in balance yet its financial statements have errors or misstatements because of the following: entire transactions were not recorded; transactions were recorded at wrong amounts; transactions were recorded in the wrong accounts; transactions were recorded in the wrong accounting period. Audits of financial statements uncover some, but obviously not all, errors or misstatements.

Answers to Self-Test Questions

1. b **2.** c **3.** d **4.** d **5.** d **6.** b **7.** a **8.** c **9.** b **10.** c **11.** d **12.** c ($16,000 − $5,000) **13.** a **14.** c **15.** a ($5,000 + $40,000 + $10,000 + $15,000 + $61,000)

A Look at IFRS

International companies use the same set of procedures and records to keep track of transaction data. Thus, the material in Chapter 2 dealing with the account, general rules of debit and credit, and steps in the recording process—the journal, ledger, chart of accounts, and trial balance—is the same under both GAAP and IFRS.

Key Points

- Transaction analysis is the same under IFRS and GAAP but, as you will see in later chapters, different standards sometimes impact how transactions are recorded.
- Rules for accounting for specific events sometimes differ across countries. For example, European companies rely less on historical cost and more on fair value than U.S. companies. Despite the differences, the double-entry accounting system is the basis of accounting systems worldwide.

- Both the IASB and FASB go beyond the basic definitions provided in this textbook for the key elements of financial statements, that is, assets, liabilities, equity, revenues, and expenses. The more substantive definitions, using the IASB definitional structure, are provided in the Chapter 1 *A Look at IFRS* discussion.
- A trial balance under IFRS follows the same format as shown in the textbook.
- As shown in the textbook, dollars signs are typically used only in the trial balance and the financial statements. The same practice is followed under IFRS, using the currency sign of the country that the reporting company is headquartered.
- In February 2010, the SEC expressed a desire to continue working toward a single set of high-quality standards. In deciding whether the United States should adopt IFRS, some of the issues the SEC said should be considered are:
    - Whether IFRS is sufficiently developed and consistent in application.
    - Whether the IASB is sufficiently independent.
    - Whether IFRS is established for the benefit of investors.
    - The issues involved in educating investors about IFRS.
    - The impact of a switch to IFRS on U.S. laws and regulations.
    - The impact on companies including changes to their accounting systems, contractual arrangements, corporate governance, and litigation.
    - The issues involved in educating accountants, so they can prepare statements under IFRS.

Looking to the Future

The basic recording process shown in this textbook is followed by companies across the globe. It is unlikely to change in the future. The definitional structure of assets, liabilities, equity, revenues, and expenses may change over time as the IASB and FASB evaluate their overall conceptual framework for establishing accounting standards.

IFRS Practice

IFRS Self-Test Questions

1. Which statement is *correct* regarding IFRS?
   (a) IFRS reverses the rules of debits and credits, that is, debits are on the right and credits are on the left.
   (b) IFRS uses the same process for recording transactions as GAAP.
   (c) The chart of accounts under IFRS is different because revenues follow assets.
   (d) None of the above statements are correct.
2. The expanded accounting equation under IFRS is as follows:
   (a) Assets = Liabilities + Common Stock + Retained Earnings + Dividends + Revenues − Expenses.
   (b) Assets + Liabilities = Common Stock + Retained Earnings − Dividends + Revenues − Expenses.
   (c) Assets = Liabilities + Common Stock + Retained Earnings − Dividends + Revenues − Expenses.
   (d) Assets = Liabilities + Common Stock + Retained Earnings − Dividends − Revenues − Expenses.
3. A trial balance:
   (a) is the same under IFRS and GAAP.
   (b) proves that transactions are recorded correctly.
   (c) proves that all transactions have been recorded.
   (d) will not balance if a correct journal entry is posted twice.

4. One difference between IFRS and GAAP is that:
   (a) GAAP uses accrual-accounting concepts and IFRS uses primarily the cash basis of accounting.
   (b) IFRS uses a different posting process than GAAP.
   (c) IFRS uses more fair value measurements than GAAP.
   (d) the limitations of a trial balance are different between IFRS and GAAP.
5. The general policy for using proper currency signs (dollar, yen, pound, etc.) is the same for both IFRS and this textbook. This policy is as follows:
   (a) Currency signs only appear in ledgers and journal entries.
   (b) Currency signs are only shown in the trial balance.
   (c) Currency signs are shown for all compound journal entries.
   (d) Currency signs are shown in trial balances and financial statements.

IFRS Exercise

IFRS2-1 Describe some of the issues the SEC must consider in deciding whether the United States should adopt IFRS.

International Financial Reporting Problem: Zetar plc

IFRS2-2 The financial statements of Zetar plc are presented in Appendix C. The company's complete annual report, including the notes to its financial statements, is available at *www.zetarplc.com*.

Instructions

Describe in which statement each of the following items is reported, and the position in the statement (e.g., current asset).

(a) Other administrative expenses.

(b) Cash at bank.

(c) Borrowings and overdrafts.

(d) Finance costs.

Answers to IFRS Self-Test Questions

1. b **2.** c **3.** a **4.** c **5.** d

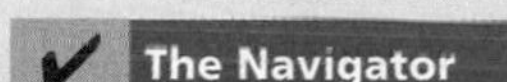

✔ Remember to go back to The Navigator box on the chapter opening page and check off your completed work.

Chapter 3 Adjusting the Accounts

Feature Story

What Was Your Profit?

The accuracy of the financial reporting system depends on answers to a few fundamental questions: At what point has revenue been recognized? At what point is the earnings process complete? When have expenses really been incurred?

During the 1990s, the stock prices of dot-com companies boomed. Most dot-coms earned most of their revenue from selling advertising space on their websites. To boost reported revenue, some dot-coms began swapping website ad space. Company A would put an ad for its website on company B's website, and company B would put an ad for its website on company A's website. No money changed hands, but each company recorded revenue (for the value of the space that it gave the other company on its site). This practice did little to boost net income, and it resulted in no additional cash flow—but it did boost *reported revenue*. Regulators eventually put an end to this misleading practice.

Another type of transgression results from companies recording revenues or expenses in the wrong year. In fact, shifting revenues and expenses is one of the most common abuses of financial accounting. Xerox admitted reporting billions of dollars of lease revenue in periods earlier than it should have been reported. And

✓ The Navigator

- Scan Learning Objectives
- Read Feature Story
- Read Preview
- Read text and answer **DO IT!** p. 104, p. 112, p. 118, p. 123
- Work Comprehensive **DO IT!** p. 124
- Review Summary of Learning Objectives
- Answer Self-Test Questions
- Complete Assignments
- Go to **WileyPLUS** for practice and tutorials

Read A Look at IFRS p. 159

Learning Objectives

After studying this chapter, you should be able to:

1. Explain the time period assumption.
2. Explain the accrual basis of accounting.
3. Explain the reasons for adjusting entries.
4. Identify the major types of adjusting entries.
5. Prepare adjusting entries for deferrals.
6. Prepare adjusting entries for accruals.
7. Describe the nature and purpose of an adjusted trial balance.

The Navigator

WorldCom stunned the financial markets with its admission that it had boosted net income by billions of dollars by delaying the recognition of expenses until later years.

Unfortunately, revelations such as these have become all too common in the corporate world. It is no wonder that a U.S. Trust survey of affluent Americans reported that 85% of respondents believed that there should be tighter regulation of financial disclosures; 66% said they did not trust the management of publicly traded companies.

Why did so many companies violate basic financial reporting rules and sound ethics? Many speculate that as stock prices climbed, executives were under increasing pressure to meet higher and higher earnings expectations. If actual results weren't as good as hoped for, some gave in to temptation and "adjusted" their numbers to meet market expectations.

✔ The Navigator

Preview of Chapter 3

In Chapter 1, you learned a neat little formula: Net income = Revenues − Expenses. In Chapter 2, you learned some rules for recording revenue and expense transactions. Guess what? Things are not really that nice and neat. In fact, it is often difficult for companies to determine in what time period they should report some revenues and expenses. In other words, in measuring net income, timing is everything.

The content and organization of Chapter 3 are as follows.

ADJUSTING THE ACCOUNTS

Timing Issues	The Basics of Adjusting Entries	The Adjusted Trial Balance and Financial Statements
• Fiscal and calendar years • Accrual- vs. cash-basis accounting • Recognizing revenues and expenses	• Types of adjusting entries • Adjusting entries for deferrals • Adjusting entries for accruals • Summary of basic relationships	• Preparing the adjusted trial balance • Preparing financial statements

✔ The Navigator

Timing Issues

LEARNING OBJECTIVE 1

Explain the time period assumption.

We would need no adjustments if we could wait to prepare financial statements until a company ended its operations. At that point, we could easily determine its final balance sheet and the amount of lifetime income it earned.

However, most companies need immediate feedback about how well they are doing. For example, management usually wants monthly financial statements, and the Internal Revenue Service requires all businesses to file annual tax returns. Therefore, **accountants divide the economic life of a business into artificial time periods**. This convenient assumption is referred to as the **time period assumption**.

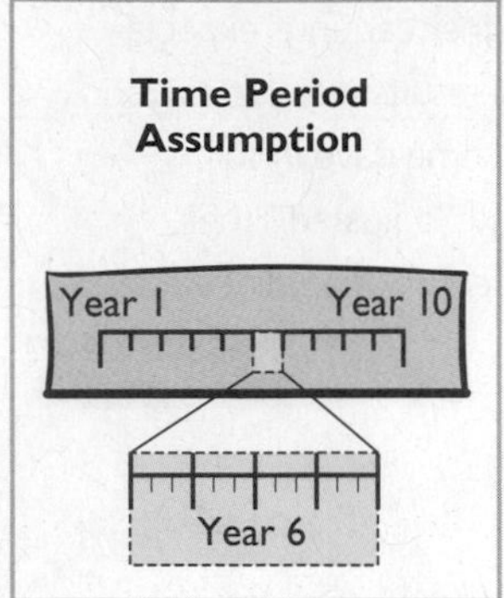

Many business transactions affect more than one of these arbitrary time periods. For example, the airplanes purchased by Southwest Airlines five years ago are still in use today. We must determine the relevance of each business transaction to specific accounting periods. (How much of the cost of an airplane contributed to operations this year?)

Fiscal and Calendar Years

Alternative Terminology The time period assumption is also called the *periodicity assumption*.

Both small and large companies prepare financial statements periodically in order to assess their financial condition and results of operations. **Accounting time periods are generally a month, a quarter, or a year.** Monthly and quarterly time periods are called **interim periods**. Most large companies must prepare both quarterly and annual financial statements.

An accounting time period that is one year in length is a **fiscal year**. A fiscal year usually begins with the first day of a month and ends twelve months later on the last day of a month. Most businesses use the **calendar year** (January 1 to December 31) as their accounting period. Some do not. Companies whose fiscal year differs from the calendar year include Delta Air Lines, June 30, and Walt Disney Productions, September 30. Sometimes a company's year-end will vary from year to year. For example, PepsiCo's fiscal year ends on the Friday closest to December 31, which was December 29 in 2009 and December 31 in 2010.

Accrual- versus Cash-Basis Accounting

LEARNING OBJECTIVE 2

Explain the accrual basis of accounting.

What you will learn in this chapter is **accrual-basis accounting**. Under the accrual basis, companies record transactions that change a company's financial statements **in the periods in which the events occur**. For example, using the accrual basis to determine net income means companies recognize revenues when they actually perform the services (rather than when they receive cash). It also means recognizing expenses when incurred (rather than when paid).

An alternative to the accrual basis is the cash basis. Under **cash-basis accounting**, companies record revenue when they receive cash. They record an expense when they pay out cash. The cash basis seems appealing due to its simplicity, but it often produces misleading financial statements. It fails to record revenue for a company that has provided services but for which it has not received the cash. As a result, it does not match expenses with earned revenues. **Cash-basis accounting is not in accordance with generally accepted accounting principles (GAAP).**

Individuals and some small companies do use cash-basis accounting. The cash basis is justified for small businesses because they often have few receivables and payables. Medium and large companies use accrual-basis accounting.

Recognizing Revenues and Expenses

It can be difficult to determine the amount of revenues and expenses to report in a given accounting period. Two principles help in this task: the revenue recognition principle and the expense recognition principle.

Revenue Recognition

Services performed

Customer requests services

Cash received

Revenue should be recognized in the accounting period in which services are performed.

REVENUE RECOGNITION PRINCIPLE

When a company agrees to perform a service or sell a product to a customer, it has a performance obligation. When the company meets this performance obligation, it recognizes revenue. The **revenue recognition principle** therefore requires that companies recognize revenue in the accounting period in which the performance obligation is satisfied.[1] To illustrate, assume that Dave's Dry Cleaning cleans clothing on June 30, but customers do not claim and pay for their clothes until the first week of July. Under the revenue recognition principle, Dave's recognizes revenue in June when it performed the service, rather than in July when it received the cash. At June 30, Dave's would report a receivable on its balance sheet and revenue in its income statement for the service performed.

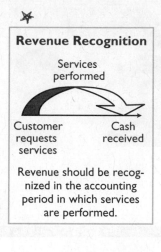

EXPENSE RECOGNITION PRINCIPLE

Accountants follow a simple rule in recognizing expenses: "Let the expenses follow the revenues." Thus, expense recognition is tied to revenue recognition. In the dry cleaning example, this means that Dave's should report the salary expense incurred in performing the June 30 cleaning service in the same period in which it recognizes the service revenue. The critical issue in expense recognition is when the expense makes its contribution to revenue. This may or may not be the same period in which the expense is paid. If Dave's does not pay the salary incurred on June 30 until July, it would report salaries payable on its June 30 balance sheet.

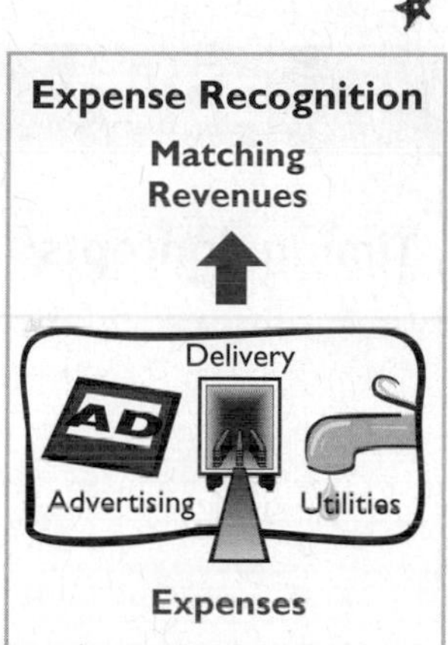

This practice of expense recognition is referred to as the **expense recognition principle** (often referred to as the **matching principle**). It dictates that efforts (expenses) be matched with results (revenues). Illustration 3-1 summarizes the revenue and expense recognition principles.

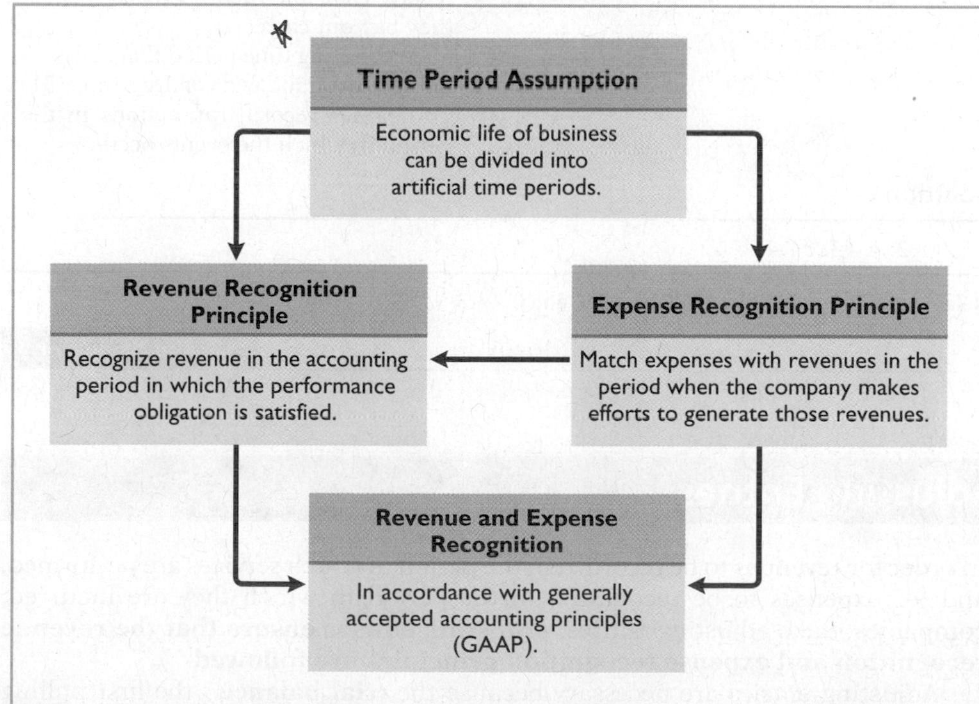

Illustration 3-1
GAAP relationships in revenue and expense recognition

[1]The defination for the revenue recognitions principle is based on the revised exposure draft issued by the FASB.

ETHICS INSIGHT

Cooking the Books?

Allegations of abuse of the revenue recognition principle have become all too common in recent years. For example, it was alleged that Krispy Kreme sometimes doubled the number of doughnuts shipped to wholesale customers at the end of a quarter to boost quarterly results. The customers shipped the unsold doughnuts back after the beginning of the next quarter for a refund. Conversely, Computer Associates International was accused of backdating sales—that is, saying that a sale that occurred at the beginning of one quarter occurred at the end of the previous quarter in order to achieve the previous quarter's sales targets.

What motivates sales executives and finance and accounting executives to participate in activities that result in inaccurate reporting of revenues? (See page 158.)

> DO IT!

Timing Concepts

Numerous timing concepts are discussed on pages 102–103. A list of concepts is provided in the left column below, with a description of the concept in the right column below. There are more descriptions provided than concepts. Match the description of the concept to the concept.

1. ____Accrual-basis accounting.
2. ____Calendar year.
3. ____Time period assumption.
4. ____Expense recognition principle.

(a) Monthly and quarterly time periods.
(b) Efforts (expenses) should be matched with results (revenues).
(c) Accountants divide the economic life of a business into artificial time periods.
(d) Companies record revenues when they receive cash and record expenses when they pay out cash.
(e) An accounting time period that starts on January 1 and ends on December 31.
(f) Companies record transactions in the period in which the events occur.

Action Plan

✔ Review the glossary terms identified on pages 102–103 and 126.

✔ Study carefully the revenue recognition principle, the expense recognition principle, and the time period assumption.

Solution

1. f 2. e 3. c 4. b

Related exercise material: **E3-1, E3-2, E3-3, and**  **3-1.**

✔ **The Navigator**

The Basics of Adjusting Entries

LEARNING OBJECTIVE 3

Explain the reasons for adjusting entries.

In order for revenues to be recorded in the period in which services are performed, and for expenses to be recognized in the period in which they are incurred, companies make adjusting entries. **Adjusting entries ensure that the revenue recognition and expense recognition principles are followed.**

Adjusting entries are necessary because the **trial balance**—the first pulling together of the transaction data—may not contain up-to-date and complete data. This is true for several reasons:

1. Some events are not recorded daily because it is not efficient to do so. Examples are the use of supplies and the earning of wages by employees.
2. Some costs are not recorded during the accounting period because these costs expire with the passage of time rather than as a result of recurring daily transactions. Examples are charges related to the use of buildings and equipment, rent, and insurance.
3. Some items may be unrecorded. An example is a utility service bill that will not be received until the next accounting period.

Adjusting entries are required every time a company prepares financial statements. The company analyzes each account in the trial balance to determine whether it is complete and up to date for financial statement purposes. **Every adjusting entry will include one income statement account and one balance sheet account.**

International Note 

Internal controls are a system of checks and balances designed to detect and prevent fraud and errors. The Sarbanes-Oxley Act requires U.S. companies to enhance their systems of internal control. However, many foreign companies do not have to meet strict internal control requirements. Some U.S. companies believe that this gives foreign firms an unfair advantage because developing and maintaining internal controls can be very expensive.

Types of Adjusting Entries

LEARNING OBJECTIVE 4

Identify the major types of adjusting entries.

Adjusting entries are classified as either **deferrals** or **accruals**. As Illustration 3-2 shows, each of these classes has two subcategories.

Illustration 3-2
Categories of adjusting entries

Deferrals:
1. Prepaid expenses: Expenses paid in cash before they are used or consumed.
2. Unearned revenues: Cash received before services are performed.

Accruals:
1. Accrued revenues: Revenues for services performed but not yet received in cash or recorded.
2. Accrued expenses: Expenses incurred but not yet paid in cash or recorded.

Subsequent sections give examples of each type of adjustment. Each example is based on the October 31 trial balance of Pioneer Advertising Agency Inc. from Chapter 2, reproduced in Illustration 3-3.

Illustration 3-3
Trial balance

Pioneer Advertising Agency Inc.
Trial Balance
October 31, 2014

	Debit	Credit
Cash	$15,200	
Supplies	2,500	
Prepaid Insurance	600	
Equipment	5,000	
Notes Payable		$ 5,000
Accounts Payable		2,500
Unearned Service Revenue		1,200
Common Stock		10,000
Retained Earnings		–0–
Dividends	500	
Service Revenue		10,000
Salaries and Wages Expense	4,000	
Rent Expense	900	
	$28,700	**$28,700**

We assume that Pioneer Advertising uses an accounting period of one month. Thus, monthly adjusting entries are made. The entries are dated October 31.

Adjusting Entries for Deferrals

LEARNING OBJECTIVE 5

Prepare adjusting entries for deferrals.

To defer means to postpone or delay. **Deferrals** are costs or revenues that are recognized at a date later than the point when cash was originally exchanged. Companies make adjusting entries for deferrals to record the portion of the deferred item that was incurred as an expense or recognized as revenue during the current accounting period. The two types of deferrals are prepaid expenses and unearned revenues.

PREPAID EXPENSES

When companies record payments of expenses that will benefit more than one accounting period, they record an asset called **prepaid expenses** or **prepayments**. When expenses are prepaid, an asset account is increased (debited) to show the service or benefit that the company will receive in the future. Examples of common prepayments are insurance, supplies, advertising, and rent. In addition, companies make prepayments when they purchase buildings and equipment.

Prepaid expenses are costs that expire either with the passage of time (e.g., rent and insurance) **or through use** (e.g., supplies). The expiration of these costs does not require daily entries, which would be impractical and unnecessary. Accordingly, companies postpone the recognition of such cost expirations until they prepare financial statements. At each statement date, they make adjusting entries to record the expenses applicable to the current accounting period and to show the remaining amounts in the asset accounts.

Prior to adjustment, assets are overstated and expenses are understated. Therefore, as shown in Illustration 3-4, **an adjusting entry for prepaid expenses results in an increase (a debit) to an expense account and a decrease (a credit) to an asset account**.

Illustration 3-4
Adjusting entries for prepaid expenses

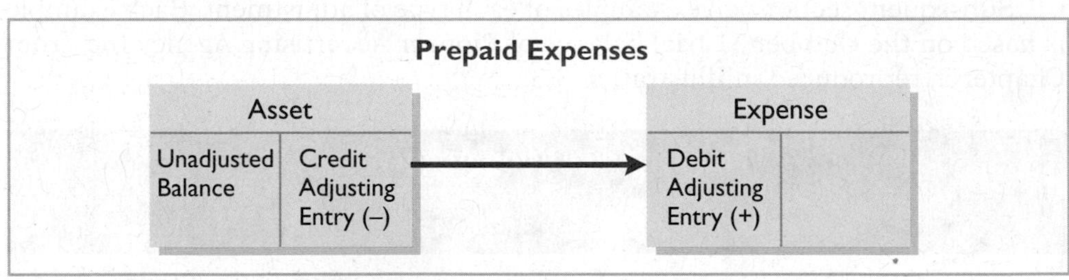

Let's look in more detail at some specific types of prepaid expenses, beginning with supplies.

SUPPLIES The purchase of supplies, such as paper and envelopes, results in an increase (a debit) to an asset account. During the accounting period, the company uses supplies. Rather than record supplies expense as the supplies are used, companies recognize supplies expense at the **end** of the accounting period. At the end of the accounting period, the company counts the remaining supplies. The difference between the unadjusted balance in the Supplies (asset) account and the actual cost of supplies on hand represents the supplies used (an expense) for that period (page 107).

Recall from Chapter 2 that Pioneer Advertising Agency Inc. purchased supplies costing $2,500 on October 5. Pioneer recorded the purchase by increasing (debiting) the asset Supplies. This account shows a balance of $2,500 in the October 31 trial balance. An inventory count at the close of business on October 31 reveals that $1,000 of supplies are still on hand. Thus, the cost of supplies used is $1,500 ($2,500 − $1,000). This use of supplies decreases an asset, Supplies. It also decreases stockholders' equity by increasing an expense account, Supplies Expense. This is shown in Illustration 3-5.

Illustration 3-5
Adjustment for supplies

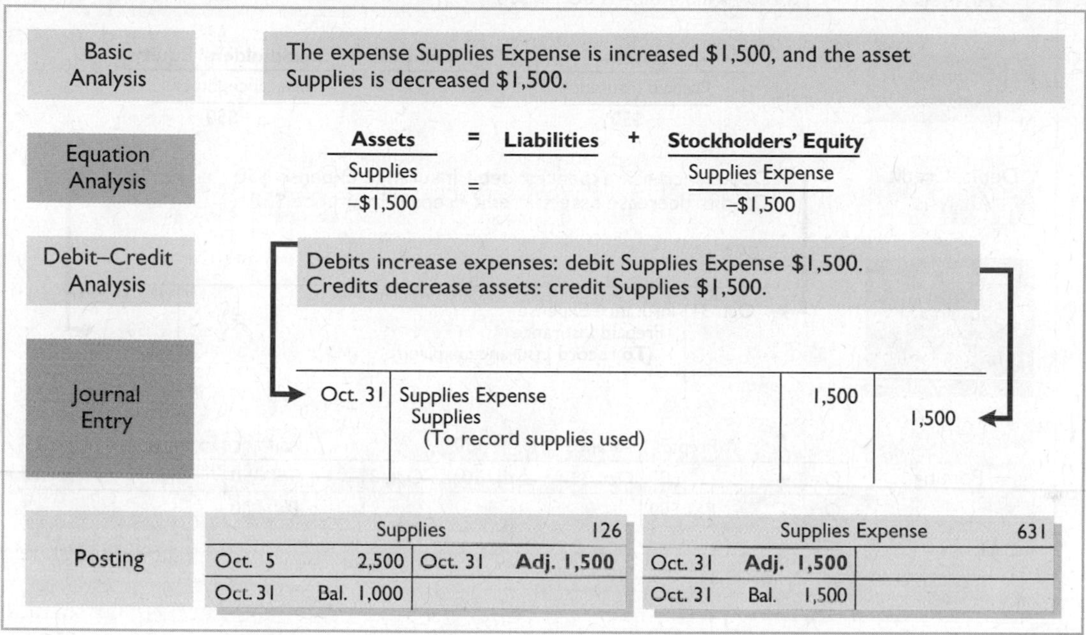

Basic Analysis
The expense Supplies Expense is increased $1,500, and the asset Supplies is decreased $1,500.
Equation Analysis
Assets = Liabilities + Stockholders' Equity
Supplies = Supplies Expense
−$1,500 −$1,500
Debit–Credit Analysis
Debits increase expenses: debit Supplies Expense $1,500.
Credits decrease assets: credit Supplies $1,500.
Journal Entry
Oct. 31 Supplies Expense 1,500
Supplies 1,500
(To record supplies used)
Posting
Supplies 126
Oct. 5 2,500 Oct. 31 Adj. 1,500
Oct. 31 Bal. 1,000
Supplies Expense 631
Oct. 31 Adj. 1,500
Oct. 31 Bal. 1,500

After adjustment, the asset account Supplies shows a balance of $1,000, which is equal to the cost of supplies on hand at the statement date. In addition, Supplies Expense shows a balance of $1,500, which equals the cost of supplies used in October. **If Pioneer does not make the adjusting entry, October expenses will be understated and net income overstated by $1,500. Moreover, both assets and stockholders' equity will be overstated by $1,500 on the October 31 balance sheet.**

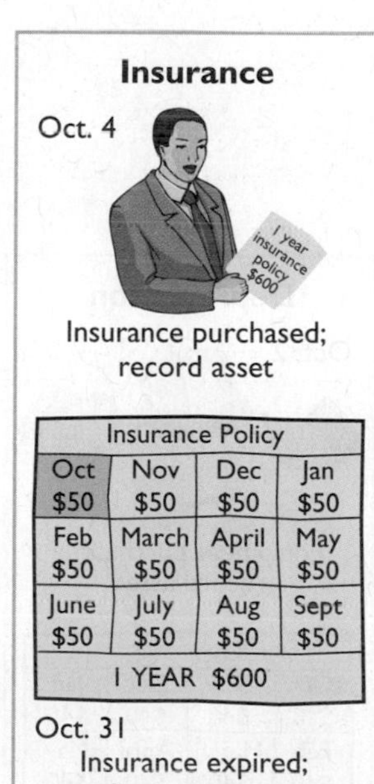

INSURANCE Companies purchase insurance to protect themselves from losses due to fire, theft, and unforeseen events. Insurance must be paid in advance, often for more than one year. The cost of insurance (premiums) paid in advance is recorded as an increase (debit) in the asset account Prepaid Insurance. At the financial statement date, companies increase (debit) Insurance Expense and decrease (credit) Prepaid Insurance for the cost of insurance that has expired during the period.

On October 4, Pioneer Advertising paid $600 for a one-year fire insurance policy. Coverage began on October 1. Pioneer recorded the payment by increasing (debiting) Prepaid Insurance. This account shows a balance of $600 in the October 31 trial balance. Insurance of $50 ($600 ÷ 12) expires each month. The expiration of prepaid insurance decreases an asset, Prepaid Insurance. It also decreases stockholders' equity by increasing an expense account, Insurance Expense.

As shown in Illustration 3-6 (page 108), the asset Prepaid Insurance shows a balance of $550, which represents the unexpired cost for the remaining 11 months of coverage. At the same time, the balance in Insurance Expense equals the insurance cost that expired in October. If Pioneer does not make this adjustment, October expenses are understated by $50 and net income is overstated by $50. Moreover, as the accounting equation shows, both assets and stockholders' equity will be overstated by $50 on the October 31 balance sheet.

Illustration 3-6
Adjustment for insurance

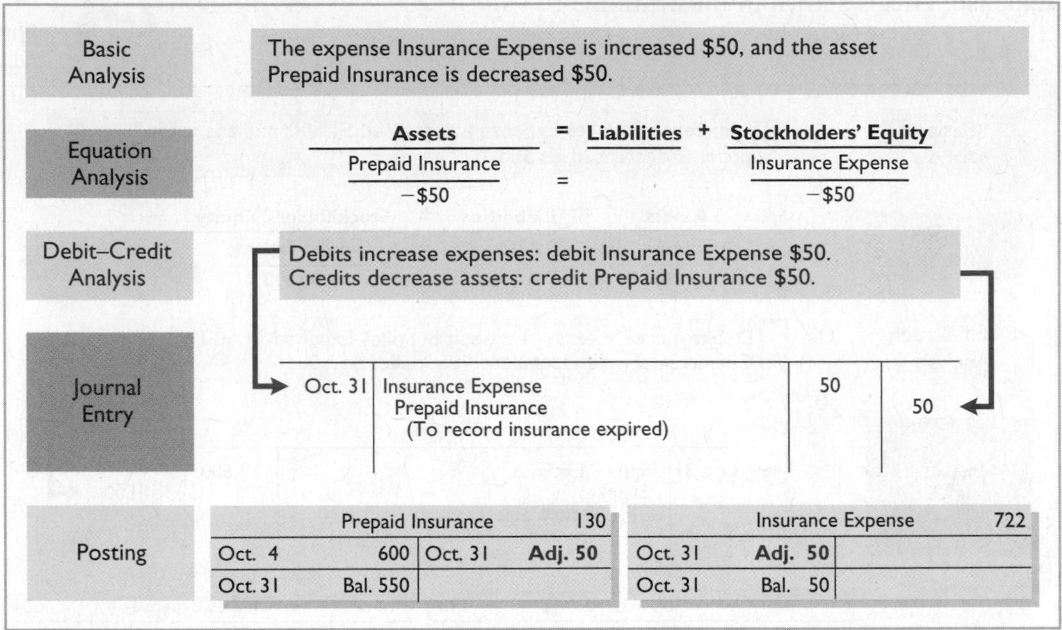

DEPRECIATION A company typically owns a variety of assets that have long lives, such as buildings, equipment, and motor vehicles. The period of service is referred to as the **useful life** of the asset. Because a building is expected to provide service for many years, it is recorded as an asset, rather than an expense, on the date it is acquired. As explained in Chapter 1, companies record such assets **at cost**, as required by the cost principle. To follow the expense recognition principle, companies allocate a portion of this cost as an expense during each period of the asset's useful life. **Depreciation** is the process of allocating the cost of an asset to expense over its useful life.

Depreciation
Oct. 2
Equipment purchased; record asset
Equipment
Oct $40 Nov $40 Dec $40 Jan $40
Feb $40 March $40 April $40 May $40
June $40 July $40 Aug $40 Sept $40
Depreciation = $480/year
Oct. 31
Depreciation recognized; record depreciation expense

Need for Adjustment. The acquisition of long-lived assets is essentially a long-term prepayment for the use of an asset. An adjusting entry for depreciation is needed to recognize the cost that has been used (an expense) during the period and to report the unused cost (an asset) at the end of the period. One very important point to understand: **Depreciation is an allocation concept, not a valuation concept.** That is, depreciation **allocates an asset's cost to the periods in which it is used. Depreciation does not attempt to report the actual change in the value of the asset**.

For Pioneer Advertising, assume that depreciation on the equipment is $480 a year, or $40 per month. As shown in Illustration 3-7 on the next page, rather than decrease (credit) the asset account directly, Pioneer instead credits Accumulated Depreciation—Equipment. Accumulated Depreciation is called a **contra asset account**. Such an account is offset against an asset account on the balance sheet. Thus, the Accumulated Depreciation—Equipment account offsets the asset Equipment. This account keeps track of the total amount of depreciation expense taken over the life of the asset. To keep the accounting equation in balance, Pioneer decreases stockholders' equity by increasing an expense account, Depreciation Expense.

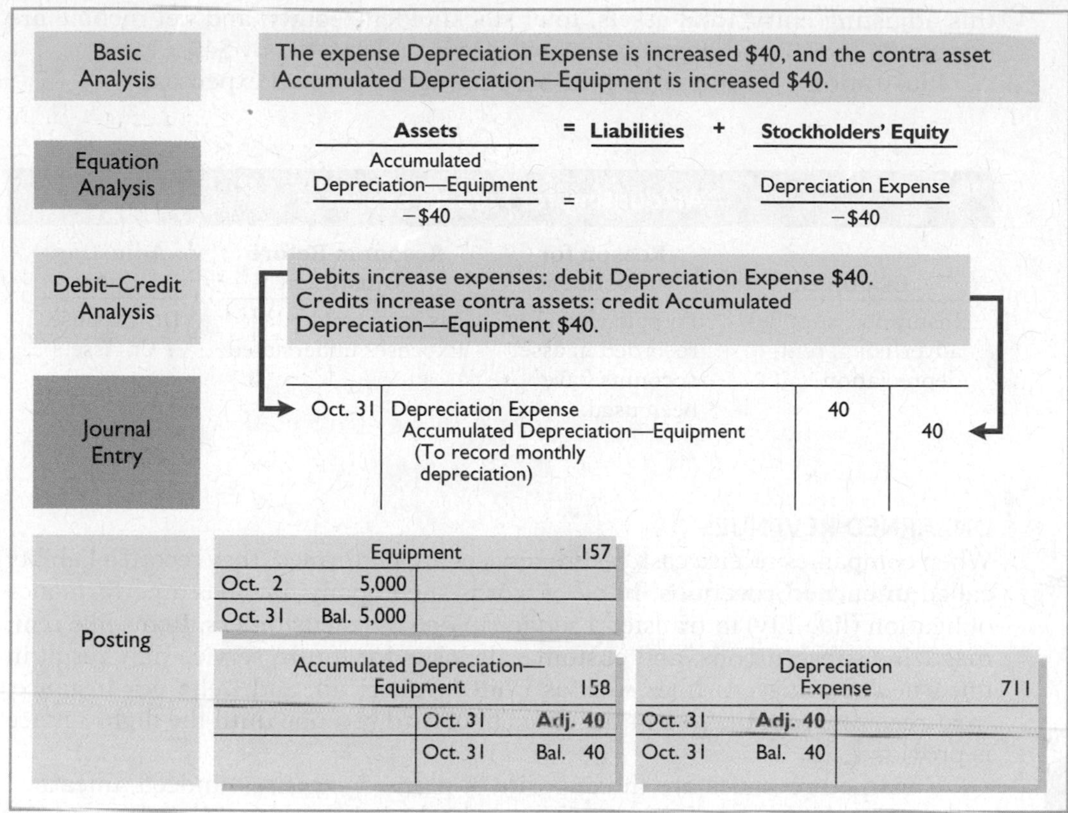
Basic Analysis
The expense Depreciation Expense is increased $40, and the contra asset Accumulated Depreciation—Equipment is increased $40.
Equation Analysis
Assets = Liabilities + Stockholders' Equity
Accumulated Depreciation—Equipment = Depreciation Expense
−$40 −$40
Debit–Credit Analysis
Debits increase expenses: debit Depreciation Expense $40.
Credits increase contra assets: credit Accumulated Depreciation—Equipment $40.
Journal Entry
Oct. 31 Depreciation Expense 40
Accumulated Depreciation—Equipment 40
(To record monthly depreciation)
Posting
Equipment 157
Oct. 2 5,000
Oct. 31 Bal. 5,000
Accumulated Depreciation—Equipment 158
Oct. 31 Adj. 40
Oct. 31 Bal. 40
Depreciation Expense 711
Oct. 31 Adj. 40
Oct. 31 Bal. 40

Illustration 3-7
Adjustment for depreciation

The balance in the Accumulated Depreciation—Equipment account will increase $40 each month, and the balance in Equipment remains $5,000.

Helpful Hint
All contra accounts have increases, decreases, and normal balances opposite to the account to which they relate.

Statement Presentation. As indicated, Accumulated Depreciation—Equipment is a contra asset account. It is offset against Equipment on the balance sheet. The normal balance of a contra asset account is a credit. A theoretical alternative to using a contra asset account would be to decrease (credit) the asset account by the amount of depreciation each period. But using the contra account is preferable for a simple reason: It discloses *both* the original cost of the equipment *and* the total cost that has expired to date. Thus, in the balance sheet, Pioneer deducts Accumulated Depreciation—Equipment from the related asset account, as shown in Illustration 3-8.

Equipment	$ 5,000
Less: Accumulated depreciation—equipment	40
	$4,960

Illustration 3-8
Balance sheet presentation of accumulated depreciation

Book value is the difference between the cost of any depreciable asset and its related accumulated depreciation. In Illustration 3-8, the book value of the equipment at the balance sheet date is $4,960. The book value and the fair value of the asset are generally two different values. As noted earlier, **the purpose of depreciation is not valuation but a means of cost allocation.**

Alternative Terminology
Book value is also referred to as *carrying value.*

Depreciation expense identifies the portion of an asset's cost that expired during the period (in this case, in October). The accounting equation shows that without this adjusting entry, total assets, total stockholders' equity, and net income are overstated by $40 and depreciation expense is understated by $40.

Illustration 3-9 summarizes the accounting for prepaid expenses.

Illustration 3-9
Accounting for prepaid expenses

Accounting for Prepaid Expenses

Examples	Reason for Adjustment	Accounts Before Adjustment	Adjusting Entry
Insurance, supplies, advertising, rent, depreciation	Prepaid expenses recorded in asset accounts have been used.	Assets overstated. Expenses understated.	Dr. Expenses Cr. Assets

UNEARNED REVENUES

Unearned Revenues

Oct. 2

Thank you in advance for your work

I will finish by Dec. 31

$1,200

Cash is received in advance; liability is recorded

Oct. 31

Some service has been performed; some revenue is recorded

When companies receive cash before services are performed, they record a liability called **unearned revenues**. In other words, a company now has a performance obligation (liability) to transfer a service to one of its customers. Items like rent, magazine subscriptions, and customer deposits for future service may result in unearned revenues. Airlines such as United, American, and Delta, for instance, treat receipts from the sale of tickets as unearned revenue until the flight service is provided.

Unearned revenues are the opposite of prepaid expenses. Indeed, unearned revenue on the books of one company is likely to be a prepaid expense on the books of the company that has made the advance payment. For example, if identical accounting periods are assumed, a landlord will have unearned rent revenue when a tenant has prepaid rent.

When a company receives payment for services to be performed in a future accounting period, it increases (credits) an unearned revenue (a liability) account to recognize the liability that exists. The company subsequently recognizes revenues when it performs the service. During the accounting period, it is not practical to make daily entries as the company provides services. Instead, the company delays recognition of revenue until the adjustment process. Then, the company makes an adjusting entry to record the revenue for services performed during the period and to show the liability that remains at the end of the accounting period. Typically, prior to adjustment, liabilities are overstated and revenues are understated. Therefore, as shown in Illustration 3-10, **the adjusting entry for unearned revenues results in a decrease (a debit) to a liability account and an increase (a credit) to a revenue account**.

Illustration 3-10
Adjusting entries for unearned revenues

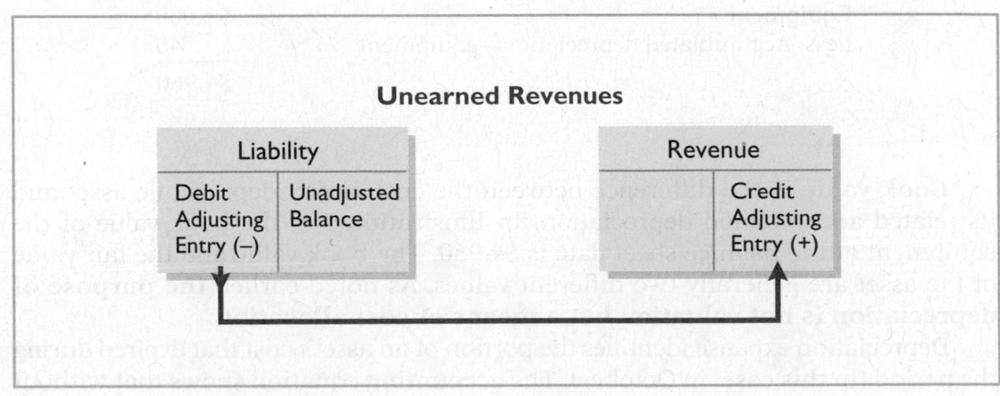

Pioneer Advertising received $1,200 on October 2 from R. Knox for advertising services expected to be completed by December 31. Pioneer credited the payment to Unearned Service Revenue, and this liability account shows a balance of $1,200 in the October 31 trial balance. From an evaluation of the service Pioneer performed for Knox during October, the company determines that it should recognize $400 of revenue in October. The liability (Unearned Service Revenue) is therefore decreased, and stockholder's equity (Service Revenue) is increased.

Alternative Terminology Unearned revenue is sometimes referred to as *deferred revenue.*

As shown in Illustration 3-11, the liability Unearned Service Revenue now shows a balance of $800. That amount represents the remaining advertising services expected to be performed in the future. At the same time, Service Revenue shows total revenue recognized in October of $10,400. **Without this adjustment, revenues and net income are understated by $400 in the income statement. Moreover, liabilities are overstated and stockholders' equity is understated by $400 on the October 31 balance sheet.**

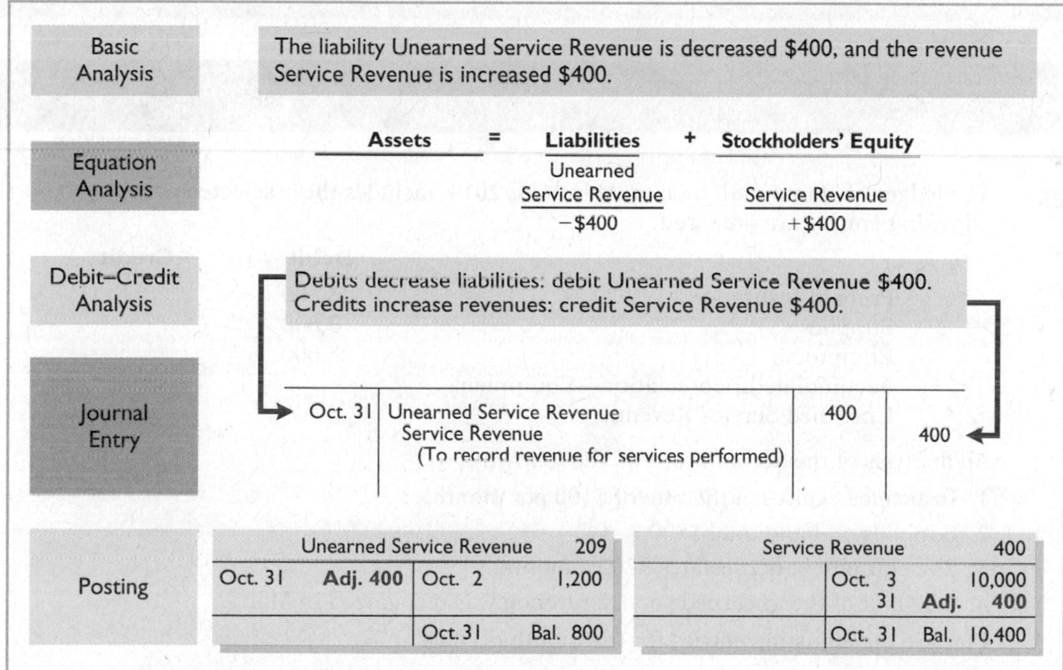

Basic Analysis
The liability Unearned Service Revenue is decreased $400, and the revenue Service Revenue is increased $400.
Equation Analysis
Assets = Liabilities + Stockholders' Equity
Unearned Service Revenue −$400
Service Revenue +$400
Debit–Credit Analysis
Debits decrease liabilities: debit Unearned Service Revenue $400.
Credits increase revenues: credit Service Revenue $400.
Journal Entry
Oct. 31 Unearned Service Revenue 400
Service Revenue 400
(To record revenue for services performed)
Posting
Unearned Service Revenue 209
Oct. 31 Adj. 400 Oct. 2 1,200
Oct. 31 Bal. 800
Service Revenue 400
Oct. 3 10,000
31 Adj. 400
Oct. 31 Bal. 10,400

Illustration 3-11
Service revenue accounts after adjustment

Illustration 3-12 summarizes the accounting for unearned revenues.

Illustration 3-12
Accounting for unearned revenues

Accounting for Unearned Revenues

Examples	Reason for Adjustment	Accounts Before Adjustment	Adjusting Entry
Rent, magazine subscriptions, customer deposits for future service	Unearned revenues recorded in liability accounts are now recognized as revenue for services performed.	Liabilities overstated. Revenues understated.	Dr. Liabilities Cr. Revenues

ACCOUNTING ACROSS THE ORGANIZATION

Turning Gift Cards into Revenue

Those of you who are marketing majors (and even most of you who are not) know that gift cards are among the hottest marketing tools in merchandising today. Customers purchase gift cards and give them to someone for later use. In a recent year, gift-card sales topped $95 billion.

Although these programs are popular with marketing executives, they create accounting questions. Should revenue be recorded at the time the gift card is sold, or when it is exercised? How should expired gift cards be accounted for? In its 2009 balance sheet, Best Buy reported unearned revenue related to gift cards of $479 million.

Source: Robert Berner, "Gift Cards: No Gift to Investors," *BusinessWeek* (March 14, 2005), p. 86.

Suppose that Robert Jones purchases a $100 gift card at Best Buy on December 24, 2013, and gives it to his wife, Mary Jones, on December 25, 2013. On January 3, 2014, Mary uses the card to purchase $100 worth of CDs. When do you think Best Buy should recognize revenue and why? **(See page 158.)**

> DO IT!

Adjusting Entries for Deferrals

The ledger of Hammond, Inc., on March 31, 2014, includes these selected accounts before adjusting entries are prepared.

	Debit	Credit
Prepaid Insurance	$ 3,600	
Supplies	2,800	
Equipment	25,000	
Accumulated Depreciation—Equipment		$5,000
Unearned Service Revenue		9,200

An analysis of the accounts shows the following.

1. Insurance expires at the rate of $100 per month.
2. Supplies on hand total $800.
3. The equipment depreciates $200 a month.
4. One-half of the unearned service revenue was recognized in March.

Prepare the adjusting entries for the month of March.

Action Plan

✔ Make adjusting entries at the end of the period for revenues recognized and expenses incurred in the period.

✔ Don't forget to make adjusting entries for deferrals. Failure to adjust for deferrals leads to overstatement of the asset or liability and understatement of the related expense or revenue.

Solution

	Debit	Credit
1. Insurance Expense	100	
Prepaid Insurance		100
(To record insurance expired)		
2. Supplies Expense	2,000	
Supplies		2,000
(To record supplies used)		
3. Depreciation Expense	200	
Accumulated Depreciation—Equipment		200
(To record monthly depreciation)		
4. Unearned Service Revenue	4,600	
Service Revenue		4,600
(To record revenue for services performed)		

Related exercise material: **BE3-3, BE3-4, BE3-5, BE3-6, and DO IT! 3-2.**

 **The Navigator**

Adjusting Entries for Accruals

LEARNING OBJECTIVE 6

Prepare adjusting entries for accruals.

The second category of adjusting entries is **accruals**. Prior to an accrual adjustment, the revenue account (and the related asset account) or the expense account (and the related liability account) are understated. Thus, the adjusting entry for accruals will **increase both a balance sheet and an income statement account.**

ACCRUED REVENUES

Revenues for services performed but not yet recorded at the statement date are **accrued revenues.** Accrued revenues may accumulate (accrue) with the passing of time, as in the case of interest revenue. These are unrecorded because the earning of interest does not involve daily transactions. Companies do not record interest revenue on a daily basis because it is often impractical to do so. Accrued revenues also may result from services that have been performed but not yet billed or collected, as in the case of commissions and fees. These may be unrecorded because only a portion of the total service has been provided and the clients won't be billed until the service has been completed.

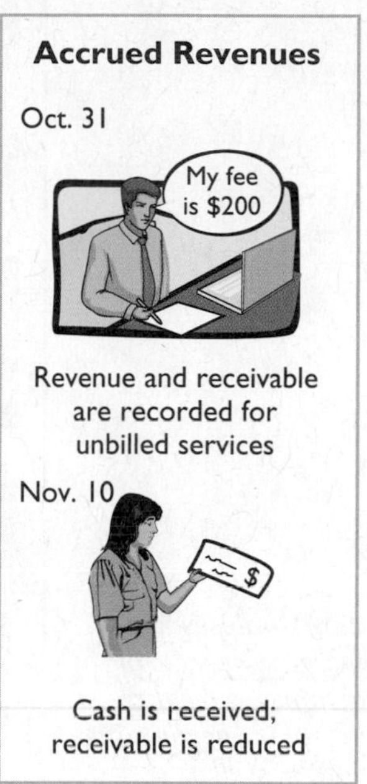

Accrued Revenues
Oct. 31
My fee is $200
Revenue and receivable are recorded for unbilled services
Nov. 10
$
Cash is received; receivable is reduced

An adjusting entry records the receivable that exists at the balance sheet date and the revenue for the services performed during the period. Prior to adjustment, both assets and revenues are understated. As shown in Illustration 3-13, **an adjusting entry for accrued revenues results in an increase (a debit) to an asset account and an increase (a credit) to a revenue account.**

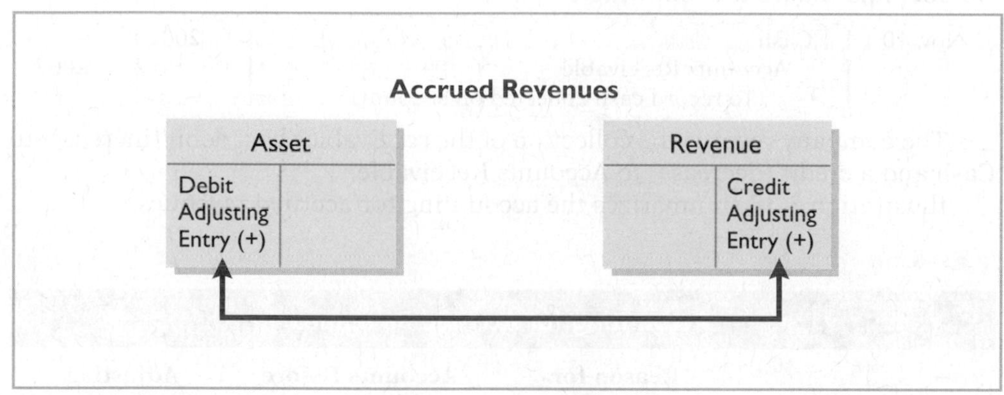

Illustration 3-13
Adjusting entries for accrued revenues

Helpful Hint
For accruals, there may have been no prior entry, and the accounts requiring adjustment may both have zero balances prior to adjustment.

In October, Pioneer Advertising Agency Inc. recognized $200 for advertising services performed that were not billed to clients on or before October 31. Because these services are not billed, they are not recorded. The accrual of unrecorded service revenue increases an asset account, Accounts Receivable. It also increases stockholders' equity by increasing a revenue account, Service Revenue, as shown in Illustration 3-14 (page 114).

The asset Accounts Receivable shows that clients owe Pioneer $200 at the balance sheet date. The balance of $10,600 in Service Revenue represents the total revenue for services performed by Pioneer during the month ($10,000 + $400 + $200). **Without the adjusting entry, assets and stockholders' equity on the balance sheet and revenues and net income on the income statement are understated.**

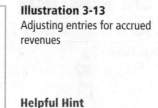

Illustration 3-14
Adjustment for accrued revenue

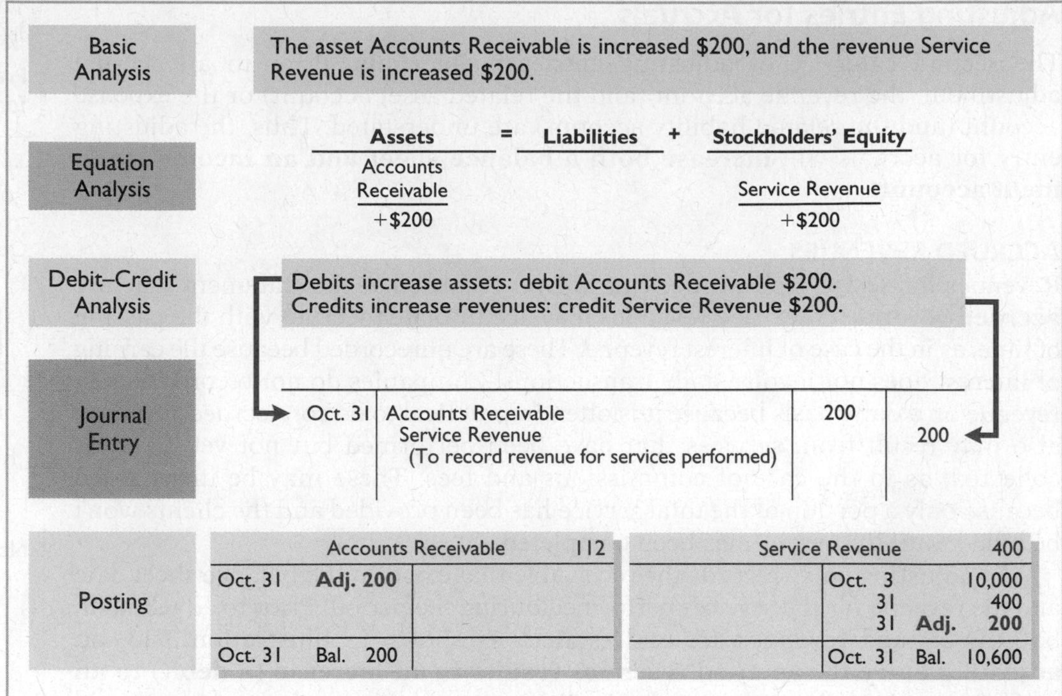
Basic Analysis
The asset Accounts Receivable is increased $200, and the revenue Service Revenue is increased $200.
Equation Analysis
Assets = Liabilities + Stockholders' Equity
Accounts Receivable +$200
Service Revenue +$200
Debit–Credit Analysis
Debits increase assets: debit Accounts Receivable $200.
Credits increase revenues: credit Service Revenue $200.
Journal Entry
Oct. 31 Accounts Receivable 200
Service Revenue 200
(To record revenue for services performed)
Posting
Accounts Receivable 112
Oct. 31 Adj. 200
Oct. 31 Bal. 200
Service Revenue 400
Oct. 3 10,000
31 400
31 Adj. 200
Oct. 31 Bal. 10,600

Equation analyses summarize the effects of transactions on the three elements of the accounting equation, as well as the effect on cash flows.

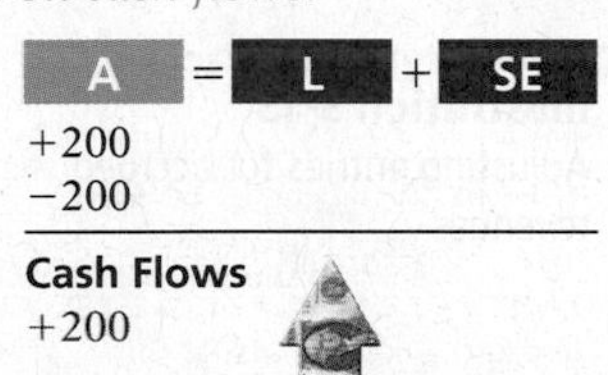
A = L + SE
+200
−200
Cash Flows
+200

On November 10, Pioneer receives cash of $200 for the services performed in October and makes the following entry.

Nov. 10	Cash	200	
	Accounts Receivable		200
	(To record cash collected on account)		

The company records the collection of the receivables by a debit (increase) to Cash and a credit (decrease) to Accounts Receivable.

Illustration 3-15 summarizes the accounting for accrued revenues.

Illustration 3-15
Accounting for accrued revenues

Accounting for Accrued Revenues

Examples	Reason for Adjustment	Accounts Before Adjustment	Adjusting Entry
Interest, rent, services performed but not collected	Services performed but not yet recorded.	Assets understated. Revenues understated.	Dr. Assets Cr. Revenues

Ethics Note

A report released by Fannie Mae's board of directors stated that improper adjusting entries at the mortgage-finance company resulted in delayed recognition of expenses caused by interest-rate changes. The motivation for such accounting apparently was the desire to hit earnings estimates.

ACCRUED EXPENSES

Expenses incurred but not yet paid or recorded at the statement date are called **accrued expenses**. Interest, taxes, and salaries are common examples of accrued expenses.

Companies make adjustments for accrued expenses to record the obligations that exist at the balance sheet date and to recognize the expenses that apply to the current accounting period. Prior to adjustment, both liabilities and expenses are understated. Therefore, as Illustration 3-16 shows, **an adjusting entry for accrued expenses results in an increase (a debit) to an expense account and an increase (a credit) to a liability account**.

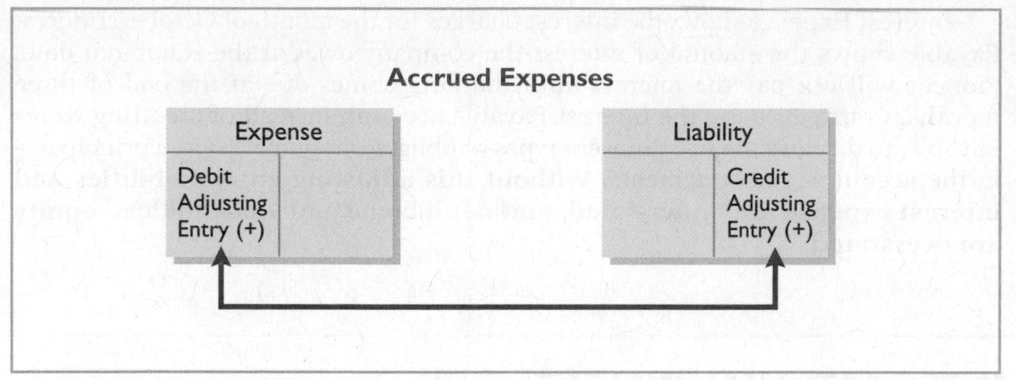

Illustration 3-16
Adjusting entries for accrued expenses

Let's look in more detail at some specific types of accrued expenses, beginning with accrued interest.

ACCRUED INTEREST Pioneer Advertising signed a three-month note payable in the amount of $5,000 on October 1. The note requires Pioneer to pay interest at an annual rate of 12%.

The amount of the interest recorded is determined by three factors: (1) the face value of the note; (2) the interest rate, which is always expressed as an annual rate; and (3) the length of time the note is outstanding. For Pioneer, the total interest due on the $5,000 note at its maturity date three months in the future is $150 ($\$5{,}000 \times 12\% \times \frac{3}{12}$), or $50 for one month. Illustration 3-17 shows the formula for computing interest and its application to Pioneer for the month of October.

Face Value of Note	×	Annual Interest Rate	×	Time in Terms of One Year	=	Interest
$5,000	×	12%	×	$\frac{1}{12}$	=	**$50**

Illustration 3-17
Formula for computing interest

Helpful Hint
In computing interest, we express the time period as a fraction of a year.

As Illustration 3-18 shows, the accrual of interest at October 31 increases a liability account, Interest Payable. It also decreases stockholders' equity by increasing an expense account, Interest Expense.

Illustration 3-18
Adjustment for accrued interest

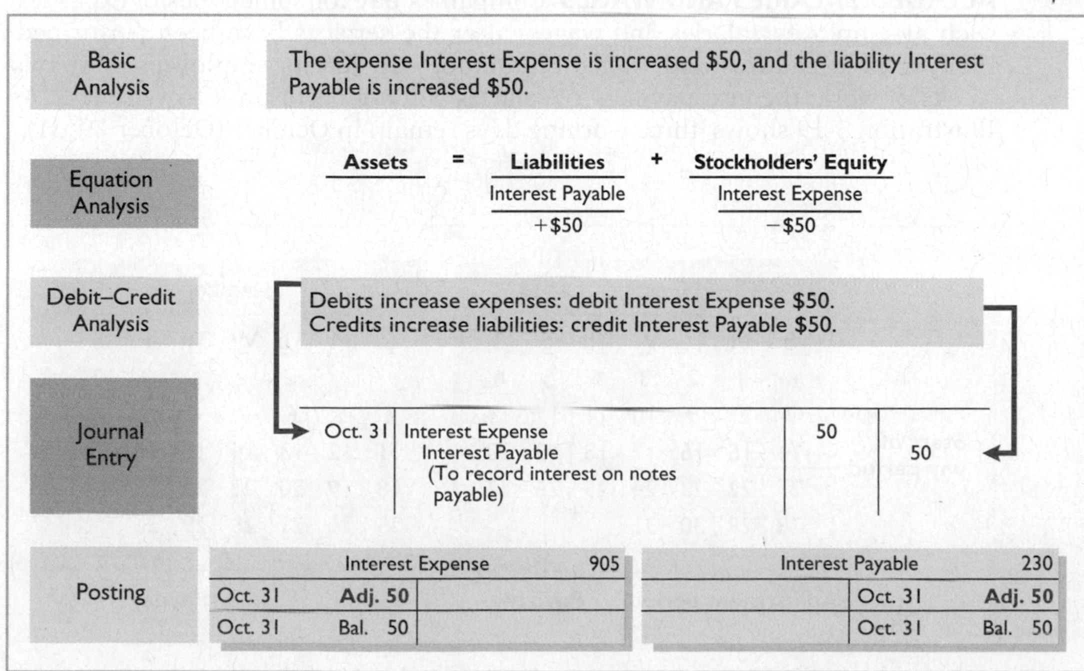

Interest Expense shows the interest charges for the month of October. Interest Payable shows the amount of interest the company owes at the statement date. Pioneer will not pay the interest until the note comes due at the end of three months. Companies use the Interest Payable account, instead of crediting Notes Payable, to disclose the two different types of obligations—interest and principal—in the accounts and statements. **Without this adjusting entry, liabilities and interest expense are understated, and net income and stockholders' equity are overstated.**

INTERNATIONAL INSIGHT

Cashing In on Accrual Accounting

The Chinese government, like most governments, uses cash accounting. A recent report, however, noted that it decided to use accrual accounting versus cash accounting for about $38 billion of expenditures in a recent budget projection. The Chinese government decided to expense the amount in the year in which the expenditures were originally allocated rather than when the payments would be made. Why did it do this? It enabled the government to keep its projected budget deficit below a 3% threshold. While the Chinese government was able to keep its projected shortfall below 3%, it did suffer some criticism for its inconsistent accounting. Critics charge that this inconsistent treatment reduces the transparency of China's accounting information. That is, it is not easy for outsiders to accurately evaluate what is really going on.

Source: Andrew Batson, "China Altered Budget Accounting to Reduce Deficit Figure," *Wall Street Journal Online* (March 15, 2010).

Accrual accounting is often considered superior to cash accounting. Why, then, were some people critical of China's use of accrual accounting in this instance? (See page 159.)

ACCRUED SALARIES AND WAGES Companies pay for some types of expenses, such as employee salaries and wages, after the services have been performed. Pioneer paid salaries and wages on October 26 for its employees' first two weeks of work; the next payment of salaries will not occur until November 9. As Illustration 3-19 shows, three working days remain in October (October 29–31).

Illustration 3-19
Calendar showing Pioneer's pay periods

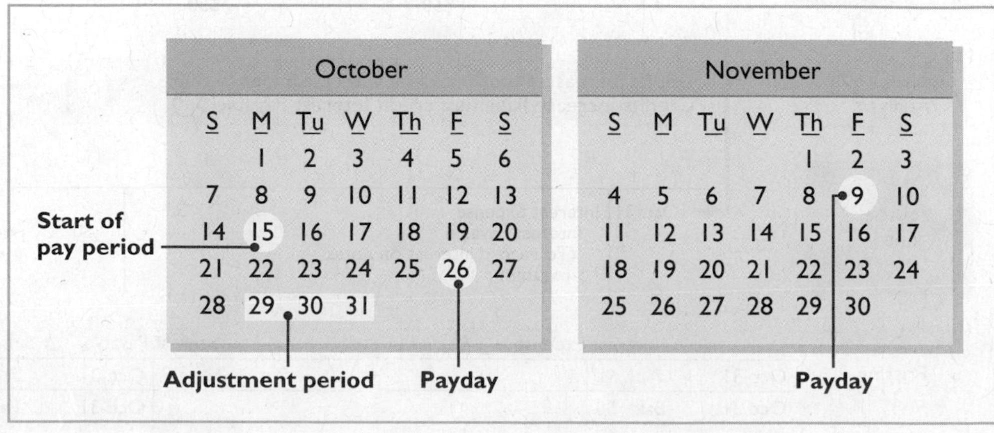

At October 31, the salaries and wages for these three days represent an accrued expense and a related liability to Pioneer. The employees receive total salaries and wages of $2,000 for a five-day work week, or $400 per day. Thus, accrued salaries and wages at October 31 are $1,200 ($400 × 3). This accrual increases a liability, Salaries and Wages Payable. It also decreases stockholders' equity by increasing an expense account, Salaries and Wages Expense, as shown in Illustration 3-20.

Illustration 3-20
Adjustment for accrued salaries and wages

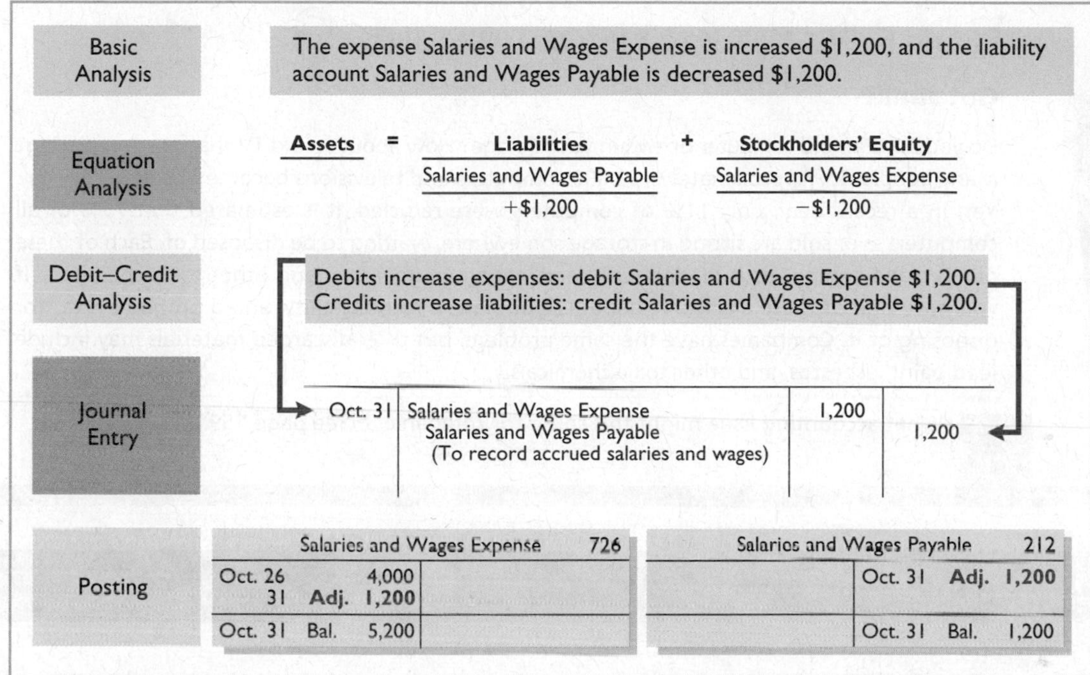
Basic Analysis
The expense Salaries and Wages Expense is increased $1,200, and the liability account Salaries and Wages Payable is decreased $1,200.
Equation Analysis
Assets = Liabilities + Stockholders' Equity
Salaries and Wages Payable
+$1,200
Salaries and Wages Expense
−$1,200
Debit–Credit Analysis
Debits increase expenses: debit Salaries and Wages Expense $1,200.
Credits increase liabilities: credit Salaries and Wages Payable $1,200.
Journal Entry
Oct. 31 Salaries and Wages Expense 1,200
Salaries and Wages Payable 1,200
(To record accrued salaries and wages)
Posting
Salaries and Wages Expense 726
Oct. 26 4,000
31 Adj. 1,200
Oct. 31 Bal. 5,200
Salaries and Wages Payable 212
Oct. 31 Adj. 1,200
Oct. 31 Bal. 1,200

After this adjustment, the balance in Salaries and Wages Expense of $5,200 (13 days × $400) is the actual salary and wages expense for October. The balance in Salaries and Wages Payable of $1,200 is the amount of the liability for salaries and wages Pioneer owes as of October 31. **Without the $1,200 adjustment for salaries and wages, Pioneer's expenses are understated $1,200 and its liabilities are understated $1,200.**

Pioneer Advertising pays salaries and wages every two weeks. Consequently, the next payday is November 9, when the company will again pay total salaries and wages of $4,000. The payment consists of $1,200 of salaries and wages payable at October 31 plus $2,800 of salaries and wages expense for November (7 working days, as shown in the November calendar × $400). Therefore, Pioneer makes the following entry on November 9.

Nov. 9	Salaries and Wages Payable	1,200	
	Salaries and Wages Expense	2,800	
	Cash		4,000
	(To record November 9 payroll)		

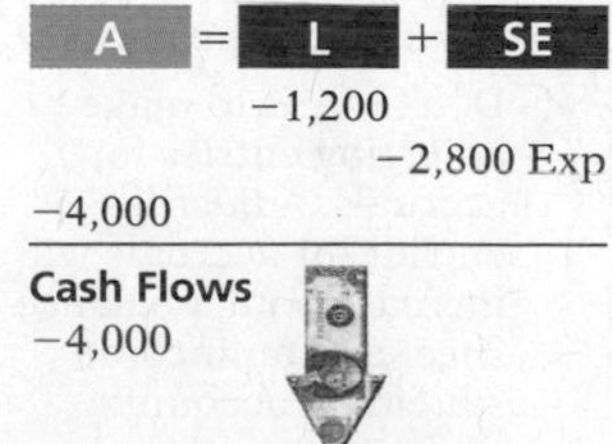
A = L + SE
−1,200
−2,800 Exp
−4,000
Cash Flows
−4,000

This entry eliminates the liability for Salaries and Wages Payable that Pioneer recorded in the October 31 adjusting entry, and it records the proper amount of Salaries and Wages Expense for the period between November 1 and November 9.

Illustration 3-21 (page 118) summarizes the accounting for accrued expenses.

Illustration 3-21
Accounting for accrued expenses

Accounting for Accrued Expenses

Examples	Reason for Adjustment	Accounts Before Adjustment	Adjusting Entry
Interest, rent, salaries	Expenses have been incurred but not yet paid in cash or recorded.	Expenses understated. Liabilities understated.	Dr. Expenses Cr. Liabilities

PEOPLE, PLANET, AND PROFIT INSIGHT

Got Junk?

Do you have an old computer or two in your garage? How about an old TV that needs replacing? Many people do. Approximately 163,000 computers and televisions become obsolete *each day*. Yet, in a recent year, only 11% of computers were recycled. It is estimated that 75% of all computers ever sold are sitting in storage somewhere, waiting to be disposed of. Each of these old TVs and computers is loaded with lead, cadmium, mercury, and other toxic chemicals. If you have one of these electronic gadgets, you have a responsibility, and a probable cost, for disposing of it. Companies have the same problem, but their discarded materials may include lead paint, asbestos, and other toxic chemicals.

What accounting issue might this cause for companies? (See page 159.)

> DO IT!

Adjusting Entries for Accruals

Micro Computer Services Inc. began operations on August 1, 2014. At the end of August 2014, management attempted to prepare monthly financial statements. The following information relates to August.

1. At August 31, the company owed its employees $800 in salaries and wages that will be paid on September 1.
2. On August 1, the company borrowed $30,000 from a local bank on a 15-year mortgage. The annual interest rate is 10%.
3. Revenue for services performed but unrecorded for August totaled $1,100.

Prepare the adjusting entries needed at August 31, 2014.

Action Plan

✔ Make adjusting entries at the end of the period for revenues recognized and expenses incurred in the period.

✔ Don't forget to make adjusting entries for accruals. Adjusting entries for accruals will increase both a balance sheet and an income statement account.

Solution

	Debit	Credit
1. Salaries and Wages Expense	800	
Salaries and Wages Payable		800
(To record accrued salaries)		
2. Interest Expense	250	
Interest Payable		250
(To record accrued interest: $\$30,000 \times 10\% \times \frac{1}{12} = \$250$)		
3. Accounts Receivable	1,100	
Service Revenue		1,100
(To record revenue for services performed)		

Related exercise material: **BE3-7, E3-5, E3-6, E3-7, E3-8, E3-9, E3-10, E3-11, E3-12, and DO IT! 3-3.**

The Navigator

Summary of Basic Relationships

Illustration 3-22 summarizes the four basic types of adjusting entries. Take some time to study and analyze the adjusting entries. Be sure to note that **each adjusting entry affects one balance sheet account and one income statement account.**

Illustration 3-22
Summary of adjusting entries

Type of Adjustment	Accounts Before Adjustment	Adjusting Entry
Prepaid expenses	Assets overstated. Expenses understated.	Dr. Expenses Cr. Assets
Unearned revenues	Liabilities overstated. Revenues understated.	Dr. Liabilities Cr. Revenues
Accrued revenues	Assets understated. Revenues understated.	Dr. Assets Cr. Revenues
Accrued expenses	Expenses understated. Liabilities understated.	Dr. Expenses Cr. Liabilities

Illustrations 3-23 (below) and 3-24 (on page 120) show the journalizing and posting of adjusting entries for Pioneer Advertising Agency Inc. on October 31. The ledger identifies all adjustments by the reference J2 because they have been recorded on page 2 of the general journal. The company may insert a center caption "Adjusting Entries" between the last transaction entry and the first adjusting entry in the journal. When you review the general ledger in Illustration 3-24, note that the entries highlighted in color are the adjustments.

Illustration 3-23
General journal showing adjusting entries

General Journal J2

Date	Account Titles and Explanation	Ref.	Debit	Credit
2014	Adjusting Entries			
Oct. 31	Supplies Expense	631	1,500	
	Supplies	126		1,500
	(To record supplies used)			
31	Insurance Expense	722	50	
	Prepaid Insurance	130		50
	(To record insurance expired)			
31	Depreciation Expense	711	40	
	Accumulated Depreciation—Equipment	158		40
	(To record monthly depreciation)			
31	Unearned Service Revenue	209	400	
	Service Revenue	400		400
	(To record revenue for services performed)			
31	Accounts Receivable	112	200	
	Service Revenue	400		200
	(To record revenue for services performed)			
31	Interest Expense	905	50	
	Interest Payable	230		50
	(To record interest on notes payable)			
31	Salaries and Wages Expense	726	1,200	
	Salaries and Wages Payable	212		1,200
	(To record accrued salaries and wages)			

Helpful Hint
1. Adjusting entries should not involve debits or credits to cash.
2. Evaluate whether the adjustment makes sense. For example, an adjustment to recognize supplies used should increase supplies expense.
3. Double-check all computations.
4. Each adjusting entry affects one balance sheet account and one income statement account.

Illustration 3-24
General ledger after adjustment

General Ledger

Cash — No. 101

Date	Explanation	Ref.	Debit	Credit	Balance
2014					
Oct. 1		J1	10,000		10,000
2		J1	1,200		11,200
3		J1		900	10,300
4		J1		600	9,700
20		J1		500	9,200
26		J1		4,000	5,200
31		J1	10,000		15,200

Accounts Receivable — No. 112

Date	Explanation	Ref.	Debit	Credit	Balance
2014					
Oct. 31	**Adj. entry**	**J2**	**200**		**200**

Supplies — No. 126

Date	Explanation	Ref.	Debit	Credit	Balance
2014					
Oct. 5		J1	2,500		2,500
31	**Adj. entry**	**J2**		**1,500**	**1,000**

Prepaid Insurance — No. 130

Date	Explanation	Ref.	Debit	Credit	Balance
2014					
Oct. 4		J1	600		600
31	**Adj. entry**	**J2**		**50**	**550**

Equipment — No. 157

Date	Explanation	Ref.	Debit	Credit	Balance
2014					
Oct. 1		J1	5,000		5,000

Accumulated Depreciation—Equipment — No. 158

Date	Explanation	Ref.	Debit	Credit	Balance
2014					
Oct. 31	**Adj. entry**	**J2**		**40**	**40**

Notes Payable — No. 200

Date	Explanation	Ref.	Debit	Credit	Balance
2014					
Oct. 1		J1		5,000	5,000

Accounts Payable — No. 201

Date	Explanation	Ref.	Debit	Credit	Balance
2014					
Oct. 5		J1		2,500	2,500

Unearned Service Revenue — No. 209

Date	Explanation	Ref.	Debit	Credit	Balance
2014					
Oct. 2		J1		1,200	1,200
31	**Adj. entry**	**J2**	**400**		**800**

Salaries and Wages Payable — No. 212

Date	Explanation	Ref.	Debit	Credit	Balance
2014					
Oct. 31	**Adj. entry**	**J2**		**1,200**	**1,200**

Interest Payable — No. 230

Date	Explanation	Ref.	Debit	Credit	Balance
2014					
Oct. 31	**Adj. entry**	**J2**		**50**	**50**

Common Stock — No. 311

Date	Explanation	Ref.	Debit	Credit	Balance
2014					
Oct. 1		J1		10,000	10,000

Retained Earnings — No. 320

Date	Explanation	Ref.	Debit	Credit	Balance
2014					

Dividends — No. 332

Date	Explanation	Ref.	Debit	Credit	Balance
2014					
Oct. 20		J1	500		500

Service Revenue — No. 400

Date	Explanation	Ref.	Debit	Credit	Balance
2014					
Oct. 31		J1		10,000	10,000
31	**Adj. entry**	**J2**		**400**	**10,400**
31	**Adj. entry**	**J2**		**200**	**10,600**

Supplies Expense — No. 631

Date	Explanation	Ref.	Debit	Credit	Balance
2014					
Oct. 31	**Adj. entry**	**J2**	**1,500**		**1,500**

Depreciation Expense — No. 711

Date	Explanation	Ref.	Debit	Credit	Balance
2014					
Oct. 31	**Adj. entry**	**J2**	**40**		**40**

Insurance Expense — No. 722

Date	Explanation	Ref.	Debit	Credit	Balance
2014					
Oct. 31	**Adj. entry**	**J2**	**50**		**50**

Salaries and Wages Expense — No. 726

Date	Explanation	Ref.	Debit	Credit	Balance
2014					
Oct. 26		J1	4,000		4,000
31	**Adj. entry**	**J2**	**1,200**		**5,200**

Rent Expense — No. 729

Date	Explanation	Ref.	Debit	Credit	Balance
2014					
Oct. 3		J1	900		900

Interest Expense — No. 905

Date	Explanation	Ref.	Debit	Credit	Balance
2014					
Oct. 31	**Adj. entry**	**J2**	**50**		**50**

The Adjusted Trial Balance and Financial Statements

LEARNING OBJECTIVE 7

Describe the nature and purpose of an adjusted trial balance.

After a company has journalized and posted all adjusting entries, it prepares another trial balance from the ledger accounts. This trial balance is called an **adjusted trial balance**. It shows the balances of all accounts, including those adjusted, at the end of the accounting period. The purpose of an adjusted trial balance is to **prove the equality** of the total debit balances and the total credit balances in the ledger after all adjustments. Because the accounts contain all data needed for financial statements, the adjusted trial balance is the **primary basis for the preparation of financial statements**.

Preparing the Adjusted Trial Balance

Illustration 3-25 presents the adjusted trial balance for Pioneer Advertising Agency Inc. prepared from the ledger accounts in Illustration 3-24. The amounts affected by the adjusting entries are highlighted in color. Compare these amounts to those in the unadjusted trial balance in Illustration 3-3 on page 105. In this comparison, you will see that there are more accounts in the adjusted trial balance as a result of the adjusting entries made at the end of the month.

Illustration 3-25
Adjusted trial balance

Pioneer Advertising Agency Inc.
Adjusted Trial Balance
October 31, 2014

	Dr.	Cr.
Cash	$15,200	
Accounts Receivable	**200**	
Supplies	**1,000**	
Prepaid Insurance	**550**	
Equipment	5,000	
Accumulated Depreciation—Equipment		$ **40**
Notes Payable		5,000
Accounts Payable		2,500
Interest Payable		**50**
Unearned Service Revenue		**800**
Salaries and Wages Payable		**1,200**
Common Stock		10,000
Retained Earnings		–0–
Dividends	500	
Service Revenue		10,600
Salaries and Wages Expense	**5,200**	
Supplies Expense	**1,500**	
Rent Expense	900	
Insurance Expense	**50**	
Interest Expense	**50**	
Depreciation Expense	**40**	
	$30,190	**$30,190**

Preparing Financial Statements

Companies can prepare financial statements directly from the adjusted trial balance. Illustrations 3-26 and 3-27 present the interrelationships of data in the adjusted trial balance and the financial statements.

As Illustration 3-26 shows, companies prepare the income statement from the revenue and expense accounts. Next, they use the Retained Earnings and Dividends accounts and the net income (or net loss) from the income statement to prepare the retained earnings statement. As Illustration 3-27 shows, companies then prepare the balance sheet from the asset and liability accounts and the ending retained earnings balance as reported in the retained earnings statement.

Illustration 3-26
Preparation of the income statement and retained earnings statement from the adjusted trial balance

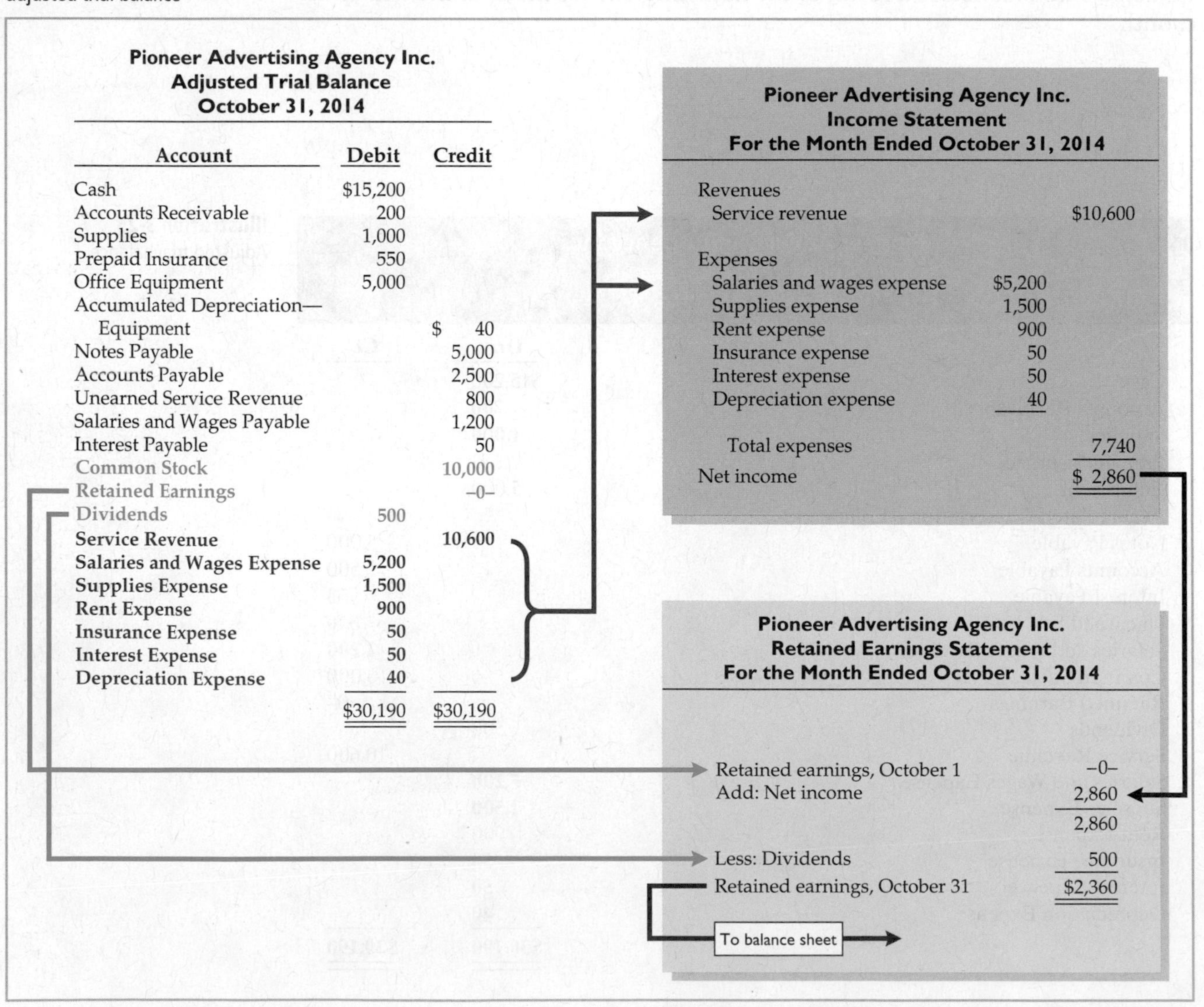

Pioneer Advertising Agency Inc.
Adjusted Trial Balance
October 31, 2014

Account	Debit	Credit
Cash	$15,200	
Accounts Receivable	200	
Supplies	1,000	
Prepaid Insurance	550	
Office Equipment	5,000	
Accumulated Depreciation—Equipment		$ 40
Notes Payable		5,000
Accounts Payable		2,500
Unearned Service Revenue		800
Salaries and Wages Payable		1,200
Interest Payable		50
Common Stock		10,000
Retained Earnings		–0–
Dividends	500	
Service Revenue		10,600
Salaries and Wages Expense	5,200	
Supplies Expense	1,500	
Rent Expense	900	
Insurance Expense	50	
Interest Expense	50	
Depreciation Expense	40	
	$30,190	$30,190

Pioneer Advertising Agency Inc.
Income Statement
For the Month Ended October 31, 2014

Revenues		
Service revenue		$10,600
Expenses		
Salaries and wages expense	$5,200	
Supplies expense	1,500	
Rent expense	900	
Insurance expense	50	
Interest expense	50	
Depreciation expense	40	
Total expenses		7,740
Net income		$ 2,860

Pioneer Advertising Agency Inc.
Retained Earnings Statement
For the Month Ended October 31, 2014

Retained earnings, October 1	–0–
Add: Net income	2,860
	2,860
Less: Dividends	500
Retained earnings, October 31	$2,360

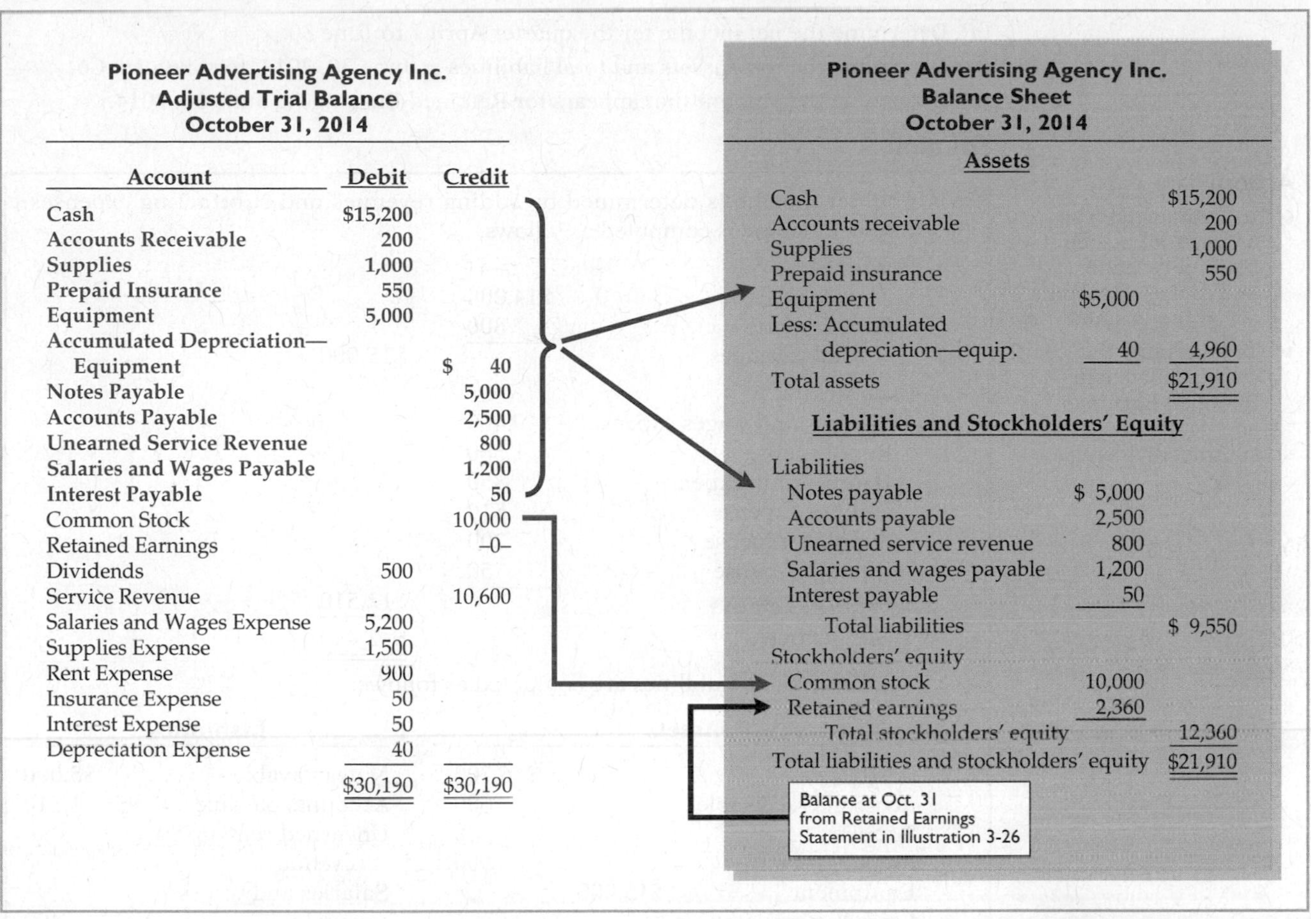

Pioneer Advertising Agency Inc.
Adjusted Trial Balance
October 31, 2014

Account	Debit	Credit
Cash	$15,200	
Accounts Receivable	200	
Supplies	1,000	
Prepaid Insurance	550	
Equipment	5,000	
Accumulated Depreciation—Equipment		$ 40
Notes Payable		5,000
Accounts Payable		2,500
Unearned Service Revenue		800
Salaries and Wages Payable		1,200
Interest Payable		50
Common Stock		10,000
Retained Earnings		-0-
Dividends	500	
Service Revenue		10,600
Salaries and Wages Expense	5,200	
Supplies Expense	1,500	
Rent Expense	900	
Insurance Expense	50	
Interest Expense	50	
Depreciation Expense	40	
	$30,190	$30,190

Pioneer Advertising Agency Inc.
Balance Sheet
October 31, 2014

Assets

Cash		$15,200
Accounts receivable		200
Supplies		1,000
Prepaid insurance		550
Equipment	$5,000	
Less: Accumulated depreciation—equip.	40	4,960
Total assets		$21,910

Liabilities and Stockholders' Equity

Liabilities		
Notes payable	$ 5,000	
Accounts payable	2,500	
Unearned service revenue	800	
Salaries and wages payable	1,200	
Interest payable	50	
Total liabilities		$ 9,550
Stockholders' equity		
Common stock	10,000	
Retained earnings	2,360	
Total stockholders' equity		12,360
Total liabilities and stockholders' equity		$21,910

Balance at Oct. 31 from Retained Earnings Statement in Illustration 3-26

Illustration 3-27
Preparation of the balance sheet from the adjusted trial balance

> DO IT!

Trial balance

Skolnick Co. was organized on April 1, 2014. The company prepares quarterly financial statements. The adjusted trial balance amounts at June 30 are shown below.

	Debits		Credits
Cash	$ 6,700	Accumulated Depreciation—Equipment	$ 850
Accounts Receivable	600	Notes Payable	5,000
Prepaid Rent	900	Accounts Payable	1,510
Supplies	1,000	Salaries and Wages Payable	400
Equipment	15,000	Interest Payable	50
Dividends	600	Unearned Rent Revenue	500
Salaries and Wages Expense	9,400	Common Stock	14,000
Rent Expense	1,500	Service Revenue	14,200
Depreciation Expense	850	Rent Revenue	800
Supplies Expense	200		
Utilities Expense	510		
Interest Expense	50		
Total debits	$37,310	Total credits	$37,310

(a) Determine the net income for the quarter April 1 to June 30.
(b) Determine the total assets and total liabilities at June 30, 2014, for Skolnick Co.
(c) Determine the amount that appears for Retained Earnings at June 30, 2014.

Solution

Action Plan

✔ In an adjusted trial balance, all assets, liability, revenue, and expense accounts are properly stated.

✔ To determine the ending balance in Retained Earnings, add net income and subtract dividends.

(a) The net income is determined by adding revenues and subtracting expenses. The net income is computed as follows.

Revenues		
Service revenue	$14,200	
Rent revenue	800	
Total revenues		$15,000
Expenses		
Salaries and wages expense	$ 9,400	
Rent expense	1,500	
Depreciation expense	850	
Utilities expense	510	
Supplies expense	200	
Interest expense	50	
Total expenses		12,510
Net income		$ 2,490

(b) Total assets and liabilities are computed as follows.

Assets			Liabilities	
Cash		$ 6,700	Notes payable	$5,000
Accounts receivable		600	Accounts payable	1,510
Supplies		1,000	Unearned rent revenue	500
Prepaid rent		900	Salaries and wages payable	400
Equipment	$15,000		Interest payable	50
Less: Accumulated depreciation—equipment	850	14,150		
Total assets		$23,350	Total liabilities	$7,460

(c)

Retained earnings, April 1	$ 0
Add: Net income	2,490
Less: Dividends	600
Retained earnings, June 30	$ 1,890

Related exercise material: **BE3-9, BE3-10, E3-11, E3-13, and DO IT! 3-4.**

✔ **The Navigator**

Comprehensive DO IT!

The Green Thumb Lawn Care Inc. began on April 1. At April 30, the trial balance shows the following balances for selected accounts.

Prepaid Insurance	$ 3,600
Equipment	28,000
Notes Payable	20,000
Unearned Service Revenue	4,200
Service Revenue	1,800

Analysis reveals the following additional data.

1. Prepaid insurance is the cost of a 2-year insurance policy, effective April 1.
2. Depreciation on the equipment is $500 per month.
3. The note payable is dated April 1. It is a 6-month, 12% note.
4. Seven customers paid for the company's 6 months' lawn service package of $600 beginning in April. The company performed services for these customers in April.
5. Lawn services provided other customers but not recorded at April 30 totaled $1,500.

Instructions

Prepare the adjusting entries for the month of April. Show computations.

Solution to Comprehensive DO IT!

Action Plan

- ✔ Note that adjustments are being made for one month.
- ✔ Make computations carefully.
- ✔ Select account titles carfully.
- ✔ Make sure debits are made first and credits are indented.
- ✔ Check that debits equal credits for each entry.

GENERAL JOURNAL **J1**

Date	Account Titles and Explanation	Ref.	Debit	Credit
	Adjusting Entries			
Apr. 30	Insurance Expense		150	
	Prepaid Insurance			150
	(To record insurance expired:			
	$3,600 ÷ 24 = $150 per month)			
30	Depreciation Expense		500	
	Accumulated Depreciation—Equipment			500
	(To record monthly depreciation)			
30	Interest Expense		200	
	Interest Payable			200
	(To record interest on notes payable:			
	$20,000 × 12% × 1/12 = $200)			
30	Unearned Service Revenue		700	
	Service Revenue			700
	(To record revenue for services performed:			
	$600 ÷ 6 = $100;			
	$100 per month × 7 = $700)			
30	Accounts Receivable		1,500	
	Service Revenue			1,500
	(To record revenue for services			
	performed)			

The Navigator

SUMMARY OF LEARNING OBJECTIVES

The Navigator

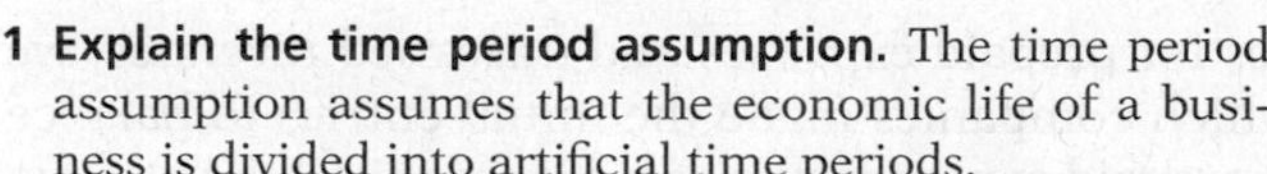

1 **Explain the time period assumption.** The time period assumption assumes that the economic life of a business is divided into artificial time periods.

2 **Explain the accrual basis of accounting.** Accrual-basis accounting means that companies record events that change a company's financial statements in the periods in which those events occur, rather than in the periods in which the company receives or pays cash.

3 **Explain the reasons for adjusting entries.** Companies make adjusting entries at the end of an accounting period. Such entries ensure that companies recognize revenues in the period in which the performance obligation is satisfied and recognize expenses in the period in which they are incurred.

4 **Identify the major types of adjusting entries.** The major types of adjusting entries are deferrals (prepaid expenses and unearned revenues) and accruals (accrued revenues and accrued expenses).

5 **Prepare adjusting entries for deferrals.** Deferrals are either prepaid expenses or unearned revenues.

Companies make adjusting entries for deferrals to record the portion of the prepayment that represents the expense incurred or the revenue for services performed in the current accounting period.

6 **Prepare adjusting entries for accruals.** Accruals are either accrued revenues or accrued expenses. Companies make adjusting entries for accruals to record revenues for services performed and expenses incurred in the current accounting period that have not been recognized through daily entries.

7 **Describe the nature and purpose of an adjusted trial balance.** An adjusted trial balance shows the balances of all accounts, including those that have been adjusted, at the end of an accounting period. Its purpose is to prove the equality of the total debit balances and total credit balances in the ledger after all adjustments.

GLOSSARY

Accrual-basis accounting Accounting basis in which companies record transactions that change a company's financial statements in the periods in which the events occur. (p. 102).

Accruals Adjusting entries for either accrued revenues or accrued expenses. (p. 105).

Accrued expenses Expenses incurred but not yet paid in cash or recorded. (p. 114).

Accrued revenues Revenues for services performed but not yet received in cash or recorded. (p. 113).

Adjusted trial balance A list of accounts and their balances after the company has made all adjustments. (p. 121).

Adjusting entries Entries made at the end of an accounting period to ensure that companies follow the revenue and expense recognition principles. (p. 104).

Book value The difference between the cost of a depreciable asset and its related accumulated depreciation. (p. 109).

Calendar year An accounting period that extends from January 1 to December 31. (p. 102).

Cash-basis accounting Accounting basis in which companies record revenue when they receive cash and an expense when they pay cash. (p. 102).

Contra asset account An account offset against an asset account on the balance sheet. (p. 108).

Deferrals Adjusting entries for either prepaid expenses or unearned revenues. (p. 105).

Depreciation The allocation of the cost of an asset to expense over its useful life in a rational and systematic manner. (p. 108).

Expense recognition (matching) principle The principle that companies match efforts (expenses) with accomplishments (revenues). (p. 103).

Fiscal year An accounting period that is one year in length. (p. 102).

Interim periods Monthly or quarterly accounting time periods. (p. 102).

Prepaid expenses (prepayments) Expenses paid in cash before they are used or consumed. (p. 106).

Revenue recognition principle The principle that companies recognize revenue in the accounting period in which the performance obligation is satisfied. (p. 103).

Time period assumption An assumption that accountants can divide the economic life of a business into artificial time periods. (p. 102).

Unearned revenues Cash received before services are performed. (p. 110).

Useful life The length of service of a long-lived asset. (p. 108).

APPENDIX 3A ALTERNATIVE TREATMENT OF PREPAID EXPENSES AND UNEARNED REVENUES

LEARNING OBJECTIVE 8

Prepare adjusting entries for the alternative treatment of deferrals.

In discussing adjusting entries for prepaid expenses and unearned revenues, we illustrated transactions for which companies made the initial entries to balance sheet accounts. In the case of prepaid expenses, the company debited the prepayment to an asset account. In the case of unearned revenue, the company credited a liability account to record the cash received.

Some companies use an alternative treatment: (1) When a company prepays an expense, it debits that amount to an expense account. (2) When it receives payment for future services, it credits the amount to a revenue account. In this appendix, we describe the circumstances that justify such entries and the different adjusting entries that may be required. This alternative treatment of prepaid expenses and unearned revenues has the same effect on the financial statements as the procedures described in the chapter.

Prepaid Expenses

Prepaid expenses become expired costs either through the passage of time (e.g., insurance) or through consumption (e.g., advertising supplies). If, at the time of purchase, the company expects to consume the supplies before the next financial statement date, **it may choose to debit (increase) an expense account rather than an asset account. This alternative treatment is simply more convenient.**

Assume that Pioneer Advertising Agency Inc. expects that it will use before the end of the month all of the supplies purchased on October 5. A debit of $2,500 to Supplies Expense (rather than to the asset account Supplies) on October 5 will eliminate the need for an adjusting entry on October 31. At October 31, the Supplies Expense account will show a balance of $2,500, which is the cost of supplies used between October 5 and October 31.

But what if the company does not use all the supplies? For example, what if an inventory of $1,000 of advertising supplies remains on October 31? Obviously, the company would need to make an adjusting entry. Prior to adjustment, the expense account Supplies Expense is overstated $1,000, and the asset account Supplies is understated $1,000. Thus, Pioneer makes the following adjusting entry.

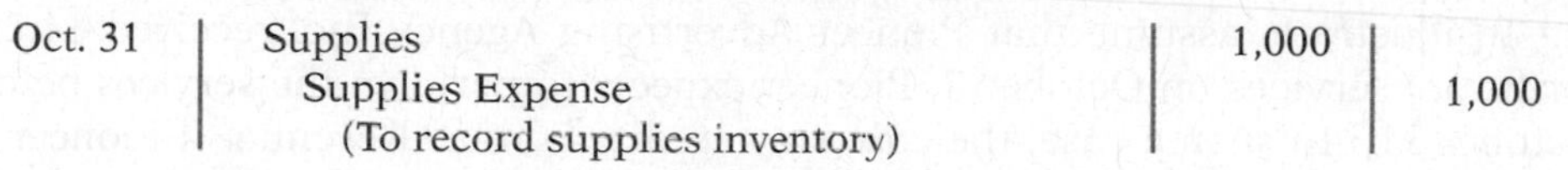

Oct. 31	Supplies	1,000	
	Supplies Expense		1,000
	(To record supplies inventory)		

A	=	L	+	SE
+1,000				
				+1,000 Exp

Cash Flows
no effect

After the company posts the adjusting entry, the accounts show:

Illustration 3A-1
Prepaid expenses accounts after adjustment

Supplies

Debit	Credit
10/31 Adj. **1,000**	

Supplies Expense

Debit	Credit
10/5 2,500	10/31 Adj. **1,000**
10/31 **Bal. 1,500**	

After adjustment, the asset account Supplies shows a balance of $1,000, which is equal to the cost of supplies on hand at October 31. In addition, Supplies Expense shows a balance of $1,500. This is equal to the cost of supplies used between October 5 and October 31. Without the adjusting entry expenses are overstated and net income is understated by $1,000 in the October income statement. Also, both assets and stockholders' equity are understated by $1,000 on the October 31 balance sheet.

Illustration 3A-2 compares the entries and accounts for advertising supplies in the two adjustment approaches.

Illustration 3A-2
Adjustment approaches—a comparison

Prepayment Initially Debited to Asset Account (per chapter)				**Prepayment Initially Debited to Expense Account (per appendix)**			
Oct. 5	Supplies	2,500		Oct. 5	Supplies Expense	2,500	
	Accounts Payable		2,500		Accounts Payable		2,500
Oct. 31	Supplies Expense	1,500		Oct. 31	Supplies	1,000	
	Supplies		1,500		Supplies Expense		1,000

After Pioneer posts the entries, the accounts appear as follows.

Illustration 3A-3
Comparison of accounts

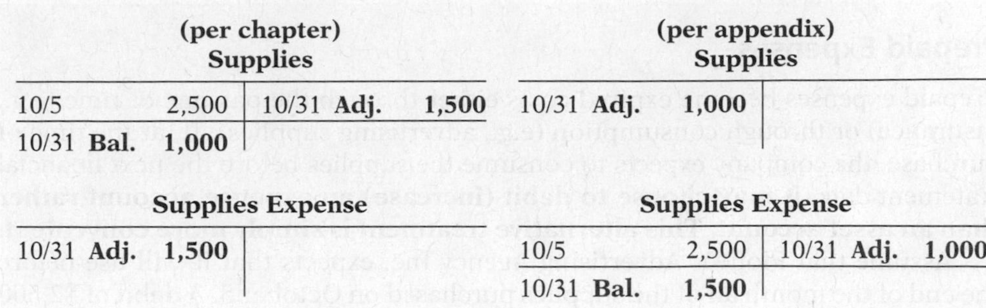

(per chapter) Supplies			
10/5	2,500	10/31 Adj.	**1,500**
10/31 **Bal.**	**1,000**		

(per appendix) Supplies			
10/31 **Adj.**	**1,000**		

(per chapter) Supplies Expense			
10/31 **Adj.**	**1,500**		

(per appendix) Supplies Expense			
10/5	2,500	10/31 **Adj.**	**1,000**
10/31 **Bal.**	**1,500**		

Note that the account balances under each alternative are the same at October 31: Supplies $1,000, and Supplies Expense $1,500.

Unearned Revenues

Unearned revenues are recognized as revenue at the time services are performed. Similar to the case for prepaid expenses, companies may credit (increase) a revenue account when they receive cash for future services.

Helpful Hint
The required adjusted balances here are Service Revenue $400 and Unearned Service Revenue $800.

To illustrate, assume that Pioneer Advertising Agency Inc. received $1,200 for future services on October 2. Pioneer expects to perform the services before October 31.[2] In such a case, the company credits Service Revenue. If Pioneer in fact performs the service before October 31, no adjustment is needed.

However, if at the statement date Pioneer has not performed $800 of the services, it would make an adjusting entry. Without the entry, the revenue account Service Revenue is overstated $800, and the liability account Unearned Service Revenue is understated $800. Thus, Pioneer makes the following adjusting entry.

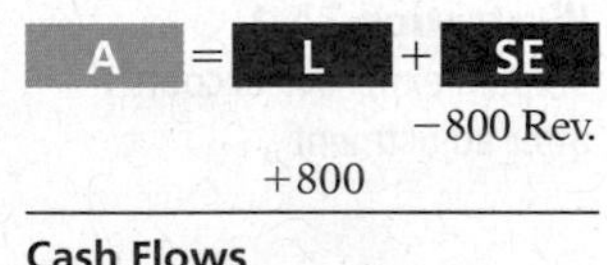

Cash Flows
no effect

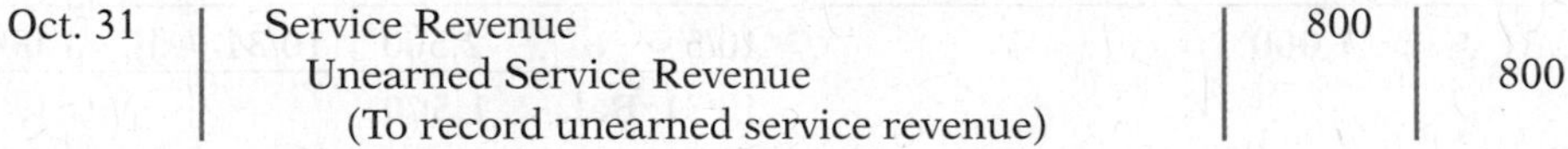

Oct. 31	Service Revenue	800	
	Unearned Service Revenue		800
	(To record unearned service revenue)		

After Pioneer posts the adjusting entry, the accounts show:

Illustration 3A-4
Unearned service revenue accounts after adjustment

Unearned Service Revenue			
		10/31 **Adj.**	**800**

Service Revenue			
10/31 **Adj.**	**800**	10/2	1,200
		10/31 **Bal.**	**400**

The liability account Unearned Service Revenue shows a balance of $800. This equals the services that will be performed in the future. In addition, the balance in Service Revenue equals the services performed in October. Without the adjusting entry, both revenues and net income are overstated by $800 in the October income statement. Also, liabilities are understated by $800, and stockholders' equity is overstated by $800 on the October 31 balance sheet.

Illustration 3A-5 compares the entries and accounts for initially recording unearned service revenue in (1) a liability account or (2) a revenue account.

[2] This example focuses only on the alternative treatment of unearned revenues. For simplicity, we have ignored the entries to Service Revenue pertaining to the immediate recognition of revenue ($10,000) and the adjusting entry for accrued revenue ($200).

Illustration 3A-5
Adjustment approaches—a comparison

Unearned Service Revenue Initially Credited to Liability Account (per chapter)			Unearned Service Revenue Initially Credited to Revenue Account (per appendix)		
Oct. 2 Cash	1,200		Oct. 2 Cash	1,200	
Unearned Service Revenue		1,200	Service Revenue		1,200
Oct. 31 Unearned Service Revenue	400		Oct. 31 Service Revenue	800	
Service Revenue		400	Unearned Service Revenue		800

After Pioneer posts the entries, the accounts appear as follows.

Illustration 3A-6
Comparison of accounts

(per chapter) Unearned Service Revenue		(per appendix) Unearned Service Revenue	
10/31 Adj. 400	10/2 1,200		10/31 Adj. 800
	10/31 Bal. 800		

Service Revenue		Service Revenue	
	10/31 Adj. 400	10/31 Adj. 800	10/2 1,200
			10/31 Bal. 400

Note that the balances in the accounts are the same under the two alternatives: Unearned Service Revenue $800, and Service Revenue $400.

Summary of Additional Adjustment Relationships

Illustration 3A-7 provides a summary of basic relationships for deferrals.

Illustration 3A-7
Summary of basic relationships for deferrals.

Type of Adjustment	Reason for Adjustment	Account Balances before Adjustment	Adjusting Entry
Prepaid expenses	(a) Prepaid expenses initially recorded in asset accounts have been used.	Assets overstated. Expenses understated.	Dr. Expenses Cr. Assets
	(b) Prepaid expenses initially recorded in expense accounts have not been used.	**Assets understated. Expenses overstated.**	**Dr. Assets Cr. Expenses**
Unearned revenues	(a) Unearned revenues initially recorded in liability accounts are now recognized as revenue.	Liabilities overstated. Revenues understated.	Dr. Liabilities Cr. Revenues
	(b) Unearned revenues initially recorded in revenue accounts are still unearned.	**Liabilities understated. Revenues overstated.**	**Dr. Revenues Cr. Liabilities**

Alternative adjusting entries **do not apply** to accrued revenues and accrued expenses because **no entries occur before companies make these types of adjusting entries.**

SUMMARY OF LEARNING OBJECTIVE FOR APPENDIX 3A

✔ The Navigator

8 Prepare adjusting entries for the alternative treatment of deferrals. Companies may initially debit prepayments to an expense account. Likewise, they may credit unearned revenues to a revenue account. At the end of the period, these accounts may be overstated. The adjusting entries for prepaid expenses are a debit to an asset account and a credit to an expense account. Adjusting entries for unearned revenues are a debit to a revenue account and a credit to a liability account.

APPENDIX 3B CONCEPTS IN ACTION

LEARNING OBJECTIVE 9

Discuss financial reporting concepts.

This appendix provides a summary of the concepts in action used in this textbook. In addition, it provides other useful concepts which accountants use as a basis for recording and reporting financial information.

Qualities of Useful Information

Recently, the FASB and IASB completed the first phase of a joint project in which they developed a conceptual framework to serve as the basis for future accounting standards. The framework begins by stating that the primary objective of financial reporting is to provide financial information that is **useful** to investors and creditors for making decisions about providing capital. According to the FASB, useful information should possess two fundamental qualities, relevance and faithful representation, as shown in Illustration 3B-1.

Illustration 3B-1
Fundamental qualities of useful information

Relevance Accounting information is considered **relevant** if it would make a difference in a business decision. Information is considered relevant if it provides information that has **predictive value**, that is, helps provide accurate expectations about the future, and has **confirmatory value**, that is, confirms or corrects prior expectations.

Faithful Representation **Faithful representation** means that information accurately depicts what really happened. To provide a faithful representation, information must be **complete** (nothing important has been omitted) and **neutral** (is not biased toward one position or another).

ENHANCING QUALITIES

In addition to the two fundamental qualities, the FASB and IASB also describe a number of enhancing qualities of useful information. These include **comparability**, **consistency**, **verifiability**, **timeliness**, and **understandability**. In accounting, **comparability** results when different companies use the same accounting principles. Another characteristic that enhances comparability is consistency. **Consistency** means that a company uses the same accounting principles and methods from year to year. Information is **verifiable** if we are able to prove that it is free from error. For accounting information to be relevant, it must be **timely**. That is, it must be available to decision-makers before it loses its capacity to influence decisions. For example, public companies like Google or Best Buy must provide their annual reports to investors within 60 days of their year-end. Information has the quality of **understandability** if it is presented in a clear and concise fashion, so that reasonably informed users of that information can interpret it and comprehend its meaning.

Assumptions in Financial Reporting

To develop accounting standards, the FASB relies on some key assumptions, as shown in Illustration 3B-2. These include assumptions about the monetary unit, economic entity, time period, going concern, and accrual basis.

Illustration 3B-2
Key assumptions in financial reporting

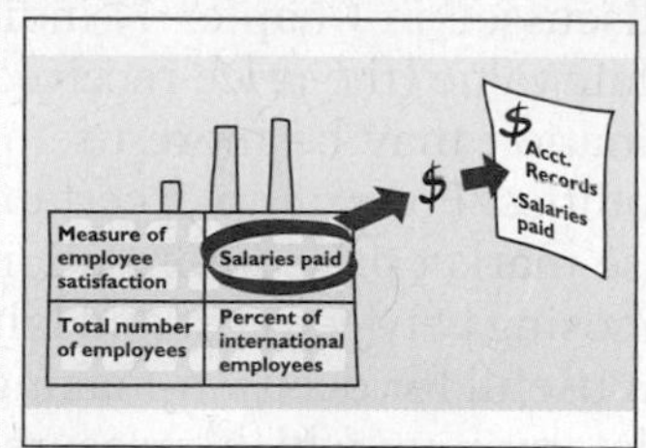

Monetary Unit Assumption The **monetary unit assumption** (discussed in Chapter 1) requires that only those things that can be expressed in money are included in the accounting records. This means that certain important information needed by investors, creditors, and managers, such as customer satisfaction, is not reported in the financial statements.

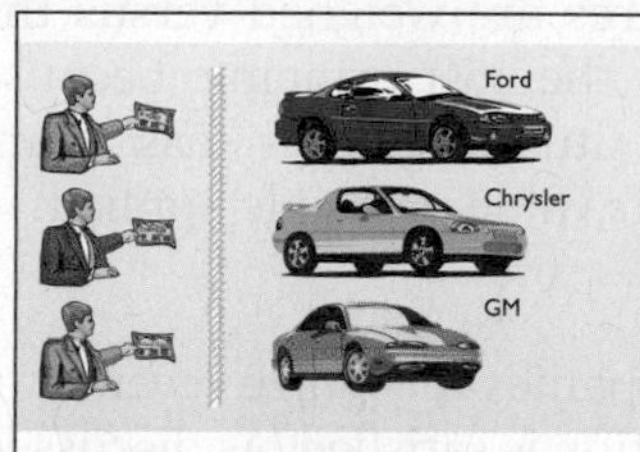

Economic Entity Assumption The **economic entity assumption** (discussed in Chapter 1) states that the activities of the entity must be kept separate and distinct from the activities of the owner. In order to assess a company's performance and financial position accurately, it is important that we not blur company transactions with personal transactions (especially those of its managers) or transactions of other companies.

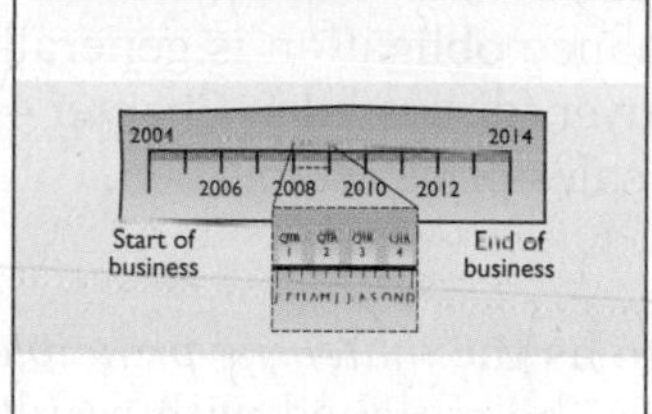

Time Period (Periodicity) Assumption Notice that the income statement, retained earnings statement, and statement of cash flows all cover periods of one year, and the balance sheet is prepared at the end of each year. The **time period assumption** (discussed in Chapter 3) states that the life of a business can be divided into artificial time periods and that useful reports covering those periods can be prepared for the business.

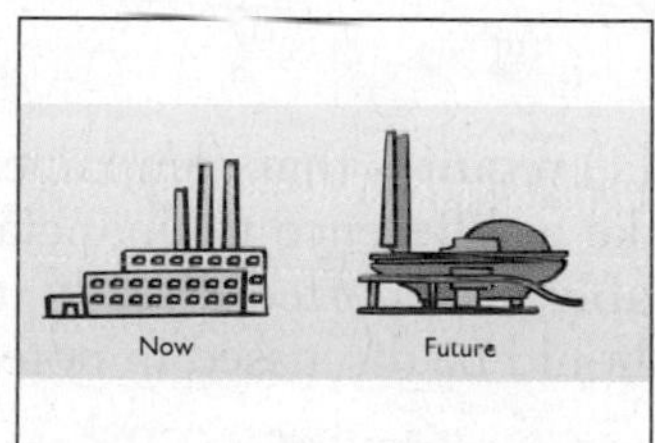

Going Concern Assumption The **going concern assumption** (discussed in Chapter 9) states that the business will remain in operation for the foreseeable future. Of course, many businesses do fail, but in general, it is reasonable to assume that the business will continue operating.

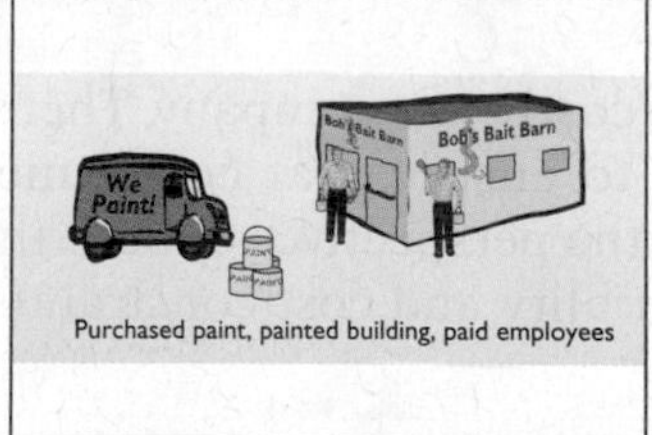

Accrual-Basis Assumption The **accrual-basis accounting assumption** (discussed in Chapter 3) means that transactions that change a company's financial statements are recorded in the periods in which the events occur. Accrual-basis accounting is addressed in more detail in Chapter 4.

Ethics Note

The importance of the economic entity assumption is illustrated by scandals involving Adelphia. In this case, senior company employees entered into transactions that blurred the line between the employees' financial interests and those of the company. For example, Adelphia guaranteed over $2 billion of loans to the founding family.

Principles in Financial Reporting

MEASUREMENT PRINCIPLES

GAAP generally uses one of two measurement principles, the cost principle or the fair value principle. Selection of which principle to follow generally relates to trade-offs between relevance and faithful representation.

COST PRINCIPLE The **cost principle** (or *historical cost principle*, discussed in Chapter 1) dictates that companies record assets at their cost. This is true not only at the time the asset is purchased but also over the time the asset is held. For example, if land that was purchased for $30,000 increases in value to $40,000, it continues to be reported at $30,000.

FAIR VALUE PRINCIPLE The **fair value principle** (discussed in Chapter 1) indicates that assets and liabilities should be reported at fair value (the price received to sell an asset or settle a liability). Fair value information may be more useful than historical cost for certain types of assets and liabilities. For example, certain investment securities are reported at fair value because market price information is often readily available for these types of assets. In choosing between cost and fair value, two qualities that make accounting information useful for decision-making are used—relevance and faithful representation. In determining which measurement principle to use, the factual nature of cost figures are weighed versus the relevance of fair value. In general, most assets follow the cost principle because market values are representationally faithful. Only in situations where assets are actively traded, such as investment securities, is the fair value principle applied.

REVENUE RECOGNITION PRINCIPLE
The **revenue recognition principle** requires that companies recognize revenue in the accounting period in which the performance obligation is satisfied. As discussed in Chapter 3, in a service company, revenue is recognized at the time the service is performed. In a merchandising company, the performance obligation is generally satisfied when the goods transfer from the seller to the buyer (discussed in Chapter 4). At this point, the sales transaction is complete and the sales price established.

EXPENSE RECOGNITION PRINCIPLE
The **expense recognition principle** (often referred to as the *matching principle*, discussed in Chapter 3) dictates that efforts (expenses) be matched with results (revenues). Thus, expenses follow revenues.

FULL DISCLOSURE PRINCIPLE
The **full disclosure principle** (discussed in Chapter 11) requires that companies disclose all circumstances and events that would make a difference to financial statement users. If an important item cannot reasonably be reported directly in one of the four types of financial statements, then it should be discussed in notes that accompany the statements.

Constraints In Financial Reporting

Efforts to provide useful financial information can be costly to a company. Therefore, the profession has agreed upon **constraints** to ensure that companies apply accounting rules in a reasonable fashion, from the perspectives of both the company and the user. The constraints are the materiality and cost constraints, as shown in Illustration 3B-3.

Illustration 3B-3
Constraints in financial reporting

Materiality Constraint The **materiality constraint** (discussed in Chapter 9) relates to a financial statement item's impact on a company's overall financial condition and operations. An item is **material** when its **size** makes it likely to influence the decision of an investor or creditor. It is **immaterial** if it is too small to impact a decision-maker. If the item does not make a difference, the company does not have to follow GAAP in reporting it.

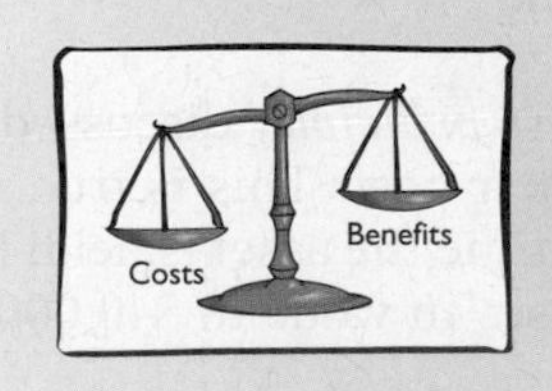

Cost Constraint The **cost constraint** (discussed in Chapter 1) relates to the fact that providing information is costly. In deciding whether companies should be required to provide a certain type of information, accounting standard-setters weigh the cost that companies will incur to provide the information against the benefit that financial statement users will gain from having the information available.

SUMMARY OF LEARNING OBJECTIVE FOR APPENDIX 3B

✔ The Navigator

9 **Discuss financial reporting concepts.** To be judged useful, information should have the primary characteristics of relevance and faithful representation. In addition, it should be comparable, consistent, verifiable, timely, and understandable.

The *monetary unit assumption* requires that companies include in the accounting records only transaction data that can be expressed in terms of money. The *economic entity assumption* states that economic events can be identified with a particular unit of accountability. The *time period assumption* states that the economic life of a business can be divided into artificial time periods and that meaningful accounting reports can be prepared for each period. The *going concern assumption* states that the company will continue in operation long enough to carry out its existing objectives and commitments. The *accrual-basis accounting assumption* means that transactions are recorded in the periods in which the events occur.

The *cost principle* states that companies should record assets at their cost. The *fair value principle* indicates that assets and liabilities should be reported at fair value. The *revenue recognition principle* requires that companies recognize revenue in the accounting period in which the performance obligation is satisfied. The *expense recognition principle* dictates that efforts (expenses) be matched with results (revenues). The *full disclosure principle* requires that companies disclose circumstances and events that matter to financial statement users.

The major constraints are materiality and cost.

GLOSSARY FOR APPENDIX 3B

Accrual-basis accounting assumption Transactions that change a company's financial statements are recorded in the periods in which the events occur. (p. 131).

Comparability Ability to compare the accounting information of different companies because they use the same accounting principles. (p. 130).

Consistency Use of the same accounting principles and methods from year to year within a company. (p. 130).

Cost constraint Constraint of determining whether the cost that companies will incur to provide the information will outweigh the benefit that financial statement users will gain from having the information available. (p. 132).

Cost principle An accounting principle that states that companies should record assets at their cost. (p. 131).

Economic entity assumption An assumption that every economic entity can be separately identified and accounted for. (p. 131).

Expense recognition principle Efforts (expenses) should be matched with results (revenues). (p. 132)

Fair value principle Assets and liabilities should be reported at fair value (the price received to sell an asset or settle a liability). (p. 132).

Faithful representation Information that is complete, neutral, and free from error. (p. 130).

Full disclosure principle Accounting principle that dictates that companies disclose circumstances and events that make a difference to financial statement users. (p. 132).

Going concern assumption The assumption that the company will continue in operation for the foreseeable future. (p. 131).

Materiality constraint The constraint of determining whether an item is large enough to likely influence the decision of an investor or creditor. (p. 132).

Monetary unit assumption An assumption that requires that only those things that can be expressed in money are included in the accounting records. (p. 131).

Relevance The quality of information that indicates the information makes a difference in a decision. (p. 130).

Revenue recognition principle Companies recognize revenue in the accounting period in which the performance obligation is satisfied. (p. 132).

Timely Information that is available to decision-makers before it loses its capacity to influence decisions. (p. 130).

Time period assumption An assumption that the life of a business can be divided into artificial time periods and that useful reports covering those periods can be prepared for the business. (p. 131).

Understandability Information presented in a clear and concise fashion so that users can interpret it and comprehend its meaning. (p. 130).

Verifiable Information that is proven to be free from error. (p. 130).

Self-Test, Brief Exercises, Exercises, Problem Set A, and many more components are available for practice in WileyPLUS.

Note: All Questions, Exercises, and Problems marked with an asterisk relate to material in the appendices to the chapter.

SELF-TEST QUESTIONS

Answers are on page 159.

(LO 1) **1.** The time period assumption states that:
(a) revenue should be recognized in the accounting period in which a performance obligation is satisfied.
(b) expenses should be matched with revenues.
(c) the economic life of a business can be divided into artificial time periods.
(d) the fiscal year should correspond with the calendar year.

(LO 1) **2.** The time period assumption states that:
(a) companies must wait until the calendar year is completed to prepare financial statements.
(b) companies use the fiscal year to report financial information.
(c) the economic life of a business can be divided into artificial time periods.
(d) companies record information in the time period in which the events occur.

(LO 2) **3.** Which of the following statements about the accrual basis of accounting is *false*?
(a) Events that change a company's financial statements are recorded in the periods in which the events occur.
(b) Revenue is recognized in the period in which services are performed.
(c) This basis is in accord with generally accepted accounting principles.
(d) Revenue is recorded only when cash is received, and expense is recorded only when cash is paid.

(LO 2) **4.** The principle or assumption dictating that efforts (expenses) be matched with accomplishments (revenues) is the:
(a) expense recognition principle.
(b) cost assumption.
(c) time period principle.
(d) revenue recognition principle.

(LO 3) **5.** Adjusting entries are made to ensure that:
(a) expenses are recognized in the period in which they are incurred.
(b) revenues are recorded in the period in which services are provided.
(c) balance sheet and income statement accounts have correct balances at the end of an accounting period.
(d) All of the above.

(LO 4) **6.** Each of the following is a major type (or category) of adjusting entries *except:*
(a) prepaid expenses.
(b) accrued revenues.
(c) accrued expenses.
(d) recognized revenues.

7. The trial balance shows Supplies $1,350 and Supplies Expense $0. If $600 of supplies are on hand at the end of the period, the adjusting entry is: (LO 5)

		Debit	Credit
(a)	Supplies	600	
	Supplies Expense		600
(b)	Supplies	750	
	Supplies Expense		750
(c)	Supplies Expense	750	
	Supplies		750
(d)	Supplies Expense	600	
	Supplies		600

8. Adjustments for prepaid expenses: (LO 5)
(a) decrease assets and increase revenues.
(b) decrease expenses and increase assets.
(c) decrease assets and increase expenses.
(d) decrease revenues and increase assets.

9. Accumulated Depreciation is: (LO 5)
(a) a contra asset account.
(b) an expense account.
(c) a stockholders' equity account.
(d) a liability account.

10. Queenan Company computes depreciation on delivery equipment at $1,000 for the month of June. The adjusting entry to record this depreciation is as follows. (LO 5)

		Debit	Credit
(a)	Depreciation Expense	1,000	
	Accumulated Depreciation—Queenan Company		1,000
(b)	Depreciation Expense	1,000	
	Equipment		1,000
(c)	Depreciation Expense	1,000	
	Accumulated Depreciation—Equipment		1,000
(d)	Equipment Expense	1,000	
	Accumulated Depreciation—Equipment		1,000

11. Adjustments for unearned revenues: (LO 5)
(a) decrease liabilities and increase revenues.
(b) have an assets and revenues account relationship.
(c) increase assets and increase revenues.
(d) decrease revenues and decrease assets.

12. Adjustments for accrued revenues: (LO 6)
(a) have a liabilities and revenues account relationship.
(b) have an assets and revenues account relationship.
(c) decrease assets and revenues.
(d) decrease liabilities and increase revenues.

13. Kathy Siska earned a salary of $400 for the last week of September. She will be paid on October 1. The adjusting entry for Kathy's employer at September 30 is: (LO 6)

(a) No entry is required.

(b) Salaries and Wages Expense	400	
Salaries and Wages Payable		400
(c) Salaries and Wages Expense	400	
Cash		400
(d) Salaries and Wages Payable	400	
Cash		400

(LO 7) **14.** Which of the following statements is *incorrect* concerning the adjusted trial balance?
(a) An adjusted trial balance proves the equality of the total debit balances and the total credit balances in the ledger after all adjustments are made.
(b) The adjusted trial balance provides the primary basis for the preparation of financial statements.
(c) The adjusted trial balance lists the account balances segregated by assets and liabilities.
(d) The adjusted trial balance is prepared after the adjusting entries have been journalized and posted.

(LO 8) ***15.** The trial balance shows Supplies $0 and Supplies Expense $1,500. If $800 of supplies are on hand at the end of the period, the adjusting entry is:
(a) Debit Supplies $800 and credit Supplies Expense $800.
(b) Debit Supplies Expense $800 and credit Supplies $800.
(c) Debit Supplies $700 and credit Supplies Expense $700.
(d) Debit Supplies Expense $700 and credit Supplies $700.

***16.** Neutrality is an ingredient of: (LO 9)

	Faithful Representation	Relevance
(a)	Yes	Yes
(b)	No	No
(c)	Yes	No
(d)	No	Yes

***17.** What accounting constraint allows a company to ignore GAAP if an item is too small to impact a decision? (LO 9)
(a) Comparability. (c) Cost.
(b) Materiality. (d) Consistency.

Go to the book's companion website, www.wiley.com/college/weygandt, for additional Self-Test Questions.

QUESTIONS

1. (a) How does the time period assumption affect an accountant's analysis of business transactions?
(b) Explain the terms *fiscal year, calendar year,* and *interim periods*.

2. State two generally accepted accounting principles that relate to adjusting the accounts.

3. Gabe Corts, a lawyer, accepts a legal engagement in March, performs the work in April, and is paid in May. If Corts' law firm prepares monthly financial statements, when should it recognize revenue from this engagement? Why?

4. Why do accrual-basis financial statements provide more useful information than cash-basis statements?

5. In completing the engagement in Question 3, Corts pays no costs in March, $2,200 in April, and $2,500 in May (incurred in April). How much expense should the firm deduct from revenues in the month when it recognizes the revenue? Why?

6. "Adjusting entries are required by the cost principle of accounting." Do you agree? Explain.

7. Why may a trial balance not contain up-to-date and complete financial information?

8. Distinguish between the two categories of adjusting entries, and identify the types of adjustments applicable to each category.

9. What is the debit/credit effect of a prepaid expense adjusting entry?

10. "Depreciation is a valuation process that results in the reporting of the fair value of the asset." Do you agree? Explain.

11. Explain the differences between depreciation expense and accumulated depreciation.

12. M. Gibbs Company purchased equipment for $18,000. By the current balance sheet date, $7,000 had been depreciated. Indicate the balance sheet presentation of the data.

13. What is the debit/credit effect of an unearned revenue adjusting entry?

14. A company fails to recognize revenue for services performed but not yet received in cash or recorded. Which of the following accounts are involved in the adjusting entry: (a) asset, (b) liability, (c) revenue, or (d) expense? For the accounts selected, indicate whether they would be debited or credited in the entry.

15. A company fails to recognize an expense incurred but not paid. Indicate which of the following accounts is debited and which is credited in the adjusting entry: (a) asset, (b) liability, (c) revenue, or (d) expense.

16. A company makes an accrued revenue adjusting entry for $900 and an accrued expense adjusting entry for $700. How much was net income understated prior to these entries? Explain.

17. On January 9, a company pays $6,000 for salaries and wages, of which $2,000 was reported as Salaries and Wages Payable on December 31. Give the entry to record the payment.

18. For each of the following items before adjustment, indicate the type of adjusting entry (prepaid expense, unearned revenue, accrued revenue, or accrued expense) that is needed to correct the misstatement. If an item could result in more than one type of adjusting entry, indicate each of the types.
(a) Assets are understated.
(b) Liabilities are overstated.

(c) Liabilities are understated.
(d) Expenses are understated.
(e) Assets are overstated.
(f) Revenue is understated.

19. One-half of the adjusting entry is given below. Indicate the account title for the other half of the entry.
(a) Salaries and Wages Expense is debited.
(b) Depreciation Expense is debited.
(c) Interest Payable is credited.
(d) Supplies is credited.
(e) Accounts Receivable is debited.
(f) Unearned Service Revenue is debited.

20. "An adjusting entry may affect more than one balance sheet or income statement account." Do you agree? Why or why not?

21. Why is it possible to prepare financial statements directly from an adjusted trial balance?

22. PEPSICO What was PepsiCo's depreciation and amortization expense for 2010 and 2009?

*23. L. Thomas Company debits Supplies Expense for all purchases of supplies and credits Rent Revenue for all advanced rentals. For each type of adjustment, give the adjusting entry.

*24. (a) What is the primary objective of financial reporting?
(b) Identify the characteristics of useful accounting information.

*25. Dan Fineman, the president of King Company, is pleased. King substantially increased its net income in 2014 while keeping its unit inventory relatively the same. Howard Gross, chief accountant, cautions Dan, however. Gross says that since King changed its method of inventory valuation, there is a consistency problem and it is difficult to determine whether King is better off. Is Gross correct? Why or why not?

*26. What is the distinction between comparability and consistency?

*27. Describe the two constraints inherent in the presentation of accounting information.

*28. Laurie Belk is president of Better Books. She has no accounting background. Belk cannot understand why fair value is not used as the basis for all accounting measurement and reporting. Discuss.

*29. What is the economic entity assumption? Give an example of its violation.

BRIEF EXERCISES

Indicate why adjusting entries are needed.
(LO 3)

BE3-1 The ledger of Basler Company includes the following accounts. Explain why each account may require adjustment.
(a) Prepaid Insurance
(b) Depreciation Expense
(c) Unearned Service Revenue
(d) Interest Payable

Identify the major types of adjusting entries.
(LO 4, 5, 6)

BE3-2 Lucci Company accumulates the following adjustment data at December 31. Indicate (a) the type of adjustment (prepaid expense, accrued revenues and so on), and (b) the status of accounts before adjustment (overstated or understated).
1. Supplies of $100 are on hand.
2. Services provided but not recorded total $870.
3. Interest of $200 has accumulated on a note payable.
4. Rent collected in advance totaling $560 has been recognized.

Prepare adjusting entry for supplies.
(LO 5)

BE3-3 Wow Advertising Company's trial balance at December 31 shows Supplies $6,700 and Supplies Expense $0. On December 31, there are $1,900 of supplies on hand. Prepare the adjusting entry at December 31, and using T-accounts, enter the balances in the accounts, post the adjusting entry, and indicate the adjusted balance in each account.

Prepare adjusting entry for depreciation.
(LO 5)

BE3-4 At the end of its first year, the trial balance of Wooster Company shows Equipment $32,000 and zero balances in Accumulated Depreciation—Equipment and Depreciation Expense. Depreciation for the year is estimated to be $6,000. Prepare the adjusting entry for depreciation at December 31, post the adjustments to T-accounts, and indicate the balance sheet presentation of the equipment at December 31.

Prepare adjusting entry for prepaid expense.
(LO 5)

BE3-5 On July 1, 2014, Pizner Co. pays $13,200 to Orlow Insurance Co. for a 3-year insurance contract. Both companies have fiscal years ending December 31. For Pizner Co., journalize and post the entry on July 1 and the adjusting entry on December 31.

Prepare adjusting entry for unearned revenue.
(LO 5)

BE3-6 Using the data in BE3-5, journalize and post the entry on July 1 and the adjusting entry on December 31 for Orlow Insurance Co. Orlow uses the accounts Unearned Service Revenue and Service Revenue.

BE3-7 The bookkeeper for Easton Company asks you to prepare the following accrued adjusting entries at December 31.

Prepare adjusting entries for accruals.

(LO 6)

1. Interest on notes payable of $360 is accrued.
2. Services provided but not recorded total $1,750.
3. Salaries earned by employees of $900 have not been recorded.

Use the following account titles: Service Revenue, Accounts Receivable, Interest Expense, Interest Payable, Salaries and Wages Expense, and Salaries and Wages Payable.

BE3-8 The trial balance of Gleason Company includes the following balance sheet accounts, which may require adjustment. For each account that requires adjustment, indicate (a) the type of adjusting entry (prepaid expenses, unearned revenues, accrued revenues, and accrued expenses) and (b) the related account in the adjusting entry.

Analyze accounts in an unadjusted trial balance.

(LO 4, 5, 6)

Accounts Receivable	Interest Payable
Prepaid Insurance	Unearned Service Revenue
Accumulated Depreciation—Equipment	

BE3-9 The adjusted trial balance of Lopez Company at December 31, 2014, includes the following accounts: Common Stock $15,600; Dividends $6,000; Service Revenue $38,400; Salaries and Wages Expense $16,000; Insurance Expense $2,000; Rent Expense $4,400; Supplies Expense $1,500; and Depreciation Expense $1,300. Prepare an income statement for the year.

Prepare an income statement from an adjusted trial balance.

(LO 7)

BE3-10 Partial adjusted trial balance data for Lopez Company is presented in BE3-9. Prepare a retained earnings statement for the year assuming net income is $13,200 for the year and Retained Earnings is $7,240 on January 1.

Prepare a retained earnings statement from an adjusted trial balance.

(LO 7)

***BE3-11** Lim Company records all prepayments in income statement accounts. At April 30, the trial balance shows Supplies Expense $2,800, Service Revenue $9,200, and zero balances in related balance sheet accounts. Prepare the adjusting entries at April 30 assuming (a) $1,000 of supplies on hand and (b) $2,000 of service revenue should be reported as unearned.

Prepare adjusting entries under alternative treatment of deferrals.

(LO 8)

***BE3-12** The accompanying chart shows the qualitative characteristics of useful accounting information. Fill in the blanks.

Identify characteristics of useful information.

(LO 9)

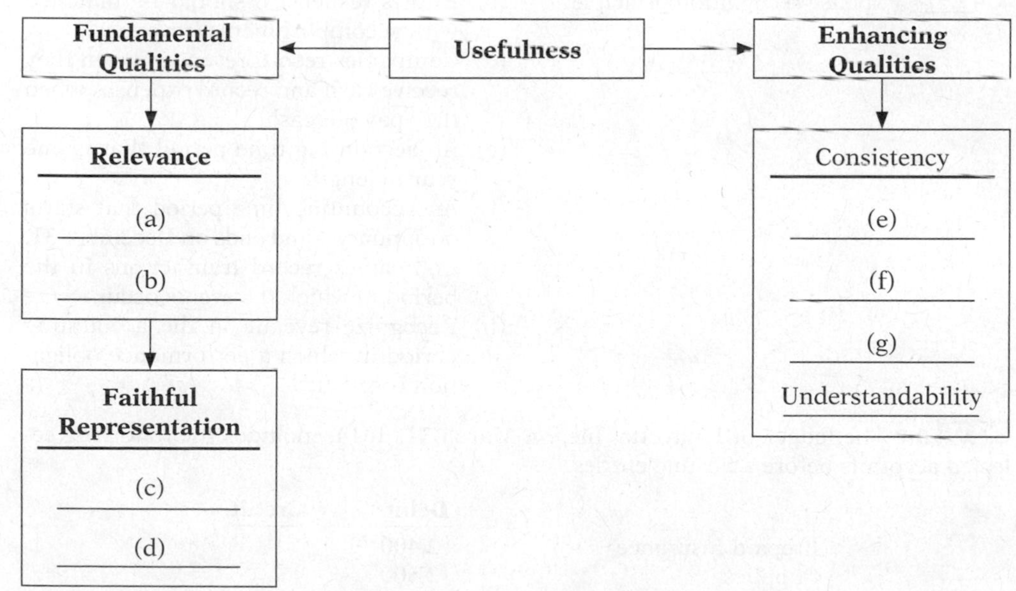

***BE3-13** Given the *characteristics* of useful accounting information, complete each of the following statements.

Identify characteristics of useful information.

(LO 9)

(a) For information to be _____, it should have predictive and confirmatory value.
(b) _____ is the quality of information that gives assurance that it is free from error and bias.
(c) _____ means using the same accounting principles and methods from year to year within a company.

Identify characteristics of useful information.
(LO 9)

***BE3-14** Here are some qualitative characteristics of useful accounting information:

1. Predictive value
2. Neutral
3. Verifiable
4. Timely

Match each qualitative characteristic to one of the following statements.

_______ (a) Accounting information should help provide accurate expectations about future events.
_______ (b) Accounting information cannot be selected, prepared, or presented to favor one set of interested users over another.
_______ (c) Accounting information must be proved to be free of error.
_______ (d) Accounting information must be available to decision-makers before it loses its capacity to influence their decisions.

Define full disclosure principle.
(LO 9)

***BE3-15** The full disclosure principle dictates that:

(a) financial statements should disclose all assets at their cost.
(b) financial statements should disclose only those events that can be measured in dollars.
(c) financial statements should disclose all events and circumstances that would matter to users of financial statements.
(d) financial statements should not be relied on unless an auditor has expressed an unqualified opinion on them.

> DO IT! REVIEW

Identify timing concepts.
(LO 1, 2)

DO IT! 3-1 Numerous timing concepts are discussed on pages 102–103. A list of concepts is provided below in the left column, with a description of the concept in the right column. There are more descriptions provided than concepts. Match the description of the concept to the concept.

1. _______ Cash-basis accounting.
2. _______ Fiscal year.
3. _______ Revenue recognition principle.
4. _______ Expense recognition principle.

(a) Monthly and quarterly time periods.
(b) Accountants divide the economic life of a business into artificial time periods.
(c) Efforts (expenses) should be matched with accomplishments (revenues).
(d) Companies record revenues when they receive cash and record expenses when they pay out cash.
(e) An accounting time period that is one year in length.
(f) An accounting time period that starts on January 1 and ends on December 31.
(g) Companies record transactions in the period in which the events occur.
(h) Recognize revenue in the accounting period in which a performance obligation is satisfied.

Prepare adjusting entries for deferrals.
(LO 5)

DO IT! 3-2 The ledger of Lafayette, Inc. on March 31, 2014, includes the following selected accounts before adjusting entries.

	Debit	Credit
Prepaid Insurance	2,400	
Supplies	2,500	
Equipment	30,000	
Unearned Service Revenue		9,000

An analysis of the accounts shows the following.

1. Insurance expires at the rate of $300 per month.
2. Supplies on hand total $1,400.
3. The equipment depreciates $200 per month.
4. 2/5 of the unearned service revenue was recognized in March.

Prepare the adjusting entries for the month of March.

DO IT! **3-3** Pegasus Computer Services began operations in July 2014. At the end of the month, the company is trying to prepare monthly financial statements. Pegasus has the following information for the month.

Prepare adjusting entries for accruals.

(LO 6)

1. At July 31, Pegasus owed employees $1,300 in salaries that the company will pay in August.
2. On July 1, Pegasus borrowed $20,000 from a local bank on a 10-year note. The annual interest rate is 9%.
3. Service revenue unrecorded in July totaled $2,400.

Prepare the adjusting entries needed at July 31, 2014.

DO IT! **3-4** Phelps Co. was organized on April 1, 2014. The company prepares quarterly financial statements. The adjusted trial balance amounts at June 30 are shown below.

Calculate amounts from trial balance.

(LO 7)

Debits		Credits	
Cash	$ 5,190	Accumulated Depreciation—Equipment	$ 700
Accounts Receivable	480	Notes Payable	4,000
Prepaid Rent	720	Accounts Payable	790
Supplies	920	Salaries and Wages Payable	300
Equipment	12,000	Interest Payable	40
Dividends	500	Unearned Rent Revenue	400
Salaries and Wages Expense	7,400	Common Stock	11,200
Rent Expense	1,200	Service Revenue	11,360
Depreciation Expense	700	Rent Revenue	900
Supplies Expense	160	Total credits	$29,690
Utilities Expense	380		
Interest Expense	40		
Total debits	$29,690		

(a) Determine the net income for the quarter April 1 to June 30.
(b) Determine the total assets and total liabilities at June 30, 2014, for Phelps Company.
(c) Determine the amount that appears for Retained Earnings at June 30, 2014.

 **The Navigator**

EXERCISES

E3-1 Fred Mosure has prepared the following list of statements about the time period assumption.

Explain the time period assumption.

(LO 1)

1. Adjusting entries would not be necessary if a company's life were not divided into artificial time periods.
2. The IRS requires companies to file annual tax returns.
3. Accountants divide the economic life of a business into artificial time periods, but each transaction affects only one of these periods.
4. Accounting time periods are generally a month, a quarter, or a year.
5. A time period lasting one year is called an interim period.
6. All fiscal years are calendar years, but not all calendar years are fiscal years.

Instructions
Identify each statement as true or false. If false, indicate how to correct the statement.

E3-2 On numerous occasions, proposals have surfaced to put the federal government on the accrual basis of accounting. This is no small issue. If this basis were used, it would mean that billions in unrecorded liabilities would have to be booked, and the federal deficit would increase substantially.

Distinguish between cash and accrual basis of accounting.

(LO 2)

Instructions

(a) What is the difference between accrual-basis accounting and cash-basis accounting?
(b) Why would politicians prefer the cash basis over the accrual basis?
(c) Write a letter to your senator explaining why the federal government should adopt the accrual basis of accounting.

Compute cash and accrual accounting income.
(LO 2)

E3-3 Concordia Industries collected $105,000 from customers in 2014. Of the amount collected, $28,000 was from revenue accrued from services performed in 2013. In addition, Concordia recognized $44,000 of revenue in 2014, which will not be collected until 2015.

Concordia Industries also paid $72,000 for expenses in 2014. Of the amount paid, $30,000 was for expenses incurred on account in 2013. In addition, Concordia incurred $37,000 of expenses in 2014, which will not be paid until 2015.

Instructions

(a) Compute 2014 cash-basis net income.
(b) Compute 2014 accrual-basis net income.

Identify the type of adjusting entry needed.
(LO 4)

E3-4 Waverly Corporation encounters the following situations:

1. Waverly collects $1,750 from a customer in 2014 for services to be performed in 2015.
2. Waverly incurs utility expense which is not yet paid in cash or recorded.
3. Waverly employees worked 3 days in 2014 but will not be paid until 2015.
4. Waverly performs services for a customer but has not yet received cash or recorded the transaction.
5. Waverly paid $2,400 rent on December 1 for the 4 months starting December 1.
6. Waverly received cash for future services and recorded a liability until the service was performed.
7. Waverly performed consulting services for a client in December 2014. On December 31, it had not billed the client for services provided of $1,200.
8. Waverly paid cash for an expense and recorded an asset until the item was used up.
9. Waverly purchased $750 of supplies in 2014; at year-end, $400 of supplies remain unused.
10. Waverly purchased equipment on January 1, 2014; the equipment will be used for 5 years.
11. Waverly borrowed $10,000 on October 1, 2014, signing an 8% one-year note payable.

Instructions

Identify what type of adjusting entry (prepaid expense, unearned revenue, accrued expense, or accrued revenue) is needed in each situation, at December 31, 2014.

Prepare adjusting entries from selected data.
(LO 5, 6)

E3-5 Dan Luther Company has the following balances in selected accounts on December 31, 2014.

Accounts Receivable	$ –0–
Accumulated Depreciation—Equipment	–0–
Equipment	7,000
Interest Payable	–0–
Notes Payable	8,000
Prepaid Insurance	2,100
Salaries and Wages Payable	–0–
Supplies	2,450
Unearned Service Revenue	30,000

All the accounts have normal balances. The information below has been gathered at December 31, 2014.

1. Dan Luther Company borrowed $8,000 by signing a 10%, one-year note on October 1, 2014.
2. A count of supplies on December 31, 2014, indicates that supplies of $780 are on hand.
3. Depreciation on the equipment for 2014 is $1,000.
4. Dan Luther Company paid $2,100 for 12 months of insurance coverage on June 1, 2014.
5. On December 1, 2014, Dan Luther collected $30,000 for consulting services to be performed from December 1, 2014, through March 31, 2015.
6. Dan Luther performed consulting services for a client in December 2014. The client will be billed $3,900.

7. Dan Luther Company pays its employees total salaries of $9,000 every Monday for the preceding 5-day week (Monday through Friday). On Monday, December 29, employees were paid for the week ending December 26. All employees worked the last 3 days of 2014.

Instructions
Prepare adjusting entries for the seven items described on page 140 and above.

E3-6 Orwell Company accumulates the following adjustment data at December 31.

Identify types of adjustments and account relationships.

(LO 4, 5, 6)

1. Services provided but not recorded total $1,420.
2. Supplies of $300 have been used.
3. Utility expenses of $225 are unpaid.
4. Unearned service revenue of $260 is recognized for services performed.
5. Salaries of $800 are unpaid.
6. Prepaid insurance totaling $380 has expired.

Instructions
For each of the above items indicate the following.

(a) The type of adjustment (prepaid expense, unearned revenue, accrued revenue, or accrued expense).
(b) The status of accounts before adjustment (overstatement or understatement).

E3-7 The ledger of Villa Rental Agency on March 31 of the current year includes the selected accounts, shown below, before adjusting entries have been prepared.

Prepare adjusting entries from selected account data.

(LO 5, 6)

	Debit	Credit
Prepaid Insurance	$ 3,600	
Supplies	2,800	
Equipment	25,000	
Accumulated Depreciation—Equipment		$ 8,400
Notes Payable		20,000
Unearned Rent Revenue		9,900
Rent Revenue		60,000
Interest Expense	–0–	
Salaries and Wages Expense	14,000	

An analysis of the accounts shows the following.

1. The equipment depreciates $300 per month.
2. One-third of the unearned rent revenue was recognized during the quarter.
3. Interest of $500 is accrued on the notes payable.
4. Supplies on hand total $650.
5. Insurance expires at the rate of $200 per month.

Instructions
Prepare the adjusting entries at March 31, assuming that adjusting entries are made **quarterly**. Additional accounts are: Depreciation Expense, Insurance Expense, Interest Payable, and Supplies Expense.

E3-8 Kari Engle, D.D.S., opened a dental practice on January 1, 2014. During the first month of operations, the following transactions occurred.

Prepare adjusting entries.

(LO 5, 6)

1. Performed services for patients who had dental plan insurance. At January 31, $875 of such services were performed but not yet recorded.
2. Utility expenses incurred but not paid prior to January 31 totaled $520.
3. Purchased dental equipment on January 1 for $80,000, paying $20,000 in cash and signing a $60,000, 3-year note payable. The equipment depreciates $400 per month. Interest is $500 per month.
4. Purchased a six-month malpractice insurance policy on January 1 for $18,000.
5. Purchased $1,600 of dental supplies. On January 31, determined that $700 of supplies were on hand.

Instructions
Prepare the adjusting entries on January 31. Account titles are: Accumulated Depreciation—Equipment, Depreciation Expense, Service Revenue, Accounts Receivable, Insurance Expense, Interest Expense, Interest Payable, Prepaid Insurance, Supplies, Supplies Expense, Utilities Expense, and Utilities Payable.

Prepare adjusting entries.
(LO 5, 6)

E3-9 The trial balance for Pioneer Advertising Agency Inc. is shown in Illustration 3-3, page 105. In lieu of the adjusting entries shown in the text at October 31, assume the following adjustment data.

1. Supplies on hand at October 31 total $800.
2. Expired insurance for the month is $100.
3. Depreciation for the month is $50.
4. Unearned service revenue recognized in October totals $600.
5. Services provided but not recorded at October 31 are $300.
6. Interest accrued at October 31 is $70.
7. Accrued salaries at October 31 are $1,200.

Instructions
Prepare the adjusting entries for the items above.

Prepare correct income statement.
(LO 2, 5, 6, 7)

E3-10 The income statement of Midland Co. for the month of July shows net income of $1,500 based on Service Revenue $5,500, Salaries and Wages Expense $2,300, Supplies Expense $1,200, and Utilities Expense $500. In reviewing the statement, you discover the following.

1. Insurance expired during July of $400 was omitted.
2. Supplies expense includes $300 of supplies that are still on hand at July 31.
3. Depreciation on equipment of $150 was omitted.
4. Accrued but unpaid salaries and wages at July 31 of $280 were not included.
5. Services performed but unrecorded totaled $920.

Instructions
Prepare a correct income statement for July 2014.

Analyze adjusted data.
(LO 4, 5, 6, 7)

E3-11 A partial adjusted trial balance of Ruiz Company at January 31, 2014, shows the following.

Ruiz Company
Adjusted Trial Balance
January 31, 2014

	Debit	Credit
Supplies	$ 850	
Prepaid Insurance	2,400	
Salaries and Wages Payable		$ 800
Unearned Service Revenue		750
Supplies Expense	950	
Insurance Expense	400	
Salaries and Wages Expense	2,500	
Service Revenue		2,000

Instructions
Answer the following questions, assuming the year begins January 1.

(a) If the amount in Supplies Expense is the January 31 adjusting entry, and $670 of supplies was purchased in January, what was the balance in Supplies on January 1?
(b) If the amount in Insurance Expense is the January 31 adjusting entry, and the original insurance premium was for one year, what was the total premium and when was the policy purchased?
(c) If $3,300 of salaries was paid in January, what was the balance in Salaries and Wages Payable at December 31, 2013?

Journalize basic transactions and adjusting entries.
(LO 5, 6, 7)

E3-12 Selected accounts of Welch Company are shown on the next page.

Supplies Expense			
7/31	800		

Supplies			
7/1 Bal.	1,100	7/31	800
7/10	200		

Salaries and Wages Payable			
		7/31	1,200

Accounts Receivable			
7/31	620		

Unearned Service Revenue			
7/31	900	7/1 Bal.	1,500
		7/20	750

Salaries and Wages Expense			
7/15	1,200		
7/31	1,200		

Service Revenue			
		7/14	2,000
		7/31	900
		7/31	620

Instructions

After analyzing the accounts, journalize (a) the July transactions and (b) the adjusting entries that were made on July 31. (*Hint:* July transactions were for cash.)

E3-13 The trial balances before and after adjustment for Matusiak Company at the end of its fiscal year are presented below.

Prepare adjusting entries from analysis of trial balances.

(LO 5, 6, 7)

Matusiak Company
Trial Balance
August 31, 2014

	Before Adjustment		After Adjustment	
	Dr.	**Cr.**	**Dr.**	**Cr.**
Cash	$10,400		$10,400	
Accounts Receivable	8,800		10,000	
Supplies	2,300		700	
Prepaid Insurance	4,000		2,500	
Equipment	14,000		14,000	
Accumulated Depreciation—Equipment		$ 3,600		$ 4,900
Accounts Payable		5,800		5,800
Salaries and Wages Payable		–0–		1,100
Unearned Rent Revenue		1,500		800
Common Stock		12,000		12,000
Retained Earnings		3,600		3,600
Service Revenue		34,000		35,200
Rent Revenue		11,000		11,700
Salaries and Wages Expense	17,000		18,100	
Supplies Expense	–0–		1,600	
Rent Expense	15,000		15,000	
Insurance Expense	–0–		1,500	
Depreciation Expense	–0–		1,300	
	$71,500	$71,500	$75,100	$75,100

Instructions

Prepare the adjusting entries that were made.

Prepare financial statements from adjusted trial balance.
(LO 7)

E3-14 The adjusted trial balance for Matusiak Company is given in E3-13.

Instructions

Prepare the income and retained earnings statements for the year and the balance sheet at August 31.

Record transactions on accrual basis; convert revenue to cash receipts.
(LO 5, 6)

E3-15 The following data are taken from the comparative balance sheets of Newman Billiards Club, which prepares its financial statements using the accrual basis of accounting.

December 31	2014	2013
Accounts receivable from members	$12,000	$ 9,000
Unearned service revenue	17,000	20,000

Members are billed based upon their use of the club's facilities. Unearned service revenues arise from the sale of gift certificates, which members can apply to their future use of club facilities. The 2014 income statement for the club showed that service revenue of $153,000 was recognized during the year.

Instructions

(*Hint:* You will probably find it helpful to use T-accounts to analyze these data.)

(a) Prepare journal entries for each of the following events that took place during 2014.
  (1) Accounts receivable from 2013 were all collected.
  (2) Gift certificates outstanding at the end of 2013 were all redeemed.
  (3) An additional $35,000 worth of gift certificates were sold during 2014. A portion of these was used by the recipients during the year; the remainder was still outstanding at the end of 2014.
  (4) Services provided to members for 2014 were billed to members.
  (5) Accounts receivable for 2014 (i.e., those billed in item [4] above) were partially collected.

(b) Determine the amount of cash received by the club, with respect to member services, during 2014.

Compute cash flow from operations and net income.
(LO 2)

E3-16 In its first year of operations, Anya Company recognized $30,000 in service revenue, $4,800 of which was on account and still outstanding at year-end. The remaining $25,200 was received in cash from customers.

The company incurred operating expenses of $17,000. Of these expenses $12,000 was paid in cash; $5,000 was still owed on account at year-end. In addition, Anya prepaid $2,600 for insurance coverage that would not be used until the second year of operations.

Instructions

(a) Compute Anya's first-year cash flow from operations.
(b) Compute Anya's first-year net income under accrual-basis accounting.
(c) Which basis of accounting (cash or accrual) provides more useful information for decision-makers?

Journalize adjusting entries.
(LO 8)

***E3-17** Rogert Company has the following balances in selected accounts on December 31, 2014.

Service Revenue	$40,000
Insurance Expense	2,880
Supplies Expense	2,450

All the accounts have normal balances. Rogert Company debits prepayments to expense accounts when paid, and credits unearned revenues to revenue accounts when received. The following information below has been gathered at December 31, 2014.

1. Rogert Company paid $2,880 for 12 months of insurance coverage on April 1, 2014.
2. On December 1, 2014, Rogert Company collected $40,000 for consulting services to be performed from December 1, 2014, through March 31, 2015.
3. A count of supplies on December 31, 2014, indicates that supplies of $420 are on hand.

Instructions

Prepare the adjusting entries needed at December 31, 2014.

***E3-18** At Beloit Company, prepayments are debited to expense when paid, and unearned revenues are credited to revenue when cash is received. During January of the current year, the following transactions occurred.

Journalize transactions and adjusting entries.

(LO 8)

Jan.	2	Paid $2,640 for fire insurance protection for the year.
	10	Paid $1,700 for supplies.
	15	Received $6,400 for services to be performed in the future.

On January 31, it is determined that $2,500 of the services were performed and that there are $650 of supplies on hand.

Instructions

(a) Journalize and post the January transactions. (Use T-accounts.)
(b) Journalize and post the adjusting entries at January 31.
(c) Determine the ending balance in each of the accounts.

***E3-19** Presented below are the assumptions and principles discussed in this chapter.

Identify accounting assumptions and principles.

(LO 9)

1. Full disclosure principle.
2. Going concern assumption.
3. Monetary unit assumption.
4. Time period assumption.
5. Cost principle.
6. Economic entity assumption.

Instructions

Identify by number the accounting assumption or principle that is described below. Do not use a number more than once.

______ (a) Is the rationale for why plant assets are not reported at liquidation value. (*Note:* Do not use the cost principle.)
______ (b) Indicates that personal and business record-keeping should be separately maintained.
______ (c) Assumes that the dollar is the "measuring stick" used to report on financial performance.
______ (d) Separates financial information into time periods for reporting purposes.
______ (e) Measurement basis used when a reliable estimate of fair value is not available.
______ (f) Dictates that companies should disclose all circumstances and events that make a difference to financial statement users.

***E3-20** Rosman Co. had three major business transactions during 2014.

Identify the assumption or principle that has been violated.

(LO 9)

(a) Reported at its fair value of $260,000 merchandise inventory with a cost of $208,000.
(b) The president of Rosman Co., Jay Rosman, purchased a truck for personal use and charged it to his expense account.
(c) Rosman Co. wanted to make its 2014 income look better, so it added 2 more weeks to the year (a 54-week year). Previous years were 52 weeks.

Instructions

In each situation, identify the assumption or principle that has been violated, if any, and discuss what the company should have done.

***E3-21** The following are characteristics, assumptions, principles, or constraints that guide the FASB when it creates accounting standards.

Identity financial accounting concepts and principles.

(LO 9)

Relevance	Expense recognition principle
Faithful representation	Time period assumption
Comparability	Going concern assumption
Consistency	Cost principle
Monetary unit assumption	Full disclosure principle
Economic entity assumption	Materiality constraint

Match each item above with a description below.

1. ________ Ability to easily evaluate one company's results relative to another's.
2. ________ Belief that a company will continue to operate for the foreseeable future.
3. ________ The judgment concerning whether an item is large enough to matter to decision-makers.

4. ________ The reporting of all information that would make a difference to financial statement users.
5. ________ The practice of preparing financial statements at regular intervals.
6. ________ The quality of information that indicates the information makes a difference in a decision.
7. ________ A belief that items should be reported on the balance sheet at the price that was paid to acquire the item.
8. ________ A company's use of the same accounting principles and methods from year to year.
9. ________ Tracing accounting events to particular companies.
10. ________ The desire to minimize errors and bias in financial statements.
11. ________ Reporting only those things that can be measured in dollars.
12. ________ Dictates that efforts (expenses) be matched with results (revenues).

Comment on the objectives and qualitative characteristics of accounting information

(LO 9)

***E3-22** Net Nanny Software International Inc., headquartered in Vancouver, specializes in Internet safety and computer security products for both the home and commercial markets. In a recent balance sheet, it reported a deficit (negative retained earnings) of US $5,678,288. It has reported only net losses since its inception. In spite of these losses, Net Nanny's common shares have traded anywhere from a high of $3.70 to a low of $0.32 on the Canadian Venture Exchange.

Net Nanny's financial statements have historically been prepared in Canadian dollars. Recently, the company adopted the U.S. dollar as its reporting currency.

Instructions

(a) What is the objective of financial reporting? How does this objective meet or not meet Net Nanny's investors' needs?
(b) Why would investors want to buy Net Nanny's shares if the company has consistently reported losses over the last few years? Include in your answer an assessment of the relevance of the information reported on Net Nanny's financial statements.
(c) Comment on how the change in reporting information from Canadian dollars to U.S. dollars likely affected the readers of Net Nanny's financial statements. Include in your answer an assessment of the comparability of the information.

Comment on the objectives and qualitative characteristics of financial reporting.

(LO 9)

***E3-23** A friend of yours, Ana Gehrig, recently completed an undergraduate degree in science and has just started working with a biotechnology company. Ana tells you that the owners of the business are trying to secure new sources of financing which are needed in order for the company to proceed with development of a new health care product. Ana said that her boss told her that the company must put together a report to present to potential investors.

Ana thought that the company should include in this package the detailed scientific findings related to the Phase I clinical trials for this product. She said, "I know that the biotech industry sometimes has only a 10% success rate with new products, but if we report all the scientific findings, everyone will see what a sure success this is going to be! The president was talking about the importance of following some set of accounting principles. Why do we need to look at some accounting rules? What they need to realize is that we have scientific results that are quite encouraging, some of the most talented employees around, and the start of some really great customer relationships. We haven't made any sales yet, but we will. We just need the funds to get through all the clinical testing and get government approval for our product. Then these investors will be quite happy that they bought in to our company early!"

Instructions

(a) What is accounting information?
(b) Comment on how Ana's suggestions for what should be reported to prospective investors conforms to the qualitative characteristics of accounting information. Do you think that the things that Ana wants to include in the information for investors will conform to financial reporting guidelines?

EXERCISES: SET B AND CHALLENGE EXERCISES

Visit the book's companion website, at **www.wiley.com/college/weygandt**, and choose the Student Companion site to access Exercise Set B and Challenge Exercises.

PROBLEMS: SET A

Prepare adjusting entries, post to ledger accounts, and prepare adjusted trial balance.

(LO 5, 6, 7)

P3-1A Joey Cuono started his own consulting firm, Cuono Company, on June 1, 2014. The trial balance at June 30 is shown below.

Cuono Company
Trial Balance
June 30, 2014

Account Number		Debit	Credit
101	Cash	$ 6,200	
112	Accounts Receivable	6,000	
126	Supplies	2,000	
130	Prepaid Insurance	3,000	
157	Equipment	14,400	
201	Accounts Payable		$ 4,700
209	Unearned Service Revenue		4,000
311	Common Stock		20,000
400	Service Revenue		7,900
726	Salaries and Wages Expense	4,000	
729	Rent Expense	1,000	
		$36,600	$36,600

In addition to those accounts listed on the trial balance, the chart of accounts for Cuono Company also contains the following accounts and account numbers: No. 158 Accumulated Depreciation—Equipment, No. 212 Salaries and Wages Payable, No. 631 Supplies Expense, No. 711 Depreciation Expense, No. 722 Insurance Expense, and No. 732 Utilities Expense.

Other data:

1. Supplies on hand at June 30 are $1,100.
2. A utility bill for $150 has not been recorded and will not be paid until next month.
3. The insurance policy is for a year.
4. $2,500 of unearned service revenue is recognized for services performed at the end of the month.
5. Salaries of $1,600 are accrued at June 30.
6. The equipment has a 4-year life with no salvage value. It is being depreciated at $300 per month for 48 months.
7. Invoices representing $2,100 of services performed during the month have not been recorded as of June 30.

Instructions

(a) Prepare the adjusting entries for the month of June. Use J3 as the page number for your journal.
(b) Post the adjusting entries to the ledger accounts. Enter the totals from the trial balance as beginning account balances and place a check mark in the posting reference column.
(c) Prepare an adjusted trial balance at June 30, 2014.

(c) Adj. trial balance $40,750

Prepare adjusting entries, post, and prepare adjusted trial balance, and financial statements.

(LO 5, 6, 7)

P3-2A Lazy River Resort opened for business on June 1 with eight air-conditioned units. Its trial balance before adjustment on August 31 is as follows.

Lazy River Resort, Inc.
Trial Balance
August 31, 2014

Account Number		Debit	Credit
101	Cash	$ 19,600	
126	Supplies	3,300	
130	Prepaid Insurance	6,000	
140	Land	25,000	
143	Buildings	125,000	
157	Equipment	26,000	
201	Accounts Payable		$ 6,500
208	Unearned Rent Revenue		7,400
275	Mortgage Payable		80,000
311	Common Stock		100,000
332	Dividends	5,000	
429	Rent Revenue		80,000
622	Maintenance and Repairs Expense	3,600	
726	Salaries and Wages Expense	51,000	
732	Utilities Expense	9,400	
		$273,900	$273,900

In addition to those accounts listed on the trial balance, the chart of accounts for Lazy River Resort also contains the following accounts and account numbers: No. 112 Accounts Receivable, No. 144 Accumulated Depreciation—Buildings, No. 158 Accumulated Depreciation—Equipment, No. 212 Salaries and Wages Payable, No. 230 Interest Payable, No. 631 Supplies Expense, No. 711 Depreciation Expense, No. 718 Interest Expense, and No. 722 Insurance Expense.

Other data:

1. Insurance expires at the rate of $400 per month.
2. A count on August 31 shows $900 of supplies on hand.
3. Annual depreciation is $4,500 on buildings and $2,400 on equipment.
4. Unearned rent revenue of $4,100 was recognized for services performed prior to August 31.
5. Salaries of $400 were unpaid at August 31.
6. Rentals of $3,700 were due from tenants at August 31. (Use Accounts Receivable.)
7. The mortgage interest rate is 9% per year. (The mortgage was taken out on August 1.)

Instructions

(a) Journalize the adjusting entries on August 31 for the 3-month period June 1–August 31.
(b) Prepare a ledger using the three-column form of account. Enter the trial balance amounts and post the adjusting entries. (Use J1 as the posting reference.)
(c) Prepare an adjusted trial balance on August 31.
(d) Prepare an income statement and a retained earnings statement for the 3 months ending August 31 and a balance sheet as of August 31.

(c) Adj. trial balance $280,325
(d) Net income $17,475
Ending retained earnings $12,475
Total assets $203,275

Prepare adjusting entries and financial statements.

(LO 5, 6, 7)

P3-3A Costello Advertising Agency Inc. was founded by Pat Costello in January of 2013. Presented on the next page are both the adjusted and unadjusted trial balances as of December 31, 2014.

Instructions

(a) Journalize the annual adjusting entries that were made.
(b) Prepare an income statement and a retained earnings statement for the year ending December 31, 2014, and a balance sheet at December 31.
(c) Answer the following questions.
  (1) If the note has been outstanding 6 months, what is the annual interest rate on that note?
  (2) If the company paid $14,500 in salaries in 2014, what was the balance in Salaries and Wages Payable on December 31, 2013?

(b) Net income $38,450
Ending retained earnings $31,950
Total assets $69,000
(c) (1) 6%
(2) $4,500

Costello Advertising Agency, Inc.
Trial Balance
December 31, 2014

	Unadjusted Dr.	Unadjusted Cr.	Adjusted Dr.	Adjusted Cr.
Cash	$11,000		$11,000	
Accounts Receivable	20,000		23,500	
Supplies	8,600		5,000	
Prepaid Insurance	3,350		2,500	
Equipment	60,000		60,000	
Accumulated Depreciation—Equipment		$ 28,000		$ 33,000
Accounts Payable		5,000		5,000
Interest Payable		-0-		150
Notes Payable		5,000		5,000
Unearned Service Revenue		7,200		5,600
Salaries and Wages Payable		-0-		1,300
Common Stock		20,000		20,000
Retained Earnings		5,500		5,500
Dividends	12,000		12,000	
Service Revenue		58,600		63,700
Salaries and Wages Expense	10,000		11,300	
Insurance Expense			850	
Interest Expense	350		500	
Depreciation Expense			5,000	
Supplies Expense			3,600	
Rent Expense	4,000		4,000	
	$129,300	$129,300	$139,250	$139,250

P3-4A A review of the ledger of Bellingham Company at December 31, 2014, produces the following data pertaining to the preparation of annual adjusting entries.

Preparing adjusting entries.

(LO 5, 6)

1. Salaries and Wages Payable $0. There are eight salaried employees. Salaries are paid every Friday for the current week. Five employees receive a salary of $800 each per week, and three employees earn $500 each per week. Assume December 31 is a Tuesday. Employees do not work weekends. All employees worked the last 2 days of December.

1. Salaries and wages expense $2,200

2. Unearned Rent Revenue $324,000. The company began subleasing office space in its new building on November 1. At December 31, the company had the following rental contracts that are paid in full for the entire term of the lease.

2. Rent revenue $74,000

Date	Term (in months)	Monthly Rent	Number of Leases
Nov. 1	6	$4,000	5
Dec. 1	6	$8,500	4

3. Prepaid Advertising $15,600. This balance consists of payments on two advertising contracts. The contracts provide for monthly advertising in two trade magazines. The terms of the contracts are as follows.

3. Advertising expense $5,200

Contract	Date	Amount	Number of Magazine Issues
A650	May 1	$6,000	12
B974	Oct. 1	9,600	24

The first advertisement runs in the month in which the contract is signed.

4. Notes Payable $100,000. This balance consists of a note for one year at an annual interest rate of 9%, dated June 1.

4. Interest expense $5,250

Instructions

Prepare the adjusting entries at December 31, 2014. (Show all computations.)

Journalize transactions and follow through accounting cycle to preparation of financial statements.

(LO 5, 6, 7)

P3-5A On September 1, 2014, the account balances of Beck Equipment Repair, Inc. were as follows.

No.	Debits		No.	Credits	
101	Cash	$ 4,880	158	Accumulated Depreciation—Equipment	$ 2,100
112	Accounts Receivable	3,520	201	Accounts Payable	3,400
126	Supplies	2,000	209	Unearned Service Revenue	1,400
157	Equipment	18,000	212	Salaries and Wages Payable	500
			311	Common Stock	10,000
			320	Retained Earnings	11,000
		$28,400			$28,400

During September, the following summary transactions were completed.

Sept. 8 Paid $1,700 for salaries due employees, of which $1,200 is for September.
10 Received $1,200 cash from customers on account.
12 Received $3,400 cash for services performed in September.
15 Purchased store equipment on account $3,000.
17 Purchased supplies on account $1,200.
20 Paid creditors $4,500 on account.
22 Paid September rent $500.
25 Paid salaries $1,050.
27 Performed services on account and billed customers for services provided $1,600.
29 Received $750 from customers for future service.

Adjustment data consist of:

1. Supplies on hand $1,700.
2. Accrued salaries payable $400.
3. Depreciation is $140 per month.
4. Unearned service revenue of $1,450 is recognized for services performed.

Instructions

(a) Enter the September 1 balances in the ledger accounts.
(b) Journalize the September transactions.
(c) Post to the ledger accounts. Use J1 for the posting reference. Use the following additional accounts: No. 400 Service Revenue, No. 631 Supplies Expense, No. 711 Depreciation Expense, No. 726 Salaries and Wages Expense, and No. 729 Rent Expense.
(d) Prepare a trial balance at September 30.
(e) Journalize and post adjusting entries.
(f) Prepare an adjusted trial balance.
(g) Prepare an income statement and a retained earnings statement for September and a balance sheet at September 30.

(d) Trial balance $33,350
(f) Adj. trial balance $33,890
(g) Net income $1,660
Ending retained earnings $12,660
Total assets $26,860

Prepare adjusting entries, adjusted trial balance, and financial statements using appendix.

(LO 5, 6, 7, 8)

***P3-6A** Alpha Graphics Company, Inc. was organized on January 1, 2014. At the end of the first 6 months of operations, the trial balance contained the accounts shown below.

Debits		Credits	
Cash	$ 8,400	Notes Payable	$ 20,000
Accounts Receivable	14,000	Accounts Payable	9,000
Equipment	45,000	Common Stock	22,000
Insurance Expense	2,880	Service Revenue	58,280
Salaries and Wages Expense	30,000		
Supplies Expense	3,900		
Advertising Expense	1,900		
Rent Expense	1,500		
Utilities Expense	1,700		
	$109,280		$109,280

Analysis reveals the following additional data.

1. The $3,900 balance in Supplies Expense represents supplies purchased in January. At June 30, $680 of supplies are on hand.
2. The note payable was issued on February 1. It is a 9%, 6-month note.
3. The balance in Insurance Expense is the premium on a one-year policy, dated March 1, 2014.
4. Service revenues are credited to revenue when received. At June 30, service revenue of $1,100 is still not performed for the customer.
5. Depreciation is $2,250 per year.

Instructions

(a) Journalize the adjusting entries at June 30. (Assume adjustments are recorded every 6 months.)
(b) Prepare an adjusted trial balance.
(c) Prepare an income statement and a retained earnings statement for the 6 months ended June 30 and a balance sheet at June 30.

(b) Adj. trial balance $111,155
(c) Net income $16,025
Ending retained earnings $16,025
Total assets $68,875

PROBLEMS: SET B

P3-1B Lynda Rigg started her own consulting firm, Vektek Consulting, Inc. on May 1, 2014. The trial balance at May 31 is as follows.

Prepare adjusting entries, post to ledger accounts, and prepare an adjusted trial balance.

(LO 5, 6, 7)

Vektek Consulting, Inc.
Trial Balance
May 31, 2014

Account Number		Debit	Credit
101	Cash	$ 7,700	
112	Accounts Receivable	4,000	
126	Supplies	1,500	
130	Prepaid Insurance	2,400	
157	Equipment	12,000	
201	Accounts Payable		$ 4,500
209	Unearned Service Revenue		2,600
311	Common Stock		16,000
400	Service Revenue		8,500
726	Salaries and Wages Expense	3,000	
729	Rent Expense	1,000	
		$31,600	$31,600

In addition to those accounts listed on the trial balance, the chart of accounts for Vektek Consulting also contains the following accounts and account numbers: No. 158 Accumulated Depreciation—Equipment, No. 212 Salaries and Wages Payable, No. 631 Supplies Expense, No. 711 Depreciation Expense, No. 722 Insurance Expense, and No. 736 Utilities Expense.

Other data:

1. $500 of supplies have been used during the month.
2. Utilities expense incurred but not paid on May 31, 2014, $200.
3. The insurance policy is for 2 years.
4. $1,000 of the balance in the Unearned Service Revenue account remains unearned at the end of the month.
5. May 31 is a Wednesday, and employees are paid on Fridays. Vektek Consulting has two employees, who are paid $500 each for a 5-day work week.
6. The office equipment has a 5-year life with no salvage value. It is being depreciated at $200 per month for 60 months.
7. Invoices representing $1,400 of services performed during the month have not been recorded as of May 31.

Instructions

(a) Prepare the adjusting entries for the month of May. Use J4 as the page number for your journal.

(b) Post the adjusting entries to the ledger accounts. Enter the totals from the trial balance as beginning account balances and place a check mark in the posting reference column.

(c) Adj. trial balance $34,000

(c) Prepare an adjusted trial balance at May 31, 2014.

Prepare adjusting entries, post, and prepare adjusted trial balance, and financial statements.

(LO 5, 6, 7)

P3-2B The Badger Motel, Inc. opened for business on May 1, 2014. Its trial balance before adjustment on May 31 is as follows.

Badger Motel, Inc.
Trial Balance
May 31, 2014

Account Number		Debit	Credit
101	Cash	$ 2,500	
126	Supplies	1,520	
130	Prepaid Insurance	2,400	
140	Land	14,000	
141	Buildings	58,000	
157	Equipment	15,000	
201	Accounts Payable		$ 4,800
208	Unearned Rent Revenue		3,300
275	Mortgage Payable		38,000
311	Common Stock		40,000
429	Rent Revenue		12,300
610	Advertising Expense	780	
726	Salaries and Wages Expense	3,300	
732	Utilities Expense	900	
		$98,400	$98,400

In addition to those accounts listed on the trial balance, the chart of accounts for Badger Motel, Inc. also contains the following accounts and account numbers: No. 142 Accumulated Depreciation—Buildings, No. 158 Accumulated Depreciation—Equipment, No. 212 Salaries and Wages Payable, No. 230 Interest Payable, No. 631 Supplies Expense, No. 711 Depreciation Expense, No. 718 Interest Expense, and No. 722 Insurance Expense.

Other data:

1. Prepaid insurance is a 1-year policy starting May 1, 2014.
2. A count of supplies shows $350 of unused supplies on May 31.
3. Annual depreciation is $2,640 on the buildings and $1,500 on equipment.
4. The mortgage interest rate is 12%. (The mortgage was taken out on May 1.)
5. Two-thirds of the unearned rent revenue has been recognized for services performed.
6. Salaries of $750 are accrued and unpaid at May 31.

Instructions

(c) Adj. trial balance $99,875

(d) Net income $6,675
Ending retained earnings $6,675
Total assets $91,705

(a) Journalize the adjusting entries on May 31.

(b) Prepare a ledger using the three-column form of account. Enter the trial balance amounts and post the adjusting entries. (Use J1 as the posting reference.)

(c) Prepare an adjusted trial balance on May 31.

(d) Prepare an income statement and a retained earnings statement for the month of May and a balance sheet at May 31.

Prepare adjusting entries and financial statements.

(LO 5, 6, 7)

P3-3B Medina Co., Inc. was organized on July 1, 2014. Quarterly financial statements are prepared. The unadjusted and adjusted trial balances as of September 30 are shown on the next page.

Medina Co., Inc.
Trial Balance
September 30, 2014

	Unadjusted		Adjusted	
	Dr.	**Cr.**	**Dr.**	**Cr.**
Cash	$ 8,700		$ 8,700	
Accounts Receivable	10,400		11,500	
Supplies	1,900		650	
Prepaid Rent	2,200		1,200	
Equipment	20,000		20,000	
Accumulated Depreciation—Equipment		$ -0-		$ 1,125
Notes Payable		10,000		10,000
Accounts Payable		3,200		3,200
Salaries and Wages Payable		-0-		725
Interest Payable		-0-		100
Unearned Rent Revenue		1,900		1,050
Common Stock		22,000		22,000
Dividends	1,000		1,000	
Service Revenue		16,800		17,900
Rent Revenue		1,710		2,560
Salaries and Wages Expense	8,000		8,725	
Rent Expense	1,900		2,900	
Depreciation Expense			1,125	
Supplies Expense			1,250	
Utilities Expense	1,510		1,510	
Interest Expense			100	
	$55,610	$55,610	$58,660	$58,660

Instructions

(a) Journalize the adjusting entries that were made.

(b) Prepare an income statement and a retained earnings statement for the 3 months ending September 30 and a balance sheet at September 30.

(c) If the note bears interest at 12%, how many months has it been outstanding?

(b) Net income $4,850
Ending retained earnings $3,850
Total assets $40,925

P3-4B A review of the ledger of Khan Company at December 31, 2014, produces the following data pertaining to the preparation of annual adjusting entries.

Prepare adjusting entries
(LO 5, 6)

1. Prepaid Insurance $9,300. The company has separate insurance policies on its buildings and its motor vehicles. Policy B4564 on the building was purchased on April 1, 2013, for $6,000. The policy has a term of 3 years. Policy A2958 on the vehicles was purchased on January 1, 2014, for $4,800. This policy has a term of 2 years.

1. Insurance expense $4,400

2. Unearned Rent Revenue $429,000. The company began subleasing office space in its new building on November 1. At December 31, the company had the following rental contracts that are paid in full for the entire term of the lease.

2. Rent revenue $84,000

Date	Term (in months)	Monthly Rent	Number of Leases
Nov. 1	9	$5,000	5
Dec. 1	6	$8,500	4

3. Notes Payable $120,000. This balance consists of a note for 9 months at an annual interest rate of 9%, dated November 1.

3. Interest expense $1,800

4. Salaries and Wages Payable $0. There are eight salaried employees. Salaries are paid every Friday for the current week. Five employees receive a salary of $640 each per week, and three employees earn $500 each per week. Assume December 31 is a Wednesday. Employees do not work weekends. All employees worked the last 3 days of December.

4. Salaries and wages expense $2,820

Instructions

Prepare the adjusting entries at December 31, 2014.

Journalize transactions and follow through accounting cycle to preparation of financial statements.

(LO 5, 6, 7)

P3-5B On November 1, 2014, the account balances of Samone Equipment Repair, Inc. were as follows.

No.	Debits		No.	Credits	
101	Cash	$ 2,400	158	Accumulated Depreciation—Equipment	$ 2,000
112	Accounts Receivable	4,450	201	Accounts Payable	2,600
126	Supplies	1,800	209	Unearned Service Revenue	1,360
157	Equipment	16,000	212	Salaries and Wages Payable	700
			311	Common Stock	10,000
			320	Retained Earnings	7,990
		$24,650			$24,650

During November, the following summary transactions were completed.

Nov. 8 Paid $1,500 for salaries due employees, of which $700 is for October salaries.
10 Received $3,420 cash from customers on account.
12 Received $3,100 cash for services performed in November.
15 Purchased equipment on account $2,000.
17 Purchased supplies on account $700.
20 Paid creditors on account $2,700.
22 Paid November rent $500.
25 Paid salaries $1,500.
27 Performed services on account and billed customers for services provided $1,900.
29 Received $350 from customers for future service.

Adjustment data consist of:

1. Supplies on hand $1,400.
2. Accrued salaries payable $350.
3. Depreciation for the month is $200.
4. Unearned service revenue of $1,380 is recognized for services performed.

Instructions

(a) Enter the November 1 balances in the ledger accounts.
(b) Journalize the November transactions.
(c) Post to the ledger accounts. Use J1 for the posting reference. Use the following additional accounts: No. 400 Service Revenue, No. 631 Supplies Expense, No. 711 Depreciation Expense, No. 726 Salaries and Wages Expense, and No. 729 Rent Expense.
(d) Prepare a trial balance at November 30.
(e) Journalize and post adjusting entries.
(f) Prepare an adjusted trial balance.
(g) Prepare an income statement and a retained earnings statement for November and a balance sheet at November 30.

(d) Trial balance $29,300
(f) Adj. trial balance $29,850
(g) Net income $1,930
Ending retained earnings $9,920
Total assets $23,200

PROBLEMS: SET C

Visit the book's companion website, at **www.wiley.com/college/weygandt**, and choose the Student Companion site to access Problem Set C.

CONTINUING COOKIE CHRONICLE

(*Note:* This is a continuation of the Cookie Chronicle from Chapters 1–2. Use the information from the previous chapters and follow the instructions on the next page using the general ledger accounts you have already prepared.)

CCC3 It is the end of November and Natalie has been in touch with her grandmother. Her grandmother asked Natalie how well things went in her first month of business. Natalie, too, would like to know if the company has been profitable or not during November.

Natalie realizes that in order to determine Cookie Creations' income, she must first make adjustments.

Natalie puts together the following additional information.

1. A count reveals that $35 of baking supplies were used during November.
2. Natalie estimates that all of her baking equipment will have a useful life of 5 years or 60 months. (Assume Natalie decides to record a full month's worth of depreciation, regardless of when the equipment was obtained by the business.)
3. Natalie's grandmother has decided to charge interest of 6% on the note payable extended on November 16. The loan plus interest is to be repaid in 24 months. (Assume that half a month of interest accrued during November.)
4. On November 30, a friend of Natalie's asks her to teach a class at the neighborhood school. Natalie agrees and teaches a group of 35 first-grade students how to make Santa Claus cookies. The next day, Natalie prepares an invoice for $300 and leaves it with the school principal. The principal says that he will pass the invoice along to the head office, and it will be paid sometime in December.
5. Natalie receives a utilities bill for $45. The bill is for utilities consumed by Natalie's business during November and is due December 15.

Instructions

Using the information that you have gathered through Chapter 2, and based on the new information above, do the following.

(a) Prepare and post the adjusting journal entries.
(b) Prepare an adjusted trial balance.
(c) Using the adjusted trial balance, calculate Cookie Creations' net income or net loss for the month of November. Do not prepare an income statement.

Broadening Your PERSPECTIVE

Financial Reporting and Analysis

Financial Reporting Problem: PepsiCo, Inc.

BYP3-1 The financial statements of PepsiCo, Inc. are presented in Appendix A at the end of this textbook.

Instructions

(a) Using the consolidated financial statements and related information, identify items that may result in adjusting entries for prepayments.
(b) Using the consolidated financial statements and related information, identify items that may result in adjusting entries for accruals.
(c) Using the Selected Financial Data and 5-Year Summary, what has been the trend since 2006 for net income?

Comparative Analysis Problem: PepsiCo, Inc. vs. The Coca-Cola Company

BYP3-2 PepsiCo's financial statements are presented in Appendix A. Financial statements for The Coca-Cola Company are presented in Appendix B.

Instructions

Based on information contained in these financial statements, determine the following for each company.

(a) Net increase (decrease) in property, plant, and equipment (net) from 2009 to 2010.
(b) Increase (decrease) in selling, general, and administrative expenses from 2009 to 2010.
(c) Increase (decrease) in long-term debt (obligations) from 2009 to 2010.

(d) Increase (decrease) in net income from 2009 to 2010.
(e) Increase (decrease) in cash and cash equivalents from 2009 to 2010.

Real-World Focus

BYP3-3 No financial decision-maker should ever rely solely on the financial information reported in the annual report to make decisions. It is important to keep abreast of financial news. This activity demonstrates how to search for financial news on the Web.

Address: http://biz.yahoo.com/i, or go to **www.wiley.com/college/weygandt**

Steps

1. Type in either Wal-Mart, Target Corp., or Kmart.
2. Choose **News**.
3. Select an article that sounds interesting to you and that would be relevant to an investor in these companies.

Instructions

(a) What was the source of the article (e.g., Reuters, Businesswire, Prnewswire)?
(b) Assume that you are a personal financial planner and that one of your clients owns stock in the company. Write a brief memo to your client summarizing the article and explaining the implications of the article for their investment.

Critical Thinking

Decision-Making Across the Organization

BYP3-4 Happy Trails Park, Inc. was organized on April 1, 2013, by Alicia Henry. Alicia is a good manager but a poor accountant. From the trial balance prepared by a part-time bookkeeper, Alicia prepared the following income statement for the quarter that ended March 31, 2014.

Happy Trails Park, Inc.
Income Statement
For the Quarter Ended March 31, 2014

Revenues		
Rent revenue		$88,000
Operating expenses		
Advertising	$ 5,200	
Salaries and wages	28,800	
Utilities	750	
Depreciation	800	
Maintenance and repairs	4,000	
Total operating expenses		39,550
Net income		$48,450

Alicia thought that something was wrong with the statement because net income had never exceeded $20,000 in any one quarter. Knowing that you are an experienced accountant, she asks you to review the income statement and other data.

You first look at the trial balance. In addition to the account balances reported above in the income statement, the ledger contains the following additional selected balances at March 31, 2014.

Supplies	$ 6,200
Prepaid Insurance	7,500
Notes Payable	12,000

You then make inquiries and discover the following.

1. Rent revenue includes advanced rentals for summer occupancy $14,000.
2. There were $1,450 of supplies on hand at March 31.
3. Prepaid insurance resulted from the payment of a one-year policy on January 1, 2014.
4. The mail on April 1, 2014, brought the following bills: advertising for week of March 24, $130; repairs made March 10, $260; and utilities, $120.
5. There are four employees, who receive wages totaling $300 per day. At March 31, 2 days' salaries and wages have been incurred but not paid.
6. The note payable is a 3-month, 10% note dated January 1, 2014.

Instructions

With the class divided into groups, answer the following.

(a) Prepare a correct income statement for the quarter ended March 31, 2014.

(b) Explain to Alicia the generally accepted accounting principles that she did not recognize in preparing her income statement and their effect on her results.

(a) Net income $26,415
(b) Effect on result is $22,035

Communication Activity

BYP3-5 In reviewing the accounts of Maribeth Co. at the end of the year, you discover that adjusting entries have not been made.

Instructions

Write a memo to Maribeth Danon, the owner of Maribeth Co., that explains the following: the nature and purpose of adjusting entries, why adjusting entries are needed, and the types of adjusting entries that may be made.

Ethics Case

BYP3-6 Watkin Company is a pesticide manufacturer. Its sales declined greatly this year due to the passage of legislation outlawing the sale of several of Watkin's chemical pesticides. In the coming year, Watkin will have environmentally safe and competitive chemicals to replace these discontinued products. Sales in the next year are expected to greatly exceed any prior year's. The decline in sales and profits appears to be a one-year aberration. But even so, the company president fears a large dip in the current year's profits. He believes that such a dip could cause a significant drop in the market price of Watkin's stock and make the company a takeover target.

To avoid this possibility, the company president calls in Diane Leno, controller, to discuss this period's year-end adjusting entries. He urges her to accrue every possible revenue and to defer as many expenses as possible. He says to Diane, "We need the revenues this year, and next year can easily absorb expenses deferred from this year. We can't let our stock price be hammered down!" Diane didn't get around to recording the adjusting entries until January 17, but she dated the entries December 31 as if they were recorded then. Diane also made every effort to comply with the president's request.

Instructions

(a) Who are the stakeholders in this situation?

(b) What are the ethical considerations of (1) the president's request and (2) Diane's dating the adjusting entries December 31?

(c) Can Diane accrue revenues and defer expenses and still be ethical?

All About You

BYP3-7 Companies must report or disclose in their financial statements information about all liabilities, including potential liabilities related to environmental clean-up. There are many situations in which you will be asked to provide personal financial information about your assets, liabilities, revenue, and expenses. Sometimes you will face difficult decisions regarding what to disclose and how to disclose it.

Instructions

Suppose that you are putting together a loan application to purchase a home. Based on your income and assets, you qualify for the mortgage loan, but just barely. How would you address each of the following situations in reporting your financial position for the loan application? Provide responses for each of the following situations.

(a) You signed a guarantee for a bank loan that a friend took out for $20,000. If your friend doesn't pay, you will have to pay. Your friend has made all of the payments so far, and it appears he will be able to pay in the future.

(b) You were involved in an auto accident in which you were at fault. There is the possibility that you may have to pay as much as $50,000 as part of a settlement. The issue will not be resolved before the bank processes your mortgage request.

(c) The company at which you work isn't doing very well, and it has recently laid off employees. You are still employed, but it is quite possible that you will lose your job in the next few months.

BYP3-8 Many companies have potential pollution or environmental-disposal problems—not only for electronic gadgets, but also for the lead paint or asbestos they sold. How do we fit these issues into the accounting equation? Are these costs and related liabilities that companies should report?

YES: As more states impose laws holding companies responsible, and as more courts levy pollution-related fines, it becomes increasingly likely that companies will have to pay large amounts in the future.

NO: The amounts still are too difficult to estimate. Putting inaccurate estimates on the financial statements reduces their usefulness. Instead, why not charge the costs later, when the actual environmental cleanup or disposal occurs, at which time the company knows the actual cost?

Instructions

Write a response indicating your position regarding this situation. Provide support for your view.

FASB Codification Activity

BYP3-9 If your school has a subscription to the FASB Codification, go to *http://aaahq.org/asclogin.cfm* to log in and prepare responses to the following.

Instructions

Access the glossary ("Master Glossary") to answer the following.

(a) What is the definition of revenue?

(b) What is the definition of compensation?

Answers to Chapter Questions

Answers to Insight and Accounting Across the Organization Questions

p. 104 Cooking the Books? Q: What motivates sales executives and finance and accounting executives to participate in activities that result in inaccurate reporting of revenues? **A:** Sales executives typically receive bonuses based on their ability to meet quarterly sales targets. In addition, they often face the possibility of losing their jobs if they miss those targets. Executives in accounting and finance are very aware of the earnings targets of Wall Street analysts and investors. If they fail to meet these targets, the company's stock price will fall. As a result of these pressures, executives sometimes knowingly engage in unethical efforts to misstate revenues. As a result of the Sarbanes-Oxley Act, the penalties for such behavior are now much more severe.

p. 112 Turning Gift Cards into Revenue Q: Suppose that Robert Jones purchases a $100 gift card at Best Buy on December 24, 2013, and gives it to his wife, Mary Jones, on December 25, 2013. On January 3, 2014, Mary uses the card to purchase $100 worth of CDs. When do you think Best Buy should recognize revenue and why? **A:** According to the revenue recognition principle, companies should recognize revenue when the performance obligation is satisfied. In this case, revenue is not recognized until Best Buy provides the goods. Thus, when Best Buy receives cash in exchange for the gift card on December 24, 2013, it should recognize a liability, Unearned Revenue, for $100. On January 3, 2014, when Mary Jones exchanges the card for merchandise, Best Buy should recognize revenue and eliminate $100 from the balance in the Unearned Revenue account.

p. 116 Cashing In on Accrual Accounting Q: Accrual accounting is often considered superior to cash accounting. Why, then, were some people critical of China's use of accrual accounting in this instance? **A:** In this case, some people were critical because, in general, China uses cash accounting. By switching to accrual accounting for this transaction, China was not being consistent in its accounting practices. Lack of consistency reduces the transparency and usefulness of accounting information.

p. 118 Got Junk? Q: What accounting issue might this cause for companies? **A:** The balance sheet should provide a fair representation of what a company owns and what it owes. If significant obligations of the company are not reported on the balance sheet, the company's net worth (its equity) will be overstated. While it is true that it is not possible to estimate the *exact* amount of future environmental cleanup costs, it is becoming clear that companies will be held accountable. Therefore, it doesn't seem reasonable to not accrue for environmental costs. Recognition of these liabilities provides a more accurate picture of the company's financial position. It also has the potential to improve the environment. As companies are forced to report these amounts on their financial statements, they will start to look for more effective and efficient means to reduce toxic waste and therefore reduce their costs.

Answers to Self-Test Questions

1. c **2.** c **3.** d **4.** a **5.** d **6.** d **7.** c ($1,350 − $600) **8.** c **9.** a **10.** c **11.** a **12.** b **13.** b **14.** c ***15.** a ***16.** c ***17.** b

A Look at IFRS

It is often difficult for companies to determine in what time period they should report particular revenues and expenses. Both the IASB and FASB are working on a joint project to develop a common conceptual framework, as well as a revenue recognition project, that will enable companies to better use the same principles to record transactions consistently over time.

Key Points

- In this chapter, you learned accrual basis accounting applied under GAAP. Companies applying IFRS also use accrual-basis accounting to ensure that they record transactions that change a company's financial statements in the period in which events occur.
- Similar to GAAP, cash-basis accounting is not in accordance with IFRS.
- IFRS also divides the economic life of companies into artificial time periods. Under both GAAP and IFRS, this is referred to as the *time period assumption*.
- IFRS requires that companies present a complete set of financial statements, including comparative information annually.
- The **general** revenue recognition principles required by GAAP that are used in this textbook are similar to those under IFRS.
- As the Feature Story illustrates, revenue recognition fraud is a major issue in U.S. financial reporting. The same situation occurs in other countries, as evidenced by revenue recognition breakdowns at Dutch software company Baan NV, Japanese electronics giant NEC, and Dutch grocer Ahold NV.
- Under IFRS, revaluation of items such as land and buildings is permitted. IFRS allows depreciation based on revaluation of assets, which is not permitted under GAAP.
- The terminology used for revenues and gains, and expenses and losses, differs somewhat between IFRS and GAAP. For example, income under IFRS is defined as:

  Increases in economic benefits during the accounting period in the form of inflows or enhancements of assets or decreases of liabilities that result in increases in equity, other than those relating to contributions from shareholders.

Income includes *both* revenues, which arise during the normal course of operating activities, and gains, which arise from activities outside of the normal sales of goods and services. The term income is not used this way under GAAP. Instead, under GAAP income refers to the net difference between revenues and expenses. Expenses under IFRS are defined as:

> Decreases in economic benefits during the accounting period in the form of outflows or depletions of assets or incurrences of liabilities that result in decreases in equity other than those relating to distributions to shareholders.

Note that under IFRS, expenses include both those costs incurred in the normal course of operations, as well as losses that are not part of normal operations. This is in contrast to GAAP, which defines each separately.

Looking to the Future

The IASB and FASB have recently completed a joint project on revenue recognition. The purpose of this project was to develop comprehensive guidance on when to recognize revenue. This approach focuses on changes in assets and liabilities as the basis for revenue recognition. It is hoped that this approach will lead to more consistent accounting in this area. For more on this topic, see *www.fasb.org/project/revenue_recognition.shtml*.

IFRS Practice

IFRS Self-Test Questions

1. GAAP:
(a) provides the same type of guidance as IFRS for revenue recognition.
(b) provides only general guidance on revenue recognition, compared to the detailed guidance provided by IFRS.
(c) allows revenue to be recognized when a customer makes an order.
(d) requires that revenue not be recognized until cash is received.

2. Which of the following statements is *false*?
(a) IFRS employs the time period assumption.
(b) IFRS employs accrual accounting.
(c) IFRS requires that revenues and costs must be capable of being measured reliably.
(d) IFRS uses the cash basis of accounting.

3. As a result of the revenue recognition project by the FASB and IASB:
(a) revenue recognition places more emphasis on when the service obligation is satisfied.
(b) revenue recognition places more emphasis on when revenue is realized.
(c) revenue recognition places more emphasis on when changes occur in assets and liabilities.
(d) revenue is no longer recorded unless cash has been received.

4. Which of the following is *false*?
(a) Under IFRS, the term *income* describes both revenues and gains.
(b) Under IFRS, the term *expenses* includes losses.
(c) Under IFRS, firms do not engage in the closing process.
(d) IFRS has fewer standards than GAAP that address revenue recognition.

5. Accrual-basis accounting:
(a) is optional under IFRS.
(b) results in companies recording transactions that change a company's financial statements in the period in which events occur.
(c) has been eliminated as a result of the IASB/FASB joint project on revenue recognition.
(d) is not consistent with the IASB conceptual framework.

IFRS Exercises

IFRS3-1 Compare and contrast the rules regarding revenue recognition under IFRS versus GAAP.

IFRS3-2 Under IFRS, do the definitions of revenues and expenses include gains and losses? Explain.

International Financial Reporting Problem: Zetar plc

IFRS3-3 The financial statements of Zetar plc are presented in Appendix C. The company's complete annual report, including the notes to its financial statements, is available at *www.zetarplc.com*.

Instructions

Visit Zetar's corporate website and answer the following questions from Zetar's 2010 annual report.

(a) From the notes to the financial statements, how does the company determine the amount of revenue to record at the time of a sale?

(b) From the notes to the financial statements, how does the company determine whether a sale has occurred?

(c) Using the consolidated income statement and consolidated statement of financial position, identify items that may result in adjusting entries for deferrals.

(d) Using the consolidated income statement, identify two items that may result in adjusting entries for accruals.

Answers to IFRS Self-Test Questions

1. a **2.** d **3.** c **4.** c **5.** b

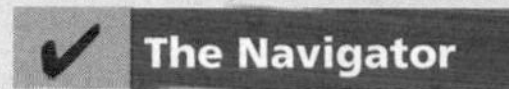

✔ Remember to go back to The Navigator box on the chapter opening page and check off your completed work.

Chapter 4

Completing the Accounting Cycle

Feature Story

Everyone Likes to Win

When Ted Castle was a hockey coach at the University of Vermont, his players were self-motivated by their desire to win. Hockey was a game you either won or lost. But at Rhino Foods, Inc., a bakery-foods company he founded in Burlington, Vermont, he discovered that manufacturing-line workers were not so self-motivated. Ted thought, what if he turned the food-making business into a game, with rules, strategies, and trophies?

Ted knew that in a game, knowing the score is all-important. He felt only if the employees know the score—know exactly how the business is doing daily, weekly, monthly—could he turn food-making into a game. But Rhino is a closely held, family-owned business, and its financial statements and profits were confidential. Ted wondered, should he open Rhino's books to the employees?

A consultant put Ted's concerns in perspective when he said, "Imagine you're playing touch football. You play for an hour or two, and the whole time I'm sitting there with a book, keeping score. All of a sudden I blow the whistle, and I say, 'OK, that's it. Everybody go home.' I close my book and walk away. How would you feel?" Ted opened his books and revealed the financial statements to his employees.

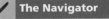

✔ The Navigator

- Scan Learning Objectives
- Read Feature Story
- Read Preview
- Read text and answer **DO IT!** p. 169 ☐ p. 173 ☐ p. 183 ☐ p. 186
- Work Comprehensive **DO IT!** p. 187
- Review Summary of Learning Objectives
- Answer Self-Test Questions
- Complete Assignments
- Go to **WileyPLUS** for practice and tutorials
-  Read A Look at IFRS p. 214

Learning Objectives

After studying this chapter, you should be able to:

1. Prepare a worksheet.
2. Explain the process of closing the books.
3. Describe the content and purpose of a post-closing trial balance.
4. State the required steps in the accounting cycle.
5. Explain the approaches to preparing correcting entries.
6. Identify the sections of a classified balance sheet.

 **The Navigator**

The next step was to teach employees the rules and strategies of how to "win" at making food. The first lesson: "Your opponent at Rhino is expenses. You must cut and control expenses." Ted and his staff distilled those lessons into daily scorecards—production reports and income statements—that keep Rhino's employees up-to-date on the game. At noon each day, Ted posts the previous day's results at the entrance to the production room. Everyone checks whether they made or lost money on what they produced the day before. And it's not just an academic exercise: There's a bonus check for each employee at the end of every four-week "game" that meets profitability guidelines.

Rhino has flourished since the first game. Employment has increased from 20 to 130 people, while both revenues and profits have grown dramatically.

Preview of Chapter 4

At Rhino Foods, Inc., financial statements help employees understand what is happening in the business. In Chapter 3, we prepared financial statements directly from the adjusted trial balance. However, with so many details involved in the end-of-period accounting procedures, it is easy to make errors. One way to minimize errors in the records and to simplify the end-of-period procedures is to use a worksheet.

In this chapter, we will explain the role of the worksheet in accounting. We also will study the remaining steps in the accounting cycle, especially the closing process, again using Pioneer Advertising Agency Inc. as an example. Then we will consider correcting entries and classified balance sheets. The content and organization of Chapter 4 are as follows.

COMPLETING THE ACCOUNTING CYCLE

Using a Worksheet	Closing the Books	Summary of Accounting Cycle	Classified Balance Sheet
• Steps in preparation • Preparing financial statements • Preparing adjusting entries	• Preparing closing entries • Posting closing entries • Preparing a post-closing trial balance	• Reversing entries—An optional step • Correcting entries—An avoidable step	• Current assets • Long-term investments • Property, plant, and equipment • Intangible assets • Current liabilities • Long-term liabilities • Stockholders' equity

✔ The Navigator

Using a Worksheet

LEARNING OBJECTIVE 1

Prepare a worksheet.

A **worksheet** is a multiple-column form used in the adjustment process and in preparing financial statements. As its name suggests, the worksheet is a working tool. **It is not a permanent accounting record**; it is neither a journal nor a part of the general ledger. The worksheet is merely a device used in preparing adjusting entries and the financial statements. Companies generally computerize worksheets using an electronic spreadsheet program such as Excel.

Illustration 4-1 shows the basic form of a worksheet and the five steps for preparing it. Each step is performed in sequence. **The use of a worksheet is optional.** When a company chooses to use one, it prepares financial statements from the worksheet. It enters the adjustments in the worksheet columns and then journalizes and posts the adjustments after it has prepared the financial statements. Thus, worksheets make it possible to provide the financial statements to management and other interested parties at an earlier date.

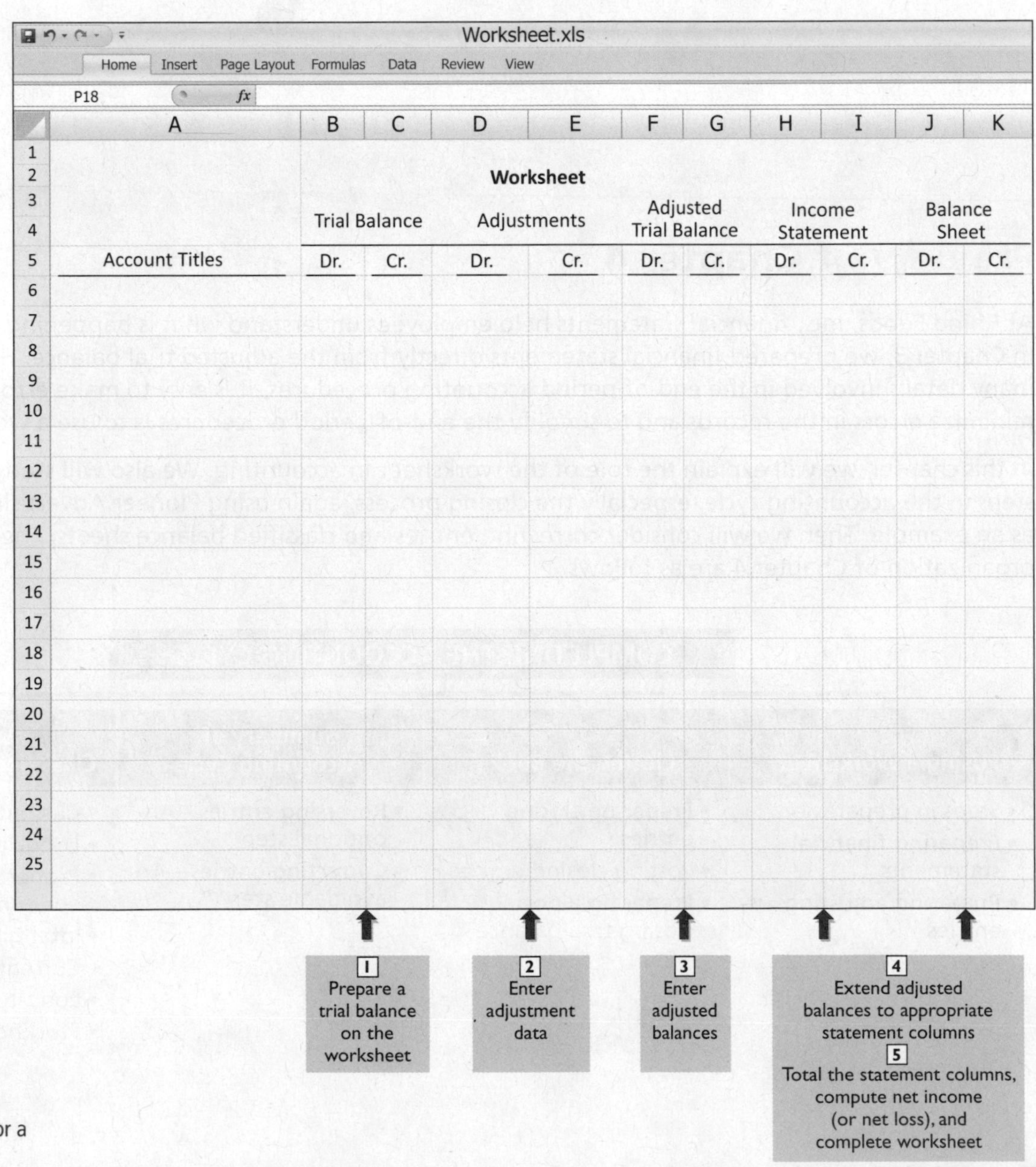

Illustration 4-1
Form and procedure for a worksheet

Steps in Preparing a Worksheet

We will use the October 31 trial balance and adjustment data of Pioneer Advertising Agency Inc., from Chapter 3, to illustrate how to prepare a worksheet. We describe each step of the process and demonstrate these steps in Illustration 4-2 (page 166) and transparencies 4-3A, B, C, and D.

STEP 1. PREPARE A TRIAL BALANCE ON THE WORKSHEET

Enter all ledger accounts with balances in the account titles space. Enter debit and credit amounts from the ledger in the trial balance columns. Illustration 4-2 shows the worksheet trial balance for Pioneer Advertising Agency Inc. This trial balance is the same one that appears in Illustration 2-32 (page 74) and Illustration 3-3 (page 105).

STEP 2. ENTER THE ADJUSTMENTS IN THE ADJUSTMENTS COLUMNS

Turn over the first transparency, Illustration 4-3A. When using a worksheet, enter all adjustments in the adjustments columns. In entering the adjustments, use applicable trial balance accounts. If additional accounts are needed, insert them on the lines immediately below the trial balance totals. A different letter identifies the debit and credit for each adjusting entry. The term used to describe this process is **keying**. **Companies do not journalize the adjustments until after they complete the worksheet and prepare the financial statements.**

The adjustments for Pioneer Advertising Agency Inc. are the same as the adjustments in Illustration 3-23 (page 119). They are keyed in the adjustments columns of the worksheet as follows.

(a) Pioneer debits an additional account, Supplies Expense, $1,500 for the cost of supplies used, and credits Supplies $1,500.

(b) Pioneer debits an additional account, Insurance Expense, $50 for the insurance that has expired, and credits Prepaid Insurance $50.

(c) The company needs two additional depreciation accounts. It debits Depreciation Expense $40 for the month's depreciation, and credits Accumulated Depreciation—Equipment $40.

(d) Pioneer debits Unearned Service Revenue $400 for services provided, and credits Service Revenue $400.

(e) Pioneer debits an additional account, Accounts Receivable, $200 for services provided but not billed, and credits Service Revenue $200.

(f) The company needs two additional accounts relating to interest. It debits Interest Expense $50 for accrued interest, and credits Interest Payable $50.

(g) Pioneer debits Salaries and Wages Expense $1,200 for accrued salaries, and credits an additional account, Salaries and Wages Payable, $1,200.

After Pioneer has entered all the adjustments, the adjustments columns are totaled to prove their equality.

STEP 3. ENTER ADJUSTED BALANCES IN THE ADJUSTED TRIAL BALANCE COLUMNS

Turn over the second transparency, Illustration 4-3B. Pioneer determines the adjusted balance of an account by combining the amounts entered in the first four columns of the worksheet for each account. For example, the Prepaid Insurance account in the trial balance columns has a $600 debit balance and a $50 credit in the adjustments columns. The result is a $550 debit balance recorded in the adjusted trial balance columns. **For each account, the amount**

(**Note:** Text continues on page 167, following acetate overlays.)

Illustration 4-2
Preparing a trial balance

Pioneer Advertising.xls

Home Insert Page Layout Formulas Data Review View

P18 fx

Pioneer Advertising Agency Inc.
Worksheet
For the Month Ended October 31, 2014

Account Titles	Trial Balance Dr.	Trial Balance Cr.	Adjustments Dr.	Adjustments Cr.	Adjusted Trial Balance Dr.	Adjusted Trial Balance Cr.	Income Statement Dr.	Income Statement Cr.	Balance Sheet Dr.	Balance Sheet Cr.
Cash	15,200									
Supplies	2,500									
Prepaid Insurance	600									
Equipment	5,000									
Notes Payable		5,000								
Accounts Payable		2,500								
Unearned Service Revenue		1,200								
Common Stock		10,000								
Dividends	500									
Service Revenue		10,000								
Salaries and Wages Expense	4,000									
Rent Expense	900									
Totals	28,700	28,700								

Include all accounts with balances from ledger.

Trial balance amounts come directly from ledger accounts.

in the adjusted trial balance columns is the balance that will appear in the ledger after journalizing and posting the adjusting entries. The balances in these columns are the same as those in the adjusted trial balance in Illustration 3-25 (page 121).

After Pioneer has entered all account balances in the adjusted trial balance columns, the columns are totaled to prove their equality. If the column totals do not agree, the financial statement columns will not balance and the financial statements will be incorrect.

STEP 4. EXTEND ADJUSTED TRIAL BALANCE AMOUNTS TO APPROPRIATE FINANCIAL STATEMENT COLUMNS

Turn over the third transparency, Illustration 4-3C. The fourth step is to extend adjusted trial balance amounts to the income statement and balance sheet columns of the worksheet. Pioneer enters balance sheet accounts in the appropriate balance sheet debit and credit columns. For instance, it enters Cash in the balance sheet debit column, and Notes Payable in the credit column. Pioneer extends Accumulated Depreciation—Equipment to the balance sheet credit column; the reason is that accumulated depreciation is a contra-asset account with a credit balance.

Helpful Hint
Every adjusted trial balance amount must be extended to one of the four statement columns.

Because the worksheet does not have columns for the retained earnings statement, Pioneer extends the balance in Common Stock and Retained Earnings, if any, to the balance sheet credit column. In addition, it extends the balance in Dividends to the balance sheet debit column because it is a stockholders' equity account with a debit balance.

The company enters the expense and revenue accounts such as Salaries and Wages Expense and Service Revenue in the appropriate income statement columns. Illustration 4-3C shows all of these extensions.

STEP 5. TOTAL THE STATEMENT COLUMNS, COMPUTE THE NET INCOME (OR NET LOSS), AND COMPLETE THE WORKSHEET

Turn over the fourth transparency, Illustration 4-3D. The company now must total each of the financial statement columns. The net income or loss for the period is the difference between the totals of the two income statement columns. If total credits exceed total debits, the result is net income. In such a case, as shown in Illustration 4-3D, the company inserts the words "Net Income" in the account titles space. It then enters the amount in the income statement debit column and the balance sheet credit column. **The debit amount balances the income statement columns; the credit amount balances the balance sheet columns.** In addition, the credit in the balance sheet column indicates the increase in stockholders' equity resulting from net income.

What if total debits in the income statement columns exceed total credits? In that case, the company has a net loss. It enters the amount of the net loss in the income statement credit column and the balance sheet debit column.

After entering the net income or net loss, the company determines new column totals. The totals shown in the debit and credit income statement columns will match. So will the totals shown in the debit and credit balance sheet columns. If either the income statement columns or the balance sheet columns are not equal after the net income or net loss has been entered, there is an error in the worksheet. Illustration 4-3D shows the completed worksheet for Pioneer Advertising Agency Inc.

Preparing Financial Statements from a Worksheet

After a company has completed a worksheet, it has at hand all the data required for preparation of financial statements. The income statement is prepared from the income statement columns. The balance sheet and retained earnings statement are prepared from the balance sheet columns. Illustration 4-4 (page 168)

Illustration 4-4
Financial statements from a worksheet

Pioneer Advertising Agency Inc.
Income Statement
For the Month Ended October 31, 2014

Revenues		
Service revenue		$10,600
Expenses		
Salaries and wages expense	$5,200	
Supplies expense	1,500	
Rent expense	900	
Insurance expense	50	
Interest expense	50	
Depreciation expense	40	
Total expenses		7,740
Net income		$ 2,860

Pioneer Advertising Agency Inc.
Retained Earnings Statement
For the Month Ended October 31, 2014

Retained earnings, October 1	$ -0-
Add: Net income	2,860
	2,860
Less: Dividends	500
Retained earnings, October 31	$2,360

Pioneer Advertising Agency Inc.
Balance Sheet
October 31, 2014

Assets

Cash		$15,200
Accounts receivable		200
Supplies		1,000
Prepaid insurance		550
Equipment	$5,000	
Less: Accumulated depreciation—equipment	40	4,960
Total assets		$21,910

Liabilities and Stockholders' Equity

Liabilities		
Notes payable	$5,000	
Accounts payable	2,500	
Interest payable	50	
Unearned service revenue	800	
Salaries and wages payable	1,200	
Total liabilities		$ 9,550
Stockholders' equity		
Common stock	10,000	
Retained earnings	2,360	
Total stockholders' equity		12,360
Total liabilities and stockholders' equity		$21,910

shows the financial statements prepared from Pioneer's worksheet. At this point, the company has not journalized or posted adjusting entries. Therefore, ledger balances for some accounts are not the same as the financial statement amounts.

The amount shown for common stock on the worksheet does not change from the beginning to the end of the period unless the company issues additional stock during the period. Because there was no balance in Pioneer's retained earnings, the account is not listed on the worksheet. Only after dividends and net income (or loss) are posted to retained earnings does this account have a balance at the end of the first year of the business.

Accounting Cycle Tutorial—Preparing Financial Statements and Closing the Books

Using a worksheet, companies can prepare financial statements before they journalize and post adjusting entries. **However, the completed worksheet is not a substitute for formal financial statements.** The format of the data in the financial statement columns of the worksheet is not the same as the format of the financial statements. **A worksheet is essentially a working tool of the accountant**; companies do not distribute it to management and other parties.

Preparing Adjusting Entries from a Worksheet

A worksheet is not a journal, and it cannot be used as a basis for posting to ledger accounts. To adjust the accounts, the company must journalize the adjustments and post them to the ledger. **The adjusting entries are prepared from the adjustments columns of the worksheet.** The reference letters in the adjustments columns and the explanations of the adjustments at the bottom of the worksheet help identify the adjusting entries. The journalizing and posting of adjusting entries **follows** the preparation of financial statements when a worksheet is used. The adjusting entries on October 31 for Pioneer Advertising Agency Inc. are the same as those shown in Illustration 3-23 (page 119).

Helpful Hint
Note that writing the explanation to the adjustment at the bottom of the worksheet is not required.

> DO IT!

Worksheet

Susan Elbe is preparing a worksheet. Explain to Susan how she should extend the following adjusted trial balance accounts to the financial statement columns of the worksheet.

Cash
Accumulated Depreciation
Accounts Payable
Dividends
Service Revenue
Salaries and Wages Expense

Action Plan

✔ Balance sheet: Extend assets to debit column. Extend liabilities to credit column. Extend contra assets to credit column. Extend dividends account to debit column.

✔ Income statement: Extend expenses to debit column. Extend revenues to credit column.

Solution

Income statement debit column—Salaries and Wages Expense
Income statement credit column—Service Revenue
Balance sheet debit column—Cash; Dividends
Balance sheet credit column—Accumulated Depreciation; Accounts Payable

Related exercise material: **BE4-1, BE4-2, BE4-3, E4-1, E4-2, E4-5, E4-6, and**  **4-1.**

✔ **The Navigator**

Closing the Books

LEARNING OBJECTIVE 2

Explain the process of closing the books.

At the end of the accounting period, the company makes the accounts ready for the next period. This is called **closing the books**. In closing the books, the company distinguishes between temporary and permanent accounts.

Temporary accounts relate only to a given accounting period. They include all income statement accounts and the Dividends account. **The company closes all temporary accounts at the end of the period.**

In contrast, **permanent accounts** relate to one or more future accounting periods. They consist of all balance sheet accounts, including stockholders' equity accounts. **Permanent accounts are not closed from period to period.** Instead, the company carries forward the balances of permanent accounts into the next accounting period. Illustration 4-5 identifies the accounts in each category.

Alternative Terminology
Temporary accounts are sometimes called *nominal accounts*, and permanent accounts are sometimes called *real accounts*.

Illustration 4-5
Temporary versus permanent accounts

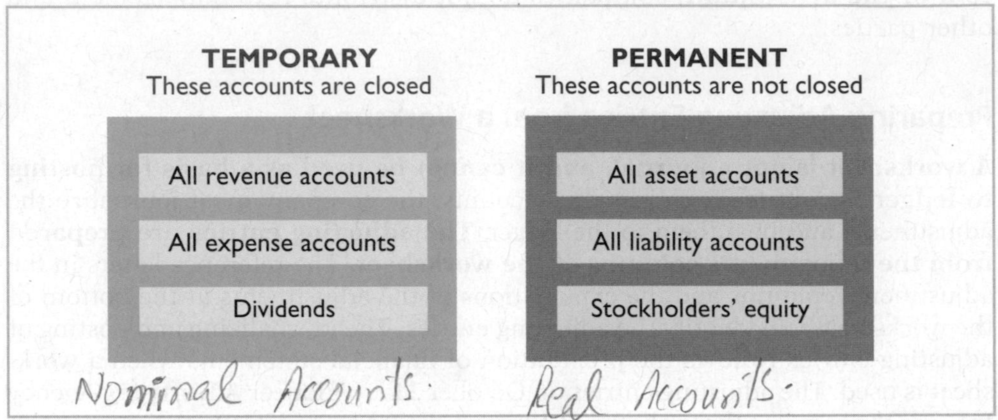

Helpful Hint
A contra-asset account, such as accumulated depreciation, is a permanent account also.

Preparing Closing Entries

At the end of the accounting period, the company transfers temporary account balances to the permanent stockholders' equity account, Retained Earnings, by means of closing entries.

Closing entries formally recognize in the ledger the transfer of net income (or net loss) and Dividends to Retained Earnings. The retained earnings statement shows the results of these entries. **Closing entries also produce a zero balance in each temporary account.** The temporary accounts are then ready to accumulate data in the next accounting period separate from the data of prior periods. Permanent accounts are not closed.

Journalizing and posting closing entries is a required step in the accounting cycle. (See Illustration 4-12 on page 177.) The company performs this step after it has prepared financial statements. In contrast to the steps in the cycle that you have already studied, companies generally journalize and post closing entries **only at the end of the annual accounting period**. Thus, all temporary accounts will contain data for the entire year.

In preparing closing entries, companies could close each income statement account directly to Retained Earnings. However, to do so would result in excessive detail in the permanent Retained Earnings account. Instead, companies close the revenue and expense accounts to another temporary account, **Income Summary**, and they transfer the resulting net income or net loss from this account to Retained Earnings.

Companies **record closing entries in the general journal**. A center caption, Closing Entries, inserted in the journal between the last adjusting entry and the first closing entry, identifies these entries. Then the company posts the closing entries to the ledger accounts.

Companies generally prepare closing entries directly from the adjusted balances in the ledger. They could prepare separate closing entries for each nominal account, but the following four entries accomplish the desired result more efficiently:

1. Debit each revenue account for its balance, and credit Income Summary for total revenues.
2. Debit Income Summary for total expenses, and credit each expense account for its balance.
3. Debit Income Summary and credit Retained Earnings for the amount of net income.
4. Debit Retained Earnings for the balance in the Dividends account, and credit Dividends for the same amount.

Helpful Hint
Dividends is closed directly to Retained Earnings and *not* to Income Summary because Dividends is not an expense.

Illustration 4-6 presents a diagram of the closing process. In it, the boxed numbers refer to the four entries required in the closing process.

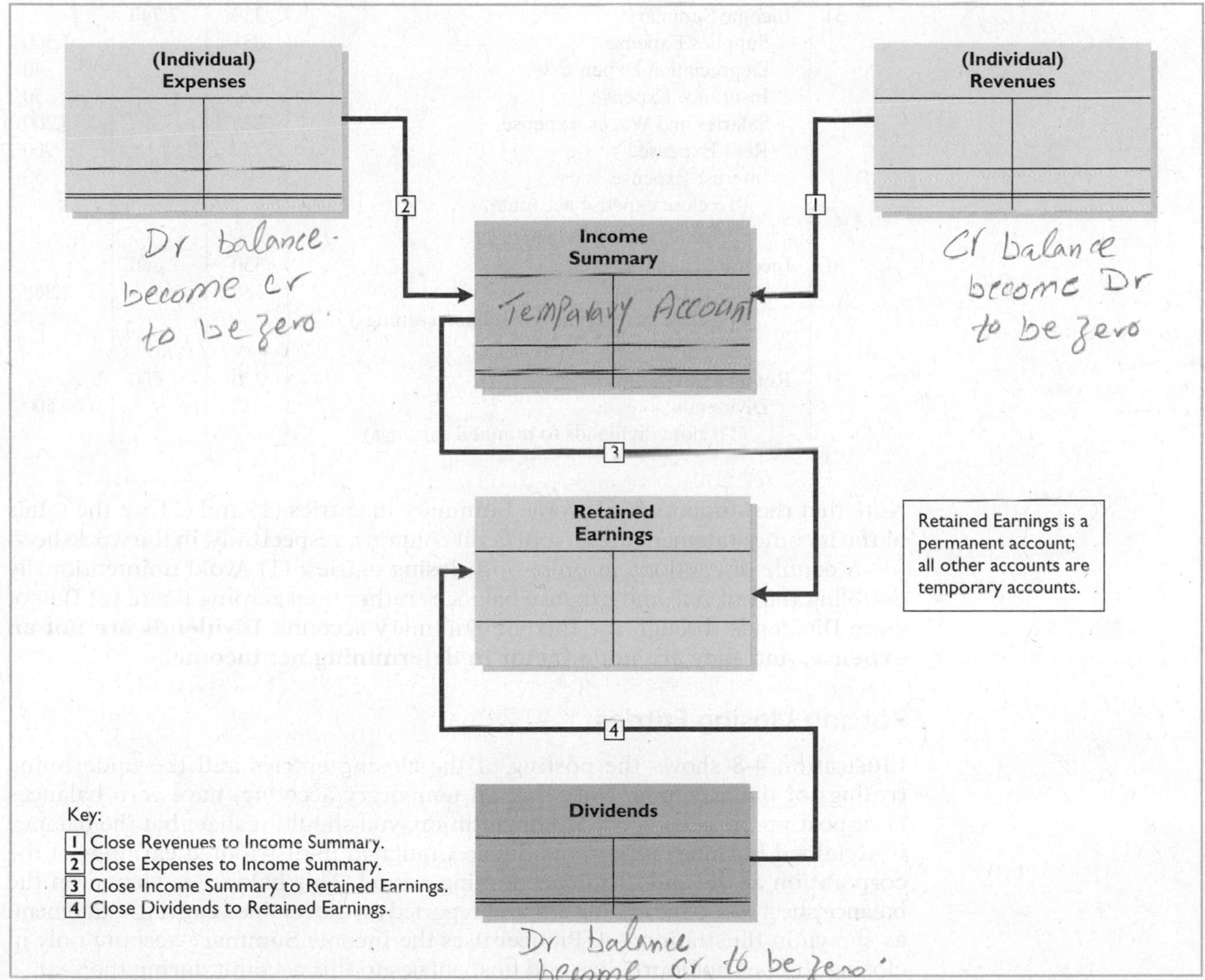

Illustration 4-6
Diagram of closing process—proprietorship

If there were a net loss (because expenses exceeded revenues), entry 3 in Illustration 4-6 would be reversed: there would be a credit to Income Summary and a debit to Retained Earnings.

CLOSING ENTRIES ILLUSTRATED

In practice, companies generally prepare closing entries only at the end of the annual accounting period. However, to illustrate the journalizing and posting of closing entries, we will assume that Pioneer Advertising Agency Inc. closes its books monthly. Illustration 4-7 shows the closing entries at October 31. (The numbers in parentheses before each entry correspond to the four entries diagrammed in Illustration 4-6.)

Illustration 4-7
Closing entries journalized

E4-7

General Journal J3

Date	Account Titles and Explanation	Ref.	Debit	Credit
	Closing Entries			
2014	(1)			
Oct. 31	Service Revenue	400	10,600	
	Income Summary	350		10,600
	(To close revenue account)			
	(2)			
31	Income Summary	350	7,740	
	Supplies Expense	631		1,500
	Depreciation Expense	711		40
	Insurance Expense	722		50
	Salaries and Wages Expense	726		5,200
	Rent Expense	729		900
	Interest Expense	905		50
	(To close expense accounts)			
	(3)			
31	Income Summary	350	2,860	
	Retained Earnings	320		2,860
	(To close net income to retained earnings)			
	(4)			
31	Retained Earnings	320	500	
	Dividends	332		500
	(To close dividends to retained earnings)			

Note that the amounts for Income Summary in entries (1) and (2) are the totals of the income statement credit and debit columns, respectively, in the worksheet.

A couple of cautions in preparing closing entries: (1) Avoid unintentionally doubling the revenue and expense balances rather than zeroing them. (2) Do not close Dividends through the Income Summary account. **Dividends are not an expense, and they are not a factor in determining net income.**

Posting Closing Entries

Illustration 4-8 shows the posting of the closing entries and the underlining (ruling) of the accounts. Note that all temporary accounts have zero balances after posting the closing entries. In addition, you should realize that the balance in Retained Earnings represents the accumulated undistributed earnings of the corporation at the end of the accounting period. This balance is shown on the balance sheet and is the ending amount reported on the retained earnings statement, as shown in Illustration 4-4. Pioneer uses the Income Summary account only in closing. It does not journalize and post entries to this account during the year.

Helpful Hint
The balance in Income Summary before it is closed must equal the net income or net loss for the period.

As part of the closing process, Pioneer totals, balances, and double-underlines its temporary accounts—revenues, expenses, and Dividends, as shown in T-account form in Illustration 4-8. It does not close its permanent accounts—assets, liabilities, and stockholders' equity (Common Stock and Retained Earnings). Instead, Pioneer draws a single underline beneath the current-period entries for the permanent accounts. The account balance is then entered below the single rule and is carried forward to the next period. (For example, see Retained Earnings.)

Supplies Expense 631

1,500	(2)	1,500

Depreciation Expense 711

40	(2)	40

Insurance Expense 722

50	(2)	50

Salaries and Wages Expense 726

4,000	(2)	5,200
1,200		
5,200		5,200

Rent Expense 729

900	(2)	900

Interest Expense 905

50	(2)	50

Service Revenue 400

(1)	10,600	10,000
		400
		200
	10,600	10,600

Income Summary 350

(2)	7,740	(1)	10,600
(3)	2,860		
	10,600		10,600

Retained Earnings 320

(4)	500	(3)	2,860
		Bal.	2,360

Dividends 332

500	(4)	500

Key:
1 Close Revenues to Income Summary.
2 Close Expenses to Income Summary.
3 Close Income Summary to Retained Earnings.
4 Close Dividends to Retained Earnings.

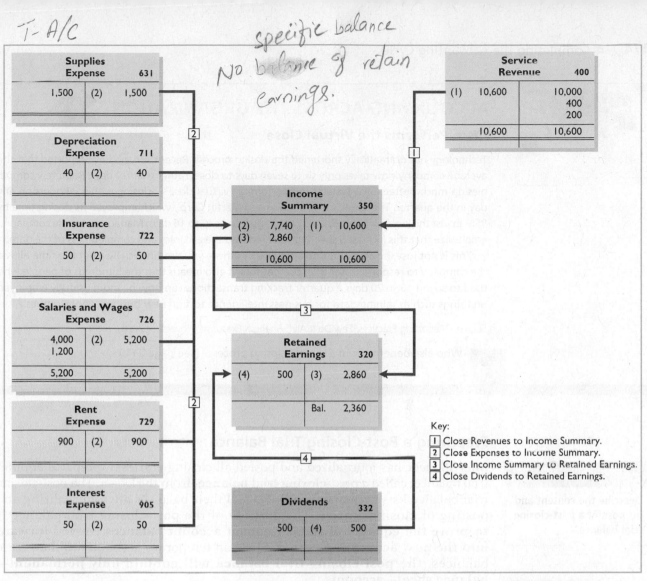

Illustration 4-8
Posting of closing entries

> DO IT!

Closing Entries

The worksheet for Hancock Company shows the following in the financial statement columns:

Dividends $15,000
Common stock $42,000
Net income $18,000

Prepare the closing entries at December 31 that affect stockholders' equity.

Action Plan

✔ Close Income Summary to Retained Earnings.

✔ Close Dividends to Retained Earnings.

Solution

Dec. 31	Income Summary	18,000	
	Retained Earnings		18,000
	(To close net income to retained earnings)		
31	Retained Earnings	15,000	
	Dividends		15,000
	(To close dividends to retained earnings)		

Related exercise material: **BE4-4, BE4-5, BE4-6, E4-4, E4-7, E4-8, E4-10, E4-11, and DO IT! 4-2.**

ACCOUNTING ACROSS THE ORGANIZATION

Cisco Performs the Virtual Close

Technology has dramatically shortened the closing process. Recent surveys have reported that the average company now takes only six to seven days to close, rather than 20 days. But a few companies do much better. Cisco Systems can perform a "virtual close"—closing within 24 hours on any day in the quarter. The same is true at Lockheed Martin Corp., which improved its closing time by 85% in just the last few years. Not very long ago it took 14 to 16 days. Managers at these companies emphasize that this increased speed has not reduced the accuracy and completeness of the data.

This is not just showing off. Knowing exactly where you are financially all of the time allows the company to respond faster than competitors. It also means that the hundreds of people who used to spend 10 to 20 days a quarter tracking transactions can now be more usefully employed on things such as mining data for business intelligence to find new business opportunities.

Source: "Reporting Practices: Few Do It All," *Financial Executive* (November 2003), p. 11.

? Who else benefits from a shorter closing process? (See page 214.)

Preparing a Post-Closing Trial Balance

LEARNING OBJECTIVE 3

Describe the content and purpose of a post-closing trial balance.

After Pioneer has journalized and posted all closing entries, it prepares another trial balance, called a **post-closing trial balance**, from the ledger. The post-closing trial balance lists permanent accounts and their balances after journalizing and posting of closing entries. The purpose of the post-closing trial balance is **to prove the equality of the permanent account balances carried forward into the next accounting period**. Since all temporary accounts will have zero balances, **the post-closing trial balance will contain only permanent—balance sheet—accounts.**

Illustration 4-9 shows the post-closing trial balance for Pioneer Advertising Agency Inc.

Illustration 4-9
Post-closing trial balance

Pioneer Advertising Agency Inc.
Post-Closing Trial Balance
October 31, 2014

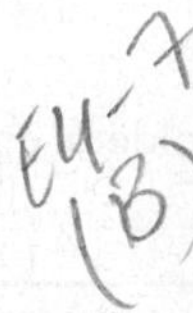

	Debit	Credit
Cash	$15,200	
Accounts Receivable	200	
Supplies	1,000	
Prepaid Insurance	550	
Equipment	5,000	
Accumulated Depreciation—Equipment		$ 40
Notes Payable		5,000
Accounts Payable		2,500
Unearned Service Revenue		800
Salaries and Wages Payable		1,200
Interest Payable		50
Common Stock		10,000
Retained Earnings		2,360
	$21,950	**$21,950**

Pioneer prepares the post-closing trial balance from the permanent accounts in the ledger. Illustration 4-10 shows the permanent accounts in Pioneer's general ledger.

Illustration 4-10
General ledger, permanent accounts

(Permanent Accounts Only)

General Ledger

Cash — No. 101

Date	Explanation	Ref.	Debit	Credit	Balance
2014					
Oct. 1		J1	10,000		10,000
2		J1	1,200		11,200
3		J1		900	10,300
4		J1		600	9,700
20		J1		500	9,200
26		J1		4,000	5,200
31		J1	10,000		**15,200**

Accounts Receivable — No. 112

Date	Explanation	Ref.	Debit	Credit	Balance
2014					
Oct. 31	Adj. entry	J2	**200**		**200**

Supplies — No. 126

Date	Explanation	Ref.	Debit	Credit	Balance
2014					
Oct. 5		J1	2,500		2,500
31	Adj. entry	J2		**1,500**	**1,000**

Prepaid Insurance — No. 130

Date	Explanation	Ref.	Debit	Credit	Balance
2014					
Oct. 4		J1	600		600
31	Adj. entry	J2		**50**	**550**

Equipment — No. 157

Date	Explanation	Ref.	Debit	Credit	Balance
2014					
Oct. 1		J1	5,000		**5,000**

Accumulated Depreciation—Equipment — No. 158

Date	Explanation	Ref.	Debit	Credit	Balance
2014					
Oct. 31	Adj. entry	J2		**40**	**40**

Notes Payable — No. 200

Date	Explanation	Ref.	Debit	Credit	Balance
2014					
Oct. 1		J1		5,000	**5,000**

Accounts Payable — No. 201

Date	Explanation	Ref.	Debit	Credit	Balance
2014					
Oct. 5		J1		2,500	**2,500**

Unearned Service Revenue — No. 209

Date	Explanation	Ref.	Debit	Credit	Balance
2014					
Oct. 2		J1		1,200	1,200
31	Adj. entry	J2	400		**800**

Salaries and Wages Payable — No. 212

Date	Explanation	Ref.	Debit	Credit	Balance
2014					
Oct. 31	Adj. entry	J2		**1,200**	**1,200**

Interest Payable — No. 230

Date	Explanation	Ref.	Debit	Credit	Balance
2014					
Oct. 31	Adj. entry	J2		**50**	**50**

Common Stock — No. 311

Date	Explanation	Ref.	Debit	Credit	Balance
2014					
Oct. 1		J1		10,000	10,000

Retained Earnings — No. 320

Date	Explanation	Ref.	Debit	Credit	Balance
2014					
Oct. 1					–0–
31	**Closing entry**	**J3**		**2,860**	**2,860**
31	**Closing entry**	**J3**	**500**		**2,360**

Note: The permanent accounts for Pioneer Advertising Agency Inc. are shown here; the temporary accounts are shown in Illustration 4-11. Both permanent and temporary accounts are part of the general ledger; we segregated them here to aid in learning.

A post-closing trial balance provides evidence that the company has properly journalized and posted the closing entries. It also shows that the accounting equation is in balance at the end of the accounting period. However, like the trial balance, it does not prove that Pioneer has recorded all transactions or that the ledger is correct.

For example, the post-closing trial balance still will balance even if a transaction is not journalized and posted or if a transaction is journalized and posted twice.

The remaining accounts in the general ledger are temporary accounts, shown in Illustration 4-11. After Pioneer correctly posts the closing entries, each temporary account has a zero balance. These accounts are double-underlined to finalize the closing process.

Illustration 4-11
General ledger, temporary accounts

(Temporary Accounts Only)

General Ledger

Dividends — No. 332

Date	Explanation	Ref.	Debit	Credit	Balance
2014					
Oct. 20		J1	500		500
31	**Closing entry**	**J3**		**500**	**–0–**

Insurance Expense — No. 722

Date	Explanation	Ref.	Debit	Credit	Balance
2014					
Oct. 31	Adj. entry	J2	**50**		50
31	**Closing entry**	**J3**		**50**	**–0–**

Income Summary — No. 350

Date	Explanation	Ref.	Debit	Credit	Balance
2014					
Oct. 31	**Closing entry**	**J3**		**10,600**	**10,600**
31	**Closing entry**	**J3**	**7,740**		**2,860**
31	**Closing entry**	**J3**	**2,860**		**–0–**

Salaries and Wages Expense — No. 726

Date	Explanation	Ref.	Debit	Credit	Balance
2014					
Oct. 26		J1	4,000		4,000
31	Adj. entry	J2	**1,200**		5,200
31	**Closing entry**	**J3**		**5,200**	**–0–**

Service Revenue — No. 400

Date	Explanation	Ref.	Debit	Credit	Balance
2014					
Oct. 31		J1		10,000	10,000
31	Adj. entry	J2		400	10,400
31	Adj. entry	J2		200	10,600
31	**Closing entry**	**J3**	**10,600**		**–0–**

Rent Expense — No. 729

Date	Explanation	Ref.	Debit	Credit	Balance
2014					
Oct. 3		J1	900		900
31	**Closing entry**	**J3**		**900**	**–0–**

Interest Expense — No. 905

Date	Explanation	Ref.	Debit	Credit	Balance
2014					
Oct. 31	Adj. entry	J2	**50**		50
31	**Closing entry**	**J3**		**50**	**–0–**

Supplies Expense — No. 631

Date	Explanation	Ref.	Debit	Credit	Balance
2014					
Oct. 31	Adj. entry	J2	1,500		1,500
31	**Closing entry**	**J3**		**1,500**	**–0–**

Depreciation Expense — No. 711

Date	Explanation	Ref.	Debit	Credit	Balance
2014					
Oct. 31	Adj. entry	J2	**40**		40
31	**Closing entry**	**J3**		**40**	**–0–**

Note: The temporary accounts for Pioneer Advertising Agency Inc. are shown here; Illustration 4-10 shows the permanent accounts. Both permanent and temporary accounts are part of the general ledger; they are segregated here to aid in learning.

Summary of the Accounting Cycle

LEARNING OBJECTIVE 4

State the required steps in the accounting cycle.

Illustration 4-12 summarizes the steps in the accounting cycle. You can see that the cycle begins with the analysis of business transactions and ends with the preparation of a post-closing trial balance.

Steps 1–3 may occur daily during the accounting period, as explained in Chapter 2. Companies perform Steps 4–7 on a periodic basis, such as monthly, quarterly, or annually. Steps 8 and 9—closing entries, and a post-closing trial balance—usually take place only at the end of a company's **annual** accounting period.

Illustration 4-12
Steps in the accounting cycle

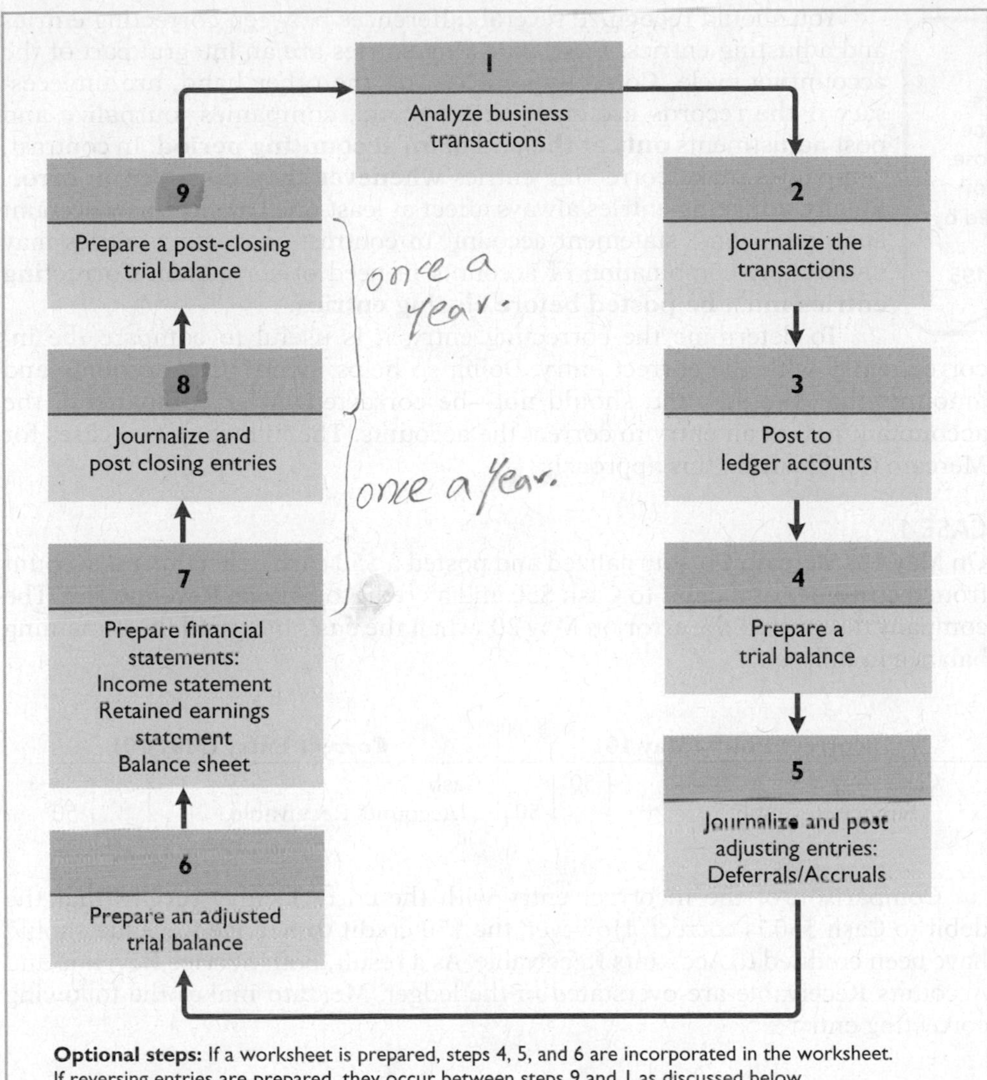

There are also two **optional steps** in the accounting cycle. As you have seen, companies may use a worksheet in preparing adjusting entries and financial statements. In addition, they may use reversing entries, as explained below.

Reversing Entries—An Optional Step

Some accountants prefer to reverse certain adjusting entries by making a **reversing entry** at the beginning of the next accounting period. A reversing entry is the exact opposite of the adjusting entry made in the previous period. **Use of reversing entries is an optional bookkeeping procedure; it is not a required step in the accounting cycle.** Accordingly, we have chosen to cover this topic in Appendix 4A at the end of the chapter.

Correcting Entries—An Avoidable Step

LEARNING OBJECTIVE 5

Explain the approaches to preparing correcting entries.

Unfortunately, errors may occur in the recording process. Companies should correct errors, **as soon as they discover them**, by journalizing and posting **correcting entries**. If the accounting records are free of errors, no correcting entries are needed.

Ethics Note

When companies find errors in previously released income statements, they restate those numbers. Perhaps because of the increased scrutiny caused by Sarbanes-Oxley, in a recent year companies filed a record 1,195 restatements.

You should recognize several differences between correcting entries and adjusting entries. First, adjusting entries are an integral part of the accounting cycle. Correcting entries, on the other hand, are unnecessary if the records are error-free. Second, companies journalize and post adjustments **only at the end of an accounting period**. In contrast, companies make correcting entries **whenever they discover an error**. Finally, adjusting entries always affect at least one balance sheet account and one income statement account. In contrast, correcting entries may involve any combination of accounts in need of correction. **Correcting entries must be posted before closing entries.**

To determine the correcting entry, it is useful to compare the incorrect entry with the correct entry. Doing so helps identify the accounts and amounts that should—and should not—be corrected. After comparison, the accountant makes an entry to correct the accounts. The following two cases for Mercato Co. illustrate this approach.

CASE 1

On May 10, Mercato Co. journalized and posted a $50 cash collection on account from a customer as a debit to Cash $50 and a credit to Service Revenue $50. The company discovered the error on May 20, when the customer paid the remaining balance in full.

Illustration 4-13
Comparison of entries

Incorrect Entry (May 10)			Correct Entry (May 10)		
Cash	50		Cash	50	
Service Revenue		50	Accounts Receivable		50

Comparison of the incorrect entry with the correct entry reveals that the debit to Cash $50 is correct. However, the $50 credit to Service Revenue should have been credited to Accounts Receivable. As a result, both Service Revenue and Accounts Receivable are overstated in the ledger. Mercato makes the following correcting entry.

Illustration 4-14
Correcting entry

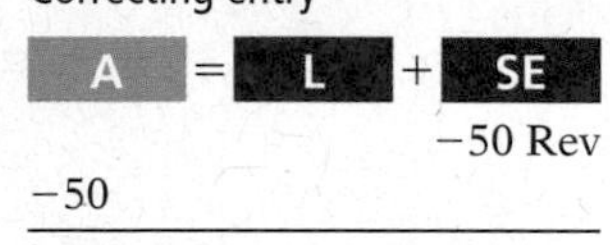

Correcting Entry

May 20	Service Revenue	50	
	Accounts Receivable		50
	(To correct entry of May 10)		

CASE 2

On May 18, Mercato purchased on account equipment costing $450. The transaction was journalized and posted as a debit to Equipment $45 and a credit to Accounts Payable $45. The error was discovered on June 3, when Mercato received the monthly statement for May from the creditor.

Illustration 4-15
Comparison of entries

Incorrect Entry (May 18)			Correct Entry (May 18)		
Equipment	45		Equipment	450	
Accounts Payable		45	Accounts Payable		450

Comparison of the two entries shows that two accounts are incorrect. Equipment is understated $405, and Accounts Payable is understated $405. Mercato makes the following correcting entry.

Correcting Entry

June 3	Equipment	405	
	Accounts Payable		405
	(To correct entry of May 18)		

A	=	L	+	SE
+405				
		+405		

Cash Flows
no effect

Illustration 4-16
Correcting entry

Instead of preparing a correcting entry, **it is possible to reverse the incorrect entry and then prepare the correct entry**. This approach will result in more entries and postings than a correcting entry, but it will accomplish the desired result.

ACCOUNTING ACROSS THE ORGANIZATION

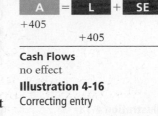

Yale Express Loses Some Transportation Bills

Yale Express, a short-haul trucking firm, turned over much of its cargo to local truckers to complete deliveries. Yale collected the entire delivery charge; when billed by the local trucker, Yale sent payment for the final phase to the local trucker. Yale used a cutoff period of 20 days into the next accounting period in making its adjusting entries for accrued liabilities. That is, it waited 20 days to receive the local truckers' bills to determine the amount of the unpaid but incurred delivery charges as of the balance sheet date.

On the other hand, Republic Carloading, a nationwide, long-distance freight forwarder, frequently did not receive transportation bills from truckers to whom it passed on cargo until months after the year-end. In making its year-end adjusting entries, Republic waited for months in order to include all of these outstanding transportation bills.

When Yale Express merged with Republic Carloading, Yale's vice president employed the 20-day cutoff procedure for both firms. As a result, millions of dollars of Republic's accrued transportation bills went unrecorded. When the company detected the error and made correcting entries, these and other errors changed a reported profit of $1.14 million into a loss of $1.88 million!

What might Yale Express's vice president have done to produce more accurate financial statements without waiting months for Republic's outstanding transportation bills? (See page 214.)

The Classified Balance Sheet

LEARNING OBJECTIVE 6

Identify the sections of a classified balance sheet.

The balance sheet presents a snapshot of a company's financial position at a point in time. To improve users' understanding of a company's financial position, companies often use a classified balance sheet. A **classified balance sheet** groups together similar assets and similar liabilities, using a number of standard classifications and sections. This is useful because items within a group have similar economic characteristics. A classified balance sheet generally contains the standard classifications listed in Illustration 4-17.

Illustration 4-17
Standard balance sheet classifications

Assets	Liabilities and Stockholders' Equity
Current assets	Current liabilities
Long-term investments	Long-term liabilities
Property, plant, and equipment	Stockholders' equity
Intangible assets	

These groupings help financial statement readers determine such things as (1) whether the company has enough assets to pay its debts as they come due, and (2) the claims of short- and long-term creditors on the company's total assets. Many of these groupings can be seen in the balance sheet of Franklin Corporation shown in Illustration 4-18 below. In the sections that follow, we explain each of these groupings.

Illustration 4-18
Classified balance sheet

Franklin Corporation
Balance Sheet
October 31, 2014

Assets			
Current assets			
Cash		$ 6,600	
Short-term investments		2,000	
Accounts receivable		7,000	
Notes receivable		1,000	
Inventory		3,000	
Supplies		2,100	
Prepaid insurance		400	
Total current assets			$22,100
Long-term investments			
Investment in stock of Walters Corp.		5,200	
Investment in real estate		2,000	7,200
Property, plant, and equipment			
Land		10,000	
Equipment	$24,000		
Less: Accumulated depreciation—equipment	5,000	19,000	29,000
Intangible assets			
Patents			3,100
Total assets			$61,400

Liabilities and Stockholders' Equity		
Current liabilities		
Notes payable	$11,000	
Accounts payable	2,100	
Salaries and wages payable	1,600	
Unearned service revenue	900	
Interest payable	450	
Total current liabilities		$16,050
Long-term liabilities		
Mortgage payable	10,000	
Notes payable	1,300	
Total long-term liabilities		11,300
Total liabilities		27,350
Stockholders' equity		
Common stock	20,000	
Retained earnings	14,050	
Total stockholders' equity		34,050
Total liabilities and stockholders' equity		$61,400

Helpful Hint
Recall that the basic accounting equation is Assets = Liabilities + Stockholders' Equity.

Current Assets

Current assets are assets that a company expects to convert to cash or use up within one year or its operating cycle, whichever is longer. In Illustration 4-18, Franklin Corporation had current assets of $22,100. For most businesses, the cutoff for classification as current assets is one year from the balance sheet date. For example, accounts receivable are current assets because the company will collect them and convert them to cash within one year. Supplies is a current asset because the company expects to use it up in operations within one year.

Some companies use a period longer than one year to classify assets and liabilities as current because they have an operating cycle longer than one year. The **operating cycle** of a company is the average time that it takes to purchase inventory, sell it on account, and then collect cash from customers. For most businesses this cycle takes less than a year, so they use a one-year cutoff. But, for some businesses, such as vineyards or airplane manufacturers, this period may be longer than a year. **Except where noted, we will assume that companies use one year to determine whether an asset or liability is current or long-term.**

Common types of current assets are (1) cash, (2) short-term investments (such as short-term U.S. government securities), (3) receivables (notes receivable, accounts receivable, and interest receivable), (4) inventories, and (5) prepaid expenses (supplies and insurance). **On the balance sheet, companies usually list these items in the order in which they expect to convert them into cash.**

Illustration 4-19 presents the current assets of Southwest Airlines Co.

Illustration 4-19
Current assets section

Southwest Airlines Co.
Balance Sheet (partial)
(in millions)

Current assets	
Cash and cash equivalents	$1,390
Short-term investments	369
Accounts receivable	241
Inventories	181
Prepaid expenses and other current assets	420
Total current assets	$2,601

As explained later in the chapter, a company's current assets are important in assessing its short-term debt-paying ability.

Long-Term Investments

Alternative Terminology
Long-term investments are often referred to simply as *investments*.

Long-term investments are generally, (1) investments in stocks and bonds of other companies that are normally held for many years, and (2) long-term assets such as land or buildings that a company is not currently using in its operating activities. In Illustration 4-18, Franklin Corporation reported total long-term investments of $7,200 on its balance sheet.

Yahoo! Inc. reported long-term investments in its balance sheet as shown in Illustration 4-20 (page 182).

Illustration 4-20
Long-term investments section

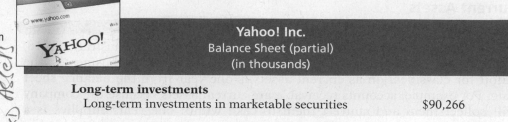

Yahoo! Inc. Balance Sheet (partial) (in thousands)	
Long-term investments	
Long-term investments in marketable securities	$90,266

Property, Plant, and Equipment

Property, plant, and equipment are assets with relatively long useful lives that a company is currently using in operating the business. This category (sometimes called *fixed assets*) includes land, buildings, machinery and equipment, delivery equipment, and furniture. In Illustration 4-18, Franklin Corporation reported property, plant, and equipment of $29,000.

> **International Note**
>
> Recently, China adopted International Financial Reporting Standards (IFRS). This was done in an effort to reduce fraud and increase investor confidence in financial reports. Under these standards, many items, such as property, plant, and equipment, may be reported at current fair values, rather than historical cost.

Depreciation is the practice of allocating the cost of assets to a number of years. Companies do this by systematically assigning a portion of an asset's cost as an expense each year (rather than expensing the full purchase price in the year of purchase). The assets that the company depreciates are reported on the balance sheet at cost less accumulated depreciation. The **accumulated depreciation** account shows the total amount of depreciation that the company has expensed thus far in the asset's life. In Illustration 4-18, Franklin Corporation reported accumulated depreciation of $5,000.

Illustration 4-21 presents the property, plant, and equipment of Cooper Tire & Rubber Company.

Illustration 4-21
Property, plant, and equipment section

Cooper Tire & Rubber Company Balance Sheet (partial) (in thousands)		
Property, plant, and equipment		
Land and land improvements	$ 41,553	
Buildings	298,706	
Machinery and equipment	1,636,091	
Molds, cores, and rings	268,158	$2,244,508
Less: Accumulated depreciation		1,252,692
		$ 991,816

Intangible Assets

> **Helpful Hint**
> Sometimes intangible assets are reported under a broader heading called *"Other assets."*

Many companies have long-lived assets that do not have physical substance yet often are very valuable. We call these assets **intangible assets**. One common intangible asset is goodwill. Others include patents, copyrights, and trademarks or trade names that give the company **exclusive right** of use for a specified period of time. In Illustration 4-18, Franklin Corporation reported intangible assets of $3,100.

Illustration 4-22 shows the intangible assets of media giant Time Warner, Inc.

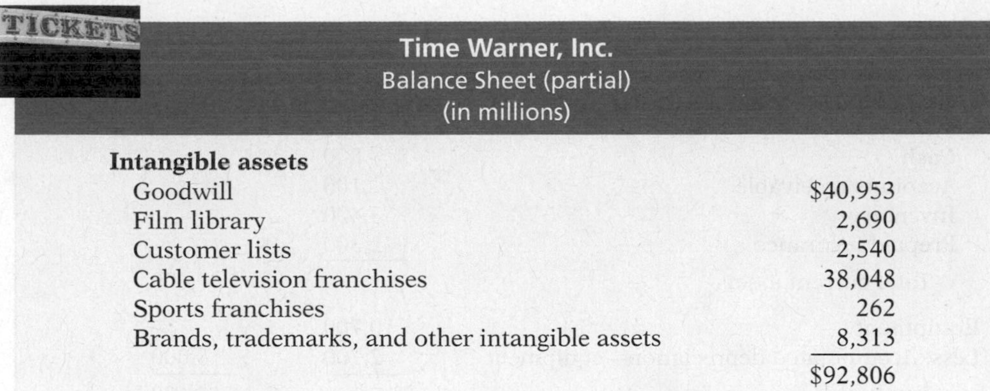

Time Warner, Inc.
Balance Sheet (partial)
(in millions)

Intangible assets	
Goodwill	$40,953
Film library	2,690
Customer lists	2,540
Cable television franchises	38,048
Sports franchises	262
Brands, trademarks, and other intangible assets	8,313
	$92,806

Illustration 4-22
Intangible assets section

PEOPLE, PLANET, AND PROFIT INSIGHT

Regaining Goodwill

After falling to unforeseen lows amidst scandals, recalls, and economic crises, the American public's positive perception of the reputation of corporate America is on the rise. Overall corporate reputation is experiencing rehabilitation as the American public gives high marks overall to corporate America, specific industries, and the largest number of individual companies in a dozen years. This is according to the findings of the 2011 Harris Interactive RQ Study, which measures the reputations of the 60 most visible companies in the U.S.

The survey focuses on six reputational dimensions that influence reputation and consumer behavior. The six dimensions, along with the five corporations that ranked highest within each, are as follows.

- **Social Responsibility:** (1) Whole Foods Market, (2) Johnson & Johnson, (3) Google, (4) The Walt Disney Company, (5) Procter & Gamble Co.
- **Emotional Appeal:** (1) Johnson & Johnson, (2) amazon.com, (3) UPS, (4) General Mills, (5) Kraft Foods
- **Financial Performance:** (1) Google, (2) Berkshire Hathaway, (3) Apple, (4) Intel, (5) The Walt Disney Company
- **Products and Services:** (1) Intel Corporation, (2) 3M Company, (3) Johnson & Johnson, (4) Google, (5) Procter & Gamble Co.

Source: www.harrisinteractive.com.

Name two industries today which are probably rated low on the reputational characteristics of "being trusted" and "having high ethical standards." (See page 214.)

> DO IT!

Asset Section of Classified Balance Sheet

Baxter Hoffman recently received the following information related to Hoffman Company's December 31, 2014, balance sheet.

Prepaid insurance	$ 2,300	Inventory	$3,400
Cash	800	Accumulated depreciation—equipment	2,700
Equipment	10,700	Accounts receivable	1,100

Prepare the asset section of Hoffman Company's classified balance sheet.

Action Plan

✔ Present current assets first. Current assets are cash and other resources that the company expects to convert to cash or use up within one year.

✔ Present current assets in the order in which the company expects to convert them into cash.

✔ Subtract accumulated depreciation—equipment from equipment to determine net equipment.

Solution

Assets

Current assets		
Cash	$ 800	
Accounts receivable	1,100	
Inventory	3,400	
Prepaid insurance	2,300	
Total current assets		$ 7,600
Equipment	10,700	
Less: Accumulated depreciation—equipment	2,700	8,000
Total assets		$15,600

Related exercise material: **BE4-10 and**  **4-3.**

✔ The Navigator

Ethics Note

A company that has more current assets than current liabilities can increase the ratio of current assets to current liabilities by using cash to pay off some current liabilities. This gives the appearance of being more liquid. Do you think this move is ethical?

Current Liabilities

In the liabilities and stockholders' equity section of the balance sheet, the first grouping is current liabilities. **Current liabilities** are obligations that the company is to pay within the coming year or its operating cycle, whichever is longer. Common examples are accounts payable, wages payable, bank loans payable, interest payable, and taxes payable. Also included as current liabilities are current maturities of long-term obligations—payments to be made within the next year on long-term obligations. In Illustration 4-18, Franklin Corporation reported five different types of current liabilities, for a total of $16,050.

Within the current liabilities section, companies usually list notes payable first, followed by accounts payable. Other items then follow in the order of their magnitude. *In your homework, you should present notes payable first, followed by accounts payable, and then other liabilities in order of magnitude.*

Illustration 4-23 shows the current liabilities section adapted from the balance sheet of Marcus Corporation.

Illustration 4-23
Current liabilities section

Marcus Corporation
Balance Sheet (partial)
(in thousands)

Current liabilities	
Notes payable	$ 239
Accounts payable	24,242
Current maturities of long-term debt	57,250
Other current liabilities	27,477
Income taxes payable	11,215
Salary and wages payable	6,720
Total current liabilities	$127,143

Users of financial statements look closely at the relationship between current assets and current liabilities. This relationship is important in evaluating a company's **liquidity**—its ability to pay obligations expected to be due within the next year. When current assets exceed current liabilities at the balance sheet date, the likelihood for paying the liabilities is favorable. When the reverse is true, short-term creditors may not be paid, and the company may ultimately be forced into bankruptcy.

ACCOUNTING ACROSS THE ORGANIZATION

Can a Company Be Too Liquid?

There actually is a point where a company can be too liquid—that is, it can have too much working capital (current assets less current liabilities). While it is important to be liquid enough to be able to pay short-term bills as they come due, a company does not want to tie up its cash in extra inventory or receivables that are not earning the company money.

By one estimate from the REL Consultancy Group, the thousand largest U.S. companies have on their books cumulative excess working capital of $764 billion. Based on this figure, companies could have reduced debt by 36% or increased net income by 9%. Given that managers throughout a company are interested in improving profitability, it is clear that they should have an eye toward managing working capital. They need to aim for a "Goldilocks solution"—not too much, not too little, but just right.

Source: K. Richardson, "Companies Fall Behind in Cash Management," *Wall Street Journal* (June 19, 2007).

What can various company managers do to ensure that working capital is managed efficiently to maximize net income? (See page 214.)

Long-Term Liabilities

Long-term liabilities are obligations that a company expects to pay **after** one year. Liabilities in this category include bonds payable, mortgages payable, long-term notes payable, lease liabilities, and pension liabilities. Many companies report long-term debt maturing after one year as a single amount in the balance sheet and show the details of the debt in notes that accompany the financial statements. Others list the various types of long-term liabilities. In Illustration 4-18, Franklin Corporation reported long-term liabilities of $11,300. *In your homework, list long-term liabilities in the order of their magnitude.*

Illustration 4-24 shows the long-term liabilities that The Procter & Gamble Company reported in its balance sheet.

Illustration 4-24
Long-term liabilities section

The Procter & Gamble Company
Balance Sheet (partial)
(in millions)

Long-term liabilities	
Long-term debt	$23,375
Deferred income taxes	12,015
Other noncurrent liabilities	5,147
Total long-term liabilities	$40,537

Stockholders' (Owners') Equity

The content of the owners' equity section varies with the form of business organization. In a proprietorship, there is one capital account. In a partnership, there is a capital account for each partner. Corporations divide owners' equity into two accounts—Common Stock (sometimes referred to as Capital Stock) and Retained Earnings. Corporations record stockholders' investments in the company by debiting an asset account and crediting the Common Stock account. They record in the Retained Earnings account income retained for use in the business. Corporations combine the Common Stock and Retained Earnings accounts and report them on the balance sheet as **stockholders' equity**. (We'll learn more about these corporation accounts in later chapters.) Nordstrom, Inc. recently reported its stockholders' equity section as follows.

Illustration 4-25
Stockholders' equity section

Nordstrom, Inc.
Balance Sheet (partial)
($ in thousands)

Stockholders' equity	
Common stock, 271,331 shares	$ 685,934
Retained earnings	1,406,747
Total stockholders' equity	$2,092,681

> DO IT!

Balance Sheet Classifications

The following accounts were taken from the financial statements of Callahan Company.

____	Salaries and wages payable	____	Investment in real estate
____	Service revenue	____	Equipment
____	Interest payable	____	Accumulated depreciation—equipment
____	Goodwill	____	Depreciation expense
____	Short-term investments	____	Common stock
____	Mortgage payable (due in 3 years)	____	Unearned service revenue

Match each of the following accounts to its proper balance sheet classification, shown below. If the item would not appear on a balance sheet, use "NA."

Current assets (CA)
Long-term investments (LTI)
Property, plant, and equipment (PPE)
Intangible assets (IA)
Current liabilities (CL)
Long-term liabilities (LTL)
Stockholders' equity (SE)

Action Plan

✔ Analyze whether each financial statement item is an asset, liability, or stockholders' equity.

✔ Determine if asset and liability items are short-term or long-term.

Solution

__CL__	Salaries and wages payable	__LTI__	Investment in real estate
__NA__	Service revenue	__PPE__	Equipment
__CL__	Interest payable	__PPE__	Accumulated depreciation—equipment
__IA__	Goodwill	__NA__	Depreciation expense
__CA__	Short-term investments	__SE__	Common stock
__LTL__	Mortgage payable (due in 3 years)	__CL__	Unearned service revenue

Related exercise material: **BE4-11, E4-14, E4-15, E4-16, E4-17, and  DO IT! 4-4.**

✔ **The Navigator**

> Comprehensive DO IT!

At the end of its first month of operations, Watson Answering Service Inc. has the following unadjusted trial balance.

Action Plan

- ✔ In completing the worksheet, be sure to (a) key the adjustments; (b) start at the top of the adjusted trial balance columns and extend adjusted balances to the correct statement columns; and (c) enter net income (or net loss) in the proper columns.
- ✔ In preparing a classified balance sheet, know the contents of each of the sections.
- ✔ In journalizing closing entries, remember that there are only four entries and that Dividends are closed to Retained Earnings.

Watson Answering Service Inc.
August 31, 2014
Trial Balance

	Debit	Credit
Cash	$ 5,400	
Accounts Receivable	2,800	
Supplies	1,300	
Prepaid Insurance	2,400	
Equipment	60,000	
Notes Payable		$40,000
Accounts Payable		2,400
Common Stock		30,000
Dividends	1,000	
Service Revenue		4,900
Salaries and Wages Expense	3,200	
Utilities Expense	800	
Advertising Expense	400	
	$77,300	$77,300

Other data:

1. Insurance expires at the rate of $200 per month.
2. $1,000 of supplies are on hand at August 31.
3. Monthly depreciation on the equipment is $900.
4. Interest of $500 on the notes payable has accrued during August.

Instructions

(a) Prepare a worksheet.
(b) Prepare a classified balance sheet assuming $35,000 of the notes payable are long-term.
(c) Journalize the closing entries.

Solution to Comprehensive DO IT!

(a)

Watson Answering Service Inc.
Worksheet for the Month Ended August 31, 2014

	Trial Balance		Adjustments		Adjusted Trial Balance		Income Statement		Balance Sheet	
Account Titles	**Dr.**	**Cr.**	**Dr.**	**Cr.**	**Dr.**	**Cr.**	**Dr.**	**Cr.**	**Dr.**	**Cr.**
Cash	5,400				5,400				5,400	
Accounts Receivable	2,800				2,800				2,800	
Supplies	1,300			(b) 300	1,000				1,000	
Prepaid Insurance	2,400			(a) 200	2,200				2,200	
Equipment	60,000				60,000				60,000	
Notes Payable		40,000				40,000				40,000
Accounts Payable		2,400				2,400				2,400
Common Stock		30,000				30,000				30,000
Dividends	1,000				1,000				1,000	
Service Revenue		4,900				4,900		4,900		
Salaries and Wages Expense	3,200				3,200		3,200			
Utilities Expense	800				800		800			
Advertising Expense	400				400		400			
Totals	77,300	77,300								

Insurance Expense	(a) 200		200		200			
Supplies Expense	(b) 300		300		300			
Depreciation Expense	(c) 900		900		900			
Accumulated Depreciation—Equipment		(c) 900		900				900
Interest Expense	(d) 500		500		500			
Interest Payable		(d) 500		500				500
Totals	1,900	1,900	78,700	78,700	6,300	4,900	72,400	73,800
Net Loss						1,400	1,400	
Totals					6,300	6,300	73,800	73,800

Explanation: (a) Insurance expired, (b) Supplies used, (c) Depreciation expensed, (d) Interest accrued.

(b)

Watson Answering Service Inc.
Balance Sheet
August 31, 2014

Assets

Current assets		
Cash	$ 5,400	
Accounts receivable	2,800	
Supplies	1,000	
Prepaid insurance	2,200	
Total current assets		$11,400
Property, plant, and equipment		
Equipment	60,000	
Less: Accumulated depreciation—equipment	900	59,100
Total assets		$70,500

Liabilities and Stockholders' Equity

Current liabilities		
Notes payable	$ 5,000	
Accounts payable	2,400	
Interest payable	500	
Total current liabilities		$ 7,900
Long-term liabilities		
Notes payable		35,000
Total liabilities		42,900
Stockholders' equity		
Common stock	30,000	
Retained earnings	(2,400)*	
Total stockholders' equity		27,600
Total liabilities and stockholders' equity		$70,500

*Net loss $1,400, plus dividends of $1,000.

(c)

Aug. 31	Service Revenue	4,900	
	Income Summary		4,900
	(To close revenue account)		
31	Income Summary	6,300	
	Salaries and Wages Expense		3,200
	Depreciation Expense		900
	Utilities Expense		800
	Interest Expense		500

Date	Account Titles and Explanation	Debit	Credit
	Advertising Expense		400
	Supplies Expense		300
	Insurance Expense		200
	(To close expense accounts)		
31	Retained Earnings	1,400	
	Income Summary		1,400
	(To close net loss to retained earnings)		
31	Retained Earnings	1,000	
	Dividends		1,000
	(To close dividends to retained earnings)		

✔ The Navigator

SUMMARY OF LEARNING OBJECTIVES

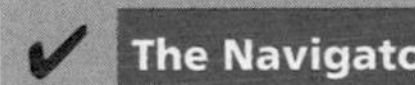

1 Prepare a worksheet. The steps in preparing a worksheet are as follows. (a) Prepare a trial balance on the worksheet. (b) Enter the adjustments in the adjustments columns. (c) Enter adjusted balances in the adjusted trial balance columns. (d) Extend adjusted trial balance amounts to appropriate financial statement columns. (e) Total the statement columns, compute net income (or net loss), and complete the worksheet.

2 Explain the process of closing the books. Closing the books occurs at the end of an accounting period. The process is to journalize and post closing entries and then underline and balance all accounts. In closing the books, companies make separate entries to close revenues and expenses to Income Summary, Income Summary to Retained Earnings, and Dividends to Retained Earnings. Only temporary accounts are closed.

3 Describe the content and purpose of a post-closing trial balance. A post-closing trial balance contains the balances in permanent accounts that are carried forward to the next accounting period. The purpose of this trial balance is to prove the equality of these balances.

4 State the required steps in the accounting cycle. The required steps in the accounting cycle are: (1) analyze business transactions, (2) journalize the transactions, (3) post to ledger accounts, (4) prepare a trial balance, (5) journalize and post adjusting entries, (6) prepare an adjusted trial balance, (7) prepare financial statements, (8) journalize and post closing entries, and (9) prepare a post-closing trial balance.

5 Explain the approaches to preparing correcting entries. One way to determine the correcting entry is to compare the incorrect entry with the correct entry. After comparison, the company makes a correcting entry to correct the accounts. An alternative to a correcting entry is to reverse the incorrect entry and then prepare the correct entry.

6 Identify the sections of a classified balance sheet. A classified balance sheet categorizes assets as current assets; long-term investments; property, plant, and equipment; and intangibles. Liabilities are classified as either current or long-term. There is also a stockholders' (owners') equity section, which varies with the form of business organization.

GLOSSARY

Classified balance sheet A balance sheet that contains standard classifications or sections. (p. 179).

Closing entries Entries made at the end of an accounting period to transfer the balances of temporary accounts to a permanent stockholders' equity account, Retained Earnings. (p. 170).

Correcting entries Entries to correct errors made in recording transactions. (p. 177).

Current assets Assets that a company expects to convert to cash or use up within one year. (p. 181).

Current liabilities Obligations that a company expects to pay within the coming year. (p. 184).

Income Summary A temporary account used in closing revenue and expense accounts. (p. 170).

Intangible assets Noncurrent assets that do not have physical substance. (p. 182).

Liquidity The ability of a company to pay obligations expected to be due within the next year. (p. 184).

Long-term investments Generally, (1) investments in stocks and bonds of other companies that companies normally hold for many years, and (2) long-term assets, such as land and buildings, not currently being used in operations. (p. 181).

Long-term liabilities Obligations that a company expects to pay after one year. (p. 185).

Operating cycle The average time that it takes to purchase inventory, sell it on account, and then collect cash from customers. (p. 181).

Permanent (real) accounts Accounts that relate to one or more accounting periods. Consist of all balance sheet accounts. Balances are carried forward to next accounting period. (p. 170).

Post-closing trial balance A list of permanent accounts and their balances after a company has journalized and posted closing entries. (p. 174).

Property, plant, and equipment Assets with relatively long useful lives and currently being used in operations. (p. 182).

Reversing entry An entry, made at the beginning of the next accounting period, that is the exact opposite of the adjusting entry made in the previous period. (p. 177).

Stockholders' equity The combination of common stock and retained earnings accounts. Often referred to as the ownership claim of shareholders on total assets. It is to a corporation what owner's equity is to a proprietorship. (p. 186).

Temporary (nominal) accounts Accounts that relate only to a given accounting period. Consist of all income statement accounts and the dividends account. All temporary accounts are closed at end of the accounting period. (p. 170).

Worksheet A multiple-column form that may be used in making adjusting entries and in preparing financial statements. (p. 164).

APPENDIX 4A REVERSING ENTRIES

LEARNING OBJECTIVE 7

Prepare reversing entries.

After preparing the financial statements and closing the books, it is often helpful to reverse some of the adjusting entries before recording the regular transactions of the next period. Such entries are **reversing entries**. Companies make **a reversing entry at the beginning of the next accounting period**. Each reversing entry **is the exact opposite of the adjusting entry made in the previous period**. The recording of reversing entries is an **optional step** in the accounting cycle.

The purpose of reversing entries is to simplify the recording of a subsequent transaction related to an adjusting entry. For example, in Chapter 3 (page 117), the payment of salaries after an adjusting entry resulted in two debits: one to Salaries and Wages Payable and the other to Salaries and Wages Expense. With reversing entries, the company can debit the entire subsequent payment to Salaries and Wages Expense. **The use of reversing entries does not change the amounts reported in the financial statements.** What it does is simplify the recording of subsequent transactions.

Reversing Entries Example

Companies most often use reversing entries to reverse two types of adjusting entries: accrued revenues and accrued expenses. To illustrate the optional use of reversing entries for accrued expenses, we will use the salaries expense transactions for Pioneer Advertising Agency Inc. as illustrated in Chapters 2, 3, and 4. The transaction and adjustment data are as follows.

1. October 26 (initial salary entry): Pioneer pays $4,000 of salaries and wages earned between October 15 and October 26.
2. October 31 (adjusting entry): Salaries and wages earned between October 29 and October 31 are $1,200. The company will pay these in the November 9 payroll.
3. November 9 (subsequent salary entry): Salaries and wages paid are $4,000. Of this amount, $1,200 applied to accrued salaries and wages payable and $2,800 was earned between November 1 and November 9.

Illustration 4A-1 shows the entries with and without reversing entries.

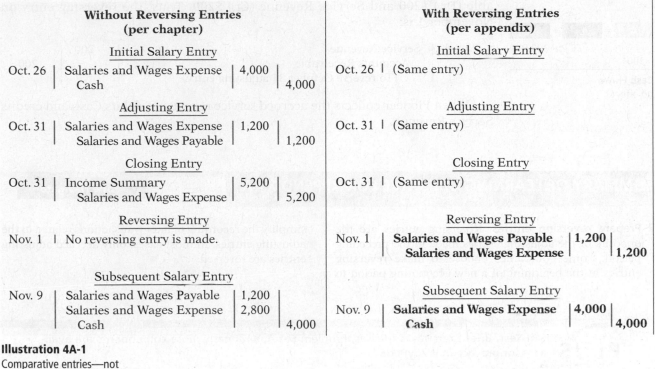

Without Reversing Entries (per chapter)				With Reversing Entries (per appendix)			
	Initial Salary Entry				**Initial Salary Entry**		
Oct. 26	Salaries and Wages Expense	4,000		Oct. 26	(Same entry)		
	Cash		4,000				
	Adjusting Entry				**Adjusting Entry**		
Oct. 31	Salaries and Wages Expense	1,200		Oct. 31	(Same entry)		
	Salaries and Wages Payable		1,200				
	Closing Entry				**Closing Entry**		
Oct. 31	Income Summary	5,200		Oct. 31	(Same entry)		
	Salaries and Wages Expense		5,200				
	Reversing Entry				**Reversing Entry**		
Nov. 1	No reversing entry is made.			Nov. 1	**Salaries and Wages Payable**	**1,200**	
					Salaries and Wages Expense		**1,200**
	Subsequent Salary Entry				**Subsequent Salary Entry**		
Nov. 9	Salaries and Wages Payable	1,200		Nov. 9	**Salaries and Wages Expense**	**4,000**	
	Salaries and Wages Expense	2,800			**Cash**		**4,000**
	Cash		4,000				

Illustration 4A-1
Comparative entries—not reversing vs. reversing

The first three entries are the same whether or not Pioneer uses reversing entries. The last two entries are different. The November 1 **reversing entry** eliminates the $1,200 balance in Salaries and Wages Payable created by the October 31 adjusting entry. The reversing entry also creates a $1,200 credit balance in the Salaries and Wages Expense account. As you know, it is unusual for an expense account to have a credit balance. The balance is correct in this instance, though, because it anticipates that the entire amount of the first salaries and wages payment in the new accounting period will be debited to Salaries and Wages Expense. This debit will eliminate the credit balance. The resulting debit balance in the expense account will equal the salaries and wages expense incurred in the new accounting period ($2,800 in this example).

If Pioneer makes reversing entries, it can debit all cash payments of expenses to the expense account. This means that on November 9 (and every payday) Pioneer can debit Salaries and Wages Expense for the amount paid, without regard to any accrued salaries and wages payable. Being able to make the **same entry each time** simplifies the recording process: The company can record subsequent transactions as if the related adjusting entry had never been made.

Illustration 4A-2 shows the posting of the entries with reversing entries.

Salaries and Wages Expense

10/26 Paid	4,000	10/31 Closing	5,200
31 Adjusting	1,200		
	5,200		5,200
11/9 Paid	4,000	**11/1 Reversing**	**1,200**

Salaries and Wages Payable

11/1 Reversing	**1,200**	10/31 Adjusting	1,200

Illustration 4A-2
Postings with reversing entries

A company can also use reversing entries for accrued revenue adjusting entries. For Pioneer Advertising Inc., the adjusting entry was Accounts Receivable (Dr.) $200 and Service Revenue (Cr.) $200. Thus, the reversing entry on November 1 is:

A	=	L	+	SE
				−200 Rev
−200				

Cash Flows
no effect

Nov. 1	Service Revenue	200	
	Accounts Receivable		200
	(To reverse October 31 adjusting entry)		

When Pioneer collects the accrued service revenue, it debits Cash and credits Service Revenue.

SUMMARY OF LEARNING OBJECTIVE FOR APPENDIX 4A

✔ The Navigator

7 Prepare reversing entries. Reversing entries are the opposite of the adjusting entries made in the preceding period. Some companies choose to make reversing entries at the beginning of a new accounting period to simplify the recording of later transactions related to the adjusting entries. In most cases, only accrued adjusting entries are reversed.

Self-Test, Brief Exercises, Exercises, Problem Set A, and many more components are available for practice in WileyPLUS

Note: All Questions, Exercises, and Problems marked with an asterisk relate to material in the appendix to the chapter.

SELF-TEST QUESTIONS

Answers are on page 214.

(LO 1) **1.** Which of the following statements is *incorrect* concerning the worksheet?
(a) The worksheet is essentially a working tool of the accountant.
(b) The worksheet is distributed to management and other interested parties.
(c) The worksheet cannot be used as a basis for posting to ledger accounts.
(d) Financial statements can be prepared directly from the worksheet before journalizing and posting the adjusting entries.

(LO 1) **2.** In a worksheet, net income is entered in the following columns:
(a) income statement (Dr) and balance sheet (Dr).
(b) income statement (Cr) and balance sheet (Dr).
(c) income statement (Dr) and balance sheet (Cr).
(d) income statement (Cr) and balance sheet (Cr).

(LO 1) **3.** In the unadjusted trial balance of its worksheet for the year ended December 31, 2014, Taitum Company reported Equipment of $120,000. The year-end adjusting entries require an adjustment of $15,000 for depreciation expense for the equipment. After adjustment, the following adjusted amount should be reported:
(a) A debit of $105,000 for Equipment in the balance sheet column.
(b) A credit of $15,000 for Depreciation Expense—Equipment in the income statement column.
(c) A debit of $120,000 for Equipment in the balance sheet column.
(d) A debit of $15,000 for Accumulated Depreciation—Equipment in the balance sheet column.

4. An account that will have a zero balance after closing entries have been journalized and posted is: (LO 2)
(a) Service Revenue.
(b) Supplies.
(c) Prepaid Insurance.
(d) Accumulated Depreciation—Equipment.

5. When a net loss has occurred, Income Summary is: (LO 2)
(a) debited and Retained Earnings is credited.
(b) credited and Retained Earnings is debited.
(c) debited and Dividends is credited.
(d) credited and Dividends is debited.

6. The closing process involves separate entries to close (1) expenses, (2) dividends, (3) revenues, and (4) income summary. The correct sequencing of the entries is: (LO 2)
(a) (4), (3), (2), (1)
(b) (1), (2), (3), (4)
(c) (3), (1), (4), (2)
(d) (3), (2), (1), (4)

(LO 3) 7. Which types of accounts will appear in the post-closing trial balance?
(a) Permanent (real) accounts.
(b) Temporary (nominal) accounts.
(c) Accounts shown in the income statement columns of a worksheet.
(d) None of the above.

(LO 4) 8. All of the following are required steps in the accounting cycle *except:*
(a) journalizing and posting closing entries.
(b) preparing financial statements.
(c) journalizing the transactions.
(d) preparing a worksheet.

(LO 4) 9. The proper order of the following steps in the accounting cycle is:
(a) prepare unadjusted trial balance, journalize transactions, post to ledger accounts, journalize and post adjusting entries.
(b) journalize transactions, prepare unadjusted trial balance, post to ledger accounts, journalize and post adjusting entries.
(c) journalize transactions, post to ledger accounts, prepare unadjusted trial balance, journalize and post adjusting entries.
(d) prepare unadjusted trial balance, journalize and post adjusting entries, journalize transactions, post to ledger accounts.

(LO 5) 10. When Alexander Company purchased supplies worth $500, it incorrectly recorded a credit to Supplies for $5,000 and a debit to Cash for $5,000. Before correcting this error:
(a) Cash is overstated and Supplies is overstated.
(b) Cash is understated and Supplies is understated.
(c) Cash is understated and Supplies is overstated.
(d) Cash is overstated and Supplies is understated.

(LO 5) 11. Cash of $100 received at the time the service was provided was journalized and posted as a debit to Cash $100 and a credit to Accounts Receivable $100. Assuming the incorrect entry is not reversed, the correcting entry is:
(a) debit Service Revenue $100 and credit Accounts Receivable $100.
(b) debit Accounts Receivable $100 and credit Service Revenue $100.
(c) debit Cash $100 and credit Service Revenue $100.
(d) debit Accounts Receivable $100 and credit Cash $100.

12. The correct order of presentation in a classified balance sheet for the following current assets is: (LO 6)
(a) accounts receivable, cash, prepaid insurance, inventory.
(b) cash, inventory, accounts receivable, prepaid insurance.
(c) cash, accounts receivable, inventory, prepaid insurance.
(d) inventory, cash, accounts receivable, prepaid insurance.

13. A company has purchased a tract of land. It expects to build a production plant on the land in approximately 5 years. During the 5 years before construction, the land will be idle. The land should be reported as: (LO 6)
(a) property, plant, and equipment.
(b) land expense.
(c) a long-term investment.
(d) an intangible asset.

14. In a classified balance sheet, assets are usually classified using the following categories: (LO 6)
(a) current assets; long-term assets; property, plant, and equipment; and intangible assets.
(b) current assets; long-term investments; property, plant, and equipment; and tangible assets.
(c) current assets; long-term investments; tangible assets; and intangible assets.
(d) current assets; long-term investments; property, plant, and equipment; and intangible assets

15. Current assets are listed: (LO 6)
(a) by expected conversion to cash.
(b) by importance.
(c) by longevity.
(d) alphabetically.

*16. On December 31, Frank Voris Company correctly made an adjusting entry to recognize $2,000 of accrued salaries payable. On January 8 of the next year, total salaries of $3,400 were paid. Assuming the correct reversing entry was made on January 1, the entry on January 8 will result in a credit to Cash $3,400 and the following debit(s): (LO 7)
(a) Salaries and Wages Payable $1,400, and Salaries and Wages Expense $2,000.
(b) Salaries and Wages Payable $2,000 and Salaries and Wages Expense $1,400.
(c) Salaries and Wages Expense $3,400.
(d) Salaries and Wages Payable $3,400.

Go to the book's companion website, www.wiley.com/college/weygandt, for additional Self-Test Questions.

✔ **The Navigator**

QUESTIONS

1. "A worksheet is a permanent accounting record and its use is required in the accounting cycle." Do you agree? Explain.
2. Explain the purpose of the worksheet.
3. What is the relationship, if any, between the amount shown in the adjusted trial balance column for an account and that account's ledger balance?

4. If a company's revenues are $125,000 and its expenses are $113,000, in which financial statement columns of the worksheet will the net income of $12,000 appear? When expenses exceed revenues, in which columns will the difference appear?
5. Why is it necessary to prepare formal financial statements if all of the data are in the statement columns of the worksheet?
6. Identify the account(s) debited and credited in each of the four closing entries, assuming the company has net income for the year.
7. Describe the nature of the Income Summary account and identify the types of summary data that may be posted to this account.
8. What are the content and purpose of a post-closing trial balance?
9. Which of the following accounts would not appear in the post-closing trial balance? Interest Payable; Equipment; Depreciation Expense; Dividends; Unearned Service Revenue; Accumulated Depreciation—Equipment; and Service Revenue.
10. Distinguish between a reversing entry and an adjusting entry. Are reversing entries required?
11. Indicate, in the sequence in which they are made, the three required steps in the accounting cycle that involve journalizing.
12. Identify, in the sequence in which they are prepared, the three trial balances that are often used to report financial information about a company.
13. How do correcting entries differ from adjusting entries?
14. What standard classifications are used in preparing a classified balance sheet?
15. What is meant by the term "operating cycle?"
16. Define current assets. What basis is used for arranging individual items within the current assets section?
17. Distinguish between long-term investments and property, plant, and equipment.
18. (a) What is the term used to describe the owners' equity section of a corporation? (b) Identify the two owners' equity accounts in a corporation and indicate the purpose of each.
19. **PEPSICO** Using PepsiCo's annual report, determine its current liabilities at December 31, 2010, and December 26, 2009. Were current liabilities higher or lower than current assets in these two years?

*20. Triumph Company prepares reversing entries. If the adjusting entry for interest payable is reversed, what type of an account balance, if any, will there be in Interest Payable and Interest Expense after the reversing entry is posted?

*21. At December 31, accrued salaries payable totaled $3,500. On January 10, total salaries of $9,200 are paid. (a) Assume that reversing entries are made at January 1. Give the January 10 entry, and indicate the Salaries and Wages Expense account balance after the entry is posted. (b) Repeat part (a) assuming reversing entries are not made.

BRIEF EXERCISES

List the steps in preparing a worksheet.
(LO 1)

BE4-1 The steps in using a worksheet are presented in random order below. List the steps in the proper order by placing numbers 1–5 in the blank spaces.

(a) _____ Prepare a trial balance on the worksheet.
(b) _____ Enter adjusted balances.
(c) _____ Extend adjusted balances to appropriate statement columns.
(d) _____ Total the statement columns, compute net income (loss), and complete the worksheet.
(e) _____ Enter adjustment data.

Prepare partial worksheet.
(LO 1)

BE4-2 The ledger of Keo Company includes the following unadjusted balances: Prepaid Insurance $3,000, Service Revenue $61,000, and Salaries and Wages Expense $25,000. Adjusting entries are required for (a) expired insurance $1,300; (b) services provided $1,100, but unbilled and uncollected; and (c) accrued salaries payable $800. Enter the unadjusted balances and adjustments into a worksheet and complete the worksheet for all accounts. *Note:* You will need to add the following accounts: Accounts Receivable, Salaries and Wages Payable, and Insurance Expense.

Identify worksheet columns for selected accounts.
(LO 1)

BE4-3 The following selected accounts appear in the adjusted trial balance columns of the worksheet for Cesar Company: Accumulated Depreciation; Depreciation Expense; Common Stock; Dividends; Service Revenue; Supplies; and Accounts Payable. Indicate the financial statement column (income statement Dr., balance sheet Cr., etc.) to which each balance should be extended.

Prepare closing entries from ledger balances.
(LO 2)

BE4-4 The ledger of Rowen Company contains the following balances: Retained Earnings $30,000; Dividends $2,000; Service Revenue $47,000; Salaries and Wages Expense $27,000; and Supplies Expense $5,000. Prepare the closing entries at December 31.

Post closing entries; underline and balance T-accounts.
(LO 2)

BE4-5 Using the data in BE4-4, enter the balances in T-accounts, post the closing entries, and underline and balance the accounts.

BE4-6 The income statement for Mosquera Golf Club for the month ending July 31 shows Service Revenue $19,200, Salaries and Wages Expense $8,800, Maintenance and Repairs Expense $2,500, and Net Income $7,900. Prepare the entries to close the revenue and expense accounts. Post the entries to the revenue and expense accounts, and complete the closing process for these accounts using the three-column form of account.

Journalize and post closing entries using the three-column form of account.

(LO 2)

BE4-7 Using the data in BE4-3, identify the accounts that would be included in a post-closing trial balance.

Identify post-closing trial balance accounts.

(LO 3)

BE4-8 The steps in the accounting cycle are listed in random order below. List the steps in proper sequence, assuming no worksheet is prepared, by placing numbers 1–9 in the blank spaces.

List the required steps in the accounting cycle in sequence.

(LO 4)

(a) _____ Prepare a trial balance.
(b) _____ Journalize the transactions.
(c) _____ Journalize and post closing entries.
(d) _____ Prepare financial statements.
(e) _____ Journalize and post adjusting entries.
(f) _____ Post to ledger accounts.
(g) _____ Prepare a post-closing trial balance.
(h) _____ Prepare an adjusted trial balance.
(i) _____ Analyze business transactions.

BE4-9 At Rafeul Company, the following errors were discovered after the transactions had been journalized and posted. Prepare the correcting entries.

Prepare correcting entries.

(LO 5)

1. A collection on account from a customer for $690 was recorded as a debit to Cash $690 and a credit to Service Revenue $690.
2. The purchase of store supplies on account for $1,580 was recorded as a debit to Supplies $1,850 and a credit to Accounts Payable $1,850.

BE4-10 The balance sheet debit column of the worksheet for Kren Company includes the following accounts: Accounts Receivable $12,500; Prepaid Insurance $3,600; Cash $6,700; Supplies $5,200; and Short-Term Investments $4,900. Prepare the current assets section of the balance sheet, listing the accounts in proper sequence.

Prepare the current assets section of a balance sheet.

(LO 6)

BE4-11 The following are the major balance sheet classifications:

Classify accounts on balance sheet.

(LO 6)

Current assets (CA)
Long-term investments (LTI)
Property, plant, and equipment (PPE)
Intangible assets (IA)
Current liabilities (CL)
Long-term liabilities (LTL)
Stockholders' equity (SE)

Match each of the following accounts to its proper balance sheet classification.

_____ Accounts payable
_____ Accounts receivable
_____ Accumulated depreciation—buildings
_____ Buildings
_____ Cash
_____ Copyrights
_____ Income taxes payable
_____ Debt investment (long-term)
_____ Land
_____ Inventory
_____ Patents
_____ Supplies

***BE4-12** At October 31, Prasad Company made an accrued expense adjusting entry of $1,680 for salaries. Prepare the reversing entry on November 1, and indicate the balances in Salaries and Wages Payable and Salaries and Wages Expense after posting the reversing entry.

Prepare reversing entries.

(LO 7)

> DO IT! REVIEW

DO IT! 4-1 Janet Adams is preparing a worksheet. Explain to Janet how she should extend the following adjusted trial balance accounts to the financial statement columns of the worksheet.

Prepare a worksheet.

(LO 1)

Service Revenue
Notes Payable
Common Stock
Accounts Receivable
Accumulated Depreciation
Utilities Expense

Prepare closing entries.
(LO 2)

DO IT! 4-2 The worksheet for Olympic Company shows the following in the financial statement columns.

Dividends	$15,000
Common Stock	70,000
Net income	47,000

Prepare the closing entries at December 31 that affect stockholders' equity.

Prepare assets section of the balance sheet.
(LO 6)

DO IT! 4-3 Tyler Pahl recently received the following information related to Pahl Company's December 31, 2014, balance sheet.

Inventory	$ 4,100	Short-term investments	$1,200
Cash	3,900	Accumulated depreciation	5,200
Equipment	21,700	Accounts receivable	4,300
Investments in stock (long-term)	6,500		

Prepare the assets section of Pahl Company's classified balance sheet.

Match accounts to balance sheet classifications.
(LO 6)

DO IT! 4-4 The following accounts were taken from the financial statements of Orville Company.

_____ Interest revenue	_____ Common stock
_____ Utilities payable	_____ Accumulated depreciation—equipment
_____ Accounts payable	_____ Equipment
_____ Supplies	_____ Salaries and wages expense
_____ Bonds payable	_____ Investment in real estate
_____ Trademarks	_____ Unearned rent revenue

Match each of the accounts to its proper balance sheet classification, as shown below. If the item would not appear on a balance sheet, use "NA."

Current assets (CA)	Current liabilities (CL)
Long-term investments (LTI)	Long-term liabilities (LTL)
Property, plant, and equipment (PPE)	Stockholders' equity (SE)
Intangible assets (IA)	

✔ The Navigator

EXERCISES

Complete the worksheet.
(LO 1)

E4-1 The trial balance columns of the worksheet for Cajon Company at June 30, 2014, are as follows.

Cajon Company
Worksheet
For the Month Ended June 30, 2014

Account Titles	Trial Balance Dr.	Trial Balance Cr.
Cash	$4,020	
Accounts Receivable	2,440	
Supplies	1,900	
Accounts Payable		$1,120
Unearned Service Revenue		240
Common Stock		5,000
Service Revenue		3,100
Salaries and Wages Expense	860	
Miscellaneous Expense	240	
	$9,460	$9,460

Other data:

1. A physical count reveals $500 of supplies on hand.
2. $100 of the unearned revenue is still unearned at month-end.
3. Accrued salaries are $250.

Instructions

Enter the trial balance on a worksheet and complete the worksheet.

Complete the worksheet.

(LO 1)

E4-2 The adjusted trial balance columns of the worksheet for Albanese Company are as follows.

Albanese Company
Worksheet (partial)
For the Month Ended April 30, 2014

Account Titles	Adjusted Trial Balance Dr.	Adjusted Trial Balance Cr.	Income Statement Dr.	Income Statement Cr.	Balance Sheet Dr.	Balance Sheet Cr.
Cash	7,442					
Accounts Receivable	7,840					
Prepaid Rent	2,280					
Equipment	23,000					
Accumulated Depreciation—Equip.		4,800				
Notes Payable		5,700				
Accounts Payable		5,672				
Common Stock		22,000				
Retained Earnings		4,000				
Dividends	3,000					
Service Revenue		12,590				
Salaries and Wages Expense	9,840					
Rent Expense	760					
Depreciation Expense	600					
Interest Expense	57					
Interest Payable		57				
Totals	54,819	54,819				

Instructions

Complete the worksheet.

Prepare financial statements from worksheet.

(LO 1, 6)

E4-3 Worksheet data for Albanese Company are presented in E4-2. No common stock was issued during April.

Instructions

Prepare an income statement, a retained earnings statement, and a classified balance sheet.

Journalize and post closing entries and prepare a post-closing trial balance.

(LO 2, 3)

E4-4 Worksheet data for Albanese Company are presented in E4-2.

Instructions

(a) Journalize the closing entries at April 30.
(b) Post the closing entries to Income Summary and Retained Earnings. Use T-accounts.
(c) Prepare a post-closing trial balance at April 30.

Prepare adjusting entries from a worksheet, and extend balances to worksheet columns.

(LO 1)

E4-5 The adjustments columns of the worksheet for Munoz Company are shown below.

Account Titles	Adjustments Debit	Adjustments Credit
Accounts Receivable	600	
Prepaid Insurance		400
Accumulated Depreciation—Equipment		900
Salaries and Wages Payable		500
Service Revenue		600
Salaries and Wages Expense	500	
Insurance Expense	400	
Depreciation Expense	900	
	2,400	2,400

Instructions

(a) Prepare the adjusting entries.

(b) Assuming the adjusted trial balance amount for each account is normal, indicate the financial statement column to which each balance should be extended.

Derive adjusting entries from worksheet data.

(LO 1)

E4-6 Selected worksheet data for Freeman Company are presented below.

Account Titles	Trial Balance		Adjusted Trial Balance	
	Dr.	**Cr.**	**Dr.**	**Cr.**
Accounts Receivable	?		34,000	
Prepaid Insurance	26,000		18,000	
Supplies	7,000		?	
Accumulated Depreciation—Equipment		12,000		?
Salaries and Wages Payable		?		5,000
Service Revenue		88,000		95,000
Insurance Expense			?	
Depreciation Expense			10,000	
Supplies Expense			4,700	
Salaries and Wages Expense	?		49,000	

Instructions

(a) Fill in the missing amounts.

(b) Prepare the adjusting entries that were made.

Prepare closing entries, and prepare a post-closing trial balance.

(LO 2, 3)

E4-7 Lanza Company had the following adjusted trial balance.

Lanza Company
Adjusted Trial Balance
For the Month Ended June 30, 2014

Account Titles	Adjusted Trial Balance	
	Debits	**Credits**
Cash	$ 3,712	
Accounts Receivable	3,904	
Supplies	480	
Accounts Payable		$ 1,556
Unearned Service Revenue		160
Common Stock		4,000
Retained Earnings		1,760
Dividends	600	
Service Revenue		4,300
Salaries and Wages Expense	1,344	
Miscellaneous Expense	180	
Supplies Expense	1,900	
Salaries and Wages Payable		344
	$12,120	$12,120

Instructions

(a) Prepare closing entries at June 30, 2014.

(b) Prepare a post-closing trial balance.

Journalize and post closing entries, and prepare a post-closing trial balance.

(LO 2, 3)

E4-8 Roth Company ended its fiscal year on July 31, 2014. The company's adjusted trial balance as of the end of its fiscal year is as shown on the next page.

Roth Company
Adjusted Trial Balance
July 31, 2014

No.	Account Titles	Debits	Credits
101	Cash	$ 9,840	
112	Accounts Receivable	8,140	
157	Equipment	15,900	
167	Accumulated Depreciation—Equip.		$ 5,400
201	Accounts Payable		2,220
208	Unearned Rent Revenue		3,800
311	Common Stock		18,000
320	Retained Earnings		20,260
332	Dividends	12,000	
404	Service Revenue		64,000
429	Rent Revenue		6,500
711	Depreciation Expense	3,700	
720	Salaries and Wages Expense	55,700	
732	Utilities Expense	14,900	
		$120,180	$120,180

Instructions

(a) Prepare the closing entries using page J15.

(b) Post to Retained Earnings and No. 350 Income Summary accounts. (Use the three-column form.)

(c) Prepare a post-closing trial balance at July 31.

E4-9 The adjusted trial balance for Roth Company is presented in E4-8.

Prepare financial statements.

(LO 6)

Instructions

(a) Prepare an income statement and a retained earnings statement for the year.

(b) Prepare a classified balance sheet at July 31.

E4-10 Patrick Kellogg has prepared the following list of statements about the accounting cycle.

Answer questions related to the accounting cycle.

(LO 4)

1. "Journalize the transactions" is the first step in the accounting cycle.
2. Reversing entries are a required step in the accounting cycle.
3. Correcting entries do not have to be part of the accounting cycle.
4. If a worksheet is prepared, some steps of the accounting cycle are incorporated into the worksheet.
5. The accounting cycle begins with the analysis of business transactions and ends with the preparation of a post-closing trial balance.
6. All steps of the accounting cycle occur daily during the accounting period.
7. The step of "post to the ledger accounts" occurs before the step of "journalize the transactions."
8. Closing entries must be prepared before financial statements can be prepared.

Instructions

Identify each statement as true or false. If false, indicate how to correct the statement.

E4-11 Selected accounts for Michelle's Salon are presented below. All June 30 postings are from closing entries.

Prepare closing entries.

(LO 2)

Salaries and Wages Expense

6/10	3,200	6/30	8,800
6/28	5,600		

Service Revenue

6/30	18,100	6/15	9,700
		6/24	8,400

Retained Earnings

6/30	2,200	6/1	12,000
		6/30	5,400
		Bal.	15,200

Supplies Expense

6/12	600	6/30	900
6/24	300		

Rent Expense

6/1	3,000	6/30	3,000

Dividends

6/13	1,000	6/30	2,200
6/25	1,200		

Instructions

(a) Prepare the closing entries that were made.
(b) Post the closing entries to Income Summary.

Prepare correcting entries.
(LO 5)

E4-12 Joshua Company discovered the following errors made in January 2014.

1. A payment of Salaries and Wages Expense of $700 was debited to Equipment and credited to Cash, both for $700.
2. A collection of $800 from a client on account was debited to Cash $300 and credited to Service Revenue $300.
3. The purchase of equipment on account for $760 was debited to Equipment $670 and credited to Accounts Payable $670.

Instructions

(a) Correct the errors by reversing the incorrect entry and preparing the correct entry.
(b) Correct the errors without reversing the incorrect entry.

Prepare correcting entries.
(LO 5)

E4-13 Kogan Company has an inexperienced accountant. During the first 2 weeks on the job, the accountant made the following errors in journalizing transactions. All entries were posted as made.

1. A payment on account of $840 to a creditor was debited to Accounts Payable $480 and credited to Cash $480.
2. The purchase of supplies on account for $380 was debited to Equipment $38 and credited to Accounts Payable $38.
3. A $500 cash dividend was debited to Salaries and Wages Expense $500 and credited to Cash $500.

Instructions

Prepare the correcting entries.

Prepare a classified balance sheet.
(LO 6)

E4-14 The adjusted trial balance for Rego Bowling Alley at December 31, 2014, contains the following accounts.

Debits		**Credits**	
Buildings	$128,000	Common Stock	$ 80,000
Accounts Receivable	7,540	Retained Earnings	28,000
Prepaid Insurance	4,680	Accumulated Depreciation—Buildings	42,600
Cash	18,040	Accounts Payable	12,300
Equipment	62,400	Notes Payable	95,000
Land	67,000	Accumulated Depreciation—Equipment	18,720
Insurance Expense	780	Interest Payable	2,600
Depreciation Expense	7,360	Service Revenue	19,180
Interest Expense	2,600		$298,400
	$298,400		

Instructions

(a) Prepare a classified balance sheet; assume that $15,000 of the note payable will be paid in 2015.
(b) Comment on the liquidity of the company.

Classify accounts on balance sheet.
(LO 6)

E4-15 The following are the major balance sheet classifications.

Current assets (CA)	Current liabilities (CL)
Long-term investments (LTI)	Long-term liabilities (LTL)
Property, plant, and equipment (PPE)	Stockholders' equity (SE)
Intangible assets (IA)	

Instructions

Classify each of the following accounts taken from Geraldo Company's balance sheet.

______ Accounts payable	______ Accumulated depreciation
______ Accounts receivable	______ Buildings
______ Cash	______ Land
______ Common stock	______ Long-term debt
______ Patents	______ Supplies
______ Salaries and wages payable	______ Equipment
______ Inventory	______ Prepaid expenses
______ Investments	

E4-16 The following items were taken from the financial statements of Sexton Company. (All dollars are in thousands.)

Prepare a classified balance sheet.

(LO 6)

Long-term debt	$ 1,000	Accumulated depreciation	$ 4,125
Prepaid insurance	680	Accounts payable	1,444
Equipment	11,500	Notes payable (due after 2015)	800
Long-term investments	1,200	Common stock	10,000
Short-term investments	3,619	Retained earnings	4,750
Notes payable (due in 2015)	500	Accounts receivable	1,696
Cash	2,668	Inventory	1,256

Instructions

Prepare a classified balance sheet in good form as of December 31, 2014.

E4-17 These financial statement items are for Emjay Company at year-end, July 31, 2014.

Prepare financial statements.

(LO 1, 6)

Salaries and wages payable	$ 2,080	Notes payable (long-term)	$ 1,800
Salaries and wages expense	50,700	Cash	14,200
Utilities expense	22,600	Accounts receivable	9,180
Equipment	30,000	Accumulated depreciation—equip.	6,000
Accounts payable	4,100	Dividends	3,000
Service revenue	62,000	Depreciation expense	2,500
Rent revenue	8,500	Retained earnings (beginning of the year)	22,700
Common stock	25,000		

Instructions

(a) Prepare an income statement and a retained earnings statement for the year.
(b) Prepare a classified balance sheet at July 31.

***E4-18** Grogan Company pays salaries of $9,000 every Monday for the preceding 5-day week (Monday through Friday). Assume December 31 falls on a Thursday, so Grogan's employees have worked 4 days without being paid.

Use reversing entries.

(LO 7)

Instructions

(a) Assume the company does not use reversing entries. Prepare the December 31 adjusting entry and the entry on Monday, January 4, when Grogan pays the payroll.
(b) Assume the company does use reversing entries. Prepare the December 31 adjusting entry, the January 1 reversing entry, and the entry on Monday, January 4, when Grogan pays the payroll.

***E4-19** On December 31, the adjusted trial balance of Select Employment Agency shows the following selected data.

Prepare closing and reversing entries.

(LO 2, 4, 7)

Accounts Receivable	$24,500	Service Revenue	$93,800
Interest Expense	8,300	Interest Payable	1,300

Analysis shows that adjusting entries were made to (1) accrue $5,000 of service revenue and (2) accrue $1,300 interest expense.

Instructions

(a) Prepare the closing entries for the temporary accounts shown above at December 31.
(b) Prepare the reversing entries on January 1.
(c) Post the entries in (a) and (b). Underline and balance the accounts. (Use T-accounts.)
(d) Prepare the entries to record (1) the collection of the accrued revenue on January 10 and (2) the payment of all interest due ($3,000) on January 15.
(e) Post the entries in (d) to the temporary accounts.

EXERCISES: SET B AND CHALLENGE EXERCISES

Visit the book's companion website, at **www.wiley.com/college/weygandt**, and choose the Student Companion site to access Exercise Set B and Challenge Exercises.

PROBLEMS: SET A

Prepare worksheet, financial statements, and adjusting and closing entries.

(LO 1, 2, 6)

P4-1A Sherlock Holmes began operations as a private investigator on January 1, 2014. The trial balance columns of the worksheet for Sherlock Holmes, P.I., Inc. at March 31 are as follows.

Sherlock Holmes P.I., Inc.
Worksheet
For the Quarter Ended March 31, 2014

	Trial Balance	
Account Titles	**Dr.**	**Cr.**
Cash	11,410	
Accounts Receivable	5,920	
Supplies	1,250	
Prepaid Insurance	2,400	
Equipment	30,000	
Notes Payable		10,000
Accounts Payable		12,350
Common Stock		20,000
Dividends	600	
Service Revenue		14,200
Salaries and Wages Expense	2,240	
Travel Expense	1,300	
Rent Expense	1,200	
Miscellaneous Expense	230	
	56,550	56,550

Other data:

1. Supplies on hand total $480.
2. Depreciation is $720 per quarter.
3. Interest accrued on 6-month note payable, issued January 1, $300.
4. Insurance expires at the rate of $200 per month.
5. Services provided but unbilled at March 31 total $1,080.

(a) Adjusted trial balance $58,650
(b) Net income $7,920
Total assets $49,970

Instructions

(a) Enter the trial balance on a worksheet and complete the worksheet.
(b) Prepare an income statement and a retained earnings statement for the quarter and a classified balance sheet at March 31.
(c) Journalize the adjusting entries from the adjustments columns of the worksheet.
(d) Journalize the closing entries from the financial statement columns of the worksheet.

Complete worksheet; prepare financial statements, closing entries, and post-closing trial balance.

(LO 1, 2, 3, 6)

GLS

P4-2A The adjusted trial balance columns of the worksheet for Watson Company are as follows.

Watson Company
Worksheet
For the Year Ended December 31, 2014

Account No.	Account Titles	Adjusted Trial Balance Dr.	Cr.
101	Cash	17,800	
112	Accounts Receivable	14,400	
126	Supplies	2,300	
130	Prepaid Insurance	4,400	
151	Equipment	46,000	
152	Accumulated Depreciation—Equipment		18,000
200	Notes Payable		20,000
201	Accounts Payable		8,000
212	Salaries and Wages Payable		2,600
230	Interest Payable		1,000
311	Common Stock		15,000
320	Retained Earnings		9,800
332	Dividends	12,000	
400	Service Revenue		86,200
610	Advertising Expense	10,000	
631	Supplies Expense	3,700	
711	Depreciation Expense	6,000	
722	Insurance Expense	4,000	
726	Salaries and Wages Expense	39,000	
905	Interest Expense	1,000	
	Totals	160,600	160,600

Instructions

(a) Complete the worksheet by extending the balances to the financial statement columns.
(b) Prepare an income statement, a retained earnings statement, and a classified balance sheet. (*Note:* $5,000 of the notes payable become due in 2015.)
(c) Prepare the closing entries. Use J14 for the journal page.
(d) Post the closing entries. Use the three-column form of account. Income Summary is account No. 350.
(e) Prepare a post-closing trial balance.

(a) Net income $22,500
(b) Current assets $38,900
Current liabilities $16,600

(e) Post-closing trial balance $84,900

P4-3A The completed financial statement columns of the worksheet for Hubbs Company are shown below and on the next page.

Prepare financial statements, closing entries, and post-closing trial balance.

(LO 1, 2, 3, 6)

Hubbs Company
Worksheet
For the Year Ended December 31, 2014

Account No.	Account Titles	Income Statement Dr.	Income Statement Cr.	Balance Sheet Dr.	Balance Sheet Cr.
101	Cash			6,200	
112	Accounts Receivable			7,500	
130	Prepaid Insurance			1,800	
157	Equipment			33,000	
167	Accumulated Depreciation—Equip.				9,900
201	Accounts Payable				11,700
212	Salaries and Wages Payable				3,000
311	Common Stock				20,000
320	Retained Earnings				9,700
332	Dividends			4,000	
400	Service Revenue		47,000		
622	Maintenance and Repairs Expense	4,100			
711	Depreciation Expense	3,300			

Account No.	Account Titles	Income Statement Dr.	Income Statement Cr.	Balance Sheet Dr.	Balance Sheet Cr.
722	Insurance Expense	2,200			
726	Salaries and Wages Expense	35,200			
732	Utilities Expense	4,000			
	Totals	48,800	47,000	52,500	54,300
	Net Loss		1,800	1,800	
		48,800	48,800	54,300	54,300

Instructions

(a) Net loss $1,800
Ending retained earnings $3,900
Total assets $38,600

(d) Post-closing trial balance $48,500

(a) Prepare an income statement, a retained earnings statement, and a classified balance sheet.
(b) Prepare the closing entries.
(c) Post the closing entries, and underline and balance the accounts. (Use T-accounts.) Income Summary is account No. 350.
(d) Prepare a post-closing trial balance.

Complete worksheet; prepare classified balance sheet, entries, and post-closing trial balance.

(LO 1, 2, 3, 6)

P4-4A Excelsior Amusement Park has a fiscal year ending on September 30. Selected data from the September 30 worksheet are presented below.

Excelsior Amusement Park
Worksheet
For the Year Ended September 30, 2014

	Trial Balance Dr.	Trial Balance Cr.	Adjusted Trial Balance Dr.	Adjusted Trial Balance Cr.
Cash	34,400		34,400	
Supplies	18,600		2,200	
Prepaid Insurance	29,900		10,900	
Land	80,000		80,000	
Equipment	120,000		120,000	
Accumulated Depreciation—Equip.		36,200		42,200
Accounts Payable		14,600		14,600
Unearned Ticket Revenue		3,900		1,000
Mortgage Payable		50,000		50,000
Common Stock		60,000		60,000
Retained Earnings		36,100		36,100
Dividends	14,000		14,000	
Ticket Revenue		277,900		280,800
Salaries and Wages Expense	98,000		98,000	
Maintenance and Repairs Expense	30,500		30,500	
Advertising Expense	9,400		9,400	
Utilities Expense	16,900		16,900	
Property Tax Expense	21,000		24,000	
Interest Expense	6,000		8,000	
Totals	478,700	478,700		
Insurance Expense			19,000	
Supplies Expense			16,400	
Interest Payable				2,000
Depreciation Expense			6,000	
Property Taxes Payable				3,000
Totals			489,700	489,700

Instructions

(a) Net income $52,600
(b) Total current assets $47,500

(e) Post-closing trial balance $247,500

(a) Prepare a complete worksheet.
(b) Prepare a classified balance sheet. (*Note:* $15,000 of the mortgage note payable is due for payment in the next fiscal year.)
(c) Journalize the adjusting entries using the worksheet as a basis.
(d) Journalize the closing entries using the worksheet as a basis.
(e) Prepare a post-closing trial balance.

P4-5A Lynda Hines opened Fresh Step Carpet Cleaners on March 1. During March, the following transactions were completed.

Complete all steps in accounting cycle.

(LO 1, 2, 3, 4, 6)

Mar.	1	Stockholders invested $14,000 cash in the business in exchange for common stock.
	1	Purchased used truck for $8,000, paying $3,000 cash and the balance on account.
	3	Purchased cleaning supplies for $1,200 on account.
	5	Paid $1,800 cash on one-year insurance policy effective March 1.
	14	Billed customers $4,800 for cleaning services.
	18	Paid $1,500 cash on amount owed on truck and $500 on amount owed on cleaning supplies.
	20	Paid $1,800 cash for employee salaries.
	21	Collected $1,600 cash from customers billed on March 14.
	28	Billed customers $2,500 for cleaning services.
	31	Paid gasoline for month on truck $320.
	31	Declared and paid $800 cash dividends.

The chart of accounts for Fresh Step Carpet Cleaners contains the following accounts: No. 101 Cash, No. 112 Accounts Receivable, No. 128 Supplies, No. 130 Prepaid Insurance, No. 157 Equipment, No. 158 Accumulated Depreciation—Equipment, No. 201 Accounts Payable, No. 212 Salaries and Wages Payable, No. 311 Common Stock, No. 320 Retained Earnings, No. 332 Dividends, No. 350 Income Summary, No. 400 Service Revenue, No. 633 Gasoline Expense, No. 634 Supplies Expense, No. 711 Depreciation Expense, No. 722 Insurance Expense, and No. 726 Salaries and Wages Expense.

Instructions

(a) Journalize and post the March transactions. Use page J1 for the journal and the three-column form of account.

(b) Prepare a trial balance at March 31 on a worksheet.

(c) Enter the following adjustments on the worksheet and complete the worksheet.
  (1) Unbilled revenue for services performed at March 31 was $750.
  (2) Depreciation on equipment for the month was $300.
  (3) One-twelfth of the insurance expired.
  (4) An inventory count shows $250 of cleaning supplies on hand at March 31.
  (5) Accrued but unpaid employee salaries were $720.

(b) Trial balance $25,500
(c) Adjusted trial balance $27,270

(d) Prepare the income statement and a retained earnings statement for March and a classified balance sheet at March 31.

(d) Net income $3,810
Total assets $21,930

(e) Journalize and post adjusting entries. Use page J2 for the journal.

(f) Journalize and post closing entries and complete the closing process. Use page J3 for the journal.

(g) Prepare a post-closing trial balance at March 31.

(g) Post-closing trial balance $22,230

P4-6A Sara Yu, CPA, was retained by Info Cable to prepare financial statements for April 2014. Yu accumulated all the ledger balances per Info's records and found the following.

Analyze errors and prepare correcting entries and trial balance.

(LO 5)

Info Cable
Trial Balance
April 30, 2014

	Debit	Credit
Cash	$ 4,100	
Accounts Receivable	3,200	
Supplies	800	
Equipment	10,600	
Accumulated Depreciation—Equip.		$ 1,250
Accounts Payable		2,100
Salaries and Wages Payable		700
Unearned Service Revenue		890
Common Stock		10,000
Retained Earnings		2,880
Service Revenue		5,450
Salaries and Wages Expense	3,300	
Advertising Expense	480	
Miscellaneous Expense	290	
Depreciation Expense	500	
	$23,270	$23,270

Sara Yu reviewed the records and found the following errors.

1. Cash received from a customer on account was recorded as $950 instead of $590.
2. A payment of $75 for advertising expense was entered as a debit to Miscellaneous Expense $75 and a credit to Cash $75.
3. The first salary payment this month was for $1,850, which included $700 of salaries payable on March 31. The payment was recorded as a debit to Salaries and Wages Expense $1,850 and a credit to Cash $1,850. (No reversing entries were made on April 1.)
4. The purchase on account of a printer costing $310 was recorded as a debit to Supplies and a credit to Accounts Payable for $310.
5. A cash payment of repair expense on equipment for $125 was recorded as a debit to Equipment $152 and a credit to Cash $152.

Instructions

(a) Prepare an analysis of each error showing (1) the incorrect entry, (2) the correct entry, and (3) the correcting entry. Items 4 and 5 occurred on April 30, 2014.

Trial balance $22,570

(b) Prepare a correct trial balance.

PROBLEMS: SET B

Prepare worksheet, financial statements, and adjusting and closing entries.

(LO 1, 2, 6)

P4-1B The trial balance columns of the worksheet for Firmament Roofing at March 31, 2014, are as follows.

Firmament Roofing
Worksheet
For the Month Ended March 31, 2014

Account Titles	Trial Balance Dr.	Trial Balance Cr.
Cash	2,720	
Accounts Receivable	2,700	
Supplies	1,500	
Equipment	11,000	
Accumulated Depreciation—Equipment		1,250
Accounts Payable		2,500
Unearned Service Revenue		550
Common Stock		10,000
Dividends	1,100	
Service Revenue		6,300
Salaries and Wages Expense	1,300	
Miscellaneous Expense	280	
	20,600	20,600

Other data:

1. A physical count reveals only $550 of roofing supplies on hand.
2. Depreciation for March is $250.
3. Unearned revenue amounted to $290 at March 31.
4. Accrued salaries are $480.

(a) Adjusted trial balance $21,330
(b) Net income $3,300
Total assets $15,470

Instructions

(a) Enter the trial balance on a worksheet and complete the worksheet.
(b) Prepare an income statement and a retained earnings statement for the month of March and a classified balance sheet at March 31. Common stock of $10,000 was issued for cash at the beginning of March.
(c) Journalize the adjusting entries from the adjustments columns of the worksheet.
(d) Journalize the closing entries from the financial statement columns of the worksheet.

Complete worksheet; prepare financial statements, closing entries, and post-closing trial balance.

(LO 1, 2, 3, 6)

GLS

P4-2B The adjusted trial balance columns of the worksheet for Eagle Company, owned by Jeff Spiegel, are as follows.

Eagle Company
Worksheet
For the Year Ended December 31, 2014

Account No.	Account Titles	Adjusted Trial Balance Dr.	Adjusted Trial Balance Cr.
101	Cash	5,300	
112	Accounts Receivable	10,800	
126	Supplies	1,500	
130	Prepaid Insurance	2,000	
151	Equipment	27,000	
152	Accumulated Depreciation—Equipment		5,600
200	Notes Payable		15,000
201	Accounts Payable		4,600
212	Salaries and Wages Payable		2,400
230	Interest Payable		600
311	Common Stock		10,000
320	Retained Earnings		4,200
332	Dividends	5,000	
400	Service Revenue		59,000
610	Advertising Expense	8,400	
631	Supplies Expense	4,000	
711	Depreciation Expense	5,600	
722	Insurance Expense	3,200	
726	Salaries and Wages Expense	28,000	
905	Interest Expense	600	
	Totals	101,400	101,400

Instructions

(a) Complete the worksheet by extending the balances to the financial statement columns.

(a) Net income $9,200

(b) Prepare an income statement, a retained earnings statement, and a classified balance sheet. (*Note:* $3,000 of the notes payable become due in 2015.)

(b) Current assets $19,600; Current liabilities $10,600

(c) Prepare the closing entries. Use J14 for the journal page.

(d) Post the closing entries. Use the three-column form of account. Income Summary is No. 350.

(e) Prepare a post-closing trial balance.

(e) Post-closing trial balance $46,600

P4-3B The completed financial statement columns of the worksheet for Lathrop Company are shown below and on the next page.

Prepare financial statements, closing entries, and post-closing trial balance.

(LO 1, 2, 3, 6)

Lathrop Company
Worksheet
For the Year Ended December 31, 2014

Account No.	Account Titles	Income Statement Dr.	Income Statement Cr.	Balance Sheet Dr.	Balance Sheet Cr.
101	Cash			8,900	
112	Accounts Receivable			10,800	
130	Prepaid Insurance			2,800	
157	Equipment			28,000	
167	Accumulated Depreciation—Equip.				4,500
201	Accounts Payable				2,000
212	Salaries and Wages Payable				2,400
311	Common Stock				12,000
320	Retained Earnings				16,400
332	Dividends			8,000	
400	Service Revenue		56,000		
622	Maintenance and Repairs Expense	1,600			

Account No.	Account Titles	Income Statement Dr.	Income Statement Cr.	Balance Sheet Dr.	Balance Sheet Cr.
711	Depreciation Expense	3,000			
722	Insurance Expense	1,800			
726	Salaries and Wages Expense	27,000			
732	Utilities Expense	1,400			
	Totals	34,800	56,000	58,500	37,300
	Net Income	21,200			21,200
		56,000	56,000	58,500	58,500

(a) Ending retained earnings $29,600;
Total current assets $22,500

(d) Post-closing trial balance $50,500

Instructions

(a) Prepare an income statement, a retained earnings statement, and a classified balance sheet.
(b) Prepare the closing entries.
(c) Post the closing entries, and underline and balance the accounts. (Use T-accounts.) Income Summary is account No. 350.
(d) Prepare a post-closing trial balance.

Complete worksheet; prepare classified balance sheet, entries, and post-closing trial balance.

(LO 1, 2, 3, 6)

P4-4B Kumar Management Services Inc. began business on January 1, 2014, with a capital investment of $120,000. The company manages condominiums for owners (Service Revenue) and rents space in its own office building (Rent Revenue). The trial balance and adjusted trial balance columns of the worksheet at the end of the first year are as follows.

Kumar Management Services Inc.
Worksheet
For the Year Ended December 31, 2014

Account Titles	Trial Balance Dr.	Trial Balance Cr.	Adjusted Trial Balance Dr.	Adjusted Trial Balance Cr.
Cash	13,800		13,800	
Accounts Receivable	26,300		26,300	
Prepaid Insurance	3,600		1,800	
Land	67,000		67,000	
Buildings	127,000		127,000	
Equipment	59,000		59,000	
Accounts Payable		12,500		12,500
Unearned Rent Revenue		8,000		3,500
Mortgage Payable		120,000		120,000
Common Stock		80,000		80,000
Retained Earnings		54,000		54,000
Dividends	16,000		16,000	
Service Revenue		90,700		90,700
Rent Revenue		26,000		30,500
Salaries and Wages Expense	42,000		42,000	
Advertising Expense	17,500		17,500	
Utilities Expense	19,000		19,000	
Totals	391,200	391,200		
Insurance Expense			1,800	
Depreciation Expense			6,600	
Accumulated Depreciation—Buildings				3,000
Accumulated Depreciation—Equipment				3,600
Interest Expense			9,600	
Interest Payable				9,600
Totals			407,400	407,400

(a) Net income $24,700
(b) Total current assets $41,900

Instructions

(a) Prepare a complete worksheet.
(b) Prepare a classified balance sheet. (*Note:* $25,000 of the mortgage note payable is due for payment next year.)

(c) Journalize the adjusting entries.
(d) Journalize the closing entries.
(e) Prepare a post-closing trial balance.

(e) Post-closing trial balance $294,900

P4-5B Tom Brennan opened Brennan's Cleaning Service on July 1, 2014. During July the following transactions were completed.

Complete all steps in accounting cycle.

(LO 1, 2, 3, 4, 6)

July	1	Stockholders invested $20,000 cash in the business in exchange for common stock.
	1	Purchased used truck for $12,000, paying $4,000 cash and the balance on account.
	3	Purchased cleaning supplies for $2,100 on account.
	5	Paid $1,800 cash on one-year insurance policy effective July 1.
	12	Billed customers $5,900 for cleaning services.
	18	Paid $1,500 cash on amount owed on truck and $1,400 on amount owed on cleaning supplies.
	20	Paid $4,500 cash for employee salaries.
	21	Collected $4,400 cash from customers billed on July 12.
	25	Billed customers $8,000 for cleaning services.
	31	Paid gasoline for month on truck $350.
	31	Declared and paid a $1,200 cash dividend.

The chart of accounts for Brennan's Cleaning Service contains the following accounts: No. 101 Cash, No. 112 Accounts Receivable, No. 128 Supplies, No. 130 Prepaid Insurance, No. 157 Equipment, No. 158 Accumulated Depreciation—Equipment, No. 201 Accounts Payable, No. 212 Salaries and Wages Payable, No. 311 Common Stock, No. 320 Retained Earnings, No. 332 Dividends, No. 350 Income Summary, No. 400 Service Revenue, No. 633 Gasoline Expense, No. 634 Supplies Expense, No. 711 Depreciation Expense, No. 722 Insurance Expense, and No. 726 Salaries and Wages Expense.

Instructions

(a) Journalize and post the July transactions. Use page J1 for the journal and the three-column form of account.
(b) Prepare a trial balance at July 31 on a worksheet.
(c) Enter the following adjustments on the worksheet and complete the worksheet.
   (1) Services provided but unbilled and uncollected at July 31 were $3,300.
   (2) Depreciation on equipment for the month was $500.
   (3) One-twelfth of the insurance expired.
   (4) An inventory count shows $600 of cleaning supplies on hand at July 31.
   (5) Accrued but unpaid employee salaries were $2,200.
(d) Prepare the income statement and retained earnings statement for July and a classified balance sheet at July 31.
(e) Journalize and post adjusting entries. Use page J2 for the journal.
(f) Journalize and post closing entries and complete the closing process. Use page J3 for the journal.
(g) Prepare a post-closing trial balance at July 31.

(b) Trial balance $41,100
(c) Adjusted trial balance $47,100
(d) Net income $8,000; Total assets $36,200
(g) Post-closing trial balance $36,700

PROBLEMS: SET C

Visit the book's companion website, at **www.wiley.com/college/weygandt**, and choose the Student Companion site to access Problem Set C.

COMPREHENSIVE PROBLEM: CHAPTERS 2 TO 4

CP4 Mary Coleman opened Mary's Maids Cleaning Service on July 1, 2014. During July, the company completed the following transactions.

July	1	Stockholders invested $15,000 cash in the business in exchange for common stock.
	1	Purchased a used truck for $10,000, paying $3,000 cash and the balance on account.

July 3 Purchased cleaning supplies for $1,700 on account.
5 Paid $1,800 on a one-year insurance policy, effective July 1.
12 Billed customers $4,200 for cleaning services.
18 Paid $1,000 of amount owed on truck, and $400 of amount owed on cleaning supplies.
20 Paid $1,900 for employee salaries.
21 Collected $2,400 from customers billed on July 12.
25 Billed customers $2,100 for cleaning services.
31 Paid gasoline for the month on the truck, $400.
31 Declared and paid a $500 cash dividend.

The chart of accounts for Mary's Maids Cleaning Service contains the following accounts: No. 101 Cash, No. 112 Accounts Receivable, No. 128 Supplies, No. 130 Prepaid Insurance, No. 157 Equipment, No. 158 Accumulated Depreciation—Equipment, No. 201 Accounts Payable, No. 212 Salaries and Wages Payable, No. 311 Common Stock, No. 320 Retained Earnings, No. 332 Dividends, No. 350 Income Summary, No. 400 Service Revenue, No. 633 Gasoline Expense, No. 634 Supplies Expense, No. 711 Depreciation Expense, No. 722 Insurance Expense, and No. 726 Salaries and Wages Expense.

Instructions

(a) Journalize and post the July transactions. Use page J1 for the journal.

(b) Trial balance totals $28,600

(b) Prepare a trial balance at July 31 on a worksheet.

(c) Enter the following adjustments on the worksheet, and complete the worksheet.
  (1) Unbilled fees for services performed at July 31 were $1,300.
  (2) Depreciation on equipment for the month was $200.
  (3) One-twelfth of the insurance expired.
  (4) An inventory count shows $280 of cleaning supplies on hand at July 31.
  (5) Accrued but unpaid employee salaries were $630.

(d) Net income $2,900
Total assets $25,330

(d) Prepare the income statement and retained earnings statement for July, and a classified balance sheet at July 31, 2014.

(e) Journalize and post the adjusting entries. Use page J2 for the journal.

(f) Journalize and post the closing entries, and complete the closing process. Use page J3 for the journal.

(g) Trial balance totals $25,530

(g) Prepare a post-closing trial balance at July 31.

CONTINUING COOKIE CHRONICLE

(*Note:* This is a continuation of the Cookie Chronicle from Chapters 1–3.)

CCC4 Natalie had a very busy December. At the end of the month, after journalizing and posting the December transactions and adjusting entries, Natalie prepared the following adjusted trial balance.

Cookie Creations
Adjusted Trial Balance
December 31, 2014

	Debit	Credit
Cash	$1,180	
Accounts Receivable	875	
Supplies	350	
Prepaid Insurance	1,210	
Equipment	1,200	
Accumulated Depreciation—Equipment		$ 40
Accounts Payable		75
Salaries and Wages Payable		56
Unearned Service Revenue		300
Notes Payable		2,000
Interest Payable		15

Common Stock		800
Dividends	500	
Service Revenue		4,515
Salaries and Wages Expense	1,006	
Utilities Expense	125	
Advertising Expense	165	
Supplies Expense	1,025	
Depreciation Expense	40	
Insurance Expense	110	
Interest Expense	15	
	$7,801	$7,801

Instructions

Using the information in the adjusted trial balance, do the following.

(a) Prepare an income statement and a retained earnings statement for the 2 months ended December 31, 2014, and a classified balance sheet at December 31, 2014. The note payable has a stated interest rate of 6%, and the principal and interest are due on November 16, 2016.

(b) Natalie has decided that her year-end will be December 31, 2014. Prepare closing entries as of December 31, 2014.

(c) Prepare a post-closing trial balance.

Broadening Your PERSPECTIVE

Financial Reporting and Analysis

Financial Reporting Problem: PepsiCo, Inc.

BYP4-1 The financial statements of PepsiCo, Inc. are presented in Appendix A at the end of this textbook.

Instructions

Answer the questions below using the Consolidated Balance Sheet and the Notes to Consolidated Financial Statements section.

(a) What were PepsiCo's total current assets at December 25, 2010, and December 26, 2009?
(b) Are assets that PepsiCo included under current assets listed in proper order? Explain.
(c) How are PepsiCo's assets classified?
(d) What are "cash equivalents"?
(e) What were PepsiCo's total current liabilities at December 25, 2010, and December 26, 2009?

Comparative Analysis Problem: PepsiCo, Inc. vs. The Coca-Cola Company

BYP4-2 PepsiCo's financial statements are presented in Appendix A. Financial statements for The Coca-Cola Company are presented in Appendix B.

Instructions

(a) Based on the information contained in these financial statements, determine each of the following for PepsiCo at December 25, 2010, and for Coca-Cola at December 31, 2010.
  (1) Total current assets.
  (2) Net amount of property, plant, and equipment (land, buildings, and equipment).
  (3) Total current liabilities.
  (4) Total equity.

(b) What conclusions concerning the companies' respective financial positions can be drawn?

Real-World Focus

BYP4-3 Numerous companies have established home pages on the Internet, e.g., Capt'n Eli Root Beer Company *(www.captneli.com/rootbeer.php)* and Kodak *(www.kodak.com)*.

Instructions

Examine the home pages of any two companies and answer the following questions.

(a) What type of information is available?
(b) Is any accounting-related information presented?
(c) Would you describe the home page as informative, promotional, or both? Why?

Critical Thinking

Decision-Making Across the Organization

BYP4-4 Everclean Janitorial Service was started 2 years ago by Lauren Baird. Because business has been exceptionally good, Lauren decided on July 1, 2014, to expand operations by acquiring an additional truck and hiring two more assistants. To finance the expansion, Lauren obtained on July 1, 2014, a $25,000, 10% bank loan, payable $10,000 on July 1, 2015, and the balance on July 1, 2016. The terms of the loan require the borrower to have $10,000 more current assets than current liabilities at December 31, 2014. If these terms are not met, the bank loan will be refinanced at 15% interest. At December 31, 2014, the accountant for Everclean Janitorial Service prepared the balance sheet shown below.

Lauren presented the balance sheet to the bank's loan officer on January 2, 2015, confident that the company had met the terms of the loan. The loan officer was not impressed. She said, "We need financial statements audited by a CPA." A CPA was hired and immediately realized that the balance sheet had been prepared from a trial balance and not from an adjusted trial balance. The adjustment data at the balance sheet date consisted of the following.

(1) Unbilled janitorial services performed were $3,900.
(2) Janitorial supplies on hand were $2,100.
(3) Prepaid insurance was a 3-year policy dated January 1, 2014.
(4) December expenses incurred but unpaid at December 31, $620.
(5) Interest on the bank loan was not recorded.
(6) The amounts for property, plant, and equipment presented in the balance sheet were reported net of accumulated depreciation (cost less accumulated depreciation). These amounts were $4,000 for cleaning equipment and $5,000 for delivery trucks as of January 1, 2014. Depreciation for 2014 was $2,000 for cleaning equipment and $5,000 for delivery trucks.

Everclean Janitorial Service
Balance Sheet
December 31, 2014

Assets		**Liabilities and Stockholders' Equity**	
Current assets		Current liabilities	
Cash	$ 5,500	Notes payable	$10,000
Accounts receivable	9,000	Accounts payable	1,500
Janitorial supplies	5,200	Total current liabilities	11,500
Prepaid insurance	4,800	Long-term liability	
Total current assets	24,500	Notes payable	15,000
Property, plant, and equipment		Total liabilities	26,500
Cleaning equipment (net)	22,000	Stockholders' equity	
Delivery trucks (net)	34,000	Common stock	30,000
Total property, plant, and equipment	56,000	Retained earnings	24,000
Total assets	$80,500	Total liabilities and stockholders' equity	$80,500

Instructions

With the class divided into groups, answer the following.

(a) Prepare a correct balance sheet.
(b) Were the terms of the bank loan met? Explain.

Communication Activity

BYP4-5 The accounting cycle is important in understanding the accounting process.

Instructions

Write a memo to your instructor that lists the steps of the accounting cycle in the order they should be completed. End with a paragraph that explains the optional steps in the cycle.

Ethics Case

BYP4-6 As the controller of Take No Prisoners Perfume Company, you discover a misstatement that overstated net income in the prior year's financial statements. The misleading financial statements appear in the company's annual report which was issued to banks and other creditors less than a month ago. After much thought about the consequences of telling the president, Phil McNally, about this misstatement, you gather your courage to inform him. Phil says, "Hey! What they don't know won't hurt them. But, just so we set the record straight, we'll adjust this year's financial statements for last year's misstatement. We can absorb that misstatement better in this year than in last year anyway! Just don't make such a mistake again."

Instructions

(a) Who are the stakeholders in this situation?
(b) What are the ethical issues in this situation?
(c) What would you do as a controller in this situation?

All About You

BYP4-7 Companies prepare balance sheets in order to know their financial position at a specific point in time. This enables them to make a comparison to their position at previous points in time, and gives them a basis for planning for the future. In order to evaluate your financial position, you need to prepare a personal balance sheet. Assume that you have compiled the following information regarding your finances. (*Hint:* Some of the items might not be used in your personal balance sheet.)

Amount owed on student loan balance (long-term)	$ 5,000
Balance in checking account	1,200
Certificate of deposit (6-month)	3,000
Annual earnings from part-time job	12,800
Automobile	7,000
Balance on automobile loan (current portion)	1,500
Balance on automobile loan (long-term portion)	4,000
Home computer	1,100
Amount owed to you by younger brother	300
Balance in money market account	1,800
Annual tuition	6,400
Video and stereo equipment	1,250
Balance owed on credit card (current portion)	190
Balance owed on credit card (long-term portion)	1,850

Instructions

Prepare a personal balance sheet using the format you have learned for a classified balance sheet for a company. For the equity account, use Owner's Equity.

FASB Codification Activity

BYP4-8 If your school has a subscription to the FASB Codification, go to *http://aaahq.org/ascLogin.cfm* to log in and prepare responses to the following.

Instructions

(a) Access the glossary ("Master Glossary") at the FASB Codification website to answer the following.
  (1) What is the definition of current assets?
  (2) What is the definition of current liabilities?
(b) A company wants to offset its accounts payable against its cash account and show a cash amount net of accounts payable on its balance sheet. Identify the criteria (found in the FASB Codification) under which a company has the right of set off. Does the company have the right to offset accounts payable against the cash account?

Answers to Chapter Questions

Answers to Insight and Accounting Across the Organization Questions

p. 174 Cisco Performs the Virtual Close Q: Who else benefits from a shorter closing process? **A:** Investors benefit from a shorter closing process. The shorter the closing, the sooner the company can report its financial results. This means that the financial information is more timely and therefore more relevant to investors.

p. 179 Yale Express Loses Some Transportation Bills Q: What might Yale Express's vice president have done to produce more accurate financial statements without waiting months for Republic's outstanding transportation bills? **A:** Yale's vice president could have engaged his accountants and auditors to prepare an adjusting entry based on an estimate of the outstanding transportation bills. (The estimate could have been made using past experience and the current volume of business.)

p. 183 Regaining Goodwill Q: Name two industries today which are probably rated low on the reputational characteristics of "being trusted" and "having high ethical standards." **A:** Two possible industries are financial companies (Goldman Sachs or AIG) or oil companies (BP).

p. 185 Can a Company Be Too Liquid? Q: What can various company managers do to ensure that working capital is managed efficiently to maximize net income? **A:** Marketing and sales managers must understand that by extending generous repayment terms, they are expanding the company's receivables balance and slowing the company's cash flow. Production managers must strive to minimize the amount of excess inventory on hand. Managers must coordinate efforts to speed up the collection of receivables, while also ensuring that the company pays its payables on time but never too early.

Answers to Self-Test Questions

1. b **2.** c **3.** c **4.** a **5.** b **6.** c **7.** a **8.** d **9.** c **10.** d **11.** b **12.** c **13.** c **14.** d **15.** a ***16.** c

A Look at IFRS

The classified balance sheet, although generally required internationally, contains certain variations in format when reporting under IFRS.

Key Points

- The procedures of the closing process are applicable to all companies, whether they are using IFRS or GAAP.
- IFRS recommends but does not require the use of the title "statement of financial position" rather than balance sheet.
- The format of statement of financial position information is often presented differently under IFRS. Although no specific format is required, most companies that follow IFRS present statement of financial position information in this order:
    - Noncurrent assets
    - Current assets
    - Equity
    - Noncurrent liabilities
    - Current liabilities
- IFRS requires a classified statement of financial position except in very limited situations. IFRS follows the same guidelines as this textbook for distinguishing between current and noncurrent assets and liabilities.

- Under IFRS, current assets are usually listed in the reverse order of liquidity. For example, under GAAP cash is listed first, but under IFRS it is listed last.
- Some companies report the subtotal *net assets,* which equals total assets minus total liabilities. See, for example, the statement of financial position of Zetar plc in Appendix C.
- IFRS has many differences in terminology that you will notice in this textbook. For example, in the sample statement of financial position illustrated below, notice in the investment category that stock is called shares.

Franklin Corporation
Statement of Financial Position
October 31, 2014

		Assets	
Intangible assets			
Patents			$ 3,100
Property, plant, and equipment			
Land		$10,000	
Equipment	$24,000		
Less: Accumulated depreciation	5,000	19,000	29,000
Long-term investments			
Investment in shares of Walters Corp.		5,200	
Investment in real estate		2,000	7,200
Current assets			
Prepaid insurance		400	
Supplies		2,100	
Inventories		3,000	
Notes receivable		1,000	
Accounts receivable		7,000	
Short-term investments		2,000	
Cash		6,600	22,100
Total assets			$61,400
		Equity and Liabilities	
Equity			
Share capital		$20,000	
Retained earnings		14,050	$34,050
Non-current liabilities			
Mortgage payable		10,000	
Notes payable		1,300	11,300
Current liabilities			
Notes payable		11,000	
Accounts payable		2,100	
Salaries payable		1,600	
Unearned service revenue		900	
Interest payable		450	16,050
Total equity and liabilities			$61,400

- Both IFRS and GAAP require disclosures about (1) accounting policies followed, (2) judgments that management has made in the process of applying the entity's accounting policies, and (3) the key assumptions and estimation uncertainty that could result in a material adjustment to the carrying amounts of assets and liabilities within the next financial year.
- Comparative prior-period information must be presented and financial statements must be prepared annually.

- Both GAAP and IFRS are increasing the use of fair value to report assets. However, at this point IFRS has adopted it more broadly. As examples, under IFRS companies can apply fair value to property, plant, and equipment; natural resources; and in some cases intangible assets.

Looking to the Future

The IASB and the FASB are working on a project to converge their standards related to financial statement presentation. A key feature of the proposed framework is that each of the statements will be organized in the same format, to separate an entity's financing activities from its operating and investing activities and, further, to separate financing activities into transactions with owners and creditors. Thus, the same classifications used in the statement of financial position would also be used in the income statement and the statement of cash flows. The project has three phases. You can follow the joint financial presentation project at the following link: *http://www.fasb.org/project/financial_statement_presentation.shtml.*

The IASB and the FASB face a difficult task in attempting to update, modify, and complete a converged conceptual framework. For example, how do companies choose between information that is highly relevant but difficult to verify versus information that is less relevant but easy to verify? How do companies define control when developing a definition of an asset? Is a liability the future sacrifice itself or the obligation to make the sacrifice? Should a single measurement method, such as historical cost or fair value, be used, or does it depend on whether it is an asset or liability that is being measured? It appears that the new document will be a significant improvement over its predecessors and will lead to principles-based standards, which will help financial statement users make better decisions.

IFRS Practice

IFRS Self-Test Questions

1. Which of the following statements is *false*?
(a) Assets equals liabilities plus equity.
(b) Under IFRS, companies sometimes net liabilities against assets to report "net assets."
(c) The FASB and IASB are working on a joint conceptual framework project.
(d) Under IFRS, the statement of financial position is usually referred to as the statement of assets and equity.

2. A company has purchased a tract of land and expects to build a production plant on the land in approximately 5 years. During the 5 years before construction, the land will be idle. Under IFRS, the land should be reported as:
(a) land expense.
(b) property, plant, and equipment.
(c) an intangible asset.
(d) a long-term investment.

3. Current assets under IFRS are listed generally:
(a) by importance.
(b) in the reverse order of their expected conversion to cash.
(c) by longevity.
(d) alphabetically.

4. Companies that use IFRS:
(a) may report all their assets on the statement of financial position at fair value.
(b) may offset assets against liabilities and show net assets and net liabilities on their statement of financial positions, rather than the underlying detailed line items.
(c) may report noncurrent assets before current assets on the statement of financial position.
(s) do not have any guidelines as to what should be reported on the statement of financial position.

5. Companies that follow IFRS to prepare a statement of financial position generally use the following order of classification:
(a) current assets, current liabilities, noncurrent assets, noncurrent liabilities, equity.
(b) noncurrent assets, noncurrent liabilities, current assets, current liabilities, equity.
(c) noncurrent assets, current assets, equity, noncurrent liabilities, current liabilities.
(d) equity, noncurrent assets, current assets, noncurrent liabilities, current liabilities.

IFRS Exercises

IFRS4-1 In what ways does the format of a statement of financial of position under IFRS often differ from a balance sheet presented under GAAP?

IFRS4-2 What term is commonly used under IFRS in reference to the balance sheet?

IFRS4-3 The statement of financial position for Diaz Company includes the following accounts (in pounds): Accounts Receivable £12,500; Prepaid Insurance £3,600; Cash £15,400; Supplies £5,200; and Short-Term Investments £6,700. Prepare the current assets section of the statement of financial position, listing the accounts in proper sequence.

IFRS4-4 Zurich Company recently received the following information (in Swiss francs) related to the company's December 31, 2014, statement of financial position.

Inventories	CHF 2,700	Short-term investments	CHF 120
Cash	13,100	Accumulated depreciation—	
Equipment	21,700	equipment	5,700
Investments in shares		Accounts receivable	4,300
(long-term)	6,500		

Prepare the assets section of the company's classified statement of financial position.

IFRS4-5 The following information is available for Rego Bowling Alley at December 31, 2014.

Buildings	$128,000	Share Capital	$90,000
Accounts Receivable	7,540	Retained Earnings	22,000
Prepaid Insurance	4,680	Accumulated Depreciation—Buildings	42,600
Cash	18,040	Accounts Payable	12,300
Equipment	62,400	Notes Payable	95,000
Land	67,000	Accumulated Depreciation—Equipment	18,720
Insurance Expense	780	Interest Payable	2,600
Depreciation Expense	7,360	Service Revenues	15,180
Interest Expense	2,600		

Prepare a classified statement of financial position; assume that $13,900 of the notes payable will be paid in 2015.

IFRS4-6 Brian Hopkins is interested in comparing the liquidity and solvency of a U.S. software company with a Chinese competitor. Is this possible if the two companies report using different currencies?

International Comparative Analysis Problem: PepsiCo vs. Zetar plc

IFRS4-7 The financial statements of Zetar plc are presented in Appendix C. The company's complete annual report, including the notes to its financial statements, is available at *www.zetarplc.com.*

Instructions

Identify five differences in the format of the statement of financial position used by Zetar plc compared to a company, such as PepsiCo, that follows GAAP. (PepsiCo's financial statements are available in Appendix A.)

Answers to IFRS Self-Test Questions

1. d **2.** d **3.** b **4.** c **5.** c

✔ Remember to go back to The Navigator box on the chapter opening page and check off your completed work.

Chapter 5

Accounting for Merchandising Operations

Feature Story

Who Doesn't Shop at Wal-Mart?

In his book *The End of Work,* Jeremy Rifkin notes that until the 20th century the word *consumption* evoked negative images. To be labeled a "consumer" was an insult. (In fact, one of the deadliest diseases in history, tuberculosis, was often referred to as "consumption.") Twentieth-century merchants realized, however, that in order to prosper, they had to convince people of the need for things not previously needed. For example, General Motors made annual changes in its cars so that people would be discontented with the cars they already owned. Thus began consumerism.

Today, consumption describes the U.S. lifestyle in a nutshell. We consume twice as much today per person as we did at the end of World War II. The amount of U.S. retail space per person is vastly greater than that of any other country. It appears that we live to shop.

The first great retail giant was Sears Roebuck. It started as a catalog company enabling people in rural areas to buy things by mail. For decades, it was the uncontested merchandising leader.

Today, Wal-Mart Stores, Inc. is the undisputed champion provider of basic (and perhaps not-so-basic) human needs. Wal-Mart opened its first store in 1962, and it now has

✔ The Navigator

- Scan Learning Objectives
- Read Feature Story
- Read Preview
- Read text and answer **DO IT!** p. 227, p. 231, p. 234, p. 239
- Work Comprehensive **DO IT!** p. 240
- Review Summary of Learning Objectives
- Answer Self-Test Questions
- Complete Assignments
- Go to **WileyPLUS** for practice and tutorials

Read A Look at IFRS p. 268

Learning Objectives

After studying this chapter, you should be able to:

1. Identify the differences between service and merchandising companies.
2. Explain the recording of purchases under a perpetual inventory system.
3. Explain the recording of sales revenues under a perpetual inventory system.
4. Explain the steps in the accounting cycle for a merchandising company.
5. Distinguish between a multiple-step and a single-step income statement.

The Navigator

more than 8,000 stores, serving more than 100 million customers every week. A key cause of Wal-Mart's incredible growth is its amazing system of inventory control and distribution. Wal-Mart has a management information system that employs six satellite channels, from which company computers receive 8.4 million updates every minute on what items customers buy and the relationship among items sold to each person.

Measured by sales revenues, Wal-Mart is the largest company in the world. In six years, it went from selling almost no groceries to being America's largest grocery retailer.

It would appear that things have never looked better at Wal-Mart. On the other hand, a *Wall Street Journal* article entitled "How to Sell More to Those Who Think It's Cool to Be Frugal" suggests that consumerism as a way of life might be dying. Don't bet your high-definition 3D TV on it though.

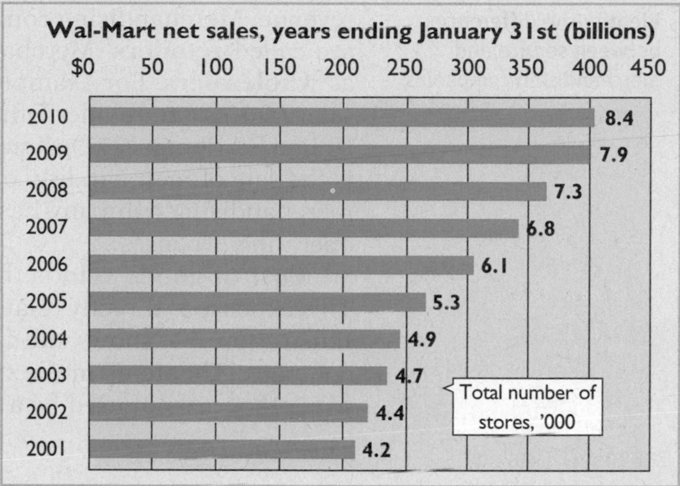

Source: "How Big Can It Grow?" *The Economist* (April 17, 2004), pp. 67–69, and *www.walmart.com* (accessed November 23, 2010).

✔ The Navigator

Preview of Chapter 5

Merchandising is one of the largest and most influential industries in the United States. It is likely that a number of you will work for a merchandiser. Therefore, understanding the financial statements of merchandising companies is important. In this chapter, you will learn the basics about reporting merchandising transactions. In addition, you will learn how to prepare and analyze a commonly used form of the income statement—the multiple-step income statement. The content and organization of the chapter are as follows.

ACCOUNTING FOR MERCHANDISING OPERATIONS

Merchandising Operations	Recording Purchases of Merchandise	Recording Sales of Merchandise	Completing the Accounting Cycle	Forms of Financial Statements
• Operating cycles • Flow of costs—perpetual and periodic inventory systems	• Freight costs • Purchase returns and allowances • Purchase discounts • Summary of purchasing transactions	• Sales returns and allowances • Sales discounts	• Adjusting entries • Closing entries • Summary of merchandising entries	• Multiple-step income statement • Single-step income statement • Classified balance sheet

✔ The Navigator

Merchandising Operations

LEARNING OBJECTIVE 1

Identify the differences between service and merchandising companies.

Wal-Mart, Kmart, and Target are called merchandising companies because they buy and sell merchandise rather than perform services as their primary source of revenue. Merchandising companies that purchase and sell directly to consumers are called **retailers**. Merchandising companies that sell to retailers are known as **wholesalers**. For example, retailer Walgreens might buy goods from wholesaler McKesson; retailer Office Depot might buy office supplies from wholesaler United Stationers. The primary source of revenues for merchandising companies is the sale of merchandise, often referred to simply as **sales revenue** or **sales**. A merchandising company has two categories of expenses: cost of goods sold and operating expenses.

Cost of goods sold is the total cost of merchandise sold during the period. This expense is directly related to the revenue recognized from the sale of goods. Illustration 5-1 shows the income measurement process for a merchandising company. The items in the two blue boxes are unique to a merchandising company; they are not used by a service company.

Illustration 5-1
Income measurement process for a merchandising company

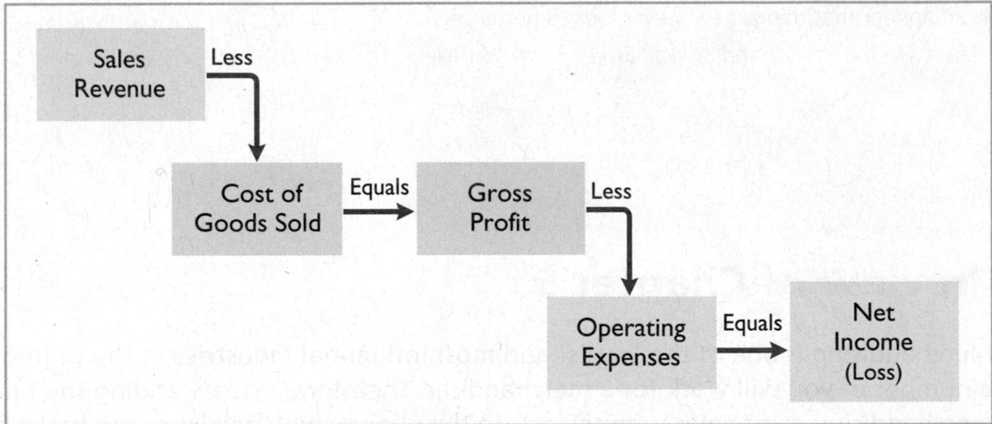

Operating Cycles

The operating cycle of a merchandising company ordinarily is longer than that of a service company. The purchase of merchandise inventory and its eventual sale lengthen the cycle. Illustration 5-2 contrasts the operating cycles of service and merchandising companies. Note that the added asset account for a merchandising company is the Inventory account. Companies report inventory as a current asset on the balance sheet.

Flow of Costs

The flow of costs for a merchandising company is as follows: Beginning inventory plus the cost of goods purchased is the cost of goods available for sale. As goods are sold, they are assigned to cost of goods sold. Those goods that are not sold by the end of the accounting period represent ending inventory. Illustration 5-3 describes these relationships. Companies use one of two systems to account for inventory: a **perpetual inventory system** or a **periodic inventory system**.

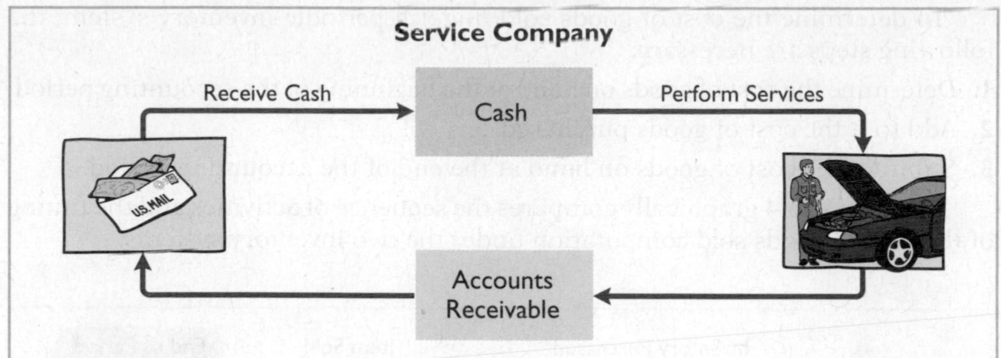

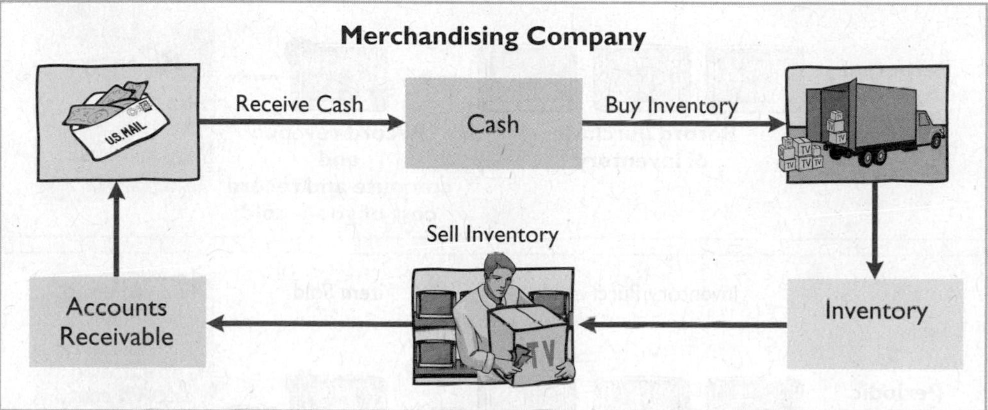

Illustration 5-2
Operating cycles for a service company and a merchandising company

PERPETUAL SYSTEM

In a **perpetual inventory system**, companies keep detailed records of the cost of each inventory purchase and sale. These records continuously—perpetually—show the inventory that should be on hand for every item. For example, a Ford dealership has separate inventory records for each automobile, truck, and van on its lot and showroom floor. Similarly, a Kroger grocery store uses bar codes and optical scanners to keep a daily running record of every box of cereal and every jar of jelly that it buys and sells. Under a perpetual inventory system, a company determines the cost of goods sold **each time a sale occurs.**

Helpful Hint
For control purposes, companies take a physical inventory count under the perpetual system, even though it is not needed to determine cost of goods sold.

PERIODIC SYSTEM

In a **periodic inventory system**, companies do not keep detailed inventory records of the goods on hand throughout the period. Instead, they determine the cost of goods sold **only at the end of the accounting period**—that is, periodically. At that point, the company takes a physical inventory count to determine the cost of goods on hand.

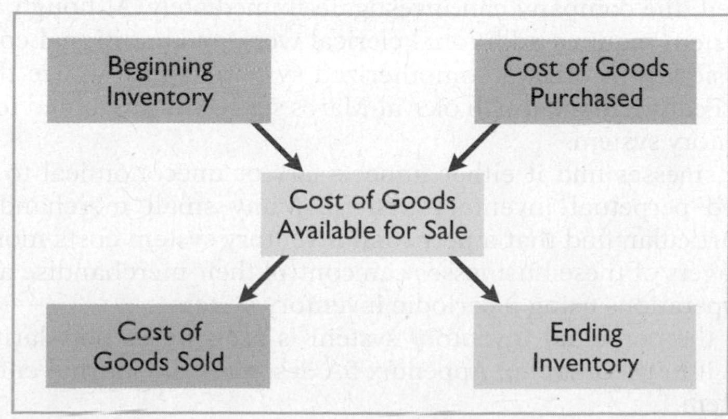

Illustration 5-3
Flow of costs

To determine the cost of goods sold under a periodic inventory system, the following steps are necessary:

1. Determine the cost of goods on hand at the beginning of the accounting period.
2. Add to it the cost of goods purchased.
3. Subtract the cost of goods on hand at the end of the accounting period.

Illustration 5-4 graphically compares the sequence of activities and the timing of the cost of goods sold computation under the two inventory systems.

Illustration 5-4
Comparing perpetual and periodic inventory systems

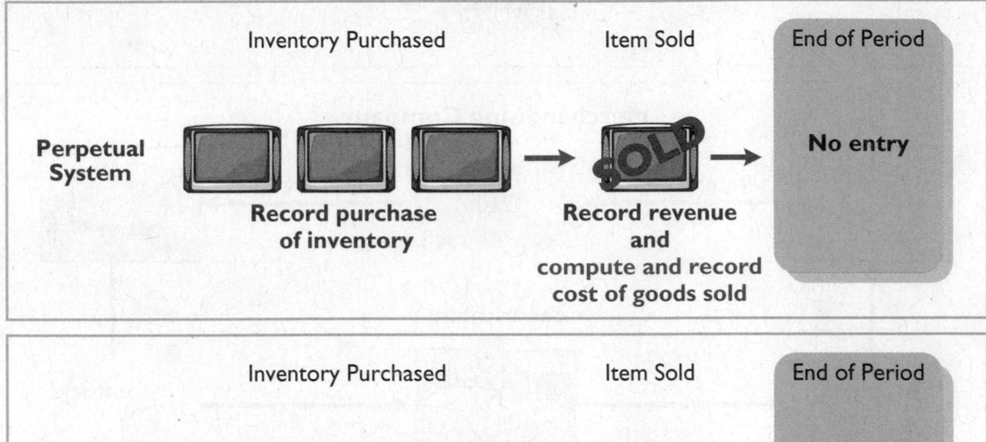

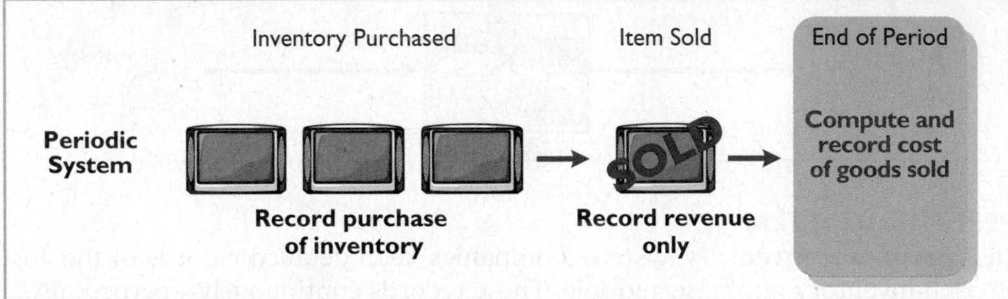

ADDITIONAL CONSIDERATIONS

Companies that sell merchandise with high unit values, such as automobiles, furniture, and major home appliances, have traditionally used perpetual systems. The growing use of computers and electronic scanners has enabled many more companies to install perpetual inventory systems. The perpetual inventory system is so named because the accounting records continuously—perpetually—show the quantity and cost of the inventory that should be on hand at any time.

A perpetual inventory system provides better control over inventories than a periodic system. Since the inventory records show the quantities that should be on hand, the company can count the goods at any time to see whether the amount of goods actually on hand agrees with the inventory records. If shortages are uncovered, the company can investigate immediately. Although a perpetual inventory system requires additional clerical work and additional cost to maintain the subsidiary records, a computerized system can minimize this cost. As noted in the Feature Story, much of Wal-Mart's success is attributed to its sophisticated inventory system.

Some businesses find it either unnecessary or uneconomical to invest in a computerized perpetual inventory system. Many small merchandising businesses, in particular, find that a perpetual inventory system costs more than it is worth. Managers of these businesses can control their merchandise and manage day-to-day operations using a periodic inventory system.

Because the perpetual inventory system is growing in popularity and use, we illustrate it in this chapter. Appendix 5A describes the journal entries for the periodic system.

INVESTOR INSIGHT

Morrow Snowboards Improves Its Stock Appeal

Investors are often eager to invest in a company that has a hot new product. However, when snowboard-maker Morrow Snowboards, Inc., issued shares of stock to the public for the first time, some investors expressed reluctance to invest in Morrow because of a number of accounting control problems. To reduce investor concerns, Morrow implemented a perpetual inventory system to improve its control over inventory. In addition, it stated that it would perform a physical inventory count every quarter until it felt that the perpetual inventory system was reliable.

? If a perpetual system keeps track of inventory on a daily basis, why do companies ever need to do a physical count? (See page 267.)

Recording Purchases of Merchandise

LEARNING OBJECTIVE 2

Explain the recording of purchases under a perpetual inventory system.

Companies purchase inventory using cash or credit (on account). They normally record purchases when they receive the goods from the seller. Business documents provide written evidence of the transaction. A canceled check or a cash register receipt, for example, indicates the items purchased and amounts paid for each cash purchase. Companies record cash purchases by an increase in Inventory and a decrease in Cash.

A **purchase invoice** should support each credit purchase. This invoice indicates the total purchase price and other relevant information. However, the purchaser does not prepare a separate purchase invoice. Instead, the purchaser uses as a purchase invoice a copy of the sales invoice sent by the seller. In Illustration 5-5 (page 224), for example, Sauk Stereo (the buyer) uses as a purchase invoice the sales invoice prepared by PW Audio Supply, Inc. (the seller).

Sauk Stereo makes the following journal entry to record its purchase from PW Audio Supply. The entry increases (debits) Inventory and increases (credits) Accounts Payable.

May 4	Inventory	3,800	
	Accounts Payable		3,800
	(To record goods purchased on account from PW Audio Supply)		

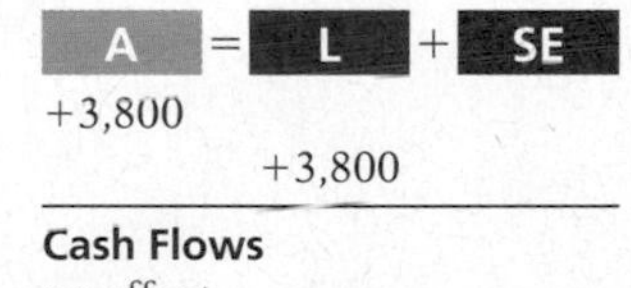

Under the perpetual inventory system, companies record purchases of merchandise for sale in the Inventory account. Thus, Wal-Mart would increase (debit) Inventory for clothing, sporting goods, and anything else purchased for resale to customers.

Not all purchases are debited to Inventory, however. Companies record purchases of assets acquired for use and not for resale, such as supplies, equipment, and similar items, as increases to specific asset accounts rather than to Inventory. For example, to record the purchase of materials used to make shelf signs or for cash register receipt paper, Wal-Mart would increase Supplies.

Freight Costs

The sales agreement should indicate who—the seller or the buyer—is to pay for transporting the goods to the buyer's place of business. When a common carrier

Illustration 5-5
Sales invoice used as purchase invoice by Sauk Stereo

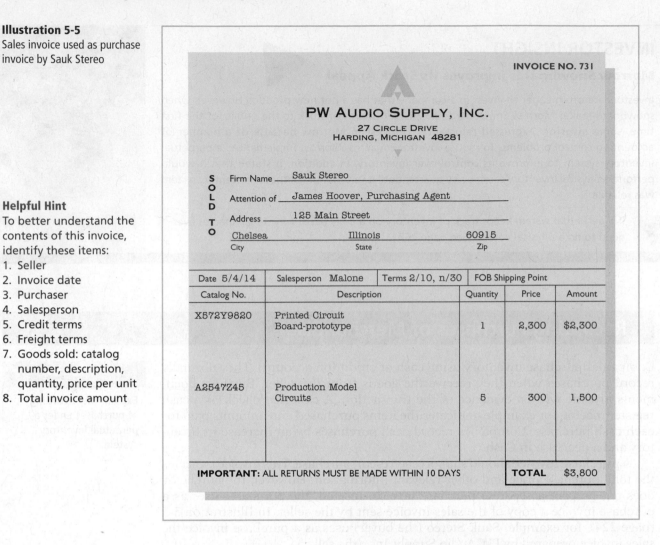

INVOICE NO. 731

PW AUDIO SUPPLY, INC.
27 CIRCLE DRIVE
HARDING, MICHIGAN 48281

SOLD TO
Firm Name: Sauk Stereo
Attention of: James Hoover, Purchasing Agent
Address: 125 Main Street
City: Chelsea State: Illinois Zip: 60915

Date 5/4/14	Salesperson Malone	Terms 2/10, n/30	FOB Shipping Point		
Catalog No.	Description		Quantity	Price	Amount
X572Y9820	Printed Circuit Board-prototype		1	2,300	$2,300
A2547Z45	Production Model Circuits		5	300	1,500
IMPORTANT: ALL RETURNS MUST BE MADE WITHIN 10 DAYS				TOTAL	$3,800

Helpful Hint
To better understand the contents of this invoice, identify these items:
1. Seller
2. Invoice date
3. Purchaser
4. Salesperson
5. Credit terms
6. Freight terms
7. Goods sold: catalog number, description, quantity, price per unit
8. Total invoice amount

such as a railroad, trucking company, or airline transports the goods, the carrier prepares a freight bill in accord with the sales agreement.

Freight terms are expressed as either FOB shipping point or FOB destination. The letters FOB mean **free on board**. Thus, **FOB shipping point** means that the seller places the goods free on board the carrier, and the buyer pays the freight costs. Conversely, **FOB destination** means that the seller places the goods free on board to the buyer's place of business, and the seller pays the freight. For example, the sales invoice in Illustration 5-5 indicates FOB shipping point. Thus, the buyer (Sauk Stereo) pays the freight charges. Illustration 5-6 illustrates these shipping terms.

Illustration 5-6
Shipping terms

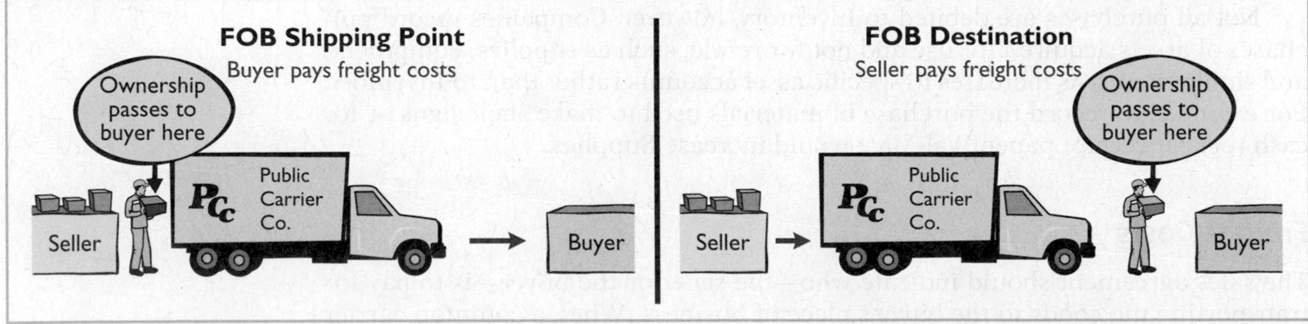

FREIGHT COSTS INCURRED BY THE BUYER

When the buyer incurs the transportation costs, these costs are considered part of the cost of purchasing inventory. Therefore, the buyer debits (increases) the account Inventory. For example, if upon delivery of the goods on May 6, Sauk Stereo (the buyer) pays Acme Freight Company $150 for freight charges, the entry on Sauk Stereo's books is:

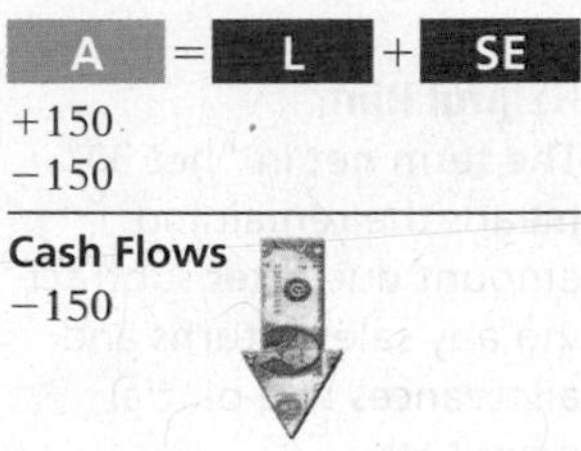

May 6	Inventory	150	
	Cash		150
	(To record payment of freight on goods purchased)		

Thus, any freight costs incurred by the buyer are part of the cost of merchandise purchased. The reason: Inventory cost should include all costs to acquire the inventory, including freight necessary to deliver the goods to the buyer. Companies recognize these costs as cost of goods sold when the inventory is sold.

FREIGHT COSTS INCURRED BY THE SELLER

In contrast, **freight costs incurred by the seller on outgoing merchandise are an operating expense to the seller**. These costs increase an expense account titled Freight-Out or Delivery Expense. If the freight terms on the invoice had required PW Audio Supply (the seller) to pay the freight charges, the entry by PW Audio Supply would be:

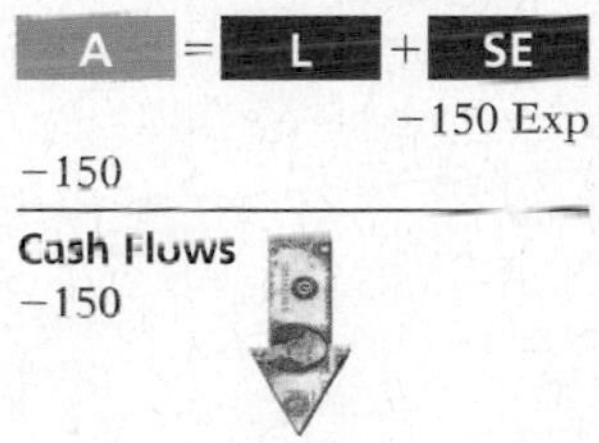

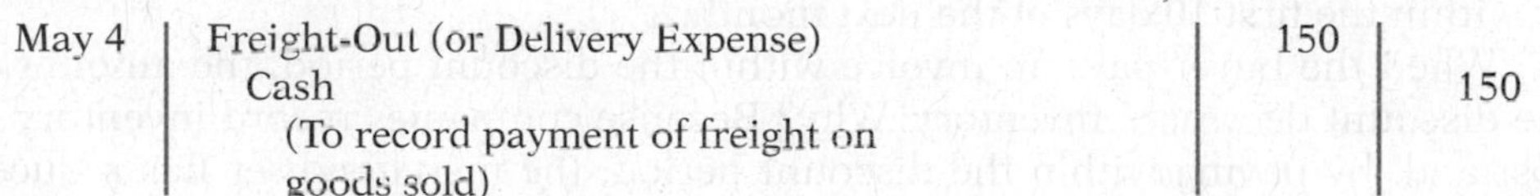

May 4	Freight-Out (or Delivery Expense)	150	
	Cash		150
	(To record payment of freight on goods sold)		

When the seller pays the freight charges, it will usually establish a higher invoice price for the goods to cover the shipping expense.

Purchase Returns and Allowances

A purchaser may be dissatisfied with the merchandise received because the goods are damaged or defective, of inferior quality, or do not meet the purchaser's specifications. In such cases, the purchaser may return the goods to the seller for credit if the sale was made on credit, or for a cash refund if the purchase was for cash. This transaction is known as a **purchase return**. Alternatively, the purchaser may choose to keep the merchandise if the seller is willing to grant an allowance (deduction) from the purchase price. This transaction is known as a **purchase allowance**.

Assume that on May 8 Sauk Stereo returned goods costing $300 to PW Audio Supply. The following entry by Sauk Stereo for the returned merchandise decreases (debits) Accounts Payable and decreases (credits) Inventory.

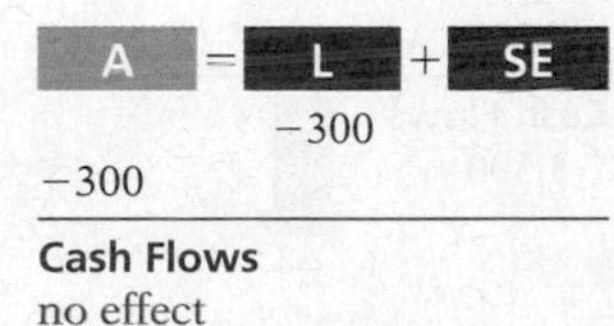

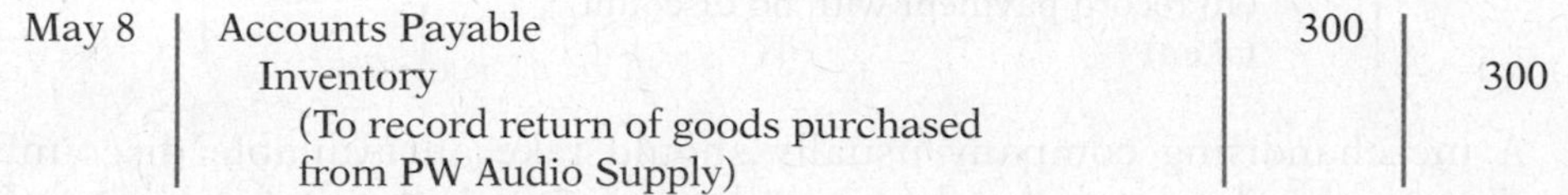

May 8	Accounts Payable	300	
	Inventory		300
	(To record return of goods purchased from PW Audio Supply)		

Because Sauk Stereo increased Inventory when the goods were received, Inventory is decreased when Sauk Stereo returns the goods (or when it is granted an allowance).

Suppose instead that Sauk Stereo chose to keep the goods after being granted a $50 allowance (reduction in price). It would reduce (debit) Accounts Payable and reduce (credit) Inventory for $50.

Purchase Discounts

The credit terms of a purchase on account may permit the buyer to claim a cash discount for prompt payment. The buyer calls this cash discount a **purchase discount**. This incentive offers advantages to both parties: The purchaser saves money, and the seller shortens the operating cycle by more quickly converting the accounts receivable into cash.

Helpful Hint
The term *net* in "net 30" means the remaining amount due after subtracting any sales returns and allowances and partial payments.

Credit terms specify the amount of the cash discount and time period in which it is offered. They also indicate the time period in which the purchaser is expected to pay the full invoice price. In the sales invoice in Illustration 5-5 (page 224), credit terms are 2/10, n/30, which is read "two-ten, net thirty." This means that the buyer may take a 2% cash discount on the invoice price less ("net of") any returns or allowances, if payment is made within 10 days of the invoice date (the **discount period**). Otherwise, the invoice price, less any returns or allowances, is due 30 days from the invoice date.

Alternatively, the discount period may extend to a specified number of days following the month in which the sale occurs. For example, 1/10 EOM (end of month) means that a 1% discount is available if the invoice is paid within the first 10 days of the next month.

When the seller elects not to offer a cash discount for prompt payment, credit terms will specify only the maximum time period for paying the balance due. For example, the invoice may state the time period as n/30, n/60, or n/10 EOM. This means, respectively, that the buyer must pay the net amount in 30 days, 60 days, or within the first 10 days of the next month.

When the buyer pays an invoice within the discount period, the amount of the discount decreases Inventory. Why? Because companies record inventory at cost and, by paying within the discount period, the merchandiser has reduced that cost. To illustrate, assume Sauk Stereo pays the balance due of \$3,500 (gross invoice price of \$3,800 less purchase returns and allowances of \$300) on May 14, the last day of the discount period. The cash discount is \$70 (\$3,500 × 2%), and Sauk Stereo pays \$3,430 (\$3,500 − \$70). The entry Sauk Stereo makes to record its May 14 payment decreases (debits) Accounts Payable by the amount of the gross invoice price, reduces (credits) Inventory by the \$70 discount, and reduces (credits) Cash by the net amount owed.

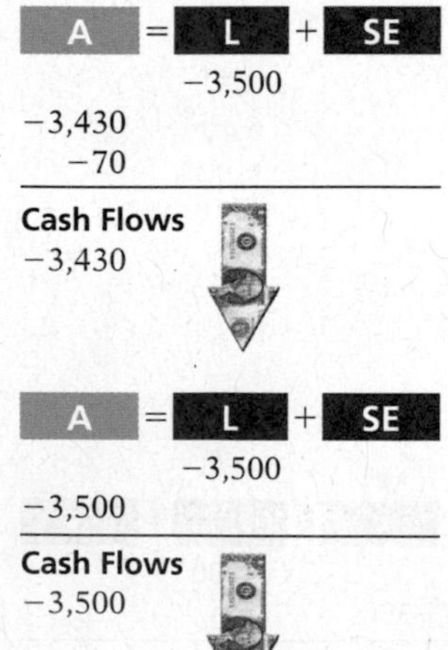

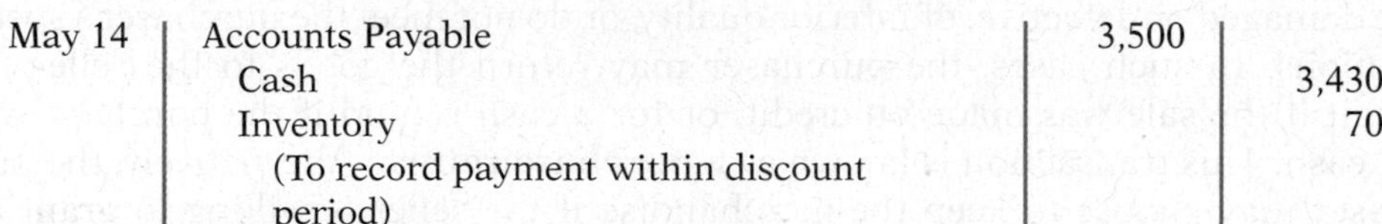

May 14	Accounts Payable	3,500	
	Cash		3,430
	Inventory		70
	(To record payment within discount period)		

If Sauk Stereo failed to take the discount, and instead made full payment of \$3,500 on June 3, it would debit Accounts Payable and credit Cash for \$3,500 each.

June 3	Accounts Payable	3,500	
	Cash		3,500
	(To record payment with no discount taken)		

A merchandising company usually should take all available discounts. Passing up the discount may be viewed as **paying interest** for use of the money. For example, passing up the discount offered by PW Audio Supply would be comparable to Sauk Stereo paying an interest rate of 2% for the use of \$3,500 for 20 days. This is the equivalent of an annual interest rate of approximately 36.5% (2% × 365/20). Obviously, it would be better for Sauk Stereo to borrow at prevailing bank interest rates of 6% to 10% than to lose the discount.

Summary of Purchasing Transactions

The following T-account (with transaction descriptions in blue) provides a summary of the effect of the previous transactions on Inventory. Sauk Stereo originally purchased $3,800 worth of inventory for resale. It then returned $300 of goods. It paid $150 in freight charges, and finally, it received a $70 discount off the balance owed because it paid within the discount period. This results in a balance in Inventory of $3,580.

	Inventory				
Purchase	May 4	3,800	May 8	300	**Purchase return**
Freight-in	6	150	14	70	**Purchase discount**
Balance		3,580			

> DO IT!

Purchase Transactions

On September 5, De La Hoya Company buys merchandise on account from Junot Diaz Company. The selling price of the goods is $1,500, and the cost to Diaz Company was $800. On September 8, De La Hoya returns defective goods with a selling price of $200. Record the transactions on the books of De La Hoya Company.

Action Plan

- ✔ Purchaser records goods at cost.
- ✔ When goods are returned, purchaser reduces Inventory.

Solution

Date	Account	Debit	Credit
Sept. 5	Inventory	1,500	
	Accounts Payable		1,500
	(To record goods purchased on account)		
8	Accounts Payable	200	
	Inventory		200
	(To record return of defective goods)		

Related exercise material: **BE5-2, BE5-4, E5-2, E5-3, E5-4, and DO IT! 5-1.**

✔ **The Navigator**

Recording Sales of Merchandise

LEARNING OBJECTIVE 3

Explain the recording of sales revenues under a perpetual inventory system.

In accordance with the revenue recognition principle, companies record sales revenue when the performance obligation is satisfied. Typically, the performance obligation is satisfied when the goods transfer from the seller to the buyer. At this point, the sales transaction is complete and the sales price established.

Sales may be made on credit or for cash. A **business document** should support every sales transaction, to provide written evidence of the sale. **Cash register tapes** provide evidence of cash sales. A **sales invoice**, like the one shown in Illustration 5-5 (page 224), provides support for a credit sale. The original copy of the invoice goes to the customer, and the seller keeps a copy for use in recording the sale. The invoice shows the date of sale, customer name, total sales price, and other relevant information.

The seller makes two entries for each sale. **The first entry records the sale**: The seller increases (debits) Cash (or Accounts Receivable, if a credit sale), and also increases (credits) Sales Revenue. **The second entry records the cost of**

the merchandise sold: The seller increases (debits) Cost of Goods Sold, and also decreases (credits) Inventory for the cost of those goods. As a result, the Inventory account will show at all times the amount of inventory that should be on hand.

To illustrate a credit sales transaction, PW Audio Supply records its May 4 sale of $3,800 to Sauk Stereo (see Illustration 5-5) as follows (assume the merchandise cost PW Audio Supply $2,400).

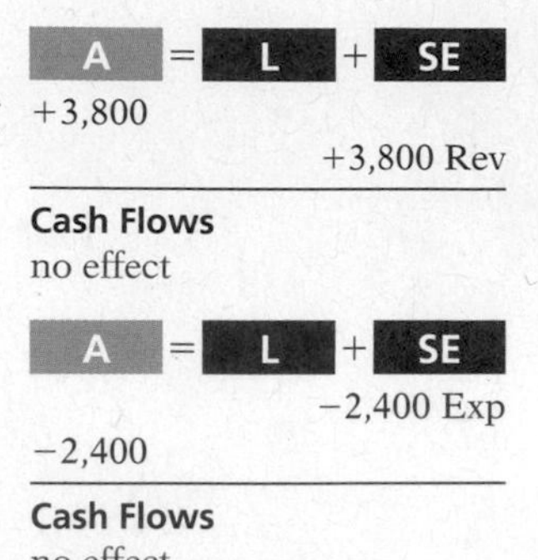

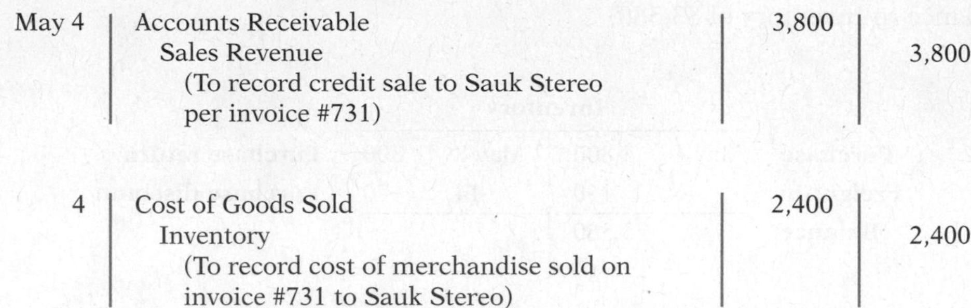

May 4	Accounts Receivable	3,800	
	Sales Revenue		3,800
	(To record credit sale to Sauk Stereo per invoice #731)		
4	Cost of Goods Sold	2,400	
	Inventory		2,400
	(To record cost of merchandise sold on invoice #731 to Sauk Stereo)		

For internal decision-making purposes, merchandising companies may use more than one sales account. For example, PW Audio Supply may decide to keep separate sales accounts for its sales of TV sets, DVD recorders, and microwave ovens. Wal-Mart might use separate accounts for sporting goods, children's clothing, and hardware—or it might have even more narrowly defined accounts. By using separate sales accounts for major product lines, rather than a single combined sales account, company management can more closely monitor sales trends and respond more strategically to changes in sales patterns. For example, if TV sales are increasing while microwave oven sales are decreasing, PW Audio Supply might reevaluate both its advertising and pricing policies on these items to ensure they are optimal.

Ethics Note

Many companies are trying to improve the quality of their financial reporting. For example, General Electric now provides more detail on its revenues and operating profits.

On its income statement presented to outside investors, a merchandising company normally would provide only a single sales figure—the sum of all of its individual sales accounts. This is done for two reasons. First, providing detail on all of its individual sales accounts would add considerable length to its income statement. Second, companies do not want their competitors to know the details of their operating results. However, Microsoft recently expanded its disclosure of revenue from three to five types. The reason: The additional categories will better enable financial statement users to evaluate the growth of the company's consumer and Internet businesses.

At the end of "Anatomy of a Fraud" stories, which describe some recent real-world frauds, we discuss the missing internal control activity that would likely have prevented or uncovered the fraud.

ANATOMY OF A FRAUD[1]

Holly Harmon was a cashier at a national superstore for only a short while when she began stealing merchandise using three methods. First, her husband or friends took UPC labels from cheaper items and put them on more expensive items. Holly then scanned the goods at the register. Second, Holly rang an item up but then voided the sale and left the merchandise in the shopping cart. A third approach was to put goods into large plastic containers. She rang up the plastic containers but not the goods within them. One day, Holly did not call in sick or show up for work. In such instances, the company reviews past surveillance tapes to look for suspicious activity by employees. This enabled the store to observe the thefts and to identify the participants.

[1]The "Anatomy of a Fraud" stories in this textbook are adapted from *Fraud Casebook: Lessons from the Bad Side of Business,* edited by Joseph T. Wells (Hoboken, NJ: John Wiley & Sons, Inc., 2007). Used by permission. The names of some of the people and organizations in the stories are fictitious, but the facts in the stories are true.

Total take: $12,000

The Missing Controls

Human resource controls. A background check would have revealed Holly's previous criminal record. She would not have been hired as a cashier.

Physical controls. Software can flag high numbers of voided transactions or a high number of sales of low-priced goods. Random comparisons of video records with cash register records can ensure that the goods reported as sold on the register are the same goods that are shown being purchased on the video recording. Finally, employees should be aware that they are being monitored.

Source: Adapted from Wells, *Fraud Casebook* (2007), pp. 251–259.

Sales Returns and Allowances

We now look at the "flipside" of purchase returns and allowances, which the seller records as **sales returns and allowances**. These are transactions where the seller either accepts goods back from the buyer (a return) or grants a reduction in the purchase price (an allowance) so the buyer will keep the goods. PW Audio Supply's entries to record credit for returned goods involve (1) an increase (debit) in Sales Returns and Allowances (a contra account to Sales Revenue) and a decrease (credit) in Accounts Receivable at the $300 selling price, and (2) an increase (debit) in Inventory (assume a $140 cost) and a decrease (credit) in Cost of Goods Sold, as shown below (assuming that the goods were not defective).

May 8	Sales Returns and Allowances	300	
	Accounts Receivable		300
	(To record credit granted to Sauk Stereo for returned goods)		
8	Inventory	140	
	Cost of Goods Sold		140
	(To record cost of goods returned)		

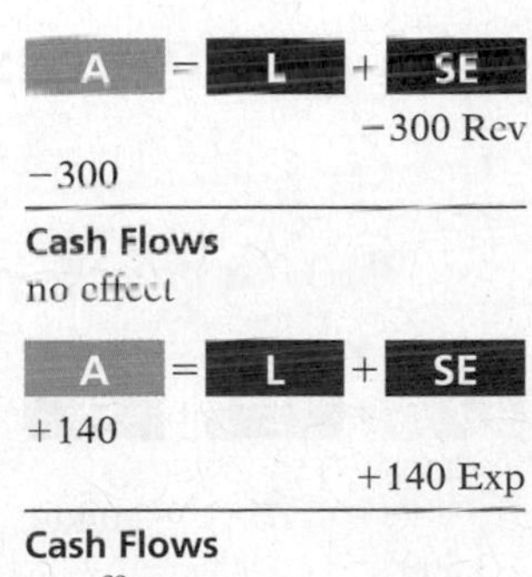

If Sauk Stereo returns goods because they are damaged or defective, then PW Audio Supply's entry to Inventory and Cost of Goods Sold should be for the fair value of the returned goods, rather than their cost. For example, if the returned goods were defective and had a fair value of $50, PW Audio Supply would debit Inventory for $50, and would credit Cost of Goods Sold for $50.

What happens if the goods are not returned but the seller grants the buyer an allowance by reducing the purchase price? In this case, the seller debits Sales Returns and Allowances and credits Accounts Receivable for the amount of the allowance.

As mentioned above, Sales Returns and Allowances is a **contra-revenue account** to Sales Revenue. The normal balance of Sales Returns and Allowances is a debit. Companies use a contra account, instead of debiting Sales Revenue, to disclose in the accounts and in the income statement the amount of sales returns and allowances. Disclosure of this information is important to management: Excessive returns and allowances may suggest problems—inferior merchandise, inefficiencies in filling orders, errors in billing customers, or delivery or shipment mistakes. Moreover, a decrease (debit) recorded directly to Sales Revenue would obscure the relative importance of sales returns and allowances as a percentage of sales. It also could distort comparisons between total sales in different accounting periods.

ACCOUNTING ACROSS THE ORGANIZATION

Should Costco Change Its Return Policy?

In most industries, sales returns are relatively minor. But returns of consumer electronics can really take a bite out of profits. Recently, the marketing executives at Costco Wholesale Corp. faced a difficult decision. Costco has always prided itself on its generous return policy. Most goods have had an unlimited grace period for returns. A new policy will require that certain electronics must be returned within 90 days of their purchase. The reason? The cost of returned products such as high-definition TVs, computers, and iPods cut an estimated 8¢ per share off Costco's earnings per share, which was $2.30.

Source: Kris Hudson, "Costco Tightens Policy on Returning Electronics," *Wall Street Journal* (February 27, 2007), p. B4.

If a company expects significant returns, what are the implications for revenue recognition? (See page 267.)

Sales Discounts

As mentioned in our discussion of purchase transactions, the seller may offer the customer a cash discount—called by the seller a **sales discount**—for the prompt payment of the balance due. Like a purchase discount, a sales discount is based on the invoice price less returns and allowances, if any. The seller increases (debits) the Sales Discounts account for discounts that are taken. For example, PW Audio Supply makes the following entry to record the cash receipt on May 14 from Sauk Stereo within the discount period.

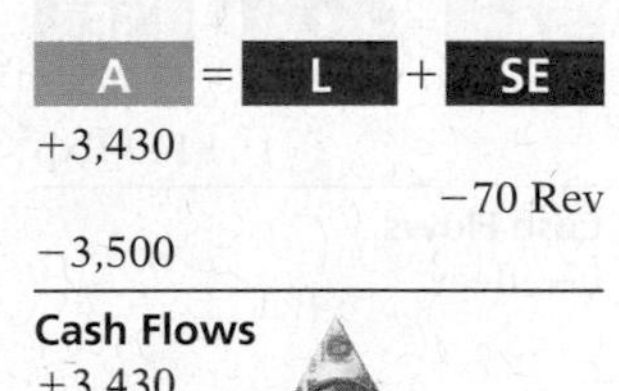

May 14	Cash	3,430	
	Sales Discounts	70	
	Accounts Receivable		3,500
	(To record collection within 2/10, n/30 discount period from Sauk Stereo)		

Like Sales Returns and Allowances, Sales Discounts is a **contra-revenue account** to Sales Revenue. Its normal balance is a debit. PW Audio Supply uses this account, instead of debiting Sales Revenue, to disclose the amount of cash discounts taken by customers. If Sauk Stereo does not take the discount, PW Audio Supply increases (debits) Cash for $3,500 and decreases (credits) Accounts Receivable for the same amount at the date of collection.

The following T-accounts summarize the three sales-related transactions and show their combined effect on net sales.

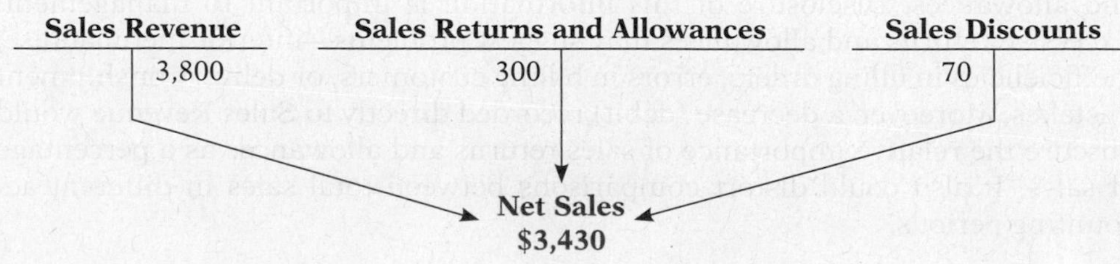

> DO IT!

Sales Transactions

On September 5, De La Hoya Company buys merchandise on account from Junot Diaz Company. The selling price of the goods is $1,500, and the cost to Diaz Company was $800. On September 8, De La Hoya returns defective goods with a selling price of $200 and a fair value of $30. Record the transactions on the books of Junot Diaz Company.

Action Plan

- ✔ Seller records both the sale and the cost of goods sold at the time of the sale.
- ✔ When goods are returned, the seller records the return in a contra account, Sales Returns and Allowances, and reduces Accounts Receivable. Any goods returned increase Inventory and reduce Cost of Goods Sold.
- ✔ Defective or damaged inventory is recorded at fair value (scrap value).

Solution

Date	Account	Debit	Credit
Sept. 5	Accounts Receivable	1,500	
	Sales Revenue		1,500
	(To record credit sale)		
5	Cost of Goods Sold	800	
	Inventory		800
	(To record cost of goods sold on account)		
8	Sales Returns and Allowances	200	
	Accounts Receivable		200
	(To record credit granted for receipt of returned goods)		
8	Inventory	30	
	Cost of Goods Sold		30
	(To record fair value of goods returned)		

Related exercise material: **BE5-2, BE5-3, E5-3, E5-4, E5-5, and DO IT! 5-2.**

✔ The Navigator

PEOPLE, PLANET, AND PROFIT INSIGHT

Selling Green

Here is a question an executive of PepsiCo was asked: Should PepsiCo market green? The executive indicated that the company should, as he believes it's the No. 1 thing consumers all over the world care about. Here are some thoughts on this issue:

If you are going to market green, what are some things we've learned? I'll share with you one thing we've learned at PepsiCo.

Sun Chips are part of the food business I run. It's a "healthy snack." We decided that Sun Chips, if it's a healthy snack, should be made in facilities that have a net-zero footprint. In other words, I want off the electric grid everywhere we make Sun Chips. We did that. Sun Chips should be made in a facility that puts back more water than it uses. It does that. And we partnered with our suppliers and came out with the world's first compostable chip package.

Now, there was an issue with this package: It was louder than the New York subway, louder than jet engines taking off. What would a company that's committed to green do: walk away or stay committed? If your people are passionate, they're going to fix it for you as long as you stay committed. Six months later, the compostable bag has half the noise of our current package.

So the view today is: we should market green, we should be proud to do it . . . it has to be a 360 process, both internal and external. And if you do that, you can monetize environmental sustainability for the shareholders.

Source: "Four Problems—and Solutions," *Wall Street Journal* (March 7, 2011), p. R2.

What is meant by "monetize environmental sustainability" for shareholders? (See page 267.)

Completing the Accounting Cycle

LEARNING OBJECTIVE 4

Explain the steps in the accounting cycle for a merchandising company.

Up to this point, we have illustrated the basic entries for transactions relating to purchases and sales in a perpetual inventory system. Now we consider the remaining steps in the accounting cycle for a merchandising company. Each of the required steps described in Chapter 4 for service companies apply to merchandising companies. Appendix 5B to this chapter shows use of a worksheet by a merchandiser (an optional step).

Adjusting Entries

A merchandising company generally has the same types of adjusting entries as a service company. However, a merchandiser using a perpetual system will require one additional adjustment to make the records agree with the actual inventory on hand. Here's why: At the end of each period, for control purposes, a merchandising company that uses a perpetual system will take a physical count of its goods on hand. The company's unadjusted balance in Inventory usually does not agree with the actual amount of inventory on hand. The perpetual inventory records may be incorrect due to recording errors, theft, or waste. Thus, the company needs to adjust the perpetual records to make the recorded inventory amount agree with the inventory on hand. **This involves adjusting Inventory and Cost of Goods Sold.**

For example, suppose that PW Audio Supply has an unadjusted balance of $40,500 in Inventory. Through a physical count, PW Audio Supply determines that its actual merchandise inventory at year-end is $40,000. The company would make an adjusting entry as follows.

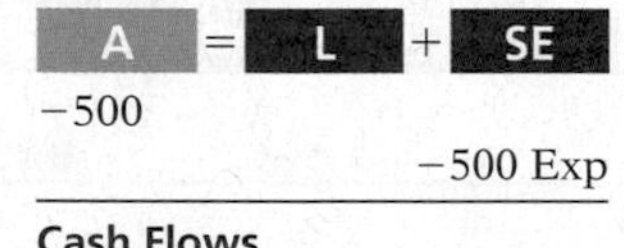

Cash Flows
no effect

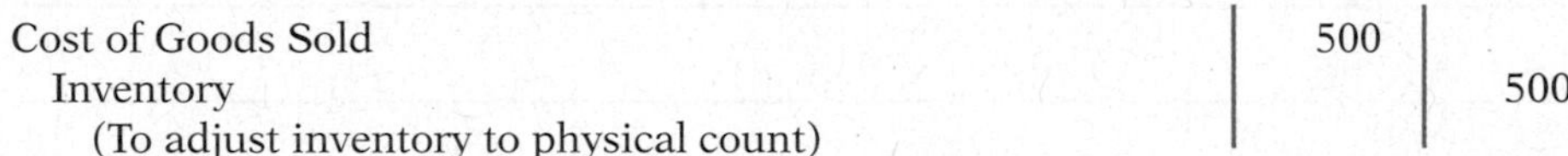

Account	Debit	Credit
Cost of Goods Sold	500	
Inventory		500
(To adjust inventory to physical count)		

Closing Entries

A merchandising company, like a service company, closes to Income Summary all accounts that affect net income. In journalizing, the company credits all temporary accounts with debit balances, and debits all temporary accounts with credit balances, as shown below for PW Audio Supply. Note that PW Audio Supply closes Cost of Goods Sold to Income Summary.

Helpful Hint
The easiest way to prepare the first two closing entries is to identify the temporary accounts by their balances and then prepare one entry for the credits and one for the debits.

Date	Account	Debit	Credit
Dec. 31	Sales Revenue	480,000	
	Income Summary		480,000
	(To close income statement accounts with credit balances)		
31	Income Summary	450,000	
	Sales Returns and Allowances		12,000
	Sales Discounts		8,000
	Cost of Goods Sold		316,000
	Salaries and Wages Expense		64,000
	Freight-Out		7,000
	Advertising Expense		16,000
	Utilities Expense		17,000
	Depreciation Expense		8,000
	Insurance Expense		2,000
	(To close income statement accounts with debit balances)		

		Dr.	Cr.
31	Income Summary	30,000	
	Retained Earnings		30,000
	(To close net income to retained earnings)		
31	Retained Earnings	15,000	
	Dividends		15,000
	(To close dividends to retained earnings)		

After PW Audio Supply has posted the closing entries, all temporary accounts have zero balances. Also, Retained Earnings has a balance that is carried over to the next period.

Summary of Merchandising Entries

Illustration 5-7 summarizes the entries for the merchandising accounts using a perpetual inventory system.

Illustration 5-7
Daily recurring and adjusting and closing entries

	Transactions	Daily Recurring Entries	Dr.	Cr.
Sales Transactions	Selling merchandise to customers.	Cash or Accounts Receivable	XX	
		Sales Revenue		XX
		Cost of Goods Sold	XX	
		Inventory		XX
	Granting sales returns or allowances to customers.	Sales Returns and Allowances	XX	
		Cash or Accounts Receivable		XX
		Inventory	XX	
		Cost of Goods Sold		XX
	Paying freight costs on sales; FOB destination.	Freight-Out	XX	
		Cash		XX
	Receiving payment from customers within discount period	Cash	XX	
		Sales Discounts	XX	
		Accounts Receivable		XX
Purchase Transactions	Purchasing merchandise for resale.	Inventory	XX	
		Cash or Accounts Payable		XX
	Paying freight costs on merchandise purchased; FOB shipping point.	Inventory	XX	
		Cash		XX
	Receiving purchase returns or allowances from suppliers.	Cash or Accounts Payable	XX	
		Inventory		XX
	Paying suppliers within discount period.	Accounts Payable	XX	
		Inventory		XX
		Cash		XX
	Events	**Adjusting and Closing Entries**		
	Adjust because book amount is higher than the inventory amount determined to be on hand.	Cost of Goods Sold	XX	
		Inventory		XX
	Closing temporary accounts with credit balances.	Sales Revenue	XX	
		Income Summary		XX
	Closing temporary accounts with debit balances.	Income Summary	XX	
		Sales Returns and Allowances		XX
		Sales Discounts		XX
		Cost of Goods Sold		XX
		Freight-Out		XX
		Expenses		XX

> DO IT!

Closing Entries

The trial balance of Celine's Sports Wear Shop at December 31 shows Inventory $25,000, Sales Revenue $162,400, Sales Returns and Allowances $4,800, Sales Discounts $3,600, Cost of Goods Sold $110,000, Rent Revenue $6,000, Freight-Out $1,800, Rent Expense $8,800, and Salaries and Wages Expense $22,000. Prepare the closing entries for the above accounts.

Action Plan

- ✔ Close all temporary accounts with credit balances to Income Summary by debiting these accounts.
- ✔ Close all temporary accounts with debit balances, except dividends, to Income Summary by crediting these accounts.

Solution

The two closing entries are:

Dec. 31	Sales Revenue	162,400	
	Rent Revenue	6,000	
	Income Summary		168,400
	(To close accounts with credit balances)		
31	Income Summary	151,000	
	Cost of Goods Sold		110,000
	Sales Returns and Allowances		4,800
	Sales Discounts		3,600
	Freight-Out		1,800
	Rent Expense		8,800
	Salaries and Wages Expense		22,000
	(To close accounts with debit balances)		

Related exercise material: **BE5-5, BE5-6, E5-6, E5-7, E5-8, and DO IT! 5-3.**

 **The Navigator**

Forms of Financial Statements

LEARNING OBJECTIVE 5

Distinguish between a multiple-step and a single-step income statement.

Merchandising companies widely use the classified balance sheet introduced in Chapter 4 and one of two forms for the income statement. This section explains the use of these financial statements by merchandisers.

Multiple-Step Income Statement

The **multiple-step income statement** is so named because it shows several steps in determining net income. Two of these steps relate to the company's principal operating activities. A multiple-step statement also distinguishes between **operating** and **nonoperating activities**. Finally, the statement also highlights intermediate components of income and shows subgroupings of expenses.

Income Statement Presentation of Sales

The multiple-step income statement begins by presenting **sales revenue**. It then deducts contra-revenue accounts—sales returns and allowances, and sales discounts—to arrive at **net sales**. Illustration 5-8 presents the sales revenues section for PW Audio Supply, using assumed data.

Illustration 5-8
Computation of net sales

PW Audio Supply, Inc. Income Statement (partial)		
Sales revenues		
Sales revenue		$ 480,000
Less: Sales returns and allowances	$12,000	
Sales discounts	8,000	20,000
Net sales		**$460,000**

This presentation discloses the key data about the company's principal revenue-producing activities.

GROSS PROFIT

From Illustration 5-1, you learned that companies deduct cost of goods sold from sales revenue in order to determine **gross profit.** For this computation, companies use **net sales** (which takes into consideration Sales Returns and Allowances and Sales Discounts) as the amount of sales revenue. On the basis of the sales data in Illustration 5-8 (net sales of $460,000) and cost of goods sold under the perpetual inventory system (assume $316,000), PW Audio Supply's gross profit is $144,000, computed as follows.

Illustration 5-9
Computation of gross profit

Net sales	$ 460,000
Cost of goods sold	316,000
Gross profit	**$144,000**

We also can express a company's gross profit as a percentage, called the **gross profit rate**. To do so, we divide the amount of gross profit by net sales. For PW Audio Supply, the **gross profit rate** is 31.3%, computed as follows.

Illustration 5-10
Gross profit rate formula and computation

Gross Profit	÷	Net Sales	=	Gross Profit Rate
$144,000	÷	$460,000	=	31.3%

Analysts generally consider the gross profit **rate** to be more useful than the gross profit **amount**. The rate expresses a more meaningful (qualitative) relationship between net sales and gross profit. For example, a gross profit of $1,000,000 may sound impressive. But if it is the result of a gross profit rate of only 7%, it is not so impressive. The gross profit rate tells how many cents of each sales dollar go to gross profit.

Gross profit represents the **merchandising profit** of a company. It is not a measure of the overall profitability, because operating expenses are not yet deducted. But managers and other interested parties closely watch the amount and trend of gross profit. They compare current gross profit with amounts reported in past periods. They also compare the company's gross profit rate with rates of competitors and with industry averages. Such comparisons provide information about the effectiveness of a company's purchasing function and the soundness of its pricing policies.

OPERATING EXPENSES AND NET INCOME

Operating expenses are the next component in measuring net income for a merchandising company. They are the expenses incurred in the process of earning sales revenue. These expenses are similar in merchandising and service companies. At PW Audio Supply, operating expenses were $114,000. The company determines its net income by subtracting operating expenses from gross profit. Thus, net income is $30,000, as shown below.

Illustration 5-11
Operating expenses in computing net income

Gross profit	$144,000
Operating expenses	**114,000**
Net income	$ 30,000

The net income amount is the so-called "bottom line" of a company's income statement.

Ethics Note

Companies manage earnings in various ways. ConAgra Foods recorded a nonrecurring gain for $186 million from the sale of Pilgrim's Pride stock to help meet an earnings projection for the quarter.

NONOPERATING ACTIVITIES

Nonoperating activities consist of various revenues and expenses and gains and losses that are unrelated to the company's main line of operations. When nonoperating items are included, the label "**Income from operations**" (or "Operating income") precedes them. This label clearly identifies the results of the company's normal operations, an amount determined by subtracting cost of goods sold and operating expenses from net sales. The results of nonoperating activities are shown in the categories "**Other revenues and gains**" and "**Other expenses and losses.**" Illustration 5-12 lists examples of each.

Illustration 5-12
Other items of nonoperating activities

Other Revenues and Gains
Interest revenue from notes receivable and marketable securities.
Dividend revenue from investments in common stock.
Rent revenue from subleasing a portion of the store.
Gain from the sale of property, plant, and equipment.

Other Expenses and Losses
Interest expense on notes and loans payable.
Casualty losses from recurring causes, such as vandalism and accidents.
Loss from the sale or abandonment of property, plant, and equipment.
Loss from strikes by employees and suppliers.

Merchandising companies report the nonoperating activities in the income statement immediately after the company's operating activities. Illustration 5-13 shows these sections for PW Audio Supply, Inc., using assumed data.

The distinction between operating and nonoperating activities is crucial to many external users of financial data. These users view operating income as sustainable and many nonoperating activities as nonrecurring. Therefore, when forecasting next year's income, analysts put the most weight on this year's operating income, and less weight on this year's nonoperating activities.

ETHICS INSIGHT

Disclosing More Details

After Enron, increased investor criticism and regulator scrutiny forced many companies to improve the clarity of their financial disclosures. For example, IBM announced that it would begin providing more detail regarding its "Other gains and losses." It had previously included these items in its selling, general, and administrative expenses, with little disclosure.

Disclosing other gains and losses in a separate line item on the income statement will not have any effect on bottom-line income. However, analysts complained that burying these details in the selling, general, and administrative expense line reduced their ability to fully understand how well IBM was performing. For example previously if IBM sold off one of its buildings at a gain, it would include this gain in the selling, general and administrative expense line item, thus reducing that expense. This made it appear that the company had done a better job of controlling operating expenses than it actually had.

Other companies that also recently announced changes to increase the informativeness of their income statements include PepsiCo and General Electric.

? Why have investors and analysts demanded more accuracy in isolating "Other gains and losses" from operating items? (See page 267.)

Illustration 5-13
Multiple-step income statement

PW Audio Supply, Inc.
Income Statement
For the Year Ended December 31, 2014

Calculation of gross profit	**Sales revenues**		
	Sales revenue		$480,000
	Less: Sales returns and allowances	$12,000	
	Sales discounts	8,000	20,000
	Net sales		460,000
	Cost of goods sold		316,000
	Gross profit		144,000
Calculation of income from operations	**Operating expenses**		
	Salaries and wages expense	64,000	
	Utilities expense	17,000	
	Advertising expense	16,000	
	Depreciation expense	8,000	
	Freight-out	7,000	
	Insurance expense	2,000	
	Total operating expenses		114,000
	Income from operations		30,000
Results of nonoperating activities	**Other revenues and gains**		
	Interest revenue	3,000	
	Gain on disposal of plant assets	600	3,600
	Other expenses and losses		
	Interest expense	1,800	
	Casualty loss from vandalism	200	2,000
	Net income		$ 31,600

Single-Step Income Statement

Another income statement format is the **single-step income statement**. The statement is so named because only one step—subtracting total expenses from total revenues—is required in determining net income.

In a single-step statement, all data are classified into two categories: (1) **revenues**, which include both operating revenues and other revenues and gains; and (2) **expenses**, which include cost of goods sold, operating expenses, and other expenses and losses. Illustration 5-14 shows a single-step statement for PW Audio Supply.

Illustration 5-14
Single-step income statement

PW Audio Supply, Inc. Income Statement For the Year Ended December 31, 2014		
Revenues		
Net sales		$460,000
Interest revenue		3,000
Gain on disposal of plant assets		600
Total revenues		463,600
Expenses		
Cost of goods sold	$316,000	
Operating expenses	114,000	
Interest expense	1,800	
Casualty loss from vandalism	200	
Total expenses		432,000
Net income		$ 31,600

There are two primary reasons for using the single-step format: (1) A company does not realize any type of profit or income until total revenues exceed total expenses, so it makes sense to divide the statement into these two categories. (2) The format is simpler and easier to read. *For homework problems, however, you should use the single-step format only when specifically instructed to do so.*

Classified Balance Sheet

In the balance sheet, merchandising companies report inventory as a current asset immediately below accounts receivable. Recall from Chapter 4 that companies generally list current asset items in the order of their closeness to cash (liquidity). Inventory is less close to cash than accounts receivable because the goods must first be sold and then collection made from the customer. Illustration 5-15 presents the assets section of a classified balance sheet for PW Audio Supply.

Illustration 5-15
Assets section of a classified balance sheet

Helpful Hint
The $40,000 is the cost of the inventory on hand, not its expected selling price.

PW Audio Supply, Inc. Balance Sheet (Partial) December 31, 2014		
Assets		
Current assets		
Cash		$ 9,500
Accounts receivable		16,100
Inventory		40,000
Prepaid insurance		1,800
Total current assets		67,400
Property, plant, and equipment		
Equipment	$80,000	
Less: Accumulated depreciation—equipment	24,000	56,000
Total assets		$123,400

> DO IT!

Financial Statement Classifications

You are presented with the following list of accounts from the adjusted trial balance for merchandiser Gorman Company. Indicate in which financial statement and under what classification each of the following would be reported.

Accounts Payable
Accounts Receivable
Accumulated Depreciation—Buildings
Accumulated Depreciation—Equipment
Advertising Expense
Buildings
Cash
Common Stock
Depreciation Expense
Dividends
Equipment
Freight-Out
Gain on Disposal of Plant Assets
Insurance Expense
Interest Expense
Interest Payable
Inventory
Land
Notes Payable (due in 3 years)
Property Taxes Payable
Salaries and Wages Expense
Salaries and Wages Payable
Sales Returns and Allowances
Sales Revenue
Utilities Expense

Action Plan

✔ Review the major sections of the income statement, sales revenues, cost of goods sold, operating expenses, other revenues and gains, and other expenses and losses.

✔ Add net income to beginning retained earnings and deduct dividends to arrive at ending retained earnings in the retained earnings statement.

✔ Review the major sections of the balance sheet, income statement, and retained earnings statement.

Solution

Account	Financial Statement	Classification
Accounts Payable	Balance sheet	Current liabilities
Accounts Receivable	Balance sheet	Current assets
Accumulated Depreciation—Buildings	Balance sheet	Property, plant, and equipment
Accumulated Depreciation—Equipment	Balance sheet	Property, plant, and equipment
Advertising Expense	Income statement	Operating expenses
Buildings	Balance sheet	Property, plant, and equipment
Cash	Balance sheet	Current assets
Common Stock	Balance sheet	Stockholders' equity
Depreciation Expense	Income statement	Operating expenses
Dividends	Retained earnings statement	Deduction section
Equipment	Balance sheet	Property, plant, and equipment
Freight-Out	Income statement	Operating expenses
Gain on Disposal of Plant Assets	Income statement	Other revenues and gains
Insurance Expense	Income statement	Operating expenses
Interest Expense	Income statement	Other expenses and losses
Interest Payable	Balance sheet	Current liabilities
Inventory	Balance sheet	Current assets
Land	Balance sheet	Property, plant, and equipment
Notes Payable	Balance sheet	Long-term liabilities
Property Taxes Payable	Balance sheet	Current liabilities
Salaries and Wages Expense	Income statement	Operating expenses
Salaries and Wages Payable	Balance sheet	Current liabilities
Sales Returns and Allowances	Income statement	Sales revenues
Sales Revenue	Income statement	Sales revenues
Utilities Expense	Income statement	Operating expenses

Related exercise material: **BE5-7, BE5-8, BE5-9, E5-9, E5-10, E5-12, E5-13, E5-14, and**  **5-4.**

✔ The Navigator

Comprehensive DO IT!

The adjusted trial balance columns of Falcetto Company's worksheet for the year ended December 31, 2014, are as follows.

Debit		Credit	
Cash	14,500	Accumulated Depreciation—Equipment	18,000
Accounts Receivable	11,100		
Inventory	29,000	Notes Payable	25,000
Prepaid Insurance	2,500	Accounts Payable	10,600
Equipment	95,000	Common Stock	50,000
Dividends	12,000	Retained Earnings	31,000
Sales Returns and Allowances	6,700	Sales Revenue	536,800
Sales Discounts	5,000	Interest Revenue	2,500
Cost of Goods Sold	363,400		673,900
Freight-Out	7,600		
Advertising Expense	12,000		
Salaries and Wages Expense	56,000		
Utilities Expense	18,000		
Rent Expense	24,000		
Depreciation Expense	9,000		
Insurance Expense	4,500		
Interest Expense	3,600		
	673,900		

Instructions

Prepare a multiple-step income statement for Falcetto Company.

Solution to Comprehensive DO IT!

Action Plan

- ✔ Remember that the key components of the income statement are net sales, cost of goods sold, gross profit, total operating expenses, and net income (loss). Report these components in the right-hand column of the income statement.
- ✔ Put nonoperating items after income from operations.

Falcetto Company
Income Statement
For the Year Ended December 31, 2014

Sales revenues		
Sales revenue		$536,800
Less: Sales returns and allowances	$ 6,700	
Sales discounts	5,000	11,700
Net sales		525,100
Cost of goods sold		363,400
Gross profit		161,700
Operating expenses		
Salaries and wages expense	56,000	
Rent expense	24,000	
Utilities expense	18,000	
Advertising expense	12,000	
Depreciation expense	9,000	
Freight-out	7,600	
Insurance expense	4,500	
Total operating expenses		131,100
Income from operations		30,600
Other revenues and gains		
Interest revenue	2,500	
Other expenses and losses		
Interest expense	3,600	1,100
Net income		$ 29,500

✔ The Navigator

SUMMARY OF LEARNING OBJECTIVES

✔ The Navigator

1 Identify the differences between service and merchandising companies. Because of inventory, a merchandising company has sales revenue, cost of goods sold, and gross profit. To account for inventory, a merchandising company must choose between a perpetual and a periodic inventory system.

2 Explain the recording of purchases under a perpetual inventory system. The company debits the Inventory account for all purchases of merchandise and freight-in, and credits it for purchase discounts and purchase returns and allowances.

3 Explain the recording of sales revenues under a perpetual inventory system. When a merchandising company sells inventory, it debits Accounts Receivable (or Cash), and credits Sales Revenue for the **selling price** of the merchandise. At the same time, it debits Cost of Goods Sold, and credits Inventory for the cost of the inventory items sold. Sales returns and allowances and sales discounts are debited.

4 Explain the steps in the accounting cycle for a merchandising company. Each of the required steps in the accounting cycle for a service company applies to a merchandising company. A worksheet is again an optional step. Under a perpetual inventory system, the company must adjust the Inventory account to agree with the physical count.

5 Distinguish between a multiple-step and a single-step income statement. A multiple-step income statement shows numerous steps in determining net income, including nonoperating activities sections. A single-step income statement classifies all data under two categories, revenues or expenses, and determines net income in one step.

GLOSSARY

Contra-revenue account An account that is offset against a revenue account on the income statement. (p. 229).

Cost of goods sold The total cost of merchandise sold during the period. (p. 220).

FOB destination Freight terms indicating that the seller places the goods free on board to the buyer's place of business, and the seller pays the freight. (p. 224).

FOB shipping point Freight terms indicating that the seller places goods free on board the carrier, and the buyer pays the freight costs. (p. 224).

Gross profit The excess of net sales over the cost of goods sold. (p. 235).

Gross profit rate Gross profit expressed as a percentage, by dividing the amount of gross profit by net sales. (p. 235).

Income from operations Income from a company's principal operating activity; determined by subtracting cost of goods sold and operating expenses from net sales. (p. 236).

Multiple-step income statement An income statement that shows several steps in determining net income. (p. 234).

Net sales Sales less sales returns and allowances and less sales discounts. (p. 234).

Nonoperating activities Various revenues, expenses, gains, and losses that are unrelated to a company's main line of operations. (p. 236).

Operating expenses Expenses incurred in the process of earning sales revenues. (p. 235).

Other expenses and losses A nonoperating-activities section of the income statement that shows expenses and losses unrelated to the company's main line of operations. (p. 236).

Other revenues and gains A nonoperating-activities section of the income statement that shows revenues and gains unrelated to the company's main line of operations. (p. 236).

Periodic inventory system An inventory system under which the company does not keep detailed inventory records throughout the accounting period but determines the cost of goods sold only at the end of an accounting period. (p. 221).

Perpetual inventory system An inventory system under which the company keeps detailed records of the cost of each inventory purchase and sale, and the records continuously show the inventory that should be on hand. (p. 221).

Purchase allowance A deduction made to the selling price of merchandise, granted by the seller so that the buyer will keep the merchandise. (p. 225).

Purchase discount A cash discount claimed by a buyer for prompt payment of a balance due. (p. 226).

Purchase invoice A document that supports each credit purchase. (p. 223).

Purchase return A return of goods from the buyer to the seller for a cash or credit refund. (p. 225).

Sales discount A reduction given by a seller for prompt payment of a credit sale. (p. 230).

Sales invoice A document that supports each credit sale. (p. 227).

Sales returns and allowances Purchase returns and allowances from the seller's perspective. See *Purchase return* and *Purchase allowance,* above. (p. 229).

Sales revenue (Sales) The primary source of revenue in a merchandising company. (p. 220).

Single-step income statement An income statement that shows only one step in determining net income. (p. 237).

APPENDIX 5A PERIODIC INVENTORY SYSTEM

LEARNING OBJECTIVE 6

Explain the recording of purchases and sales of inventory under a periodic inventory system.

As described in this chapter, companies may use one of two basic systems of accounting for inventories: (1) the perpetual inventory system or (2) the periodic inventory system. In the chapter, we focused on the characteristics of the perpetual inventory system. In this appendix, we discuss and illustrate the **periodic inventory system**. One key difference between the two systems is the point at which the company computes cost of goods sold. For a visual reminder of this difference, refer back to Illustration 5-4 (page 222).

Determining Cost of Goods Sold Under a Periodic System

Determining cost of goods sold is different when a periodic inventory system is used rather than a perpetual system. As you have seen, a company using a **perpetual system** makes an entry to record cost of goods sold and to reduce inventory *each time a sale is made*. A company using a **periodic system** does not determine cost of goods sold *until the end of the period*. At the end of the period the company performs a count to determine the ending balance of inventory. It then **calculates cost of goods sold by subtracting ending inventory from the goods available for sale**. Goods available for sale is the sum of beginning inventory plus purchases, as shown in Illustration 5A-1.

Illustration 5A-1
Basic formula for cost of goods sold using the periodic system

	Beginning Inventory
+	Cost of Goods Purchased
	Cost of Goods Available for Sale
−	Ending Inventory
	Cost of Goods Sold

Another difference between the two approaches is that the perpetual system directly adjusts the Inventory account for any transaction that affects inventory (such as freight costs, returns, and discounts). The periodic system does not do this. Instead, it creates different accounts for purchases, freight costs, returns, and discounts. These various accounts are shown in Illustration 5A-2, which presents the calculation of cost of goods sold for PW Audio Supply using the periodic approach.

Illustration 5A-2
Cost of goods sold for a merchandiser using a periodic inventory system

PW Audio Supply, Inc.
Cost of Goods Sold
For the Year Ended December 31, 2014

Cost of goods sold			
Inventory, January 1			$ 36,000
Purchases		$325,000	
Less: Purchase returns and allowances	$10,400		
Purchase discounts	6,800	17,200	
Net purchases		307,800	
Add: Freight-in		12,200	
Cost of goods purchased			320,000
Cost of goods available for sale			356,000
Inventory, December 31			40,000
Cost of goods sold			$316,000

Helpful Hint
The far right column identifies the primary items that make up cost of goods sold of $316,000. The middle column explains cost of goods purchased of $320,000. The left column reports contra purchase items of $17,200.

Note that the basic elements from Illustration 5A-1 are highlighted in Illustration 5A-2. You will learn more in Chapter 6 about how to determine cost of goods sold using the periodic system.

The use of the periodic inventory system does not affect the form of presentation in the balance sheet. As under the perpetual system, a company reports inventory in the current assets section.

Recording Merchandise Transactions

In a **periodic inventory system**, companies record revenues from the sale of merchandise when sales are made, just as in a perpetual system. Unlike the perpetual system, however, companies **do not attempt on the date of sale to record the cost of the merchandise sold**. Instead, they take a physical inventory count at the **end of the period** to determine (1) the cost of the merchandise then on hand and (2) the cost of the goods sold during the period. And, **under a periodic system, companies record purchases of merchandise in the Purchases account rather than the Inventory account**. Also, in a periodic system, purchase returns and allowances, purchase discounts, and freight costs on purchases are recorded in separate accounts.

To illustrate the recording of merchandise transactions under a periodic inventory system, we will use purchase/sale transactions between PW Audio Supply, Inc. and Sauk Stereo, as illustrated for the perpetual inventory system in this chapter.

Recording Purchases of Merchandise

On the basis of the sales invoice (Illustration 5-5, shown on page 224) and receipt of the merchandise ordered from PW Audio Supply, Sauk Stereo records the $3,800 purchase as follows.

Helpful Hint
Be careful not to debit purchases of equipment or supplies to a Purchases account.

May 4	Purchases	3,800	
	Accounts Payable		3,800
	(To record goods purchased on account from PW Audio Supply)		

Purchases is a temporary account whose normal balance is a debit.

FREIGHT COSTS

When the purchaser directly incurs the freight costs, it debits the account Freight-In (or Transportation-In). For example, if Sauk Stereo pays Acme Freight Company $150 for freight charges on its purchase from PW Audio Supply on May 6, the entry on Sauk Stereo's books is:

May 6	Freight-In (Transportation-In)	150	
	Cash		150
	(To record payment of freight on goods purchased)		

Like Purchases, Freight-In is a temporary account whose normal balance is a debit. **Freight-In is part of cost of goods purchased.** The reason is that cost of goods purchased should include any freight charges necessary to bring the goods to the purchaser. Freight costs are not subject to a purchase discount. Purchase discounts apply only to the invoice cost of the merchandise.

Alternative Terminology
Freight-in is also called *transportation-in*.

PURCHASE RETURNS AND ALLOWANCES

Sauk Stereo returns $300 of goods to PW Audio Supply and prepares the following entry to recognize the return.

May 8	Accounts Payable	300	
	Purchase Returns and Allowances		300
	(To record return of goods purchased from PW Audio Supply)		

Purchase Returns and Allowances is a temporary account whose normal balance is a credit.

PURCHASE DISCOUNTS

On May 14, Sauk Stereo pays the balance due on account to PW Audio Supply, taking the 2% cash discount allowed by PW Audio Supply for payment within 10 days. Sauk Stereo records the payment and discount as follows.

May 14	Accounts Payable ($3,800 − $300)	3,500	
	Purchase Discounts ($3,500 × .02)		70
	Cash		3,430
	(To record payment within the discount period)		

Purchase Discounts is a temporary account whose normal balance is a credit.

Recording Sales of Merchandise

The seller, PW Audio Supply, records the sale of $3,800 of merchandise to Sauk Stereo on May 4 (sales invoice No. 731, Illustration 5-5, page 224) as follows.

May 4	Accounts Receivable	3,800	
	Sales Revenue		3,800
	(To record credit sales per invoice #731 to Sauk Stereo)		

SALES RETURNS AND ALLOWANCES

To record the returned goods received from Sauk Stereo on May 8, PW Audio Supply records the $300 sales return as follows.

May 8	Sales Returns and Allowances	300	
	Accounts Receivable		300
	(To record credit granted to Sauk Stereo for returned goods)		

SALES DISCOUNTS

On May 14, PW Audio Supply receives payment of $3,430 on account from Sauk Stereo. PW Audio Supply honors the 2% cash discount and records the payment of Sauk Stereo's account receivable in full as follows.

May 14	Cash	3,430	
	Sales Discounts ($3,500 × .02)	70	
	Accounts Receivable ($3,800 − $300)		3,500
	(To record collection within 2/10, n/30 discount period from Sauk Stereo)		

COMPARISON OF ENTRIES—PERPETUAL VS. PERIODIC

Illustration 5A-3 summarizes the periodic inventory entries shown in this appendix and compares them to the perpetual-system entries from the chapter. Entries that differ in the two systems are shown in color.

Entries on Sauk Stereo's Books

Transaction		Perpetual Inventory System			Periodic Inventory System		
May 4	Purchase of merchandise on credit.	**Inventory**	**3,800**		**Purchases**	**3,800**	
		Accounts Payable		3,800	Accounts Payable		3,800
6	Freight costs on purchases.	**Inventory**	**150**		**Freight-In**	**150**	
		Cash		150	Cash		150
8	Purchase returns and allowances.	Accounts Payable	300		Accounts Payable	300	
		Inventory		**300**	**Purchase Returns and Allowances**		**300**
14	Payment on account with a discount.	Accounts Payable	3,500		Accounts Payable	3,500	
		Cash		3,430	Cash		3,430
		Inventory		**70**	**Purchase Discounts**		**70**

Entries on PW Audio Supply's Books

Transaction		Perpetual Inventory System			Periodic Inventory System		
May 4	Sale of merchandise on credit.	Accounts Receivable	3,800		Accounts Receivable	3,800	
		Sales Revenue		3,800	Sales Revenue		3,800
		Cost of Goods Sold	**2,400**		**No entry for cost of goods sold**		
		Inventory		**2,400**			
8	Return of merchandise sold.	Sales Returns and Allowances	300		Sales Returns and Allowances	300	
		Accounts Receivable		300	Accounts Receivable		300
		Inventory	**140**		**No entry**		
		Cost of Goods Sold		**140**			
14	Cash received on account with a discount.	Cash	3,430		Cash	3,430	
		Sales Discounts	70		Sales Discounts	70	
		Accounts Receivable		3,500	Accounts Receivable		3,500

Illustration 5A-3
Comparison of entries for perpetual and periodic inventory systems

SUMMARY OF LEARNING OBJECTIVE FOR APPENDIX 5A

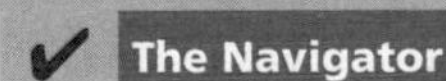

6 Explain the recording of purchases and sales of inventory under a periodic inventory system. In recording purchases under a periodic system, companies must make entries for (a) cash and credit purchases, (b) purchase returns and allowances, (c) purchase discounts, and (d) freight costs. In recording sales, companies must make entries for (a) cash and credit sales, (b) sales returns and allowances, and (c) sales discounts.

APPENDIX 5B WORKSHEET FOR A MERCHANDISING COMPANY

Using a Worksheet

LEARNING OBJECTIVE 7

Prepare a worksheet for a merchandising company.

As indicated in Chapter 4, a worksheet enables companies to prepare financial statements before they journalize and post adjusting entries. The steps in preparing a worksheet for a merchandising company are the same as for a service company (see pages 164–167). Illustration 5B-1 (page 246) shows the worksheet for PW Audio Supply (excluding nonoperating items). The unique accounts for a merchandiser using a perpetual inventory system are in boldface letters and in red.

PW Audio Supply.xls

Home Insert Page Layout Formulas Data Review View

P18 *fx*

PW Audio Supply, Inc.
Worksheet
For the Year Ended December 31, 2014

	A	B	C	D	E	F	G	H	I	J	K
5		Trial Balance		Adjustments		Adjusted Trial Balance		Income Statement		Balance Sheet	
7	Accounts	Dr.	Cr.	Dr.	Cr.	Dr.	Cr.	Dr.	Cr.	Dr.	Cr.
8	Cash	9,500				9,500				9,500	
9	Accounts Receivable	16,100				16,100				16,100	
10	**Inventory**	**40,500**			(a) 500	**40,000**				**40,000**	
11	Prepaid Insurance	3,800			(b) 2,000	1,800				1,800	
12	Equipment	80,000				80,000				80,000	
13	Accumulated Depreciation—Equipment		16,000		(c) 8,000		24,000				24,000
14	Accounts Payable		20,400				20,400				20,400
15	Common Stock		50,000				50,000				50,000
16	Retained Earnings		33,000				33,000				33,000
17	Dividends	15,000				15,000				15,000	
18	**Sales Revenue**		**480,000**				**480,000**		**480,000**		
19	**Sales Returns and Allowances**	**12,000**				**12,000**		**12,000**			
20	**Sales Discounts**	**8,000**				**8,000**		**8,000**			
21	**Cost of Goods Sold**	**315,500**		(a) 500		**316,000**		**316,000**			
22	Freight-Out	7,000				7,000		7,000			
23	Advertising Expense	16,000				16,000		16,000			
24	Salaries and Wages Expense	59,000		(d) 5,000		64,000		64,000			
25	Utilities Expense	17,000				17,000		17,000			
26	Totals	599,400	599,400								
27	Insurance Expense			(b) 2,000		2,000		2,000			
28	Depreciation Expense			(c) 8,000		8,000		8,000			
29	Salaries and Wages Payable				(d) 5,000		5,000				5,000
30	Totals			15,500	15,500	612,400	612,400	450,000	480,000	162,400	132,400
31	Net Income							30,000			30,000
32	Totals							480,000	480,000	162,400	162,400

Key: (a) Adjustment to inventory on hand. (b) Insurance expired. (c) Depreciation expense. (d) Salaries accrued.

Illustration 5B-1
Worksheet for merchandising company

TRIAL BALANCE COLUMNS

Data for the trial balance come from the ledger balances of PW Audio Supply at December 31. The amount shown for Inventory, $40,500, is the year-end inventory amount from the perpetual inventory system.

ADJUSTMENTS COLUMNS

A merchandising company generally has the same types of adjustments as a service company. As you see in the worksheet, adjustments (b), (c), and (d) are for insurance, depreciation, and salaries. Pioneer Advertising Agency Inc. as illustrated in Chapters 3 and 4, also had these adjustments. Adjustment (a) was required to adjust the perpetual inventory carrying amount to the actual count.

After PW Audio Supply enters all adjustments data on the worksheet, it establishes the equality of the adjustments column totals. It then extends the balances in all accounts to the adjusted trial balance columns.

ADJUSTED TRIAL BALANCE

The adjusted trial balance shows the balance of all accounts after adjustment at the end of the accounting period.

INCOME STATEMENT COLUMNS

Next, the merchandising company transfers the accounts and balances that affect the income statement from the adjusted trial balance columns to the income statement columns. PW Audio Supply shows sales of $480,000 in the credit column. It shows the contra-revenue accounts Sales Returns and Allowances $12,000 and Sales Discounts $8,000 in the debit column. The difference of $460,000 is the net sales shown on the income statement (Illustration 5-13, page 237).

Finally, the company totals all the credits in the income statement column and compares those totals to the total of the debits in the income statement column. If the credits exceed the debits, the company has net income. PW Audio Supply has net income of $30,000. If the debits exceed the credits, the company would report a net loss.

BALANCE SHEET COLUMNS

The major difference between the balance sheets of a service company and a merchandiser is inventory. PW Audio Supply shows the ending inventory amount of $40,000 in the balance sheet debit column. The information to prepare the retained earnings statement is also found in these columns. That is, the retained earnings beginning balance is $33,000. The dividends are $15,000. Net income results when the total of the debit column exceeds the total of the credit column in the balance sheet columns. A net loss results when the total of the credits exceeds the total of the debit balances.

SUMMARY OF LEARNING OBJECTIVE FOR APPENDIX 5B

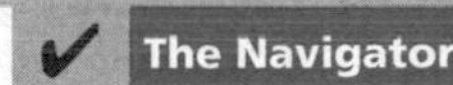

7 Prepare a worksheet for a merchandising company. The steps in preparing a worksheet for a merchandising company are the same as for a service company. The unique accounts for a merchandiser are Inventory, Sales Revenue, Sales Returns and Allowances, Sales Discounts, and Cost of Goods Sold.

Self-Test, Brief Exercises, Exercises, Problem Set A, and many more components are available for practice in WileyPLUS.

**Note:* All asterisked Questions, Exercises, and Problems relate to material in the appendix to the chapter.

SELF-TEST QUESTIONS

Answers are on page 267.

(LO 1) 1. Gross profit will result if:
(a) operating expenses are less than net income.
(b) sales revenues are greater than operating expenses.
(c) sales revenues are greater than cost of goods sold.
(d) operating expenses are greater than cost of goods sold.

2. Under a perpetual inventory system, when goods are purchased for resale by a company: (LO 2)
(a) purchases on account are debited to Inventory.
(b) purchases on account are debited to Purchases.
(c) purchase returns are debited to Purchase Returns and Allowances.
(d) freight costs are debited to Freight-Out.

(LO 3) **3.** The sales accounts that normally have a debit balance are:
(a) Sales Discounts.
(b) Sales Returns and Allowances.
(c) Both (a) and (b).
(d) Neither (a) nor (b).

(LO 3) **4.** A credit sale of $750 is made on June 13, terms 2/10, net/30. A return of $50 is granted on June 16. The amount received as payment in full on June 23 is:
(a) $700. (c) $685.
(b) $686. (d) $650.

(LO 2) **5.** Which of the following accounts will normally appear in the ledger of a merchandising company that uses a perpetual inventory system?
(a) Purchases. (c) Cost of Goods Sold.
(b) Freight-In. (d) Purchase Discounts.

(LO 3) **6.** To record the sale of goods for cash in a perpetual inventory system:
(a) only one journal entry is necessary to record cost of goods sold and reduction of inventory.
(b) only one journal entry is necessary to record the receipt of cash and the sales revenue.
(c) two journal entries are necessary: one to record the receipt of cash and sales revenue, and one to record the cost of goods sold and reduction of inventory.
(d) two journal entries are necessary: one to record the receipt of cash and reduction of inventory, and one to record the cost of goods sold and sales revenue.

(LO 4) **7.** The steps in the accounting cycle for a merchandising company are the same as those in a service company *except*:
(a) an additional adjusting journal entry for inventory may be needed in a merchandising company.
(b) closing journal entries are not required for a merchandising company.
(c) a post-closing trial balance is not required for a merchandising company.
(d) a multiple-step income statement is required for a merchandising company.

(LO 5) **8.** The multiple-step income statement for a merchandising company shows each of the following features *except*:
(a) gross profit.
(b) cost of goods sold.
(c) a sales revenue section.
(d) investing activities section.

9. If sales revenues are $400,000, cost of goods sold is $310,000, and operating expenses are $60,000, the gross profit is: (LO 5)
(a) $30,000. (c) $340,000.
(b) $90,000. (d) $400,000.

10. A single-step income statement: (LO 5)
(a) reports gross profit.
(b) does not report cost of goods sold.
(c) reports sales revenues and "Other revenues and gains" in the revenues section of the income statement.
(d) reports operating income separately.

11. Which of the following appears on both a single-step and a multiple-step income statement? (LO 5)
(a) inventory.
(b) gross profit.
(c) income from operations.
(d) cost of goods sold.

***12.** In determining cost of goods sold: (LO 6)
(a) purchase discounts are deducted from net purchases.
(b) freight-out is added to net purchases.
(c) purchase returns and allowances are deducted from net purchases.
(d) freight-in is added to net purchases.

***13.** If beginning inventory is $60,000, cost of goods purchased is $380,000, and ending inventory is $50,000, cost of goods sold is: (LO 6)
(a) $390,000. (c) $330,000.
(b) $370,000. (d) $420,000.

***14.** When goods are purchased for resale by a company using a periodic inventory system: (LO 6)
(a) purchases on account are debited to Inventory.
(b) purchases on account are debited to Purchases.
(c) purchase returns are debited to Purchase Returns and Allowances.
(d) freight costs are debited to Purchases.

***15.** In a worksheet, Inventory is shown in the following columns: (LO 7)
(a) Adjusted trial balance debit and balance sheet debit.
(b) Income statement debit and balance sheet debit.
(c) Income statement credit and balance sheet debit.
(d) Income statement credit and adjusted trial balance debit.

Go to the book's companion website, www.wiley.com/college/weygandt, for additional Self-Test Questions.

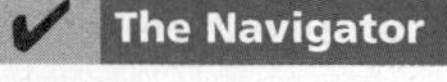

QUESTIONS

1. (a) "The steps in the accounting cycle for a merchandising company are different from the accounting cycle for a service company." Do you agree or disagree? (b) Is the measurement of net income for a merchandising company conceptually the same as for a service company? Explain.

2. Why is the normal operating cycle for a merchandising company likely to be longer than for a service company?

3. (a) How do the components of revenues and expenses differ between merchandising and service companies? (b) Explain the income measurement process in a merchandising company.

4. How does income measurement differ between a merchandising and a service company?

5. When is cost of goods sold determined in a perpetual inventory system?

6. Distinguish between FOB shipping point and FOB destination. Identify the freight terms that will result in a debit to Inventory by the buyer and a debit to Freight-Out by the seller.
7. Explain the meaning of the credit terms 2/10, n/30.
8. Goods costing $2,500 are purchased on account on July 15 with credit terms of 2/10, n/30. On July 18, a $200 credit memo is received from the supplier for damaged goods. Give the journal entry on July 24 to record payment of the balance due within the discount period using a perpetual inventory system.
9. Karen Lloyd believes revenues from credit sales may be earned before they are collected in cash. Do you agree? Explain.
10. (a) What is the primary source document for recording (1) cash sales, (2) credit sales. (b) Using XXs for amounts, give the journal entry for each of the transactions in part (a).
11. A credit sale is made on July 10 for $700, terms 2/10, n/30. On July 12, $100 of goods are returned for credit. Give the journal entry on July 19 to record the receipt of the balance due within the discount period.
12. Explain why the Inventory account will usually require adjustment at year-end.
13. Prepare the closing entries for the Sales Revenue account, assuming a balance of $180,000 and the Cost of Goods Sold account with a $125,000 balance.
14. What merchandising account(s) will appear in the post-closing trial balance?
15. Regis Co. has sales revenue of $109,000, cost of goods sold of $70,000, and operating expenses of $23,000. What is its gross profit and its gross profit rate?
16. Kathy Ho Company reports net sales of $800,000, gross profit of $570,000, and net income of $240,000. What are its operating expenses?
17. Identify the distinguishing features of an income statement for a merchandising company.
18. Identify the sections of a multiple-step income statement that relate to (a) operating activities, and (b) nonoperating activities.
19. How does the single-step form of income statement differ from the multiple-step form?
20. **PEPSICO** Determine PepsiCo's gross profit rate for 2010 and 2009. Indicate whether it increased or decreased from 2009 to 2010.
*21. Identify the accounts that are added to or deducted from Purchases to determine the cost of goods purchased. For each account, indicate whether it is added or deducted.
*22. Goods costing $2,000 are purchased on account on July 15 with credit terms of 2/10, n/30. On July 18, a $200 credit was received from the supplier for damaged goods. Give the journal entry on July 24 to record payment of the balance due within the discount period, assuming a periodic inventory system.
*23. Indicate the columns of the worksheet in which (a) inventory and (b) cost of goods sold will be shown.

BRIEF EXERCISES

Compute missing amounts in determining net income. (LO 1)

BE5-1 Presented below are the components in Clearwater Company's income statement. Determine the missing amounts.

	Sales Revenue	Cost of Goods Sold	Gross Profit	Operating Expenses	Net Income
(a)	$75,000	?	$30,000	?	$10,800
(b)	$108,000	$55,000	?	?	$29,500
(c)	?	$83,900	$79,600	$39,500	?

Journalize perpetual inventory entries. (LO 2, 3)

BE5-2 Giovanni Company buys merchandise on account from Gordon Company. The selling price of the goods is $780, and the cost of the goods is $560. Both companies use perpetual inventory systems. Journalize the transaction on the books of both companies.

Journalize sales transactions. (LO 3)

BE5-3 Prepare the journal entries to record the following transactions on Benson Company's books using a perpetual inventory system.

(a) On March 2, Benson Company sold $800,000 of merchandise to Edgebrook Company, terms 2/10, n/30. The cost of the merchandise sold was $620,000.
(b) On March 6, Edgebrook Company returned $120,000 of the merchandise purchased on March 2. The cost of the returned merchandise was $90,000.
(c) On March 12, Benson Company received the balance due from Edgebrook Company.

Journalize purchase transactions. (LO 2)

BE5-4 From the information in BE5-3, prepare the journal entries to record these transactions on Edgebrook Company's books under a perpetual inventory system.

Prepare adjusting entry for merchandise inventory. (LO 4)

BE5-5 At year-end, the perpetual inventory records of Salsa Company showed merchandise inventory of $98,000. The company determined, however, that its actual inventory on hand was $94,600. Record the necessary adjusting entry.

Prepare closing entries for merchandise accounts. (LO 4)

BE5-6 Orlaida Company has the following merchandise account balances: Sales Revenue $192,000, Sales Discounts $2,000, Cost of Goods Sold $105,000, and Inventory $40,000. Prepare the entries to record the closing of these items to Income Summary.

Prepare sales revenues section of income statement.

(LO 5)

BE5-7 Piccola Company provides the following information for the month ended October 31, 2014: sales on credit $280,000, cash sales $100,000, sales discounts $5,000, sales returns and allowances $18,000. Prepare the sales revenues section of the income statement based on this information.

Contrast presentation in multiple-step and single-step income statements.

(LO 5)

BE5-8 Explain where each of the following items would appear on (1) a multiple-step income statement, and on (2) a single-step income statement: (a) gain on sale of equipment, (b) interest expense, (c) casualty loss from vandalism, and (d) cost of goods sold.

Compute net sales, gross profit, income from operations, and gross profit rate.

(LO 5)

BE5-9 Assume Jose Company has the following reported amounts: Sales revenue $506,000, Sales returns and allowances $13,000, Cost of goods sold $330,000, Operating expenses $110,000. Compute the following: (a) net sales, (b) gross profit, (c) income from operations, and (d) gross profit rate. (Round to one decimal place.)

Compute net purchases and cost of goods purchased.

(LO 6)

***BE5-10** Assume that Guardian Company uses a periodic inventory system and has these account balances: Purchases $430,000; Purchase Returns and Allowances $13,000; Purchase Discounts $8,000; and Freight-In $16,000. Determine net purchases and cost of goods purchased.

Compute cost of goods sold and gross profit.

(LO 6)

***BE5-11** Assume the same information as in BE5-10 and also that Guardian Company has beginning inventory of $60,000, ending inventory of $90,000, and net sales of $680,000. Determine the amounts to be reported for cost of goods sold and gross profit.

Journalize purchase transactions.

(LO 6)

***BE5-12** Prepare the journal entries to record these transactions on Huntington Company's books using a periodic inventory system.

(a) On March 2, Huntington Company purchased $900,000 of merchandise from Saunder Company, terms 2/10, n/30.

(b) On March 6, Huntington Company returned $184,000 of the merchandise purchased on March 2.

(c) On March 12, Huntington Company paid the balance due to Saunder Company.

Identify worksheet columns for selected accounts.

(LO 7)

***BE5-13** Presented below is the format of the worksheet presented in the chapter.

Trial Balance		Adjustments		Adjusted Trial Balance		Income Statement		Balance Sheet	
Dr.	Cr.	Dr.	Cr.	Dr.	Cr.	Dr.	Cr.	Dr.	Cr.

Indicate where the following items will appear on the worksheet: (a) Cash, (b) Inventory, (c) Sales revenue, and (d) Cost of goods sold.

Example:
Cash: Trial balance debit column; Adjusted trial balance debit column; and Balance sheet debit column.

> DO IT! REVIEW

Record transactions of purchasing company.

(LO 2)

DO IT! 5-1 On October 5, Gibson Company buys merchandise on account from Quincy Company. The selling price of the goods is $4,700, and the cost to Quincy Company is $3,100. On October 8, Gibson returns defective goods with a selling price of $650 and a fair value of $160. Record the transactions on the books of Gibson Company.

Record transactions of selling company.

(LO 3)

DO IT! 5-2 Assume information similar to that in **DO IT! 5-1**. That is: On October 5, Gibson Company buys merchandise on account from Quincy Company. The selling price of the goods is $4,700, and the cost to Quincy Company is $3,100. On October 8, Gibson returns defective goods with a selling price of $650 and a fair value of $160. Record the transactions on the books of Quincy Company.

Prepare closing entries for a merchandising company.

(LO 4)

DO IT! 5-3 The trial balance of Optique's Boutique at December 31 shows Inventory $21,000, Sales Revenue $156,000, Sales Returns and Allowances $4,000, Sales Discounts $3,000, Cost of Goods Sold $92,400, Interest Revenue $3,000, Freight-Out $1,900, Utilities Expense $7,400, and Salaries and Wages Expense $19,500. Prepare the closing entries for Optique.

DO IT! 5-4 Dorothea Company is preparing its multiple-step income statement, retained earnings statement, and classified balance sheet. Using the column heads *Account*, *Financial Statement*, and *Classification*, indicate in which financial statement and under what classification each of the following would be reported.

Classify financial statement accounts.

(LO 5)

Account	Financial Statement	Classification
Accounts Payable		
Accounts Receivable		
Accumulated Depreciation—Buildings		
Cash		
Casualty Loss from Vandalism		
Common Stock		
Cost of Goods Sold		
Depreciation Expense		
Dividends		
Equipment		
Freight-Out		
Insurance Expense		
Interest Payable		
Inventory		
Land		
Notes Payable (due in 5 years)		
Property Taxes Payable		
Salaries and Wages Expense		
Salaries and Wages Payable		
Sales Returns and Allowances		
Sales Revenue		
Unearned Rent Revenue		
Utilities Expense		

 The Navigator

EXERCISES

E5-1 Mr. Soukup has prepared the following list of statements about service companies and merchandisers.

Answer general questions about merchandisers.

(LO 1)

1. Measuring net income for a merchandiser is conceptually the same as for a service company.
2. For a merchandiser, sales less operating expenses is called gross profit.
3. For a merchandiser, the primary source of revenues is the sale of inventory.
4. Sales salaries and wages is an example of an operating expense.
5. The operating cycle of a merchandiser is the same as that of a service company.
6. In a perpetual inventory system, no detailed inventory records of goods on hand are maintained.
7. In a periodic inventory system, the cost of goods sold is determined only at the end of the accounting period.
8. A periodic inventory system provides better control over inventories than a perpetual system.

Instructions

Identify each statement as true or false. If false, indicate how to correct the statement.

E5-2 Information related to Duffy Co. is presented below.

Journalize purchases transactions.

(LO 2)

1. On April 5, purchased merchandise from Thomas Company for $25,000, terms 2/10, net/30, FOB shipping point.
2. On April 6, paid freight costs of $900 on merchandise purchased from Thomas.
3. On April 7, purchased equipment on account for $26,000.

4. On April 8, returned damaged merchandise to Thomas Company and was granted a $2,600 credit for returned merchandise.
5. On April 15, paid the amount due to Thomas Company in full.

Instructions

(a) Prepare the journal entries to record these transactions on the books of Duffy Co. under a perpetual inventory system.

(b) Assume that Duffy Co. paid the balance due to Thomas Company on May 4 instead of April 15. Prepare the journal entry to record this payment.

Journalize perpetual inventory entries.

(LO 2, 3)

E5-3 On September 1, Roshek Office Supply had an inventory of 30 calculators at a cost of $22 each. The company uses a perpetual inventory system. During September, the following transactions occurred.

Sept. 6 Purchased 90 calculators at $20 each from Harlow Co., terms 2/10, n/30.
9 Paid freight of $180 on calculators purchased from Harlow Co.
10 Returned 3 calculators to Harlow Co. for $66 credit (including freight) because they did not meet specifications.
12 Sold 26 calculators costing $22 (including freight) for $33 each to Village Book Store, terms n/30.
14 Granted credit of $33 to Village Book Store for the return of one calculator that was not ordered.
20 Sold 40 calculators costing $22 for $32 each to Dixie Card Shop, terms n/30.

Instructions

Journalize the September transactions.

Prepare purchase and sale entries.

(LO 2, 3)

E5-4 On June 10, Rebecca Company purchased $7,600 of merchandise from Clinton Company, FOB shipping point, terms 2/10, n/30. Rebecca pays the freight costs of $400 on June 11. Damaged goods totaling $300 are returned to Clinton for credit on June 12. The fair value of these goods is $70. On June 19, Rebecca pays Clinton Company in full, less the purchase discount. Both companies use a perpetual inventory system.

Instructions

(a) Prepare separate entries for each transaction on the books of Rebecca Company.

(b) Prepare separate entries for each transaction for Clinton Company. The merchandise purchased by Rebecca on June 10 had cost Clinton $4,300.

Journalize sales transactions.

(LO 3)

E5-5 Presented below are transactions related to Yarrow Company.

1. On December 3, Yarrow Company sold $570,000 of merchandise to Lampkins Co., terms 1/10, n/30, FOB shipping point. The cost of the merchandise sold was $364,800.
2. On December 8, Lampkins Co. was granted an allowance of $20,000 for merchandise purchased on December 3.
3. On December 13, Yarrow Company received the balance due from Lampkins Co.

Instructions

(a) Prepare the journal entries to record these transactions on the books of Yarrow Company using a perpetual inventory system.

(b) Assume that Yarrow Company received the balance due from Lampkins Co. on January 2 of the following year instead of December 13. Prepare the journal entry to record the receipt of payment on January 2.

Prepare sales revenues section and closing entries.

(LO 4, 5)

E5-6 The adjusted trial balance of Mendoza Company shows the following data pertaining to sales at the end of its fiscal year October 31, 2014: Sales Revenue $820,000, Freight-Out $16,000, Sales Returns and Allowances $28,000, and Sales Discounts $13,000.

Instructions

(a) Prepare the sales revenues section of the income statement.

(b) Prepare separate closing entries for (1) sales, and (2) the contra accounts to sales.

Prepare adjusting and closing entries.

(LO 4)

E5-7 Twix Company had the following account balances at year-end: Cost of Goods Sold $60,000; Inventory $15,000; Operating Expenses $29,000; Sales Revenue $115,000; Sales Discounts $1,300; and Sales Returns and Allowances $1,700. A physical count of inventory determines that merchandise inventory on hand is $13,600.

Instructions

(a) Prepare the adjusting entry necessary as a result of the physical count.

(b) Prepare closing entries.

E5-8 Presented below is information related to Taylor Co. for the month of January 2014.

Prepare adjusting and closing entries.

(LO 4)

Ending inventory per perpetual records	$ 21,600	Insurance expense	$ 12,000
Ending inventory actually on hand	21,000	Rent expense	20,000
Cost of goods sold	208,000	Salaries and wages expense	59,000
Freight-out	7,000	Sales discounts	8,000
		Sales returns and allowances	13,000
		Sales revenue	378,000

Instructions

(a) Prepare the necessary adjusting entry for inventory.
(b) Prepare the necessary closing entries.

E5-9 Presented below is information for Bach Company for the month of March 2014.

Prepare multiple-step income statement.

(LO 5)

Cost of goods sold	$212,000	Rent expense	$ 32,000
Freight-out	9,000	Sales discounts	6,600
Insurance expense	6,000	Sales returns and allowances	13,000
Salaries and wages expense	58,000	Sales revenue	380,000

Instructions

(a) Prepare a multiple-step income statement.
(b) Compute the gross profit rate.

E5-10 In its income statement for the year ended December 31, 2014, Michael Company reported the following condensed data.

Prepare multiple-step and single-step income statements.

(LO 5)

Operating expenses	$ 725,000	Interest revenue	$ 33,000
Cost of goods sold	1,256,000	Loss on disposal of plant assets	17,000
Interest expense	70,000	Net sales	2,200,000

Instructions

(a) Prepare a multiple-step income statement.
(b) Prepare a single-step income statement.

E5-11 An inexperienced accountant for Gulliver Company made the following errors in recording merchandising transactions.

Prepare correcting entries for sales and purchases.

(LO 2, 3)

1. A $175 refund to a customer for faulty merchandise was debited to Sales Revenue $175 and credited to Cash $175.
2. A $150 credit purchase of supplies was debited to Inventory $150 and credited to Cash $150.
3. A $215 sales discount was debited to Sales Revenue.
4. A cash payment of $20 for freight on merchandise purchases was debited to Freight-Out $200 and credited to Cash $200.

Instructions

Prepare separate correcting entries for each error, assuming that the incorrect entry is not reversed. (Omit explanations.)

E5-12 In 2014, Endeaver Company had net sales of $860,000 and cost of goods sold of $533,200. Operating expenses were $221,000, and interest expense was $7,000. Endeaver prepares a multiple-step income statement.

Compute various income measures.

(LO 5)

Instructions

(a) Compute Endeaver's gross profit.
(b) Compute the gross profit rate. Why is this rate computed by financial statement users?
(c) What is Endeaver's income from operations and net income?
(d) If Endeaver prepared a single-step income statement, what amount would it report for net income?
(e) In what section of its classified balance sheet should Endeaver report merchandise inventory?

E5-13 Presented below is financial information for two different companies.

Compute missing amounts and compute gross profit rate.

(LO 5)

	Lee Company	Chan Company
Sales revenue	$90,000	(d)
Sales returns	(a)	$ 5,000
Net sales	81,000	98,000
Cost of goods sold	56,000	(e)
Gross profit	(b)	37,500
Operating expenses	12,000	(f)
Net income	(c)	15,000

Instructions

(a) Determine the missing amounts.

(b) Determine the gross profit rates. (Round to one decimal place.)

Compute missing amounts.

(LO 5)

E5-14 Financial information is presented below for three different companies.

	Athena Cosmetics	Harry Grocery	Panama Wholesalers
Sales revenue	$90,000	$ (e)	$122,000
Sales returns and allowances	(a)	5,000	12,000
Net sales	86,000	95,000	(i)
Cost of goods sold	56,000	(f)	(j)
Gross profit	(b)	22,000	24,000
Operating expenses	15,000	(g)	18,000
Income from operations	(c)	(h)	(k)
Other expenses and losses	4,000	3,000	(l)
Net income	(d)	11,000	5,000

Instructions

Determine the missing amounts.

Prepare cost of goods sold section.

(LO 6)

***E5-15** The trial balance of Roman Company at the end of its fiscal year, August 31, 2014, includes these accounts: Inventory $17,200; Purchases $149,000; Sales Revenue $190,000; Freight-In $5,000; Sales Returns and Allowances $3,000; Freight-Out $1,000; and Purchase Returns and Allowances $6,000. The ending inventory is $14,000.

Instructions

Prepare a cost of goods sold section for the year ending August 31 (periodic inventory).

Compute various income statement items.

(LO 6)

***E5-16** On January 1, 2014, Clover Corporation had inventory of $50,000. At December 31, 2014, Clover had the following account balances.

Freight-in	$ 4,000
Purchases	509,000
Purchase discounts	6,000
Purchase returns and allowances	8,000
Sales revenue	840,000
Sales discounts	7,000
Sales returns and allowances	11,000

At December 31, 2014, Clover determines that its ending inventory is $60,000.

Instructions

(a) Compute Clover's 2014 gross profit.

(b) Compute Clover's 2014 operating expenses if net income is $130,000 and there are no nonoperating activities.

Prepare cost of goods sold section.

(LO 6)

***E5-17** Below is a series of cost of goods sold sections for companies Alpha, Beta, Chi, and Decca.

	Alpha	Beta	Chi	Decca
Beginning inventory	$ 150	$ 70	$1,000	$ (j)
Purchases	1,620	1,060	(g)	43,590
Purchase returns and allowances	40	(d)	290	(k)
Net purchases	(a)	1,030	6,210	41,090
Freight-in	95	(e)	(h)	2,240
Cost of goods purchased	(b)	1,280	7,940	(l)
Cost of goods available for sale	1,825	1,350	(i)	49,530
Ending inventory	310	(f)	1,450	6,230
Cost of goods sold	(c)	1,260	7,490	43,300

Instructions

Fill in the lettered blanks to complete the cost of goods sold sections.

Journalize purchase transactions.

(LO 6)

***E5-18** This information relates to Olaf Co.

1. On April 5, purchased merchandise from DeVito Company for $18,000, terms 2/10, net/30, FOB shipping point.
2. On April 6, paid freight costs of $820 on merchandise purchased from DeVito Company.
3. On April 7, purchased equipment on account for $30,000.

4. On April 8, returned some of April 5 merchandise, which cost $2,800, to DeVito Company.
5. On April 15, paid the amount due to DeVito Company in full.

Instructions

(a) Prepare the journal entries to record these transactions on the books of Olaf Co. using a periodic inventory system.
(b) Assume that Olaf Co. paid the balance due to DeVito Company on May 4 instead of April 15. Prepare the journal entry to record this payment.

***E5-19** Presented below is information related to Chile Co.

Journalize purchase transactions.

(LO 6)

1. On April 5, purchased merchandise from Graham Company for $16,000, terms 2/10, net/30, FOB shipping point.
2. On April 6, paid freight costs of $800 on merchandise purchased from Graham.
3. On April 7, purchased equipment on account from Reed Mfg. Co. for $27,000.
4. On April 8, returned merchandise, which cost $4,000, to Graham Company.
5. On April 15, paid the amount due to Graham Company in full.

Instructions

(a) Prepare the journal entries to record these transactions on the books of Chile Co. using a periodic inventory system.
(b) Assume that Chile Co. paid the balance due to Graham Company on May 4 instead of April 15. Prepare the journal entry to record this payment.

***E5-20** Presented below are selected accounts for Higley Company as reported in the worksheet at the end of May 2014.

Complete worksheet.

(LO 7)

Accounts	Adjusted Trial Balance		Income Statement		Balance Sheet	
	Dr.	Cr.	Dr.	Cr.	Dr.	Cr.
Cash	9,000					
Inventory	76,000					
Sales Revenue		460,000				
Sales Returns and Allowances	10,000					
Sales Discounts	9,000					
Cost of Goods Sold	288,000					

Instructions

Complete the worksheet by extending amounts reported in the adjusted trial balance to the appropriate columns in the worksheet. Do not total individual columns.

***E5-21** The trial balance columns of the worksheet for Adelle Company at June 30, 2014, are as follows.

Prepare a worksheet.

(LO 7)

Adelle Company
Worksheet
For the Month Ended June 30, 2014

Account Titles	Trial Balance Debit	Trial Balance Credit
Cash	$ 2,120	
Accounts Receivable	2,440	
Inventory	11,640	
Accounts Payable		$ 1,120
Common Stock		4,000
Sales Revenue		42,500
Cost of Goods Sold	20,560	
Operating Expenses	10,860	
	$47,620	$47,620

Other data:
Operating expenses incurred on account, but not yet recorded, total $1,500.

Instructions

Enter the trial balance on a worksheet and complete the worksheet.

EXERCISES: SET B AND CHALLENGE EXERCISES

Visit the book's companion website, at **www.wiley.com/college/weygandt**, and choose the Student Companion site to access Exercise Set B and Challenge Exercises.

PROBLEMS: SET A

Journalize purchase and sales transactions under a perpetual inventory system.

(LO 2, 3)

P5-1A Ready-Set-Go Co. distributes suitcases to retail stores and extends credit terms of 1/10, n/30 to all of its customers. At the end of June, Ready-Set-Go's inventory consisted of suitcases costing $1,200. During the month of July, the following merchandising transactions occurred.

July 1 Purchased suitcases on account for $1,500 from Trunk Manufacturers, FOB destination, terms 2/10, n/30. The appropriate party also made a cash payment of $100 for freight on this date.
3 Sold suitcases on account to Satchel World for $2,200. The cost of suitcases sold is $1,400.
9 Paid Trunk Manufacturers in full.
12 Received payment in full from Satchel World.
17 Sold suitcases on account to Lady GoGo for $1,400. The cost of the suitcases sold was $1,010.
18 Purchased suitcases on account for $1,900 from Holiday Manufacturers, FOB shipping point, terms 1/10, n/30. The appropriate party also made a cash payment of $125 for freight on this date.
20 Received $300 credit (including freight) for suitcases returned to Holiday Manufacturers.
21 Received payment in full from Lady GoGo.
22 Sold suitcases on account to Vagabond for $2,250. The cost of suitcases sold was $1,350.
30 Paid Holiday Manufacturers in full.
31 Granted Vagabond $200 credit for suitcases returned costing $120.

Ready-Set-Go's chart of accounts includes the following: No. 101 Cash, No. 112 Accounts Receivable, No. 120 Inventory, No. 201 Accounts Payable, No. 401 Sales Revenue, No. 412 Sales Returns and Allowances, No. 414 Sales Discounts, and No. 505 Cost of Goods Sold.

Instructions

Journalize the transactions for the month of July for Ready-Set-Go using a perpetual inventory system.

Journalize, post, and prepare a partial income statement.

(LO 2, 3, 5)

P5-2A Shmi Distributing Company completed the following merchandising transactions in the month of April. At the beginning of April, the ledger of Shmi showed Cash of $8,000 and Common Stock of $8,000.

Apr. 2 Purchased merchandise on account from Walker Supply Co. $6,200, terms 1/10, n/30.
4 Sold merchandise on account $5,500, FOB destination, terms 1/10, n/30. The cost of the merchandise sold was $3,400.
5 Paid $240 freight on April 4 sale.
6 Received credit from Walker Supply Co. for merchandise returned $500.
11 Paid Walker Supply Co. in full, less discount.
13 Received collections in full, less discounts, from customers billed on April 4.
14 Purchased merchandise for cash $3,800.
16 Received refund from supplier for returned goods on cash purchase of April 14, $500.
18 Purchased merchandise from Benjamin Distributors $4,500, FOB shipping point, terms 2/10, n/30.
20 Paid freight on April 18 purchase $160.
23 Sold merchandise for cash $7,400. The merchandise sold had a cost of $4,120.

Apr. 26 Purchased merchandise for cash $2,300.
27 Paid Benjamin Distributors in full, less discount.
29 Made refunds to cash customers for defective merchandise $90. The returned merchandise had a fair value of $30.
30 Sold merchandise on account $3,400, terms n/30. The cost of the merchandise sold was $1,900.

Shmi Distributing Company's chart of accounts includes the following: No. 101 Cash, No. 112 Accounts Receivable, No. 120 Inventory, No. 201 Accounts Payable, No. 311 Common Stock, No. 401 Sales Revenue, No. 412 Sales Returns and Allowances, No. 414 Sales Discounts, No. 505 Cost of Goods Sold, and No. 644 Freight-Out.

Instructions

(a) Journalize the transactions using a perpetual inventory system.
(b) Enter the beginning cash and capital balances, and post the transactions. (Use J1 for the journal reference.)
(c) Prepare the income statement through gross profit for the month of April 2014.

(c) Gross profit $6,765

Prepare financial statements and adjusting and closing entries.

(LO 4, 5)

P5-3A Starz Department Store is located near the Towne Shopping Mall. At the end of the company's calendar year on December 31, 2014, the following accounts appeared in two of its trial balances.

	Unadjusted	Adjusted		Unadjusted	Adjusted
Accounts Payable	$ 79,300	$ 80,300	Interest Revenue	$ 4,000	$ 4,000
Accounts Receivable	50,300	50,300	Inventory	75,000	75,000
Accumulated Depr.—Buildings	42,100	52,500	Mortgage Payable	80,000	80,000
Accumulated Depr.—Equipment	29,600	42,900	Prepaid Insurance	9,600	2,400
Buildings	290,000	290,000	Property Tax Expense		4,800
Cash	23,800	23,800	Property Taxes Payable		4,800
Common Stock	112,000	112,000	Retained Earnings	64,600	64,600
Cost of Goods Sold	412,700	412,700	Salaries and Wages Expense	108,000	108,000
Depreciation Expense		23,700	Sales Commissions Expense	10,200	14,500
Dividends	24,000	24,000	Sales Commissions Payable		4,300
Equipment	110,000	110,000	Sales Returns and Allowances	8,000	8,000
Insurance Expense		7,200	Sales Revenue	724,000	724,000
Interest Expense	3,000	8,600	Utilities Expense	11,000	12,000
Interest Payable		5,600			

Instructions

(a) Prepare a multiple-step income statement, a retained earnings statement, and a classified balance sheet. $16,000 of the mortgage payable is due for payment next year.
(b) Journalize the adjusting entries that were made.
(c) Journalize the closing entries that are necessary.

(a) Net income $128,500
Retained earnings $169,100
Total assets $456,100

Journalize, post, and prepare a trial balance.

(LO 2, 3, 4)

P5-4A J. Ackbar, a former professional tennis star, operates Ackbar's Tennis Shop at the Miller Lake Resort. At the beginning of the current season, the ledger of Ackbar's Tennis Shop showed Cash $2,200, Inventory $1,800, and Common Stock $4,000. The following transactions were completed during April.

Apr. 4 Purchased racquets and balls from Jay-Mac Co. $760, FOB shipping point, terms 2/10, n/30.
6 Paid freight on purchase from Jay-Mac Co. $40.
8 Sold merchandise to members $1,150, terms n/30. The merchandise sold had a cost of $790.
10 Received credit of $60 from Jay-Mac Co. for a racquet that was returned.
11 Purchased tennis shoes from Venus Sports for cash, $420.
13 Paid Jay-Mac Co. in full.
14 Purchased tennis shirts and shorts from Everett Sportswear $800, FOB shipping point, terms 3/10, n/60.
15 Received cash refund of $50 from Venus Sports for damaged merchandise that was returned.
17 Paid freight on Everett Sportswear purchase $30.
18 Sold merchandise to members $980, terms n/30. The cost of the merchandise sold was $520.

Apr. 20 Received $600 in cash from members in settlement of their accounts.
21 Paid Everett Sportswear in full.
27 Granted an allowance of $40 to members for tennis clothing that did not fit properly.
30 Received cash payments on account from members, $820.

The chart of accounts for the tennis shop includes the following: No. 101 Cash, No. 112 Accounts Receivable, No. 120 Inventory, No. 201 Accounts Payable, No. 311 Common Stock, No. 401 Sales Revenue, No. 412 Sales Returns and Allowances, and No. 505 Cost of Goods Sold.

Instructions

(a) Journalize the April transactions using a perpetual inventory system.
(b) Enter the beginning balances in the ledger accounts and post the April transactions. (Use J1 for the journal reference.)
(c) Prepare a trial balance on April 30, 2014.

(c) Total debits $6,130

Determine cost of goods sold and gross profit under periodic approach.

(LO 6)

***P5-5A** At the end of Apex Department Store's fiscal year on December 31, 2014, these accounts appeared in its adjusted trial balance.

Freight-In	$ 5,600
Inventory	40,500
Purchases	442,000
Purchase Discounts	12,000
Purchase Returns and Allowances	6,400
Sales Revenue	718,000
Sales Returns and Allowances	18,000

Additional facts:

1. Merchandise inventory on December 31, 2014, is $65,000.
2. Apex Department Store uses a periodic system.

Instructions

Prepare an income statement through gross profit for the year ended December 31, 2014.

Gross profit $295,300

Calculate missing amounts and assess profitability.

(LO 6)

***P5-6A** Valerie Fons operates a retail clothing operation. She purchases all merchandise inventory on credit and uses a periodic inventory system. The Accounts Payable account is used for recording inventory purchases only; all other current liabilities are accrued in separate accounts. You are provided with the following selected information for the fiscal years 2011–2014.

	2011	2012	2013	2014
Inventory (ending)	$13,000	$ 11,300	$ 14,700	$ 12,200
Accounts payable (ending)	20,000			
Sales revenue		225,700	240,300	235,000
Purchases of merchandise inventory on account		141,000	150,000	132,000
Cash payments to suppliers		135,000	161,000	127,000

Instructions

(a) Calculate cost of goods sold for each of the 2012, 2013, and 2014 fiscal years.
(b) Calculate the gross profit for each of the 2012, 2013, and 2014 fiscal years.
(c) Calculate the ending balance of accounts payable for each of the 2012, 2013, and 2014 fiscal years.
(d) Sales declined in fiscal 2014. Does that mean that profitability, as measured by the gross profit rate, necessarily also declined? Explain, calculating the gross profit rate for each fiscal year to help support your answer. (Round to one decimal place.)

(a) 2013 $146,600

(c) 2013 Ending accts payable $16,000

Journalize, post, and prepare trial balance and partial income statement using periodic approach.

(LO 6)

GLS

***P5-7A** At the beginning of the current season, the ledger of Village Tennis Shop showed Cash $2,500; Inventory $1,700; and Common Stock $4,200. The following transactions were completed during April.

Apr. 4 Purchased racquets and balls from Lowell Co. $860, terms 3/10, n/30.
6 Paid freight on Lowell Co. purchase $74.
8 Sold merchandise to members $900, terms n/30.
10 Received credit of $60 from Lowell Co. for a racquet that was returned.

Apr. 11 Purchased tennis shoes from Volker Sports for cash $300.
13 Paid Lowell Co. in full.
14 Purchased tennis shirts and shorts from Linzey Sportswear $700, terms 2/10, n/60.
15 Received cash refund of $50 from Volker Sports for damaged merchandise that was returned.
17 Paid freight on Linzey Sportswear purchase $30.
18 Sold merchandise to members $1,200, terms n/30.
20 Received $500 in cash from members in settlement of their accounts.
21 Paid Linzey Sportswear in full.
27 Granted an allowance of $25 to members for tennis clothing that did not fit properly.
30 Received cash payments on account from members $620.

The chart of accounts for the tennis shop includes Cash, Accounts Receivable, Inventory, Accounts Payable, Common Stock, Sales Revenue, Sales Returns and Allowances, Purchases, Purchase Returns and Allowances, Purchase Discounts, and Freight-In.

Instructions

(a) Journalize the April transactions using a periodic inventory system.
(b) Using T-accounts, enter the beginning balances in the ledger accounts and post the April transactions.
(c) Prepare a trial balance on April 30, 2014.
(d) Prepare an income statement through gross profit, assuming inventory on hand at April 30 is $2,296.

(c) Tot. trial balance $6,448
(d) Gross profit $855

***P5-8A** The trial balance of Mr. Rosiak Fashion Center contained the following accounts at November 30, the end of the company's fiscal year.

Complete accounting cycle beginning with a worksheet.

(LO 4, 5, 7)

Mr. Rosiak Fashion Center
Trial Balance
November 30, 2014

	Debit	Credit
Cash	$ 8,700	
Accounts Receivable	27,700	
Inventory	44,700	
Supplies	6,200	
Equipment	133,000	
Accumulated Depreciation—Equipment		$ 23,000
Notes Payable		51,000
Accounts Payable		48,500
Common Stock		50,000
Retained Earnings		38,000
Dividends	8,000	
Sales Revenue		755,200
Sales Returns and Allowances	12,800	
Cost of Goods Sold	497,400	
Salaries and Wages Expense	136,000	
Advertising Expense	24,400	
Utilities Expense	14,000	
Maintenance and Repairs Expense	12,100	
Freight-Out	16,700	
Rent Expense	24,000	
Totals	$965,700	$965,700

Adjustment data:

1. Supplies on hand totaled $2,100.
2. Depreciation is $11,500 on the equipment.
3. Interest of $4,000 is accrued on notes payable at November 30.
4. Inventory actually on hand is $44,520.

(a) Adj. trial balance $981,200
Net loss $1,980
(b) Gross profit $244,820
Total assets $181,520

Instructions

(a) Enter the trial balance on a worksheet, and complete the worksheet.
(b) Prepare a multiple-step income statement and a retained earnings statement for the year, and a classified balance sheet as of November 30, 2014. Notes payable of $6,000 are due in January 2015.
(c) Journalize the adjusting entries.
(d) Journalize the closing entries.
(e) Prepare a post-closing trial balance.

PROBLEMS: SET B

Journalize purchase and sales transactions under a perpetual inventory system.

(LO 2, 3)

P5-1B Book Nook Warehouse distributes hardcover books to retail stores and extends credit terms of 2/10, n/30 to all of its customers. At the end of May, Book Nook's inventory consisted of books purchased for $1,800. During June, the following merchandising transactions occurred.

June 1 Purchased books on account for $1,850 from Phantom Publishers, FOB destination, terms 2/10, n/30. The appropriate party also made a cash payment of $50 for the freight on this date.
3 Sold books on account to Ex Libris for $2,500. The cost of the books sold was $1,440.
6 Received $150 credit for books returned to Phantom Publishers.
9 Paid Phantom Publishers in full, less discount.
15 Received payment in full from Ex Libris.
17 Sold books on account to Bargain Books for $1,800. The cost of the books sold was $1,020.
20 Purchased books on account for $1,500 from Bookem Publishers, FOB destination, terms 2/15, n/30. The appropriate party also made a cash payment of $50 for the freight on this date.
24 Received payment in full from Bargain Books.
26 Paid Bookem Publishers in full, less discount.
28 Sold books on account to Corner Bookstore for $1,300. The cost of the books sold was $850.
30 Granted Corner Bookstore $120 credit for books returned costing $72.

Book Nook Warehouse's chart of accounts includes the following: No. 101 Cash, No. 112 Accounts Receivable, No. 120 Inventory, No. 201 Accounts Payable, No. 401 Sales Revenue, No. 412 Sales Returns and Allowances, No. 414 Sales Discounts, and No. 505 Cost of Goods Sold.

Instructions

Journalize the transactions for the month of June for Book Nook Warehouse using a perpetual inventory system.

Journalize, post, and prepare a partial income statement.

(LO 2, 3, 5)

P5-2B Copple Hardware Store completed the following merchandising transactions in the month of May. At the beginning of May, the ledger of Copple showed Cash of $5,000 and Common Stock of $5,000.

May 1 Purchased merchandise on account from Nute's Wholesale Supply $4,200, terms 2/10, n/30.
2 Sold merchandise on account $2,300, terms 1/10, n/30. The cost of the merchandise sold was $1,300.
5 Received credit from Nute's Wholesale Supply for merchandise returned $500.
9 Received collections in full, less discounts, from customers billed on sales of $2,300 on May 2.
10 Paid Nute's Wholesale Supply in full, less discount.
11 Purchased supplies for cash $400.
12 Purchased merchandise for cash $1,400.
15 Received refund for poor quality merchandise from supplier on cash purchase $150.
17 Purchased merchandise from Sherrick Distributors $1,300, FOB shipping point, terms 2/10, n/30.

May 19 Paid freight on May 17 purchase $130.
24 Sold merchandise for cash $3,200. The merchandise sold had a cost of $2,000.
25 Purchased merchandise from Herbert, Inc. $620, FOB destination, terms 2/10, n/30.
27 Paid Sherrick Distributors in full, less discount.
29 Made refunds to cash customers for defective merchandise $90. The returned merchandise had a fair value of $40.
31 Sold merchandise on account $1,000 terms n/30. The cost of the merchandise sold was $560.

Copple Hardware's chart of accounts includes the following: No. 101 Cash, No. 112 Accounts Receivable, No. 120 Inventory, No. 126 Supplies, No. 201 Accounts Payable, No. 311 Common Stock, No. 401 Sales Revenue, No. 412 Sales Returns and Allowances, No. 414 Sales Discounts, and No. 505 Cost of Goods Sold.

Instructions

(a) Journalize the transactions using a perpetual inventory system.
(b) Enter the beginning cash and common stock balances and post the transactions. (Use J1 for the journal reference.)
(c) Prepare an income statement through gross profit for the month of May 2014.

(c) Gross profit $2,567

P5-3B The Moulton Store is located in midtown Metropolis. During the past several years, net income has been declining because of suburban shopping centers. At the end of the company's fiscal year on November 30, 2014, the following accounts appeared in two of its trial balances.

Prepare financial statements and adjusting and closing entries.

(LO 4, 5)

	Unadjusted	**Adjusted**		**Unadjusted**	**Adjusted**
Accounts Payable	$ 25,200	$ 25,200	Notes Payable	$ 37,000	$ 37,000
Accounts Receivable	30,500	30,500	Prepaid Insurance	10,500	3,500
Accumulated Depr.—Equip.	22,000	33,000	Property Tax Expense		3,500
Cash	26,000	26,000	Property Taxes Payable		3,500
Common Stock	50,000	50,000	Rent Expense	15,000	15,000
Cost of Goods Sold	507,000	507,000	Retained Earnings	61,700	61,700
Depreciation Expense		11,000	Salaries and Wages Expense	96,000	96,000
Dividends	8,000	8,000	Sales Commissions Expense	6,500	13,500
Equipment	154,300	154,300	Sales Commissions Payable		7,000
Freight-Out	6,500	6,500	Sales Returns and Allowances	9,000	9,000
Insurance Expense		7,000	Sales Revenue	706,000	706,000
Interest Expense	6,100	6,100	Utilities Expense	8,500	8,500
Interest Revenue	8,000	8,000			
Inventory	26,000	26,000			

Instructions

(a) Prepare a multiple-step income statement, a retained earnings statement, and a classified balance sheet. Notes payable are due in 2017.
(b) Journalize the adjusting entries that were made.
(c) Journalize the closing entries that are necessary.

(a) Net income $30,900
Retained earnings $84,600
Total assets $207,300

P5-4B Bill Kokott, a former disc golf star, operates Bill's Discorama. At the beginning of the current season on April 1, the ledger of Bill's Discorama showed Cash $1,850, Inventory $2,150, and Common Stock $4,000. The following transactions were completed during April.

Journalize, post, and prepare a trial balance.

(LO 2, 3, 4)

Apr. 5 Purchased golf discs, bags, and other inventory on account from Ellis Co. $1,200, FOB shipping point, terms 2/10, n/60.
7 Paid freight on the Ellis purchase $75.
9 Received credit from Ellis Co. for merchandise returned $100.
10 Sold merchandise on account for $930, terms n/30. The merchandise sold had a cost of $540.
12 Purchased disc golf shirts and other accessories on account from Penguin Sportswear $720, terms 1/10, n/30.
14 Paid Ellis Co. in full, less discount.
17 Received credit from Penguin Sportswear for merchandise returned $120.
20 Made sales on account for $610, terms n/30. The cost of the merchandise sold was $370.

Apr. 21 Paid Penguin Sportswear in full, less discount.
27 Granted an allowance to members for clothing that was flawed $20.
30 Received payments on account from customers $960.

The chart of accounts for the store includes the following: No. 101 Cash, No. 112 Accounts Receivable, No. 120 Inventory, No. 201 Accounts Payable, No. 311 Common Stock, No. 401 Sales Revenue, No. 412 Sales Returns and Allowances, and No. 505 Cost of Goods Sold.

Instructions

(a) Journalize the April transactions using a perpetual inventory system.
(b) Enter the beginning balances in the ledger accounts and post the April transactions. (Use J1 for the journal reference.)
(c) Prepare a trial balance on April 30, 2014.

(c) Total debits $5,540

Determine cost of goods sold and gross profit under periodic approach.

(LO 6)

***P5-5B** At the end of Stampfer Department Store's fiscal year on November 30, 2014, these accounts appeared in its adjusted trial balance.

Freight-In	$ 7,500
Inventory	40,000
Purchases	585,000
Purchase Discounts	5,300
Purchase Returns and Allowances	2,900
Sales Revenue	1,000,000
Sales Returns and Allowances	28,000

Additional facts:

1. Merchandise inventory on November 30, 2014, is $54,600.
2. Stampfer Department Store uses a periodic system.

Instructions

Prepare an income statement through gross profit for the year ended November 30, 2014.

Gross profit $402,300

Calculate missing amounts and assess profitability.

(LO 6)

***P5-6B** Psang Inc. operates a retail operation that purchases and sells home entertainment products. The company purchases all merchandise inventory on credit and uses a periodic inventory system. The Accounts Payable account is used for recording inventory purchases only; all other current liabilities are accrued in separate accounts. You are provided with the following selected information for the fiscal years 2011 through 2014, inclusive.

	2011	2012	2013	2014
Income Statement Data				
Sales revenue		$53,000	$ (e)	$46,000
Cost of goods sold		(a)	13,800	14,300
Gross profit		38,300	35,200	(i)
Operating expenses		35,900	(f)	28,600
Net income		$ (b)	$ 2,500	$ (j)
Balance Sheet Data				
Inventory	$7,200	$ (c)	$ 8,100	$ (k)
Accounts payable	3,200	3,400	2,500	(l)
Additional Information				
Purchases of merchandise inventory on account		$14,200	$ (g)	$13,200
Cash payments to suppliers		(d)	(h)	13,600

(c) $6,700
(g) $15,200
(i) $31,700

Instructions

(a) Calculate the missing amounts.
(b) Sales declined over the 3-year fiscal period, 2012–2014. Does that mean that profitability necessarily also declined? Explain, computing the gross profit rate and the profit margin ratio for each fiscal year to help support your answer. (Round to one decimal place.)

Journalize, post, and prepare trial balance and partial income statement using periodic approach.

(LO 6)

GLS

***P5-7B** At the beginning of the current season on April 1, the ledger of Tri-State Pro Shop showed Cash $3,000; Inventory $4,000; and Common Stock $7,000. These transactions occurred during April 2014.

Apr. 5 Purchased golf bags, clubs, and balls on account from Balata Co. $1,300, FOB shipping point, terms 2/10, n/60.
7 Paid freight on Balata Co. purchases $70.
9 Received credit from Balata Co. for merchandise returned $100.
10 Sold merchandise on account to members $670, terms n/30.
12 Purchased golf shoes, sweaters, and other accessories on account from Arrow Sportswear $450, terms 1/10, n/30.
14 Paid Balata Co. in full.
17 Received credit from Arrow Sportswear for merchandise returned $50.
20 Made sales on account to members $600, terms n/30.
21 Paid Arrow Sportswear in full.
27 Granted credit to members for clothing that had flaws $55.
30 Received payments on account from members $630.

The chart of accounts for the pro shop includes Cash, Accounts Receivable, Inventory, Accounts Payable, Common Stock, Sales Revenue, Sales Returns and Allowances, Purchases, Purchase Returns and Allowances, Purchase Discounts, and Freight-In.

Instructions

(a) Journalize the April transactions using a periodic inventory system.

(b) Using T-accounts, enter the beginning balances in the ledger accounts and post the April transactions.

(c) Prepare a trial balance on April 30, 2014.

(d) Prepare an income statement through gross profit, assuming merchandise inventory on hand at April 30 is $4,824.

(c) Tot. trial balance $8,448
Gross profit $397

PROBLEMS: SET C

Visit the book's companion website, at **www.wiley.com/college/weygandt**, and choose the Student Companion site to access Problem Set C.

COMPREHENSIVE PROBLEM

CP5 On December 1, 2014, Jurczyk Distributing Company had the following account balances.

	Debits		Credits
Cash	$ 7,200	Accumulated Depreciation—Equipment	$ 2,200
Accounts Receivable	4,600	Accounts Payable	4,500
Inventory	12,000	Salaries and Wages Payable	1,000
Supplies	1,200	Common Stock	30,000
Equipment	22,000	Retained Earnings	9,300
	$47,000		$47,000

During December, the company completed the following summary transactions.

Dec. 6 Paid $1,600 for salaries and wages due employees, of which $600 is for December and $1,000 is for November salaries and wages payable.
8 Received $2,100 cash from customers in payment of account (no discount allowed).
10 Sold merchandise for cash $6,600. The cost of the merchandise sold was $4,100.
13 Purchased merchandise on account from Gong Co. $9,000, terms 2/10, n/30.
15 Purchased supplies for cash $2,000.
18 Sold merchandise on account $12,000, terms 3/10, n/30. The cost of the merchandise sold was $8,400.
20 Paid salaries and wages $1,800.
23 Paid Gong Co. in full, less discount.
27 Received collections in full, less discounts, from customers billed on December 18.

Adjustment data:

1. Accrued salaries and wages payable $800.
2. Depreciation $200 per month.
3. Supplies on hand $1,700.

Instructions

(a) Journalize the December transactions using a perpetual inventory system.

(b) Enter the December 1 balances in the ledger T-accounts and post the December transactions. Use Cost of Goods Sold, Depreciation Expense, Salaries and Wages Expense, Sales Revenue, Sales Discounts, and Supplies Expense.

(c) Journalize and post adjusting entries.

(d) Totals $65,600

(e) Net income $840

(d) Prepare an adjusted trial balance.

(e) Prepare an income statement and a retained earnings statement for December and a classified balance sheet at December 31.

CONTINUING COOKIE CHRONICLE

(*Note:* This is a continuation of the Cookie Chronicle from Chapters 1–4.)

CCC5 Because Natalie has had such a successful first few months, she is considering other opportunities to develop her business. One opportunity is the sale of fine European mixers. The owner of Kzinski Supply Company has approached Natalie to become the exclusive U.S. distributor of these fine mixers in her state. The current cost of a mixer is approximately $575 (U.S.), and Natalie would sell each one for $1,150. Natalie comes to you for advice on how to account for these mixers.

Go to the book's companion website, www.wiley.com/college/weygandt, to see the completion of this problem.

Broadening Your PERSPECTIVE

Financial Reporting and Analysis

Financial Reporting Problem: PepsiCo, Inc.

BYP5-1 The financial statements of PepsiCo, Inc. are presented in Appendix A at the end of this textbook.

Instructions

Answer the following questions using PepsiCo's Consolidated Statement of Income.

(a) What was the percentage change in (1) sales and in (2) net income from 2008 to 2009 and from 2009 to 2010?

(b) What was the company's gross profit rate in 2008, 2009, and 2010?

(c) What was the company's percentage of net income to net sales in 2008, 2009, and 2010? Comment on any trend in this percentage.

Comparative Analysis Problem: PepsiCo, Inc. vs. The Coca-Cola Company

BYP5-2 PepsiCo's financial statements are presented in Appendix A. Financial statements of The Coca-Cola Company are presented in Appendix B.

Instructions

(a) Based on the information contained in these financial statements, determine each of the following for each company.
  (1) Gross profit for 2010.
  (2) Gross profit rate for 2010.
  (3) Operating income for 2010.
  (4) Percentage change in operating income from 2009 to 2010.

(b) What conclusions concerning the relative profitability of the two companies can you draw from these data?

Real-World Focus

BYP5-3 No financial decision-maker should ever rely solely on the financial information reported in the annual report to make decisions. It is important to keep abreast of financial news. This activity demonstrates how to search for financial news on the Web.

Address: **biz.yahoo.com/i,** or go to **www.wiley.com/college/weygandt**

Steps

1. Type in either PepsiCo or Coca-Cola.
2. Choose **News**.
3. Select an article that sounds interesting to you.

Instructions

(a) What was the source of the article (e.g., Reuters, Businesswire, PR Newswire)?

(b) Assume that you are a personal financial planner and that one of your clients owns stock in the company. Write a brief memo to your client, summarizing the article and explaining the implications of the article for their investment.

Critical Thinking

Decision-Making Across the Organization

BYP5-4 Three years ago, Debbie Sells and her brother-in-law Mike Mooney opened Family Department Store. For the first two years, business was good, but the following condensed income results for 2013 were disappointing.

Family Department Store
Income Statement
For the Year Ended December 31, 2013

Net sales		$700,000
Cost of goods sold		553,000
Gross profit		147,000
Operating expenses		
Selling expenses	$100,000	
Administrative expenses	20,000	120,000
Net income		$ 27,000

Debbie believes the problem lies in the relatively low gross profit rate (gross profit divided by net sales) of 21%. Mike believes the problem is that operating expenses are too high.

Debbie thinks the gross profit rate can be improved by making both of the following changes. She does not anticipate that these changes will have any effect on operating expenses.

1. Increase average selling prices by 20%. This increase is expected to lower sales volume so that total sales will increase only 5%.
2. Buy merchandise in larger quantities and take all purchase discounts. These changes are expected to increase the gross profit rate by 3 percentage points.

Mike thinks expenses can be cut by making both of the following changes. He feels that these changes will not have any effect on net sales.

1. Cut 2013 sales salaries of $60,000 in half and give sales personnel a commission of 2% of net sales.
2. Reduce store deliveries to one day per week rather than twice a week; this change will reduce 2013 delivery expenses of $30,000 by 40%.

Debbie and Mike come to you for help in deciding the best way to improve net income.

Instructions

With the class divided into groups, answer the following.

(a) Prepare a condensed income statement for 2014, assuming (1) Debbie's changes are implemented and (2) Mike's ideas are adopted.

(b) What is your recommendation to Debbie and Mike?

(c) Prepare a condensed income statement for 2014, assuming both sets of proposed changes are made.

Communication Activity

BYP5-5 The following situation is in chronological order.

1. Dexter decides to buy a surfboard.
2. He calls Boardin USA Co. to inquire about their surfboards.
3. Two days later, he requests Boardin USA Co. to make him a surfboard.
4. Three days later, Boardin USA Co. sends Dexter a purchase order to fill out.
5. He sends back the purchase order.
6. Boardin USA Co. receives the completed purchase order.
7. Boardin USA Co. completes the surfboard.
8. Dexter picks up the surfboard.
9. Boardin USA Co. bills Dexter.
10. Boardin USA Co. receives payment from Dexter.

Instructions

In a memo to the president of Boardin USA Co., answer the following.

(a) When should Boardin USA Co. record the sale?

(b) Suppose that with his purchase order, Dexter is required to make a down payment. Would that change your answer?

Ethics Case

BYP5-6 Anita Zurbrugg was just hired as the assistant treasurer of Yorktown Stores. The company is a specialty chain store with nine retail stores concentrated in one metropolitan area. Among other things, the payment of all invoices is centralized in one of the departments Anita will manage. Her primary responsibility is to maintain the company's high credit rating by paying all bills when due and to take advantage of all cash discounts.

Chris Dadian, the former assistant treasurer who has been promoted to treasurer, is training Anita in her new duties. He instructs Anita that she is to continue the practice of preparing all checks "net of discount" and dating the checks the last day of the discount period. "But," Chris continues, "we always hold the checks at least 4 days beyond the discount period before mailing them. That way, we get another 4 days of interest on our money. Most of our creditors need our business and don't complain. And, if they scream about our missing the discount period, we blame it on the mail room or the post office. We've only lost one discount out of every hundred we take that way. I think everybody does it. By the way, welcome to our team!"

Instructions

(a) What are the ethical considerations in this case?

(b) Who are the stakeholders that are harmed or benefitted in this situation?

(c) Should Anita continue the practice started by Chris? Does she have any choice?

All About You

BYP5-7 There are many situations in business where it is difficult to determine the proper period in which to record revenue. Suppose that after graduation with a degree in finance, you take a job as a manager at a consumer electronics store called Pacifica Electronics. The company has expanded rapidly in order to compete with Best Buy. Pacifica has also begun selling gift cards for its electronic products. The cards are available in any dollar amount and allow the holder of the card to purchase an item for up to 2 years from the time the card is purchased. If the card is not used during that 2 years, it expires.

Instructions
Answer the following questions.

At what point should the revenue from the gift cards be recognized? Should the revenue be recognized at the time the card is sold, or should it be recorded when the card is redeemed? Explain the reasoning to support your answers.

FASB Codification Activity

BYP5-8 If your school has a subscription to the FASB Codification, go to *http://aaahq.org/ascLogin.cfm* to log in and prepare responses to the following

(a) Access the glossary ("Master Glossary") to answer the following.
  (1) What is the definition provided for inventory?
  (2) What is a customer?

(b) What guidance does the Codification provide concerning reporting inventories above cost?

Answers to Chapter Questions

Answers to Insight and Accounting Across the Organization Questions

p. 223 Morrow Snowboards Improves Its Stock Appeal Q: If a perpetual system keeps track of inventory on a daily basis, why do companies ever need to do a physical count? **A:** A perpetual system keeps track of all sales and purchases on a continuous basis. This provides a constant record of the number of units in the inventory. However, if employees make errors in recording sales or purchases, or if there is theft, the inventory value will not be correct. As a consequence, all companies do a physical count of inventory at least once a year.

p. 230 Should Costco Change Its Return Policy? Q: If a company expects significant returns, what are the implications for revenue recognition? **A:** If a company expects significant returns, it should make an adjusting entry at the end of the year reducing sales by the estimated amount of sales returns. This is necessary so as not to overstate the amount of revenue recognized in the period.

p. 231 Selling Green Q: What is meant by "monetize environmental sustainability" for shareholders? **A:** By marketing green, not only does PepsiCo help the environment in the long run, but it also leads to long-term profitability as well. In other words, sound sustainability practices are good business and lead to sound financial results.

p. 237 Disclosing More Details Q: Why have investors and analysts demanded more accuracy in isolating "Other gains and losses" from operating items? **A:** Greater accuracy in the classification of operating versus nonoperating ("Other gains and losses") items permits investors and analysts to judge the real operating margin, the results of continuing operations, and management's ability to control operating expenses.

Answers to Self-Test Questions

1. c **2.** a **3.** c **4.** b (($750 − $50) × .98) **5.** c **6.** c **7.** a **8.** d **9.** b ($400,000 − $310,000) **10.** c **11.** d ***12.** d ***13.** a ($60,000 + $380,000 − $50,000) ***14.** b ***15.** a

A Look at IFRS

The basic accounting entries for merchandising are the same under both GAAP and IFRS. The income statement is a required statement under both sets of standards. The basic format is similar although some differences do exist.

Key Points

- Under both GAAP and IFRS, a company can choose to use either a perpetual or a periodic system.
- Inventories are defined by IFRS as held-for-sale in the ordinary course of business, in the process of production for such sale, or in the form of materials or supplies to be consumed in the production process or in the providing of services.
- Under GAAP, companies generally classify income statement items by function. Classification by function leads to descriptions like administration, distribution, and manufacturing. Under IFRS, companies must classify expenses by either nature or function. Classification by nature leads to descriptions such as the following: salaries, depreciation expense, and utilities expense. If a company uses the functional-expense method on the income statement, disclosure by nature is required in the notes to the financial statements.
- Presentation of the income statement under GAAP follows either a single-step or multiple-step format. IFRS does not mention a single-step or multiple-step approach.
- Under IFRS, revaluation of land, buildings, and intangible assets is permitted. The initial gains and losses resulting from this revaluation are reported as adjustments to equity, often referred to as *other comprehensive income*. The effect of this difference is that the use of IFRS results in more transactions affecting equity (other comprehensive income) but not net income.
- *IAS 1*, "Presentation of Financial Statements," provides general guidelines for the reporting of income statement information. Subsequently, a number of international standards have been issued that provide additional guidance to issues related to income statement presentation.
- Similar to GAAP, comprehensive income under IFRS includes unrealized gains and losses (such as those on so-called "non-trading" securities) that are not included in the calculation of net income.
- IFRS requires that two years of income statement information be presented, whereas GAAP requires three years.

Looking to the Future

The IASB and FASB are working on a project that would rework the structure of financial statements. Specifically, this project will address the issue of how to classify various items in the income statement. A main goal of this new approach is to provide information that better represents how businesses are run. In addition, this approach draws attention away from just one number—net income. It will adopt major groupings similar to those currently used by the statement of cash flows (operating, investing, and financing), so that numbers can be more readily traced across statements. For example, the amount of income that is generated by operations would be traceable to the assets and liabilities used to generate the income. Finally, this approach would also provide detail, beyond that currently seen in most statements (either GAAP or IFRS), by requiring that line items be presented both by function and by nature. The new financial statement format was heavily influenced by suggestions from financial statement analysts.

IFRS Practice

IFRS Self-Test Questions

1. Which of the following would *not* be included in the definition of inventory under IFRS?
   (a) Photocopy paper held for sale by an office-supply store.
   (b) Stereo equipment held for sale by an electronics store.
   (c) Used office equipment held for sale by the human relations department of a plastics company.
   (d) All of the above would meet the definition.

2. Which of the following would *not* be a line item of a company reporting costs by nature?
   (a) Depreciation expense.
   (b) Salaries expense.
   (c) Interest expense.
   (d) Manufacturing expense
3. Which of the following would *not* be a line item of a company reporting costs by function?
   (a) Administration.
   (b) Manufacturing.
   (c) Utilities expense.
   (d) Distribution.
4. Which of the following statements is *false*?
   (a) IFRS specifically requires use of a multiple-step income statement.
   (b) Under IFRS, companies can use either a perpetual or periodic system.
   (c) The proposed new format for financial statements was heavily influenced by the suggestions of financial statement analysts.
   (d) The new income statement format will try to de-emphasize the focus on the "net income" line item.
5. Under the new format for financial statements being proposed under a joint IASB/FASB project:
   (a) all financial statements would adopt headings similar to the current format of the balance sheet.
   (b) financial statements would be presented consistent with the way management usually run companies.
   (c) companies would be required to report income statement line items by function only.
   (d) the amount of detail shown in the income statement would decrease compared to current presentations.

IFRS Exercises

IFRS5-1 Explain the difference between the "nature-of-expense" and "function-of-expense" classifications.

IFRS5-2 For each of the following income statement line items, state whether the item is a "by nature" expense item or a "by function" expense item.

_______ Cost of goods sold
_______ Depreciation expense
_______ Salaries and wages expense
_______ Selling expenses
_______ Utilities expense
_______ Delivery expense
_______ General and administrative expenses

IFRS5-3 Atlantis Company reported the following amounts (in euros) in 2014: net income, €150,000; unrealized gain related to revaluation of buildings, €10,000; and unrealized loss on non-trading securities, €(35,000). Determine Atlantis's total comprehensive income for 2014.

International Financial Reporting Problem: Zetar plc

IFRS5-4 The financial statements of Zetar plc are presented in Appendix C. The company's complete annual report, including the notes to its financial statements, is available at *www.zetarplc.com*.

Instructions

(a) Is Zetar using a multiple-step or a single-step income statement format? Explain how you made your determination.

(b) Instead of "interest expense," what label does Zetar use for interest costs that it incurs?

(c) Using the notes to the company's financial statements, explain what each of the following are:
   (1) Adjusted results.
   (2) One-off items.

Answers to IFRS Self-Test Questions

1. c **2.** d **3.** c **4.** a **5.** b

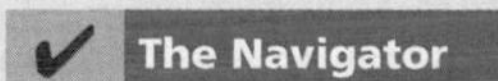

Remember to go back to The Navigator box on the chapter opening page and check off your completed work.

Chapter 6 Inventories

Feature Story

"Where Is That Spare Bulldozer Blade?"

Let's talk inventory—big, bulldozer-size inventory. Caterpillar Inc. is the world's largest manufacturer of construction and mining equipment, diesel and natural gas engines, and industrial gas turbines. It sells its products in over 200 countries, making it one of the most successful U.S. exporters. More than 70% of its productive assets are located domestically, and nearly 50% of its sales are foreign.

During the 1980s, Caterpillar's profitability suffered, but today it is very successful. A big part of this turnaround can be attributed to effective management of its inventory. Imagine what it costs Caterpillar to have too many bulldozers sitting around in inventory—a situation the company definitely wants to avoid. Conversely, Caterpillar must make sure it has enough inventory to meet demand.

At one time during a 7-year period, Caterpillar's sales increased by 100%, while its inventory increased by only 50%. To achieve this dramatic reduction in the amount of resources tied up in inventory, while continuing to meet customers' needs, Caterpillar used a two-pronged approach. First, it completed a factory modernization program, which dramatically increased its production efficiency. The program

✔ The Navigator

- Scan Learning Objectives
- Read Feature Story
- Read Preview
- Read text and answer **DO IT!** p. 275 / p. 281 / p. 287 / p. 290
- Work Comprehensive **DO IT!** **1** p. 290 / **2** p. 295
- Review Summary of Learning Objectives
- Answer Self-Test Questions
- Complete Assignments
- Go to **WileyPLUS** for practice and tutorials

Read A Look at IFRS p. 321

Learning Objectives

After studying this chapter, you should be able to:

1. Describe the steps in determining inventory quantities.
2. Explain the accounting for inventories and apply the inventory cost flow methods.
3. Explain the financial effects of the inventory cost flow assumptions.
4. Explain the lower-of-cost-or-market basis of accounting for inventories.
5. Indicate the effects of inventory errors on the financial statements.
6. Compute and interpret the inventory turnover ratio.

The Navigator

reduced by 60% the amount of inventory the company processed at any one time. It also reduced by an incredible 75% the time it takes to manufacture a part.

Second, Caterpillar dramatically improved its parts distribution system. It ships more than 100,000 items daily from its 23 distribution centers strategically located around the world (10 *million* square feet of warehouse space—remember, we're talking bulldozers). The company can virtually guarantee that it can get any part to anywhere in the world within 24 hours.

After these changes, Caterpillar had record exports, profits, and revenues. It would seem that things couldn't be better. But industry analysts, as well as the company's managers, thought otherwise. In order to maintain Caterpillar's position as the industry leader, management began another major overhaul of inventory production and inventory management processes. The goal: to cut the number of repairs in half, increase productivity by 20%, and increase inventory turnover by 40%.

In short, Caterpillar's ability to manage its inventory has been a key reason for its past success, and inventory management will very likely play a huge part in its ability to succeed in the future.

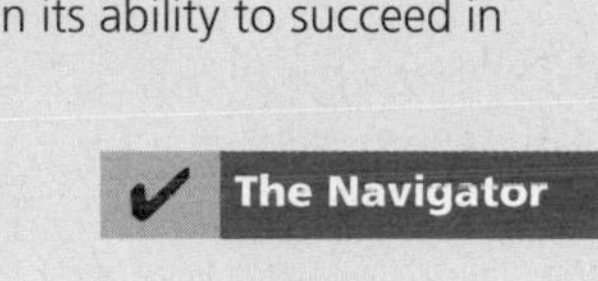

Preview of Chapter 6

In the previous chapter, we discussed the accounting for merchandise inventory using a perpetual inventory system. In this chapter, we explain the methods used to calculate the cost of inventory on hand at the balance sheet date and the cost of goods sold.

The content and organization of this chapter are as follows.

INVENTORIES

Classifying Inventory	Determining Inventory Quantities	Inventory Costing	Inventory Errors	Statement Presentation and Analysis
• Finished goods • Work in process • Raw materials	• Taking a physical inventory • Determining ownership of goods	• Specific identification • Cost flow assumptions • Financial statement and tax effects • Consistent use • Lower-of-cost-or-market	• Income statement effects • Balance sheet effects	• Presentation • Analysis

✔ The Navigator

Classifying Inventory

How a company classifies its inventory depends on whether the firm is a merchandiser or a manufacturer. In a *merchandising* company, such as those described in Chapter 5, inventory consists of many different items. For example, in a grocery store, canned goods, dairy products, meats, and produce are just a few of the inventory items on hand. These items have two common characteristics: (1) They are owned by the company, and (2) they are in a form ready for sale to customers in the ordinary course of business. Thus, merchandisers need only one inventory classification, **merchandise inventory**, to describe the many different items that make up the total inventory.

In a *manufacturing* company, some inventory may not yet be ready for sale. As a result, manufacturers usually classify inventory into three categories: finished goods, work in process, and raw materials. **Finished goods inventory** is manufactured items that are completed and ready for sale. **Work in process** is that portion of manufactured inventory that has been placed into the production process but is not yet complete. **Raw materials** are the basic goods that will be used in production but have not yet been placed into production.

Helpful Hint
Regardless of the classification, companies report all inventories under Current Assets on the balance sheet.

For example, Caterpillar classifies earth-moving tractors completed and ready for sale as **finished goods**. It classifies the tractors on the assembly line in various stages of production as **work in process**. The steel, glass, tires, and other components that are on hand waiting to be used in the production of tractors are identified as **raw materials**.

By observing the levels and changes in the levels of these three inventory types, financial statement users can gain insight into management's production plans. For example, low levels of raw materials and high levels of finished goods suggest that management believes it has enough inventory on hand, and production will be slowing down—perhaps in anticipation of a recession. On the other hand, high levels of raw materials and low levels of finished goods probably signal that management is planning to step up production.

Many companies have significantly lowered inventory levels and costs using **just-in-time (JIT) inventory** methods. Under a just-in-time method, companies manufacture or purchase goods just in time for use. Dell is famous for having developed a system for making computers in response to individual customer requests. Even though it makes each computer to meet each customer's particular specifications, Dell is able to assemble the computer and put it on a truck in less than 48 hours. The success of the JIT system depends on reliable suppliers. By integrating its information systems with those of its suppliers, Dell reduced its inventories to nearly zero. This is a huge advantage in an industry where products become obsolete nearly overnight.

The accounting concepts discussed in this chapter apply to the inventory classifications of both merchandising and manufacturing companies. Our focus here is on merchandise inventory.

ACCOUNTING ACROSS THE ORGANIZATION

A Big Hiccup

JIT can save a company a lot of money, but it isn't without risk. An unexpected disruption in the supply chain can cost a company a lot of money. Japanese automakers experienced just such a disruption when a 6.8-magnitude earthquake caused major damage to the company that produces 50% of their piston rings. The rings themselves cost only $1.50, but without them you cannot make a car. No other supplier could quickly begin producing sufficient quantities of the rings to match the desired specifications. As a result, the automakers were forced to shut down production for a few days—a loss of tens of thousands of cars.

Source: Amy Chozick, "A Key Strategy of Japan's Car Makers Backfires," *Wall Street Journal* (July 20, 2007).

? What steps might the companies take to avoid such a serious disruption in the future? (See page 320.)

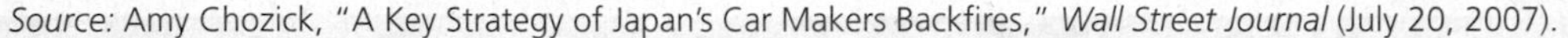

Determining Inventory Quantities

LEARNING OBJECTIVE 1

Describe the steps in determining inventory quantities.

No matter whether they are using a periodic or perpetual inventory system, all companies need to determine inventory quantities at the end of the accounting period. If using a perpetual system, companies take a physical inventory for two reasons:

1. To check the accuracy of their perpetual inventory records.
2. To determine the amount of inventory lost due to wasted raw materials, shoplifting, or employee theft.

Companies using a periodic inventory system take a physical inventory to determine the inventory on hand at the balance sheet date, and to determine the cost of goods sold for the period.

Determining inventory quantities involves two steps: (1) taking a physical inventory of goods on hand and (2) determining the ownership of goods.

Taking a Physical Inventory

Companies take a physical inventory at the end of the accounting period. Taking a physical inventory involves actually counting, weighing, or measuring each kind of inventory on hand. In many companies, taking an inventory is a formidable task. Retailers such as Target, True Value Hardware, or Home Depot have thousands of different inventory items. An inventory count is generally more accurate when goods are not being sold or received during the counting. Consequently, companies often "take inventory" when the business is closed or when business is slow. Many retailers close early on a chosen day in January—after the holiday sales and returns, when inventories are at their lowest level—to count inventory. Recall from Chapter 5 that Wal-Mart Stores, Inc. has a year-end of January 31.

Ethics Note

In a famous fraud, a salad oil company filled its storage tanks mostly with water. The oil rose to the top, so auditors thought the tanks were full of oil. The company also said it had more tanks than it really did: It repainted numbers on the tanks to confuse auditors.

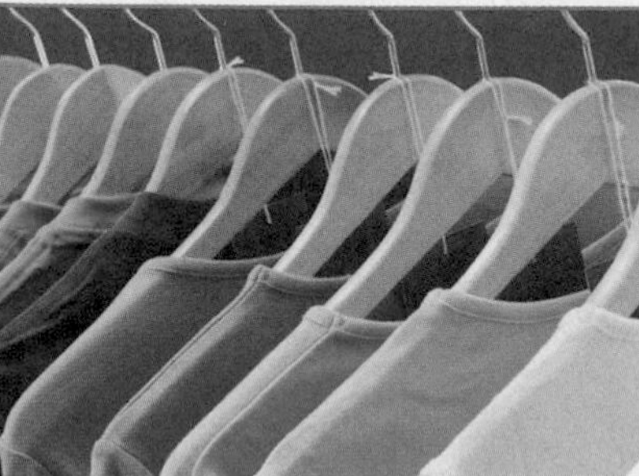

ETHICS INSIGHT

Falsifying Inventory to Boost Income

Managers at women's apparel maker Leslie Fay were convicted of falsifying inventory records to boost net income—and consequently to boost management bonuses. In another case, executives at Craig Consumer Electronics were accused of defrauding lenders by manipulating inventory records. The indictment said the company classified "defective goods as new or refurbished" and claimed that it owned certain shipments "from overseas suppliers" when, in fact, Craig either did not own the shipments or the shipments did not exist.

What effect does an overstatement of inventory have on a company's financial statements? (See page 320.)

Determining Ownership of Goods

One challenge in computing inventory quantities is determining what inventory a company owns. To determine ownership of goods, two questions must be answered: Do all of the goods included in the count belong to the company? Does the company own any goods that were not included in the count?

GOODS IN TRANSIT

A complication in determining ownership is **goods in transit** (on board a truck, train, ship, or plane) at the end of the period. The company may have purchased goods that have not yet been received, or it may have sold goods that have not yet been delivered. To arrive at an accurate count, the company must determine ownership of these goods.

Goods in transit should be included in the inventory of the company that has legal title to the goods. Legal title is determined by the terms of the sale, as shown in Illustration 6-1 and described below.

Illustration 6-1
Terms of sale

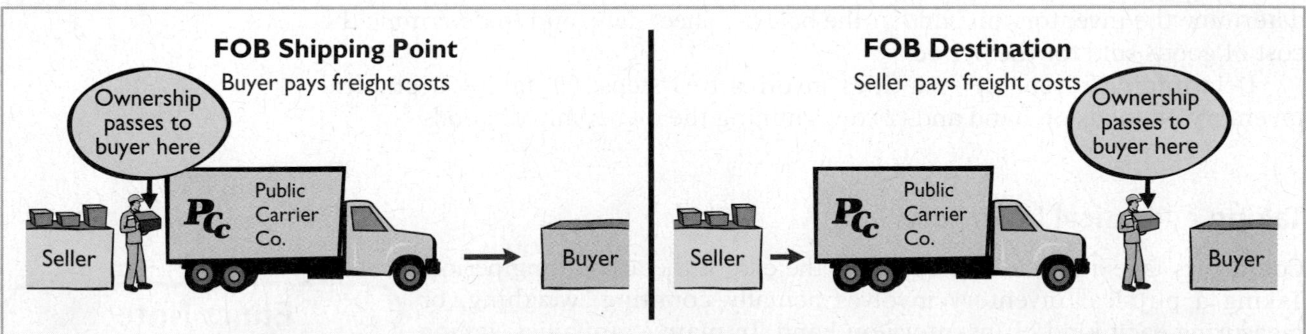

1. When the terms are **FOB (free on board) shipping point**, ownership of the goods passes to the buyer when the public carrier accepts the goods from the seller.
2. When the terms are **FOB destination**, ownership of the goods remains with the seller until the goods reach the buyer.

If goods in transit at the statement date are ignored, inventory quantities may be seriously miscounted. Assume, for example, that Hargrove Company has

20,000 units of inventory on hand on December 31. It also has the following goods in transit:

1. Sales of 1,500 units shipped December 31 FOB destination.
2. Purchases of 2,500 units shipped FOB shipping point by the seller on December 31.

Hargrove has legal title to both the 1,500 units sold and the 2,500 units purchased. If the company ignores the units in transit, it would understate inventory quantities by 4,000 units (1,500 + 2,500).

As we will see later in the chapter, inaccurate inventory counts affect not only the inventory amount shown on the balance sheet but also the cost of goods sold calculation on the income statement.

CONSIGNED GOODS

In some lines of business, it is common to hold the goods of other parties and try to sell the goods for them for a fee, but without taking ownership of the goods. These are called **consigned goods**.

For example, you might have a used car that you would like to sell. If you take the item to a dealer, the dealer might be willing to put the car on its lot and charge you a commission if it is sold. Under this agreement, the dealer **would not take ownership** of the car, which would still belong to you. Therefore, if an inventory count were taken, the car would not be included in the dealer's inventory.

Many car, boat, and antique dealers sell goods on consignment to keep their inventory costs down and to avoid the risk of purchasing an item that they will not be able to sell. Today, even some manufacturers are making consignment agreements with their suppliers in order to keep their inventory levels low.

> DO IT!

Rules of Ownership

Hasbeen Company completed its inventory count. It arrived at a total inventory value of $200,000. As a new member of Hasbeen's accounting department, you have been given the information listed below. Discuss how this information affects the reported cost of inventory.

1. Hasbeen included in the inventory goods held on consignment for Falls Co., costing $15,000.
2. The company did not include in the count purchased goods of $10,000 which were in transit (terms: FOB shipping point).
3. The company did not include in the count sold inventory with a cost of $12,000 which was in transit (terms: FOB shipping point).

Action Plan

✔ Apply the rules of ownership to goods held on consignment.

✔ Apply the rules of ownership to goods in transit.

Solution

The goods of $15,000 held on consignment should be deducted from the inventory count. The goods of $10,000 purchased FOB shipping point should be added to the inventory count. Sold goods of $12,000 which were in transit FOB shipping point should not be included in the ending inventory. Thus, inventory should be carried at $195,000 ($200,000 − $15,000 + $10,000).

Related exercise material: **BE6-1, E6-1, E6-2, and DO IT! 6-1.**

 **The Navigator**

ANATOMY OF A FRAUD

Ted Nickerson, CEO of clock manufacturer Dally Industries, was feared by all of his employees. Ted also had expensive tastes. To support his expensive tastes, Ted took out large loans, which he collateralized with his shares of Dally Industries stock. If the price of Dally's stock fell, he was required to provide the bank with more shares of stock. To achieve target net income figures and thus maintain the stock price, Ted coerced employees in the company to alter inventory figures. Inventory quantities were manipulated by changing the amounts on inventory control tags after the year-end physical inventory count. For example, if a tag said there were 20 units of a particular item, the tag was changed to 220. Similarly, the unit costs that were used to determine the value of ending inventory were increased from, for example, $125 per unit to $1,250. Both of these fraudulent changes had the effect of increasing the amount of reported ending inventory. This reduced cost of goods sold and increased net income.

Total take: $245,000

The Missing Control

Independent internal verification. The company should have spot-checked its inventory records periodically, verifying that the number of units in the records agreed with the amount on hand and that the unit costs agreed with vendor price sheets.

Source: Adapted from Wells, *Fraud Casebook* (2007), pp. 502–509.

Inventory Costing

LEARNING OBJECTIVE 2

Explain the accounting for inventories and apply the inventory cost flow methods.

Inventory is accounted for at cost. Cost includes all expenditures necessary to acquire goods and place them in a condition ready for sale. For example, freight costs incurred to acquire inventory are added to the cost of inventory, but the cost of shipping goods to a customer are a selling expense.

After a company has determined the quantity of units of inventory, it applies unit costs to the quantities to compute the total cost of the inventory and the cost of goods sold. This process can be complicated if a company has purchased inventory items at different times and at different prices.

For example, assume that Crivitz TV Company purchases three identical 50-inch TVs on different dates at costs of $700, $750, and $800. During the year, Crivitz sold two sets at $1,200 each. These facts are summarized in Illustration 6-2.

Illustration 6-2
Data for inventory costing example

Purchases			
February 3	1 TV	at	$700
March 5	1 TV	at	$750
May 22	1 TV	at	$800
Sales			
June 1	2 TVs	for	$2,400 ($1,200 × 2)

Cost of goods sold will differ depending on which two TVs the company sold. For example, it might be $1,450 ($700 + $750), or $1,500 ($700 + $800), or $1,550 ($750 + $800). In this section, we discuss alternative costing methods available to Crivitz.

Specific Identification

If Crivitz can positively identify which particular units it sold and which are still in ending inventory, it can use the **specific identification method** of inventory costing. For example, if Crivitz sold the TVs it purchased on February 3 and May 22, then its cost of goods sold is $1,500 ($700 + $800), and its ending inventory is $750 (see Illustration 6-3). Using this method, companies can accurately determine ending inventory and cost of goods sold.

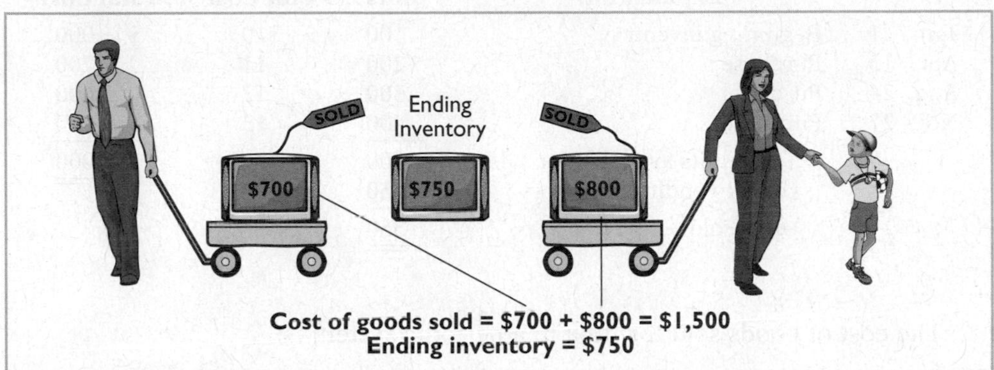

Illustration 6-3
Specific identification method

Specific identification requires that companies keep records of the original cost of each individual inventory item. Historically, specific identification was possible only when a company sold a limited variety of high-unit-cost items that could be identified clearly from the time of purchase through the time of sale. Examples of such products are cars, pianos, or expensive antiques.

Today, bar coding, electronic product codes, and radio frequency identification make it theoretically possible to do specific identification with nearly any type of product. The reality is, however, that this practice is still relatively rare. Instead, rather than keep track of the cost of each particular item sold, most companies make assumptions, called **cost flow assumptions**, about which units were sold.

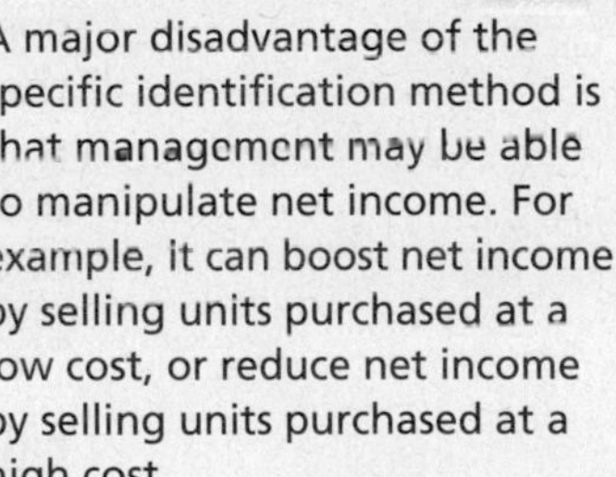

Ethics Note

A major disadvantage of the specific identification method is that management may be able to manipulate net income. For example, it can boost net income by selling units purchased at a low cost, or reduce net income by selling units purchased at a high cost.

Cost Flow Assumptions

Because specific identification is often impractical, other cost flow methods are permitted. These differ from specific identification in that they **assume** flows of costs that may be unrelated to the physical flow of goods. There are three assumed cost flow methods:

1. First-in, first-out (FIFO)
2. Last-in, first-out (LIFO)
3. Average-cost

There is no accounting requirement that the cost flow assumption be consistent with the physical movement of the goods. Company management selects the appropriate cost flow method.

To demonstrate the three cost flow methods, we will use a ***periodic*** inventory system. We assume a periodic system for two main reasons. First, many small companies use periodic rather than perpetual systems. Second, **very few companies use *perpetual* LIFO, FIFO, or average-cost** to cost their inventory and related cost of goods sold. Instead, companies that use perpetual systems often use an assumed cost (called a standard cost) to record cost of goods sold at the time of sale. Then, at the end of the period when they count their inventory, they

recalculate cost of goods sold using *periodic* FIFO, LIFO, or average-cost and adjust cost of goods sold to this recalculated number.[1]

To illustrate the three inventory cost flow methods, we will use the data for Houston Electronics' Astro condensers, shown in Illustration 6-4.

Illustration 6-4
Data for Houston Electronics

Houston Electronics
Astro Condensers

Date	Explanation	Units	Unit Cost	Total Cost
Jan. 1	Beginning inventory	100	$10	$ 1,000
Apr. 15	Purchase	200	11	2,200
Aug. 24	Purchase	300	12	3,600
Nov. 27	Purchase	400	13	5,200
	Total units available for sale	1,000		$12,000
	Units in ending inventory	450		
	Units sold	550		

The cost of goods sold formula in a periodic system is:

(Beginning Inventory + Purchases) − Ending Inventory = Cost of Goods Sold

Houston Electronics had a total of 1,000 units available to sell during the period (beginning inventory plus purchases). The total cost of these 1,000 units is $12,000, referred to as *cost of goods available for sale*. A physical inventory taken at December 31 determined that there were 450 units in ending inventory. Therefore, Houston sold 550 units (1,000 − 450) during the period. To determine the cost of the 550 units that were sold (the cost of goods sold), we assign a cost to the ending inventory and subtract that value from the cost of goods available for sale. The value assigned to the ending inventory **will depend on which cost flow method we use.** No matter which cost flow assumption we use, though, the sum of cost of goods sold plus the cost of the ending inventory must equal the cost of goods available for sale—in this case, $12,000.

FIRST-IN, FIRST-OUT (FIFO)

The **first-in, first-out (FIFO) method** assumes that the **earliest goods** purchased are the first to be sold. FIFO often parallels the actual physical flow of merchandise. That is, it generally is good business practice to sell the oldest units first. Under the FIFO method, therefore, the **costs** of the earliest goods purchased are the first to be recognized in determining cost of goods sold. (This does not necessarily mean that the oldest units *are* sold first, but that the costs of the oldest units are *recognized* first. In a bin of picture hangers at the hardware store, for example, no one really knows, nor would it matter, which hangers are sold first.) Illustration 6-5 shows the allocation of the cost of goods available for sale at Houston Electronics under FIFO.

[1]Also, some companies use a perpetual system to keep track of units, but they do not make an entry for perpetual cost of goods sold. In addition, firms that employ LIFO tend to use *dollar-value LIFO*, a method discussed in upper-level courses. FIFO periodic and FIFO perpetual give the same result. Therefore, firms should not incur the additional cost to use FIFO perpetual. Few firms use perpetual average-cost because of the added cost of record-keeping. Finally, for instructional purposes, we believe it is easier to demonstrate the cost flow assumptions under the periodic system, which makes it more pedagogically appropriate.

Illustration 6-5
Allocation of costs—FIFO method

Cost of Goods Available for Sale

Date	Explanation	Units	Unit Cost	Total Cost
Jan. 1	Beginning inventory	100	$10	$ 1,000
Apr. 15	Purchase	200	11	2,200
Aug. 24	Purchase	300	12	3,600
Nov. 27	Purchase	400	13	5,200
	Total	1,000		$12,000

Step 1: Ending Inventory

Date	Units	Unit Cost	Total Cost
Nov. 27	400	$13	$5,200
Aug. 24	50	12	600
Total	450		$5,800

Step 2: Cost of Goods Sold

Cost of goods available for sale	$12,000
Less: Ending inventory	5,800
Cost of goods sold	$ 6,200

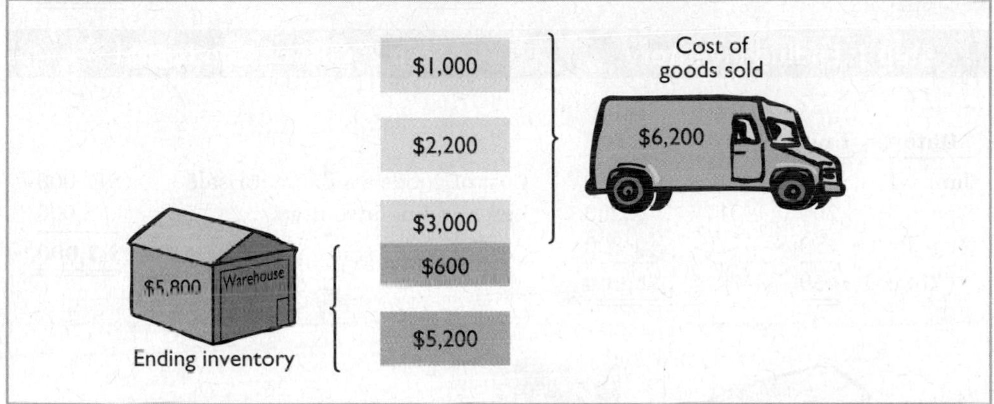

Helpful Hint
Note the sequencing of the allocation: (1) Compute ending inventory, and (2) determine cost of goods sold.

Helpful Hint
Another way of thinking about the calculation of FIFO ending inventory is the *LISH assumption*—last in still here.

Under FIFO, since it is assumed that the first goods purchased were the first goods sold, ending inventory is based on the prices of the most recent units purchased. That is, **under FIFO, companies obtain the cost of the ending inventory by taking the unit cost of the most recent purchase and working backward until all units of inventory have been costed**. In this example, Houston Electronics prices the 450 units of ending inventory using the *most recent* prices. The last purchase was 400 units at $13 on November 27. The remaining 50 units are priced using the unit cost of the second most recent purchase, $12, on August 24. Next, Houston Electronics calculates cost of goods sold by subtracting the cost of the units **not sold** (ending inventory) from the cost of all goods available for sale.

Illustration 6-6 demonstrates that companies also can calculate cost of goods sold by pricing the 550 units sold using the prices of the first 550 units acquired. Note that of the 300 units purchased on August 24, only 250 units are assumed sold. This agrees with our calculation of the cost of ending inventory, where 50 of these units were assumed unsold and thus included in ending inventory.

Illustration 6-6
Proof of cost of goods sold

Date	Units	Unit Cost	Total Cost
Jan. 1	100	$10	$ 1,000
Apr. 15	200	11	2,200
Aug. 24	250	12	3,000
Total	550		$6,200

LAST-IN, FIRST-OUT (LIFO)

The **last-in, first-out (LIFO) method** assumes that the **latest goods** purchased are the first to be sold. LIFO seldom coincides with the actual physical flow of inventory. (Exceptions include goods stored in piles, such as coal or hay, where goods are removed from the top of the pile as they are sold.) Under the LIFO method, the **costs** of the latest goods purchased are the first to be recognized in determining cost of goods sold. Illustration 6-7 shows the allocation of the cost of goods available for sale at Houston Electronics under LIFO.

Illustration 6-7
Allocation of costs—LIFO method

Cost of Goods Available for Sale

Date	Explanation	Units	Unit Cost	Total Cost
Jan. 1	Beginning inventory	100	$10	$ 1,000
Apr. 15	Purchase	200	11	2,200
Aug. 24	Purchase	300	12	3,600
Nov. 27	Purchase	400	13	5,200
	Total	1,000		**$12,000**

Step 1: Ending Inventory

Date	Units	Unit Cost	Total Cost
Jan. 1	100	$10	$ 1,000
Apr. 15	200	11	2,200
Aug. 24	150	12	1,800
Total	450		**$5,000**

Step 2: Cost of Goods Sold

Cost of goods available for sale	$12,000
Less: Ending inventory	5,000
Cost of goods sold	**$ 7,000**

Helpful Hint
Another way of thinking about the calculation of LIFO ending inventory is the *FISH assumption*—first in still here.

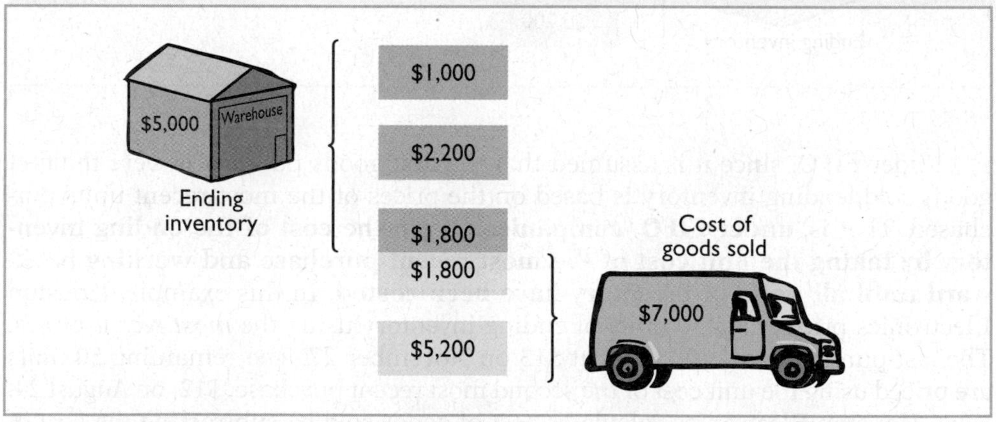

Under LIFO, since it is assumed that the first goods sold were those that were most recently purchased, ending inventory is based on the prices of the oldest units purchased. That is, **under LIFO, companies obtain the cost of the ending inventory by taking the unit cost of the earliest goods available for sale and working forward until all units of inventory have been costed**. In this example, Houston Electronics prices the 450 units of ending inventory using the *earliest* prices. The first purchase was 100 units at $10 in the January 1 beginning inventory. Then, 200 units were purchased at $11. The remaining 150 units needed are priced at $12 per unit (August 24 purchase). Next, Houston Electronics calculates cost of goods sold by subtracting the cost of the units **not sold** (ending inventory) from the cost of all goods available for sale.

Illustration 6-8 demonstrates that companies also can calculate cost of goods sold by pricing the 550 units sold using the prices of the last 550 units acquired. Note that of the 300 units purchased on August 24, only 150 units are assumed sold. This agrees with our calculation of the cost of ending inventory, where 150 of these units were assumed unsold and thus included in ending inventory.

Date	Units	Unit Cost	Total Cost
Nov. 27	400	$13	$ 5,200
Aug. 24	150	12	1,800
Total	550		**$7,000**

Illustration 6-8
Proof of cost of goods sold

Under a periodic inventory system, which we are using here, **all goods purchased during the period are assumed to be available for the first sale, regardless of the date of purchase**.

AVERAGE-COST

The **average-cost method** allocates the cost of goods available for sale on the basis of the **weighted-average unit cost** incurred. The average-cost method assumes that goods are similar in nature. Illustration 6-9 presents the formula and a sample computation of the weighted-average unit cost.

Cost of Goods Available for Sale	÷	Total Units Available for Sale	=	Weighted-Average Unit Cost
$12,000	÷	1,000	=	**$12.00**

Illustration 6-9
Formula for weighted-average unit cost

The company then applies the weighted-average unit cost to the units on hand to determine the cost of the ending inventory. Illustration 6-10 (page 282) shows the allocation of the cost of goods available for sale at Houston Electronics using average-cost.

We can verify the cost of goods sold under this method by multiplying the units sold times the weighted-average unit cost (550 × $12 = $6,600). Note that this method does not use the average of the unit costs. That average is $11.50 ($10 + $11 + $12 + $13 = $46; $46 ÷ 4). The average-cost method instead uses the average **weighted by** the quantities purchased at each unit cost.

> DO IT!

Cost Flow Methods

The accounting records of Shumway Ag Implement show the following data.

Beginning inventory	4,000 units at $ 3
Purchases	6,000 units at $ 4
Sales	7,000 units at $12

Determine the cost of goods sold during the period under a periodic inventory system using (a) the FIFO method, (b) the LIFO method, and (c) the average-cost method.

Action Plan

✔ Understand the periodic inventory system.

✔ Allocate costs between goods sold and goods on hand (ending inventory) for each cost flow method.

✔ Compute cost of goods sold for each method.

Solution

Cost of goods available for sale = (4,000 × $3) + (6,000 × $4) = $36,000
Ending inventory = 10,000 − 7,000 = 3,000 units

(a) FIFO: $36,000 − (3,000 × $4) = $24,000

(b) LIFO: $36,000 − (3,000 × $3) = $27,000

(c) Average cost per unit: [(4,000 @ $3) + (6,000 @ $4)] ÷ 10,000 = $3.60
Average-cost: $36,000 − (3,000 × $3.60) = $25,200

Related exercise material: **BE6-3, BE6-4, BE6-5, E6-3, E6-4, E6-5, E6-6, E6-7, E6-8, and DO IT! 6-2.**

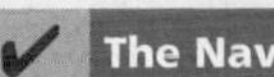
✔ The Navigator

Illustration 6-10
Allocation of costs—average-cost method

Cost of Goods Available for Sale

Date	Explanation	Units	Unit Cost	Total Cost
Jan. 1	Beginning inventory	100	$10	$ 1,000
Apr. 15	Purchase	200	11	2,200
Aug. 24	Purchase	300	12	3,600
Nov. 27	Purchase	400	13	5,200
	Total	1,000		**$12,000**

Step 1: Ending Inventory

$12,000 ÷ 1,000 = $12.00

Units	Unit Cost	Total Cost
450	$12.00	**$5,400**

Step 2: Cost of Goods Sold

Cost of goods available for sale	$12,000
Less: Ending inventory	5,400
Cost of goods sold	**$ 6,600**

$12,000 / 1,000 units = $12 per unit
Cost per unit
450 units × $12 = $5,400
Warehouse
Ending inventory
$12,000 – $5,400 = $6,600
Cost of goods sold

Financial Statement and Tax Effects of Cost Flow Methods

LEARNING OBJECTIVE 3

Explain the financial effects of the inventory cost flow assumptions.

Each of the three assumed cost flow methods is acceptable for use. For example, Reebok International Ltd. and Wendy's International currently use the FIFO method of inventory costing. Campbell Soup Company, Krogers, and Walgreen Drugs use LIFO for part or all of their inventory. Bristol-Myers Squibb, Starbucks, and Motorola use the average-cost method. In fact, a company may also use more than one cost flow method at the same time. Stanley Black & Decker Manufacturing Company, for example, uses LIFO for domestic inventories and FIFO for foreign inventories. Illustration 6-11 (in the margin) shows the use of the three cost flow methods in the 500 largest U.S. companies.

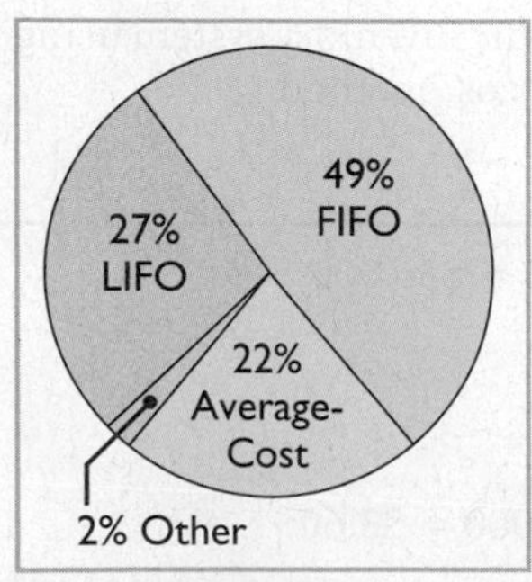

Illustration 6-11
Use of cost flow methods in major U.S. companies

The reasons companies adopt different inventory cost flow methods are varied, but they usually involve one of three factors: (1) income statement effects, (2) balance sheet effects, or (3) tax effects.

INCOME STATEMENT EFFECTS

To understand why companies might choose a particular cost flow method, let's examine the effects of the different cost flow assumptions on the financial statements of Houston Electronics. The condensed income statements in Illustration 6-12 assume that Houston sold its 550 units for $11,500, had operating expenses of $2,000, and is subject to an income tax rate of 30%.

Illustration 6-12
Comparative effects of cost flow methods

Houston Electronics
Condensed Income Statements

	FIFO	LIFO	Average-Cost
Sales revenue	$11,500	$11,500	$11,500
Beginning inventory	1,000	1,000	1,000
Purchases	11,000	11,000	11,000
Cost of goods available for sale	12,000	12,000	12,000
Ending inventory	**5,800**	**5,000**	**5,400**
Cost of goods sold	6,200	7,000	6,600
Gross profit	5,300	4,500	4,900
Operating expenses	2,000	2,000	2,000
Income before income taxes*	3,300	2,500	2,900
Income tax expense (30%)	990	750	870
Net income	**$ 2,310**	**$ 1,750**	**$ 2,030**

*We are assuming that Houston Electronics is a corporation, and corporations are required to pay income taxes.

Note the cost of goods available for sale ($12,000) is the same under each of the three inventory cost flow methods. However, the ending inventories and the costs of goods sold are different. This difference is due to the unit costs that the company allocated to cost of goods sold and to ending inventory. Each dollar of difference in ending inventory results in a corresponding dollar difference in income before income taxes. For Houston, an $800 difference exists between FIFO and LIFO cost of goods sold.

In periods of changing prices, the cost flow assumption can have a significant impact on income and on evaluations based on income. In most instances, prices are rising (inflation). In a period of inflation, FIFO produces a higher net income because the lower unit costs of the first units purchased are matched against revenues. In a period of rising prices (as is the case in the Houston example), FIFO reports the highest net income ($2,310) and LIFO the lowest ($1,750); average-cost falls in the middle ($2,030). If prices are falling, the results from the use of FIFO and LIFO are reversed. FIFO will report the lowest net income and LIFO the highest.

To management, higher net income is an advantage. It causes external users to view the company more favorably. In addition, management bonuses, if based on net income, will be higher. Therefore, when prices are rising (which is usually the case), companies tend to prefer FIFO because it results in higher net income.

Some argue that the use of LIFO in a period of inflation enables the company to avoid reporting **paper** (or **phantom**) **profit** as economic gain. To illustrate, assume that Kralik Company buys 200 units of a product at $20 per unit on January 10 and 200 more on December 31 at $24 each. During the year, Kralik sells 200 units at $30 each. Illustration 6-13 shows the results under FIFO and LIFO.

Illustration 6-13
Income statement effects compared

	FIFO	LIFO
Sales (200 × $30)	$6,000	$6,000
Cost of goods sold	**4,000 (200 × $20)**	**4,800 (200 × $24)**
Gross profit	$2,000	$1,200

Under LIFO, Kralik Company has recovered the current replacement cost ($4,800) of the units sold. Thus, the gross profit in economic terms is real. However, under FIFO, the company has recovered only the January 10 cost ($4,000). To replace the units sold, it must reinvest $800 (200 × $4) of the gross profit. Thus, $800 of the gross profit is said to be phantom or illusory. As a result, reported net income is also overstated in real terms.

BALANCE SHEET EFFECTS

A major advantage of the FIFO method is that in a period of inflation, the costs allocated to ending inventory will approximate their current cost. For example, for Houston Electronics, 400 of the 450 units in the ending inventory are costed under FIFO at the higher November 27 unit cost of $13.

Conversely, a major shortcoming of the LIFO method is that in a period of inflation, the costs allocated to ending inventory may be significantly understated in terms of current cost. The understatement becomes greater over prolonged periods of inflation if the inventory includes goods purchased in one or more prior accounting periods. For example, Caterpillar has used LIFO for 50 years. Its balance sheet shows ending inventory of $6,360 million. But, the inventory's actual current cost if FIFO had been used is $9,363 million.

Helpful Hint
A tax rule, often referred to as the *LIFO conformity rule*, requires that if companies use LIFO for tax purposes they must also use it for financial reporting purposes. This means that if a company chooses the LIFO method to reduce its tax bills, it will also have to report lower net income in its financial statements.

TAX EFFECTS

We have seen that both inventory on the balance sheet and net income on the income statement are higher when companies use FIFO in a period of inflation. Yet, many companies have selected LIFO. Why? The reason is that LIFO results in the lowest income taxes (because of lower net income) during times of rising prices. For example, at Houston Electronics, income taxes are $750 under LIFO, compared to $990 under FIFO. The tax savings of $240 makes more cash available for use in the business.

Using Inventory Cost Flow Methods Consistently

Whatever cost flow method a company chooses, it should use that method consistently from one accounting period to another. This approach is often referred to as the concept of **consistency**, which means that a company uses the same accounting principles and methods from year to year. Consistent application enhances the comparability of financial statements over successive time periods. In contrast, using the FIFO method one year and the LIFO method the next year would make it difficult to compare the net incomes of the two years.

Although consistent application is preferred, it does not mean that a company may *never* change its inventory costing method. When a company adopts a different method, it should disclose in the financial statements the change and its effects on net income. Illustration 6-14 shows a typical disclosure, using information from the financial statements of Quaker Oats (now a unit of PepsiCo).

Illustration 6-14
Disclosure of change in cost flow method

Quaker Oats
Notes to the Financial Statements

Note 1: Effective July 1, the Company adopted the LIFO cost flow assumption for valuing the majority of U.S. Grocery Products inventories. The Company believes that the use of the LIFO method better matches current costs with current revenues. The effect of this change on the current year was to decrease net income by $16.0 million.

INTERNATIONAL INSIGHT 

Is LIFO Fair?

ExxonMobil Corporation, like many U.S. companies, uses LIFO to value its inventory for financial reporting and tax purposes. In one recent year, this resulted in a cost of goods sold figure that was $5.6 billion higher than under FIFO. By increasing cost of goods sold, ExxonMobil reduces net income, which reduces taxes. Critics say that LIFO provides an unfair "tax dodge." As Congress looks for more sources of tax revenue, some lawmakers favor the elimination of LIFO. Supporters of LIFO argue that the method is conceptually sound because it matches current costs with current revenues. In addition, they point out that this matching provides protection against inflation.

International accounting standards do not allow the use of LIFO. Because of this, the net income of foreign oil companies such as BP and Royal Dutch Shell are not directly comparable to U.S. companies, which makes analysis difficult.

Source: David Reilly, "Big Oil's Accounting Methods Fuel Criticism," *Wall Street Journal* (August 8, 2006), p. C1.

What are the arguments for and against the use of LIFO? (See page 320.)

Lower-of-Cost-or-Market

LEARNING OBJECTIVE 4

Explain the lower-of-cost-or-market basis of accounting for inventories.

The value of inventory for companies selling high-technology or fashion goods can drop very quickly due to changes in technology or fashion. These circumstances sometimes call for inventory valuation methods other than those presented so far. For example, at one time purchasing managers at Ford decided to make a large purchase of palladium, a precious metal used in vehicle emission devices. They made this purchase because they feared a future shortage. The shortage did not materialize, and by the end of the year the price of palladium had plummeted. Ford's inventory was then worth $1 billion less than its original cost. Do you think Ford's inventory should have been stated at cost, in accordance with the cost principle, or at its lower replacement cost?

International Note 

Under U.S. GAAP, companies cannot reverse inventory write-downs if inventory increases in value in subsequent periods. IFRS permits companies to reverse write-downs in some circumstances.

As you probably reasoned, this situation requires a departure from the cost basis of accounting. When the value of inventory is lower than its cost, companies can "write down" the inventory to its market value. This is done by valuing the inventory at the **lower-of-cost-or-market (LCM)** in the period in which the price decline occurs. LCM is an example of the accounting concept of conservatism, which means that the best choice among accounting alternatives is the method that is least likely to overstate assets and net income.

Companies apply LCM to the items in inventory after they have used one of the cost flow methods (specific identification, FIFO, LIFO, or average-cost) to determine cost. Under the LCM basis, market is defined as **current replacement cost**, not selling price. For a merchandising company, market is the cost of purchasing the same goods at the present time from the usual suppliers in the usual quantities. Current replacement cost is used because a decline in the replacement cost of an item usually leads to a decline in the selling price of the item.

To illustrate the application of LCM, assume that Ken Tuckie TV has the following lines of merchandise with costs and market values as indicated. LCM produces the results shown in Illustration 6-15 (page 286). Note that the amounts shown in the final column are the lower-of-cost-or-market amounts for each item.

Illustration 6-15
Computation of lower-of-cost-or-market

	Cost	Market	Lower-of-Cost-or-Market
Flat-screen TVs	$60,000	$55,000	$ 55,000
Satellite radios	45,000	52,000	45,000
DVD recorders	48,000	45,000	45,000
DVDs	15,000	14,000	14,000
Total inventory			**$159,000**

Inventory Errors

LEARNING OBJECTIVE 5

Indicate the effects of inventory errors on the financial statements.

Unfortunately, errors occasionally occur in accounting for inventory. In some cases, errors are caused by failure to count or price the inventory correctly. In other cases, errors occur because companies do not properly recognize the transfer of legal title to goods that are in transit. When errors occur, they affect both the income statement and the balance sheet.

Income Statement Effects

Under a periodic inventory system, both the beginning and ending inventories appear in the income statement. The ending inventory of one period automatically becomes the beginning inventory of the next period. Thus, inventory errors affect the computation of cost of goods sold and net income in two periods.

The effects on cost of goods sold can be computed by entering incorrect data in the formula in Illustration 6-16 and then substituting the correct data.

Illustration 6-16
Formula for cost of goods sold

Beginning Inventory	+	Cost of Goods Purchased	−	Ending Inventory	=	Cost of Goods Sold

If the error understates *beginning* inventory, cost of goods sold will be understated. If the error understates *ending* inventory, cost of goods sold will be overstated. Illustration 6-17 shows the effects of inventory errors on the current year's income statement.

Illustration 6-17
Effects of inventory errors on current year's income statement

When Inventory Error:	Cost of Goods Sold Is:	Net Income Is:
Understates beginning inventory	Understated	Overstated
Overstates beginning inventory	Overstated	Understated
Understates ending inventory	Overstated	Understated
Overstates ending inventory	Understated	Overstated

Ethics Note

Inventory fraud increases during recessions. Such fraud includes pricing inventory at amounts in excess of its actual value, or claiming to have inventory when no inventory exists. Inventory fraud usually overstates ending inventory, thereby understating cost of goods sold and creating higher income.

So far, the effects of inventory errors are fairly straightforward. Now, though, comes the (at first) surprising part: An error in the ending inventory of the current period will have a **reverse effect on net income of the next accounting period**. Illustration 6-18 shows this effect. As you study the illustration, you will see that the reverse effect comes from the fact that understating ending inventory in 2013 results in understating beginning inventory in 2014 and overstating net income in 2014.

Over the two years, though, total net income is correct because the errors **offset each other**. Notice that total income using incorrect data is $35,000 ($22,000 + $13,000), which is the same as the total income of $35,000 ($25,000 + $10,000) using correct data. Also note in this example

Sample Company
Condensed Income Statements

	2013				2014			
	Incorrect		Correct		Incorrect		Correct	
Sales revenue		$80,000		$80,000		$90,000		$90,000
Beginning inventory	$20,000		$20,000		**$12,000**		**$15,000**	
Cost of goods purchased	40,000		40,000		68,000		68,000	
Cost of goods available for sale	60,000		60,000		80,000		83,000	
Ending inventory	**12,000**		**15,000**		23,000		23,000	
Cost of goods sold		48,000		45,000		57,000		60,000
Gross profit		32,000		35,000		33,000		30,000
Operating expenses		10,000		10,000		20,000		20,000
Net income		$22,000		$25,000		$13,000		$10,000

$(3,000) Net income understated

$3,000 Net income overstated

The errors cancel. Thus the combined total income for the 2-year period is correct.

Illustration 6-18
Effects of inventory errors on two years' income statements

that an error in the beginning inventory does not result in a corresponding error in the ending inventory for that period. The correctness of the ending inventory depends entirely on the accuracy of taking and costing the inventory at the balance sheet date under the periodic inventory system.

Balance Sheet Effects

Companies can determine the effect of ending inventory errors on the balance sheet by using the basic accounting equation: Assets = Liabilities + Stockholders' Equity. Errors in the ending inventory have the effects shown in Illustration 6-19.

Illustration 6-19
Effects of ending inventory errors on balance sheet

Ending Inventory Error	Assets	Liabilities	Stockholders' Equity
Overstated	Overstated	No effect	Overstated
Understated	Understated	No effect	Understated

The effect of an error in ending inventory on the subsequent period was shown in Illustration 6-18. Recall that if the error is not corrected, the combined total net income for the two periods would be correct. Thus, total stockholders' equity reported on the balance sheet at the end of 2014 will also be correct.

> DO IT!

LCM Basis; Inventory Errors

(a) Tracy Company sells three different types of home heating stoves (gas, wood, and pellet). The cost and market value of its inventory of stoves are as follows.

	Cost	Market
Gas	$ 84,000	$ 79,000
Wood	250,000	280,000
Pellet	112,000	101,000

Action Plan

✔ Determine whether cost or market value is lower for each inventory type.

✔ Sum the lowest value of each inventory type to determine the total value of inventory.

Determine the value of the company's inventory under the lower-of-cost-or-market approach.

Solution

The lowest value for each inventory type is gas $79,000, wood $250,000, and pellet $101,000. The total inventory value is the sum of these amounts, $430,000.

Action Plan

✔ An ending inventory error in one period will have an equal and opposite effect on cost of goods sold and net income in the next period.

✔ After two years, the errors have offset each other.

(b) Visual Company overstated its 2013 ending inventory by $22,000. Determine the impact this error has on ending inventory, cost of goods sold, and stockholders' equity in 2013 and 2014.

Solution

	2013	2014
Ending inventory	$22,000 overstated	No effect
Cost of goods sold	$22,000 understated	$22,000 overstated
Stockholders' equity	$22,000 overstated	No effect

Related exercise material: **BE6-7, BE6-8, E6-9, E6-10, E6-11, E6-12, and**  **6-3.**

✔ **The Navigator**

Statement Presentation and Analysis

Presentation

As indicated in Chapter 5, inventory is classified in the balance sheet as a current asset immediately below receivables. In a multiple-step income statement, cost of goods sold is subtracted from sales. There also should be disclosure of (1) the major inventory classifications, (2) the basis of accounting (cost, or lower-of-cost-or-market), and (3) the cost method (FIFO, LIFO, or average).

Wal-Mart Stores, Inc., for example, in its January 31, 2011, balance sheet reported inventories of $36,318 million under current assets. The accompanying notes to the financial statements, as shown in Illustration 6-20, disclosed the following information.

Illustration 6-20
Inventory disclosures by Wal-Mart

Wal-Mart Stores, Inc.
Notes to the Financial Statements

Note 1: Summary of Significant Accounting Policies

Inventories

The Company values inventories at the lower of cost or market as determined primarily by the retail method of accounting, using the last-in, first-out ("LIFO") method for substantially all of the Walmart U.S. segment's merchandise inventories. The retail method of accounting results in inventory being valued at the lower of cost or market since permanent markdowns are currently taken as a reduction of the retail value of inventory. The Sam's Club segment's merchandise is valued based on the weighted-average cost using the LIFO method. Inventories for the Walmart International operations are primarily valued by the retail method of accounting and are stated using the first-in, first-out ("FIFO") method. At January 31, 2011 and 2010, our inventories valued at LIFO approximate those inventories as if they were valued at FIFO.

As indicated in this note, Wal-Mart values its inventories at the lower-of-cost-or-market using LIFO and FIFO.

Analysis

LEARNING OBJECTIVE 6

Compute and interpret the inventory turnover ratio.

The amount of inventory carried by a company has significant economic consequences. And inventory management is a double-edged sword that requires constant attention. On the one hand, management wants to have a great variety and quantity on hand so that customers have a wide selection and items are always in stock. But, such a policy may incur high carrying costs (e.g., investment, storage, insurance, obsolescence, and damage). On the other hand, low inventory levels lead to stock-outs and lost sales. Common ratios used to manage and evaluate inventory levels are inventory turnover and a related measure, days in inventory.

Inventory turnover measures the number of times on average the inventory is sold during the period. Its purpose is to measure the liquidity of the inventory. The inventory turnover is computed by dividing cost of goods sold by the average inventory during the period. Unless seasonal factors are significant, average inventory can be computed from the beginning and ending inventory balances. For example, Wal-Mart reported in its 2011 annual report a beginning inventory of $32,713 million, an ending inventory of $36,318 million, and cost of goods sold for the year ended January 31, 2011, of $315,287 million. The inventory turnover formula and computation for Wal-Mart are shown below.

Illustration 6-21
Inventory turnover formula and computation for Wal-Mart

Cost of Goods Sold	÷	Average Inventory	=	Inventory Turnover
$315,287	÷	$\frac{\$36,318 + \$32,713}{2}$	=	**9.13 times**

A variant of the inventory turnover ratio is **days in inventory**. This measures the average number of days inventory is held. It is calculated as 365 divided by the inventory turnover ratio. For example, Wal-Mart's inventory turnover of 9.13 times divided into 365 is approximately 40 days. This is the approximate time that it takes a company to sell the inventory once it arrives at the store.

There are typical levels of inventory in every industry. Companies that are able to keep their inventory at lower levels and higher turnovers and still satisfy customer needs are the most successful.

ACCOUNTING ACROSS THE ORGANIZATION

Improving Inventory Control with RFID

Wal-Mart improved its inventory control with the introduction of radio frequency identification (RFID). Much like bar codes, which tell a retailer the number of boxes of a specific product it has, RFID goes a step farther, helping to distinguish one box of a specific product from another. RFID uses technology similar to that used by keyless remotes that unlock car doors.

Companies currently use RFID to track shipments from supplier to distribution center to store. Other potential uses include monitoring product expiration dates and acting quickly on product recalls. Wal-Mart also anticipates faster returns and warranty processing using RFID. This technology will further assist Wal-Mart managers in their efforts to ensure that their store has just the right type of inventory, in just the right amount, in just the right place. Other companies are also interested in RFID. Best Buy has spent millions researching possible applications in its stores.

? Why is inventory control important to managers such as those at Wal-Mart and Best Buy? (See page 320.)

DO IT!

Inventory Turnover

Early in 2014, Westmoreland Company switched to a just-in-time inventory system. Its sales, cost of goods sold, and inventory amounts for 2013 and 2014 are shown below.

	2013	2014
Sales revenue	$2,000,000	$1,800,000
Cost of goods sold	1,000,000	910,000
Beginning inventory	290,000	210,000
Ending inventory	210,000	50,000

Determine the inventory turnover and days in inventory for 2013 and 2014. Discuss the changes in the amount of inventory, the inventory turnover and days in inventory, and the amount of sales across the two years.

Action Plan

- ✔ To find the inventory turnover ratio, divide cost of goods sold by average inventory.
- ✔ To determine days in inventory, divide 365 days by the inventory turnover ratio.
- ✔ Just-in-time inventory reduces the amount of inventory on hand, which reduces carrying costs. Reducing inventory levels by too much has potential negative implications for sales.

Solution

	2013	2014
Inventory turnover ratio	$\frac{\$1{,}000{,}000}{(\$290{,}000 + \$210{,}000)/2} = 4$	$\frac{\$910{,}000}{(\$210{,}000 + \$50{,}000)/2} = 7$
Days in inventory	365 ÷ 4 = 91.3 days	365 ÷ 7 = 52.1 days

The company experienced a very significant decline in its ending inventory as a result of the just-in-time inventory. This decline improved its inventory turnover ratio and its days in inventory. However, its sales declined by 10%. It is possible that this decline was caused by the dramatic reduction in the amount of inventory that was on hand, which increased the likelihood of "stock-outs." To determine the optimal inventory level, management must weigh the benefits of reduced inventory against the potential lost sales caused by stock-outs.

Related exercise material: **BE6-9, E6-13, E6-14, and DO IT! 6-4.**

 **The Navigator**

Comprehensive DO IT! 1

Gerald D. Englehart Company has the following inventory, purchases, and sales data for the month of March.

Inventory:	March 1	200 units @ $4.00	$ 800
Purchases:			
	March 10	500 units @ $4.50	2,250
	March 20	400 units @ $4.75	1,900
	March 30	300 units @ $5.00	1,500
Sales:			
	March 15	500 units	
	March 25	400 units	

The physical inventory count on March 31 shows 500 units on hand.

Instructions

Under a **periodic inventory system**, determine the cost of inventory on hand at March 31 and the cost of goods sold for March under (a) (FIFO), (b) (LIFO), and (c) average-cost.

Solution to Comprehensive DO IT! 1

Action Plan

- ✔ Compute the total goods available for sale, in both units and dollars.
- ✔ Compute the cost of ending inventory under the periodic FIFO method by allocating to the units on hand the **latest costs**.
- ✔ Compute the cost of ending inventory under the periodic LIFO method by allocating to the units on hand the **earliest costs**.
- ✔ Compute the cost of ending inventory under the periodic average-cost method by allocating to the units on hand a **weighted-average cost**.

The cost of goods available for sale is $6,450, as follows.

Inventory:		200 units @ $4.00	$ 800
Purchases:			
	March 10	500 units @ $4.50	2,250
	March 20	400 units @ $4.75	1,900
	March 30	300 units @ $5.00	1,500
Total:		1,400	$6,450

Under a **periodic inventory system**, the cost of goods sold under each cost flow method is as follows.

FIFO Method

Ending inventory:

Date	Units	Unit Cost	Total Cost	
March 30	300	$5.00	$1,500	
March 20	200	4.75	950	$2,450

Cost of goods sold: $6,450 − $2,450 = $4,000

LIFO Method

Ending inventory:

Date	Units	Unit Cost	Total Cost	
March 1	200	$4.00	$ 800	
March 10	300	4.50	1,350	$2,150

Cost of goods sold: $6,450 − $2,150 = $4,300

Average-Cost Method

Average unit cost: $6,450 ÷ 1,400 = $4.607

Ending inventory: 500 × $4.607 = $2,303.50

Cost of goods sold: $6,450 − $2,303.50 = $4,146.50

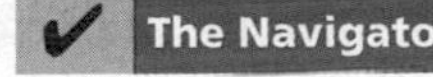

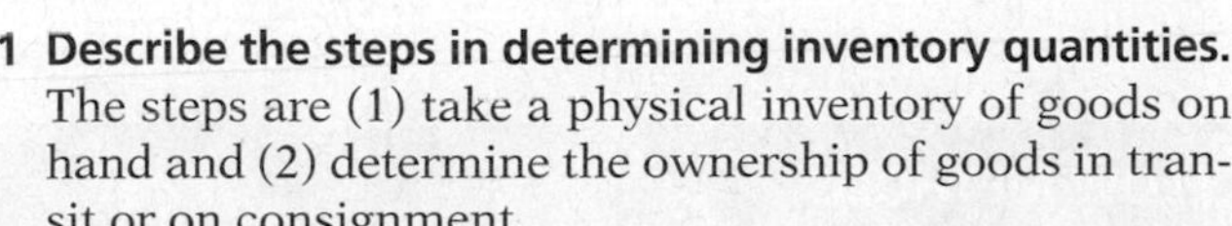

✔ The Navigator

1 Describe the steps in determining inventory quantities. The steps are (1) take a physical inventory of goods on hand and (2) determine the ownership of goods in transit or on consignment.

2 Explain the accounting for inventories and apply the inventory cost flow methods. The primary basis of accounting for inventories is cost. Cost of goods available for sale includes (a) cost of beginning inventory and (b) cost of goods purchased. The inventory cost flow methods are specific identification and three assumed cost flow methods—FIFO, LIFO, and average-cost.

3 Explain the financial effects of the inventory cost flow assumptions. Companies may allocate the cost of goods available for sale to cost of goods sold and ending inventory by specific identification or by a method based on an assumed cost flow. When prices are rising, the first-in, first-out (FIFO) method results in lower cost of goods sold and higher net income than the other methods. The reverse is true when prices are falling. In the balance sheet, FIFO results in an ending inventory that is closest to current value; inventory under LIFO is the farthest from current value. LIFO results in the lowest income taxes.

4 Explain the lower-of-cost-or-market basis of accounting for inventories. Companies may use the lower-of-cost-or-market (LCM) basis when the current replacement cost (market) is less than cost. Under LCM, companies recognize the loss in the period in which the price decline occurs.

5 Indicate the effects of inventory errors on the financial statements. *In the income statement of the current year:* (a) An error in beginning inventory will have a reverse effect on net income. (b) An error in ending inventory will have a similar effect on net income. In the following period, its effect on net income for that period is reversed, and total net income for the two years will be correct.

In the balance sheet: Ending inventory errors will have the same effect on total assets and total stockholders' equity and no effect on liabilities.

6 Compute and interpret the inventory turnover ratio. The inventory turnover ratio is cost of goods sold divided by average inventory. To convert it to average days in inventory, divide 365 days by the inventory turnover ratio.

GLOSSARY

Average-cost method Inventory costing method that uses the weighted-average unit cost to allocate to ending inventory and cost of goods sold the cost of goods available for sale. (p. 281).

Consigned goods Goods held for sale by one party although ownership of the goods is retained by another party. (p. 275).

Consistency concept Dictates that a company use the same accounting principles and methods from year to year. (p. 284).

Current replacement cost The current cost to replace an inventory item. (p. 285).

Days in inventory Measure of the average number of days inventory is held; calculated as 365 divided by inventory turnover ratio. (p. 289).

Finished goods inventory Manufactured items that are completed and ready for sale. (p. 272).

First-in, first-out (FIFO) method Inventory costing method that assumes that the costs of the earliest goods purchased are the first to be recognized as cost of goods sold. (p. 278).

FOB (free on board) destination Freight terms indicating that ownership of the goods remains with the seller until the goods reach the buyer. (p. 274).

FOB (free on board) shipping point Freight terms indicating that ownership of the goods passes to the buyer when the public carrier accepts the goods from the seller. (p. 274).

Inventory turnover A ratio that measures the number of times on average the inventory sold during the period; computed by dividing cost of goods sold by the average inventory during the period. (p. 289).

Just-in-time (JIT) inventory method Inventory system in which companies manufacture or purchase goods just in time for use. (p. 272).

Last-in, first-out (LIFO) method Inventory costing method that assumes the costs of the latest units purchased are the first to be allocated to cost of goods sold. (p. 280).

Lower-of-cost-or-market (LCM) basis A basis whereby inventory is stated at the lower of either its cost or its market value as determined by current replacement cost. (p. 285).

Raw materials Basic goods that will be used in production but have not yet been placed into production. (p. 272).

Specific identification method An actual physical flow costing method in which items still in inventory are specifically costed to arrive at the total cost of the ending inventory. (p. 277).

Weighted-average unit cost Average cost that is weighted by the number of units purchased at each unit cost. (p. 281).

Work in process That portion of manufactured inventory that has been placed into the production process but is not yet complete. (p. 272).

APPENDIX 6A INVENTORY COST FLOW METHODS IN PERPETUAL INVENTORY SYSTEMS

LEARNING OBJECTIVE 7

Apply the inventory cost flow methods to perpetual inventory records.

What inventory cost flow methods do companies employ if they use a perpetual inventory system? Simple—they can use any of the inventory cost flow methods described in the chapter. To illustrate the application of the three assumed cost flow methods (FIFO, LIFO, and average-cost), we will use the data shown in Illustration 6A-1 and in this chapter for Houston Electronics' Astro Condenser.

Illustration 6A-1
Inventoriable units and costs

Houston Electronics
Astro Condensers

Date	Explanation	Units	Units Cost	Total Cost	Balance in Units
1/1	Beginning inventory	100	$10	$ 1,000	100
4/15	Purchases	200	11	2,200	300
8/24	Purchases	300	12	3,600	600
9/10	Sale	550			50
11/27	Purchases	400	13	5,200	450
				$12,000	

First-In, First-Out (FIFO)

Under FIFO, the company charges to cost of goods sold the cost of the earliest goods on hand **prior to each sale**. Therefore, the cost of goods sold on September 10 consists of the units on hand January 1 and the units purchased April 15 and August 24. Illustration 6A-2 shows the inventory under a FIFO method perpetual system.

Illustration 6A-2
Perpetual system—FIFO

Date	Purchases		Cost of Goods Sold	Balance (in units and cost)	
January 1				(100 @ $10)	$1,000
April 15	(200 @ $11)	$2,200		(100 @ $10) (200 @ $11)	$3,200
August 24	(300 @ $12)	$3,600		(100 @ $10) (200 @ $11) (300 @ $12)	$6,800
September 10			(100 @ $10) (200 @ $11) (250 @ $12) **$6,200** — Cost of goods sold	(50 @ $12)	$ 600
November 27	(400 @ $13)	$5,200		(50 @ $12) (400 @ $13)	**$5,800** — Ending inventory

The ending inventory in this situation is $5,800, and the cost of goods sold is $6,200 [(100 @ $10) + (200 @ $11) + (250 @ $12)].

Compare Illustrations 6-5 (page 279) and 6A-2. You can see that the results under FIFO in a perpetual system are the **same as in a periodic system**. In both cases, the ending inventory is $5,800 and cost of goods sold is $6,200. Regardless of the system, the first costs in are the costs assigned to cost of goods sold.

Last-In, First-Out (LIFO)

Under the LIFO method using a perpetual system, the company charges to cost of goods sold the cost of the most recent purchase prior to sale. Therefore, the cost of the goods sold on September 10 consists of all the units from the August 24 and April 15 purchases plus 50 of the units in beginning inventory. Illustration 6A-3 (page 294) shows the computation of the ending inventory under the LIFO method.

Illustration 6A-3
Perpetual system—LIFO

Date	Purchases		Cost of Goods Sold	Balance (in units and cost)	
January 1				(100 @ $10)	$1,000
April 15	(200 @ $11)	$2,200		(100 @ $10) (200 @ $11)	$3,200
August 24	(300 @ $12)	$3,600		(100 @ $10) (200 @ $11) (300 @ $12)	$6,800
September 10			(300 @ $12) (200 @ $11) (50 @ $10)	(50 @ $10)	$ 500
Cost of goods sold			**$6,300**		
November 27	(400 @ $13)	$5,200		(50 @ $10) (400 @ $13)	**$5,700**
Ending inventory					**$5,700**

The use of LIFO in a perpetual system will usually produce cost allocations that differ from those using LIFO in a periodic system. In a perpetual system, the company allocates the latest units purchased *prior to each sale* to cost of goods sold. In contrast, in a periodic system, the latest units purchased *during the period* are allocated to cost of goods sold. Thus, when a purchase is made after the last sale, the LIFO periodic system will apply this purchase to the previous sale. Compare Illustrations 6-7 (page 280) and 6A-3. Illustration 6-7 shows that the 400 units at $13 purchased on November 27 applied to the sale of 550 units (on September 10). Under the LIFO perpetual system in Illustration 6A-3, the 400 units at $13 purchased on November 27 are all applied to the ending inventory.

The ending inventory in this LIFO perpetual illustration is $5,700, and cost of goods sold is $6,300, as compared to the LIFO periodic Illustration 6-7 (on page 280) where the ending inventory is $5,000 and cost of goods sold is $7,000.

Average-Cost

The average-cost method in a perpetual inventory system is called the **moving-average method.** Under this method, the company computes a new average **after each purchase**, by dividing the cost of goods available for sale by the units on hand. The average cost is then applied to (1) the units sold, to determine the cost of goods sold, and (2) the remaining units on hand, to determine the ending inventory amount. Illustration 6A-4 shows the application of the moving-average cost method by Houston Electronics.

Illustration 6A-4
Perpetual system—average-cost method

Date	Purchases		Cost of Goods Sold	Balance (in units and cost)	
January 1				(100 @ $10)	$ 1,000
April 15	(200 @ $11)	$2,200		(300 @ $10.667)	$ 3,200
August 24	(300 @ $12)	$3,600		(600 @ $11.333)	$ 6,800
September 10			(550 @ $11.333)	(50 @ $11.333)	$ 567
Cost of goods sold			**$6,233**		
November 27	(400 @ $13)	$5,200		(450 @ $12.816)	**$5,767**
Ending inventory					**$5,767**

As indicated, Houston Electronics computes **a new average each time it makes a purchase**. On April 15, after it buys 200 units for $2,200, a total of 300 units costing $3,200 ($1,000 + $2,200) are on hand. The average unit cost is $10.667 ($3,200 ÷ 300). On August 24, after Houston Electronics buys 300 units for $3,600, a total of 600 units costing $6,800 ($1,000 + $2,200 + $3,600) are on hand, at an average cost per unit of $11.333 ($6,800 ÷ 600). Houston Electronics uses this unit cost of $11.333 in costing sales until it makes another purchase, when the company computes a new unit cost. Accordingly, the unit cost of the 550 units sold (on September 10) is $11.333, and the total cost of goods sold is $6,233. On November 27, following the purchase of 400 units for $5,200, there are 450 units on hand costing $5,767 ($567 + $5,200) with a new average cost of $12.816 ($5,767 ÷ 450).

Compare this moving-average cost under the perpetual inventory system to Illustration 6-10 (on page 282) showing the average-cost method under a periodic inventory system.

> Comprehensive DO IT! 2

Comprehensive DO IT! 1 on page 290 showed cost of goods sold computations under a periodic inventory system. Now let's assume that Gerald D. Englehart Company uses a perpetual inventory system. The company has the same inventory, purchases, and sales data for the month of March as shown earlier:

Inventory:	March 1	200 units @ $4.00	$ 800
Purchases:	March 10	500 units @ $4.50	2,250
	March 20	400 units @ $4.75	1,900
	March 30	300 units @ $5.00	1,500
Sales:	March 15	500 units	
	March 25	400 units	

The physical inventory count on March 31 shows 500 units on hand.

Instructions

Under a **perpetual inventory system**, determine the cost of inventory on hand at March 31 and the cost of goods sold for March under (a) FIFO, (b) LIFO, and (c) average-cost.

Solution to Comprehensive DO IT! 2

Action Plan

- ✔ Compute the cost of goods sold under the perpetual FIFO method by allocating to the goods sold the **earliest** cost of goods purchased.
- ✔ Compute the cost of goods sold under the perpetual LIFO method by allocating to the goods sold the **latest** cost of goods purchased.
- ✔ Compute the cost of goods sold under the perpetual average-cost method by allocating to the goods sold a **moving-average** cost.

The cost of goods available for sale is $6,450, as follows.

Inventory:		200 units @ $4.00	$ 800
Purchases:	March 10	500 units @ $4.50	2,250
	March 20	400 units @ $4.75	1,900
	March 30	300 units @ $5.00	1,500
Total:		1,400	$6,450

Under a **perpetual inventory system**, the cost of goods sold under each cost flow method is as follows.

FIFO Method

Date	Purchases		Cost of Goods Sold	Balance	
March 1				(200 @ $4.00)	$ 800
March 10	(500 @ $4.50)	$2,250		(200 @ $4.00) (500 @ $4.50)	$3,050
March 15			(200 @ $4.00) (300 @ $4.50) $2,150	(200 @ $4.50)	$ 900

Date	Purchases		Cost of Goods Sold		Balance	
March 20	(400 @ \$4.75)	\$1,900			(200 @ \$4.50) (400 @ \$4.75)	\$2,800
March 25			(200 @ \$4.50) (200 @ \$4.75)	\$1,850	(200 @ \$4.75)	\$ 950
March 30	(300 @ \$5.00)	\$1,500			(200 @ \$4.75) (300 @ \$5.00)	\$2,450
	Ending inventory \$2,450		Cost of goods sold: \$2,150 + \$1,850 = \$4,000			

LIFO Method

Date	Purchases		Cost of Goods Sold		Balance	
March 1					(200 @ \$4.00)	\$ 800
March 10	(500 @ \$4.50)	\$2,250			(200 @ \$4.00) (500 @ \$4.50)	\$3,050
March 15			(500 @ \$4.50)	\$2,250	(200 @ \$4.00)	\$ 800
March 20	(400 @ \$4.75)	\$1,900			(200 @ \$4.00) (400 @ \$4.75)	\$2,700
March 25			(400 @ \$4.75)	\$1,900	(200 @ \$4.00)	\$ 800
March 30	(300 @ \$5.00)	\$1,500			(200 @ \$4.00) (300 @ \$5.00)	\$2,300
	Ending inventory \$2,300		Cost of goods sold: \$2,250 + \$1,900 = \$4,150			

Moving-Average Cost Method

Date	Purchases		Cost of Goods Sold		Balance	
March 1					(200 @ \$4.00)	\$ 800
March 10	(500 @ \$4.50)	\$2,250			(700 @ \$4.357)	\$3,050
March 15			(500 @ \$4.357)	\$ 2,179	(200 @ \$4.357)	\$ 871
March 20	(400 @ \$4.75)	\$1,900			(600 @ \$4.618)	\$2,771
March 25			(400 @ \$4.618)	\$ 1,847	(200 @ \$4.618)	\$ 924
March 30	(300 @ \$5.00)	\$1,500			(500 @ \$4.848)	\$2,424
	Ending inventory \$2,424		Cost of goods sold: \$2,179 + \$1,847 = \$4,026			

The Navigator

SUMMARY OF LEARNING OBJECTIVE FOR APPENDIX 6A

The Navigator

7 Apply the inventory cost flow methods to perpetual inventory records. Under FIFO and a perpetual inventory system, companies charge to cost of goods sold the cost of the earliest goods on hand prior to each sale. Under LIFO and a perpetual system, companies charge to cost of goods sold the cost of the most recent purchase prior to sale. Under the moving-average (average cost) method and a perpetual system, companies compute a new average cost after each purchase.

APPENDIX 6B ESTIMATING INVENTORIES

LEARNING OBJECTIVE 8

Describe the two methods of estimating inventories.

In the chapter, we assumed that a company would be able to physically count its inventory. What if it cannot? What if the inventory were destroyed by fire or flood, for example? In that case, the company would use an estimate.

Two circumstances explain why companies sometimes estimate inventories. First, a casualty such as fire, flood, or earthquake may make it impossible to take a physical inventory. Second, managers may want monthly or quarterly financial statements, but a physical inventory is taken only annually. The need for estimating inventories occurs primarily with a periodic inventory system because of the absence of perpetual inventory records.

There are two widely used methods of estimating inventories: (1) the gross profit method, and (2) the retail inventory method.

Gross Profit Method

The **gross profit method** estimates the cost of ending inventory by applying a gross profit rate to net sales. This method is relatively simple but effective. Accountants, auditors, and managers frequently use the gross profit method to test the reasonableness of the ending inventory amount. It will detect large errors.

To use this method, a company needs to know its net sales, cost of goods available for sale, and gross profit rate. The company then can estimate its gross profit for the period. Illustration 6B-1 shows the formulas for using the gross profit method.

Illustration 6B-1
Gross profit method formulas

Step 1:	**Net Sales**	**−**	**Estimated Gross Profit**	**=**	**Estimated Cost of Goods Sold**
Step 2:	**Cost of Goods Available for Sale**	**−**	**Estimated Cost of Goods Sold**	**=**	**Estimated Cost of Ending Inventory**

To illustrate, assume that Kishwaukee Company wishes to prepare an income statement for the month of January. Its records show net sales of $200,000, beginning inventory $40,000, and cost of goods purchased $120,000. In the preceding year, the company realized a 30% gross profit rate. It expects to earn the same rate this year. Given these facts and assumptions, Kishwaukee can compute the estimated cost of the ending inventory at January 31 under the gross profit method as follows.

Illustration 6B-2
Example of gross profit method

Step 1:	
Net sales	$ 200,000
Less: Estimated gross profit (30% × $200,000)	60,000
Estimated cost of goods sold	**$140,000**
Step 2:	
Beginning inventory	$ 40,000
Cost of goods purchased	120,000
Cost of goods available for sale	160,000
Less: Estimated cost of goods sold	140,000
Estimated cost of ending inventory	**$ 20,000**

The gross profit method is based on the assumption that the gross profit rate will remain constant. But, it may not remain constant, due to a change in merchandising policies or in market conditions. In such cases, the company should adjust the rate to reflect current operating conditions. In some cases, companies can obtain a more accurate estimate by applying this method on a department or product-line basis.

Note that companies should not use the gross profit method to prepare financial statements at the end of the year. These statements should be based on a physical inventory count.

Retail Inventory Method

A retail store such as Home Depot, Ace Hardware, or Wal-Mart has thousands of different types of merchandise at low unit costs. In such cases, it is difficult and time-consuming to apply unit costs to inventory quantities. An alternative is to use the **retail inventory method** to estimate the cost of inventory. Most retail companies can establish a relationship between cost and sales price. The company then applies the cost-to-retail percentage to the ending inventory at retail prices to determine inventory at cost.

Under the retail inventory method, a company's records must show both the cost and retail value of the goods available for sale. Illustration 6B-3 presents the formulas for using the retail inventory method.

Illustration 6B-3
Retail inventory method formulas

Step 1:	**Goods Available for Sale at Retail**	**−**	**Net Sales**	**=**	**Ending Inventory at Retail**
Step 2:	**Goods Available for Sale at Cost**	**÷**	**Goods Available for Sale at Retail**	**=**	**Cost-to-Retail Ratio**
Step 3:	**Ending Inventory at Retail**	**×**	**Cost-to-Retail Ratio**	**=**	**Estimated Cost of Ending Inventory**

We can demonstrate the logic of the retail method by using unit-cost data. Assume that Ortiz Inc. has marked 10 units purchased at \$7 to sell for \$10 per unit. Thus, the cost-to-retail ratio is 70% (\$70 ÷ \$100). If four units remain unsold, their retail value is \$40 (4 × \$10), and their cost is \$28 (\$40 × 70%). This amount agrees with the total cost of goods on hand on a per unit basis (4 × \$7).

Illustration 6B-4 shows application of the retail method for Valley West Co. Note that it is not necessary to take a physical inventory to determine the estimated cost of goods on hand at any given time.

Illustration 6B-4
Application of retail inventory method

	At Cost	At Retail
Beginning inventory	$14,000	$ 21,500
Goods purchased	61,000	78,500
Goods available for sale	$75,000	100,000
Net sales		70,000
Step (1) Ending inventory at retail =		**$ 30,000**

Step (2) Cost-to-retail ratio = \$75,000 ÷ \$100,000 = 75%
Step (3) Estimated cost of ending inventory = \$30,000 × 75% = \$22,500

The retail inventory method also facilitates taking a physical inventory at the end of the year. Valley West can value the goods on hand at the prices marked on the merchandise and then apply the cost-to-retail ratio to the goods on hand at retail to determine the ending inventory at cost.

Helpful Hint In determining inventory at retail, companies use selling prices of the units.

The major disadvantage of the retail method is that it is an averaging technique. Thus, it may produce an incorrect inventory valuation if the mix of the ending inventory is not representative of the mix in the goods available for sale. Assume, for example, that the cost-to-retail ratio of 75% for Valley West consists of equal proportions of inventory items that have cost-to-retail ratios of 70%, 75%, and 80%. If the ending inventory contains only items with a 70% ratio, an incorrect inventory cost will result. Companies can minimize this problem by applying the retail method on a department or product-line basis.

SUMMARY OF LEARNING OBJECTIVE FOR APPENDIX 6B

The Navigator

8 Describe the two methods of estimating inventories. The two methods of estimating inventories are the gross profit method and the retail inventory method. Under the gross profit method, companies apply a gross profit rate to net sales to determine estimated cost of goods sold. They then subtract estimated cost of goods sold from cost of goods available for sale to determine the estimated cost of the ending inventory.

Under the retail inventory method, companies compute a cost-to-retail ratio by dividing the cost of goods available for sale by the retail value of the goods available for sale. They then apply this ratio to the ending inventory at retail to determine the estimated cost of the ending inventory.

GLOSSARY FOR APPENDIX 6B

Gross profit method A method for estimating the cost of the ending inventory by applying a gross profit rate to net sales and subtracting estimated cost of goods sold from cost of goods available for sale. (p. 297).

Retail inventory method A method for estimating the cost of the ending inventory by applying a cost-to-retail ratio to the ending inventory at retail. (p. 298).

Self-Test, Brief Exercises, Exercises, Problem Set A, and many more components are available for practice in WileyPLUS.

**Note:* All asterisked Questions, Exercises, and Problems relate to material in the appendices to the chapter.

SELF-TEST QUESTIONS

Answers are on page 320.

(LO 1) **1.** Which of the following should *not* be included in the physical inventory of a company?
- (a) Goods held on consignment from another company.
- (b) Goods shipped on consignment to another company.
- (c) Goods in transit from another company shipped FOB shipping point.
- (d) None of the above.

(LO 1) **2.** As a result of a thorough physical inventory, Railway Company determined that it had inventory worth $180,000 at December 31, 2014. This count did not take into consideration the following facts. Rogers Consignment store currently has goods worth $35,000 on its sales floor that belong to Railway but are being sold on consignment by Rogers. The selling price of these goods is $50,000. Railway purchased $13,000 of goods that were shipped on December 27, FOB destination, that will be received by Railway on January 3. Determine the correct amount of inventory that Railway should report.
- (a) $230,000.
- (b) $215,000.
- (c) $228,000.
- (d) $193,000.

(LO 2) 3. Cost of goods available for sale consists of two elements: beginning inventory and:
(a) ending inventory.
(b) cost of goods purchased.
(c) cost of goods sold.
(d) All of the above.

(LO 2) 4. Tinker Bell Company has the following:

	Units	Unit Cost
Inventory, Jan. 1	8,000	$11
Purchase, June 19	13,000	12
Purchase, Nov. 8	5,000	13

If Tinker Bell has 9,000 units on hand at December 31, the cost of the ending inventory under FIFO is:
(a) $99,000. (c) $113,000.
(b) $108,000. (d) $117,000.

(LO 2) 5. Using the data in Question 4 above, the cost of the ending inventory under LIFO is:
(a) $113,000. (c) $99,000.
(b) $108,000. (d) $100,000.

(LO 2) 6. Davidson Electronics has the following:

	Units	Unit Cost
Inventory, Jan. 1	5,000	$ 8
Purchase, April 2	15,000	$10
Purchase, Aug. 28	20,000	$12

If Davidson has 7,000 units on hand at December 31, the cost of ending inventory under the average-cost method is:
(a) $84,000. (c) $56,000.
(b) $70,000. (d) $75,250.

(LO 3) 7. In periods of rising prices, LIFO will produce:
(a) higher net income than FIFO.
(b) the same net income as FIFO.
(c) lower net income than FIFO.
(d) higher net income than average-cost.

(LO 3) 8. Factors that affect the selection of an inventory costing method do *not* include:
(a) tax effects.
(b) balance sheet effects.
(c) income statement effects.
(d) perpetual vs. periodic inventory system.

(LO 4) 9. Rickety Company purchased 1,000 widgets and has 200 widgets in its ending inventory at a cost of $91 each and a current replacement cost of $80 each. The ending inventory under lower-of-cost-or-market is:
(a) $91,000. (c) $18,200.
(b) $80,000. (d) $16,000.

10. Atlantis Company's ending inventory is understated $4,000. The effects of this error on the current year's cost of goods sold and net income, respectively, are: (LO 5)
(a) understated, overstated.
(b) overstated, understated.
(c) overstated, overstated.
(d) understated, understated.

11. Harold Company overstated its inventory by $15,000 at December 31, 2013. It did not correct the error in 2013 or 2014. As a result, Harold's stockholders' equity was: (LO 4)
(a) overstated at December 31, 2013, and understated at December 31, 2014.
(b) overstated at December 31, 2013, and properly stated at December 31, 2014.
(c) understated at December 31, 2013, and understated at December 31, 2014.
(d) overstated at December 31, 2013, and overstated at December 31, 2014.

12. Which of these would cause the inventory turnover ratio to increase the most? (LO 6)
(a) Increasing the amount of inventory on hand.
(b) Keeping the amount of inventory on hand constant but increasing sales.
(c) Keeping the amount of inventory on hand constant but decreasing sales.
(d) Decreasing the amount of inventory on hand and increasing sales.

13. Carlos Company had beginning inventory of $80,000, ending inventory of $110,000, cost of goods sold of $285,000, and sales of $475,000. Carlos's days in inventory is: (LO 5)
(a) 73 days. (c) 102.5 days.
(b) 121.7 days. (d) 84.5 days.

*14. Songbird Company has sales of $150,000 and cost of goods available for sale of $135,000. If the gross profit rate is 30%, the estimated cost of the ending inventory under the gross profit method is: (LO 8)
(a) $15,000. (c) $45,000.
(b) $30,000. (d) $75,000.

*15. In a perpetual inventory system: (LO 7)
(a) LIFO cost of goods sold will be the same as in a periodic inventory system.
(b) average costs are based entirely on unit cost averages.
(c) a new average is computed under the average-cost method after each sale.
(d) FIFO cost of goods sold will be the same as in a periodic inventory system.

Go to the book's companion website, www.wiley.com/college/weygandt, for additional Self-Test Questions.

✔ The Navigator

QUESTIONS

1. "The key to successful business operations is effective inventory management." Do you agree? Explain.
2. An item must possess two characteristics to be classified as inventory by a merchandiser. What are these two characteristics?
3. Your friend Art Mega has been hired to help take the physical inventory in Jaegar Hardware Store. Explain to Art Mega what this job will entail.
4. (a) Hanson Company ships merchandise to Fox Company on December 30. The merchandise

reaches the buyer on January 6. Indicate the terms of sale that will result in the goods being included in (1) Hanson's December 31 inventory, and (2) Fox's December 31 inventory.

(b) Under what circumstances should Hanson Company include consigned goods in its inventory?

5. Topp Hat Shop received a shipment of hats for which it paid the wholesaler $2,970. The price of the hats was $3,000 but Topp was given a $30 cash discount and required to pay freight charges of $80. In addition, Topp paid $130 to cover the travel expenses of an employee who negotiated the purchase of the hats. What amount will Topp record for inventory? Why?

6. Explain the difference between the terms FOB shipping point and FOB destination.

7. Jason Bradley believes that the allocation of inventoriable costs should be based on the actual physical flow of the goods. Explain to Jason why this may be both impractical and inappropriate.

8. What is a major advantage and a major disadvantage of the specific identification method of inventory costing?

9. "The selection of an inventory cost flow method is a decision made by accountants." Do you agree? Explain. Once a method has been selected, what accounting requirement applies?

10. Which assumed inventory cost flow method:

(a) usually parallels the actual physical flow of merchandise?

(b) assumes that goods available for sale during an accounting period are identical?

(c) assumes that the latest units purchased are the first to be sold?

11. In a period of rising prices, the inventory reported in Barto Company's balance sheet is close to the current cost of the inventory. Phelan Company's inventory is considerably below its current cost. Identify the inventory cost flow method being used by each company. Which company has probably been reporting the higher gross profit?

12. Olsen Company has been using the FIFO cost flow method during a prolonged period of rising prices. During the same time period, Olsen has been paying out all of its net income as dividends. What adverse effects may result from this policy?

13. Steve Kerns is studying for the next accounting midterm examination. What should Steve know about (a) departing from the cost basis of accounting for inventories and (b) the meaning of "market" in the lower-of-cost-or-market method?

14. Steering Music Center has 5 CD players on hand at the balance sheet date. Each cost $100. The current replacement cost is $90 per unit. Under the lower-of-cost-or-market basis of accounting for inventories, what value should be reported for the CD players on the balance sheet? Why?

15. Maggie Stores has 20 toasters on hand at the balance sheet date. Each cost $28. The current replacement cost is $30 per unit. Under the lower-of-cost-or-market basis of accounting for inventories, what value should Maggie report for the toasters on the balance sheet? Why?

16. Cohen Company discovers in 2014 that its ending inventory at December 31, 2013, was $7,600 understated. What effect will this error have on (a) 2013 net income, (b) 2014 net income, and (c) the combined net income for the 2 years?

17. Raglan Company's balance sheet shows Inventory $162,800. What additional disclosures should be made?

18. Under what circumstances might inventory turnover be too high? That is, what possible negative consequences might occur?

19. **PEPSICO** What inventory cost flow does PepsiCo use for its inventories? (*Hint:* you will need to examine the notes for PepsiCo's financial statements.)

***20.** "When perpetual inventory records are kept, the results under the FIFO and LIFO methods are the same as they would be in a periodic inventory system." Do you agree? Explain.

***21.** How does the average-cost method of inventory costing differ between a perpetual inventory system and a periodic inventory system?

***22.** When is it necessary to estimate inventories?

***23.** Both the gross profit method and the retail inventory method are based on averages. For each method, indicate the average used, how it is determined, and how it is applied.

***24.** Edmonds Company has net sales of $400,000 and cost of goods available for sale of $300,000. If the gross profit rate is 40%, what is the estimated cost of the ending inventory? Show computations.

***25.** Park Shoe Shop had goods available for sale in 2014 with a retail price of $120,000. The cost of these goods was $84,000. If sales during the period were $90,000, what is the ending inventory at cost using the retail inventory method?

BRIEF EXERCISES

BE6-1 Dayne Company identifies the following items for possible inclusion in the taking of a physical inventory. Indicate whether each item should be included or excluded from the inventory taking.

Identify items to be included in taking a physical inventory.

(LO 1)

(a) Goods shipped on consignment by Dayne to another company.

(b) Goods in transit from a supplier shipped FOB destination.

(c) Goods sold but being held for customer pickup.
(d) Goods held on consignment from another company.

Identify the components of goods available for sale.
(LO 2)

BE6-2 The ledger of Perez Company includes the following items: (a) Freight-In, (b) Purchase Returns and Allowances, (c) Purchases, (d) Sales Discounts, and (e) Purchase Discounts. Identify which items are included in goods available for sale.

Compute ending inventory using FIFO and LIFO.
(LO 2)

BE6-3 In its first month of operations, Rusch Company made three purchases of merchandise in the following sequence: (1) 300 units at $6, (2) 400 units at $7, and (3) 200 units at $8. Assuming there are 450 units on hand, compute the cost of the ending inventory under the (a) FIFO method and (b) LIFO method. Rusch uses a periodic inventory system.

Compute the ending inventory using average-cost.
(LO 2)

BE6-4 Data for Rusch Company are presented in BE6-3. Compute the cost of the ending inventory under the average-cost method, assuming there are 450 units on hand.

Explain the financial statement effect of inventory cost flow assumptions.
(LO 3)

BE6-5 The management of Muni Corp. is considering the effects of various inventory-costing methods on its financial statements and its income tax expense. Assuming that the price the company pays for inventory is increasing, which method will:
(a) Provide the highest net income?
(b) Provide the highest ending inventory?
(c) Result in the lowest income tax expense?
(d) Result in the most stable earnings over a number of years?

Explain the financial statement effect of inventory cost flow assumptions.
(LO 3)

BE6-6 In its first month of operation, Marquis Company purchased 100 units of inventory for $6, then 200 units for $7, and finally 150 units for $8. At the end of the month, 200 units remained. Compute the amount of phantom profit that would result if the company used FIFO rather than LIFO. Explain why this amount is referred to as *phantom profit*. The company uses the periodic method.

Determine the LCM valuation using inventory categories.
(LO 4)

BE6-7 Pena Appliance Center accumulates the following cost and market data at December 31.

Inventory Categories	Cost Data	Market Data
Cameras	$12,000	$12,100
Camcorders	9,500	9,200
DVD players	14,000	12,800

Compute the lower-of-cost-or-market valuation for the company's total inventory.

Determine correct income statement amounts.
(LO 5)

BE6-8 Farr Company reports net income of $90,000 in 2014. However, ending inventory was understated $5,000. What is the correct net income for 2014? What effect, if any, will this error have on total assets as reported in the balance sheet at December 31, 2014?

Compute inventory turnover and days in inventory.
(LO 6)

BE6-9 At December 31, 2014, the following information was available for J. Simon Company: ending inventory $40,000, beginning inventory $60,000, cost of goods sold $300,000, and sales revenue $380,000. Calculate inventory turnover and days in inventory for J. Simon Company.

Apply cost flow methods to perpetual inventory records.
(LO 7)

***BE6-10** Abbott's Department Store uses a perpetual inventory system. Data for product E2-D2 include the following purchases.

Date	Number of Units	Unit Price
May 7	50	$11
July 28	30	13

On June 1, Abbott's sold 30 units, and on August 27, 35 more units. Prepare the perpetual inventory schedule for the above transactions using (a) FIFO, (b) LIFO, and (c) moving-average cost.

Apply the gross profit method.
(LO 8)

***BE6-11** At May 31, Stuart Company has net sales of $330,000 and cost of goods available for sale of $230,000. Compute the estimated cost of the ending inventory, assuming the gross profit rate is 40%.

Apply the retail inventory method.
(LO 8)

***BE6-12** On June 30, Dusto Fabrics has the following data pertaining to the retail inventory method: Goods available for sale: at cost $35,000, at retail $50,000; net sales $42,000; and ending inventory at retail $8,000. Compute the estimated cost of the ending inventory using the retail inventory method.

> DO IT! REVIEW

DO IT! 6-1 Brazille Company just took its physical inventory. The count of inventory items on hand at the company's business locations resulted in a total inventory cost of $300,000. In reviewing the details of the count and related inventory transactions, you have discovered the following.

Apply rules of ownership to determine inventory cost.

(LO 1)

1. Brazille has sent inventory costing $21,000 on consignment to Nikki Company. All of this inventory was at Nikki's showrooms on December 31.
2. The company did not include in the count inventory (cost, $20,000) that was purchased on December 28, terms FOB shipping point. The goods were in transit on December 31.
3. The company did not include in the count inventory (cost, $17,000) that was sold with terms of FOB shipping point. The goods were in transit on December 31.

Compute the correct December 31 inventory.

DO IT! 6-2 The accounting records of Connor Electronics show the following data.

Compute cost of goods sold under different cost flow methods.

(LO 2)

Beginning inventory	3,000 units at $5
Purchases	8,000 units at $7
Sales	9,400 units at $10

Determine cost of goods sold during the period under a periodic inventory system using (a) the FIFO method, (b) the LIFO method, and (c) the average-cost method. (Round unit cost to nearest tenth of a cent.)

DO IT! 6-3 (a) Wahl Company sells three different categories of tools (small, medium, and large). The cost and market value of its inventory of tools are as follows.

Compute inventory value under LCM.

(LO 4)

	Cost	Market Value
Small	$ 64,000	$ 73,000
Medium	290,000	260,000
Large	152,000	149,000

Determine the value of the company's inventory under the lower-of-cost-or-market approach.

(b) Rhodee Company understated its 2013 ending inventory by $28,000. Determine the impact this error has on ending inventory, cost of goods sold, and stockholders' equity in 2013 and 2014.

DO IT! 6-4 Early in 2014, Racine Company switched to a just-in-time inventory system. Its sales, cost of goods sold, and inventory amounts for 2013 and 2014 are shown below.

Compute inventory turnover ratio and assess inventory level.

(LO 6)

	2013	2014
Sales	$3,120,000	$3,713,000
Cost of goods sold	1,200,000	1,425,000
Beginning inventory	180,000	220,000
Ending inventory	220,000	100,000

Determine the inventory turnover and days in inventory for 2013 and 2014. Discuss the changes in the amount of inventory, the inventory turnover and days in inventory, and the amount of sales across the two years.

EXERCISES

E6-1 Premier Bank and Trust is considering giving Alou Company a loan. Before doing so, management decides that further discussions with Alou's accountant may be desirable. One area of particular concern is the inventory account, which has a year-end balance of $297,000. Discussions with the accountant reveal the following

Determine the correct inventory amount.

(LO 1)

1. Alou sold goods costing $38,000 to Comerico Company, FOB shipping point, on December 28. The goods are not expected to arrive at Comerico until January 12. The goods were not included in the physical inventory because they were not in the warehouse.
2. The physical count of the inventory did not include goods costing $95,000 that were shipped to Alou FOB destination on December 27 and were still in transit at year-end.
3. Alou received goods costing $19,000 on January 2. The goods were shipped FOB shipping point on December 26 by Grant Co. The goods were not included in the physical count.
4. Alou sold goods costing $35,000 to Emerick Co., FOB destination, on December 30. The goods were received at Emerick on January 8. They were not included in Alou's physical inventory.
5. Alou received goods costing $44,000 on January 2 that were shipped FOB shipping point on December 29. The shipment was a rush order that was supposed to arrive December 31. This purchase was included in the ending inventory of $297,000.

Instructions

Determine the correct inventory amount on December 31.

Determine the correct inventory amount.

(LO 1)

E6-2 Kale Wilson, an auditor with Sneed CPAs, is performing a review of Platinum Company's inventory account. Platinum did not have a good year, and top management is under pressure to boost reported income. According to its records, the inventory balance at year-end was $740,000. However, the following information was not considered when determining that amount.

1. Included in the company's count were goods with a cost of $250,000 that the company is holding on consignment. The goods belong to Superior Corporation.
2. The physical count did not include goods purchased by Platinum with a cost of $40,000 that were shipped FOB destination on December 28 and did not arrive at Platinum's warehouse until January 3.
3. Included in the inventory account was $17,000 of office supplies that were stored in the warehouse and were to be used by the company's supervisors and managers during the coming year.
4. The company received an order on December 29 that was boxed and sitting on the loading dock awaiting pick-up on December 31. The shipper picked up the goods on January 1 and delivered them on January 6. The shipping terms were FOB shipping point. The goods had a selling price of $49,000 and a cost of $33,000. The goods were not included in the count because they were sitting on the dock.
5. On December 29, Platinum shipped goods with a selling price of $80,000 and a cost of $60,000 to District Sales Corporation FOB shipping point. The goods arrived on January 3. District Sales had only ordered goods with a selling price of $10,000 and a cost of $8,000. However, a sales manager at Platinum had authorized the shipment and said that if District wanted to ship the goods back next week, it could.
6. Included in the count was $48,000 of goods that were parts for a machine that the company no longer made. Given the high-tech nature of Platinum's products, it was unlikely that these obsolete parts had any other use. However, management would prefer to keep them on the books at cost, "since that is what we paid for them, after all."

Instructions

Prepare a schedule to determine the correct inventory amount. Provide explanations for each item above, saying why you did or did not make an adjustment for each item.

Calculate cost of goods sold using specific identification and FIFO.

(LO 2, 3)

E6-3 On December 1, Discount Electronics Ltd. has three DVD players left in stock. All are identical, all are priced to sell at $150. One of the three DVD players left in stock, with serial #1012, was purchased on June 1 at a cost of $100. Another, with serial #1045, was purchased on November 1 for $90. The last player, serial #1056, was purchased on November 30 for $84.

Instructions

(a) Calculate the cost of goods sold using the FIFO periodic inventory method assuming that two of the three players were sold by the end of December, Discount Electronics' year-end.

(b) If Discount Electronics used the specific identification method instead of the FIFO method, how might it alter its earnings by "selectively choosing" which particular players to sell to the two customers? What would Discount's cost of goods sold be if the company wished to minimize earnings? Maximize earnings?

(c) Which of the two inventory methods do you recommend that Discount use? Explain why.

Compute inventory and cost of goods sold using FIFO and LIFO.

(LO 2)

E6-4 Sherper's Boards sells a snowboard, Xpert, that is popular with snowboard enthusiasts. Information relating to Sherper's purchases of Xpert snowboards during September is shown below. During the same month, 121 Xpert snowboards were sold. Sherper's uses a periodic inventory system.

Date	Explanation	Units	Unit Cost	Total Cost
Sept. 1	Inventory	23	$ 97	$ 2,231
Sept. 12	Purchases	45	102	4,590
Sept. 19	Purchases	20	104	2,080
Sept. 26	Purchases	44	105	4,620
	Totals	132		$13,521

Instructions

(a) Compute the ending inventory at September 30 and cost of goods sold using the FIFO and LIFO methods. Prove the amount allocated to cost of goods sold under each method.

(b) For both FIFO and LIFO, calculate the sum of ending inventory and cost of goods sold. What do you notice about the answers you found for each method?

Compute inventory and cost of goods sold using FIFO and LIFO.

(LO 2)

E6-5 Zambian Co. uses a periodic inventory system. Its records show the following for the month of May, in which 68 units were sold.

		Units	Unit Cost	Total Cost
May 1	Inventory	30	$ 9	$270
15	Purchases	25	11	275
24	Purchases	35	12	420
	Totals	90		$965

Instructions

Compute the ending inventory at May 31 and cost of goods sold using the FIFO and LIFO methods. Prove the amount allocated to cost of goods sold under each method.

Compute inventory and cost of goods sold using FIFO and LIFO.

(LO 2, 3)

E6-6 Eastland Company reports the following for the month of June.

		Units	Unit Cost	Total Cost
June 1	Inventory	200	$5	$1,000
12	Purchase	300	6	1,800
23	Purchase	500	7	3,500
30	Inventory	160		

Instructions

(a) Compute the cost of the ending inventory and the cost of goods sold under (1) FIFO and (2) LIFO.

(b) Which costing method gives the higher ending inventory? Why?

(c) Which method results in the higher cost of goods sold? Why?

Compute inventory under FIFO, LIFO, and average-cost.

(LO 2, 3)

E6-7 Givens Company had 100 units in beginning inventory at a total cost of $10,000. The company purchased 200 units at a total cost of $26,000. At the end of the year, Givens had 75 units in ending inventory.

Instructions

(a) Compute the cost of the ending inventory and the cost of goods sold under (1) FIFO, (2) LIFO, and (3) average-cost.

(b) Which cost flow method would result in the highest net income?

(c) Which cost flow method would result in inventories approximating current cost in the balance sheet?

(d) Which cost flow method would result in Givens paying the least taxes in the first year?

Compute inventory and cost of goods sold using average-cost.

(LO 2, 3)

E6-8 Inventory data for Eastland Company are presented in E6-6.

Instructions

(a) Compute the cost of the ending inventory and the cost of goods sold using the average-cost method.

(b) Will the results in (a) be higher or lower than the results under (1) FIFO and (2) LIFO?

(c) Why is the average unit cost not $6?

Determine ending inventory under LCM.

(LO 4)

E6-9 Kinshasa Camera Shop uses the lower-of-cost-or-market basis for its inventory. The following data are available at December 31.

Item	Units	Unit Cost	Market
Cameras:			
Minolta	8	$170	$156
Canon	6	150	152
Light meters:			
Vivitar	12	125	115
Kodak	14	115	135

Instructions

Determine the amount of the ending inventory by applying the lower-of-cost-or-market basis.

Compute lower-of-cost-or-market.

(LO 4)

E6-10 Fenton Company applied FIFO to its inventory and got the following results for its ending inventory.

Cameras	100 units at a cost per unit of $68
DVD players	150 units at a cost per unit of $75
iPods	125 units at a cost per unit of $80

The cost of purchasing units at year-end was cameras $70, DVD players $69, and iPods $78.

Instructions

Determine the amount of ending inventory at lower-of-cost-or-market.

Determine effects of inventory errors.

(LO 5)

E6-11 Delhi Hardware reported cost of goods sold as follows.

	2013	2014
Beginning inventory	$ 20,000	$ 30,000
Cost of goods purchased	150,000	175,000
Cost of goods available for sale	170,000	205,000
Ending inventory	30,000	35,000
Cost of goods sold	$140,000	$170,000

Delhi made two errors: (1) 2013 ending inventory was overstated $2,000, and (2) 2014 ending inventory was understated $6,000.

Instructions

Compute the correct cost of goods sold for each year.

Prepare correct income statements.

(LO 5)

E6-12 Horner Watch Company reported the following income statement data for a 2-year period.

	2013	2014
Sales revenue	$210,000	$250,000
Cost of goods sold		
Beginning inventory	32,000	44,000
Cost of goods purchased	173,000	202,000
Cost of goods available for sale	205,000	246,000
Ending inventory	44,000	52,000
Cost of goods sold	161,000	194,000
Gross profit	$ 49,000	$ 56,000

Horner uses a periodic inventory system. The inventories at January 1, 2013, and December 31, 2014, are correct. However, the ending inventory at December 31, 2013, was understated $6,000.

Instructions

(a) Prepare correct income statement data for the 2 years.

(b) What is the cumulative effect of the inventory error on total gross profit for the 2 years?

(c) Explain in a letter to the president of Horner Watch Company what has happened, i.e., the nature of the error and its effect on the financial statements.

E6-13 This information is available for Sepia Photo Corporation for 2012, 2013, and 2014.

Compute inventory turnover, days in inventory, and gross profit rate.

(LO 6)

	2012	2013	2014
Beginning inventory	$ 100,000	$ 330,000	$ 400,000
Ending inventory	330,000	400,000	480,000
Cost of goods sold	900,000	1,120,000	1,300,000
Sales revenue	1,200,000	1,600,000	1,900,000

Instructions

Calculate inventory turnover, days in inventory, and gross profit rate (from Chapter 5) for Sepia's Photo Corporation for 2012, 2013, and 2014. Comment on any trends.

E6-14 The cost of goods sold computations for Silver Company and Gold Company are shown below.

Compute inventory turnover and days in inventory.

(LO 6)

	Silver Company	Gold Company
Beginning inventory	$ 47,000	$ 71,000
Cost of goods purchased	200,000	290,000
Cost of goods available for sale	247,000	361,000
Ending inventory	55,000	69,000
Cost of goods sold	$192,000	$292,000

Instructions

(a) Compute inventory turnover and days in inventory for each company.
(b) Which company moves its inventory more quickly?

***E6-15** Roselle Appliance uses a perpetual inventory system. For its flat-screen television sets, the January 1 inventory was 3 sets at $600 each. On January 10, Roselle purchased 6 units at $648 each. The company sold 2 units on January 8 and 4 units on January 15.

Apply cost flow methods to perpetual records.

(LO 7)

Instructions

Compute the ending inventory under (1) FIFO, (2) LIFO, and (3) moving-average cost.

***E6-16** Eastland Company reports the following for the month of June.

Calculate inventory and cost of goods sold using three cost flow methods in a perpetual inventory system.

(LO 7)

Date	Explanation	Units	Unit Cost	Total Cost
June 1	Inventory	200	$5	$1,000
12	Purchase	300	6	1,800
23	Purchase	500	7	3,500
30	Inventory	160		

Instructions

(a) Calculate the cost of the ending inventory and the cost of goods sold for each cost flow assumption, using a perpetual inventory system. Assume a sale of 400 units occurred on June15 for a selling price of $8 and a sale of 440 units on June 27 for $9.
(b) How do the results differ from E6-6 and E6-8?
(c) Why is the average unit cost not $6 [($5 + $6 + $7) ÷ 3 = $6]?

***E6-17** Information about Sherper's Boards is presented in E6-4. Additional data regarding Sherper's sales of Xpert snowboards are provided below. Assume that Sherper's uses a perpetual inventory system.

Apply cost flow methods to perpetual records.

(LO 7)

Date		Units	Unit Price	Total Revenue
Sept. 5	Sale	12	$199	$ 2,388
Sept. 16	Sale	50	203	10,150
Sept. 29	Sale	59	209	12,331
	Totals	121		$24,869

Instructions

(a) Compute ending inventory at September 30 using FIFO, LIFO, and moving-average cost.
(b) Compare ending inventory using a perpetual inventory system to ending inventory using a periodic inventory system (from E6-4).
(c) Which inventory cost flow method (FIFO, LIFO) gives the same ending inventory value under both periodic and perpetual? Which method gives different ending inventory values?

Use the gross profit method to estimate inventory.

(LO 8)

***E6-18** Adler Company reported the following information for November and December 2014.

	November	December
Cost of goods purchased	$500,000	$ 610,000
Inventory, beginning-of-month	100,000	120,000
Inventory, end-of-month	120,000	????
Sales revenue	750,000	1,000,000

Adler's ending inventory at December 31 was destroyed in a fire.

Instructions

(a) Compute the gross profit rate for November.

(b) Using the gross profit rate for November, determine the estimated cost of inventory lost in the fire.

Determine merchandise lost using the gross profit method of estimating inventory.

(LO 8)

***E6-19** The inventory of Florence Company was destroyed by fire on March 1. From an examination of the accounting records, the following data for the first 2 months of the year are obtained: Sales Revenue $51,000, Sales Returns and Allowances $1,000, Purchases $31,200, Freight-In $1,200, and Purchase Returns and Allowances $1,800.

Instructions

Determine the merchandise lost by fire, assuming:

(a) A beginning inventory of $20,000 and a gross profit rate of 40% on net sales.

(b) A beginning inventory of $30,000 and a gross profit rate of 32% on net sales.

Determine ending inventory at cost using retail method.

(LO 8)

***E6-20** Peacock Shoe Store uses the retail inventory method for its two departments, Women's Shoes and Men's Shoes. The following information for each department is obtained.

Item	Women's Shoes	Men's Shoes
Beginning inventory at cost	$ 36,500	$ 45,000
Cost of goods purchased at cost	148,000	136,300
Net sales	178,000	185,000
Beginning inventory at retail	46,000	60,000
Cost of goods purchased at retail	179,000	185,000

Instructions

Compute the estimated cost of the ending inventory for each department under the retail inventory method.

EXERCISES: SET B AND CHALLENGE EXERCISES

Visit the book's companion website, at **www.wiley.com/college/weygandt**, and choose the Student Companion site to access Exercise Set B and Challenge Exercises.

PROBLEMS: SET A

Determine items and amounts to be recorded in inventory.

(LO 1)

P6-1A Columbus Limited is trying to determine the value of its ending inventory at February 28, 2014, the company's year-end. The accountant counted everything that was in the warehouse as of February 28, which resulted in an ending inventory valuation of $48,000. However, she didn't know how to treat the following transactions so she didn't record them.

(a) On February 26, Columbus shipped to a customer goods costing $800. The goods were shipped FOB shipping point, and the receiving report indicates that the customer received the goods on March 2.

(b) On February 26, Shira Inc. shipped goods to Columbus FOB destination. The invoice price was $350. The receiving report indicates that the goods were received by Columbus on March 2.

(c) Columbus had $620 of inventory at a customer's warehouse "on approval." The customer was going to let Columbus know whether it wanted the merchandise by the end of the week, March 4.

(d) Columbus also had $400 of inventory on consignment at a Palletine craft shop.

(e) On February 26, Columbus ordered goods costing $750. The goods were shipped FOB shipping point on February 27. Columbus received the goods on March 1.
(f) On February 28, Columbus packaged goods and had them ready for shipping to a customer FOB destination. The invoice price was $350; the cost of the items was $220. The receiving report indicates that the goods were received by the customer on March 2.
(g) Columbus had damaged goods set aside in the warehouse because they are no longer saleable. These goods cost $400 and Columbus originally expected to sell these items for $600.

Instructions

For each of the above transactions, specify whether the item in question should be included in ending inventory and, if so, at what amount. For each item that is not included in ending inventory, indicate who owns it and what account, if any, it should have been recorded in.

P6-2A Dyna Distribution markets CDs of the performing artist King James. At the beginning of March, Dyna had in beginning inventory 1,500 King James CDs with a unit cost of $7. During March, Dyna made the following purchases of King James CDs.

Determine cost of goods sold and ending inventory using FIFO, LIFO, and average-cost with analysis.

(LO 2, 3)

March 5	3,500 @ $8	March 21	2,000 @ $10
March 13	4,000 @ $9	March 26	2,000 @ $11

During March, 10,000 units were sold. Dyna uses a periodic inventory system.

Instructions

(a) Determine the cost of goods available for sale.
(b) Determine (1) the ending inventory and (2) the cost of goods sold under each of the assumed cost flow methods (FIFO, LIFO, and average-cost). Prove the accuracy of the cost of goods sold under the FIFO and LIFO methods.
(c) Which cost flow method results in (1) the highest inventory amount for the balance sheet and (2) the highest cost of goods sold for the income statement?

(b) (2) Cost of goods sold:
FIFO $84,500
LIFO $94,000
Average $89,615

P6-3A Milo Company had a beginning inventory of 400 units of Product Kimbo at a cost of $8 per unit. During the year, purchases were:

Determine cost of goods sold and ending inventory using FIFO, LIFO, and average-cost with analysis.

(LO 2, 3)

Feb. 20	300 units at $9	Aug. 12	600 units at $11
May 5	500 units at $10	Dec. 8	200 units at $12

Milo Company uses a periodic inventory system. Sales totaled 1,500 units.

Instructions

(a) Determine the cost of goods available for sale.
(b) Determine (1) the ending inventory and (2) the cost of goods sold under each of the assumed cost flow methods (FIFO, LIFO, and average-cost). Prove the accuracy of the cost of goods sold under the FIFO and LIFO methods.
(c) Which cost flow method results in (1) the lowest inventory amount for the balance sheet, and (2) the lowest cost of goods sold for the income statement?

(b) Cost of goods sold:
FIFO $14,200
LIFO $15,800
Average $14,925

P6-4A The management of Red Robin Co. is reevaluating the appropriateness of using its present inventory cost flow method, which is average-cost. They request your help in determining the results of operations for 2014 if either the FIFO method or the LIFO method had been used. For 2014, the accounting records show the following data.

Compute ending inventory, prepare income statements, and answer questions using FIFO and LIFO.

(LO 2, 3)

Inventories		Purchases and Sales	
Beginning (10,000 units)	$22,800	Total net sales (225,000 units)	$865,000
Ending (15,000 units)		Total cost of goods purchased (230,000 units)	578,500

Purchases were made quarterly as follows.

Quarter	Units	Unit Cost	Total Cost
1	60,000	$2.30	$138,000
2	50,000	2.50	125,000
3	50,000	2.60	130,000
4	70,000	2.65	185,500
	230,000		$578,500

Operating expenses were $147,000, and the company's income tax rate is 32%.

(a) Net income
FIFO $106,386
LIFO $102,680
(b)(4) $1,744

Instructions

(a) Prepare comparative condensed income statements for 2014 under FIFO and LIFO. (Show computations of ending inventory.)

(b) Answer the following questions for management.
   (1) Which cost flow method (FIFO or LIFO) produces the more meaningful inventory amount for the balance sheet? Why?
   (2) Which cost flow method (FIFO or LIFO) produces the more meaningful net income? Why?
   (3) Which cost flow method (FIFO or LIFO) is more likely to approximate actual physical flow of the goods? Why?
   (4) How much additional cash will be available for management under LIFO than under FIFO? Why?
   (5) Will gross profit under the average-cost method be higher or lower than (i) FIFO and (ii) LIFO? (*Note:* It is not necessary to quantify your answer.)

Calculate ending inventory, cost of goods sold, gross profit, and gross profit rate under periodic method; compare results.

(LO 2, 3)

P6-5A You are provided with the following information for Matthew Inc. for the month ended October 31, 2014. Matthew uses a periodic method for inventory.

Date	Description	Units	Unit Cost or Selling Price
October 1	Beginning inventory	60	$24
October 9	Purchase	120	26
October 11	Sale	100	35
October 17	Purchase	70	27
October 22	Sale	65	40
October 25	Purchase	80	28
October 29	Sale	120	40

(a)(iii) Gross profit:
LIFO $3,290
FIFO $3,470
Average $3,395

Instructions

(a) Calculate (i) ending inventory, (ii) cost of goods sold, (iii) gross profit, and (iv) gross profit rate under each of the following methods.
   (1) LIFO.
   (2) FIFO.
   (3) Average-cost.

(b) Compare results for the three cost flow assumptions.

Compare specific identification, FIFO and LIFO under periodic method; use cost flow assumption to influence earnings.

(LO 2, 3)

P6-6A You have the following information for Greco Diamonds. Greco Diamonds uses the periodic method of accounting for its inventory transactions. Greco only carries one brand and size of diamonds—all are identical. Each batch of diamonds purchased is carefully coded and marked with its purchase cost.

March 1	Beginning inventory 150 diamonds at a cost of $310 per diamond.
March 3	Purchased 200 diamonds at a cost of $350 each.
March 5	Sold 180 diamonds for $600 each.
March 10	Purchased 350 diamonds at a cost of $380 each.
March 25	Sold 400 diamonds for $650 each.

(a) Gross profit:
(1) Maximum $164,100
(2) Minimum $155,700

Instructions

(a) Assume that Greco Diamonds uses the specific identification cost flow method.
   (1) Demonstrate how Greco Diamonds could maximize its gross profit for the month by specifically selecting which diamonds to sell on March 5 and March 25.
   (2) Demonstrate how Greco Diamonds could minimize its gross profit for the month by selecting which diamonds to sell on March 5 and March 25.

(b) Assume that Greco Diamonds uses the FIFO cost flow assumption. Calculate cost of goods sold. How much gross profit would Greco Diamonds report under this cost flow assumption?

(c) Assume that Greco Diamonds uses the LIFO cost flow assumption. Calculate cost of goods sold. How much gross profit would the company report under this cost flow assumption?

(d) Which cost flow method should Greco Diamonds select? Explain.

Compute ending inventory, prepare income statements, and answer questions using FIFO and LIFO.

(LO 2, 3)

P6-7A The management of Mumba Inc. asks your help in determining the comparative effects of the FIFO and LIFO inventory cost flow methods. For 2014, the accounting records provide the data shown at the top of the next page.

Inventory, January 1 (10,000 units)	$ 35,000
Cost of 120,000 units purchased	501,000
Selling price of 100,000 units sold	665,000
Operating expenses	130,000

Units purchased consisted of 40,000 units at $4.00 on May 10; 60,000 units at $4.20 on August 15; and 20,000 units at $4.45 on November 20. Income taxes are 28%.

Instructions

(a) Prepare comparative condensed income statements for 2014 under FIFO and LIFO. (Show computations of ending inventory.)

Gross profit:
FIFO $260,000
LIFO $244,000

(b) Answer the following questions for management in the form of a business letter.
  (1) Which inventory cost flow method produces the most meaningful inventory amount for the balance sheet? Why?
  (2) Which inventory cost flow method produces the most meaningful net income? Why?
  (3) Which inventory cost flow method is most likely to approximate the actual physical flow of the goods? Why?
  (4) How much more cash will be available for management under LIFO than under FIFO? Why?
  (5) How much of the gross profit under FIFO is illusionary in comparison with the gross profit under LIFO?

***P6-8A** Tempo Ltd. is a retailer operating in Dartmouth, Nova Scotia. Tempo uses the perpetual inventory method. All sales returns from customers result in the goods being returned to inventory; the inventory is not damaged. Assume that there are no credit transactions; all amounts are settled in cash. You are provided with the following information for Tempo Ltd. for the month of January 2014.

Calculate cost of goods sold and ending inventory for FIFO, moving-average cost, and LIFO under the perpetual system; compare gross profit under each assumption.

(LO 7)

Date	Description	Quantity	Unit Cost or Selling Price
December 31	Ending inventory	150	$19
January 2	Purchase	100	21
January 6	Sale	150	40
January 9	Sale return	10	40
January 9	Purchase	75	24
January 10	Purchase return	15	24
January 10	Sale	50	45
January 23	Purchase	100	26
January 30	Sale	160	50

Instructions

(a) For each of the following cost flow assumptions, calculate (i) cost of goods sold, (ii) ending inventory, and (iii) gross profit.
  (1) LIFO. (2) FIFO. (3) Moving-average cost.

(b) Compare results for the three cost flow assumptions.

Gross profit:
LIFO $8,000
FIFO $8,420
Average $8,266

***P6-9A** Dominican Appliance Mart began operations on May 1. It uses a perpetual inventory system. During May, the company had the following purchases and sales for its Model 25 Sureshot camera.

Determine ending inventory under a perpetual inventory system.

(LO 7)

Date	Purchases: Units	Purchases: Unit Cost	Sales Units
May 1	7	$155	
4			4
8	8	$170	
12			5
15	6	$185	
20			3
25			5

Instructions

(a) Determine the ending inventory under a perpetual inventory system using (1) FIFO, (2) moving-average cost, and (3) LIFO.

(a) FIFO $740
Average $702
LIFO $635

(b) Which costing method produces (1) the highest ending inventory valuation and (2) the lowest ending inventory valuation?

Estimate inventory loss using gross profit method.

(LO 8)

***P6-10A** Fram Company lost 70% of its inventory in a fire on March 25, 2014. The accounting records showed the following gross profit data for February and March.

	February	March (to 3/25)
Net sales	$300,000	$260,000
Net purchases	197,800	191,000
Freight-in	2,900	4,000
Beginning inventory	4,500	25,200
Ending inventory	25,200	?

Fram Company is fully insured for fire losses but must prepare a report for the insurance company.

Instructions

(a) Compute the gross profit rate for the month of February.
(b) Using the gross profit rate for February, determine both the estimated total inventory and inventory lost in the fire in March.

Compute ending inventory using retail method.

(LO 8)

***P6-11A** Thai Department Store uses the retail inventory method to estimate its monthly ending inventories. The following information is available for two of its departments at August 31, 2014.

	Sporting Goods		Jewelry and Cosmetics	
	Cost	Retail	Cost	Retail
Net sales		$1,010,000		$1,150,000
Purchases	$675,000	1,066,000	$741,000	1,158,000
Purchase returns	(26,000)	(40,000)	(12,000)	(20,000)
Purchase discounts	(12,360)	—	(2,440)	—
Freight-in	9,000	—	14,000	—
Beginning inventory	47,360	74,000	39,440	62,000

At December 31, Thai Department Store takes a physical inventory at retail. The actual retail values of the inventories in each department are Sporting Goods $85,000, and Jewelry and Cosmetics $54,000.

Instructions

(a) Determine the estimated cost of the ending inventory for each department on August 31, 2014, using the retail inventory method.
(b) Compute the ending inventory at cost for each department at **December 31**, assuming the cost-to-retail ratios are 60% for Sporting Goods and 64% for Jewelry and Cosmetics.

PROBLEMS: SET B

Determine items and amounts to be recorded in inventory.

(LO 1)

P6-1B Banff Limited is trying to determine the value of its ending inventory as of February 28, 2014, the company's year-end. The following transactions occurred, and the accountant asked your help in determining whether they should be recorded or not.

(a) On February 26, Banff shipped goods costing $800 to a customer and charged the customer $1,000. The goods were shipped with terms FOB shipping point and the receiving report indicates that the customer received the goods on March 2.
(b) On February 26, Vendor Inc. shipped goods to Banff under terms FOB shipping point. The invoice price was $450 plus $30 for freight. The receiving report indicates that the goods were received by Banff on March 2.
(c) Banff had $720 of inventory isolated in the warehouse. The inventory is designated for a customer who has requested that the goods be shipped on March 10.
(d) Also included in Banff's warehouse is $700 of inventory that Jasper Producers shipped to Banff on consignment.

(e) On February 26, Banff issued a purchase order to acquire goods costing $900. The goods were shipped with terms FOB destination on February 27. Banff received the goods on March 2.

(f) On February 26, Banff shipped goods to a customer under terms FOB destination. The invoice price was $350; the cost of the items was $200. The receiving report indicates that the goods were received by the customer on February 28.

Instructions

For each of the above transactions, specify whether the item in question should be included in ending inventory, and if so, at what amount.

Determine cost of goods sold and ending inventory using FIFO, LIFO, and average-cost with analysis.

(LO 2, 3)

P6-2B Doom's Day Distribution markets CDs of the performing artist Marilynn. At the beginning of October, Doom's Day had in beginning inventory 2,000 of Marilynn's CDs with a unit cost of $7. During October, Doom's Day made the following purchases of Marilynn's CDs.

Oct. 3	3,000 @ $8	Oct. 19	4,000 @ $10
Oct. 9	5,500 @ $9	Oct. 25	2,000 @ $11

During October, 13,500 units were sold. Doom's Day uses a periodic inventory system.

Instructions

(a) Determine the cost of goods available for sale.

(b) Determine (1) the ending inventory and (2) the cost of goods sold under each of the assumed cost flow methods (FIFO, LIFO, and average-cost). Prove the accuracy of the cost of goods sold under the FIFO and LIFO methods.

(c) Which cost flow method results in (1) the highest inventory amount for the balance sheet and (2) the highest cost of goods sold for the income statement?

(b)(2) Cost of goods sold:
FIFO $117,500
LIFO $127,500
Average $122,317

Determine cost of goods sold and ending inventory, using FIFO, LIFO, and average-cost with analysis.

(LO 2, 3)

P6-3B Collins Company had a beginning inventory on January 1 of 100 units of Product 4-18-15 at a cost of $21 per unit. During the year, the following purchases were made.

Mar. 15	300 units at $24	Sept. 4	300 units at $28
July 20	200 units at $25	Dec. 2	100 units at $30

700 units were sold. Collins Company uses a periodic inventory system.

Instructions

(a) Determine the cost of goods available for sale.

(b) Determine (1) the ending inventory, and (2) the cost of goods sold under each of the assumed cost flow methods (FIFO, LIFO, and average-cost). Prove the accuracy of the cost of goods sold under the FIFO and LIFO methods.

(c) Which cost flow method results in (1) the highest inventory amount for the balance sheet, and (2) the highest cost of goods sold for the income statement?

(b)(2) Cost of goods sold:
FIFO $17,100
LIFO $18,800
Average $17,990

Compute ending inventory, prepare income statements, and answer questions using FIFO and LIFO.

(LO 2, 3)

P6-4B The management of Gilbert Inc. is reevaluating the appropriateness of using its present inventory cost flow method, which is average-cost. The company requests your help in determining the results of operations for 2014 if either the FIFO or the LIFO method had been used. For 2014, the accounting records show these data:

Inventories		**Purchases and Sales**	
Beginning (8,000 units)	$16,000	Total net sales (188,000 units)	$780,000
Ending (15,000 units)		Total cost of goods purchased (195,000 units)	480,500

Purchases were made quarterly as follows.

Quarter	Units	Unit Cost	Total Cost
1	50,000	$2.20	$110,000
2	40,000	2.40	96,000
3	45,000	2.50	112,500
4	60,000	2.70	162,000
	195,000		$480,500

Operating expenses were $130,000, and the company's income tax rate is 36%.

(a) Gross profit:
FIFO $324,000
LIFO $314,900

Instructions

(a) Prepare comparative condensed income statements for 2014 under FIFO and LIFO. (Show computations of ending inventory.)

(b) Answer the following questions for management.

(1) Which cost flow method (FIFO or LIFO) produces the more meaningful inventory amount for the balance sheet? Why?

(2) Which cost flow method (FIFO or LIFO) produces the more meaningful net income? Why?

(3) Which cost flow method (FIFO or LIFO) is more likely to approximate the actual physical flow of goods? Why?

(4) How much more cash will be available for management under LIFO than under FIFO? Why?

(5) Will gross profit under the average-cost method be higher or lower than FIFO? Than LIFO? (*Note:* It is not necessary to quantify your answer.)

Calculate ending inventory, cost of goods sold, gross profit, and gross profit rate under periodic method; compare results.

(LO 2, 3)

P6-5B You are provided with the following information for Lahti Inc. for the month ended June 30, 2014. Lahti uses the periodic method for inventory.

Date	Description	Quantity	Unit Cost or Selling Price
June 1	Beginning inventory	40	$40
June 4	Purchase	135	43
June 10	Sale	110	70
June 11	Sale return	15	70
June 18	Purchase	55	46
June 18	Purchase return	10	46
June 25	Sale	60	75
June 28	Purchase	30	50

(a)(iii) Gross profit:
LIFO $4,140
FIFO $4,605
Average $4,345.50

Instructions

(a) Calculate (i) ending inventory, (ii) cost of goods sold, (iii) gross profit, and (iv) gross profit rate under each of the following methods.
(1) LIFO. (2) FIFO. (3) Average-cost.

(b) Compare results for the three cost flow assumptions.

Compare specific identification, FIFO, and LIFO under periodic method; use cost flow assumption to justify price increase.

(LO 2, 3)

P6-6B You are provided with the following information for Gas Guzzlers. Gas Guzzlers uses the periodic method of accounting for its inventory transactions.

March 1 Beginning inventory 2,200 liters at a cost of 60¢ per liter.
March 3 Purchased 2,500 liters at a cost of 65¢ per liter.
March 5 Sold 2,200 liters for $1.05 per liter.
March 10 Purchased 4,000 liters at a cost of 72¢ per liter.
March 20 Purchased 2,500 liters at a cost of 80¢ per liter.
March 30 Sold 5,500 liters for $1.25 per liter.

Instructions

(a) Prepare partial income statements through gross profit, and calculate the value of ending inventory that would be reported on the balance sheet, under each of the following cost flow assumptions. (Round ending inventory and cost of goods sold to the nearest dollar.)

(1) Specific identification method assuming:

(i) The March 5 sale consisted of 1,100 liters from the March 1 beginning inventory and 1,100 liters from the March 3 purchase; and

(ii) The March 30 sale consisted of the following number of units sold from beginning inventory and each purchase: 450 liters from March 1; 850 liters from March 3; 2,900 liters from March 10; 1,300 liters from March 20.

(2) FIFO.

(3) LIFO.

(b) How can companies use a cost flow method to justify price increases? Which cost flow method would best support an argument to increase prices?

(a)(1) Gross profit:
Specific identification $3,860
(2) FIFO $4,080
(3) LIFO $3,525

Compute ending inventory, prepare income statements, and answer questions using FIFO and LIFO.

(LO 2, 3)

P6-7B The management of Creek Co. asks your help in determining the comparative effects of the FIFO and LIFO inventory cost flow methods. For 2014, the accounting records provide the data shown at the top of the next page.

Inventory, January 1 (10,000 units)	$ 47,000
Cost of 100,000 units purchased	532,000
Selling price of 85,000 units sold	740,000
Operating expenses	140,000

Units purchased consisted of 35,000 units at $5.10 on May 10; 35,000 units at $5.30 on August 15; and 30,000 units at $5.60 on November 20. Income taxes are 32%.

Instructions

(a) Prepare comparative condensed income statements for 2014 under FIFO and LIFO. (Show computations of ending inventory.)

(b) Answer the following questions for management.

(1) Which inventory cost flow method produces the most meaningful inventory amount for the balance sheet? Why?

(2) Which inventory cost flow method produces the most meaningful net income? Why?

(3) Which inventory cost flow method is most likely to approximate actual physical flow of the goods? Why?

(4) How much additional cash will be available for management under LIFO than under FIFO? Why?

(5) How much of the gross profit under FIFO is illusory in comparison with the gross profit under LIFO?

(a) Net income
FIFO $109,480
LIFO $98,260

***P6-8B** Yuan Li Inc. is a retailer operating in Edmonton, Alberta. Yuan Li uses the perpetual inventory method. All sales returns from customers result in the goods being returned to inventory; the inventory is not damaged. Assume that there are no credit transactions; all amounts are settled in cash. You are provided with the following information for Yuan Li Inc. for the month of January 2014.

Calculate cost of goods sold and ending inventory under LIFO, FIFO, and moving-average cost under the perpetual system; compare gross profit under each assumption.

(LO 7)

Date	Description	Quantity	Unit Cost or Selling Price
January 1	Beginning inventory	100	$14
January 5	Purchase	150	17
January 8	Sale	110	28
January 10	Sale return	10	28
January 15	Purchase	55	19
January 16	Purchase return	5	19
January 20	Sale	80	32
January 25	Purchase	30	22

Instructions

(a) For each of the following cost flow assumptions, calculate (i) cost of goods sold, (ii) ending inventory, and (iii) gross profit.
(1) LIFO. (2) FIFO. (3) Moving-average cost.

(b) Compare results for the three cost flow assumptions.

Gross profit:
LIFO $2,200
FIFO $2,600
Average $2,452

***P6-9B** Lemansky Co. began operations on July 1. It uses a perpetual inventory system. During July, the company had the following purchases and sales.

Determine ending inventory under a perpetual inventory system.

(LO 7)

	Purchases		
Date	Units	Unit Cost	Sales Units
July 1	5	$120	
July 6			3
July 11	6	$136	
July 14			4
July 21	8	$147	
July 27			6

Instructions

(a) Determine the ending inventory under a perpetual inventory system using (1) FIFO, (2) moving-average cost, and (3) LIFO.

(b) Which costing method produces the highest ending inventory valuation?

(a) Ending inventory
FIFO $882
Avg $852
LIFO $806

Compute gross profit rate and inventory loss using gross profit method.

(LO 8)

***P6-10B** Bristol Company lost all of its inventory in a fire on December 26, 2014. The accounting records showed the following gross profit data for November and December.

	November	December (to 12/26)
Net sales	$600,000	$700,000
Beginning inventory	30,000	33,000
Purchases	368,000	420,000
Purchase returns and allowances	13,300	14,900
Purchase discounts	8,500	9,500
Freight-in	4,800	5,900
Ending inventory	33,000	?

Bristol is fully insured for fire losses but must prepare a report for the insurance company.

Instructions

(a) Compute the gross profit rate for November.

(b) Using the gross profit rate for November, determine the estimated cost of the inventory lost in the fire.

Compute ending inventory using retail method.

(LO 8)

***P6-11B** Hooked on Books uses the retail inventory method to estimate its monthly ending inventories. The following information is available for two of its departments at October 31, 2014.

	Hardcovers		Paperbacks	
	Cost	Retail	Cost	Retail
Beginning inventory	$ 420,000	$ 700,000	$ 280,000	$ 360,000
Purchases	2,094,000	3,200,000	1,155,000	1,540,000
Freight-in	26,000		12,000	
Purchase discounts	44,000		22,000	
Net sales		3,100,000		1,570,000

At December 31, Hooked on Books takes a physical inventory at retail. The actual retail values of the inventories in each department are Hardcovers $790,000 and Paperbacks $335,000.

Instructions

(a) Determine the estimated cost of the ending inventory for each department at October 31, 2014, using the retail inventory method.

(b) Compute the ending inventory at cost for each department at December 31, assuming the cost-to-retail ratios for the year are 65% for Hardcovers and 77% for Paperbacks.

PROBLEMS: SET C

Visit the book's companion website, at **www.wiley.com/college/weygandt**, and choose the Student Companion site to access Problem Set C.

COMPREHENSIVE PROBLEM

CP6 On December 1, 2014, Seattle Company had the account balances shown below.

	Debits		Credits
Cash	$ 4,650	Accumulated Depreciation—Equipment	$ 1,500
Accounts Receivable	3,900	Accounts Payable	3,000
Inventory	1,950*	Common Stock	20,000
Equipment	21,000	Retained Earnings	7,000
	$31,500		$31,500

*(3,000 × $0.65)

The following transactions occurred during December.

Dec. 3 Purchased 4,000 units of inventory on account at a cost of $0.72 per unit.
5 Sold 4,400 units of inventory on account for $0.92 per unit. (It sold 3,000 of the $0.65 units and 1,400 of the $0.72.)
7 Granted the December 5 customer $180 credit for 200 units of inventory returned costing $150. These units were returned to inventory.
17 Purchased 2,200 units of inventory for cash at $0.78 each.
22 Sold 2,000 units of inventory on account for $0.95 per unit. (It sold 2,000 of the $0.72 units.)

Adjustment data:

1. Accrued salaries payable $400.
2. Depreciation $200 per month.

Instructions

(a) Journalize the December transactions and adjusting entries, assuming Seattle uses the perpetual inventory method.
(b) Enter the December 1 balances in the ledger T-accounts and post the December transactions. In addition to the accounts mentioned above, use the following additional accounts: Cost of Goods Sold, Depreciation Expense, Salaries and Wages Expense, Salaries and Wages Payable, Sales Revenue, and Sales Returns and Allowances.
(c) Prepare an adjusted trial balance as of December 31, 2014.
(d) Prepare an income statement for December 2014 and a classified balance sheet at December 31, 2014.
(e) Compute ending inventory and cost of goods sold under FIFO, assuming Seattle Company uses the periodic inventory system.
(f) Compute ending inventory and cost of goods sold under LIFO, assuming Seattle Company uses the periodic inventory system.

CONTINUING COOKIE CHRONICLE

(*Note:* This is a continuation of the Cookie Chronicle from Chapters 1–5.)

CCC6 Natalie is busy establishing both divisions of her business (cookie classes and mixer sales) and completing her business degree. Her goals for the next 11 months are to sell one mixer per month and to give two to three classes per week.

The cost of the fine European mixers is expected to increase. Natalie has just negotiated new terms with Kzinski that include shipping costs in the negotiated purchase price (mixers will be shipped FOB destination). Natalie must choose a cost flow assumption for her mixer inventory.

Go to the book's companion website, www.wiley.com/college/weygandt, to see the completion of this problem.

Broadening Your PERSPECTIVE

Financial Reporting and Analysis

Financial Reporting Problem: PepsiCo, Inc.

BYP6-1 The notes that accompany a company's financial statements provide informative details that would clutter the amounts and descriptions presented in the statements. Refer to the financial statements of PepsiCo, Inc. and the Notes to Consolidated Financial Statements in Appendix A.

Instructions

Answer the following questions. Complete the requirements in millions of dollars, as shown in PepsiCo's annual report.

(a) What did PepsiCo report for the amount of inventories in its consolidated balance sheet at December 25, 2010? At December 26, 2009?

(b) Compute the dollar amount of change and the percentage change in inventories between 2009 and 2010. Compute inventory as a percentage of current assets at December 25, 2010.

(c) How does PepsiCo value its inventories? Which inventory cost flow method does PepsiCo use? (See Notes to the Financial Statements.)

(d) What is the cost of sales (cost of goods sold) reported by PepsiCo for 2010, 2009, and 2008? Compute the percentage of cost of sales to net sales in 2010.

Comparative Analysis Problem: PepsiCo, Inc. vs. The Coca-Cola Company

BYP6-2 PepsiCo's financial statements are presented in Appendix A. Financial statements of The Coca-Cola Company are presented in Appendix B.

Instructions

(a) Based on the information contained in these financial statements, compute the following 2010 ratios for each company.

(1) Inventory turnover ratio.

(2) Days in inventory.

(b) What conclusions concerning the management of the inventory can you draw from these data?

Real-World Focus

BYP6-3 A company's annual report usually will identify the inventory method used. Knowing that, you can analyze the effects of the inventory method on the income statement and balance sheet.

Address: **www.cisco.com,** or go to **www.wiley.com/college/weygandt**

Instructions

Answer the following questions based on the current year's annual report on Cisco's website.

(a) At Cisco's fiscal year-end, what was the inventory on the balance sheet?

(b) How has this changed from the previous fiscal year-end?

(c) How much of the inventory was finished goods?

(d) What inventory method does Cisco use?

Critical Thinking

Decision-Making Across the Organization

BYP6-4 On April 10, 2014, fire damaged the office and warehouse of Ehlert Company. Most of the accounting records were destroyed, but the following account balances were determined as of March 31, 2014: Inventory (January 1, 2014), $80,000; Sales Revenue (January 1–March 31, 2014), $180,000; Purchases (January 1–March 31, 2014), $94,000.

The company's fiscal year ends on December 31. It uses a periodic inventory system.

From an analysis of the April bank statement, you discover cancelled checks of $4,200 for cash purchases during the period April 1–10. Deposits during the same period totaled $20,500. Of that amount, 60% were collections on accounts receivable, and the balance was cash sales.

Correspondence with the company's principal suppliers revealed $12,400 of purchases on account from April 1 to April 10. Of that amount, $1,900 was for merchandise in transit on April 10 that was shipped FOB destination.

Correspondence with the company's principal customers produced acknowledgments of credit sales totaling $37,000 from April 1 to April 10. It was estimated that $5,600 of credit sales will never be acknowledged or recovered from customers.

Ehlert Company reached an agreement with the insurance company that its fire-loss claim should be based on the average of the gross profit rates for the preceding 2 years. The financial statements for 2012 and 2013 showed the following data.

	2013	2012
Net sales	$600,000	$480,000
Cost of goods purchased	404,000	346,400
Beginning inventory	60,000	40,000
Ending inventory	80,000	60,000

Inventory with a cost of $17,000 was salvaged from the fire.

Instructions
With the class divided into groups, answer the following.

(a) Determine the balances in (1) Sales Revenue and (2) Purchases at April 10.
*(b) Determine the average gross profit rate for the years 2012 and 2013. (*Hint:* Find the gross profit rate for each year and divide the sum by 2.)
*(c) Determine the inventory loss as a result of the fire, using the gross profit method.

Communication Activity

BYP6-5 You are the controller of Classic Toys Inc. Kathy McDonnell, the president, recently mentioned to you that she found an error in the 2013 financial statements which she believes has corrected itself. She determined, in discussions with the Purchasing Department, that 2013 ending inventory was overstated by $1 million. Kathy says that the 2014 ending inventory is correct. Thus, she assumes that 2014 income is correct. Kathy says to you, "What happened has happened—there's no point in worrying about it anymore."

Instructions
You conclude that Kathy is incorrect. Write a brief, tactful memo to Kathy, clarifying the situation.

Ethics Case

BYP6-6 Paeth Wholesale Corp. uses the LIFO method of inventory costing. In the current year, profit at Paeth is running unusually high. The corporate tax rate is also high this year, but it is scheduled to decline significantly next year. In an effort to lower the current year's net income and to take advantage of the changing income tax rate, the president of Paeth Wholesale instructs the plant accountant to recommend to the purchasing department a large purchase of inventory for delivery 3 days before the end of the year. The price of the inventory to be purchased has doubled during the year, and the purchase will represent a major portion of the ending inventory value.

Instructions

(a) What is the effect of this transaction on this year's and next year's income statement and income tax expense? Why?
(b) If Paeth Wholesale had been using the FIFO method of inventory costing, would the president give the same directive?
(c) Should the plant accountant order the inventory purchase to lower income? What are the ethical implications of this order?

All About You

BYP6-7 Some of the largest business frauds ever perpetrated have involved the misstatement of inventory. Two classics were at Leslie Fay and McKesson Corporation.

Instructions
There is considerable information regarding inventory frauds available on the Internet. Search for information about one of the two cases mentioned above, or inventory fraud at any other company, and prepare a short explanation of the nature of the inventory fraud.

BYP6-8 Suppose you own a number of wine shops selling mid-level as well as expensive bottled wine. You have been experiencing significant losses from theft at your stores. You suspect that it is a combination of both employee and customer theft. Assuming that it would be cost-effective, would you install video cameras to reduce both employee theft and customer theft?

YES: Most employees and customers are honest. However, some will steal if given the opportunity. Management has a responsibility to employ reasonable, cost-effective approaches to safeguard company assets.

NO: The use of video technology to monitor employees and customers sends a message of distrust. You run the risk of alienating your employees (who may well figure out a way around the cameras anyway). Cameras might also reduce the welcoming atmosphere for your customers, who might find the cameras offensive.

Instructions

Write a response indicating your position regarding the situation, provide support for your view.

FASB Codification Activity

BYP6-9 If your school has a subscription to the FASB Codification, go to *http://aaahq.org/ascLogin.cfm* to log in and prepare responses to the following.

(a) The primary basis for accounting for inventories is cost. How is cost defined in the Codification?

(b) What does the Codification state regarding the use of consistency in the selection or employment of a basis for inventory?

(c) What does the Codification indicate is a justification for the use of the lower-of-cost-or-market for inventory valuation?

Answers to Chapter Questions

Answers to Insight and Accounting Across the Organization Questions

p. 273 A Big Hiccup Q: What steps might the companies take to avoid such a serious disruption in the future? **A:** The manufacturer of the piston rings should spread its manufacturing facilities across a few locations that are far enough apart that they would not all be at risk at once. In addition, the automakers might consider becoming less dependent on a single supplier.

p. 274 Falsifying Inventory to Boost Income Q: What effect does an overstatement of inventory have on a company's financial statements? **A:** The balance sheet looks stronger because inventory and retained earnings are overstated. The income statement looks better because cost of goods sold is understated and income is overstated.

p. 285 Is LIFO Fair? Q: What are the arguments for and against the use of LIFO? **A:** Proponents of LIFO argue that it is conceptually superior because it matches the most recent cost with the most recent selling price. Critics contend that it artificially understates the company's net income and consequently reduces tax payments. Also, because most foreign companies are not allowed to use LIFO, its use by U.S. companies reduces the ability of investors to compare U.S. companies with foreign companies.

p. 289 Improving Inventory Control with RFID Q: Why is inventory control important to managers such as those at Wal-Mart and Best Buy? **A:** In the very competitive environment of discount retailing, where Wal-Mart and Best Buy are major players, small differences in price matter to the customer. Wal-Mart sells a high volume of inventory at a low gross profit rate. When operating in a high-volume, low-margin environment, small cost savings can mean the difference between being profitable or going out of business.

Answers to Self-Test Questions

1. a **2.** b ($180,000 + $35,000) **3.** b **4.** c [(5,000 × $13) + (4,000 × $12)] **5.** d [(8,000 × $11) + (1,000 × $12)] **6.** d ((5,000 × $8) + (15,000 × $10) + (20,000 × $12)) ÷ 40,000 = $10.75; $10.75 × 7,000 **7.** c **8.** d **9.** d (200 × $80) **10.** b **11.** b **12.** d **13.** b $285,000 ÷ [($80,000 + $110,000) ÷ 2] = 3; 365 ÷ 3 ***14.** b [$150,000 − (30% × $150,000)] = $105,000; $135,000 − $105,000 ***15.** d

A Look at IFRS

The major IFRS requirements related to accounting and reporting for inventories are the same as GAAP. The major differences are that IFRS prohibits the use of the LIFO cost flow assumption and determines market in the lower-of-cost-or-market inventory valuation differently.

Key Points

- The requirements for accounting for and reporting inventories are more principles-based under IFRS. That is, GAAP provides more detailed guidelines in inventory accounting.
- The definitions for inventory are essentially similar under IFRS and GAAP. Both define inventory as assets held-for-sale in the ordinary course of business, in the process of production for sale (work in process), or to be consumed in the production of goods or services (e.g., raw materials).
- Who owns the goods—goods in transit or consigned goods—as well as the costs to include in inventory, are accounted for the same under IFRS and GAAP.
- Both GAAP and IFRS permit specific identification where appropriate. IFRS actually requires that the specific identification method be used where the inventory items are not interchangeable (i.e., can be specifically identified). If the inventory items are not specifically identifiable, a cost flow assumption is used. GAAP does not specify situations in which specific identification must be used.
- A major difference between IFRS and GAAP relates to the LIFO cost flow assumption. GAAP permits the use of LIFO for inventory valuation. IFRS prohibits its use. FIFO and average-cost are the only two acceptable cost flow assumptions permitted under IFRS.
- IFRS requires companies to use the same cost flow assumption for all goods of a similar nature. GAAP has no specific requirement in this area.
- In the lower-of-cost-or-market test for inventory valuation, IFRS defines market as net realizable value. Net realizable value is the estimated selling price in the ordinary course of business, less the estimated costs of completion and estimated selling expenses. In other words, net realizable value is the best estimate of the net amounts that inventories are expected to realize. GAAP, on the other hand, defines market as essentially replacement cost.
- Under GAAP, if inventory is written down under the lower-of-cost-or-market valuation, the new basis is now considered its cost. As a result, the inventory may not be written back up to its original cost in a subsequent period. Under IFRS, the write-down may be reversed in a subsequent period up to the amount of the previous write-down. Both the write-down and any subsequent reversal should be reported on the income statement as an expense. An item-by-item approach is generally followed under IFRS.
- An example of the use of lower-of-cost-or-net realizable value under IFRS follows.

Mendel Company has the following four items in its ending inventory as of December 31, 2014. The company uses the lower-of-cost-or-net realizable value approach for inventory valuation following IFRS.

Item No.	Cost	Net Realizable Value
1320	$3,600	$3,400
1333	4,000	4,100
1428	2,800	2,100
1510	5,000	4,700

The computation of the ending inventory value to be reported in the financial statements at December 31, 2014, is as follows.

Item No.	Cost	Net Realizable Value	LCNRV
1320	$ 3,600	$ 3,400	$ 3,400
1333	4,000	4,100	4,000
1428	2,800	2,100	2,100
1510	5,000	4,700	4,700
Total	$15,400	$14,300	$14,200

- Unlike property, plant, and equipment, IFRS does not permit the option of valuing inventories at fair value. As indicated above, IFRS requires inventory to be written down, but inventory cannot be written up above its original cost.
- Similar to GAAP, certain agricultural products and mineral products can be reported at net realizable value using IFRS.

Looking to the Future

One convergence issue that will be difficult to resolve relates to the use of the LIFO cost flow assumption. As indicated, IFRS specifically prohibits its use. Conversely, the LIFO cost flow assumption is widely used in the United States because of its favorable tax advantages. In addition, many argue that LIFO from a financial reporting point of view provides a better matching of current costs against revenue and, therefore, enables companies to compute a more realistic income.

IFRS Practice

IFRS Self-Test Questions

1. Which of the following should *not* be included in the inventory of a company using IFRS?
   (a) Goods held on consignment from another company.
   (b) Goods shipped on consignment to another company.
   (c) Goods in transit from another company shipped FOB shipping point.
   (d) None of the above.
2. Which method of inventory costing is prohibited under IFRS?
   (a) Specific identification.
   (c) FIFO.
   (b) LIFO.
   (d) Average-cost.
3. Yang Company purchased 2,000 widgets and has 400 widgets in its ending inventory at a cost of $90 each and a current replacement cost of $80 each. The net realizable value of each unit in the ending inventory is $70. The ending inventory under lower-of-cost-or-net realizable value is:
   (a) $36,000.
   (c) $28,000.
   (b) $32,000.
   (d) None of the above.
4. Specific identification:
   (a) must be used under IFRS if the inventory items are not interchangeable.
   (b) cannot be used under IFRS.
   (c) cannot be used under GAAP.
   (d) must be used under IFRS if it would result in the most conservative net income.
5. IFRS requires the following:
   (a) Ending inventory is written up and down to net realizable value each reporting period.
   (b) Ending inventory is written down to net realizable value but cannot be written up.
   (c) Ending inventory is written down to net realizable value and may be written up in future periods to its net realizable value but not above its original cost.
   (d) Ending inventory is written down to net realizable value and may be written up in future periods to its net realizable value.

IFRS Exercises

IFRS6-1 Briefly describe some of the similarities and differences between GAAP and IFRS with respect to the accounting for inventories.

IFRS6-2 LaTour Inc. is based in France and prepares its financial statements in accordance with IFRS. In 2014, it reported (in euros) cost of goods sold of €578 million and average inventory of €154 million. Briefly discuss how analysis of LaTour's inventory turnover ratio (and comparisons to a company using GAAP) might be affected by differences in inventory accounting between IFRS and GAAP.

IFRS6-3 Franklin Company has the following four items in its ending inventory as of December 31, 2014. The company uses the lower-of-cost-or-net realizable value approach for inventory valuation following IFRS.

Item No.	Cost	Net Realizable Value
AB	$1,700	$1,400
TRX	2,200	2,300
NWA	7,800	7,100
SGH	3,000	3,700

Compute the lower-of-cost-or-net realizable value.

International Financial Reporting Problem: Zetar plc

IFRS6-4 The financial statements of Zetar plc are presented in Appendix C. The company's complete annual report, including the notes to its financial statements, is available at *www.zetarplc.com.*

Instructions

Using the notes to the company's financial statements, answer the following questions.

(a) What cost flow assumption does the company use to value inventory?

(b) What was the amount of expense that the company reported for inventory write-downs during 2010?

(c) What amount of raw materials, work in process, and finished goods inventory did the company report at April 30, 2010?

Answers to IFRS Self-Test Questions

1. a **2.** b **3.** c **4.** a **5.** c

✔ Remember to go back to The Navigator box on the chapter opening page and check off your completed work.

Chapter 7

Fraud, Internal Control, and Cash

Feature Story

Minding the Money in Moose Jaw

If you're ever looking for a cappuccino in Moose Jaw, Saskatchewan, stop by Stephanie's Gourmet Coffee and More, located on Main Street. Staff there serve, on average, 650 cups of coffee a day, including both regular and specialty coffees, not to mention soups, Italian sandwiches, and a wide assortment of gourmet cheesecakes.

"We've got high school students who come here, and students from the community college," says owner/manager Stephanie Mintenko, who has run the place since opening it in 1995. "We have customers who are retired, and others who are working people and have only 30 minutes for lunch. We have to be pretty quick."

That means that the cashiers have to be efficient. Like most businesses where purchases are low-cost and high-volume, cash control has to be simple.

"We have an electronic cash register, but it's not the fancy new kind where you just punch in the item," explains Ms. Mintenko. "You have to punch in the prices." The machine does keep track of sales in several categories, however. Cashiers punch a button to indicate whether each item is a beverage, a meal, or a Wi-Fi charge for the cafe's Internet service. An internal tape in the machine keeps a record of

✔ The Navigator

- Scan Learning Objectives
- Read Feature Story
- Read Preview
- Read text and answer **DO IT!** p. 335 p. 338 p. 343 p. 351
- Work Comprehensive **DO IT!** p. 353
- Review Summary of Learning Objectives
- Answer Self-Test Questions
- Complete Assignments
- Go to **WileyPLUS** for practice and tutorials
-  Read A Look at IFRS p. 375

Learning Objectives

After studying this chapter, you should be able to:

1. Define fraud and internal control.
2. Identify the principles of internal control activities.
3. Explain the applications of internal control principles to cash receipts.
4. Explain the applications of internal control principles to cash disbursements.
5. Describe the operation of a petty cash fund.
6. Indicate the control features of a bank account.
7. Prepare a bank reconciliation.
8. Explain the reporting of cash.

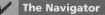

 **The Navigator**

all transactions; the customer receives a receipt only upon request.

There is only one cash register. "Up to three of us might operate it on any given shift, including myself," says Ms. Mintenko.

She and her staff do two "cashouts" each day—one with the shift change at 5:00 p.m. and one when the shop closes at 10:00 p.m. At each cashout, they count the cash in the register drawer. That amount, minus the cash change carried forward (the float), should match the shift total on the register tape. If there's a discrepancy, they do another count. Then, if necessary, "we go through the whole tape to find the mistake," she explains. "It usually turns out to be someone who punched in $18 instead of $1.80, or something like that."

Ms. Mintenko sends all the cash tapes and float totals to a bookkeeper, who double-checks everything and provides regular reports. "We try to keep the accounting simple, so we can concentrate on making great coffee and food."

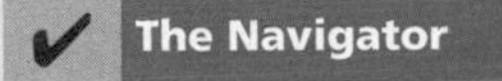

Preview of Chapter 7

As the story about recording cash sales at Stephanie's Gourmet Coffee and More indicates, control of cash is important to ensure that fraud does not occur. Companies also need controls to safeguard other types of assets. For example, Stephanie's undoubtedly has controls to prevent the theft of food and supplies, and controls to prevent the theft of tableware and dishes from its kitchen.

In this chapter, we explain the essential features of an internal control system and how it prevents fraud. We also describe how those controls apply to a specific asset—cash. The applications include some controls with which you may be already familiar, such as the use of a bank.

The content and organization of Chapter 7 are as follows.

FRAUD, INTERNAL CONTROL, AND CASH

Fraud and Internal Control	Cash Controls	Control Features: Use of a Bank	Reporting Cash
• Fraud • The Sarbanes-Oxley Act • Internal control • Principles of internal control activities • Limitations	• Cash receipts controls • Cash disbursements controls	• Making deposits • Writing checks • Bank statements • Reconciling the bank account • Electronic funds transfer (EFT) system	• Cash equivalents • Restricted cash

✔ The Navigator

Fraud and Internal Control

LEARNING OBJECTIVE 1

Define fraud and internal control.

The Feature Story describes many of the internal control procedures used by Stephanie's Gourmet Coffee and More. These procedures are necessary to discourage employees from fraudulent activities.

Fraud

A **fraud** is a dishonest act by an employee that results in personal benefit to the employee at a cost to the employer. Examples of fraud reported in the financial press include:

- A bookkeeper in a small company diverted $750,000 of bill payments to a personal bank account over a three-year period.
- A shipping clerk with 28 years of service shipped $125,000 of merchandise to himself.
- A computer operator embezzled $21 million from Wells Fargo Bank over a two-year period.
- A church treasurer "borrowed" $150,000 of church funds to finance a friend's business dealings.

Why does fraud occur? The three main factors that contribute to fraudulent activity are depicted by the **fraud triangle** in Illustration 7-1 (in the margin).

Illustration 7-1
Fraud triangle

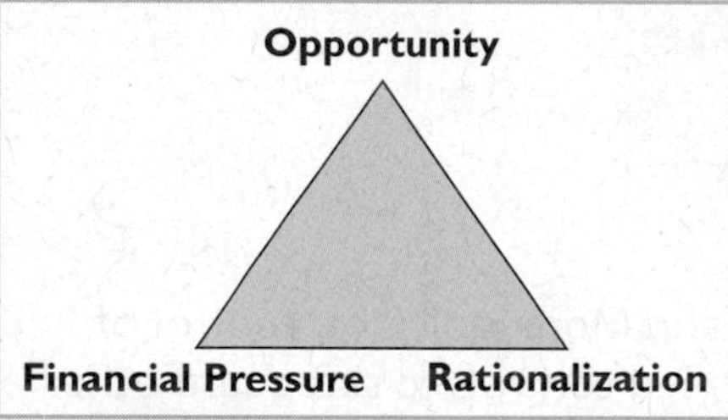

The most important element of the fraud triangle is **opportunity**. For an employee to commit fraud, the workplace environment must provide opportunities that an employee can take advantage of. Opportunities occur when the workplace lacks sufficient controls to deter and detect fraud. For example, inadequate monitoring of employee actions can create opportunities for theft and can embolden employees because they believe they will not be caught.

A second factor that contributes to fraud is **financial pressure**. Employees sometimes commit fraud because of personal financial problems caused by too much debt. Or, they might commit fraud because they want to lead a lifestyle that they cannot afford on their current salary.

The third factor that contributes to fraud is **rationalization**. In order to justify their fraud, employees rationalize their dishonest actions. For example, employees sometimes justify fraud because they believe they are underpaid while the employer is making lots of money. Employees feel justified in stealing because they believe they deserve to be paid more.

The Sarbanes-Oxley Act

What can be done to prevent or to detect fraud? After numerous corporate scandals came to light in the early 2000s, Congress addressed this issue by passing the **Sarbanes-Oxley Act (SOX)**. Under SOX, all publicly traded U.S. corporations are required to maintain an adequate system of internal control. Corporate executives and boards of directors must ensure that these controls are reliable and effective. In addition, independent outside auditors must attest to the adequacy of the internal control system. Companies that fail to comply are subject to fines, and company officers can be imprisoned. SOX also created the Public Company Accounting Oversight Board (PCAOB), to establish auditing standards and regulate auditor activity.

One poll found that 60% of investors believe that SOX helps safeguard their stock investments. Many say they would be unlikely to invest in a company that fails to follow SOX requirements. Although some corporate executives have criticized the time and expense involved in following the SOX requirements, SOX appears to be working well. For example, the chief accounting officer of Eli Lily noted that SOX triggered a comprehensive review of how the company documents controls. This review uncovered redundancies and pointed out controls that needed to be added. In short, it added up to time and money well spent. And the finance chief at General Electric noted, "We have seen value in SOX. It helps build investors' trust and gives them more confidence."[1]

Internal Control

Internal control consists of all the related methods and measures adopted within an organization to safeguard its assets, enhance the reliability of its accounting records, increase efficiency of operations, and ensure compliance with laws and regulations. Internal control systems have five primary components as listed below.[2]

- **A control environment.** It is the responsibility of top management to make it clear that the organization values integrity and that unethical activity will not be tolerated. This component is often referred to as the "tone at the top."
- **Risk assessment.** Companies must identify and analyze the various factors that create risk for the business and must determine how to manage these risks.
- **Control activities.** To reduce the occurrence of fraud, management must design policies and procedures to address the specific risks faced by the company.
- **Information and communication.** The internal control system must capture and communicate all pertinent information both down and up the organization, as well as communicate information to appropriate external parties.
- **Monitoring.** Internal control systems must be monitored periodically for their adequacy. Significant deficiencies need to be reported to top management and/or the board of directors.

PEOPLE, PLANET, AND PROFIT INSIGHT

And the Controls Are . . .

Internal controls are important for an effective financial reporting system. The same is true for sustainability reporting. An effective system of internal controls for sustainability reporting will help in the following ways: (1) prevent the unauthorized use of data; (2) provide reasonable assurance that the information is accurate, valid, and complete; and (3) report information that is consistent with the overall sustainability accounting policies. With these types of controls, users will have the confidence that they can use the sustainability information effectively.

Some regulators are calling for even more assurance through audits of this information. Companies that potentially can cause environmental damage through greenhouse gases are subject to reporting requirements as well as companies in the mining and extractive industries. And, as demand for more information in the sustainability area expands, the need for audits of this information will grow.

Why is sustainability information important to investors? (See page 374.)

[1]"Corporate Regulation Must Be Working—There's a Backlash," *Wall Street Journal*, (June 16, 2004), p. C1; and Judith Burns, "Is Sarbanes-Oxley Working?" *Wall Street Journal*, (June 21, 2004), pp. R8–R9.

[2]The Committee of Sponsoring Organizations of the Treadway Commission, "Internal Control—Integrated Framework," *www.coso.org/publications/executive_summary_integrated_framework.htm* (accessed March 2008).

LEARNING OBJECTIVE 2

Identify the principles of internal control activities.

Principles of Internal Control Activities

Each of the five components of an internal control system is important. Here, we will focus on one component, the control activities. The reason? These activities are the backbone of the company's efforts to address the risks it faces, such as fraud. The specific control activities used by a company will vary, depending on management's assessment of the risks faced. This assessment is heavily influenced by the size and nature of the company.

The six principles of control activities are as follows.

- Establishment of responsibility
- Segregation of duties
- Documentation procedures
- Physical controls
- Independent internal verification
- Human resource controls

We explain these principles in the following sections. You should recognize that they apply to most companies and are relevant to both manual and computerized accounting systems.

It's your shift now. I'm turning in my cash drawer and heading home.

Transfer of Cash Drawers

ESTABLISHMENT OF RESPONSIBILITY

An essential principle of internal control is to assign responsibility to specific employees. **Control is most effective when only one person is responsible for a given task.**

To illustrate, assume that the cash on hand at the end of the day in a Safeway supermarket is $10 short of the cash rung up on the cash register. If only one person has operated the register, the shift manager can quickly determine responsibility for the shortage. If two or more individuals have worked the register, it may be impossible to determine who is responsible for the error. In the Feature Story, the principle of establishing responsibility does not appear to be strictly applied by Stephanie's Gourmet Coffee and More, since three people operate the cash register on any given shift.

Establishing responsibility often requires limiting access only to authorized personnel, and then identifying those personnel. For example, the automated systems used by many companies have mechanisms such as identifying passcodes that keep track of who made a journal entry, who rang up a sale, or who entered an inventory storeroom at a particular time. Use of identifying passcodes enables the company to establish responsibility by identifying the particular employee who carried out the activity.

ANATOMY OF A FRAUD

Maureen Frugali was a training supervisor for claims processing at Colossal Healthcare. As a standard part of the claims processing training program, Maureen created fictitious claims for use by trainees. These fictitious claims were then sent to the accounts payable department. After the training claims had been processed, she was to notify Accounts Payable of all fictitious claims, so that they would not be paid. However, she did not inform Accounts Payable about every fictitious claim. She created some fictitious claims for entities that she controlled (that is, she would receive the payment), and she let Accounts Payable pay her.

Total take: $11 million

The Missing Control

Establishment of responsibility. The health-care company did not adequately restrict the responsibility for authoring and approving claims transactions. The training supervisor should not have been authorized to create claims in the company's "live" system.

Source: Adapted from Wells, *Fraud Casebook* (2007), pp. 61–70.

SEGREGATION OF DUTIES

Segregation of duties is indispensable in an internal control system. There are two common applications of this principle:

1. Different individuals should be responsible for related activities.
2. The responsibility for record-keeping for an asset should be separate from the physical custody of that asset.

The rationale for segregation of duties is this: **The work of one employee should, without a duplication of effort, provide a reliable basis for evaluating the work of another employee.** For example, the personnel that design and program computerized systems should not be assigned duties related to day-to-day use of the system. Otherwise, they could design the system to benefit them personally and conceal the fraud through day-to-day use.

SEGREGATION OF RELATED ACTIVITIES **Making one individual responsible for related activities increases the potential for errors and irregularities.** For example, companies should assign related *purchasing activities* to different individuals. Related purchasing activities include ordering merchandise, order approval, receiving goods, authorizing payment, and paying for goods or services. Various frauds are possible when one person handles related purchasing activities. For example:

- If a purchasing agent is allowed to order goods without obtaining supervisory approval, the likelihood of the purchasing agent receiving kickbacks from suppliers increases.
- If an employee who orders goods also handles receipt of the goods and invoice, as well as payment authorization, he or she might authorize payment for a fictitious invoice.

These abuses are less likely to occur when companies divide the purchasing tasks.

Similarly, companies should assign related *sales activities* to different individuals. Related selling activities include making a sale, shipping (or delivering) the goods to the customer, billing the customer, and receiving payment. Various frauds are possible when one person handles related sales transactions. For example:

- If a salesperson can make a sale without obtaining supervisory approval, he or she might make sales at unauthorized prices to increase sales commissions.
- A shipping clerk who also has access to accounting records could ship goods to himself.
- A billing clerk who handles billing and receipt could understate the amount billed for sales made to friends and relatives.

These abuses are less likely to occur when companies divide the sales tasks: The salespeople make the sale; the shipping department ships the goods on the basis of the sales order; and the billing department prepares the sales invoice after comparing the sales order with the report of goods shipped.

ANATOMY OF A FRAUD

Lawrence Fairbanks, the assistant vice-chancellor of communications at Aesop University, was allowed to make purchases of under $2,500 for his department without external approval. Unfortunately, he also sometimes bought items for himself, such as expensive antiques and other collectibles. How did he do it? He replaced the vendor invoices he received with fake vendor invoices that he created. The fake invoices had descriptions that were more consistent with the communications department's purchases. He submitted these fake invoices to the accounting department as the basis for their journal entries and to the accounts payable department as the basis for payment.

Total take: $475,000

The Missing Control

Segregation of duties. The university had not properly segregated related purchasing activities. Lawrence was ordering items, receiving the items, and receiving the invoice. By receiving the invoice, he had control over the documents that were used to account for the purchase and thus was able to substitute a fake invoice.

Source: Adapted from Wells, *Fraud Casebook* (2007), pp. 3–15.

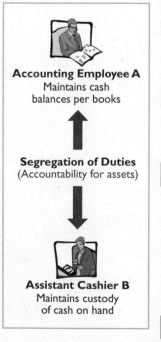

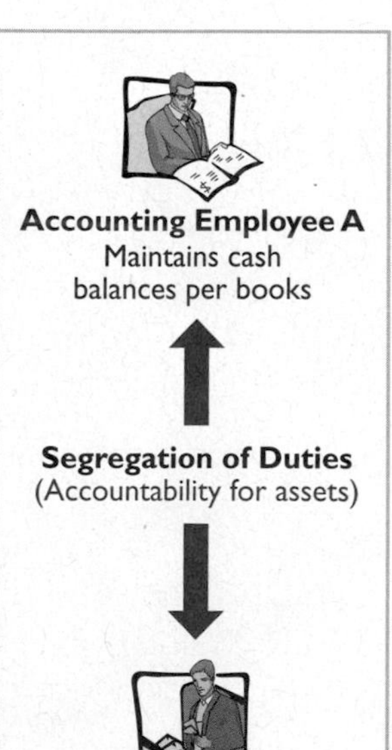

SEGREGATION OF RECORD-KEEPING FROM PHYSICAL CUSTODY The accountant should have neither physical custody of the asset nor access to it. Likewise, the custodian of the asset should not maintain or have access to the accounting records. **The custodian of the asset is not likely to convert the asset to personal use when one employee maintains the record of the asset, and a different employee has physical custody of the asset.** The separation of accounting responsibility from the custody of assets is especially important for cash and inventories because these assets are very vulnerable to fraud.

ANATOMY OF A FRAUD

Angela Bauer was an accounts payable clerk for Aggasiz Construction Company. She prepared and issued checks to vendors and reconciled bank statements. Angela perpetrated a fraud in this way: She wrote checks for costs that the company had not actually incurred (e.g., fake taxes). A supervisor then approved and signed the checks. Before issuing the check, though, Angela would "white-out" the payee line on the check and change it to personal accounts that she controlled. She was able to conceal the theft because she also reconciled the bank account. That is, nobody else ever saw that the checks had been altered.

Total take: $570,000

The Missing Control

Segregation of duties. Aggasiz Construction Company did not properly segregate record-keeping from physical custody. Angela had physical custody of the checks, which essentially was control of the cash. She also had record-keeping responsibility because she prepared the bank reconciliation.

Source: Adapted from Wells, *Fraud Casebook* (2007), pp. 100–107.

DOCUMENTATION PROCEDURES

Documents provide evidence that transactions and events have occurred. At Stephanie's Gourmet Coffee and More, the cash register tape is the restaurant's documentation for the sale and the amount of cash received. Similarly, a shipping document indicates that the goods have been shipped, and a sales invoice indicates that the company has billed the customer for the goods. By requiring signatures (or initials) on the documents, the company can identify the individual(s) responsible for the transaction or event. Companies should document transactions when the transaction occurs.

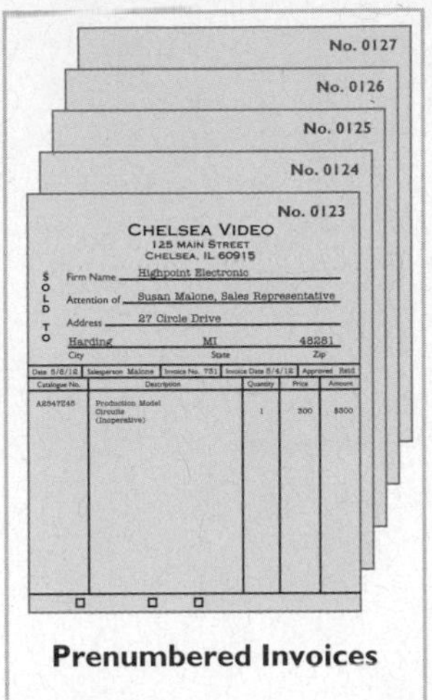

Prenumbered Invoices

Companies should establish procedures for documents. First, whenever possible, companies should use **prenumbered documents, and all documents should be accounted for**. Prenumbering helps to prevent a transaction from being recorded more than once, or conversely, from not being recorded at all. Second, the control system should require that employees **promptly forward source documents for accounting entries to the accounting department. This control measure helps to ensure timely recording of the transaction** and contributes directly to the accuracy and reliability of the accounting records.

ANATOMY OF A FRAUD

To support their reimbursement requests for travel costs incurred, employees at Mod Fashions Corporation's design center were required to submit receipts. The receipts could include the detailed bill provided for a meal, or the credit card receipt provided when the credit card payment is made, or a copy of the employee's monthly credit card bill that listed the item. A number of the designers who frequently traveled together came up with a fraud scheme: They submitted claims for the same expenses. For example, if they had a meal together that cost $200, one person submitted the detailed meal bill, another submitted the credit card receipt, and a third submitted a monthly credit card bill showing the meal as a line item. Thus, all three received a $200 reimbursement.

Total take: $75,000

The Missing Control

Documentation procedures. Mod Fashions should require the original, detailed receipt. It should not accept photocopies, and it should not accept credit card statements. In addition, documentation procedures could be further improved by requiring the use of a corporate credit card (rather than a personal credit card) for all business expenses.

Source: Adapted from Wells, *Fraud Casebook* (2007), pp. 79–90.

PHYSICAL CONTROLS

Use of physical controls is essential. *Physical controls* relate to the safeguarding of assets and enhance the accuracy and reliability of the accounting records. Illustration 7-2 shows examples of these controls.

Illustration 7-2
Physical controls

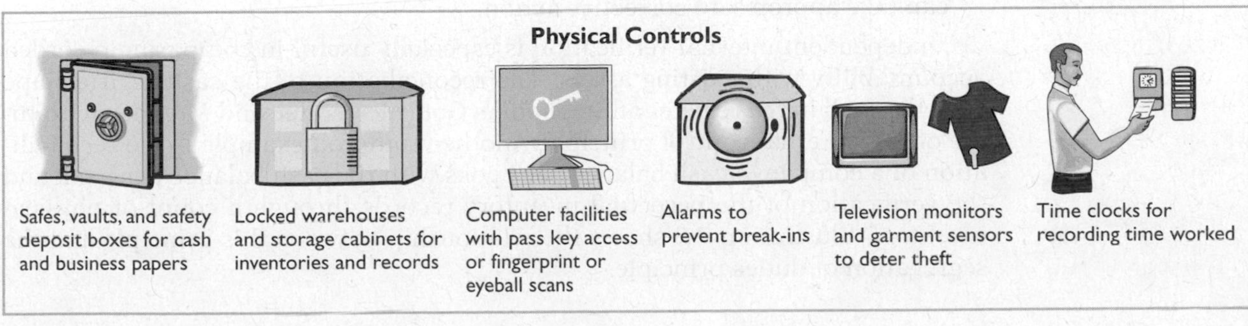

Physical Controls
Safes, vaults, and safety deposit boxes for cash and business papers
Locked warehouses and storage cabinets for inventories and records
Computer facilities with pass key access or fingerprint or eyeball scans
Alarms to prevent break-ins
Television monitors and garment sensors to deter theft
Time clocks for recording time worked

ANATOMY OF A FRAUD

At Centerstone Health, a large insurance company, the mailroom each day received insurance applications from prospective customers. Mailroom employees scanned the applications into electronic documents before the applications were processed. Once the applications are scanned they can be accessed online by authorized employees.

Insurance agents at Centerstone Health earn commissions based upon successful applications. The sales agent's name is listed on the application. However, roughly 15% of the applications are from customers who did not work with a sales agent. Two friends—Alex, an employee in record-keeping, and Parviz, a sales agent—thought up a way to perpetrate a fraud. Alex identified scanned applications that did not list a sales agent. After business hours, he entered the mailroom and found the hard-copy applications that did not show a sales agent. He wrote in Parviz's name as the sales agent and then rescanned the application for processing. Parviz received the commission, which the friends then split.

Total take: $240,000

The Missing Control

Physical controls. Centerstone Health lacked two basic physical controls that could have prevented this fraud. First, the mailroom should have been locked during nonbusiness hours, and access during business hours should have been tightly controlled. Second, the scanned applications supposedly could be accessed only by authorized employees using their passwords. However, the password for each employee was the same as the employee's user ID. Since employee user-ID numbers were available to all other employees, all employees knew all other employees' passwords. Unauthorized employees could access the scanned applications. Thus, Alex could enter the system using another employee's password and access the scanned applications.

Source: Adapted from Wells, *Fraud Casebook* (2007), pp. 316–326.

INDEPENDENT INTERNAL VERIFICATION

Most internal control systems provide for **independent internal verification**. This principle involves the review of data prepared by employees. To obtain maximum benefit from independent internal verification:

1. Companies should verify records periodically or on a surprise basis.
2. An employee who is independent of the personnel responsible for the information should make the verification.
3. Discrepancies and exceptions should be reported to a management level that can take appropriate corrective action.

Independent internal verification is especially useful in comparing recorded accountability with existing assets. The reconciliation of the cash register tape with the cash in the register at Stephanie's Gourmet Coffee and More is an example of this internal control principle. Another common example is the reconciliation of a company's cash balance per books with the cash balance per bank and the verification of the perpetual inventory records through a count of physical inventory. Illustration 7-3 shows the relationship between this principle and the segregation of duties principle.

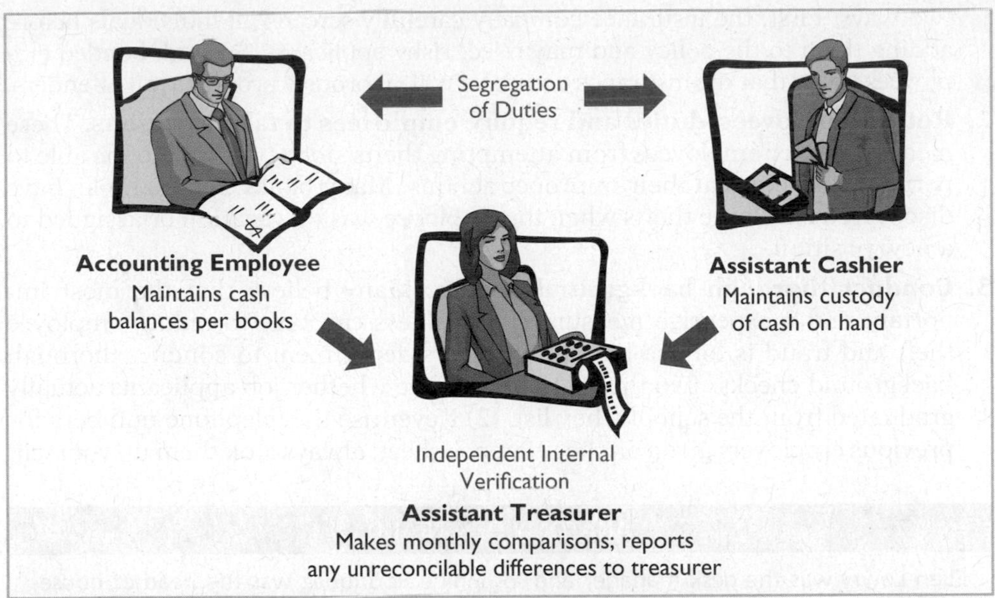

Illustration 7-3
Comparison of segregation of duties principle with independent internal verification principle

ANATOMY OF A FRAUD

Bobbi Jean Donnelly, the office manager for Mod Fashions Corporations design center, was responsible for preparing the design center budget and reviewing expense reports submitted by design center employees. Her desire to upgrade her wardrobe got the better of her, and she enacted a fraud that involved filing expense-reimbursement requests for her own personal clothing purchases. She was able to conceal the fraud because she was responsible for reviewing all expense reports, including her own. In addition, she sometimes was given ultimate responsibility for signing off on the expense reports when her boss was "too busy." Also, because she controlled the budget, when she submitted her expenses, she coded them to budget items that she knew were running under budget, so that they would not catch anyone's attention.

Total take: $275,000

The Missing Control

Independent internal verification. Bobbi Jean's boss should have verified her expense reports. When asked what he thought her expenses for a year were, the boss said about $10,000. At $115,000 per year, her actual expenses were more than 10 times what would have been expected. However, because he was "too busy" to verify her expense reports or to review the budget, he never noticed.

Source: Adapted from Wells, *Fraud Casebook* (2007), pp. 79–90.

Large companies often assign independent internal verification to internal auditors. **Internal auditors** are company employees who continuously evaluate the effectiveness of the company's internal control systems. They review the activities of departments and individuals to determine whether prescribed internal controls are being followed. They also recommend improvements when needed. In fact, most fraud is discovered by the company through internal mechanisms such as existing internal controls and internal audits. For example, the alleged fraud at WorldCom, involving billions of dollars, was uncovered by an internal auditor.

HUMAN RESOURCE CONTROLS

Human resource control activities include the following.

1. **Bond employees who handle cash. Bonding** involves obtaining insurance protection against theft by employees. It contributes to the safeguarding of cash in

two ways: First, the insurance company carefully screens all individuals before adding them to the policy and may reject risky applicants. Second, bonded employees know that the insurance company will vigorously prosecute all offenders.

2. **Rotate employees' duties and require employees to take vacations.** These measures deter employees from attempting thefts since they will not be able to permanently conceal their improper actions. Many banks, for example, have discovered employee thefts when the employee was on vacation or assigned to a new position.
3. **Conduct thorough background checks.** Many believe that the most important and inexpensive measure any business can take to reduce employee theft and fraud is for the human resources department to conduct thorough background checks. Two tips: (1) Check to see whether job applicants actually graduated from the schools they list. (2) Never use the telephone numbers for previous employers given on the reference sheet; always look them up yourself.

ANATOMY OF A FRAUD

Ellen Lowry was the desk manager and Josephine Rodriquez was the head of housekeeping at the Excelsior Inn, a luxury hotel. The two best friends were so dedicated to their jobs that they never took vacations, and they frequently filled in for other employees. In fact, Ms. Rodriquez, whose job as head of housekeeping did not include cleaning rooms, often cleaned rooms herself, "just to help the staff keep up." These two "dedicated" employees, working as a team, found a way to earn a little more cash. Ellen, the desk manager, provided significant discounts to guests who paid with cash. She kept the cash and did not register the guest in the hotel's computerized system. Instead, she took the room out of circulation "due to routine maintenance." Because the room did not show up as being used, it did not receive a normal housekeeping assignment. Instead, Josephine, the head of housekeeping, cleaned the rooms during the guests' stay.

Total take: $95,000

The Missing Control

Human resource controls. Ellen, the desk manager, had been fired by a previous employer after being accused of fraud. If the Excelsior Inn had conducted a thorough background check, it would not have hired her. The hotel fraud was detected when Ellen missed work for a few days due to illness. A system of mandatory vacations and rotating days off would have increased the chances of detecting the fraud before it became so large.

Source: Adapted from Wells, *Fraud Casebook* (2007), pp. 145–155.

ACCOUNTING ACROSS THE ORGANIZATION

SOX Boosts the Role of Human Resources

Under SOX, a company needs to keep track of employees' degrees and certifications to ensure that employees continue to meet the specified requirements of a job. Also, to ensure proper employee supervision and proper separation of duties, companies must develop and monitor an organizational chart. When one corporation went through this exercise, it found that out of 17,000 employees, there were 400 people who did not report to anyone. The corporation also had 35 people who reported to each other. In addition, if an employee complains of an unfair firing and mentions financial issues at the company, HR must refer the case to the company audit committee and possibly to its legal counsel.

Why would unsupervised employees or employees who report to each other represent potential internal control threats? (See page 374.)

Limitations of Internal Control

Companies generally design their systems of internal control to provide **reasonable assurance** of proper safeguarding of assets and reliability of the accounting records. The concept of reasonable assurance rests on the premise that the costs of establishing control procedures should not exceed their expected benefit.

To illustrate, consider shoplifting losses in retail stores. Stores could eliminate such losses by having a security guard stop and search customers as they leave the store. But, store managers have concluded that the negative effects of such a procedure cannot be justified. Instead, they have attempted to control shoplifting losses by less costly procedures. They post signs saying, "We reserve the right to inspect all packages" and "All shoplifters will be prosecuted." They use hidden TV cameras and store detectives to monitor customer activity, and they install sensor equipment at exits.

Helpful Hint
Controls may vary with the risk level of the activity. For example, management may consider cash to be high risk and maintaining inventories in the stockroom as low risk. Thus, management would have stricter controls for cash.

The **human element** is an important factor in every system of internal control. A good system can become ineffective as a result of employee fatigue, carelessness, or indifference. For example, a receiving clerk may not bother to count goods received and may just "fudge" the counts. Occasionally, two or more individuals may work together to get around prescribed controls. Such **collusion** can significantly reduce the effectiveness of a system, eliminating the protection offered by segregation of duties. No system of internal control is perfect.

The size of the business also may impose limitations on internal control. A small company, for example, may find it difficult to segregate duties or to provide for independent internal verification.

ETHICS INSIGHT

Big Theft at Small Companies

A study by the Association of Certified Fraud Examiners indicates that businesses with fewer than 100 employees are most at risk for employee theft. In fact, 38% of frauds occurred at companies with fewer than 100 employees. The median loss at small companies was $200,000, which was higher than the median fraud at companies with more than 10,000 employees ($147,000). A $200,000 loss can threaten the very existence of a small company.

Source: 2008 Report to the Nation on Occupational Fraud and Abuse, Association of Certified Fraud Examiners, *www.acfe.com/documents/2008-rttn.pdf*, p. 26.

Why are small companies more susceptible to employee theft? (See page 374.)

> DO IT!

Control Activities

Identify which control activity is violated in each of the following situations, and explain how the situation creates an opportunity for a fraud.

1. The person with primary responsibility for reconciling the bank account is also the company's accountant and makes all bank deposits.
2. Wellstone Company's treasurer received an award for distinguished service because he had not taken a vacation in 30 years.
3. In order to save money spent on order slips and to reduce time spent keeping track of order slips, a local bar/restaurant does not buy prenumbered order slips.

Action Plan

✔ Familiarize yourself with each of the control activities summarized on page 328.

✔ Understand the nature of the frauds that each control activity is intended to address.

Solution

1. Violates the control activity of segregation of duties. Record-keeping should be separate from physical custody. As a consequence, the employee could embezzle cash and make journal entries to hide the theft.
2. Violates the control activity of human resource controls. Key employees must take vacations. Otherwise, the treasurer, who manages the company's cash, might embezzle cash and use his position to conceal the theft.
3. Violates the control activity of documentation procedures. If prenumbered documents are not used, then it is virtually impossible to account for the documents. As a consequence, an employee could write up a dinner sale, receive the cash from the customer, and then throw away the order slip and keep the cash.

Related exercise material: **BE7-1, BE7-2, BE7-3, BE7-4, E7-1,** and  **7-1.**

✔ **The Navigator**

Cash Controls

LEARNING OBJECTIVE 3

Explain the applications of internal control principles to cash receipts.

Cash is the one asset that is readily convertible into any other type of asset. It also is easily concealed and transported, and is highly desired. Because of these characteristics, **cash is the asset most susceptible to fraudulent activities.** In addition, because of the large volume of cash transactions, numerous errors may occur in executing and recording them. To safeguard cash and to ensure the accuracy of the accounting records for cash, effective internal control over cash is critical.

Cash Receipts Controls

Illustration 7-4 shows how the internal control principles explained earlier apply to cash receipts transactions. As you might expect, companies vary considerably

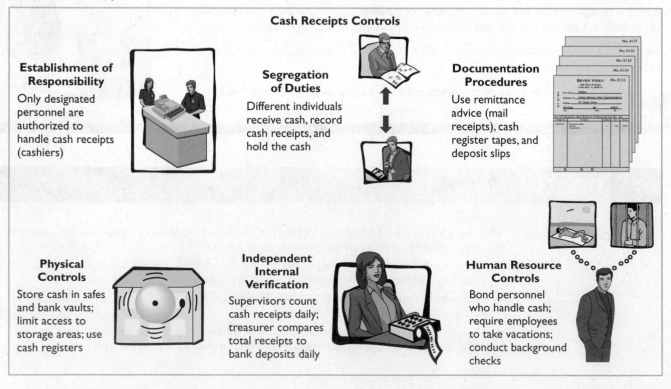

Illustration 7-4
Application of internal control principles to cash receipts

Cash Receipts Controls

Establishment of Responsibility
Only designated personnel are authorized to handle cash receipts (cashiers)

Segregation of Duties
Different individuals receive cash, record cash receipts, and hold the cash

Documentation Procedures
Use remittance advice (mail receipts), cash register tapes, and deposit slips

Physical Controls
Store cash in safes and bank vaults; limit access to storage areas; use cash registers

Independent Internal Verification
Supervisors count cash receipts daily; treasurer compares total receipts to bank deposits daily

Human Resource Controls
Bond personnel who handle cash; require employees to take vacations; conduct background checks

in how they apply these principles. To illustrate internal control over cash receipts, we will examine control activities for a retail store with both over-the-counter and mail receipts.

OVER-THE-COUNTER RECEIPTS

In retail businesses, control of over-the-counter receipts centers on cash registers that are visible to customers. A cash sale is rung up on a cash register, with the amount clearly visible to the customer. This activity prevents the cashier from ringing up a lower amount and pocketing the difference. The customer receives an itemized cash register receipt slip and is expected to count the change received. The cash register's tape is locked in the register until a supervisor removes it. This tape accumulates the daily transactions and totals.

At the end of the clerk's shift, the clerk counts the cash and sends the cash and the count to the cashier. The cashier counts the cash, prepares a deposit slip, and deposits the cash at the bank. The cashier also sends a duplicate of the deposit slip to the accounting department to indicate cash received. The supervisor removes the cash register tape and sends it to the accounting department as the basis for a journal entry to record the cash received. Illustration 7-5 summarizes this process.

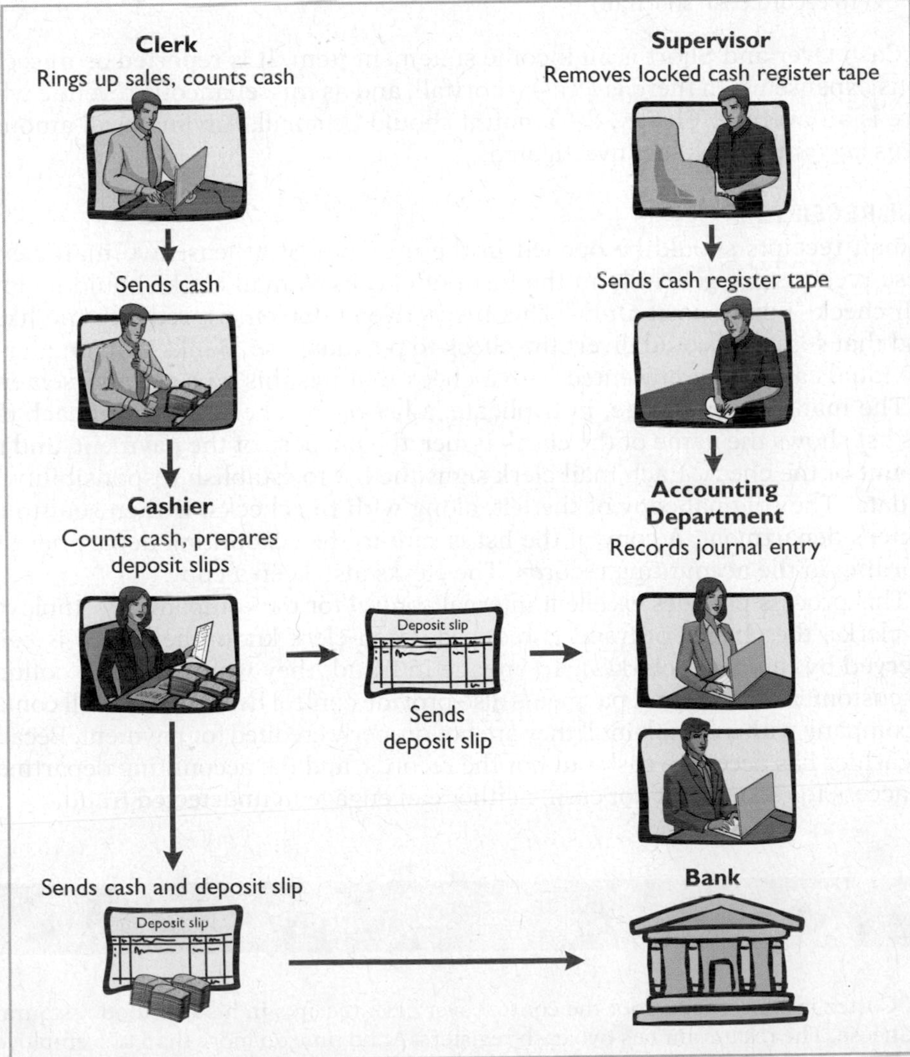

Illustration 7-5
Control of over-the-counter receipts

Helpful Hint
Flowcharts such as this one enhance the understanding of the flow of documents, the processing steps, and the internal control procedures.

This system for handling cash receipts uses an important internal control principle—segregation of record-keeping from physical custody. The supervisor has access to the cash register tape but **not** to the cash. The clerk and the cashier have access to the cash but **not** to the register tape. In addition, the cash register tape provides documentation and enables independent internal verification. Use of these three principles of internal control (segregation of record-keeping from physical custody, documentation, and independent internal verification) provides an effective system of internal control. Any attempt at fraudulent activity should be detected unless there is collusion among the employees.

In some instances, the amount deposited at the bank will not agree with the cash recorded in the accounting records based on the cash register tape. These differences often result because the clerk hands incorrect change back to the retail customer. In this case, the difference between the actual cash and the amount reported on the cash register tape is reported in a Cash Over and Short account. For example, suppose that the cash register tape indicated sales of $6,956.20 but the amount of cash was only $6,946.10. A cash shortfall of $10.10 exists. To account for this cash shortfall and related cash, the company makes the following entry.

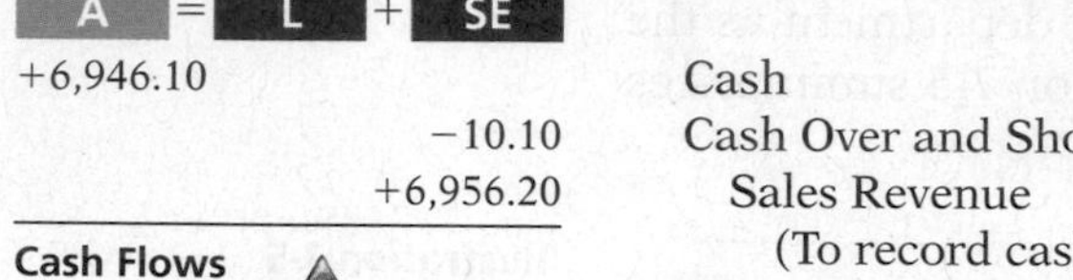

Cash Flows
+6,946.10

Cash	6,946.10	
Cash Over and Short	10.10	
Sales Revenue		6,956.20
(To record cash shortfall)		

Cash Over and Short is an income statement item. It is reported as miscellaneous expense when there is a cash shortfall, and as miscellaneous revenue when there is an overage. Clearly, the amount should be small. Any material amounts in this account should be investigated.

MAIL RECEIPTS

All mail receipts should be opened in the presence of at least two mail clerks. These receipts are generally in the form of checks. A mail clerk should endorse each check "For Deposit Only." This restrictive endorsement reduces the likelihood that someone could divert the check to personal use. Banks will not give an individual cash when presented with a check that has this type of endorsement.

The mail clerks prepare, in triplicate, a list of the checks received each day. This list shows the name of the check issuer, the purpose of the payment, and the amount of the check. Each mail clerk signs the list to establish responsibility for the data. The original copy of the list, along with the checks, is then sent to the cashier's department. A copy of the list is sent to the accounting department for recording in the accounting records. The clerks also keep a copy.

This process provides excellent internal control for the company. By employing two clerks, the chance of fraud is reduced. Each clerk knows he or she is being observed by the other clerk(s). To engage in fraud, they would have to collude. The customers who submit payments also provide control because they will contact the company with a complaint if they are not properly credited for payment. Because the cashier has access to cash but not the records, and the accounting department has access to records but not cash, neither can engage in undetected fraud.

> DO IT!

Control over Cash Receipts

L. R. Cortez is concerned about the control over cash receipts in his fast-food restaurant, Big Cheese. The restaurant has two cash registers. At no time do more than two employees take customer orders and ring up sales. Work shifts for employees range from 4 to 8 hours. Cortez asks your help in installing a good system of internal control over cash receipts.

Action Plan

- ✔ Differentiate among the internal control principles of (1) establishing responsibility, (2) using physical controls, and (3) independent internal verification.
- ✔ Design an effective system of internal control over cash receipts.

Solution

Cortez should assign a cash register to each employee at the start of each work shift, with register totals set at zero. Each employee should be instructed to use only the assigned register and to ring up all sales. Each customer should be given a receipt. At the end of the shift, the employee should do a cash count. A separate employee should compare the cash count with the register tape, to be sure they agree. In addition, Cortez should install an automated system that would enable the company to compare orders rung up on the register to orders processed by the kitchen.

Related exercise material: **BE7-5, E7-2, and DO IT! 7-2.**

 **The Navigator**

Cash Disbursements Controls

LEARNING OBJECTIVE 4

Explain the applications of internal control principles to cash disbursements.

Companies disburse cash for a variety of reasons, such as to pay expenses and liabilities or to purchase assets. **Generally, internal control over cash disbursements is more effective when companies pay by check rather than by cash.** One exception is **for incidental amounts that are paid out of petty cash.**[3]

Companies generally issue checks only after following specified control procedures. Illustration 7-6 (page 340) shows how principles of internal control apply to cash disbursements.

VOUCHER SYSTEM CONTROLS

Most medium and large companies use vouchers as part of their internal control over cash disbursements. A **voucher system** is a network of approvals by authorized individuals, acting independently, to ensure that all disbursements by check are proper.

The system begins with the authorization to incur a cost or expense. It ends with the issuance of a check for the liability incurred. A **voucher** is an authorization form prepared for each expenditure. Companies require vouchers for all types of cash disbursements except those from petty cash.

The starting point in preparing a voucher is to fill in the appropriate information about the liability on the face of the voucher. The vendor's invoice provides most of the needed information. Then, an employee in accounts payable records the voucher (in a journal called a **voucher register**) and files it according to the date on which it is to be paid. The company issues and sends a check on that date, and stamps the voucher "paid." The paid voucher is sent to the accounting department for recording (in a journal called the **check register**). A voucher system involves two journal entries, one to record the liability when the voucher is issued and a second to pay the liability that relates to the voucher.

The use of a voucher system improves internal control over cash disbursements. First, the authorization process inherent in a voucher system establishes responsibility. Each individual has responsibility to review the underlying documentation to ensure that it is correct. In addition, the voucher system keeps track of the documents that back up each transaction. By keeping these documents in one place, a supervisor can independently verify the authenticity of each transaction. Consider, for example, the case of Aesop University presented on page 330. Aesop did not use a voucher system for transactions under $2,500. As a consequence,

[3]We explain the operation of a petty cash fund on pages 340–342.

Cash Disbursements Controls

Establishment of Responsibility
Only designated personnel are authorized to sign checks (treasurer) and approve vendors

Physical Controls
Store blank checks in safes, with limited access; print check amounts by machine in indelible ink

Segregation of Duties
Different individuals approve and make payments; check signers do not record disbursements

Independent Internal Verification
Compare checks to invoices; reconcile bank statement monthly

Documentation Procedures
Use prenumbered checks and account for them in sequence; each check must have an approved invoice; require employees to use corporate credit cards for reimbursable expenses; stamp invoices "paid"

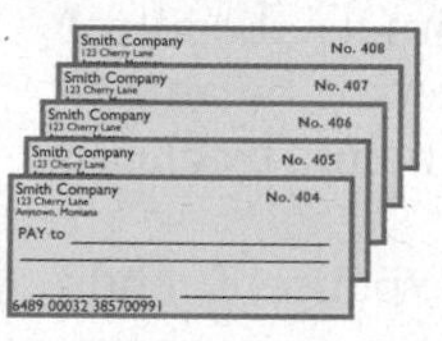

Human Resource Controls
Bond personnel who handle cash; require employees to take vacations; conduct background checks

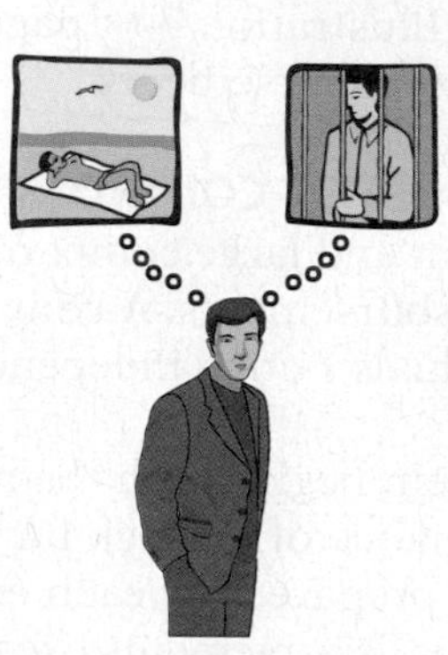

Illustration 7-6
Application of internal control principles to cash disbursements

there was no independent verification of the documents, which enabled the employee to submit fake invoices to hide his unauthorized purchases.

PETTY CASH FUND CONTROLS

LEARNING OBJECTIVE 5
Describe the operation of a petty cash fund.

As you learned earlier in the chapter, better internal control over cash disbursements is possible when companies make payments by check. However, using checks to pay small amounts is both impractical and a nuisance. For instance, a company would not want to write checks to pay for postage due, working lunches, or taxi fares. A common way of handling such payments, while maintaining satisfactory control, is to use a **petty cash fund** to pay relatively small amounts. The operation of a petty cash fund, often called an **imprest system**, involves (1) establishing the fund, (2) making payments from the fund, and (3) replenishing the fund.[4]

[4]The term "imprest" means an advance of money for a designated purpose.

ESTABLISHING THE PETTY CASH FUND Two essential steps in establishing a petty cash fund are: (1) appointing a petty cash custodian who will be responsible for the fund, and (2) determining the size of the fund. Ordinarily, a company expects the amount in the fund to cover anticipated disbursements for a three- to four-week period.

To establish the fund, a company issues a check payable to the petty cash custodian for the stipulated amount. For example, if Laird Company decides to establish a $100 fund on March 1, the general journal entry is:

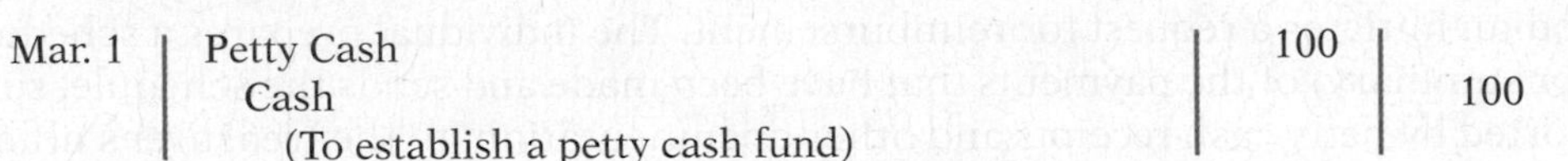

Mar. 1	Petty Cash	100	
	Cash		100
	(To establish a petty cash fund)		

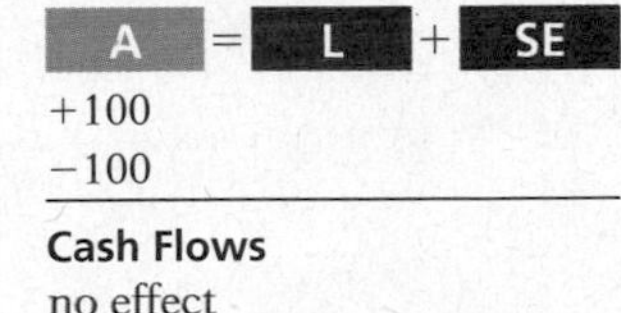

A = L + SE
+100
−100
Cash Flows
no effect

The fund custodian cashes the check and places the proceeds in a locked petty cash box or drawer. Most petty cash funds are established on a fixed-amount basis. The company will make no additional entries to the Petty Cash account unless management changes the stipulated amount of the fund. For example, if Laird Company decides on July 1 to increase the size of the fund to $250, it would debit Petty Cash $150 and credit Cash $150.

Ethics Note
Petty cash funds are authorized and legitimate. In contrast, "slush" funds are unauthorized and hidden (under the table).

MAKING PAYMENTS FROM THE PETTY CASH FUND The petty cash custodian has the authority to make payments from the fund that conform to prescribed management policies. Usually, management limits the size of expenditures that come from petty cash. Likewise, it may not permit use of the fund for certain types of transactions (such as making short-term loans to employees).

Each payment from the fund must be documented on a prenumbered petty cash receipt (or petty cash voucher), as shown in Illustration 7-7. The signatures of both the fund custodian and the person receiving payment are required on the receipt. If other supporting documents such as a freight bill or invoice are available, they should be attached to the petty cash receipt.

Helpful Hint
The petty cash receipt satisfies two internal control procedures: (1) establishing responsibility (signature of custodian), and (2) documentation procedures.

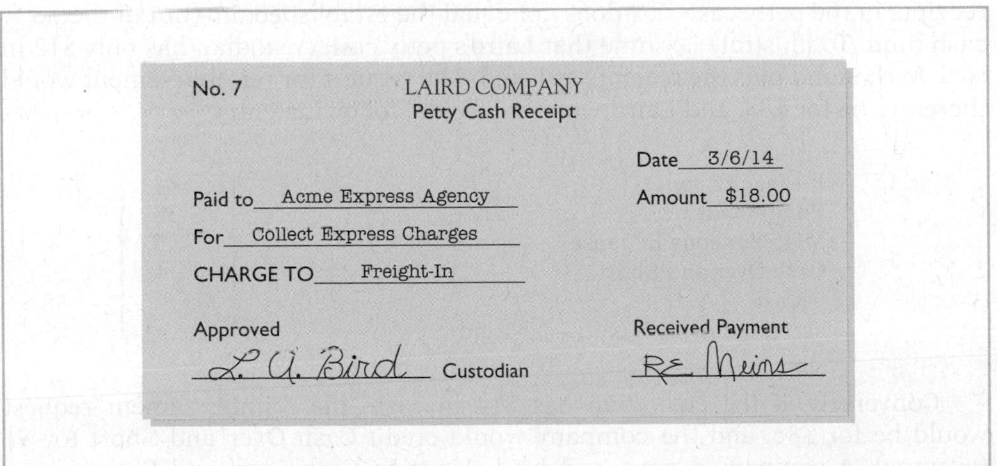
No. 7
LAIRD COMPANY
Petty Cash Receipt

Date 3/6/14

Paid to Acme Express Agency
Amount $18.00

For Collect Express Charges

CHARGE TO Freight-In

Approved
L. A. Bird Custodian

Received Payment
R E Meins

Illustration 7-7
Petty cash receipt

The fund custodian keeps the receipts in the petty cash box until the fund is replenished. The sum of the petty cash receipts and the money in the fund should equal the established total at all times. Management can (and should) make surprise counts at any time to determine whether the fund is being maintained correctly.

Ethics Note
Internal control over a petty cash fund is strengthened by: (1) having a supervisor make surprise counts of the fund to confirm whether the paid petty cash receipts and fund cash equal the imprest amount, and (2) canceling or mutilating the paid petty cash receipts so they cannot be resubmitted for reimbursement.

The company does not make an accounting entry to record a payment when it is made from petty cash. It is considered both inexpedient and unnecessary to do so. Instead, the company recognizes the accounting effects of each payment when it replenishes the fund.

REPLENISHING THE PETTY CASH FUND When the money in the petty cash fund reaches a minimum level, the company replenishes the fund. The petty cash custodian initiates a request for reimbursement. The individual prepares a schedule (or summary) of the payments that have been made and sends the schedule, supported by petty cash receipts and other documentation, to the treasurer's office. The treasurer's office examines the receipts and supporting documents to verify that proper payments from the fund were made. The treasurer then approves the request and issues a check to restore the fund to its established amount. At the same time, all supporting documentation is stamped "paid" so that it cannot be submitted again for payment.

To illustrate, assume that on March 15 Laird's petty cash custodian requests a check for $87. The fund contains $13 cash and petty cash receipts for postage $44, freight-out $38, and miscellaneous expenses $5. The general journal entry to record the check is:

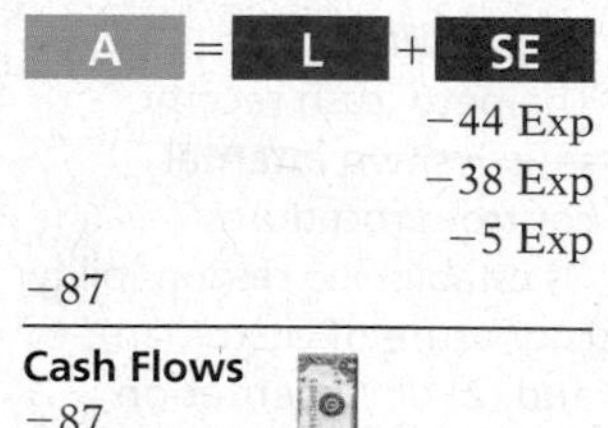

Mar. 15	Postage Expense	44	
	Freight-Out	38	
	Miscellaneous Expense	5	
	Cash		87
	(To replenish petty cash fund)		

Note that the reimbursement entry does not affect the Petty Cash account. Replenishment changes the composition of the fund by replacing the petty cash receipts with cash. It does not change the balance in the fund.

Occasionally, in replenishing a petty cash fund, the company may need to recognize a cash shortage or overage. This results when the total of the cash plus receipts in the petty cash box does not equal the established amount of the petty cash fund. To illustrate, assume that Laird's petty cash custodian has only $12 in cash in the fund plus the receipts as listed. The request for reimbursement would therefore be for $88, and Laird would make the following entry.

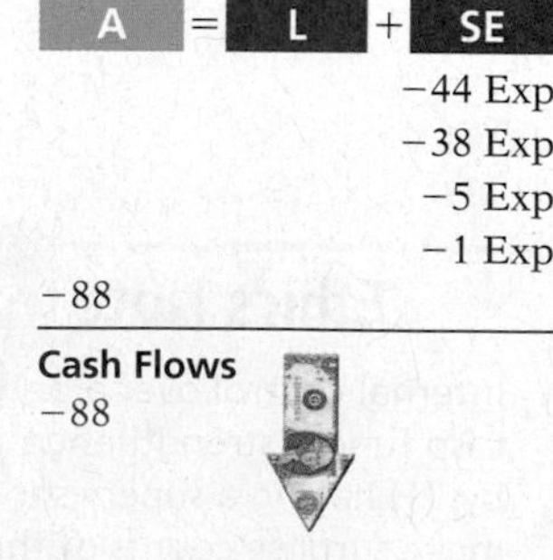

Mar. 15	Postage Expense	44	
	Freight-Out	38	
	Miscellaneous Expense	5	
	Cash Over and Short	1	
	Cash		88
	(To replenish petty cash fund)		

Conversely, if the custodian has $14 in cash, the reimbursement request would be for $86, and the company would credit Cash Over and Short for $1 (overage). A company reports a debit balance in Cash Over and Short in the income statement as miscellaneous expense. It reports a credit balance in the account as miscellaneous revenue. The company closes Cash Over and Short to Income Summary at the end of the year.

Companies should replenish a petty cash fund at the end of the accounting period, regardless of the cash in the fund. Replenishment at this time is necessary in order to recognize the effects of the petty cash payments on the financial statements.

Helpful Hint
Cash over and short situations result from mathematical errors or from failure to keep accurate records.

ETHICS INSIGHT

How Employees Steal

A recent study by the Association of Certified Fraud Examiners found that two-thirds of all employee thefts involved a fraudulent disbursement by an employee. The most common form (28.3% of cases) was fraudulent billing schemes. In these, the employee causes the company to issue a payment to the employee by submitting a bill for nonexistent goods or services, purchases of personal goods by the employee, or inflated invoices. The following graph shows various types of fraudulent disbursements and the median loss from each.

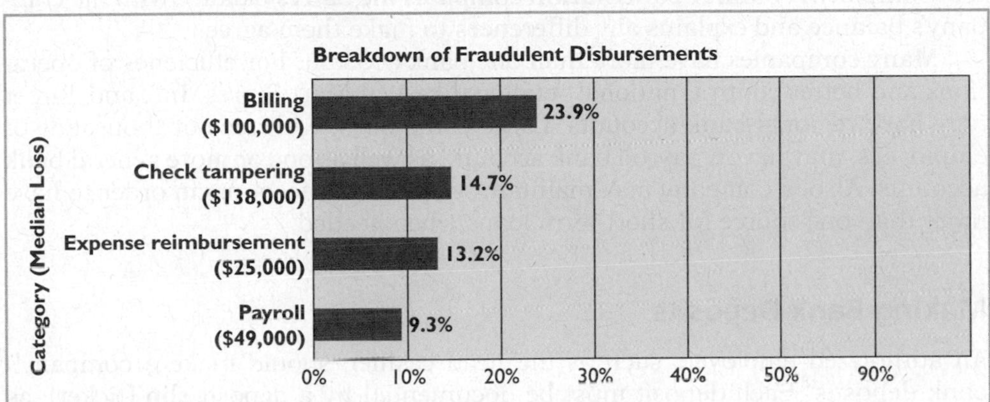

Source: *2008 Report to the Nation on Occupational Fraud and Abuse*, Association of Certified Fraud Examiners, *www.acfe.com/documents/2008_rttn.pdf*, p. 13.

? How can companies reduce the likelihood of fraudulent disbursements? (See page 375.)

> DO IT!

Petty Cash Fund

Action Plan

- ✔ To establish the fund, set up a separate general ledger account.
- ✔ Determine how much cash is needed to replenish the fund: subtract the cash remaining from the petty cash fund balance.
- ✔ Total the petty cash receipts. Determine any cash over or short—the difference between the cash needed to replenish the fund and the total of the petty cash receipts.
- ✔ Record the expenses incurred according to the petty cash receipts when replenishing the fund.

Bateer Company established a $50 petty cash fund on July 1. On July 30, the fund had $12 cash remaining and petty cash receipts for postage $14, office supplies $10, and delivery expense $15. Prepare journal entries to establish the fund on July 1 and to replenish the fund on July 30.

Solution

Date	Account	Debit	Credit
July 1	Petty Cash	50	
	Cash		50
	(To establish petty cash fund)		
30	Postage Expense	14	
	Supplies	10	
	Delivery Expense	15	
	Cash Over and Short		1
	Cash ($50 – $12)		38
	(To replenish petty cash)		

Related exercise material: **BE7-9, E7-7, E7-8,** and **DO IT! 7-3.**

 **The Navigator**

Control Features: Use of a Bank

LEARNING OBJECTIVE 6

Indicate the control features of a bank account.

The use of a bank contributes significantly to good internal control over cash. A company can safeguard its cash by using a bank as a depository and as a clearing house for checks received and written. Use of a bank minimizes the amount of currency that a company must keep on hand. Also, use of a bank facilitates the control of cash because it creates a double record of all bank transactions—one by the company and the other by the bank. The asset account Cash maintained by the company should have the same balance as the bank's liability account for that company. A **bank reconciliation** compares the bank's balance with the company's balance and explains any differences to make them agree.

Many companies have more than one bank account. For efficiency of operations and better control, national retailers like Wal-Mart Stores, Inc. and Target may have regional bank accounts. Large companies, with tens of thousands of employees, may have a payroll bank account, as well as one or more general bank accounts. Also, a company may maintain several bank accounts in order to have more than one source for short-term loans when needed.

Making Bank Deposits

An authorized employee, such as the head cashier, should make a company's bank deposits. Each deposit must be documented by a deposit slip (ticket), as shown in Illustration 7-8.

Illustration 7-8
Deposit slip

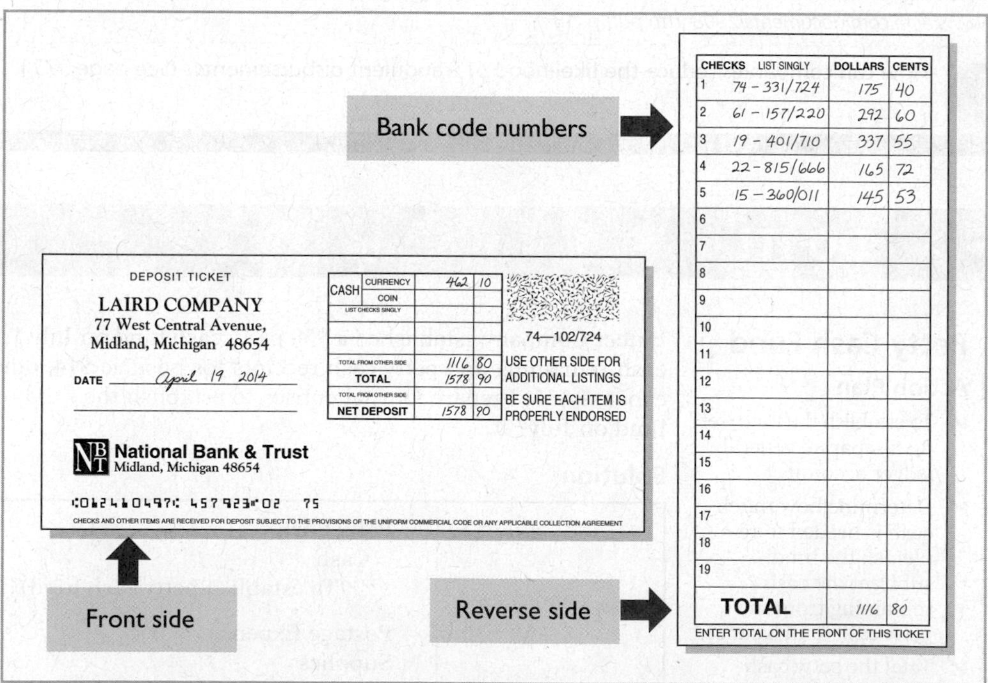

DEPOSIT TICKET
LAIRD COMPANY
77 West Central Avenue,
Midland, Michigan 48654
DATE April 19 2014

CASH	CURRENCY	462	10
	COIN		
LIST CHECKS SINGLY			
TOTAL FROM OTHER SIDE		1116	80
TOTAL		1578	90
TOTAL FROM OTHER SIDE			
NET DEPOSIT		1578	90

74—102/724
USE OTHER SIDE FOR ADDITIONAL LISTINGS
BE SURE EACH ITEM IS PROPERLY ENDORSED

National Bank & Trust
Midland, Michigan 48654

CHECKS AND OTHER ITEMS ARE RECEIVED FOR DEPOSIT SUBJECT TO THE PROVISIONS OF THE UNIFORM COMMERCIAL CODE OR ANY APPLICABLE COLLECTION AGREEMENT

	CHECKS LIST SINGLY	DOLLARS	CENTS
1	74 - 331/724	175	40
2	61 - 157/220	292	60
3	19 - 401/710	337	55
4	22 - 815/666	165	72
5	15 - 360/011	145	53
6			
7			
8			
9			
10			
11			
12			
13			
14			
15			
16			
17			
18			
19			
TOTAL		1116	80

ENTER TOTAL ON THE FRONT OF THIS TICKET

Deposit slips are prepared in duplicate. The bank retains the original; the depositor keeps the duplicate, machine-stamped by the bank to establish its authenticity.

Writing Checks

Most of us write checks without thinking very much about them. A **check** is a written order signed by the depositor directing the bank to pay a specified sum of money to a designated recipient. There are three parties to a check: (1) the **maker** (or drawer) who issues the check, (2) the **bank** (or payer) on which the check is drawn, and (3) the **payee** to whom the check is payable. A check is a **negotiable instrument** that one party can transfer to another party by endorsement. Each check should be accompanied by an explanation of its purpose. In many companies, a remittance advice attached to the check, as shown in Illustration 7-9, explains the check's purpose.

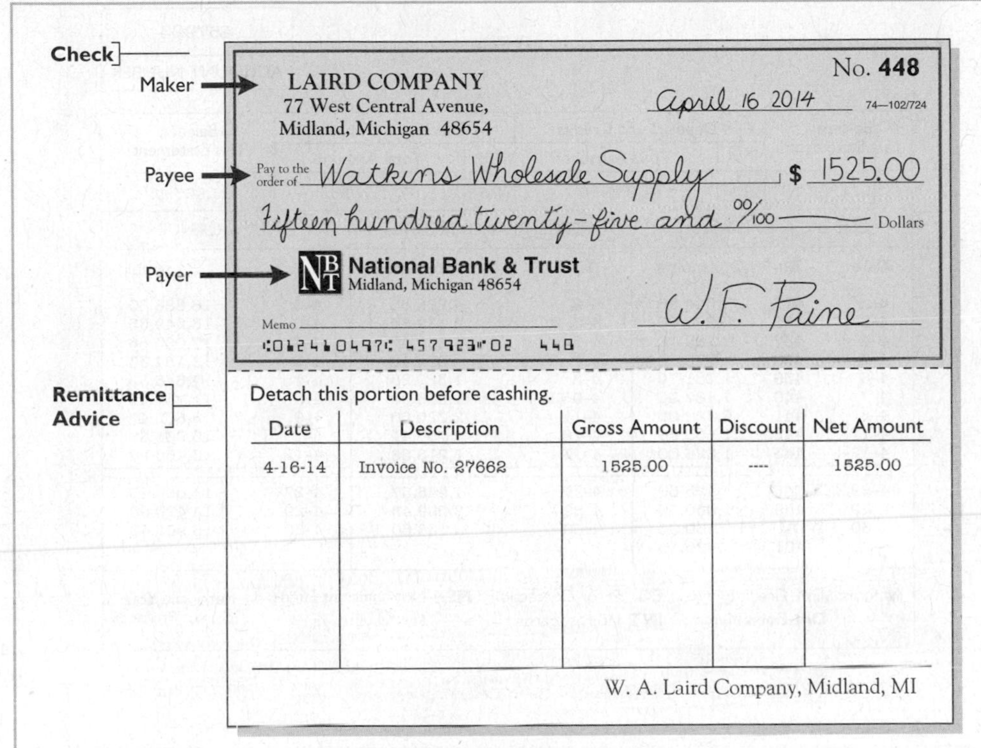

Check — Maker — Payee — Payer

LAIRD COMPANY
77 West Central Avenue,
Midland, Michigan 48654

No. **448**

April 16 2014 74—102/724

Pay to the order of Watkins Wholesale Supply $ 1525.00

Fifteen hundred twenty-five and 00/100 —— Dollars

National Bank & Trust
Midland, Michigan 48654

Memo

W.F. Paine

⑆0124104971⑆ 457923⑈02 448

Remittance Advice

Detach this portion before cashing.

Date	Description	Gross Amount	Discount	Net Amount
4-16-14	Invoice No. 27662	1525.00	----	1525.00

W. A. Laird Company, Midland, MI

Illustration 7-9
Check with remittance advice

It is important to know the balance in the checking account at all times. To keep the balance current, the depositor should enter each deposit and check on running-balance memo forms (or online statements) provided by the bank or on the check stubs in the checkbook.

Bank Statements

If you have a personal checking account, you are probably familiar with bank statements. A **bank statement** shows the depositor's bank transactions and balances.[5] Each month, a depositor receives a statement from the bank. Illustration 7-10 (page 346) presents a typical bank statement. It shows (1) checks paid and other debits that reduce the balance in the depositor's account, (2) deposits and other credits that increase the balance in the account, and (3) the account balance after each day's transactions.

Helpful Hint
Essentially, the bank statement is a copy of the bank's records sent to the customer (or available online) for review.

The bank statement lists in numerical sequence all "paid" checks, along with the date the check was paid and its amount. Upon paying a check, the bank

[5]Our presentation assumes that the depositor makes all adjustments at the end of the month. In practice, a company may also make journal entries during the month as it reviews information from the bank regarding its account.

Illustration 7-10
Bank statement

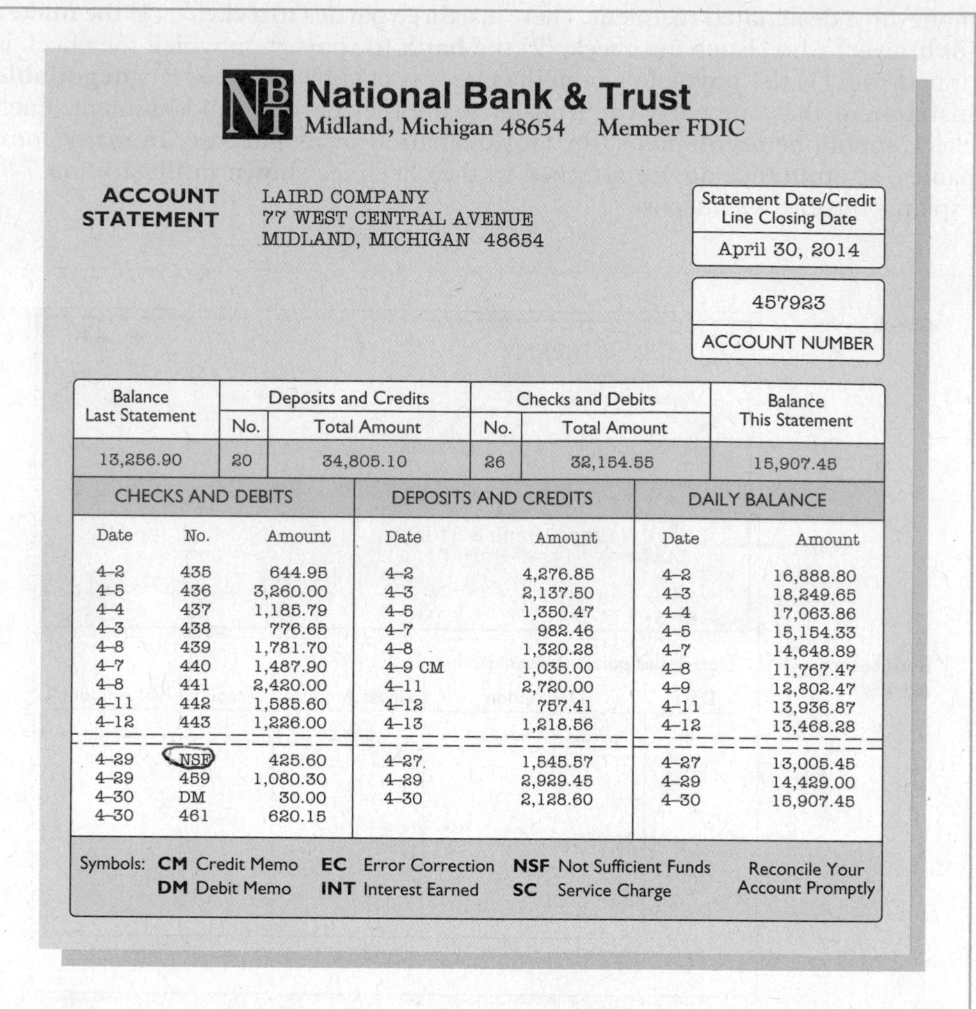

National Bank & Trust
Midland, Michigan 48654 Member FDIC

ACCOUNT STATEMENT

LAIRD COMPANY
77 WEST CENTRAL AVENUE
MIDLAND, MICHIGAN 48654

Statement Date/Credit Line Closing Date: April 30, 2014

457923
ACCOUNT NUMBER

Balance Last Statement	Deposits and Credits		Checks and Debits		Balance This Statement
	No.	Total Amount	No.	Total Amount	
13,256.90	20	34,805.10	26	32,154.55	15,907.45

CHECKS AND DEBITS			DEPOSITS AND CREDITS		DAILY BALANCE	
Date	No.	Amount	Date	Amount	Date	Amount
4-2	435	644.95	4-2	4,276.85	4-2	16,888.80
4-5	436	3,260.00	4-3	2,137.50	4-3	18,249.65
4-4	437	1,185.79	4-5	1,350.47	4-4	17,063.86
4-3	438	776.65	4-7	982.46	4-5	15,154.33
4-8	439	1,781.70	4-8	1,320.28	4-7	14,648.89
4-7	440	1,487.90	4-9 CM	1,035.00	4-8	11,767.47
4-8	441	2,420.00	4-11	2,720.00	4-9	12,802.47
4-11	442	1,585.60	4-12	757.41	4-11	13,936.87
4-12	443	1,226.00	4-13	1,218.56	4-12	13,468.28
4-29	NSF	425.60	4-27	1,545.57	4-27	13,005.45
4-29	459	1,080.30	4-29	2,929.45	4-29	14,429.00
4-30	DM	30.00	4-30	2,128.60	4-30	15,907.45
4-30	461	620.15				

Symbols: **CM** Credit Memo **EC** Error Correction **NSF** Not Sufficient Funds
DM Debit Memo **INT** Interest Earned **SC** Service Charge

Reconcile Your Account Promptly

Helpful Hint
The bank *credits* to the customer's account every deposit it receives. The reverse occurs when the bank "pays" a check issued by a company on its checking account balance. Payment reduces the bank's liability. Thus, the bank *debits* check payments to the customer's account with the bank.

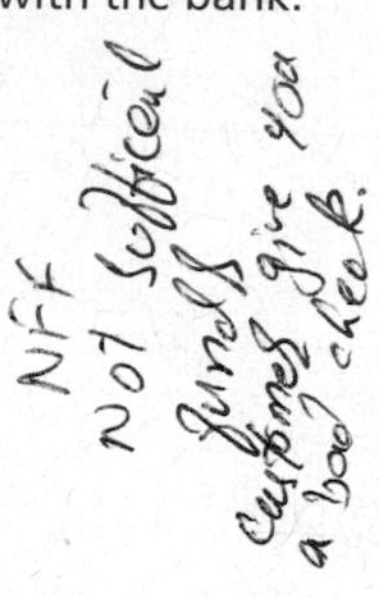

stamps the check "paid"; a paid check is sometimes referred to as a **canceled** check. On the statement, the bank also includes memoranda explaining other debits and credits it made to the depositor's account.

DEBIT MEMORANDUM

Some banks charge a monthly fee for their services. Often, they charge this fee only when the average monthly balance in a checking account falls below a specified amount. They identify the fee, called a **bank service charge**, on the bank statement by a symbol such as **SC**. The bank also sends with the statement a debit memorandum explaining the charge noted on the statement. Other debit memoranda may also be issued for other bank services such as the cost of printing checks, issuing traveler's checks, and wiring funds to other locations. The symbol **DM** is often used for such charges.

Banks also use a debit memorandum when a deposited check from a customer "bounces" because of insufficient funds. For example, assume that Scott Company, a customer of Laird Company, sends a check for $800 to Laird Company for services provided. Unfortunately, Scott does not have sufficient funds at its bank to pay for these services. In such a case, Scott's bank marks the check **NSF** (not sufficient funds) and returns it to Laird's (the depositor's) bank. Laird's bank then debits Laird's account, as shown by the symbol NSF on the bank statement in Illustration 7-10. The bank sends the NSF check and debit memorandum to Laird as notification of the charge. Laird then records an Account Receivable from Scott Company (the writer of the bad check) and reduces cash for the NSF check.

CREDIT MEMORANDUM

Sometimes a depositor asks the bank to collect its notes receivable. In such a case, the bank will credit the depositor's account for the cash proceeds of the note. This is illustrated by the symbol **CM** on the Laird Company bank statement. The bank issues and sends with the statement a credit memorandum to explain the entry. Many banks also offer interest on checking accounts. The interest earned may be indicated on the bank statement by the symbol **CM** or **INT**.

Reconciling the Bank Account

LEARNING OBJECTIVE 7

Prepare a bank reconciliation.

The bank and the depositor maintain independent records of the depositor's checking account. People tend to assume that the respective balances will always agree. In fact, the two balances are seldom the same at any given time, and both balances differ from the "correct" or "true" balance. Therefore, it is necessary to make the balance per books and the balance per bank agree with the correct or true amount—a process called **reconciling the bank account**. The need for agreement has two causes:

1. **Time lags** that prevent one of the parties from recording the transaction in the same period as the other party.
2. **Errors** by either party in recording transactions.

Time lags occur frequently. For example, several days may elapse between the time a company mails a check to a payee and the date the bank pays the check. Similarly, when the depositor uses the bank's night depository to make its deposits, there will be a difference of at least one day between the time the depositor records the deposit and the time the bank does so. A time lag also occurs whenever the bank mails a debit or credit memorandum to the depositor.

The incidence of errors depends on the effectiveness of the internal controls of the depositor and the bank. Bank errors are infrequent. However, either party could accidentally record a $450 check as $45 or $540. In addition, the bank might mistakenly charge a check to a wrong account by keying in an incorrect account name or number.

RECONCILIATION PROCEDURE

The bank reconciliation should be prepared by an employee who has no other responsibilities pertaining to cash. If a company fails to follow this internal control principle of independent internal verification, cash embezzlements may go unnoticed. For example, a cashier who prepares the reconciliation can embezzle cash and conceal the embezzlement by misstating the reconciliation. Thus, the bank accounts would reconcile, and the embezzlement would not be detected.

In reconciling the bank account, it is customary to reconcile the balance per books and balance per bank to their adjusted (correct or true) cash balances. The starting point in preparing the reconciliation is to enter the balance per bank statement and balance per books on the reconciliation schedule. The company then makes various adjustments, as shown in Illustration 7-11 (page 348).

The following steps should reveal all the reconciling items that cause the difference between the two balances.

Step 1. Deposits in transit. Compare the individual deposits listed on the bank statement with deposits in transit from the preceding bank reconciliation and with the deposits per company records or duplicate deposit slips. Deposits recorded by the depositor that have not been recorded by the bank are the **deposits in transit**. Add these deposits to the balance per bank.

Helpful Hint
Deposits in transit and outstanding checks are reconciling items because of time lags.

Illustration 7-11
Bank reconciliation adjustments

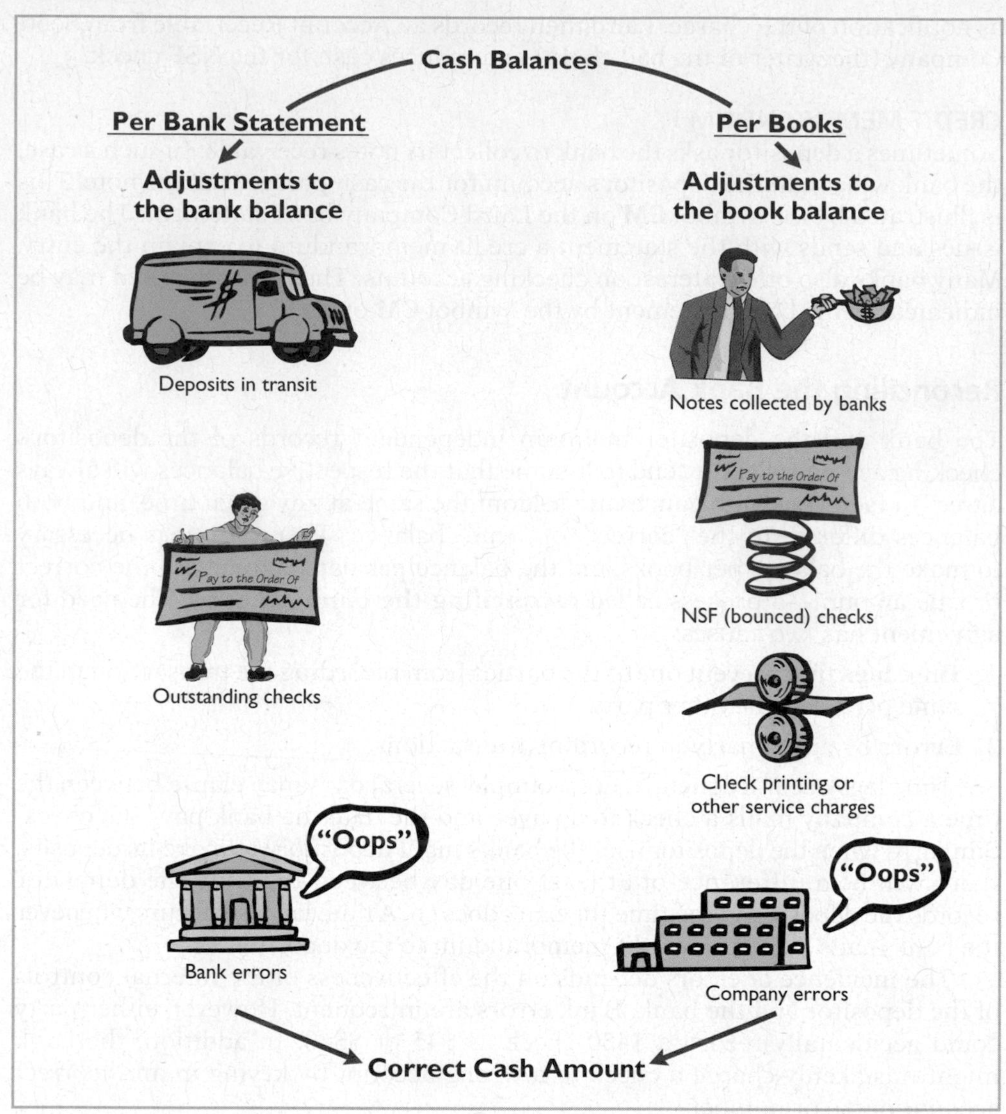

Step 2. Outstanding checks. Compare the paid checks shown on the bank statement with (a) checks outstanding from the previous bank reconciliation, and (b) checks issued by the company as recorded in the cash payments journal (or in the check register in your personal checkbook). Issued checks recorded by the company but that have not yet been paid by the bank are **outstanding checks**. Deduct outstanding checks from the balance per the bank.

Step 3. Errors. Note any errors discovered in the foregoing steps and list them in the appropriate section of the reconciliation schedule. For example, if the company mistakenly recorded as $169 a paid check correctly written for $196, it would deduct the error of $27 from the balance per books. All errors made by the depositor are reconciling items in determining the adjusted cash balance per books. In contrast, all errors made by the bank are reconciling items in determining the adjusted cash balance per the bank.

Step 4. Bank memoranda. Trace bank memoranda to the depositor's records. List in the appropriate section of the reconciliation schedule any unrecorded memoranda. For example, the company would deduct from the balance per books a $5 debit memorandum for bank service charges. Similarly, it would add to the balance per books $32 of interest earned.

BANK RECONCILIATION ILLUSTRATED

The bank statement for Laird Company, in Illustration 7-10, shows a balance per bank of $15,907.45 on April 30, 2014. On this date the balance of cash per books is $11,589.45. Using the four reconciliation steps, Laird determines the following reconciling items.

Step 1. Deposits in transit: April 30 deposit (received by bank on May 1).	$2,201.40
Step 2. Outstanding checks: No. 453, $3,000.00; no. 457, $1,401.30; no. 460, $1,502.70.	5,904.00
Step 3. Errors: Laird wrote check no. 443 for $1,226.00 and the bank correctly paid that amount. However, Laird recorded the check as $1,262.00.	36.00
Step 4. Bank memoranda:	
a. Debit—NSF check from J. R. Baron for $425.60	425.60
b. Debit—Charge for printing company checks $30.00	30.00
c. Credit—Collection of note receivable for $1,000 plus interest earned $50, less bank collection fee $15.00	1,035.00

Illustration 7-12 shows Laird's bank reconciliation.

Helpful Hint
Note in the bank statement on page 346 that checks no. 459 and 461 have been paid but check no. 460 is not listed. Thus, this check is outstanding. If a complete bank statement were provided, checks no. 453 and 457 would also not be listed. The amounts for these three checks are obtained from the company's cash payments records.

Illustration 7-12
Bank reconciliation

Laird Company Bank Reconciliation April 30, 2014		
Cash balance per bank statement		$ 15,907.45
Add: Deposits in transit		2,201.40
		18,108.85
Less: Outstanding checks		
No. 453	$3,000.00	
No. 457	1,401.30	
No. 460	1,502.70	5,904.00
Adjusted cash balance per bank		**$12,204.85**
Cash balance per books		$ 11,589.45
Add: Collection of note receivable $1,000, plus interest earned $50, less collection fee $15	$1,035.00	
Error in recording check no. 443	36.00	1,071.00
		12,660.45
Less: NSF check	425.60	
Bank service charge	30.00	455.60
Adjusted cash balance per books		**$12,204.85**

Alternative Terminology
The terms *adjusted cash balance, true cash balance,* and *correct cash balance* are used interchangeably.

Helpful Hint
The entries that follow are adjusting entries. In prior chapters, Cash was an account that did not require adjustment. That was a simplifying assumption for learning purposes because we had not yet explained a bank reconciliation.

ENTRIES FROM BANK RECONCILIATION

The company records each reconciling item used to determine the **adjusted cash balance per books. If the company does not journalize and post these items, the Cash account will not show the correct balance.** Laird Company would make the following entries on April 30.

A	=	L	+	SE
+1,035				
				−15 Exp
−1,000				
				+50 Rev

Cash Flows
+1,035

COLLECTION OF NOTE RECEIVABLE This entry involves four accounts. Assuming that the interest of $50 has not been accrued and the collection fee is charged to Miscellaneous Expense, the entry is:

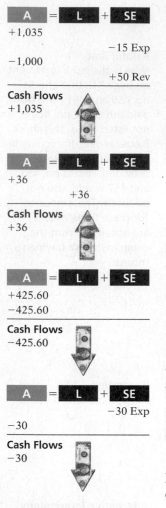

Apr. 30	Cash	1,035.00	
	Miscellaneous Expense	15.00	
	Notes Receivable		1,000.00
	Interest Revenue		50.00
	(To record collection of note receivable by bank)		

A	=	L	+	SE
+36				
		+36		

Cash Flows
+36

BOOK ERROR The cash disbursements journal shows that check no. 443 was a payment on account to Andrea Company, a supplier. The correcting entry is:

Apr. 30	Cash	36.00	
	Accounts Payable—Andrea Company		36.00
	(To correct error in recording check no. 443)		

A	=	L	+	SE
+425.60				
−425.60				

Cash Flows
−425.60

NSF CHECK As indicated earlier, an NSF check becomes an account receivable to the depositor. The entry is:

Apr. 30	Accounts Receivable—J. R. Baron	425.60	
	Cash		425.60
	(To record NSF check)		

A	=	L	+	SE
				−30 Exp
−30				

Cash Flows
−30

BANK SERVICE CHARGES Depositors debit check printing charges (DM) and other bank service charges (SC) to Miscellaneous Expense because they are usually nominal in amount. The entry is:

Apr. 30	Miscellaneous Expense	30.00	
	Cash		30.00
	(To record charge for printing company checks)		

Instead of making four separate entries, Laird could combine them into one compound entry.

After Laird has posted the entries, the Cash account will show the following.

Illustration 7-13
Adjusted balance in cash account

Cash			
Apr. 30 Bal.	11,589.45	Apr. 30	425.60
30	1,035.00	30	30.00
30	36.00		
Apr. 30 Bal.	**12,204.85**		

The adjusted cash balance in the ledger should agree with the adjusted cash balance per books in the bank reconciliation in Illustration 7-12 (page 349).

What entries does the bank make? If the company discovers any bank errors in preparing the reconciliation, it should notify the bank. The bank then can make the necessary corrections in its records. The bank does not make any entries for deposits in transit or outstanding checks. Only when these items reach the bank will the bank record these items.

Electronic Funds Transfer (EFT) System

It is not surprising that companies and banks have developed approaches to transfer funds among parties without the use of paper (deposit tickets, checks, etc.). Such procedures, called **electronic funds transfers (EFT)**, are disbursement systems that use wire, telephone, or computers to transfer cash balances from one location to another. Use of EFT is quite common. For example, many employees receive no formal payroll checks from their employers. Instead, employers send electronic payroll data to the appropriate banks. Also, individuals now frequently make regular payments such as those for house, car, and utilities by EFT.

EFT transfers normally result in better internal control since no cash or checks are handled by company employees. This does not mean that opportunities for fraud are eliminated. In fact, the same basic principles related to internal control apply to EFT transfers. For example, without proper segregation of duties and authorizations, an employee might be able to redirect electronic payments into a personal bank account and conceal the theft with fraudulent accounting entries.

INVESTOR INSIGHT

Madoff's Ponzi Scheme

No recent fraud has generated more interest and rage than the one perpetrated by Bernard Madoff. Madoff was an elite New York investment fund manager who was highly regarded by securities regulators. Investors flocked to him because he delivered very steady returns of between 10% and 15%, no matter whether the market was going up or going down. However, for many years, Madoff did not actually invest the cash that people gave to him. Instead, he was running a Ponzi scheme: He paid returns to existing investors using cash received from new investors. As long as the size of his investment fund continued to grow from new investments at a rate that exceeded the amounts that he needed to pay out in returns, Madoff was able to operate his fraud smoothly. To conceal his misdeeds, he fabricated false investment statements that were provided to investors. In addition, Madoff hired an auditor that never verified the accuracy of the investment records but automatically issued unqualified opinions each year. Although a competing fund manager warned the SEC a number of times over a nearly 10-year period that he thought Madoff was engaged in fraud, the SEC never aggressively investigated the allegations. Investors, many of which were charitable organizations, lost more than $18 billion. Madoff was sentenced to a jail term of 150 years.

? How was Madoff able to conceal such a giant fraud? (See page 375.)

> DO IT!

Bank Reconciliation

Sally Kist owns Linen Kist Fabrics. Sally asks you to explain how she should treat the following reconciling items when reconciling the company's bank account: (1) a debit memorandum for an NSF check, (2) a credit memorandum for a note collected by the bank, (3) outstanding checks, and (4) a deposit in transit.

Action Plan

✔ Understand the purpose of a bank reconciliation.

✔ Identify time lags and explain how they cause reconciling items.

Solution

Sally should treat the reconciling items as follows.

(1) NSF check: Deduct from balance per books.

(2) Collection of note: Add to balance per books.

(3) Outstanding checks: Deduct from balance per bank.

(4) Deposit in transit: Add to balance per bank.

Related exercise material: **BE7-11, BE7-12, BE7-13, BE7-14, E7-9, E7-10, E7-11, E7-12, E7-13, and DO IT! 7-4.**

 **The Navigator**

Reporting Cash

LEARNING OBJECTIVE 8

Explain the reporting of cash.

Cash consists of coins, currency (paper money), checks, money orders, and money on hand or on deposit in a bank or similar depository. Companies report cash in two different statements: the balance sheet and the statement of cash flows. The balance sheet reports the amount of cash available at a given point in time. The statement of cash flows shows the sources and uses of cash during a period of time. The statement of cash flows was introduced in Chapter 1 and will be discussed in much detail in Chapter 13. In this section, we discuss some important points regarding the presentation of cash in the balance sheet.

When presented in a balance sheet, cash on hand, cash in banks, and petty cash are often combined and reported simply as **Cash**. Because it is the most liquid asset owned by the company, cash is listed first in the current assets section of the balance sheet.

Cash Equivalents

Many companies use the designation "Cash and cash equivalents" in reporting cash. (See Illustration 7-14 for an example.) **Cash equivalents** are short-term, highly liquid investments that are both:

1. Readily convertible to known amounts of cash, and
2. So near their maturity that their market value is relatively insensitive to changes in interest rates.

Illustration 7-14
Balance sheet presentation of cash

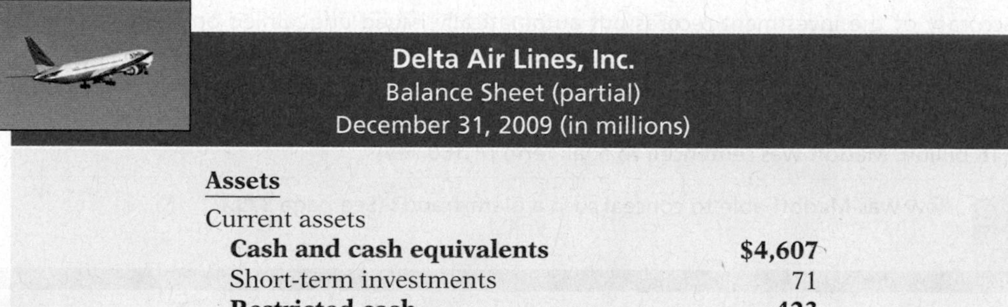

Delta Air Lines, Inc.
Balance Sheet (partial)
December 31, 2009 (in millions)

Assets	
Current assets	
Cash and cash equivalents	**$4,607**
Short-term investments	71
Restricted cash	**423**
Accounts receivable and other net	1,360
Parts inventories	327
Prepaid expenses and other	953
Total current assets	$ 7,741

Examples of cash equivalents are Treasury bills, commercial paper (short-term corporate notes), and money market funds. All typically are purchased with cash that is in excess of immediate needs.

Ethics Note

Recently, some companies were forced to restate their financial statements because they had too broadly interpreted which types of investments could be treated as cash equivalents. By reporting these items as cash equivalents, the companies made themselves look more liquid.

Occasionally, a company will have a net negative balance in its bank account. In this case, the company should report the negative balance among current liabilities. For example, farm equipment manufacturer Ag-Chem recently reported "Checks outstanding in excess of cash balances" of $2,145,000 among its current liabilities.

Restricted Cash

A company may have **restricted cash**, cash that is not available for general use but rather is restricted for a special purpose. For example, landfill companies are often required to maintain a fund of restricted cash to ensure they will have adequate resources to cover closing and clean-up costs at the end of a landfill site's useful life. McKessor Corp. recently reported restricted cash of $962 million to be paid out as the result of investor lawsuits.

Cash restricted in use should be reported separately on the balance sheet as restricted cash. If the company expects to use the restricted cash within the next year, it reports the amount as a current asset. When this is not the case, it reports the restricted funds as a noncurrent asset.

Illustration 7-14 shows restricted cash reported in the financial statements of Delta Air Lines. The company is required to maintain restricted cash as collateral to support insurance obligations related to workers' compensation claims. Delta does not have access to these funds for general use, and so it must report them separately, rather than as part of cash and cash equivalents.

> Comprehensive DO IT!

Poorten Company's bank statement for May 2014 shows the following data.

Balance 5/1	$12,650	Balance 5/31	$14,280
Debit memorandum:		Credit memorandum:	
NSF check	$175	Collection of note receivable	$505

The cash balance per books at May 31 is $13,319. Your review of the data reveals the following.

1. The NSF check was from Copple Co., a customer.
2. The note collected by the bank was a $500, 3-month, 12% note. The bank charged a $10 collection fee. No interest has been accrued.
3. Outstanding checks at May 31 total $2,410.
4. Deposits in transit at May 31 total $1,752.
5. A Poorten Company check for $352, dated May 10, cleared the bank on May 25. The company recorded this check, which was a payment on account, for $325.

Instructions

(a) Prepare a bank reconciliation at May 31.
(b) Journalize the entries required by the reconciliation.

Solution to Comprehensive DO IT!

Action Plan

- ✔ Follow the four steps in the reconciliation procedure (pp. 347–349).
- ✔ Work carefully to minimize mathematical errors in the reconciliation.
- ✔ Prepare entries from reconciling items per books.
- ✔ Make sure the cash ledger balance after posting the reconciling entries agrees with the adjusted cash balance per books.

(a)

Poorten Company
Bank Reconciliation
May 31, 2014

Cash balance per bank statement		$14,280
Add: Deposits in transit		1,752
		16,032
Less: Outstanding checks		2,410
Adjusted cash balance per bank		$13,622
Cash balance per books		$13,319
Add: Collection of note receivable $500, plus $15 interest, less collection fee $10		505
		13,824
Less: NSF check	$175	
Error in recording check	27	202
Adjusted cash balance per books		$13,622

(b)

Date	Account	Debit	Credit
May 31	Cash	505	
	Miscellaneous Expense	10	
	Notes Receivable		500
	Interest Revenue		15
	(To record collection of note by bank)		
31	Accounts Receivable—Copple Co.	175	
	Cash		175
	(To record NSF check from Copple Co.)		
31	Accounts Payable	27	
	Cash		27
	(To correct error in recording check)		

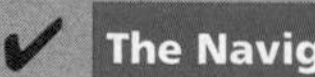

SUMMARY OF LEARNING OBJECTIVES

✔ The Navigator

1 Define fraud and internal control. A fraud is a dishonest act by an employee that results in personal benefit to the employee at a cost to the employer. The fraud triangle refers to the three factors that contribute to fraudulent activity by employees: opportunity, financial pressure, and rationalization. Internal control consists of all the related methods and measures adopted within an organization to safeguard its assets, enhance the reliability of its accounting records, increase efficiency of operations, and ensure compliance with laws and regulations.

2 Identify the principles of internal control activities. The principles of internal control are establishment of responsibility; segregation of duties; documentation procedures; physical controls; independent internal verification; and human resource controls such as bonding and requiring employees to take vacations.

3 Explain the applications of internal control principles to cash receipts. Internal controls over cash receipts include: (a) designating specific personnel to handle cash; (b) assigning different individuals to receive cash, record cash, and maintain custody of cash; (c) using remittance advices for mail receipts, cash register tapes for over-the-counter receipts, and deposit slips for bank deposits; (d) using company safes and bank vaults to store cash with access limited to authorized personnel, and using cash registers in executing over-the-counter receipts; (e) making independent daily counts of register receipts and daily comparison of total receipts with total deposits; and (f) bonding personnel that handle cash and requiring them to take vacations.

4 Explain the applications of internal control principles to cash disbursements. Internal controls over cash disbursements include: (a) having specific individuals such as the treasurer authorized to sign checks and approve invoices; (b) assigning different individuals to approve items for payment, pay the items, and record the payment; (c) using prenumbered checks and accounting for all checks, with each check supported by an approved invoice (d) storing blank checks in a safe or vault with access restricted to authorized personnel, and using a checkwriting machine to imprint amounts on checks; (e) comparing each check with the approved invoice before issuing the check, and making monthly reconciliations of bank and book balances; and (f) bonding personnel who handle cash, requiring employees to take vacations, and conducting background checks.

5 Describe the operation of a petty cash fund. Companies operate a petty cash fund to pay relatively small amounts of cash. They must establish the fund, make payments from the fund, and replenish the fund when the cash in the fund reaches a minimum level.

6 Indicate the control features of a bank account. A bank account contributes to good internal control by providing physical controls for the storage of cash. It minimizes the amount of currency that a company must keep on hand, and it creates a double record of a depositor's bank transactions.

7 Prepare a bank reconciliation. It is customary to reconcile the balance per books and balance per bank to their adjusted balances. The steps in the reconciling process are to determine deposits in transit, outstanding checks, errors by the depositor or the bank, and unrecorded bank memoranda.

8 Explain the reporting of cash. Companies list cash first in the current assets section of the balance sheet. In some cases, they report cash together with cash equivalents. Cash restricted for a special purpose is reported separately as a current asset or as a noncurrent asset, depending on when the cash is expected to be used.

GLOSSARY

Bank reconciliation The process of comparing the bank's balance of an account with the company's balance and explaining any differences to make them agree. (p. 344).

Bank service charge A fee charged by a bank for the use of its services. (p. 346).

Bank statement A monthly statement from the bank that shows the depositor's bank transactions and balances. (p. 345).

Bonding Obtaining insurance protection against misappropriation of assets by employees. (p. 333).

Cash Resources that consist of coins, currency, checks, money orders, and money on hand or on deposit in a bank or similar depository. (p. 352).

Cash equivalents Short-term, highly liquid investments that can be converted to a specific amount of cash. (p. 352).

Check A written order signed by a bank depositor, directing the bank to pay a specified sum of money to a designated recipient. (p. 344).

Deposits in transit Deposits recorded by the depositor but not yet been recorded by the bank. (p. 347).

Electronic funds transfer (EFT) A disbursement system that uses wire, telephone, or computers to transfer funds from one location to another. (p. 350).

Fraud A dishonest act by an employee that results in personal benefit to the employee at a cost to the employer. (p. 326).

Fraud triangle The three factors that contribute to fraudulent activity by employees: opportunity, financial pressure, and rationalization. (p. 326).

Internal auditors Company employees who continuously evaluate the effectiveness of the company's internal control system. (p. 333).

Internal control All of the related methods and activities adopted within an organization to safeguard its assets and enhance the accuracy and reliability of its accounting records. (p. 327).

NSF check A check that is not paid by a bank because of insufficient funds in a customer's bank account. (p. 346).

Outstanding checks Checks issued and recorded by a company but not yet paid by the bank. (p. 348).

Petty cash fund A cash fund used to pay relatively small amounts. (p. 340).

Restricted cash Cash that must be used for a special purpose. (p. 352).

Sarbanes-Oxley Act (SOX) Regulations passed by Congress to try to reduce unethical corporate behavior. (p. 326).

Voucher An authorization form prepared for each payment in a voucher system. (p. 339).

Voucher system A network of approvals by authorized individuals acting independently to ensure that all disbursements by check are proper. (p. 339).

Self-Test, Brief Exercises, Exercises, Problem Set A, and many more components are available for practice in WileyPLUS.

SELF-TEST QUESTIONS

Answers are on page 375.

(LO 1) **1.** Which of the following is *not* an element of the fraud triangle?
- (a) Rationalization.
- (b) Financial pressure.
- (c) Segregation of duties.
- (d) Opportunity.

(LO 1) **2.** An organization uses internal control to enhance the accuracy and reliability of its accounting records and to:
- (a) safeguard its assets.
- (b) prevent fraud.
- (c) produce correct financial statements.
- (d) deter employee dishonesty.

(LO 1) **3.** Which of the following was *not* a result of the Sarbanes-Oxley Act?
- (a) Companies must file financial statements with the Internal Revenue Service.
- (b) All publicly traded companies must maintain adequate internal controls.
- (c) The Public Company Accounting Oversight Board was created to establish auditing standards and regulate auditor activity.
- (d) Corporate executives and board of directors must ensure that controls are reliable and effective, and they can be fined or imprisoned for failure to do so.

4. The principles of internal control do *not* include: (LO 2)
- (a) establishment of responsibility.
- (b) documentation procedures.
- (c) management responsibility.
- (d) independent internal verification.

5. Physical controls do *not* include: (LO 2)
- (a) safes and vaults to store cash.
- (b) independent bank reconciliations.

(c) locked warehouses for inventories.
(d) bank safety deposit boxes for important papers.

(LO 3) **6.** Permitting only designated personnel to handle cash receipts is an application of the principle of:
(a) segregation of duties.
(b) establishment of responsibility.
(c) independent check.
(d) human resource controls.

(LO 3) **7.** Which of the following control activities is *not* relevant to when a company uses a computerized (rather than manual) accounting system?
(a) Establishment of responsibility.
(b) Segregation of duties.
(c) Independent internal verification.
(d) All of these control activities are relevant to a computerized system.

(LO 4) **8.** The use of prenumbered checks in disbursing cash is an application of the principle of:
(a) establishment of responsibility.
(b) segregation of duties.
(c) physical controls.
(d) documentation procedures.

(LO 5) **9.** A company writes a check to replenish a $100 petty cash fund when the fund contains receipts of $94 and $4 in cash. In recording the check, the company should:
(a) debit Cash Over and Short for $2.
(b) debit Petty Cash for $94.
(c) credit Cash for $94.
(d) credit Petty Cash for $2.

10. The control features of a bank account do *not* include: (LO 6)
(a) having bank auditors verify the correctness of the bank balance per books.
(b) minimizing the amount of cash that must be kept on hand.
(c) providing a double record of all bank transactions.
(d) safeguarding cash by using a bank as a depository.

11. In a bank reconciliation, deposits in transit are: (LO 7)
(a) deducted from the book balance.
(b) added to the book balance.
(c) added to the bank balance.
(d) deducted from the bank balance.

12. The reconciling item in a bank reconciliation that will result in an adjusting entry by the depositor is: (LO 7)
(a) outstanding checks.
(b) deposit in transit.
(c) a bank error.
(d) bank service charges.

13. Which of the following items in a cash drawer at November 30 is *not* cash? (LO 8)
(a) Money orders.
(b) Coins and currency.
(c) A customer check dated December 1.
(d) A customer check dated November 28.

14. Which of the following statements correctly describes the reporting of cash? (LO 8)
(a) Cash cannot be combined with cash equivalents.
(b) Restricted cash funds may be combined with cash.
(c) Cash is listed first in the current assets section.
(d) Restricted cash funds cannot be reported as a current asset.

Go to the book's companion website, www.wiley.com/college/weygandt, for additional Self-Test Questions.

✔ **The Navigator**

QUESTIONS

1. A local bank reported that it lost $150,000 as the result of an employee fraud. Travis Witt is not clear on what is meant by an "employee fraud." Explain the meaning of fraud to Travis and give an example of frauds that might occur at a bank.

2. Fraud experts often say that there are three primary factors that contribute to employee fraud. Identify the three factors and explain what is meant by each.

3. Identify and describe the five components of a good internal control system.

4. "Internal control is concerned only with enhancing the accuracy of the accounting records." Do you agree? Explain.

5. What principles of internal control apply to most organizations?

6. At the corner grocery store, all sales clerks make change out of one cash register drawer. Is this a violation of internal control? Why?

7. Pam Duffy is reviewing the principle of segregation of duties. What are the two common applications of this principle?

8. How do documentation procedures contribute to good internal control?

9. What internal control objectives are met by physical controls?

10. (a) Explain the control principle of independent internal verification. (b) What practices are important in applying this principle?

11. The management of Yeager Company asks you, as the company accountant, to explain (a) the concept of reasonable assurance in internal control and (b) the importance of the human factor in internal control.

12. Yorkville Fertilizer Co. owns the following assets at the balance sheet date.

Cash in bank savings account	$ 6,000
Cash on hand	850
Cash refund due from the IRS	1,000
Checking account balance	12,000
Postdated checks	500

What amount should Yorkville report as cash in the balance sheet?

13. What principle(s) of internal control is (are) involved in making daily cash counts of over-the-counter receipts?
14. Aurora Department Stores has just installed new electronic cash registers in its stores. How do cash registers improve internal control over cash receipts?
15. At Oswego Wholesale Company, two mail clerks open all mail receipts. How does this strengthen internal control?
16. "To have maximum effective internal control over cash disbursements, all payments should be made by check." Is this true? Explain.
17. Ted Rampolla Company's internal controls over cash disbursements provide for the treasurer to sign checks imprinted by a check-writing machine in indelible ink after comparing the check with the approved invoice. Identify the internal control principles that are present in these controls.
18. How do the principles of (a) physical controls and (b) documentation controls apply to cash disbursements?
19. (a) What is a voucher system? (b) What principles of internal control apply to a voucher system?
20. What is the essential feature of an electronic funds transfer (EFT) procedure?
21. (a) Identify the three activities that pertain to a petty cash fund, and indicate an internal control principle that is applicable to each activity. (b) When are journal entries required in the operation of a petty cash fund?
22. "The use of a bank contributes significantly to good internal control over cash." Is this true? Why or why not?
23. Faye Uhlik is confused about the lack of agreement between the cash balance per books and the balance per bank. Explain the causes for the lack of agreement to Faye, and give an example of each cause.
24. What are the four steps involved in finding differences between the balance per books and balance per bank?
25. Pauline Duche asks your help concerning an NSF check. Explain to Pauline (a) what an NSF check is, (b) how it is treated in a bank reconciliation, and (c) whether it will require an adjusting entry.
26. (a) "Cash equivalents are the same as cash." Do you agree? Explain. (b) How should restricted cash funds be reported on the balance sheet?
27. PEPSICO At what amount does PepsiCo report cash and cash equivalents in its 2010 consolidated balance sheet?

BRIEF EXERCISES

Identify fraud triangle concepts. (LO 1)

BE7-1 Match each situation with the fraud triangle factor"—opportunity, financial pressure, or rationalization"—that best describes it.

1. An employee's monthly credit card payments are nearly 75% of his or her monthly earnings.
2. An employee earns minimum wage at a firm that has reported record earnings for each of the last five years.
3. An employee has an expensive gambling habit.
4. An employee has check-writing and signing responsibilities for a small company, as well as reconciling the bank account.

Indicate internal control concepts. (LO 1)

BE7-2 Bridget Harrard has prepared the following list of statements about internal control.

1. One of the objectives of internal control is to safeguard assets from employee theft, robbery, and unauthorized use.
2. One of the objectives of internal control is to enhance the accuracy and reliability of the accounting records.
3. No laws require U.S. corporations to maintain an adequate system of internal control.

Identify each statement as true or false. If false, indicate how to correct the statement.

Explain the importance of internal control. (LO 1)

BE7-3 Emily Cooper is the new owner of Preferred Parking. She has heard about internal control but is not clear about its importance for her business. Explain to Emily the four purposes of internal control and give her one application of each purpose for Preferred Parking.

Identify internal control principles. (LO 2)

BE7-4 The internal control procedures in Naperville Company provide that:

1. Employees who have physical custody of assets do not have access to the accounting records.
2. Each month, the assets on hand are compared to the accounting records by an internal auditor.
3. A prenumbered shipping document is prepared for each shipment of goods to customers.

Identify the principles of internal control that are being followed.

Identify the internal control principles applicable to cash receipts. (LO 3)

BE7-5 Syracuse Company has the following internal control procedures over cash receipts. Identify the internal control principle that is applicable to each procedure.

1. All over-the-counter receipts are entered on cash registers.
2. All cashiers are bonded.
3. Daily cash counts are made by cashier department supervisors.

4. The duties of receiving cash, recording cash, and custody of cash are assigned to different individuals.
5. Only cashiers may operate cash registers.

Make journal entries for cash overage and shortfall.

(LO 3)

BE7-6 The cash register tape for Goodmood Industries reported sales of $6,891.50. Record the journal entry that would be necessary for each of the following situations. (a) Cash to be accounted for exceeds cash on hand by $46.25. (b) Cash on hand exceeds cash to be accounted for by $28.32.

Make journal entry using cash count sheet.

(LO 3)

BE7-7 While examining cash receipts information, the accounting department determined the following information: opening cash balance $180, cash on hand $1,125.74, and cash sales per register tape $950.83. Prepare the required journal entry based upon the cash count sheet.

Identify the internal control principles applicable to cash disbursements.

(LO 4)

BE7-8 Helena Company has the following internal control procedures over cash disbursements. Identify the internal control principle that is applicable to each procedure.

1. Company checks are prenumbered.
2. The bank statement is reconciled monthly by an internal auditor.
3. Blank checks are stored in a safe in the treasurer's office.
4. Only the treasurer or assistant treasurer may sign checks.
5. Check signers are not allowed to record cash disbursement transactions.

Prepare entry to replenish a petty cash fund.

(LO 5)

BE7-9 On March 20, Batavia's petty cash fund of $100 is replenished when the fund contains $9 in cash and receipts for postage $52, freight-out $26, and travel expense $10. Prepare the journal entry to record the replenishment of the petty cash fund.

Identify the control features of a bank account.

(LO 6)

BE7-10 Louis Whited is uncertain about the control features of a bank account. Explain the control benefits of (a) a check and (b) a bank statement.

Indicate location of reconciling items in a bank reconciliation.

(LO 7)

BE7-11 The following reconciling items are applicable to the bank reconciliation for Hinckley Company: (1) outstanding checks, (2) bank debit memorandum for service charge, (3) bank credit memorandum for collecting a note for the depositor, and (4) deposits in transit. Indicate how each item should be shown on a bank reconciliation.

Identify reconciling items that require adjusting entries.

(LO 7)

BE7-12 Using the data in BE7-11, indicate (a) the items that will result in an adjustment to the depositor's records and (b) why the other items do not require adjustment.

Prepare partial bank reconciliation.

(LO 7)

BE7-13 At July 31, Shabbona Company has the following bank information: cash balance per bank $7,420, outstanding checks $762, deposits in transit $1,620, and a bank service charge $20. Determine the adjusted cash balance per bank at July 31.

Prepare partial bank reconciliation.

(LO 7)

BE7-14 At August 31, DeKalb Company has a cash balance per books of $8,900 and the following additional data from the bank statement: charge for printing DeKalb Company checks $35, interest earned on checking account balance $40, and outstanding checks $800. Determine the adjusted cash balance per books at August 31.

Explain the statement presentation of cash balances.

(LO 8)

BE7-15 Plano Company has the following cash balances: Cash in Bank $15,742, Payroll Bank Account $5,000, and Plant Expansion Fund Cash $45,000. Explain how each balance should be reported on the balance sheet.

> DO IT! REVIEW

Identify violations of control activities.

(LO 2)

DO IT! 7-1 Identify which control activity is violated in each of the following situations, and explain how the situation creates an opportunity for fraud or inappropriate accounting practices.

1. Once a month, the sales department sends sales invoices to the accounting department to be recorded.
2. Sam Hustad orders merchandise for Green Lake Company; he also receives merchandise and authorizes payment for merchandise.
3. Several clerks at Ralph's Foods use the same cash register drawer.

DO IT! 7-2 Jerry Holman is concerned with control over mail receipts at Midtown Sporting Goods. All mail receipts are opened by Don Judd. Don sends the checks to the accounting department, where they are stamped "For Deposit Only." The accounting department records and deposits the mail receipts weekly. Jerry asks for your help in installing a good system of internal control over mail receipts.

Design system of internal control over cash receipts.

(LO 3)

DO IT! 7-3 Markee Company established a $100 petty cash fund on August 1. On August 31, the fund had $6 cash remaining and petty cash receipts for postage $31, office supplies $42, and miscellaneous expense $16. Prepare journal entries to establish the fund on August 1 and replenish the fund on August 31.

Make journal entries for petty cash fund.

(LO 5)

DO IT! 7-4 Jon Rapp owns Rapp Blankets. Jon asks you to explain how he should treat the following reconciling items when reconciling the company's bank account.

Explain treatment of items in bank reconciliation.

(LO 7)

1. Outstanding checks.
2. A deposit in transit.
3. The bank charged to our account a check written by another company.
4. A debit memorandum for a bank service charge.

✔ The Navigator

EXERCISES

E7-1 Sue Ernesto is the owner of Ernesto's Pizza. Ernesto's is operated strictly on a carryout basis. Customers pick up their orders at a counter where a clerk exchanges the pizza for cash. While at the counter, the customer can see other employees making the pizzas and the large ovens in which the pizzas are baked.

Identify the principles of internal control.

(LO 2)

Instructions
Identify the six principles of internal control and give an example of each principle that you might observe when picking up your pizza. (*Note:* It may not be possible to observe all the principles.)

E7-2 The following control procedures are used at Aldean Company for over-the-counter cash receipts.

Identify internal control weaknesses over cash receipts and suggest improvements.

(LO 2, 3)

1. To minimize the risk of robbery, cash in excess of $100 is stored in an unlocked attaché case in the stock room until it is deposited in the bank.
2. All over-the-counter receipts are registered by three clerks who use a cash register with a single cash drawer.
3. The company accountant makes the bank deposit and then records the day's receipts.
4. At the end of each day, the total receipts are counted by the cashier on duty and reconciled to the cash register total.
5. Cashiers are experienced; they are not bonded.

Instructions
(a) For each procedure, explain the weakness in internal control, and identify the control principle that is violated.
(b) For each weakness, suggest a change in procedure that will result in good internal control.

E7-3 The following control procedures are used in Morgan's Boutique Shoppe for cash disbursements.

Identify internal control weaknesses over cash disbursements and suggest improvements.

(LO 2, 4)

1. The company accountant prepares the bank reconciliation and reports any discrepancies to the owner.
2. The store manager personally approves all payments before signing and issuing checks.
3. Each week, 100 company checks are left in an unmarked envelope on a shelf behind the cash register.
4. After payment, bills are filed in a paid invoice folder.
5. The company checks are unnumbered.

Instructions

(a) For each procedure, explain the weakness in internal control, and identify the internal control principle that is violated.

(b) For each weakness, suggest a change in the procedure that will result in good internal control.

Identify internal control weaknesses for cash disbursements and suggest improvements.

(LO 4)

E7-4 At Teresa Company, checks are not prenumbered because both the purchasing agent and the treasurer are authorized to issue checks. Each signer has access to unissued checks kept in an unlocked file cabinet. The purchasing agent pays all bills pertaining to goods purchased for resale. Prior to payment, the purchasing agent determines that the goods have been received and verifies the mathematical accuracy of the vendor's invoice. After payment, the invoice is filed by vendor name, and the purchasing agent records the payment in the cash disbursements journal. The treasurer pays all other bills following approval by authorized employees. After payment, the treasurer stamps all bills PAID, files them by payment date, and records the checks in the cash disbursements journal. Teresa Company maintains one checking account that is reconciled by the treasurer.

Instructions

(a) List the weaknesses in internal control over cash disbursements.

(b) Write a memo to the company treasurer indicating your recommendations for improvement.

Indicate whether procedure is good or weak internal control.

(LO 2, 3, 4)

E7-5 Listed below are five procedures followed by Parson Company.

1. Several individuals operate the cash register using the same register drawer.
2. A monthly bank reconciliation is prepared by someone who has no other cash responsibilities.
3. Fran Vorbeck writes checks and also records cash payment journal entries.
4. One individual orders inventory, while a different individual authorizes payments.
5. Unnumbered sales invoices from credit sales are forwarded to the accounting department every four weeks for recording.

Instructions

Indicate whether each procedure is an example of good internal control or of weak internal control. If it is an example of good internal control, indicate which internal control principle is being followed. If it is an example of weak internal control, indicate which internal control principle is violated. Use the table below.

Procedure	IC Good or Weak?	Related Internal Control Principle
1.		
2.		
3.		
4.		
5.		

Indicate whether procedure is good or weak internal control.

(LO 2, 3, 4)

E7-6 Listed below are five procedures followed by Bingham Company.

1. Employees are required to take vacations.
2. Any member of the sales department can approve credit sales.
3. Blake Nayak ships goods to customers, bills customers, and receives payment from customers.
4. Total cash receipts are compared to bank deposits daily by someone who has no other cash responsibilities.
5. Time clocks are used for recording time worked by employees.

Instructions

Indicate whether each procedure is an example of good internal control or of weak internal control. If it is an example of good internal control, indicate which internal control principle is being followed. If it is an example of weak internal control, indicate which internal control principle is violated. Use the table below.

Procedure	IC Good or Weak?	Related Internal Control Principle
1.		
2.		
3.		
4.		
5.		

E7-7 LaSalle Company established a petty cash fund on May 1, cashing a check for $100. The company reimbursed the fund on June 1 and July 1 with the following results.

Prepare journal entries for a petty cash fund.

(LO 5)

June 1: Cash in fund $1.75. Receipts: delivery expense $31.25; postage expense $41.00; and miscellaneous expense $25.00.
July 1: Cash in fund $3.25. Receipts: delivery expense $21.00; entertainment expense $51.00; and miscellaneous expense $24.75.

On July 10, LaSalle increased the fund from $100 to $150.

Instructions

Prepare journal entries for LaSalle Company for May 1, June 1, July 1, and July 10.

E7-8 Kickapoo Company uses an imprest petty cash system. The fund was established on March 1 with a balance of $100. During March, the following petty cash receipts were found in the petty cash box.

Prepare journal entries for a petty cash fund.

(LO 5)

Date	Receipt No.	For	Amount
3/5	1	Stamp Inventory	$39
7	2	Freight-Out	17
9	3	Miscellaneous Expense	6
11	4	Travel Expense	24
14	5	Miscellaneous Expense	7

The fund was replenished on March 15 when the fund contained $4 in cash. On March 20, the amount in the fund was increased to $150.

Instructions

Journalize the entries in March that pertain to the operation of the petty cash fund.

E7-9 Lisa Ceja is unable to reconcile the bank balance at January 31. Lisa's reconciliation is as follows.

Prepare bank reconciliation and adjusting entries.

(LO 7)

Cash balance per bank	$3,660.20
Add: NSF check	590.00
Less: Bank service charge	25.00
Adjusted balance per bank	$4,225.20
Cash balance per books	$3,825.20
Less: Deposits in transit	480.00
Add: Outstanding checks	930.00
Adjusted balance per books	$4,275.20

Instructions

(a) Prepare a correct bank reconciliation.
(b) Journalize the entries required by the reconciliation.

E7-10 On April 30, the bank reconciliation of Perrin Company shows three outstanding checks: no. 254, $650; no. 255, $720; and no. 257, $410. The May bank statement and the May cash payments journal show the following.

Determine outstanding checks.

(LO 7)

Bank Statement			Cash Payments Journal		
Checks Paid			Checks Issued		
Date	Check No.	Amount	Date	Check No.	Amount
5/4	254	650	5/2	258	159
5/2	257	410	5/5	259	275
5/17	258	159	5/10	260	820
5/12	259	275	5/15	261	500
5/20	261	500	5/22	262	750
5/29	263	480	5/24	263	480
5/30	264	560	5/29	264	560

Instructions

Using step 2 in the reconciliation procedure, list the outstanding checks at May 31.

Prepare bank reconciliation and adjusting entries.

(LO 7)

E7-11 The following information pertains to Worthy Video Company.

1. Cash balance per bank, July 31, $7,293.
2. July bank service charge not recorded by the depositor $28.
3. Cash balance per books, July 31, $7,384.
4. Deposits in transit, July 31, $1,500.
5. Bank collected $800 note for Worthy in July, plus interest $36, less fee $20. The collection has not been recorded by Worthy, and no interest has been accrued.
6. Outstanding checks, July 31, $621.

Instructions

(a) Prepare a bank reconciliation at July 31.
(b) Journalize the adjusting entries at July 31 on the books of Worthy Video Company.

Prepare bank reconciliation and adjusting entries.

(LO 7)

E7-12 The information below relates to the Cash account in the ledger of Wasson Company.

Balance September 1—$17,150; Cash deposited—$64,000.
Balance September 30—$17,404; Checks written—$63,746.

The September bank statement shows a balance of $16,122 on September 30 and the following memoranda.

Credits		Debits	
Collection of $1,500 note plus interest $30	$1,530	NSF check: Violet Jones	$725
Interest earned on checking account	$45	Safety deposit box rent	$65

At September 30, deposits in transit were $4,450, and outstanding checks totaled $2,383.

Instructions

(a) Prepare the bank reconciliation at September 30.
(b) Prepare the adjusting entries at September 30, assuming (1) the NSF check was from a customer on account, and (2) no interest had been accrued on the note.

Compute deposits in transit and outstanding checks for two bank reconciliations.

(LO 7)

E7-13 The cash records of Satter Company show the following four situations.

1. The June 30 bank reconciliation indicated that deposits in transit total $920. During July, the general ledger account Cash shows deposits of $15,750, but the bank statement indicates that only $15,600 in deposits were received during the month.
2. The June 30 bank reconciliation also reported outstanding checks of $880. During the month of July, Satter Company books show that $17,200 of checks were issued. The bank statement showed that $16,400 of checks cleared the bank in July.
3. In September, deposits per the bank statement totaled $26,700, deposits per books were $25,400, and deposits in transit at September 30 were $2,600.
4. In September, cash disbursements per books were $23,700, checks clearing the bank were $24,000, and outstanding checks at September 30 were $2,100.

There were no bank debit or credit memoranda. No errors were made by either the bank or Satter Company.

Instructions

Answer the following questions.

(a) In situation (1), what were the deposits in transit at July 31?
(b) In situation (2), what were the outstanding checks at July 31?
(c) In situation (3), what were the deposits in transit at August 31?
(d) In situation (4), what were the outstanding checks at August 31?

Show presentation of cash in financial statements.

(LO 8)

E7-14 Nayak Company has recorded the following items in its financial records.

Cash in bank	$ 41,000
Cash in plant expansion fund	100,000
Cash on hand	8,000
Highly liquid investments	34,000
Petty cash	500
Receivables from customers	89,000
Stock investments	61,000

The cash in bank is subject to a compensating balance of $5,000. The highly liquid invest ments had maturities of 3 months or less when they were purchased. The stock investments will be sold in the next 6 to 12 months. The plant expansion project will begin in 3 years.

Instructions

(a) What amount should Nayak report as "Cash and cash equivalents" on its balance sheet?

(b) Where should the items not included in part (a) be reported on the balance sheet?

(c) What disclosures should Nayak make in its financial statements concerning "cash and cash equivalents"?

EXERCISES: SET B AND CHALLENGE EXERCISES

Visit the book's companion website, at **www.wiley.com/college/weygandt**, and choose the Student Companion site to access Exercise Set B and Challenge Exercises.

PROBLEMS: SET A

Identify internal control principles over cash disbursements.

(LO 2, 4)

P7-1A Mainland Supply Company recently changed its system of internal control over cash disbursements. The system includes the following features.

Instead of being unnumbered and manually prepared, all checks must now be prenumbered and written by using the new checkwriting machine purchased by the company. Before a check can be issued, each invoice must have the approval of Erin McGarry, the purchasing agent, and Barb Speas, the receiving department supervisor. Checks must be signed by either Amaika Blake, the treasurer, or Ken Yost, the assistant treasurer. Before signing a check, the signer is expected to compare the amount of the check with the amount on the invoice.

After signing a check, the signer stamps the invoice PAID and inserts within the stamp, the date, check number, and amount of the check. The "paid" invoice is then sent to the accounting department for recording.

Blank checks are stored in a safe in the treasurer's office. The combination to the safe is known only by the treasurer and assistant treasurer. Each month, the bank statement is reconciled with the bank balance per books by the assistant chief accountant. All employees who handle or account for cash are bonded.

Instructions

Identify the internal control principles and their application to cash disbursements of Mainland Supply Company.

Journalize and post petty cash fund transactions.

(LO 5)

P7-2A Arial Company maintains a petty cash fund for small expenditures. The following transactions occurred over a 2-month period.

July 1 Established petty cash fund by writing a check on Coulter Bank for $200.

15 Replenished the petty cash fund by writing a check for $198.00. On this date the fund consisted of $2.00 in cash and the following petty cash receipts: freight-out $87.00, postage expense $51.40, entertainment expense $46.60, and miscellaneous expense $11.20.

31 Replenished the petty cash fund by writing a check for $192.00. At this date, the fund consisted of $8.00 in cash and the following petty cash receipts: freight-out $82.10, charitable contributions expense $45.00, postage expense $25.50, and miscellaneous expense $39.40.

Aug. 15 Replenished the petty cash fund by writing a check for $187.00. On this date, the fund consisted of $13.00 in cash and the following petty cash receipts: freight-out $75.60, entertainment expense $43.00, postage expense $33.00, and miscellaneous expense $37.00.

16 Increased the amount of the petty cash fund to $300 by writing a check for $100.

31 Replenished petty cash fund by writing a check for $277.00. On this date, the fund consisted of $23 in cash and the following petty cash receipts: postage expense $133.00, travel expense $95.60, and freight-out $47.10.

Instructions

(a) Journalize the petty cash transactions.
(b) Post to the Petty Cash account.
(c) What internal control features exist in a petty cash fund?

(a) July 15, Cash short $1.80
(b) Aug. 31 balance $300

Prepare a bank reconciliation and adjusting entries.
(LO 7)

P7-3A On May 31, 2014, Terrell Company had a cash balance per books of $6,781.50. The bank statement from Home Town State Bank on that date showed a balance of $6,804.60. A comparison of the statement with the cash account revealed the following facts.

1. The statement included a debit memo of $40 for the printing of additional company checks.
2. Cash sales of $836.15 on May 12 were deposited in the bank. The cash receipts journal entry and the deposit slip were incorrectly made for $886.15. The bank credited Terrell Company for the correct amount.
3. Outstanding checks at May 31 totaled $276.25. Deposits in transit were $1,916.15.
4. On May 18, the company issued check No. 1181 for $685 to Barry Dietz on account. The check, which cleared the bank in May, was incorrectly journalized and posted by Terrell Company for $658.
5. A $3,000 note receivable was collected by the bank for Terrell Company on May 31 plus $80 interest. The bank charged a collection fee of $20. No interest has been accrued on the note.
6. Included with the cancelled checks was a check issued by Bridges Company to Jon Newton for $600 that was incorrectly charged to Terrell Company by the bank.
7. On May 31, the bank statement showed an NSF charge of $680 for a check issued by Sandy Grifton, a customer, to Terrell Company on account.

Instructions

(a) Prepare the bank reconciliation at May 31, 2014.
(b) Prepare the necessary adjusting entries for Terrell Company at May 31, 2014.

(a) Adjusted cash balance per bank $9,044.50

Prepare a bank reconciliation and adjusting entries from detailed data.
(LO 7)

P7-4A The bank portion of the bank reconciliation for Rintala Company at November 30, 2014, was as follows.

Rintala Company
Bank Reconciliation
November 30, 2014

Cash balance per bank			$14,367.90
Add: Deposits in transit			2,530.20
			16,898.10
Less: Outstanding checks			
	Check Number	Check Amount	
	3451	$2,260.40	
	3470	720.10	
	3471	844.50	
	3472	1,426.80	
	3474	1,050.00	6,301.80
Adjusted cash balance per bank			$10,596.30

The adjusted cash balance per bank agreed with the cash balance per books at November 30.

The December bank statement showed the following checks and deposits.

Bank Statement

Checks			Deposits	
Date	**Number**	**Amount**	**Date**	**Amount**
12-1	3451	$ 2,260.40	12-1	$ 2,530.20
12-2	3471	844.50	12-4	1,211.60
12-7	3472	1,426.80	12-8	2,365.10
12-4	3475	1,640.70	12-16	2,672.70
12-8	3476	1,300.00	12-21	2,945.00
12-10	3477	2,130.00	12-26	2,567.30
12-15	3479	3,080.00	12-29	2,836.00
12-27	3480	600.00	12-30	1,025.00
12-30	3482	475.50	Total	$18,152.90
12-29	3483	1,140.00		
12-31	3485	540.80		
	Total	$15,438.70		

The cash records per books for December showed the following.

Cash Payments Journal

Date	Number	Amount	Date	Number	Amount
12-1	3475	$1,640.70	12-20	3482	$ 475.50
12-2	3476	1,300.00	12-22	3483	1,140.00
12-2	3477	2,130.00	12-23	3484	798.00
12-4	3478	621.30	12-24	3485	450.80
12-8	3479	3,080.00	12-30	3486	1,889.50
12-10	3480	600.00	Total		$14,933.20
12-17	3481	807.40			

Cash Receipts Journal

Date	Amount
12-3	$ 1,211.60
12-7	2,365.10
12-15	2,672.70
12-20	2,954.00
12-25	2,567.30
12-28	2,836.00
12-30	1,025.00
12-31	1,190.40
Total	$16,822.10

The bank statement contained two memoranda:

1. A credit of $3,645 for the collection of a $3,500 note for Rintala Company plus interest of $160 and less a collection fee of $15. Rintala Company has not accrued any interest on the note.
2. A debit of $572.80 for an NSF check written by D. Chagnon, a customer. At December 31, the check had not been redeposited in the bank.

At December 31, the cash balance per books was $12,485.20, and the cash balance per the bank statement was $20,154.30. The bank did not make any errors, but two errors were made by Rintala Company.

Instructions

(a) Using the four steps in the reconciliation procedure, prepare a bank reconciliation at December 31.

(a) Adjusted balance per books $15,458.40

(b) Prepare the adjusting entries based on the reconciliation. (*Hint:* The correction of any errors pertaining to recording checks should be made to Accounts Payable. The correction of any errors relating to recording cash receipts should be made to Accounts Receivable.)

Prepare a bank reconciliation and adjusting entries.

(LO 7)

P7-5A Cayemberg Company maintains a checking account at the Commerce Bank. At July 31, selected data from the ledger balance and the bank statement are shown below.

	Cash in Bank	
	Per Books	**Per Bank**
Balance, July 1	$17,600	$16,800
July receipts	81,400	
July credits		82,470
July disbursements	77,150	
July debits		74,756
Balance, July 31	$21,850	$24,514

Analysis of the bank data reveals that the credits consist of $81,000 of July deposits and a credit memorandum of $1,470 for the collection of a $1,400 note plus interest revenue of $70. The July debits per bank consist of checks cleared $74,700 and a debit memorandum of $56 for printing additional company checks.

You also discover the following errors involving July checks: (1) A check for $230 to a creditor on account that cleared the bank in July was journalized and posted as $320. (2) A salary check to an employee for $255 was recorded by the bank for $155.

The June 30 bank reconciliation contained only two reconciling items: deposits in transit $7,000 and outstanding checks of $6,200.

Instructions

(a) Adjusted balance per books $23,354

(a) Prepare a bank reconciliation at July 31, 2014.

(b) Journalize the adjusting entries to be made by Cayemberg Company. Assume that interest on the note has not been accrued.

Identify internal control weaknesses in cash receipts and cash disbursements.

(LO 2, 3, 4)

P7-6A Nature Hill Middle School wants to raise money for a new sound system for its auditorium. The primary fund-raising event is a dance at which the famous disc jockey Obnoxious Al will play classic and not-so-classic dance tunes. Rob Drexler, the music and theater instructor, has been given the responsibility for coordinating the fund-raising efforts. This is Rob's first experience with fund-raising. He decides to put the eighth-grade choir in charge of the event; he will be a relatively passive observer.

Rob had 500 unnumbered tickets printed for the dance. He left the tickets in a box on his desk and told the choir students to take as many tickets as they thought they could sell for $5 each. In order to ensure that no extra tickets would be floating around, he told them to dispose of any unsold tickets. When the students received payment for the tickets, they were to bring the cash back to Rob and he would put it in a locked box in his desk drawer.

Some of the students were responsible for decorating the gymnasium for the dance. Rob gave each of them a key to the money box and told them that if they took money out to purchase materials, they should put a note in the box saying how much they took and what it was used for. After 2 weeks the money box appeared to be getting full, so Rob asked Erik Radley to count the money, prepare a deposit slip, and deposit the money in a bank account Rob had opened.

The day of the dance, Rob wrote a check from the account to pay the DJ. Obnoxious Al, however, said that he accepted only cash and did not give receipts. So Rob took $200 out of the cash box and gave it to Al. At the dance, Rob had Sobia Hamm working at the entrance to the gymnasium, collecting tickets from students, and selling tickets to those who had not prepurchased them. Rob estimated that 400 students attended the dance.

The following day, Rob closed out the bank account, which had $250 in it, and gave that amount plus the $180 in the cash box to Principal Coleman. Principal Coleman seemed surprised that, after generating roughly $2,000 in sales, the dance netted only $430 in cash. Rob did not know how to respond.

Instructions

Identify as many internal control weaknesses as you can in this scenario, and suggest how each could be addressed.

PROBLEMS: SET B

P7-1B Orpheum Theater is located in the Brooklyn Mall. A cashier's booth is located near the entrance to the theater. Three cashiers are employed. One works from 1–5 P.M., another from 5–9 P.M. The shifts are rotated among the three cashiers. The cashiers receive cash from customers and operate a machine that ejects serially numbered tickets. The rolls of tickets are inserted and locked into the machine by the theater manager at the beginning of each cashier's shift.

Identify internal control weaknesses over cash receipts.

(LO 2, 3)

After purchasing a ticket, the customer takes the ticket to an usher stationed at the entrance of the theater lobby some 60 feet from the cashier's booth. The usher tears the ticket in half, admits the customer, and returns the ticket stub to the customer. The other half of the ticket is dropped into a locked box by the usher.

At the end of each cashier's shift, the theater manager removes the ticket rolls from the machine and makes a cash count. The cash count sheet is initialed by the cashier. At the end of the day, the manager deposits the receipts in total in a bank night deposit vault located in the mall. The manager also sends copies of the deposit slip and the initialed cash count sheets to the theater company treasurer for verification and to the company's accounting department. Receipts from the first shift are stored in a safe located in the manager's office.

Instructions

(a) Identify the internal control principles and their application to the cash receipts transactions of the Orpheum Theater.

(b) If the usher and cashier decide to collaborate to misappropriate cash, what actions might they take?

P7-2B McArtor Company maintains a petty cash fund for small expenditures. The following transactions occurred over a 2-month period.

Journalize and post petty cash fund transactions.

(LO 5)

July 1 Established petty cash fund by writing a check on Star Bank for $100.

15 Replenished the petty cash fund by writing a check for $94.90. On this date, the fund consisted of $5.10 in cash and the following petty cash receipts: freight-out $51.00, postage expense $20.50, entertainment expense $23.10, and miscellaneous expense $4.10.

31 Replenished the petty cash fund by writing a check for $92.90. At this date, the fund consisted of $7.10 in cash and the following petty cash receipts: freight-out $43.50, charitable contributions expense $20.00, postage expense $20.10, and miscellaneous expense $9.30.

Aug. 15 Replenished the petty cash fund by writing a check for $98.00. On this date, the fund consisted of $2.00 in cash and the following petty cash receipts: freight-out $40.20, entertainment expense $21.00, postage expense $14.00, and miscellaneous expense $19.80.

16 Increased the amount of the petty cash fund to $150 by writing a check for $50.

31 Replenished the petty cash fund by writing a check for $137.00. On this date, the fund consisted of $13 in cash and the following petty cash receipts: freight-out $74.00, entertainment expense $43.20, and postage expense $17.70.

Instructions

(a) Journalize the petty cash transactions.

(b) Post to the Petty Cash account.

(c) What internal control features exist in a petty cash fund?

(a) July 15 Cash over $3.80
(b) Aug. 31 balance $150

P7-3B Aglife Genetics Company of Lancaster, Wisconsin, spreads herbicides and applies liquid fertilizer for local farmers. On May 31, 2014, the company's Cash account per its general ledger showed the following balance.

Prepare a bank reconciliation and adjusting entries.

(LO 7)

CASH NO. 101

Date	Explanation	Ref.	Debit	Credit	Balance
May 31	Balance				13,287

The bank statement from Lancaster State Bank on that date showed the following balance.

Lancaster State Bank		
Checks and Debits	**Deposits and Credits**	**Daily Balance**
XXX	XXX	5/31 12,732

A comparison of the details on the bank statement with the details in the cash account revealed the following facts.

1. The statement included a debit memo of $35 for the printing of additional company checks.
2. Cash sales of $1,720 on May 12 were deposited in the bank. The cash receipts journal entry and the deposit slip were incorrectly made for $1,820. The bank credited Aglife Genetics Company for the correct amount.
3. Outstanding checks at May 31 totaled $1,425, and deposits in transit were $2,100.
4. On May 18, the company issued check no. 1181 for $1,102 to M. Datz on account. The check, which cleared the bank in May, was incorrectly journalized and posted by Aglife Genetics Company for $110.
5. A $4,000 note receivable was collected by the bank for Aglife Genetics Company on May 31 plus $80 interest. The bank charged a collection fee of $25. No interest has been accrued on the note.
6. Included with the cancelled checks was a check issued by Bohr Company to Carol Mertz for $900 that was incorrectly charged to Aglife Genetics Company by the bank.
7. On May 31, the bank statement showed an NSF charge of $1,908 for a check issued by Tyler Gricius, a customer, to Aglife Genetics Company on account.

Instructions

(a) Adj. cash bal. $14,307

(a) Prepare the bank reconciliation at May 31, 2014.

(b) Prepare the necessary adjusting entries for Aglife Genetics Company at May 31, 2014.

Prepare a bank reconciliation and adjusting entries from detailed data.

(LO 7)

P7-4B The bank portion of the bank reconciliation for Goulet Company at October 31, 2014, was as follows.

Goulet Company
Bank Reconciliation
October 31, 2014

Cash balance per bank		$6,000
Add: Deposits in transit		842
		6,842
Less: Outstanding checks		
Check Number	Check Amount	
2451	$700	
2470	396	
2471	464	
2472	170	
2474	578	2,308
Adjusted cash balance per bank		$4,534

The adjusted cash balance per bank agreed with the cash balance per books at October 31.

The November bank statement showed the following checks and deposits:

Bank Statement

Checks			Deposits	
Date	**Number**	**Amount**	**Date**	**Amount**
11-1	2470	$ 396	11-1	$ 842
11-2	2471	464	11-4	666
11-5	2474	578	11-8	545
11-4	2475	903	11-13	1,416
11-8	2476	1,556	11-18	810
11-10	2477	330	11-21	1,624
11-15	2479	980	11-25	1,412
11-18	2480	714	11-28	908
11-27	2481	382	11-30	652
11-30	2483	317	Total	$8,875
11-29	2486	495		
	Total	$7,115		

The cash records per books for November showed the following.

Cash Payments Journal

Date	Number	Amount	Date	Number	Amount
11-1	2475	$ 903	11-20	2483	$ 317
11-2	2476	1,556	11-22	2484	460
11-2	2477	330	11-23	2485	525
11-4	2478	300	11-24	2486	495
11-8	2479	890	11-29	2487	340
11-10	2480	714	11-30	2488	635
11-15	2481	382	Total		$8,197
11-18	2482	350			

Cash Receipts Journal

Date	Amount
11-3	$ 666
11-7	545
11-12	1,416
11-17	810
11-20	1,642
11-24	1,412
11-27	908
11-29	652
11-30	1,581
Total	$9,632

The bank statement contained two bank memoranda:

1. A credit of $1,375 for the collection of a $1,300 note for Goulet Company plus interest of $91 and less a collection fee of $16. Goulet Company has not accrued any interest on the note.
2. A debit for the printing of additional company checks $35.

At November 30, the cash balance per books was $5,969, and the cash balance per the bank statement was $9,100. The bank did not make any errors, but two errors were made by Goulet Company.

Instructions

(a) Using the four steps in the reconciliation procedure described on pages 347–349, prepare a bank reconciliation at November 30.

(a) Adjusted cash balance per bank $7,201

(b) Prepare the adjusting entries based on the reconciliation. (*Hint:* The correction of any errors pertaining to recording checks should be made to Accounts Payable. The correction of any errors relating to recording cash receipts should be made to Accounts Receivable).

P7-5B Tizani Company's bank statement from Eastern National Bank at August 31, 2014, shows the information below.

Prepare a bank reconciliation and adjusting entries.

(LO 7)

Balance, August 1	$11,284	Bank credit memoranda:	
August deposits	47,521	Collection of note	
Checks cleared in August	46,175	receivable plus $105	
Balance, August 31	17,146	interest	$4,505
		Interest earned	41
		Bank debit memorandum:	
		Safety deposit box rent	30

A summary of the Cash account in the ledger for August shows: Balance, August 1, $10,559; receipts $50,050; disbursements $47,794; and balance, August 31, $12,815. Analysis reveals that the only reconciling items on the July 31 bank reconciliation were a deposit in transit for $2,200 and outstanding checks of $2,925. The deposit in transit was the first deposit recorded by the bank in August. In addition, you determine that there were two errors involving company checks drawn in August: (1) A check for $340 to a creditor on account that cleared the bank in August was journalized and posted for $430. (2) A salary check to an employee for $275 was recorded by the bank for $277.

Instructions

(a) Adjusted balance per books $17,421

(a) Prepare a bank reconciliation at August 31.
(b) Journalize the adjusting entries to be made by Tizani Company at August 31. Assume that interest on the note has not been accrued by the company.

Prepare a comprehensive bank reconciliation with theft and internal control deficiencies.

(LO 2, 3, 4, 7)

P7-6B Stupendous Company is a very profitable small business. It has not, however, given much consideration to internal control. For example, in an attempt to keep clerical and office expenses to a minimum, the company has combined the jobs of cashier and bookkeeper. As a result, Jake Burnett handles all cash receipts, keeps the accounting records, and prepares the monthly bank reconciliations.

The balance per the bank statement on October 31, 2014, was $15,313. Outstanding checks were: no. 62 for $107.74, no. 183 for $127.50, no. 284 for $215.26, no. 862 for $132.10, no. 863 for $192.78, and no. 864 for $140.49. Included with the statement was a credit memorandum of $460 indicating the collection of a note receivable for Stupendous Company by the bank on October 25. This memorandum has not been recorded by Stupendous Company.

The company's ledger showed one cash account with a balance of $18,608.81. The balance included undeposited cash on hand. Because of the lack of internal controls, Burnett took for personal use all of the undeposited receipts in excess of $3,226.18. He then prepared the following bank reconciliation in an effort to conceal his theft of cash.

Bank Reconciliation

Cash balance per books, October 31		$18,608.81
Add: Outstanding checks		
No. 862	$132.10	
No. 863	192.78	
No. 864	140.49	390.37
		18,999.18
Less: Undeposited receipts		3,226.18
Unadjusted balance per bank, October 31		15,773.00
Less: Bank credit memorandum		460.00
Cash balance per bank statement, October 31		$15,313.00

Instructions

(a) Adjusted balance per books $17,623.31

(a) Prepare a correct bank reconciliation. (*Hint:* Deduct the amount of the theft from the adjusted balance per books.)
(b) Indicate the three ways that Burnett attempted to conceal the theft and the dollar amount pertaining to each method.
(c) What principles of internal control were violated in this case?

PROBLEMS: SET C

Visit the book's companion website, at **www.wiley.com/college/weygandt**, and choose the Student Companion site to access Problem Set C.

COMPREHENSIVE PROBLEM

CP7 On December 1, 2014, Westmoreland Company had the following account balances.

	Debits		**Credits**
Cash	$18,200	Accumulated Depreciation— Equipment	$ 3,000
Notes Receivable	2,000	Accounts Payable	6,100
Accounts Receivable	7,500	Common Stock	50,000
Inventory	16,000	Retained Earnings	14,200
Prepaid Insurance	1,600		$73,300
Equipment	28,000		
	$73,300		

During December, the company completed the following transactions.

Dec. 7 Received $3,600 cash from customers in payment of account (no discount allowed).
12 Purchased merchandise on account from Alice Co. $12,000, terms 1/10, n/30.
17 Sold merchandise on account $16,000, terms 2/10, n/30. The cost of the merchandise sold was $10,000.
19 Paid salaries $2,200.
22 Paid Alice Co. in full, less discount.
26 Received collections in full, less discounts, from customers billed on December 17.
31 Received $2,700 cash from customers in payment of account (no discount allowed).

Adjustment data:

1. Depreciation $200 per month.
2. Insurance expired $400.

Instructions

(a) Journalize the December transactions. (Assume a perpetual inventory system.)
(b) Enter the December 1 balances in the ledger T-accounts and post the December transactions. Use Cost of Goods Sold, Depreciation Expense, Insurance Expense, Salaries and Wages Expense, Sales Revenue, and Sales Discounts.
(c) The statement from Dodge County Bank on December 31 showed a balance of $25,930. A comparison of the bank statement with the Cash account revealed the following facts.
   1. The bank collected a note receivable of $2,000 for Westmoreland Company on December 15.
   2. The December 31 receipts were deposited in a night deposit vault on December 31. These deposits were recorded by the bank in January.
   3. Checks outstanding on December 31 totaled $1,210.
   4. On December 31, the bank statement showed a NSF charge of $680 for a check received by the company from K. Quinn, a customer, on account.

   Prepare a bank reconciliation as of December 31 based on the available information. (*Hint:* The cash balance per books is $26,100. This can be proven by finding the balance in the Cash account from parts (a) and (b).)
(d) Journalize the adjusting entries resulting from the bank reconciliation and adjustment data.
(e) Post the adjusting entries to the ledger T-accounts.
(f) Prepare an adjusted trial balance.
(g) Prepare an income statement for December and a classified balance sheet at December 31.

CONTINUING COOKIE CHRONICLE

(*Note:* This is a continuation of the Cookie Chronicle from Chapters 1–6.)

CCC7 Part 1 Natalie is struggling to keep up with the recording of her accounting transactions. She is spending a lot of time marketing and selling mixers and giving her cookie classes. Her friend John is an accounting student who runs his own accounting service. He has asked Natalie if she would like to have him do her accounting. John and Natalie meet and discuss her business.

Part 2 Natalie decides that she cannot afford to hire John to do her accounting. One way that she can ensure that her cash account does not have any errors and is accurate and up-to-date is to prepare a bank reconciliation at the end of each month. Natalie would like you to help her.

Go to the book's companion website, www.wiley.com/college/weygandt, to see the completion of this problem.

Broadening Your PERSPECTIVE

Financial Reporting and Analysis

Financial Reporting Problem: PepsiCo, Inc.

BYP7-1 The financial statements of PepsiCo, Inc. are presented in Appendix A at the end of this textbook.

Instructions

(a) What comments, if any, are made about cash in the report of the independent registered public accounting firm?
(b) What data about cash and cash equivalents are shown in the consolidated balance sheet?
(c) In its notes to Consolidated Financial Statements, how does PepsiCo define cash equivalents?
(d) In the section "Management's Report on Internal Control Over Financial Reporting," what does PepsiCo's management say about internal control? (See page A-35 in Appendix A of the back of the book.)

Comparative Analysis Problem: PepsiCo, Inc. vs. The Coca-Cola Company

BYP7-2 PepsiCo's financial statements are presented in Appendix A. Financial statements of The Coca-Cola Company are presented in Appendix B.

Instructions

(a) Based on the information contained in these financial statements, determine each of the following for each company:
 (1) Cash and cash equivalents balance at December 25, 2010, for PepsiCo and at December 31, 2010, for Coca-Cola.
 (2) Increase (decrease) in cash and cash equivalents from 2009 to 2010.
 (3) Cash provided by operating activities during the year ended December 2010 (from statement of cash flows).
(b) What conclusions concerning the management of cash can be drawn from these data?

Real-World Focus

BYP7-3 All organizations should have systems of internal control. Universities are no exception. This site discusses the basics of internal control in a university setting.

Address: **www.bc.edu/offices/audit/controls,** or go to **www.wiley.com/college/weygandt**

Steps: Go to the site shown above.

Instructions

The front page of this site provides links to pages that answer six critical questions. Use these links to answer the following questions.

(a) In a university setting, who has responsibility for evaluating the adequacy of the system of internal control?
(b) What do reconciliations ensure in the university setting? Who should review the reconciliation?
(c) What are some examples of physical controls?
(d) What are two ways to accomplish inventory counts?

Critical Thinking

Decision-Making Across the Organization

BYP7-4 The board of trustees of a local church is concerned about the internal accounting controls for the offering collections made at weekly services. The trustees ask you to serve on a three-person audit team with the internal auditor of a local college and a CPA who has just joined the church.

At a meeting of the audit team and the board of trustees, you learn the following.

1. The church's board of trustees has delegated responsibility for the financial management and audit of the financial records to the finance committee. This group prepares the annual budget and approves major disbursements. It is not involved in collections or record-keeping. No audit has been made in recent years because the same trusted employee has kept church records and served as financial secretary for 15 years. The church does not carry any fidelity insurance.
2. The collection at the weekly service is taken by a team of ushers who volunteer to serve one month. The ushers take the collection plates to a basement office at the rear of the church. They hand their plates to the head usher and return to the church service. After all plates have been turned in, the head usher counts the cash received. The head usher then places the cash in the church safe along with a notation of the amount counted. The head usher volunteers to serve for 3 months.
3. The next morning, the financial secretary opens the safe and recounts the collection. The secretary withholds $150–$200 in cash, depending on the cash expenditures expected for the week, and deposits the remainder of the collections in the bank. To facilitate the deposit, church members who contribute by check are asked to make their checks payable to "Cash."
4. Each month, the financial secretary reconciles the bank statement and submits a copy of the reconciliation to the board of trustees. The reconciliations have rarely contained any bank errors and have never shown any errors per books.

Instructions
With the class divided into groups, answer the following.

(a) Indicate the weaknesses in internal accounting control over the handling of collections.
(b) List the improvements in internal control procedures that you plan to make at the next meeting of the audit team for (1) the ushers, (2) the head usher, (3) the financial secretary, and (4) the finance committee.
(c) What church policies should be changed to improve internal control?

Communication Activity

BYP7-5 As a new auditor for the CPA firm of Murphy, Mooney, and Feeney, you have been assigned to review the internal controls over mail cash receipts of Stillwater Company. Your review reveals the following: Checks are promptly endorsed "For Deposit Only," but no list of the checks is prepared by the person opening the mail. The mail is opened either by the cashier or by the employee who maintains the accounts receivable records. Mail receipts are deposited in the bank weekly by the cashier.

Instructions
Write a letter to Jack Meyer, owner of Stillwater Company, explaining the weaknesses in internal control and your recommendations for improving the system.

Ethics Case

BYP7-6 You are the assistant controller in charge of general ledger accounting at Springtime Bottling Company. Your company has a large loan from an insurance company. The loan agreement requires that the company's cash account balance be maintained at $200,000 or more, as reported monthly.

At June 30, the cash balance is $80,000, which you report to Anne Shirley, the financial vice president. Anne excitedly instructs you to keep the cash receipts book open for one additional day for purposes of the June 30 report to the insurance company. Anne says, "If we don't get that cash balance over $200,000, we'll default on our loan agreement. They could close us down, put us all out of our jobs!" Anne continues, "I talked to Oconto Distributors (one of Springtime's largest customers) this morning. They said they sent us a check for $150,000 yesterday. We should receive it tomorrow. If we include just that one check in our cash balance, we'll be in the clear. It's in the mail!"

Instructions

(a) Who will suffer negative effects if you do not comply with Anne Shirley's instructions? Who will suffer if you do comply?
(b) What are the ethical considerations in this case?
(c) What alternatives do you have?

All About You

BYP7-7 As you may already know, potential security risks may arise from your personal computer. It is important to keep in mind, however, that there are also many other ways that your identity can be stolen other than from your computer. The federal government provides many resources to help protect you from identity thieves.

Instructions

Go to **http://onguardonline.gov/idtheft.html**, and click on **ID Theft Faceoff**. Complete the quiz provided there.

BYP7-8 Identity thieves determine your identity by going through your mail or trash, stealing your credit cards, redirecting mail through change of address forms, or acquiring personal information you share on unsecured sites. In a recent year, more than 7 million people were victims of identity theft.

Do you feel it is safe to store personal financial data (such as Social Security numbers and bank and credit account numbers) on your computer?

YES: I have anti-virus software that will detect and stop any intruder.

NO: Even the best anti-virus software does not detect every kind of intruder.

Instructions

Write a response indicating your position regarding the situation. Provide support for your view.

FASB Codification Activity

BYP7-9 If your school has a subscription to the FASB Codification, go to *http://aaahq.org/ascLogin.cfm* to log in and prepare responses to the following.

(a) How is cash defined in the Codification?
(b) How are cash equivalents defined in the Codification?
(c) What are the disclosure requirements related to cash and cash equivalents?

Answers to Chapter Questions

Answers to Insight and Accounting Across the Organization Questions

p. 327 And the Controls Are... Q: Why is sustainability information important to investors? **A:** Investors, customers, suppliers, and employees want more information about companies' long-term impact on society. There is a growing awareness that sustainability issues can affect a company's financial performance. Proper reporting on sustainability issues develops a solid reputation for transparency and provides confidence to shareholders.

p. 334 SOX Boosts the Role of Human Resources Q: Why would unsupervised employees or employees who report to each other represent potential internal control threats? **A:** An unsupervised employee may have a fraudulent job (or may even be a fictitious person), e.g., a person drawing a paycheck without working. Or, if two employees supervise each other, there is no real separation of duties, and they can conspire to defraud the company.

p. 335 Big Theft at Small Companies Q: Why are small companies more susceptible to employee theft? **A:** The high degree of trust often found in small companies makes them more vulnerable. Also, small companies tend to have less sophisticated systems of internal control, and they usually lack internal auditors. In addition, it is very hard to achieve some internal control features, such as segregation of duties, when you have very few employees.

p. 343 How Employees Steal Q: How can companies reduce the likelihood of fraudulent disbursements? **A:** To reduce the occurrence of fraudulent disbursements, a company should follow the procedures discussed in this chapter. These include having only designated personnel sign checks; having different personnel approve payments and make payments; ensuring that check signers do not record disbursements; using prenumbered checks and matching each check to an approved invoice; storing blank checks securely; reconciling the bank statement; and stamping invoices PAID.

p. 351 Madoff's Ponzi Scheme Q: How was Madoff able to conceal such a giant fraud? **A:** Madoff fabricated false investment statements that were provided to investors. In addition, his auditor never verified these investment statements even though the auditor gave him an unqualified opinion each year.

Answers to Self-Test Questions

1. c **2.** a **3.** a **4.** c **5.** b **6.** b **7.** d **8.** d **9.** a ($100 − ($94 + $4)) **10.** a **11.** c **12.** d **13.** c **14.** c

A Look at IFRS

Fraud can occur anywhere. And because the three main factors that contribute to fraud are universal in nature, the principles of internal control activities are used globally by companies. While Sarbanes-Oxley (SOX) does not apply to international companies, most large international companies have internal controls similar to those indicated in the chapter. IFRS and GAAP are very similar in accounting for cash. *IAS No. 1 (revised)*, "Presentation of Financial Statements," is the only standard that discusses issues specifically related to cash.

Key Points

- The fraud triangle discussed in this chapter is applicable to all international companies. Some of the major frauds on an international basis are Parmalat (Italy), Royal Ahold (the Netherlands), and Satyam Computer Services (India).
- Rising economic crime poses a growing threat to companies, with nearly half of all organizations worldwide being victims of fraud in a recent two-year period (*PricewaterhouseCoopers' Global Economic Crime Survey*, 2005). Specifically, 44% of Romanian companies surveyed experienced fraud in the past two years.
- Globally, the number of companies reporting fraud increased from 37% to 45% since 2003, a 22% increase. The cost to companies was an average US$1.7 million in losses from "tangible frauds," that is, those that result in an immediate and direct financial loss. These include asset misappropriation, false pretenses, and counterfeiting (*PricewaterhouseCoopers' Global Economic Crime Survey*, 2005).
- Accounting scandals both in the United States and internationally have re-ignited the debate over the relative merits of GAAP, which takes a "rules-based" approach to accounting, versus IFRS, which takes a "principles-based" approach. The FASB announced that it intends to introduce more principles-based standards.
- On a lighter note, at one time Ig Nobel Prize in Economics went to the CEOs of those companies involved in the corporate accounting scandals of that year for "adapting the mathematical concept of imaginary numbers for use in the business world." A parody of the Nobel Prizes, the Ig Nobel Prizes (read Ignoble, as not noble) are given each year in early October for 10 achievements that "first make people laugh, and then make them think." Organized by the scientific humor magazine *Annals of Improbable Research (AIR)*, they are presented by a group that includes genuine Nobel laureates at a ceremony at Harvard University's Sanders Theater. (See *en.wikipedia.org/wiki/Ig_Nobel_Prize*.)

- Internal controls are a system of checks and balances designed to prevent and detect fraud and errors. While most companies have these systems in place, many have never completely documented them, nor had an independent auditor attest to their effectiveness. Both of these actions are required under SOX.
- Companies find that internal control review is a costly process but badly needed. One study estimates the cost of SOX compliance for U.S. companies at over $35 billion, with audit fees doubling in the first year of compliance. At the same time, examination of internal controls indicates lingering problems in the way companies operate. One study of first compliance with the internal-control testing provisions documented material weaknesses for about 13% of companies reporting in a two-year period (*PricewaterhouseCoopers' Global Economic Crime Survey*, 2005).
- The SOX internal control standards apply only to companies listed on U.S. exchanges. There is continuing debate over whether foreign issuers should have to comply with this extra layer of regulation.
- The accounting and internal control procedures related to cash are essentially the same under both IFRS and this textbook. In addition, the definition used for cash equivalents is the same.
- Most companies report cash and cash equivalents together under IFRS, as shown in this textbook. In addition, IFRS follows the same accounting policies related to the reporting of restricted cash.
- IFRS defines cash and cash equivalents as follows.
  - **Cash** is comprised of cash on hand and demand deposits.
  - **Cash equivalents** are short-term, highly liquid investments that are readily convertible to known amounts of cash and which are subject to an insignificant risk of changes in value.
- Under IFRS, cash and cash equivalents are often shown last in the statement of financial position.

Looking to the Future

Ethics has become a very important aspect of reporting. Different cultures have different perspectives on bribery and other questionable activities, and consequently penalties for engaging in such activities vary considerably across countries.

High-quality international accounting requires both high-quality accounting standards and high-quality auditing. Similar to the convergence of GAAP and IFRS, there is movement to improve international auditing standards. The International Auditing and Assurance Standards Board (IAASB) functions as an independent standard-setting body. It works to establish high-quality auditing and assurance and quality-control standards throughout the world. Whether the IAASB adopts internal control provisions similar to those in SOX remains to be seen. You can follow developments in the international audit arena at *http://www.ifac.org/iaasb/*.

Under proposed new standards for financial statements, companies would not be allowed to combine cash equivalents with cash.

IFRS Practice

IFRS Self-Test Questions

1. Non-U.S companies that follow IFRS:
   (a) do not normally use the principles of internal control activities described in this textbook.
   (b) often offset cash with accounts payable on the balance sheet.
   (c) are not required to follow SOX.
   (d) None of the above.
2. Which of the following is the correct accounting under IFRS for cash?
   (a) Cash cannot be combined with cash equivalents.
   (b) Restricted cash funds may be reported as a current or non-current asset depending on the circumstances.
   (c) Restricted cash funds cannot be reported as a current asset.
   (d) Cash on hand is not reported on the balance sheet as Cash.

3. The Sarbanes-Oxley Act applies to:
   (a) all U.S. companies listed on U.S. exchanges.
   (b) all companies that list stock on any stock exchange in any country.
   (c) all European companies listed on European exchanges.
   (d) Both (a) and (c).
4. High-quality international accounting requires both high-quality accounting standards and:
   (a) a reconsideration of SOX to make it less onerous.
   (b) high-quality auditing standards.
   (c) government intervention to ensure that the public interest is protected.
   (d) the development of new principles of internal control activities.
5. Cash equivalents under IFRS:
   (a) are significantly different than the cash equivalents discussed in the textbook.
   (b) are generally disclosed separately from cash.
   (c) may be required to be reported separately from cash in the future.
   (d) None of the above.

IFRS Exercises

IFRS7-1 Some people argue that the internal control requirements of the Sarbanes-Oxley Act (SOX) put U.S. companies at a competitive disadvantage to companies outside the United States. Discuss the competitive implications (both pros and cons) of SOX.

IFRS7-2 State whether each of the following is true or false. For those that are false, explain why.

(a) A proposed new financial accounting standard would not allow cash equivalents to be reported in combination with cash.

(b) Perspectives on bribery and penalties for engaging in bribery are the same across all countries.

(c) Cash equivalents are comprised of cash on hand and demand deposits.

(d) SOX was created by the International Accounting Standards Board.

International Financial Reporting Problem: Zetar plc

IFRS7-3 The financial statements of Zetar plc are presented in Appendix C. The company's complete annual report, including the notes to its financial statements, is available at *www.zetarplc.com.*

Instructions

Using the notes to the company's financial statements, answer the following questions.

(a) Which committee of the board of directors is responsible for considering management's reports on internal control?

(b) What are the company's key control procedures?

(c) Does the company have an internal audit department?

(d) In what section or sections does Zetar report its bank overdrafts?

Answers to IFRS Self-Test Questions

1. c **2.** b **3.** a **4.** b **5.** c

✔ Remember to go back to The Navigator box on the chapter opening page and check off your completed work.

Chapter 8

Accounting for Receivables

Feature Story

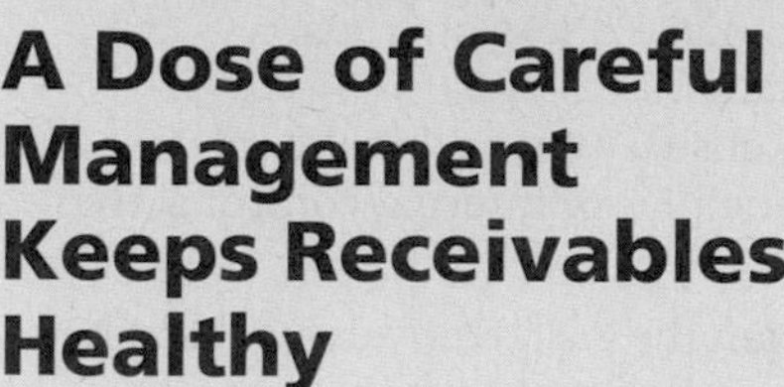

A Dose of Careful Management Keeps Receivables Healthy

"Sometimes you have to know when to be very tough, and sometimes you can give them a bit of a break," says Vivi Su. She's not talking about her children, but about the customers of a subsidiary of pharmaceutical company Whitehall-Robins, where she works as supervisor of credit and collections.

For example, while the company's regular terms are 1/15, n/30 (1% discount if paid within 15 days), a customer might ask for and receive a few days of grace and still get the discount. Or a customer might place orders above its credit limit, in which case, depending on its payment history and the circumstances, Ms. Su might authorize shipment of the goods anyway.

"It's not about drawing a line in the sand, and that's all," she explains. "You want a good relationship with your customers—but you also need to bring in the money."

"The money," in Whitehall-Robins's case, amounts to some $170 million in sales a year. Nearly all of it comes in through the credit accounts Ms. Su manages. The process starts with the decision to grant a customer an account in the first place, Ms. Su explains. The sales rep gives the customer a credit application. "My

The Navigator

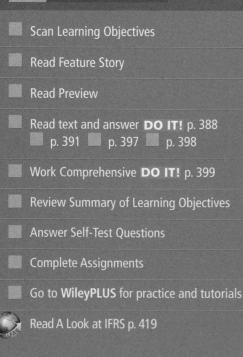

- Scan Learning Objectives
- Read Feature Story
- Read Preview
- Read text and answer **DO IT!** p. 388, p. 391, p. 397, p. 398
- Work Comprehensive **DO IT!** p. 399
- Review Summary of Learning Objectives
- Answer Self-Test Questions
- Complete Assignments
- Go to **WileyPLUS** for practice and tutorials
-  Read A Look at IFRS p. 419

Learning Objectives

After studying this chapter, you should be able to:

1. Identify the different types of receivables.
2. Explain how companies recognize accounts receivable.
3. Distinguish between the methods and bases companies use to value accounts receivable.
4. Describe the entries to record the disposition of accounts receivable.
5. Compute the maturity date of and interest on notes receivable.
6. Explain how companies recognize notes receivable.
7. Describe how companies value notes receivable.
8. Describe the entries to record the disposition of notes receivable.
9. Explain the statement presentation and analysis of receivables.

 **The Navigator**

department reviews this application very carefully; a customer needs to supply three good references, and we also run a check with a credit firm like Equifax. If we accept them, then based on their size and history, we assign a credit limit."

Once accounts are established, the company supervises them very carefully. "I get an aging report every single day," says Ms. Su.

"The rule of thumb is that we should always have at least 85% of receivables current—meaning they were billed less than 30 days ago," she continues. "But we try to do even better than that—I like to see 90%." Similarly, her guideline is never to have more than 5% of receivables at over 90 days. But long before that figure is reached, "we jump on it," she says firmly.

At 15 days overdue, Whitehall-Robins phones the client. Often there's a reasonable explanation for the delay—an invoice may have gone astray, or the payables clerk is away. "But if a customer keeps on delaying, and tells us several times that it'll only be a few more days, we know there's a problem," says Ms. Su. After 45 days, "I send a letter. Then a second notice is sent in writing. After the third and final notice, the client has 10 days to pay, and then I hand it over to a collection agency, and it's out of my hands."

Ms. Su's boss, Terry Norton, records an estimate for bad debts every year, based on a percentage of receivables. The percentage depends on the current aging history. He also calculates and monitors the company's receivables turnover ratio, which the company reports in its financial statements. "I think of it in terms of collection period of DSO—days of sales outstanding," he explains.

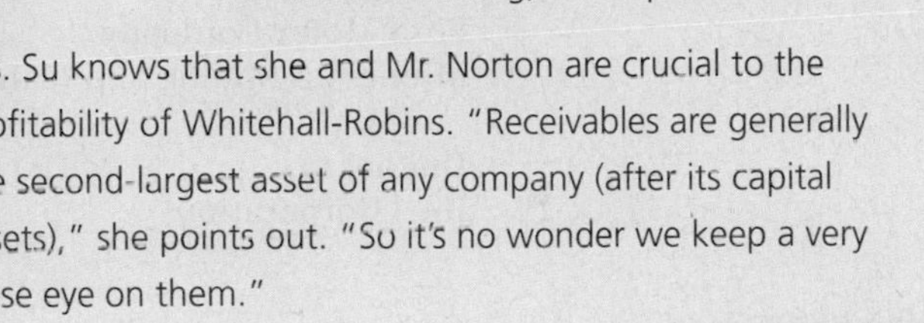

Ms. Su knows that she and Mr. Norton are crucial to the profitability of Whitehall-Robins. "Receivables are generally the second-largest asset of any company (after its capital assets)," she points out. "So it's no wonder we keep a very close eye on them."

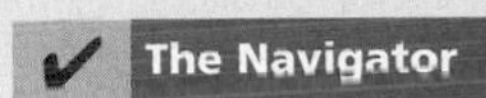

✓ The Navigator

Preview of Chapter 8

As indicated in the Feature Story, receivables are a significant asset for many pharmaceutical companies. Because a large portion of sales in the United States are done on credit, receivables are important to companies in other industries as well. As a consequence, companies must pay close attention to their receivables and manage them carefully. In this chapter, you will learn what journal entries companies make when they sell products, when they collect cash from those sales, and when they write off accounts they cannot collect.

The content and organization of the chapter are as follows.

ACCOUNTING FOR RECEIVABLES

Types of Receivables	Accounts Receivable	Notes Receivable	Statement Presentation and Analysis
• Accounts receivable • Notes receivable • Other receivables	• Recognizing accounts receivable • Valuing accounts receivable • Disposing of accounts receivable	• Determining maturity date • Computing interest • Recognizing notes receivable • Valuing notes receivable • Disposing of notes receivable	• Presentation • Analysis

✓ The Navigator

Types of Receivables

LEARNING OBJECTIVE 1

Identify the different types of receivables.

The term **receivables** refers to amounts due from individuals and companies. Receivables are claims that are expected to be collected in cash. The management of receivables is a very important activity for any company that sells goods or services on credit.

Receivables are important because they represent one of a company's most liquid assets. For many companies, receivables are also one of the largest assets. For example, receivables represented 21.9% of the current assets of pharmaceutical giant Rite Aid in 2011. Illustration 8-1 lists receivables as a percentage of total assets for five other well-known companies in a recent year.

Illustration 8-1
Receivables as a percentage of assets

Company	Receivables as a Percentage of Total Assets
General Electric	52%
Ford Motor Company	42%
Minnesota Mining and Manufacturing Company (3M)	14%
DuPont Co.	17%
Intel Corporation	5%

The relative significance of a company's receivables as a percentage of its assets depends on various factors: its industry, the time of year, whether it extends long-term financing, and its credit policies. To reflect important differences among receivables, they are frequently classified as (1) accounts receivable, (2) notes receivable, and (3) other receivables.

Accounts receivable are amounts customers owe on account. They result from the sale of goods and services. Companies generally expect to collect accounts receivable within 30 to 60 days. They are usually the most significant type of claim held by a company.

Notes receivable are a written promise (as evidenced by a formal instrument) for amounts to be received. The note normally requires the collection of interest and extends for time periods of 60–90 days or longer. Notes and accounts receivable that result from sales transactions are often called **trade receivables.**

Ethics Note

Companies report receivables from employees separately in the financial statements. The reason: Sometimes those assets are not the result of an "arm's-length" transaction.

Other receivables include nontrade receivables such as interest receivable, loans to company officers, advances to employees, and income taxes refundable. These do not generally result from the operations of the business. Therefore, they are generally classified and reported as separate items in the balance sheet.

Accounts Receivable

Three accounting issues associated with accounts receivable are:

1. **Recognizing** accounts receivable.
2. **Valuing** accounts receivable.
3. **Disposing** of accounts receivable.

Recognizing Accounts Receivable

Recognizing accounts receivable is relatively straightforward. A service organization records a receivable when it provides service on account. A merchandiser records accounts receivable at the point of sale of merchandise on account. When a merchandiser sells goods, it increases (debits) Accounts Receivable and increases (credits) Sales Revenue.

LEARNING OBJECTIVE 2

Explain how companies recognize accounts receivable.

The seller may offer terms that encourage early payment by providing a discount. Sales returns also reduce receivables. The buyer might find some of the goods unacceptable and choose to return the unwanted goods.

Ethics Note

In exchange for lower interest rates, some companies have eliminated the 25-day grace period before finance charges kick in. Be sure you read the fine print in any credit agreement you sign.

To review, assume that Jordache Co. on July 1, 2014, sells merchandise on account to Polo Company for $1,000, terms 2/10, n/30. On July 5, Polo returns merchandise worth $100 to Jordache Co. On July 11, Jordache receives payment from Polo Company for the balance due. The journal entries to record these transactions on the books of Jordache Co. are as follows. **(Cost of goods sold entries are omitted.)**

Date	Account	Debit	Credit
July 1	Accounts Receivable—Polo Company	1,000	
	Sales Revenue		1,000
	(To record sales on account)		
July 5	Sales Returns and Allowances	100	
	Accounts Receivable—Polo Company		100
	(To record merchandise returned)		
July 11	Cash ($900 − $18)	882	
	Sales Discounts ($900 × .02)	18	
	Accounts Receivable—Polo Company		900
	(To record collection of accounts receivable)		

Helpful Hint
These entries are the same as those described in Chapter 5. For simplicity, we have omitted inventory and cost of goods sold from this set of journal entries and from end-of-chapter material.

Some retailers issue their own credit cards. When you use a retailer's credit card (JCPenney, for example), the retailer charges interest on the balance due if not paid within a specified period (usually 25–30 days).

To illustrate, assume that you use your JCPenney credit card to purchase clothing with a sales price of $300 on June 1, 2014. JCPenney will increase (debit) Accounts Receivable for $300 and increase (credit) Sales Revenue for $300 (cost of goods sold entry omitted) as follows.

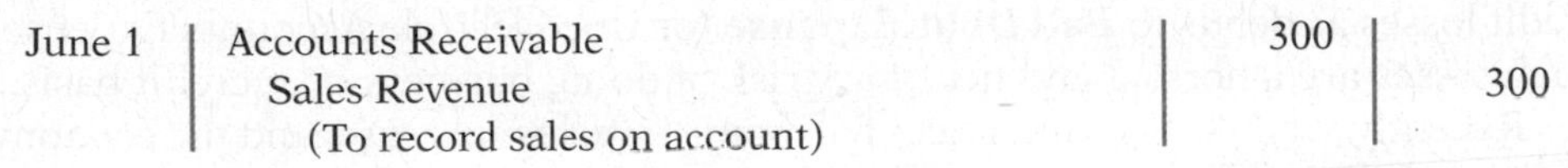

Date	Account	Debit	Credit
June 1	Accounts Receivable	300	
	Sales Revenue		300
	(To record sales on account)		

A	=	L	+	SE
+300				
				+300 Rev

Cash Flows
no effect

Assuming that you owe $300 at the end of the month, and JCPenney charges 1.5% per month on the balance due, the adjusting entry that JCPenney makes to record interest revenue of $4.50 ($300 × 1.5%) on June 30 is as follows.

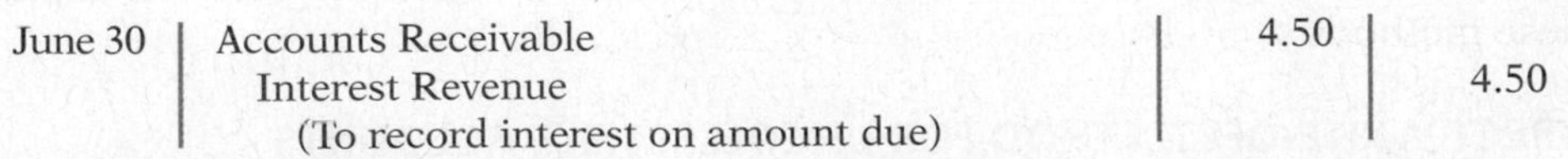

Date	Account	Debit	Credit
June 30	Accounts Receivable	4.50	
	Interest Revenue		4.50
	(To record interest on amount due)		

A	=	L	+	SE
+4.50				
				+4.50 Rev

Cash Flows
no effect

Interest revenue is often substantial for many retailers.

ANATOMY OF A FRAUD

Tasanee was the accounts receivable clerk for a large non-profit foundation that provided performance and exhibition space for the performing and visual arts. Her responsibilities included activities normally assigned to an accounts receivable clerk, such as recording revenues from various sources that included donations, facility rental fees, ticket revenue, and bar receipts. However, she was also responsible for handling all cash and checks from the time they were received until the time she deposited them, as well as preparing the bank reconciliation. Tasanee took advantage of her situation by falsifying bank deposits and bank reconciliations so that she could steal cash from the bar receipts. Since nobody else logged the donations or matched the donation receipts to pledges prior to Tasanee receiving them, she was able to offset the cash that was stolen against donations that she received but didn't record. Her crime was made easier by the fact that her boss, the company's controller, only did a very superficial review of the bank reconciliation and thus didn't notice that some numbers had been cut out from other documents and taped onto the bank reconciliation.

Total take: $1.5 million

The Missing Controls

Segregation of duties. The foundation should not have allowed an accounts receivable clerk, whose job was to record receivables, to also handle cash, record cash, make deposits, and especially prepare the bank reconciliation.

Independent internal verification. The controller was supposed to perform a thorough review of the bank reconciliation. Because he did not, he was terminated from his position.

Source: Adapted from Wells, *Fraud Casebook* (2007), pp. 183–194.

Valuing Accounts Receivable

LEARNING OBJECTIVE 3

Distinguish between the methods and bases companies use to value accounts receivable.

Once companies record receivables in the accounts, the next question is: How should they report receivables in the financial statements? Companies report accounts receivable on the balance sheet as an asset. But determining the **amount** to report is sometimes difficult because some receivables will become uncollectible.

Each customer must satisfy the credit requirements of the seller before the credit sale is approved. Inevitably, though, some accounts receivable become uncollectible. For example, a customer may not be able to pay because of a decline in its sales revenue due to a downturn in the economy. Similarly, individuals may be laid off from their jobs or faced with unexpected hospital bills. Companies record credit losses as debits to **Bad Debt Expense** (or Uncollectible Accounts Expense). Such losses are a normal and necessary risk of doing business on a credit basis.

Alternative Terminology
You will sometimes see *Bad Debt Expense* called *Uncollectible Accounts Expense.*

Recently, when U.S. home prices fell, home foreclosures rose, and the economy in general slowed, lenders experienced huge increases in their bad debt expense. For example, during a recent quarter Wachovia (a large U.S. bank now owned be Wells Fargo) increased bad debt expense from $108 million to $408 million. Similarly, American Express increased its bad debt expense by 70%.

Two methods are used in accounting for uncollectible accounts: (1) the direct write-off method and (2) the allowance method. The following sections explain these methods.

DIRECT WRITE-OFF METHOD FOR UNCOLLECTIBLE ACCOUNTS

Under the **direct write-off method**, when a company determines a particular account to be uncollectible, it charges the loss to Bad Debt Expense. Assume, for example, that Warden Co. writes off as uncollectible M. E. Doran's $200 balance on December 12. Warden's entry is:

Dec. 12	Bad Debt Expense	200	
	Accounts Receivable—M. E. Doran		200
	(To record write-off of M. E. Doran account)		

A	=	L	+	SE
				−200 Exp
−200				

Cash Flows
no effect

Under this method, Bad Debt Expense will show only **actual losses** from uncollectibles. The company will report accounts receivable at its gross amount.

Although this method is simple, its use can reduce the usefulness of both the income statement and balance sheet. Consider the following example. Assume that in 2014, Quick Buck Computer Company decided it could increase its revenues by offering computers to college students without requiring any money down and with no credit-approval process. On campuses across the country, it distributed one million computers with a selling price of $800 each. This increased Quick Buck's revenues and receivables by $800 million. The promotion was a huge success! The 2014 balance sheet and income statement looked great. Unfortunately, during 2015, nearly 40% of the customers defaulted on their loans. This made the 2015 income statement and balance sheet look terrible. Illustration 8-2 shows the effect of these events on the financial statements if the direct write-off method is used.

Illustration 8-2
Effects of direct write-off method

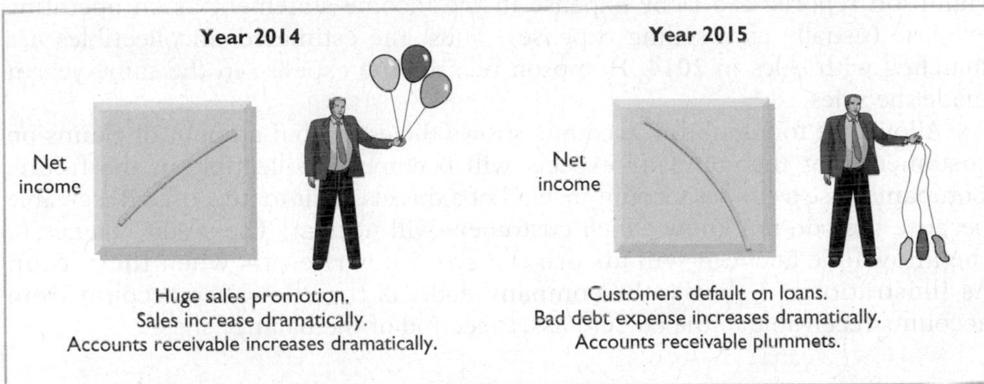

Under the direct write-off method, companies often record bad debt expense in a period different from the period in which they record the revenue. The method does not attempt to match bad debt expense to sales revenues in the income statement. Nor does the direct write-off method show accounts receivable in the balance sheet at the amount the company actually expects to receive. **Consequently, unless bad debt losses are insignificant, the direct write-off method is not acceptable for financial reporting purposes.**

ALLOWANCE METHOD FOR UNCOLLECTIBLE ACCOUNTS

The **allowance method** of accounting for bad debts involves estimating uncollectible accounts at the end of each period. This provides better matching on the income statement. It also ensures that companies state receivables on the balance sheet at their cash (net) realizable value. **Cash (net) realizable value** is the net amount the company expects to receive in cash. It excludes amounts that the company estimates it will not collect. Thus, this method reduces receivables in the balance sheet by the amount of estimated uncollectible receivables.

GAAP requires the allowance method for financial reporting purposes when bad debts are material in amount. This method has three essential features:

Helpful Hint
In this context, *material* means significant or important to financial statement users.

1. Companies **estimate** uncollectible accounts receivable. They match this estimated expense **against revenues** in the same accounting period in which they record the revenues.

2. Companies debit estimated uncollectibles to Bad Debt Expense and credit them to Allowance for Doubtful Accounts through an adjusting entry at the end of each period. Allowance for Doubtful Accounts is a contra account to Accounts Receivable.
3. When companies write off a specific account, they debit actual uncollectibles to Allowance for Doubtful Accounts and credit that amount to Accounts Receivable.

RECORDING ESTIMATED UNCOLLECTIBLES To illustrate the allowance method, assume that Hampson Furniture has credit sales of $1,200,000 in 2014. Of this amount, $200,000 remains uncollected at December 31. The credit manager estimates that $12,000 of these sales will be uncollectible. The adjusting entry to record the estimated uncollectibles increases (debits) Bad Debt Expense and increases (credits) Allowance for Doubtful Accounts, as follows.

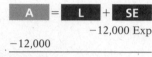

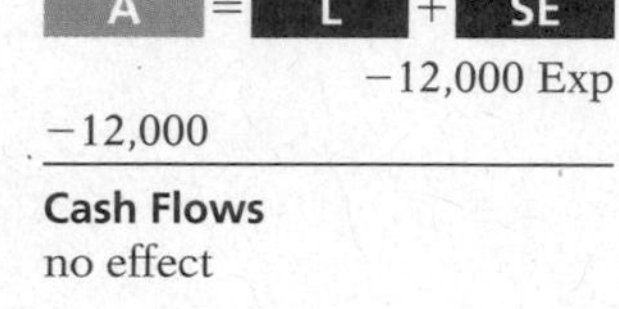

Dec. 31	Bad Debt Expense	12,000	
	Allowance for Doubtful Accounts		12,000
	(To record estimate of uncollectible accounts)		

Hampson reports Bad Debt Expense in the income statement as an operating expense (usually as a selling expense). Thus, the estimated uncollectibles are matched with sales in 2014. Hampson records the expense in the same year it made the sales.

Allowance for Doubtful Accounts shows the estimated amount of claims on customers that the company expects will become uncollectible in the future. Companies use a contra account instead of a direct credit to Accounts Receivable because they do not know *which* customers will not pay. The credit balance in the allowance account will absorb the specific write-offs when they occur. As Illustration 8-3 shows, the company deducts the allowance account from accounts receivable in the current assets section of the balance sheet.

Illustration 8-3
Presentation of allowance for doubtful accounts

Hampson Furniture
Balance Sheet (partial)

Current assets		
Cash		$ 14,800
Accounts receivable	**$200,000**	
Less: Allowance for doubtful accounts	**12,000**	**188,000**
Inventory		310,000
Supplies		25,000
Total current assets		$537,800

Helpful Hint
Cash realizable value is sometimes referred to as *accounts receivable (net)*.

The amount of $188,000 in Illustration 8-3 represents the expected **cash realizable value** of the accounts receivable at the statement date. **Companies do not close Allowance for Doubtful Accounts at the end of the fiscal year.**

RECORDING THE WRITE-OFF OF AN UNCOLLECTIBLE ACCOUNT As described in the Feature Story, companies use various methods of collecting past-due accounts, such as letters, calls, and legal action. When they have exhausted all means of collecting a past-due account and collection appears impossible, the company should write off the account. In the credit card industry, for example, it is standard practice to write off accounts that are 210 days past due. To prevent premature or unauthorized write-offs, authorized management personnel should formally approve each write-off. To maintain good internal control, companies should not authorize someone to write off accounts who also has daily responsibilities related to cash or receivables.

To illustrate a receivables write-off, assume that the financial vice president of Hampson Furniture authorizes a write-off of the $500 balance owed by R. A. Ware on March 1, 2015. The entry to record the write-off is:

Mar. 1	Allowance for Doubtful Accounts	500	
	Accounts Receivable—R. A. Ware		500
	(Write-off of R. A. Ware account)		

A	=	L	+	SE
+500				
−500				

Cash Flows
no effect

Bad Debt Expense does not increase when the write-off occurs. **Under the allowance method, companies debit every bad debt write-off to the allowance account rather than to Bad Debt Expense.** A debit to Bad Debt Expense would be incorrect because the company has already recognized the expense when it made the adjusting entry for estimated bad debts. Instead, the entry to record the write-off of an uncollectible account reduces both Accounts Receivable and Allowance for Doubtful Accounts. After posting, the general ledger accounts will appear as in Illustration 8-4.

Illustration 8-4
General ledger balances after write-off

Accounts Receivable

Jan. 1 Bal. 200,000	Mar. 1 **500**
Mar. 1 Bal. 199,500	

Allowance for Doubtful Accounts

Mar. 1 **500**	Jan. 1 Bal. 12,000
	Mar. 1 Bal. 11,500

A write-off affects **only balance sheet accounts**—not income statement accounts. The write-off of the account reduces both Accounts Receivable and Allowance for Doubtful Accounts. Cash realizable value in the balance sheet, therefore, remains the same, as Illustration 8-5 shows.

Illustration 8-5
Cash realizable value comparison

	Before Write-Off	After Write-Off
Accounts receivable	$ 200,000	$ 199,500
Allowance for doubtful accounts	12,000	11,500
Cash realizable value	**$188,000**	**$188,000**

RECOVERY OF AN UNCOLLECTIBLE ACCOUNT Occasionally, a company collects from a customer after it has written off the account as uncollectible. The company makes two entries to record the recovery of a bad debt: (1) It reverses the entry made in writing off the account. This reinstates the customer's account. (2) It journalizes the collection in the usual manner.

To illustrate, assume that on July 1, R. A. Ware pays the $500 amount that Hampson had written off on March 1. Hampson makes these entries:

(1)

July 1	Accounts Receivable—R. A. Ware	500	
	Allowance for Doubtful Accounts		500
	(To reverse write-off of R. A. Ware account)		

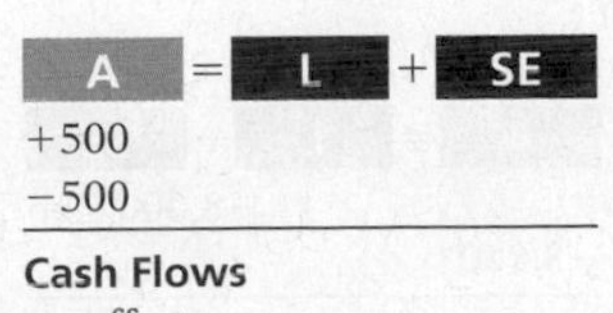

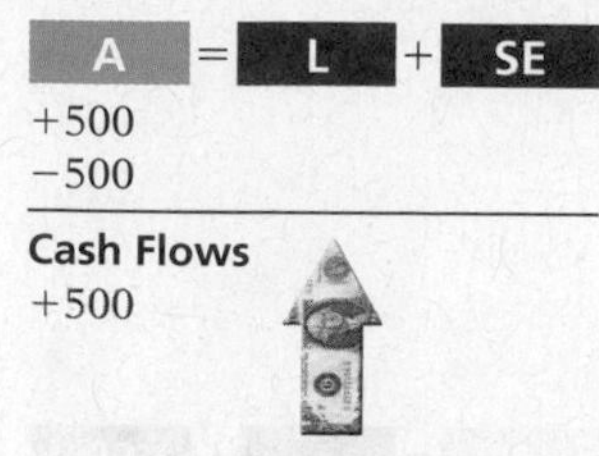

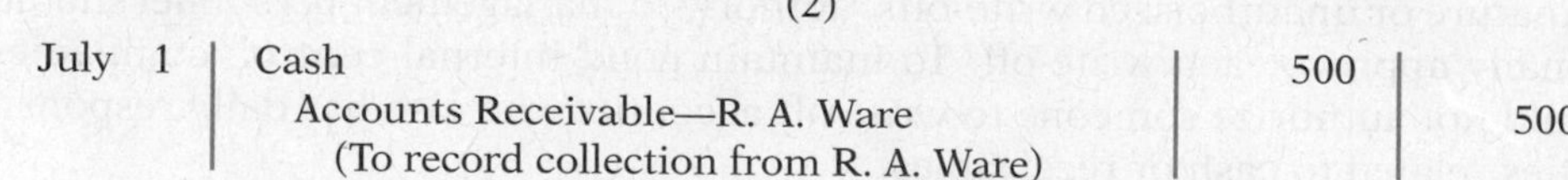

(2)

July 1	Cash	500	
	Accounts Receivable—R. A. Ware		500
	(To record collection from R. A. Ware)		

Note that the recovery of a bad debt, like the write-off of a bad debt, affects **only balance sheet accounts**. The net effect of the two entries above is a debit to Cash and a credit to Allowance for Doubtful Accounts for $500. Accounts Receivable and the Allowance for Doubtful Accounts both increase in entry (1) for two reasons. First, the company made an error in judgment when it wrote off the account receivable. Second, after R. A. Ware did pay, Accounts Receivable in the general ledger and Ware's account in the subsidiary ledger should show the collection for possible future credit purposes.

ESTIMATING THE ALLOWANCE For Hampson Furniture in Illustration 8-3, the amount of the expected uncollectibles was given. However, in "real life," companies must estimate that amount when they use the allowance method. Two bases are used to determine this amount: **(1) percentage of sales**, and **(2) percentage of receivables**. Both bases are generally accepted. The choice is a management decision. It depends on the relative emphasis that management wishes to give to expenses and revenues on the one hand or to cash realizable value of the accounts receivable on the other. The choice is whether to emphasize income statement or balance sheet relationships. Illustration 8-6 compares the two bases.

Illustration 8-6
Comparison of bases for estimating uncollectibles

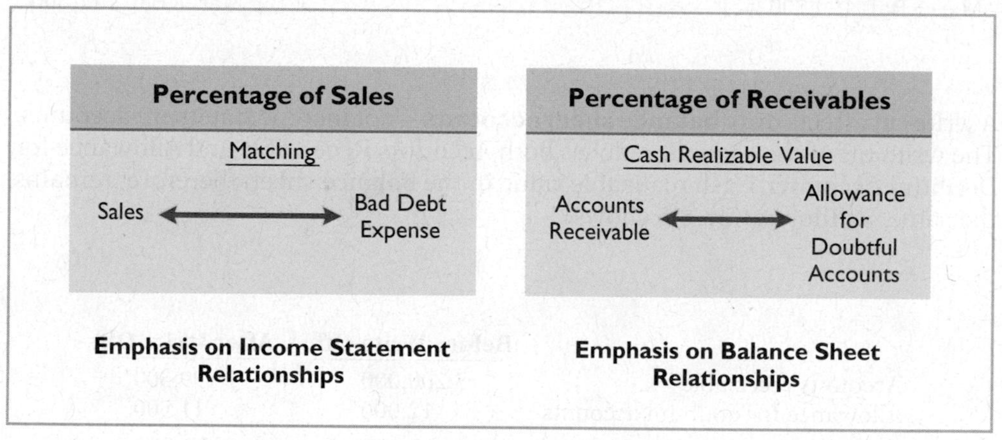

The percentage-of-sales basis results in a better matching of expenses with revenues—an income statement viewpoint. The percentage-of-receivables basis produces the better estimate of cash realizable value—a balance sheet viewpoint. Under both bases, the company must determine its past experience with bad debt losses.

Percentage-of-Sales. In the **percentage-of-sales basis**, management estimates what percentage of credit sales will be uncollectible. This percentage is based on past experience and anticipated credit policy.

The company applies this percentage to either total credit sales or net credit sales of the current year. To illustrate, assume that Gonzalez Company elects to use the percentage-of-sales basis. It concludes that 1% of net credit sales will become uncollectible. If net credit sales for 2014 are $800,000, the estimated bad debt expense is $8,000 (1% × $800,000). The adjusting entry is:

A = L + SE
−8,000 Exp
−8,000
Cash Flows
no effect

Dec. 31	Bad Debt Expense	8,000	
	Allowance for Doubtful Accounts		8,000
	(To record estimated bad debts for year)		

After the adjusting entry is posted, assuming the allowance account already has a credit balance of $1,723, the accounts of Gonzalez Company will show the following:

Illustration 8-7
Bad debt accounts after posting

Bad Debt Expense		Allowance for Doubtful Accounts	
Dec. 31 Adj. **8,000**			Jan. 1 Bal. 1,723
			Dec. 31 Adj. **8,000**
			Dec. 31 Bal. 9,723

This basis of estimating uncollectibles emphasizes the matching of expenses with revenues. As a result, Bad Debt Expense will show a direct percentage relationship to the sales base on which it is computed. **When the company makes the adjusting entry, it disregards the existing balance in Allowance for Doubtful Accounts.** The adjusted balance in this account should be a reasonable approximation of the realizable value of the receivables. If actual write-offs differ significantly from the amount estimated, the company should modify the percentage for future years.

Percentage-of-Receivables. Under the **percentage-of-receivables basis**, management estimates what percentage of receivables will result in losses from uncollectible accounts. The company prepares an **aging schedule**, in which it classifies customer balances by the length of time they have been unpaid. Because of its emphasis on time, the analysis is often called **aging the accounts receivable.** In the Feature Story, Whitehall-Robins prepared an aging report daily.

Helpful Hint
Where appropriate, the percentage-of-receivables basis may use only a single percentage rate.

After the company arranges the accounts by age, it determines the expected bad debt losses. It applies percentages based on past experience to the totals in each category. The longer a receivable is past due, the less likely it is to be collected. Thus, the estimated percentage of uncollectible debts increases as the number of days past due increases. Illustration 8-8 shows an aging schedule for Dart Company. Note that the estimated percentage uncollectible increases from 2% to 40% as the number of days past due increases.

Illustration 8-8
Aging schedule

Worksheet.xls

Home Insert Page Layout Formulas Data Review View

P18 fx

	A	B	C	D	E	F	G
1					Number of Days Past Due		
2			Not				
3	Customer	Total	Yet Due	1–30	31–60	61–90	Over 90
4	T. E. Adert	$ 600		$ 300		$ 200	$ 100
5	R. C. Bortz	300	$ 300				
6	B. A. Carl	450		200	$ 250		
7	O. L. Diker	700	500			200	
8	T. O. Ebbet	600			300		300
9	Others	36,950	26,200	5,200	2,450	1,600	1,500
10		$39,600	$27,000	$5,700	$3,000	$2,000	$1,900
11	Estimated Percentage Uncollectible		2%	4%	10%	20%	40%
12	Total Estimated Bad Debts	$ 2,228	$ 540	$ 228	$ 300	$ 400	$ 760
13							

Helpful Hint
The older categories have higher percentages because the longer an account is past due, the less likely it is to be collected.

Total estimated bad debts for Dart Company ($2,228) represent the amount of existing customer claims the company expects will become uncollectible in the future. This amount represents the **required balance** in Allowance for Doubtful

Accounts at the balance sheet date. **The amount of the bad debt adjusting entry is the difference between the required balance and the existing balance in the allowance account.** If the trial balance shows Allowance for Doubtful Accounts with a credit balance of $528, the company will make an adjusting entry for $1,700 ($2,228 − $528), as shown here.

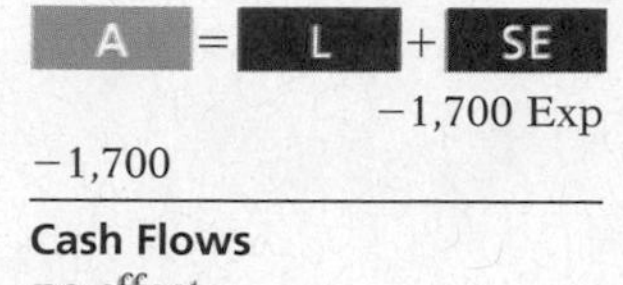

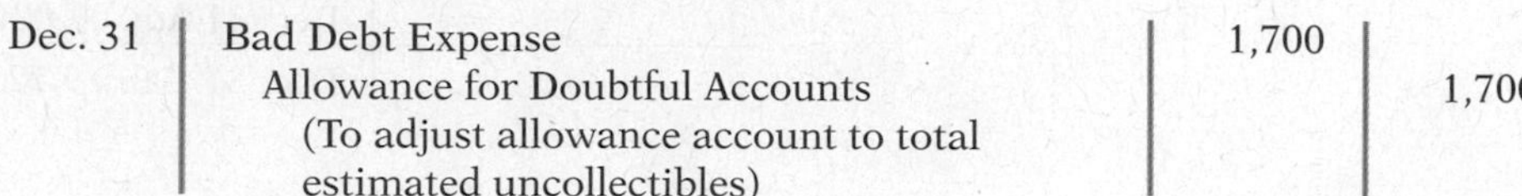

Dec. 31	Bad Debt Expense	1,700	
	Allowance for Doubtful Accounts		1,700
	(To adjust allowance account to total estimated uncollectibles)		

After Dart posts its adjusting entry, its accounts will appear as follows.

Illustration 8-9
Bad debt accounts after posting

Bad Debt Expense			Allowance for Doubtful Accounts	
Dec. 31 Adj.	**1,700**		Bal.	528
			Dec. 31 Adj.	**1,700**
			Bal.	2,228

Occasionally, the allowance account will have a **debit balance** prior to adjustment. This occurs when write-offs during the year have exceeded previous provisions for bad debts. In such a case, the company **adds the debit balance to the required balance** when it makes the adjusting entry. Thus, if there had been a $500 debit balance in the allowance account before adjustment, the adjusting entry would have been for $2,728 ($2,228 + $500) to arrive at a credit balance of $2,228. The percentage-of-receivables basis will normally result in the better approximation of cash realizable value.

> DO IT!

Uncollectible Accounts Receivable

Brule Co. has been in business five years. The ledger at the end of the current year shows:

Accounts Receivable	$30,000 Dr.
Sales Revenue	$180,000 Cr.
Allowance for Doubtful Accounts	$2,000 Dr.

Bad debts are estimated to be 10% of receivables. Prepare the entry to adjust Allowance for Doubtful Accounts.

Action Plan

✔ Report receivables at their cash (net) realizable value.

✔ Estimate the amount the company does not expect to collect.

✔ Consider the existing balance in the allowance account when using the percentage-of-receivables basis.

Solution

The following entry should be made to bring the balance in Allowance for Doubtful Accounts up to a balance of $3,000 (10% × $30,000):

Bad Debt Expense [(10% × $30,000) + $2,000]	5,000	
Allowance for Doubtful Accounts		5,000
(To record estimate of uncollectible accounts)		

Related exercise material: **BE8-3, BE8-6, BE8-7, E8-3, E8-4, E8-5, and DO IT! 8-1.**

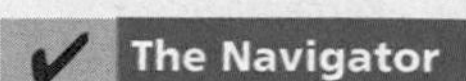

LEARNING OBJECTIVE 4

Describe the entries to record the disposition of accounts receivable.

Disposing of Accounts Receivable

In the normal course of events, companies collect accounts receivable in cash and remove the receivables from the books. However, as credit sales and receivables have grown in significance, the "normal course of events" has changed.

Companies now frequently sell their receivables to another company for cash, thereby shortening the cash-to-cash operating cycle.

Companies sell receivables for two major reasons. First, **they may be the only reasonable source of cash**. When money is tight, companies may not be able to borrow money in the usual credit markets. Or, if money is available, the cost of borrowing may be prohibitive.

A second reason for selling receivables is that **billing and collection are often time-consuming and costly**. It is often easier for a retailer to sell the receivables to another party with expertise in billing and collection matters. Credit card companies such as MasterCard, Visa, and Discover specialize in billing and collecting accounts receivable.

SALE OF RECEIVABLES

A common sale of receivables is a sale to a factor. A **factor** is a finance company or bank that buys receivables from businesses and then collects the payments directly from the customers. Factoring is a multibillion dollar business.

Factoring arrangements vary widely. Typically, the factor charges a commission to the company that is selling the receivables. This fee ranges from 1–3% of the amount of receivables purchased. To illustrate, assume that Hendredon Furniture factors $600,000 of receivables to Federal Factors. Federal Factors assesses a service charge of 2% of the amount of receivables sold. The journal entry to record the sale by Hendredon Furniture is as follows.

	Debit	Credit
Cash	588,000	
Service Charge Expense (2% × $600,000)	12,000	
Accounts Receivable		600,000
(To record the sale of accounts receivable)		

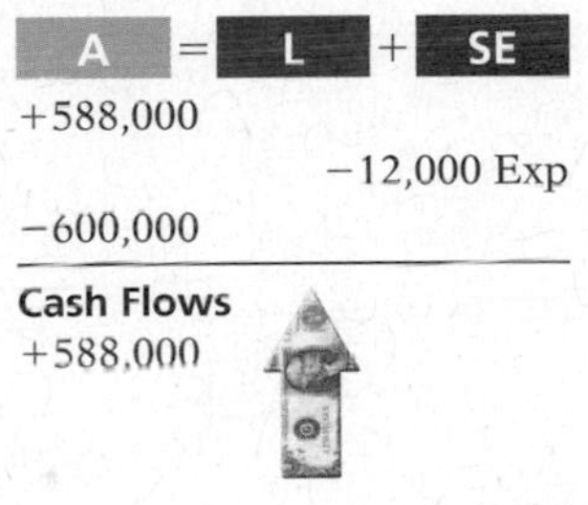

If the company often sells its receivables, it records the service charge expense (such as that incurred by Hendredon) as selling expense. If the company infrequently sells receivables, it may report this amount in the "Other expenses and losses" section of the income statement.

CREDIT CARD SALES

Over one billion credit cards are in use in the United States—more than three credit cards for every man, woman, and child in this country. Visa, MasterCard, and American Express are the national credit cards that most individuals use. Three parties are involved when national credit cards are used in retail sales: (1) the credit card issuer, who is independent of the retailer; (2) the retailer; and (3) the customer. A retailer's acceptance of a national credit card is another form of selling (factoring) the receivable.

Illustration 8-10 (page 390) shows the major advantages of national credit cards to the retailer. In exchange for these advantages, the retailer pays the credit card issuer a fee of 2–6% of the invoice price for its services.

ACCOUNTING FOR CREDIT CARD SALES The retailer generally considers sales from the use of national credit card sales as *cash sales*. The retailer must pay to the bank that issues the card a fee for processing the transactions. The retailer records the credit card slips in a similar manner as checks deposited from a cash sale.

To illustrate, Anita Ferreri purchases $1,000 of compact discs for her restaurant from Karen Kerr Music Co., using her Visa First Bank Card. First Bank charges a service fee of 3%. The entry to record this transaction by Karen Kerr Music is as follows.

	Debit	Credit
Cash	970	
Service Charge Expense	30	
Sales Revenue		1,000
(To record Visa credit card sales)		

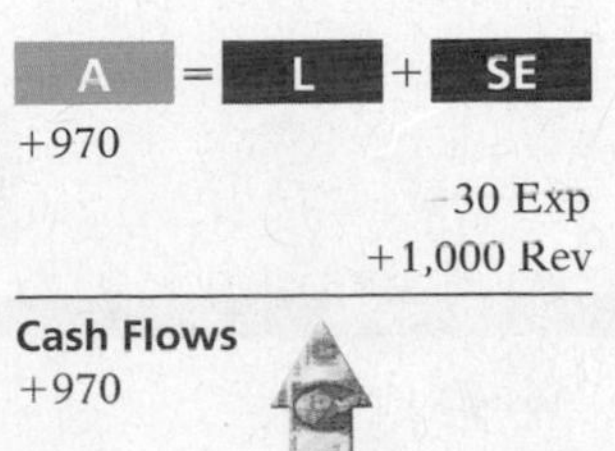

Illustration 8-10
Advantages of credit cards to the retailer

ACCOUNTING ACROSS THE ORGANIZATION

How Does a Credit Card Work?

Most of you know how to *use* a credit card, but do you know what happens in the transaction and how the transaction is processed? Suppose that you use a Visa card to purchase some new ties at Nordstrom. The salesperson swipes your card, which allows the information on the magnetic strip on the back of the card to be read. The salesperson then enters the amount of the purchase. The machine contacts the Visa computer, which routes the call back to the bank that issued your Visa card. The issuing bank verifies that the account exists, that the card is not stolen, and that you have not exceeded your credit limit. At this point, the slip is printed, which you sign.

Visa acts as the clearing agent for the transaction. It transfers funds from the issuing bank to Nordstrom's bank account. Generally this transfer of funds, from sale to the receipt of funds in the merchant's account, takes two to three days.

In the meantime, Visa puts a pending charge on your account for the amount of the tie purchase; that amount counts immediately against your available credit limit. At the end of the billing period, Visa sends you an invoice (your credit card bill) which shows the various charges you made, and the amounts that Visa expended on your behalf, for the month. You then must "pay the piper" for your stylish new ties.

Assume that Nordstrom prepares a bank reconciliation at the end of each month. If some credit card sales have not been processed by the bank, how should Nordstrom treat these transactions on its bank reconciliation? (See page 418.)

> DO IT!

Disposition of Accounts Receivable

Mehl Wholesalers Co. has been expanding faster than it can raise capital. According to its local banker, the company has reached its debt ceiling. Mehl's suppliers (creditors) are demanding payment within 30 days of the invoice date for goods acquired, but Mehl's customers are slow in paying (60–90 days). As a result, Mehl has a cash flow problem.

Mehl needs $120,000 in cash to safely cover next Friday's payroll. Its balance of outstanding accounts receivables totals $750,000. What might Mehl do to alleviate this cash crunch? Record the entry that Mehl would make when it raises the needed cash.

Action Plan

✔ To speed up the collection of cash, sell receivables to a factor.

✔ Calculate service charge expense as a percentage of the factored receivables.

Solution

Assuming that Mehl Wholesalers factors $125,000 of its accounts receivable at a 1% service charge, it would make the following entry.

Cash	123,750	
Service Charge Expense (1% × $125,000)	1,250	
Accounts Receivable		125,000
(To record sale of receivables to factor)		

Related exercise material: **BE8-8, E8-7, E8-8, E8-9, and DO IT! 8-2.**

 **The Navigator**

Notes Receivable

Companies may also grant credit in exchange for a formal credit instrument known as a promissory note. A **promissory note** is a written promise to pay a specified amount of money on demand or at a definite time. Promissory notes may be used (1) when individuals and companies lend or borrow money, (2) when the amount of the transaction and the credit period exceed normal limits, or (3) in settlement of accounts receivable.

In a promissory note, the party making the promise to pay is called the **maker**. The party to whom payment is to be made is called the **payee**. The note may specifically identify the payee by name or may designate the payee simply as the bearer of the note.

In the note shown in Illustration 8-11 (page 392), Calhoun Company is the maker, and Wilma Company is the payee. To Wilma Company, the promissory note is a note receivable. To Calhoun Company, it is a note payable.

Notes receivable give the holder a stronger legal claim to assets than do accounts receivable. Like accounts receivable, notes receivable can be readily sold to another party. Promissory notes are negotiable instruments (as are checks), which means that they can be transferred to another party by endorsement.

Companies frequently accept notes receivable from customers who need to extend the payment of an outstanding account receivable. They often require such notes from high-risk customers. In some industries (such as the pleasure and sport boat industry), all credit sales are supported by notes. The majority of notes, however, originate from loans.

Illustration 8-11
Promissory note

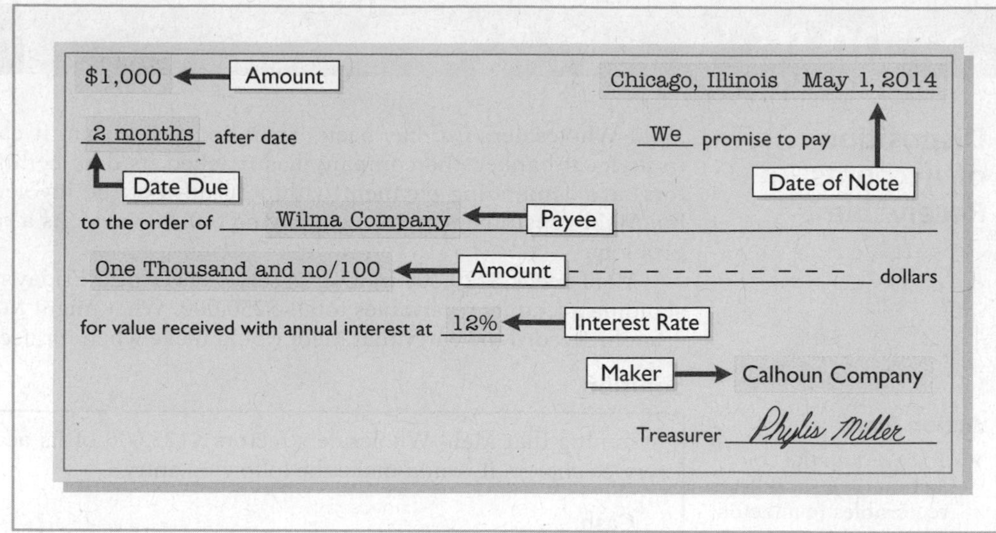
$1,000 ← Amount | Chicago, Illinois May 1, 2014 ↑ Date of Note

2 months after date ↑ Date Due | We promise to pay

to the order of Wilma Company ← Payee

One Thousand and no/100 ← Amount ------------ dollars

for value received with annual interest at 12% ← Interest Rate

Maker → Calhoun Company

Treasurer Phylis Miller

Helpful Hint
Who are the two key parties to a note, and what entry does each party make when the note is issued?

Answer:
1. The maker, Calhoun Company, credits Notes Payable.
2. The payee, Wilma Company, debits Notes Receivable.

The basic issues in accounting for notes receivable are the same as those for accounts receivable:

1. **Recognizing** notes receivable.
2. **Valuing** notes receivable.
3. **Disposing** of notes receivable.

On the following pages, we will look at these issues. Before we do, we need to consider two issues that do not apply to accounts receivable: maturity date and computing interest.

Determining the Maturity Date

LEARNING OBJECTIVE 5

Compute the maturity date of and interest on notes receivable.

When the life of a note is expressed in terms of months, you find the date when it matures by counting the months from the date of issue. For example, the maturity date of a three-month note dated May 1 is August 1. A note drawn on the last day of a month matures on the last day of a subsequent month. That is, a July 31 note due in two months matures on September 30.

When the due date is stated in terms of days, you need to count the exact number of days to determine the maturity date. In counting, **omit the date the note is issued but include the due date**. For example, the maturity date of a 60-day note dated July 17 is September 15, computed as follows.

Illustration 8-12
Computation of maturity date

Term of note		60 days
July (31–17)	14	
August	31	45
Maturity date: September		**15**

Illustration 8-13 shows three ways of stating the maturity date of a promissory note.

Illustration 8-13
Maturity date of different notes

Computing Interest

Illustration 8-14 gives the basic formula for computing interest on an interest-bearing note.

Face Value of Note	×	Annual Interest Rate	×	Time in Terms of One Year	=	Interest

Illustration 8-14
Formula for computing interest

The interest rate specified in a note is an **annual** rate of interest. The time factor in the computation in Illustration 8-14 expresses the fraction of a year that the note is outstanding. When the maturity date is stated in days, the time factor is often the number of days divided by 360. When counting days, omit the date that the note is issued but include the due date. When the due date is stated in months, the time factor is the number of months divided by 12. Illustration 8-15 shows computation of interest for various time periods.

Helpful Hint
The interest rate specified is the *annual* rate.

Illustration 8-15
Computation of interest

Terms of Note	Interest Computation
	Face × Rate × Time = Interest
$ 730, 18%, 120 days	$ 730 × 18% × 120/360 = $ 43.80
$1,000, 15%, 6 months	$1,000 × 15% × 6/12 = $ 75.00
$2,000, 12%, 1 year	$2,000 × 12% × 1/1 = $240.00

There are different ways to calculate interest. For example, the computation in Illustration 8-15 assumes 360 days for the length of the year. Most financial instruments use 365 days to compute interest. *For homework problems, assume 360 days to simplify computations*.

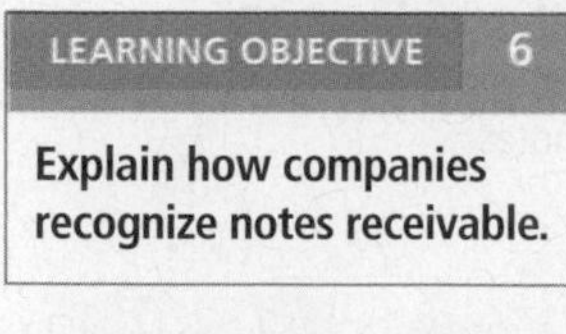

LEARNING OBJECTIVE 6
Explain how companies recognize notes receivable.

Recognizing Notes Receivable

To illustrate the basic entry for notes receivable, we will use Calhoun Company's $1,000, two-month, 12% promissory note dated May 1. Assuming that Calhoun Company wrote the note to settle an open account, Wilma Company makes the following entry for the receipt of the note.

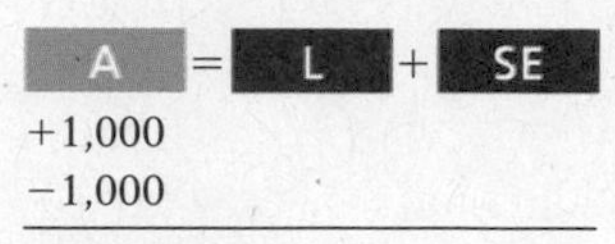

+1,000
−1,000

Cash Flows
no effect

May 1	Notes Receivable	1,000	
	Accounts Receivable—Calhoun Company		1,000
	(To record acceptance of Calhoun Company note)		

The company records the note receivable at its **face value**, the amount shown on the face of the note. No interest revenue is reported when the note is accepted because the revenue recognition principle does not recognize revenue until the performance obligation is satisfied. Interest is earned (accrued) as time passes.

If a company lends money using a note, the entry is a debit to Notes Receivable and a credit to Cash in the amount of the loan.

Valuing Notes Receivable

LEARNING OBJECTIVE 7

Describe how companies value notes receivable.

Valuing short-term notes receivable is the same as valuing accounts receivable. Like accounts receivable, companies report short-term notes receivable at their **cash (net) realizable value**. The notes receivable allowance account is Allowance for Doubtful Accounts. The estimations involved in determining cash realizable value and in recording bad debt expense and the related allowance are done similarly to accounts receivable.

INTERNATIONAL INSIGHT

Can Fair Value Be Unfair?

The FASB and the International Accounting Standards Board (IASB) are considering proposals for how to account for financial instruments. The FASB has proposed that loans and receivables be accounted for at their fair value (the amount they could currently be sold for), as are most investments. The FASB believes that this would provide a more accurate view of a company's financial position. It might be especially useful as an early warning when a bank is in trouble because of poor-quality loans. But, banks argue that fair values are difficult to estimate accurately. They are also concerned that volatile fair values could cause large swings in a bank's reported net income.

Source: David Reilly, "Banks Face a Mark-to-Market Challenge," *Wall Street Journal Online* (March 15, 2010).

? What are the arguments in favor of and against fair value accounting for loans and receivables? (See page 418.)

Disposing of Notes Receivable

LEARNING OBJECTIVE 8

Describe the entries to record the disposition of notes receivable.

Notes may be held to their maturity date, at which time the face value plus accrued interest is due. In some situations, the maker of the note defaults, and the payee must make an appropriate adjustment. In other situations, similar to accounts receivable, the holder of the note speeds up the conversion to cash by selling the receivables (described later in this chapter).

HONOR OF NOTES RECEIVABLE

A note is **honored** when its maker pays in full at its maturity date. For each interest-bearing note, the **amount due at maturity** is the face value of the note plus interest for the length of time specified on the note.

To illustrate, assume that Wolder Co. lends Higley Co. $10,000 on June 1, accepting a five-month, 9% interest note. In this situation, interest is $375 ($10,000 × 9% × $\frac{5}{12}$). The amount due, the maturity value, is $10,375 ($10,000 + $375). To obtain payment, Wolder (the payee) must present the note either to Higley Co. (the maker) or to the maker's agent, such as a bank. If Wolder presents the note to Higley Co. on November 1, the maturity date, Wolder's entry to record the collection is:

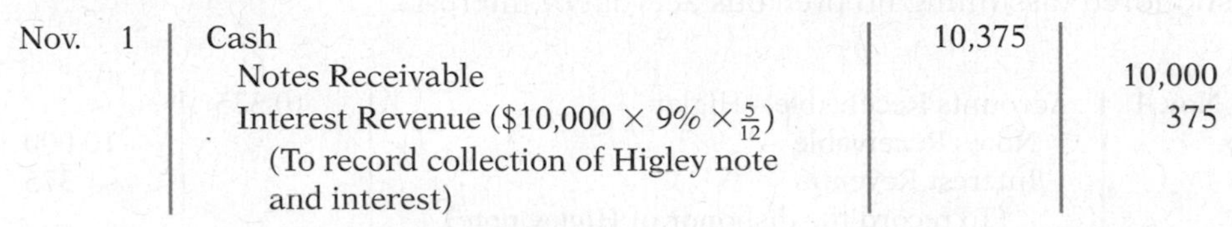

Nov. 1	Cash	10,375	
	Notes Receivable		10,000
	Interest Revenue ($10,000 × 9% × $\frac{5}{12}$)		375
	(To record collection of Higley note and interest)		

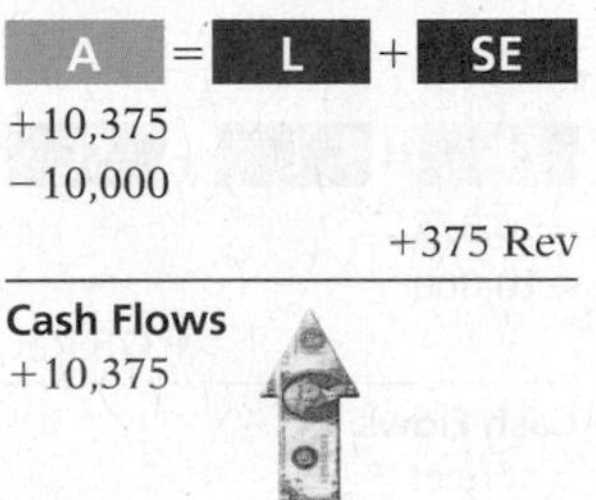

ACCRUAL OF INTEREST RECEIVABLE

Suppose instead that Wolder Co. prepares financial statements as of September 30. The timeline in Illustration 8-16 presents this situation.

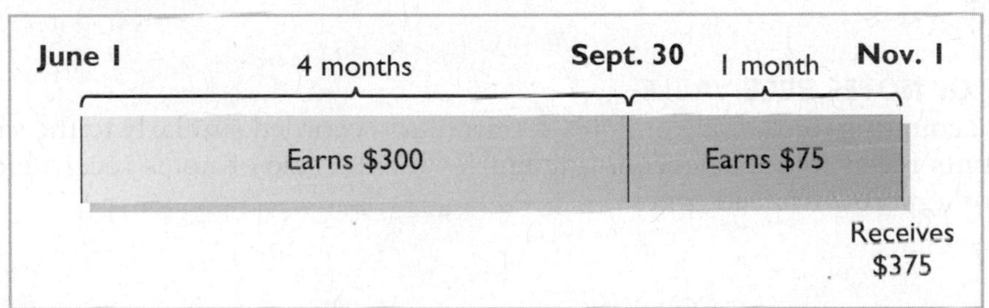

Illustration 8-16
Timeline of interest earned

To reflect interest earned but not yet received, Wolder must accrue interest on September 30. In this case, the adjusting entry by Wolder is for four months of interest, or $300, as shown below.

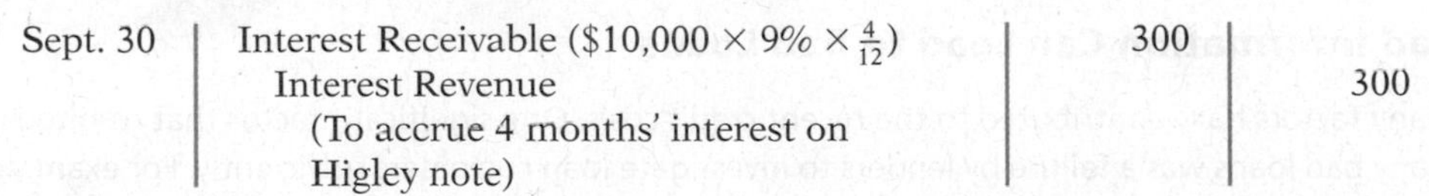

Sept. 30	Interest Receivable ($10,000 × 9% × $\frac{4}{12}$)	300	
	Interest Revenue		300
	(To accrue 4 months' interest on Higley note)		

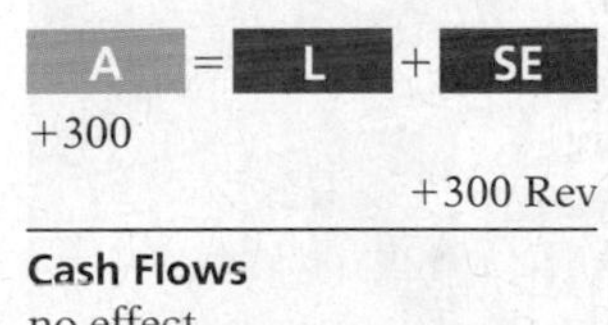

At the note's maturity on November 1, Wolder receives $10,375. This amount represents repayment of the $10,000 note as well as five months of interest, or $375, as shown below. The $375 is comprised of the $300 Interest Receivable accrued on September 30 plus $75 earned during October. Wolder's entry to record the honoring of the Higley note on November 1 is:

Nov. 1	Cash [$10,000 + ($10,000 × 9% × $\frac{5}{12}$)]	10,375	
	Notes Receivable		10,000
	Interest Receivable		300
	Interest Revenue ($10,000 × 9% × $\frac{1}{12}$)		75
	(To record collection of Higley note and interest)		

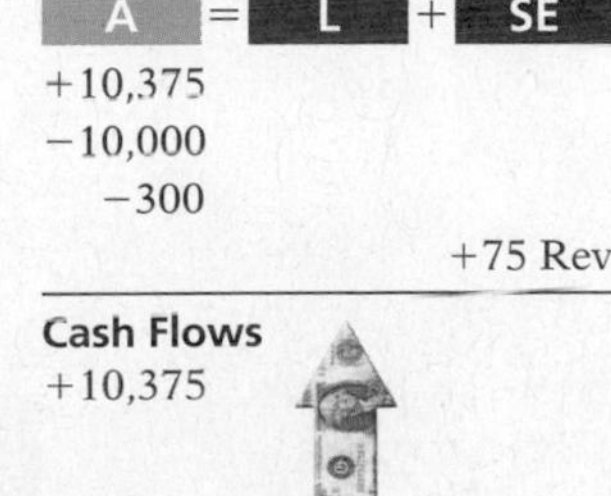

In this case, Wolder credits Interest Receivable because the receivable was established in the adjusting entry on September 30.

DISHONOR OF NOTES RECEIVABLE

A **dishonored (defaulted) note** is a note that is not paid in full at maturity. A dishonored note receivable is no longer negotiable. However, the payee still has a claim against the maker of the note for both the note and the interest. Therefore, the note holder usually transfers the Notes Receivable account to an account receivable.

To illustrate, assume that Higley Co. on November 1 indicates that it cannot pay at the present time. The entry to record the dishonor of the note depends on whether Wolder Co. expects eventual collection. If it does expect eventual collection, Wolder Co. debits the amount due (face value and interest) on the note to Accounts Receivable. It would make the following entry at the time the note is dishonored (assuming no previous accrual of interest).

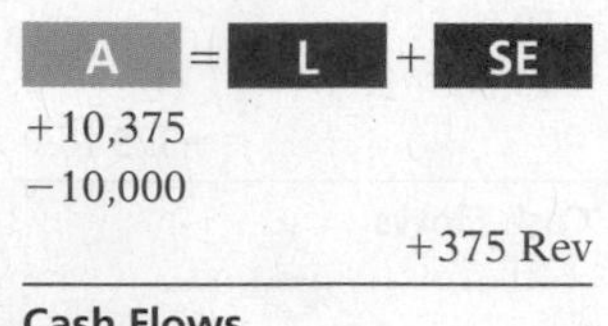

+10,375
−10,000
+375 Rev

Cash Flows
no effect

Nov. 1	Accounts Receivable—Higley	10,375	
	Notes Receivable		10,000
	Interest Revenue		375
	(To record the dishonor of Higley note)		

If instead, on November 1, there is no hope of collection, the note holder would write off the face value of the note by debiting Allowance for Doubtful Accounts. No interest revenue would be recorded because collection will not occur.

SALE OF NOTES RECEIVABLE

The accounting for the sale of notes receivable is recorded similarly to the sale of accounts receivable. The accounting entries for the sale of notes receivable are left for a more advanced course.

ACCOUNTING ACROSS THE ORGANIZATION

Bad Information Can Lead to Bad Loans

Many factors have contributed to the recent credit crisis. One significant factor that resulted in many bad loans was a failure by lenders to investigate loan customers sufficiently. For example, Countrywide Financial Corporation wrote many loans under its "Fast and Easy" loan program. That program allowed borrowers to provide little or no documentation for their income or their assets. Other lenders had similar programs, which earned the nickname "liars' loans." One study found that in these situations, 60% of applicants overstated their incomes by more than 50% in order to qualify for a loan. Critics of the banking industry say that because loan officers were compensated for loan volume, and because banks were selling the loans to investors rather than holding them, the lenders had little incentive to investigate the borrowers' creditworthiness.

Source: Glenn R. Simpson and James R. Hagerty, "Countrywide Loss Focuses Attention on Underwriting," *Wall Street Journal* (April 30, 2008), p. B1; and Michael Corkery, "Fraud Seen as Driver in Wave of Foreclosures," *Wall Street Journal* (December 21, 2007), p. A1.

What steps should the banks have taken to ensure the accuracy of financial information provided on loan applications? (See page 418.)

> **DO IT!**

Notes Receivable

Gambit Stores accepts from Leonard Co. a $3,400, 90-day, 6% note dated May 10 in settlement of Leonard's overdue account. (a) What is the maturity date of the note? (b) What entry does Gambit make at the maturity date, assuming Leonard pays the note and interest in full at that time?

Action Plan

- ✔ Count the exact number of days to determine the maturity date. Omit the date the note is issued, but include the due date.
- ✔ Determine whether interest was accrued.
- ✔ Compute the accrued interest.
- ✔ Prepare the entry for payment of the note and interest.
- ✔ The entry to record interest at maturity in this solution assumes no interest has been previously accrued on this note.

Solution

(a) The maturity date is August 8, computed as follows.

Term of note:		90 days
May (31–10)	21	
June	30	
July	31	82
Maturity date: August		8

(b) The interest payable at the maturity date is $51, computed as follows.

Face	×	Rate	×	Time	=	Interest
$3,400	×	6%	×	90/360	=	$51

The entry recorded by Gambit Stores at the maturity date is:

Cash	3,451	
Notes Receivable		3,400
Interest Revenue		51
(To record collection of Leonard note)		

Related exercise material: **BE8-9, BE8-10, BE8-11, E8-10, E8-11, E8-12, E8-13, and DO IT! 8-3.**

Statement Presentation and Analysis

Presentation

LEARNING OBJECTIVE 9

Explain the statement presentation and analysis of receivables.

Companies should identify in the balance sheet or in the notes to the financial statements each of the major types of receivables. Short-term receivables appear in the current assets section of the balance sheet. Short-term investments appear before short-term receivables because these investments are more liquid (nearer to cash). Companies report both the gross amount of receivables and the allowance for doubtful accounts.

In a multiple-step income statement, companies report bad debt expense and service charge expense as selling expenses in the operating expenses section. Interest revenue appears under "Other revenues and gains" in the nonoperating activities section of the income statement.

Analysis

Investors and corporate managers compute financial ratios to evaluate the liquidity of a company's accounts receivable. They use the **accounts receivable turnover ratio** to assess the liquidity of the receivables. This ratio measures the number of times, on average, the company collects accounts receivable during the period. It is computed by dividing net credit sales (net sales less cash sales) by the average net accounts receivable during the year. Unless seasonal factors are significant, average net accounts receivable outstanding can be computed from the beginning and ending balances of net accounts receivable.

For example, in 2009 Cisco Systems had net sales of $32,420 million for the year. It had a beginning accounts receivable (net) balance of $3,177 million and an ending accounts receivable (net) balance of $4,929 million. Assuming that Cisco's sales were all on credit, its accounts receivable turnover ratio is computed as follows.

Illustration 8-17
Accounts receivable turnover ratio and computation

Net Credit Sales	÷	Average Net Accounts Receivable	=	Accounts Receivable Turnover
$32,420	÷	$\frac{\$3,177 + \$4,929}{2}$	=	**8 times**

The result indicates an accounts receivable turnover ratio of 8 times per year. The higher the turnover ratio, the more liquid the company's receivables.

A variant of the accounts receivable turnover ratio that makes the liquidity even more evident is its conversion into an **average collection period** in terms of days. This is done by dividing the turnover ratio into 365 days. For example, Cisco's turnover of 8 times is divided into 365 days, as shown in Illustration 8-18, to obtain approximately 46 days. This means that it takes Cisco 46 days to collect its accounts receivable.

Illustration 8-18
Average collection period for receivables formula and computation

Days in Year	÷	Accounts Receivable Turnover	=	Average Collection Period in Days
365 days	÷	8 times	=	**46 days**

Companies frequently use the average collection period to assess the effectiveness of a company's credit and collection policies. The general rule is that the collection period should not greatly exceed the credit term period (that is, the time allowed for payment).

> DO IT!

Analysis of Receivables

In 2014, Phil Mickelson Company has net credit sales of $923,795 for the year. It had a beginning accounts receivable (net) balance of $38,275 and an ending accounts receivable (net) balance of $35,988. Compute Phil Mickelson Company's (a) accounts receivable turnover and (b) average collection period in days.

Action Plan

- ✔ Review the formula to compute the accounts receivable turnover.
- ✔ Make sure that both the beginning and ending accounts receivable balances are considered in the computation.
- ✔ Review the formula to compute the average collection period in days.

Solution

(a)	Net credit sales	÷	Average net accounts receivable	=	Accounts receivable turnover
	$923,795	÷	$\frac{38,275 + 35,988}{2}$	=	24.9 times
(b)	Days in year	÷	Accounts receivable turnover	=	Average collection period in days
	365	÷	24.9 times	=	14.7 days

Related exercise material: **BE8-12, E8-14, and DO IT! 8-4.**

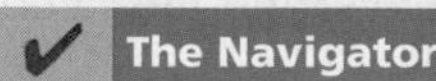

> Comprehensive DO IT!

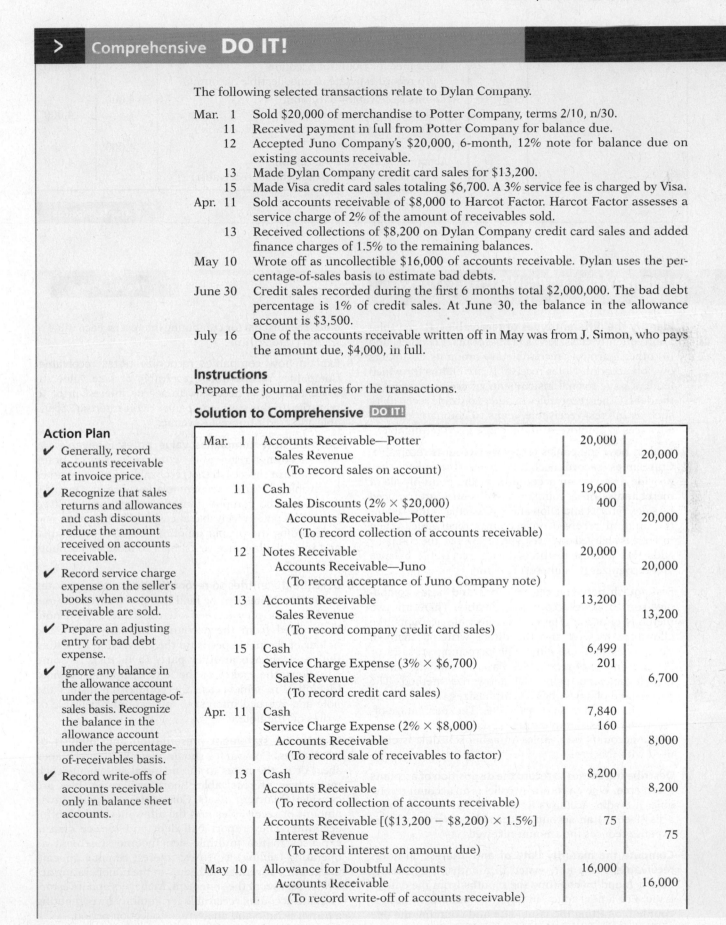

The following selected transactions relate to Dylan Company.

Mar.	1	Sold $20,000 of merchandise to Potter Company, terms 2/10, n/30.
	11	Received payment in full from Potter Company for balance due.
	12	Accepted Juno Company's $20,000, 6-month, 12% note for balance due on existing accounts receivable.
	13	Made Dylan Company credit card sales for $13,200.
	15	Made Visa credit card sales totaling $6,700. A 3% service fee is charged by Visa.
Apr.	11	Sold accounts receivable of $8,000 to Harcot Factor. Harcot Factor assesses a service charge of 2% of the amount of receivables sold.
	13	Received collections of $8,200 on Dylan Company credit card sales and added finance charges of 1.5% to the remaining balances.
May	10	Wrote off as uncollectible $16,000 of accounts receivable. Dylan uses the percentage-of-sales basis to estimate bad debts.
June	30	Credit sales recorded during the first 6 months total $2,000,000. The bad debt percentage is 1% of credit sales. At June 30, the balance in the allowance account is $3,500.
July	16	One of the accounts receivable written off in May was from J. Simon, who pays the amount due, $4,000, in full.

Instructions

Prepare the journal entries for the transactions.

Solution to Comprehensive DO IT!

Date		Account	Debit	Credit
Mar.	1	Accounts Receivable—Potter	20,000	
		Sales Revenue		20,000
		(To record sales on account)		
	11	Cash	19,600	
		Sales Discounts (2% × $20,000)	400	
		Accounts Receivable—Potter		20,000
		(To record collection of accounts receivable)		
	12	Notes Receivable	20,000	
		Accounts Receivable—Juno		20,000
		(To record acceptance of Juno Company note)		
	13	Accounts Receivable	13,200	
		Sales Revenue		13,200
		(To record company credit card sales)		
	15	Cash	6,499	
		Service Charge Expense (3% × $6,700)	201	
		Sales Revenue		6,700
		(To record credit card sales)		
Apr.	11	Cash	7,840	
		Service Charge Expense (2% × $8,000)	160	
		Accounts Receivable		8,000
		(To record sale of receivables to factor)		
	13	Cash	8,200	
		Accounts Receivable		8,200
		(To record collection of accounts receivable)		
		Accounts Receivable [($13,200 − $8,200) × 1.5%]	75	
		Interest Revenue		75
		(To record interest on amount due)		
May	10	Allowance for Doubtful Accounts	16,000	
		Accounts Receivable		16,000
		(To record write-off of accounts receivable)		

Action Plan

- ✔ Generally, record accounts receivable at invoice price.
- ✔ Recognize that sales returns and allowances and cash discounts reduce the amount received on accounts receivable.
- ✔ Record service charge expense on the seller's books when accounts receivable are sold.
- ✔ Prepare an adjusting entry for bad debt expense.
- ✔ Ignore any balance in the allowance account under the percentage-of-sales basis. Recognize the balance in the allowance account under the percentage-of-receivables basis.
- ✔ Record write-offs of accounts receivable only in balance sheet accounts.

June 30	Bad Debt Expense ($2,000,000 × 1%)	20,000	
	Allowance for Doubtful Accounts		20,000
	(To record estimate of uncollectible accounts)		
July 16	Accounts Receivable—J. Simon	4,000	
	Allowance for Doubtful Accounts		4,000
	(To reverse write-off of accounts receivable)		
	Cash	4,000	
	Accounts Receivable—J. Simon		4,000
	(To record collection of accounts receivable)		

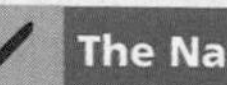

SUMMARY OF LEARNING OBJECTIVES

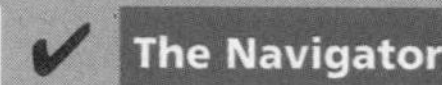

1 **Identify the different types of receivables.** Receivables are frequently classified as (1) accounts, (2) notes, and (3) other. Accounts receivable are amounts customers owe on account. Notes receivable are claims for which lenders issue formal instruments of credit as proof of the debt. Other receivables include nontrade receivables such as interest receivable, loans to company officers, advances to employees, and income taxes refundable.

2 **Explain how companies recognize accounts receivable.** Companies record accounts receivable when they provide a service on account or at the point-of-sale of merchandise on account. Sales revenues are reduced by sales returns and allowances. Cash discounts reduce the amount received on accounts receivable. When interest is charged on a past due receivable, the company adds this interest to the accounts receivable balance and recognizes it as interest revenue.

3 **Distinguish between the methods and bases companies use to value accounts receivable.** There are two methods of accounting for uncollectible accounts: the allowance method and the direct write-off method. Companies may use either the percentage-of-sales or the percentage-of-receivables basis to estimate uncollectible accounts using the allowance method. The percentage-of-sales basis emphasizes the expense recognition (matching) principle. The percentage-of-receivables basis emphasizes the cash realizable value of the accounts receivable. An aging schedule is often used with this basis.

4 **Describe the entries to record the disposition of accounts receivable.** When a company collects an account receivable, it credits Accounts Receivable. When a company sells (factors) an account receivable, a service charge expense reduces the amount received.

5 **Compute the maturity date of and interest on notes receivable.** For a note stated in months, the maturity date is found by counting the months from the date of issue. For a note stated in days, the number of days is counted, omitting the issue date and counting the due date. The formula for computing interest is: Face value × Interest rate × Time.

6 **Explain how companies recognize notes receivable.** Companies record notes receivable at face value. In some cases, it is necessary to accrue interest prior to maturity. In this case, companies debit Interest Receivable and credit Interest Revenue.

7 **Describe how companies value notes receivable.** As with accounts receivable, companies report notes receivable at their cash (net) realizable value. The notes receivable allowance account is Allowance for Doubtful Accounts. The computation and estimations involved in valuing notes receivable at cash realizable value, and in recording the proper amount of bad debt expense and related allowance, are similar to those for accounts receivable.

8 **Describe the entries to record the disposition of notes receivable.** Notes can be held to maturity. At that time the face value plus accrued interest is due, and the note is removed from the accounts. In many cases, the holder of the note speeds up the conversion by selling the receivable to another party (a factor). In some situations, the maker of the note dishonors the note (defaults), in which case the company transfers the note and accrued interest to an account receivable or writes off the note.

9 **Explain the statement presentation and analysis of receivables.** Companies should identify in the balance sheet or in the notes to the financial statements each major type of receivable. Short-term receivables are considered current assets. Companies report the gross amount of receivables and the allowance for doubtful accounts. They report bad debt and service charge expenses in the multiple-step income statement as operating (selling) expenses; interest revenue appears under other revenues and gains in the nonoperating activities section of the statement. Managers and investors evaluate accounts receivable for liquidity by computing a turnover ratio and an average collection period.

GLOSSARY

Accounts receivable Amounts owed by customers on account. (p. 380).

Accounts receivable turnover ratio A measure of the liquidity of accounts receivable; computed by dividing net credit sales by average net accounts receivable. (p. 397).

Aging the accounts receivable The analysis of customer balances by the length of time they have been unpaid. (p. 387).

Allowance method A method of accounting for bad debts that involves estimating uncollectible accounts at the end of each period. (p. 383).

Average collection period The average amount of time that a receivable is outstanding; calculated by dividing 365 days by the accounts receivable turnover ratio. (p. 398).

Bad Debt Expense An expense account to record uncollectible receivables. (p. 382).

Cash (net) realizable value The net amount a company expects to receive in cash. (p. 383).

Direct write-off method A method of accounting for bad debts that involves expensing accounts at the time they are determined to be uncollectible. (p. 382).

Dishonored (defaulted) note A note that is not paid in full at maturity. (p. 396).

Factor A finance company or bank that buys receivables from businesses and then collects the payments directly from the customers. (p. 389).

Maker The party in a promissory note who is making the promise to pay. (p. 391).

Notes receivable Written promise (as evidenced by a formal instrument) for amounts to be received. (p. 380).

Other receivables Various forms of nontrade receivables, such as interest receivable and income taxes refundable. (p. 380).

Payee The party to whom payment of a promissory note is to be made. (p. 391).

Percentage-of-receivables basis Management estimates what percentage of receivables will result in losses from uncollectible accounts. (p. 387).

Percentage-of-sales basis Management estimates what percentage of credit sales will be uncollectible. (p. 386).

Promissory note A written promise to pay a specified amount of money on demand or at a definite time. (p. 391).

Receivables Amounts due from individuals and other companies. (p. 380).

Trade receivables Notes and accounts receivable that result from sales transactions. (p. 380).

Self-Test, Brief Exercises, Exercises, Problem Set A, and many more components are available for practice in WileyPLUS.

SELF-TEST QUESTIONS

Answers are on page 419.

(LO 1) **1.** Receivables are frequently classified as:
(a) accounts receivable, company receivables, and other receivables.
(b) accounts receivable, notes receivable, and employee receivables.
(c) accounts receivable and general receivables.
(d) accounts receivable, notes receivable, and other receivables.

(LO 2) **2.** Buehler Company on June 15 sells merchandise on account to Chaz Co. for $1,000, terms 2/10, n/30. On June 20, Chaz Co. returns merchandise worth $300 to Buehler Company. On June 24, payment is received from Chaz Co. for the balance due. What is the amount of cash received?
(a) $700. (c) $686.
(b) $680. (d) None of the above.

(LO 3) **3.** Which of the following approaches for bad debts is best described as a balance sheet method?
(a) Percentage-of-receivables basis.
(b) Direct write-off method.
(c) Percentage-of-sales basis.
(d) Both a and b.

4. Hughes Company has a credit balance of $5,000 in its Allowance for Doubtful Accounts before any adjustments are made at the end of the year. Based on review and aging of its accounts receivable at the end of the year, Hughes estimates that $60,000 of its receivables are uncollectible. The amount of bad debt expense which should be reported for the year is: (LO 3)
(a) $5,000. (c) $60,000.
(b) $55,000. (d) $65,000.

5. Use the same information as in question 4, except that Hughes has a debit balance of $5,000 in its Allowance for Doubtful Accounts before any adjustments are made at the end of the year. In this situation, the amount of bad debt expense that should be reported for the year is: (LO 3)
(a) $5,000. (c) $60,000.
(b) $55,000. (d) $65,000.

6. Net sales for the month are $800,000, and bad debts are expected to be 1.5% of net sales. The company uses the percentage-of-sales basis. If Allowance for Doubtful Accounts has a credit balance of $15,000 before adjustment, what is the balance after adjustment? (LO 3)
(a) $15,000. (c) $23,000.
(b) $27,000. (d) $31,000.

(LO 3) **7.** In 2014, Roso Carlson Company had net credit sales of $750,000. On January 1, 2014, Allowance for Doubtful Accounts had a credit balance of $18,000. During 2014, $30,000 of uncollectible accounts receivable were written off. Past experience indicates that 3% of net credit sales become uncollectible. What should be the adjusted balance of Allowance for Doubtful Accounts at December 31, 2014?
(a) $10,050. (c) $22,500.
(b) $10,500. (d) $40,500.

(LO 3) **8.** An analysis and aging of the accounts receivable of Prince Company at December 31 reveals the following data.

Accounts receivable	$800,000
Allowance for doubtful accounts per books before adjustment	50,000
Amounts expected to become uncollectible	65,000

The cash realizable value of the accounts receivable at December 31, after adjustment, is:
(a) $685,000. (c) $800,000.
(b) $750,000. (d) $735,000.

(LO 6) **9.** One of the following statements about promissory notes is incorrect. The *incorrect* statement is:
(a) The party making the promise to pay is called the maker.
(b) The party to whom payment is to be made is called the payee.
(c) A promissory note is not a negotiable instrument.
(d) A promissory note is often required from high-risk customers.

(LO 4) **10.** Which of the following statements about Visa credit card sales is *incorrect*?
(a) The credit card issuer makes the credit investigation of the customer.
(b) The retailer is not involved in the collection process.
(c) Two parties are involved.
(d) The retailer receives cash more quickly than it would from individual customers on account.

(LO 4) **11.** Blinka Retailers accepted $50,000 of Citibank Visa credit card charges for merchandise sold on July 1. Citibank charges 4% for its credit card use. The entry to record this transaction by Blinka Retailers will include a credit to Sales Revenue of $50,000 and a debit(s) to:
(a) Cash $48,000
and Service Charge Expense $2,000
(b) Accounts Receivable $48,000
and Service Charge Expense $2,000
(c) Cash $50,000
(d) Accounts Receivable $50,000

12. Foti Co. accepts a $1,000, 3-month, 6% promissory note in settlement of an account with Bartelt Co. The entry to record this transaction is as follows. (LO 6)

(a) Notes Receivable	1,015	
Accounts Receivable		1,015
(b) Notes Receivable	1,000	
Accounts Receivable		1,000
(c) Notes Receivable	1,000	
Sales Revenue		1,000
(d) Notes Receivable	1,030	
Accounts Receivable		1,030

13. Ginter Co. holds Kolar Inc.'s $10,000, 120-day, 9% note. The entry made by Ginter Co. when the note is collected, assuming no interest has been previously accrued, is: (LO 8)

(a) Cash	10,300	
Notes Receivable		10,300
(b) Cash	10,000	
Notes Receivable		10,000
(c) Accounts Receivable	10,300	
Notes Receivable		10,000
Interest Revenue		300
(d) Cash	10,300	
Notes Receivable		10,000
Interest Revenue		300

14. Accounts and notes receivable are reported in the current assets section of the balance sheet at: (LO 9)
(a) cash (net) realizable value
(b) net book value.
(c) lower-of-cost-or-market value.
(d) invoice cost.

15. Oliveras Company had net credit sales during the year of $800,000 and cost of goods sold of $500,000. The balance in accounts receivable at the beginning of the year was $100,000, and the end of the year it was $150,000. What were the accounts receivable turnover ratio and the average collection period in days? (LO 9)
(a) 4.0 and 91.3 days. (c) 6.4 and 57 days.
(b) 5.3 and 68.9 days. (d) 8.0 and 45.6 days.

Go to the book's companion website, www.wiley.com/college/weygandt, for additional Self-Test Questions.

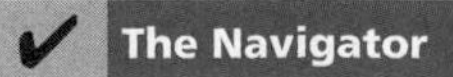

QUESTIONS

1. What is the difference between an account receivable and a note receivable?

2. What are some common types of receivables other than accounts receivable and notes receivable?

3. Texaco Oil Company issues its own credit cards. Assume that Texaco charges you $40 interest on an unpaid balance. Prepare the journal entry that Texaco makes to record this revenue.

4. What are the essential features of the allowance method of accounting for bad debts?

5. Roger Holloway cannot understand why cash realizable value does not decrease when an uncollectible account is written off under the allowance method. Clarify this point for Roger Holloway.

6. Distinguish between the two bases that may be used in estimating uncollectible accounts.
7. Borke Company has a credit balance of $3,200 in Allowance for Doubtful Accounts. The estimated bad debt expense under the percentage-of-sales basis is $3,700. The total estimated uncollectibles under the percentage-of-receivables basis is $5,800. Prepare the adjusting entry under each basis.
8. How are bad debts accounted for under the direct write-off method? What are the disadvantages of this method?
9. Freida Company accepts both its own credit cards and national credit cards. What are the advantages of accepting both types of cards?
10. An article recently appeared in the *Wall Street Journal* indicating that companies are selling their receivables at a record rate. Why are companies selling their receivables?
11. WestSide Textiles decides to sell $800,000 of its accounts receivable to First Factors Inc. First Factors assesses a service charge of 3% of the amount of receivables sold. Prepare the journal entry that WestSide Textiles makes to record this sale.
12. Your roommate is uncertain about the advantages of a promissory note. Compare the advantages of a note receivable with those of an account receivable.
13. How may the maturity date of a promissory note be stated?
14. Indicate the maturity date of each of the following promissory notes:

Date of Note	Terms
(a) March 13	one year after date of note
(b) May 4	3 months after date
(c) June 20	30 days after date
(d) July 1	60 days after date

15. Compute the missing amounts for each of the following notes.

Principal	Annual Interest Rate	Time	Total Interest
(a) ?	9%	120 days	$ 450
(b) $30,000	10%	3 years	?
(c) $60,000	?	5 months	$3,000
(d) $45,000	8%	?	$1,200

16. In determining interest revenue, some financial institutions use 365 days per year and others use 360 days. Why might a financial institution use 360 days?
17. Jana Company dishonors a note at maturity. What are the options available to the lender?
18. General Motors Corporation has accounts receivable and notes receivable. How should the receivables be reported on the balance sheet?
19. The accounts receivable turnover ratio is 8.14, and average net receivables during the period are $400,000. What is the amount of net credit sales for the period?
20. PEPSICO What percentage does PepsiCo's allowance for doubtful accounts represent as a percentage of its gross receivables?

BRIEF EXERCISES

BE8-1 Presented below are three receivables transactions. Indicate whether these receivables are reported as accounts receivable, notes receivable, or other receivables on a balance sheet.

Identify different types of receivables. (LO 1)

(a) Sold merchandise on account for $64,000 to a customer.
(b) Received a promissory note of $57,000 for services performed.
(c) Advanced $8,000 to an employee.

BE8-2 Record the following transactions on the books of Galaxy Co.

Record basic accounts receivable transactions. (LO 2)

(a) On July 1, Galaxy Co. sold merchandise on account to Kingston Inc. for $17,200, terms 2/10, n/30.
(b) On July 8, Kingston Inc. returned merchandise worth $3,800 to Galaxy Co.
(c) On July 11, Kingston Inc. paid for the merchandise.

BE8-3 During its first year of operations, Energy Company had credit sales of $3,000,000; $600,000 remained uncollected at year-end. The credit manager estimates that $31,000 of these receivables will become uncollectible.

Prepare entry for allowance method and partial balance sheet. (LO 3, 9)

(a) Prepare the journal entry to record the estimated uncollectibles.
(b) Prepare the current assets section of the balance sheet for Energy Company. Assume that in addition to the receivables it has cash of $90,000, inventory of $118,000, and prepaid insurance of $7,500.

BE8-4 At the end of 2014, Endrun Co. has accounts receivable of $700,000 and an allowance for doubtful accounts of $54,000. On January 24, 2015, the company learns that its receivable from Marcello is not collectible, and management authorizes a write-off of $6,200.

Prepare entry for write-off; determine cash realizable value. (LO 3)

(a) Prepare the journal entry to record the write-off.
(b) What is the cash realizable value of the accounts receivable (1) before the write-off and (2) after the write-off?

Prepare entries for collection of bad debt write-off.
(LO 3)

BE8-5 Assume the same information as BE8-4. On March 4, 2015, Endrun Co. receives payment of $6,200 in full from Marcello. Prepare the journal entries to record this transaction.

Prepare entry using percentage-of-sales method.
(LO 3)

BE8-6 Hamblin Co. elects to use the percentage-of-sales basis in 2014 to record bad debt expense. It estimates that 2% of net credit sales will become uncollectible. Sales revenues are $800,000 for 2014, sales returns and allowances are $38,000, and the allowance for doubtful accounts has a credit balance of $9,000. Prepare the adjusting entry to record bad debt expense in 2014.

Prepare entry using percentage-of-receivables method.
(LO 3)

BE8-7 Gleason Co. uses the percentage-of-receivables basis to record bad debt expense. It estimates that 1% of accounts receivable will become uncollectible. Accounts receivable are $420,000 at the end of the year, and the allowance for doubtful accounts has a credit balance of $1,500.

(a) Prepare the adjusting journal entry to record bad debt expense for the year.
(b) If the allowance for doubtful accounts had a debit balance of $740 instead of a credit balance of $1,500, determine the amount to be reported for bad debt expense.

Prepare entries to dispose of accounts receivable.
(LO 4)

BE8-8 Presented below are two independent transactions.

(a) Fiesta Restaurant accepted a Visa card in payment of a $175 lunch bill. The bank charges a 4% fee. What entry should Fiesta make?
(b) St. Charles Company sold its accounts receivable of $70,000. What entry should St. Charles make, given a service charge of 3% on the amount of receivables sold?

Compute interest and determine maturity dates on notes.
(LO 5)

BE8-9 Compute interest and find the maturity date for the following notes.

	Date of Note	Principal	Interest Rate (%)	Terms
(a)	June 10	$80,000	6%	60 days
(b)	July 14	$64,000	7%	90 days
(c)	April 27	$12,000	8%	75 days

Determine maturity dates and compute interest and rates on notes.
(LO 5)

BE8-10 Presented below are data on three promissory notes. Determine the missing amounts.

	Date of Note	Terms	Maturity Date	Principal	Annual Interest Rate	Total Interest
(a)	April 1	60 days	?	$600,000	5%	?
(b)	July 2	30 days	?	90,000	?	$600
(c)	March 7	6 months	?	120,000	10%	?

Prepare entry for notes receivable exchanged for account receivable.
(LO 6)

BE8-11 On January 10, 2014, Wilfer Co. sold merchandise on account to Elgin Co. for $11,600, n/30. On February 9, Elgin Co. gave Wilfer Co. a 9% promissory note in settlement of this account. Prepare the journal entry to record the sale and the settlement of the account receivable.

Compute ratios to analyze receivables.
(LO 9)

BE8-12 The financial statements of Minnesota Mining and Manufacturing Company (3M) report net sales of $20.0 billion. Accounts receivable (net) are $2.7 billion at the beginning of the year and $2.8 billion at the end of the year. Compute 3M's accounts receivable turnover ratio. Compute 3M's average collection period for accounts receivable in days.

> DO IT! REVIEW

Prepare entry for uncollectible accounts.
(LO 3)

DO IT! 8-1 Todd Company has been in business several years. At the end of the current year, the ledger shows:

Accounts Receivable	$ 310,000 Dr.
Sales Revenue	2,200,000 Cr.
Allowance for Doubtful Accounts	4,700 Cr.

Bad debts are estimated to be 5% of receivables. Prepare the entry to adjust Allowance for Doubtful Accounts.

DO IT! 8-2 Paltrow Distributors is a growing company whose ability to raise capital has not been growing as quickly as its expanding assets and sales. Paltrow's local banker has indicated that the company cannot increase its borrowing for the foreseeable future. Paltrow's suppliers are demanding payment for goods acquired within 30 days of the invoice date, but Paltrow's customers are slow in paying for their purchases (60–90 days). As a result, Paltrow has a cash flow problem.

Prepare entry for factored accounts.

(LO 4)

Paltrow needs $160,000 to cover next Friday's payroll. Its balance of outstanding accounts receivable totals $1,000,000. What might Paltrow do to alleviate this cash crunch? Record the entry that Paltrow would make when it raises the needed cash. (Assume a 3% service charge.)

DO IT! 8-3 Karbon Wholesalers accepts from Bazaar Stores a $6,200, 4-month, 9% note dated May 31 in settlement of Bazaar's overdue account. (a) What is the maturity date of the note? (b) What is the entry made by Karbon at the maturity date, assuming Bazaar pays the note and interest in full at that time?

Prepare entries for notes receivable.

(LO 5, 8)

DO IT! 8-4 In 2014, Lauren Company has net credit sales of $1,480,000 for the year. It had a beginning accounts receivable (net) balance of $112,000 and an ending accounts receivable (net) balance of $108,000. Compute Lauren Company's (a) accounts receivable turnover and (b) average collection period in days.

Compute ratios for receivables.

(LO 9)

 The Navigator

EXERCISES

E8-1 Presented below are selected transactions of Menge Company. Menge sells in large quantities to other companies and also sells its product in a small retail outlet.

Journalize entries related to accounts receivable.

(LO 2)

March 1 Sold merchandise on account to Lynda Company for $3,800, terms 2/10, n/30.
3 Lynda Company returned merchandise worth $500 to Menge.
9 Menge collected the amount due from Lynda Company from the March 1 sale.
15 Menge sold merchandise for $200 in its retail outlet. The customer used his Menge credit card.
31 Menge added 1.5% monthly interest to the customer's credit card balance.

Instructions

Prepare journal entries for the transactions above.

E8-2 Presented below are two independent situations.

Journalize entries for recognizing accounts receivable.

(LO 2)

(a) On January 6, Bennett Co. sells merchandise on account to Jackie Inc. for $7,000, terms 2/10, n/30. On January 16, Jackie Inc. pays the amount due. Prepare the entries on Bennett's books to record the sale and related collection.

(b) On January 10, Connor Bybee uses his Sheridan Co. credit card to purchase merchandise from Sheridan Co. for $9,000. On February 10, Bybee is billed for the amount due of $9,000. On February 12, Bybee pays $6,000 on the balance due. On March 10, Bybee is billed for the amount due, including interest at 2% per month on the unpaid balance as of February 12. Prepare the entries on Sheridan Co.'s books related to the transactions that occurred on January 10, February 12, and March 10.

E8-3 The ledger of Elburn Company at the end of the current year shows Accounts Receivable $110,000, Sales Revenue $840,000, and Sales Returns and Allowances $28,000.

Journalize entries to record allowance for doubtful accounts using two different bases.

(LO 3)

Instructions

(a) If Elburn uses the direct write-off method to account for uncollectible accounts, journalize the adjusting entry at December 31, assuming Elburn determines that T. Thum's $1,400 balance is uncollectible.

(b) If Allowance for Doubtful Accounts has a credit balance of $2,100 in the trial balance, journalize the adjusting entry at December 31, assuming bad debts are expected to be (1) 1% of net sales, and (2) 10% of accounts receivable.

(c) If Allowance for Doubtful Accounts has a debit balance of $200 in the trial balance, journalize the adjusting entry at December 31, assuming bad debts are expected to be (1) 0.75% of net sales and (2) 6% of accounts receivable.

Determine bad debt expense; prepare the adjusting entry for bad debt expense.

(LO 3)

E8-4 Leland Company has accounts receivable of $98,100 at March 31. An analysis of the accounts shows the following information.

Month of Sale	Balance, March 31
March	$65,000
February	17,600
January	8,500
Prior to January	7,000
	$98,100

Credit terms are 2/10, n/30. At March 31, Allowance for Doubtful Accounts has a credit balance of $900 prior to adjustment. The company uses the percentage-of-receivables basis for estimating uncollectible accounts. The company's estimate of bad debts is shown below.

Age of Accounts	Estimated Percentage Uncollectible
1–30 days	2.0%
31–60 days	5.0%
61–90 days	30.0%
Over 90 days	50.0%

Instructions

(a) Determine the total estimated uncollectibles.

(b) Prepare the adjusting entry at March 31 to record bad debt expense.

Journalize write-off and recovery.

(LO 3)

E8-5 At December 31, 2013, Crawford Company had a balance of $15,000 in Allowance for Doubtful Accounts. During 2014, Crawford wrote off accounts totaling $14,100. One of those accounts ($1,800) was later collected. At December 31, 2014, an aging schedule indicated that the balance in Allowance for Doubtful Accounts should be $19,000.

Instructions

Prepare journal entries to record the 2014 transactions of Crawford Company.

Journalize percentage-of-sales basis, write-off, recovery.

(LO 3)

E8-6 On December 31, 2013, Russell Co. estimated that 2% of its net sales of $360,000 will become uncollectible. The company recorded this amount as an addition to Allowance for Doubtful Accounts. On May 11, 2014, Russell Co. determined that the B. Vetter account was uncollectible and wrote off $1,100. On June 12, 2014, Vetter paid the amount previously written off.

Instructions

Prepare the journal entries on December 31, 2013, May 11, 2014, and June 12, 2014.

Journalize entries for the sale of accounts receivable.

(LO 4)

E8-7 Presented below are two independent situations.

(a) On March 3, Hinckley Appliances sells $620,000 of its receivables to Universal Factors Inc. Universal Factors assesses a finance charge of 3% of the amount of receivables sold. Prepare the entry on Hinckley Appliances' books to record the sale of the receivables.

(b) On May 10, Cody Company sold merchandise for $3,500 and accepted the customer's America Bank MasterCard. America Bank charges a 5% service charge for credit card sales. Prepare the entry on Cody Company's books to record the sale of merchandise.

Journalize entries for credit card sales.

(LO 4)

E8-8 Presented below are two independent situations.

(a) On April 2, Julie Keiser uses her JCPenney Company credit card to purchase merchandise from a JCPenney store for $1,500. On May 1, Keiser is billed for the $1,500 amount due. Keiser pays $900 on the balance due on May 3. On June 1, Keiser receives a bill for the amount due, including interest at 1.0% per month on the unpaid balance as of May 3. Prepare the entries on JCPenney Co.'s books related to the transactions that occurred on April 2, May 3, and June 1.

(b) On July 4, Avalon Restaurant accepts a Visa card for a $200 dinner bill. Visa charges a 3% service fee. Prepare the entry on Avalon's books related to this transaction.

E8-9 Burtonville Stores accepts both its own and national credit cards. During the year, the following selected summary transactions occurred.

Journalize credit card sales, and indicate the statement presentation of financing charges and service charge expense.

(LO 4)

Jan. 15	Made Burtonville credit card sales totaling $18,000. (There were no balances prior to January 15.)
20	Made Visa credit card sales (service charge fee 2%) totaling $4,800.
Feb. 10	Collected $10,000 on Burtonville credit card sales.
15	Added finance charges of 1.5% to Burtonville credit card account balances.

Instructions

(a) Journalize the transactions for Burtonville Stores.
(b) Indicate the statement presentation of the financing charges and the credit card service charge expense for Burtonville Stores.

E8-10 Reeves Supply Co. has the following transactions related to notes receivable during the last 2 months of 2014.

Journalize entries for notes receivable transactions.

(LO 5, 6)

Nov. 1	Loaned $15,000 cash to Norma Jeanne on a 1-year, 9% note.
Dec. 11	Sold goods to Bob Sharbo, Inc., receiving a $6,750, 90-day, 8% note.
16	Received a $4,400, 6-month, 12% note in exchange for Richard Russo's outstanding accounts receivable.
31	Accrued interest revenue on all notes receivable.

Instructions

(a) Journalize the transactions for Reeves Supply Co.
(b) Record the collection of the Jeanne note at its maturity in 2015.

E8-11 Record the following transactions for Taylor Co. in the general journal.

Journalize entries for notes receivable.

(LO 5, 6)

2014

May 1	Received a $7,500, 1-year, 9% note in exchange for Len Monroe's outstanding accounts receivable.
Dec. 31	Accrued interest on the Monroe note.
Dec. 31	Closed the interest revenue account.

2015

May 1	Received principal plus interest on the Monroe note. (No interest has been accrued in 2015.)

E8-12 Bieber Company had the following select transactions.

Prepare entries for note receivable transactions.

(LO 5, 6, 8)

May 1, 2014	Accepted Crane Company's 1-year, 12% note in settlement of a $16,000 account receivable.
July 1, 2014	Loaned $25,000 cash to Sam Howard on a 9-month, 10% note.
Dec. 31, 2014	Accrued interest on all notes receivable.
Apr. 1, 2015	Sam Howard dishonored its note; Bieber expects it will eventually collect.
May 1, 2015	Received principal plus interest on the Crane note.

Instructions

Prepare journal entries to record the transactions. Bieber prepares adjusting entries once a year on December 31.

E8-13 On May 2, Ottawa Company lends $7,600 to Cortland, Inc., issuing a 6-month, 8% note. At the maturity date, November 2, Cortland indicates that it cannot pay.

Journalize entries for dishonor of notes receivable.

(LO 5, 8)

Instructions

(a) Prepare the entry to record the issuance of the note.
(b) Prepare the entry to record the dishonor of the note, assuming that Ottawa Company expects collection will occur.
(c) Prepare the entry to record the dishonor of the note, assuming that Ottawa Company does not expect collection in the future.

E8-14 Lashkova Company had accounts receivable of $100,000 on January 1, 2014. The only transactions that affected accounts receivable during 2014 were net credit sales of $1,000,000, cash collections of $920,000, and accounts written off of $30,000.

Compute accounts receivable turnover and average collection period.

(LO 9)

Instructions

(a) Compute the ending balance of accounts receivable.
(b) Compute the accounts receivable turnover ratio for 2014.
(c) Compute the average collection period in days.

EXERCISES: SET B AND CHALLENGE EXERCISES

Visit the book's companion website, at **www.wiley.com/college/weygandt**, and choose the Student Companion site to access Exercise Set B and Challenge Exercises.

PROBLEMS: SET A

Prepare journal entries related to bad debt expense.

(LO 2, 3, 9)

P8-1A At December 31, 2013, Dean Co. reported the following information on its balance sheet.

Accounts receivable	$960,000
Less: Allowance for doubtful accounts	70,000

During 2014, the company had the following transactions related to receivables.

1. Sales on account	$3,315,000
2. Sales returns and allowances	50,000
3. Collections of accounts receivable	2,810,000
4. Write-offs of accounts receivable deemed uncollectible	90,000
5. Recovery of bad debts previously written off as uncollectible	29,000

Instructions

(a) Prepare the journal entries to record each of these five transactions. Assume that no cash discounts were taken on the collections of accounts receivable.

(b) Accounts receivable $1,325,000 ADA $9,000

(c) Bad debt expense $116,000

(b) Enter the January 1, 2014, balances in Accounts Receivable and Allowance for Doubtful Accounts, post the entries to the two accounts (use T-accounts), and determine the balances.

(c) Prepare the journal entry to record bad debt expense for 2014, assuming that an aging of accounts receivable indicates that expected bad debts are $125,000.

(d) Compute the accounts receivable turnover ratio for 2014.

Compute bad debt amounts.

(LO 3)

P8-2A Information related to Hamilton Company for 2014 is summarized below.

Total credit sales	$2,500,000
Accounts receivable at December 31	970,000
Bad debts written off	66,000

Instructions

(a) What amount of bad debt expense will Hamilton Company report if it uses the direct write-off method of accounting for bad debts?

(b) Assume that Hamilton Company estimates its bad debt expense to be 3% of credit sales. What amount of bad debt expense will Hamilton record if it has an Allowance for Doubtful Accounts credit balance of $4,000?

(c) Assume that Hamilton Company estimates its bad debt expense based on 7% of accounts receivable. What amount of bad debt expense will Hamilton record if it has an Allowance for Doubtful Accounts credit balance of $3,000?

(d) Assume the same facts as in (c), except that there is a $3,000 debit balance in Allowance for Doubtful Accounts. What amount of bad debt expense will Hamilton record?

(e) What is the weakness of the direct write-off method of reporting bad debt expense?

P8-3A Presented below is an aging schedule for Sycamore Company.

Journalize entries to record transactions related to bad debts.

(LO 2, 3)

Worksheet.xls

	A	B	C	D	E	F	G
1				Number of Days Past Due			
2			Not				
3	Customer	Total	Yet Due	1–30	31–60	61–90	Over 90
4	Anders	$ 28,000		$12,000	$16,000		
5	Blake	40,000	$ 40,000				
6	Cyrs	57,000	16,000	6,000		$35,000	
7	De Jong	34,000					$34,000
8	Others	132,000	96,000	16,000	14,000		6,000
9		$291,000	$152,000	$34,000	$30,000	$35,000	$40,000
10	Estimated percentage uncollectible		2%	6%	13%	25%	60%
11	Total estimated bad debts	$ 41,730	$ 3,040	$ 2,040	$ 3,900	$ 8,750	$24,000
12							

At December 31, 2014, the unadjusted balance in Allowance for Doubtful Accounts is a credit of $9,000.

Instructions

(a) Journalize and post the adjusting entry for bad debts at December 31, 2014.

(a) Bad debt expense $32,730

(b) Journalize and post to the allowance account the following events and transactions in the year 2015.

(1) On March 31, a $1,000 customer balance originating in 2014 is judged uncollectible.

(2) On May 31, a check for $1,000 is received from the customer whose account was written off as uncollectible on March 31.

(c) Journalize the adjusting entry for bad debts on December 31, 2015, assuming that the unadjusted balance in Allowance for Doubtful Accounts is a debit of $800 and the aging schedule indicates that total estimated bad debts will be $31,600.

(c) Bad debt expense $32,400

P8-4A Mineo Inc. uses the allowance method to estimate uncollectible accounts receivable. The company produced the following aging of the accounts receivable at year-end.

Journalize transactions related to bad debts.

(LO 2, 3)

Worksheet.xls

	A	B	C	D	E	F	G
1			Number of Days Outstanding				
2							
3		Total	0–30	31–60	61–90	91–120	Over 120
4	Accounts receivable	193,000	70,000	46,000	39,000	23,000	$15,000
5	% uncollectible		1%	3%	5%	8%	10%
6	Estimated bad debts						
7							

Instructions

(a) Calculate the total estimated bad debts based on the above information.

(a) Tot. est. bad debts $7,370

(b) Prepare the year-end adjusting journal entry to record the bad debts using the aged uncollectible accounts receivable determined in (a). Assume the current balance in Allowance for Doubtful Accounts is a $3,000 debit.

(c) Of the above accounts, $5,000 is determined to be specifically uncollectible. Prepare the journal entry to write off the uncollectible account.

(d) The company collects $5,000 subsequently on a specific account that had previously been determined to be uncollectible in (c). Prepare the journal entry(ies) necessary to restore the account and record the cash collection.

(e) Comment on how your answers to (a)–(d) would change if Mineo Inc. used 3% of *total* accounts receivable, rather than aging the accounts receivable. What are the advantages to the company of aging the accounts receivable rather than applying a percentage to total accounts receivable?

Journalize entries to record transactions related to bad debts.

(LO 3)

P8-5A At December 31, 2014, the trial balance of Roberto Company contained the following amounts before adjustment.

	Debits	Credits
Accounts Receivable	$385,000	
Allowance for Doubtful Accounts		$ 800
Sales Revenue		918,000

Instructions

(a) Based on the information given, which method of accounting for bad debts is Roberto Company using—the direct write-off method or the allowance method? How can you tell?

(b) Prepare the adjusting entry at December 31, 2014, for bad debt expense under each of the following independent assumptions.

(1) An aging schedule indicates that $11,750 of accounts receivable will be uncollectible.

(b) (2) $9,180

(2) The company estimates that 1% of sales will be uncollectible.

(c) Repeat part (b) assuming that instead of a credit balance there is an $800 debit balance in Allowance for Doubtful Accounts.

(d) During the next month, January 2015, a $3,000 account receivable is written off as uncollectible. Prepare the journal entry to record the write-off.

(e) Repeat part (d) assuming that Roberto uses the direct write-off method instead of the allowance method in accounting for uncollectible accounts receivable.

(f) What type of account is Allowance for Doubtful Accounts? How does it affect how accounts receivable is reported on the balance sheet at the end of the accounting period?

Prepare entries for various notes receivable transactions.

(LO 2, 4, 5, 8, 9)

P8-6A Hilo Company closes its books monthly. On September 30, selected ledger account balances are:

Notes Receivable	$31,000
Interest Receivable	170

Notes Receivable include the following.

Date	Maker	Face	Term	Interest
Aug. 16	Demaster Inc.	$ 8,000	60 days	8%
Aug. 25	Skinner Co.	9,000	60 days	10%
Sept. 30	Almer Corp.	14,000	6 months	9%

Interest is computed using a 360-day year. During October, the following transactions were completed.

Oct. 7	Made sales of $6,300 on Hilo credit cards.
12	Made sales of $1,200 on MasterCard credit cards. The credit card service charge is 3%.
15	Added $460 to Hilo customer balance for finance charges on unpaid balances.
15	Received payment in full from Demaster Inc. on the amount due.
24	Received notice that the Skinner note has been dishonored. (Assume that Skinner is expected to pay in the future.)

Instructions

(a) Journalize the October transactions and the October 31 adjusting entry for accrued interest receivable.

(b) Accounts receivable $15,910

(c) Total receivables $30,015

(b) Enter the balances at October 1 in the receivable accounts. Post the entries to all of the receivable accounts.

(c) Show the balance sheet presentation of the receivable accounts at October 31.

P8-7A On January 1, 2014, Derek Company had Accounts Receivable $139,000, Notes Receivable $30,000, and Allowance for Doubtful Accounts $13,200. The note receivable is from Kaye Noonan Company. It is a 4-month, 12% note dated December 31, 2013. Derek Company prepares financial statements annually. During the year, the following selected transactions occurred.

Prepare entries for various receivable transactions.

(LO 2, 4, 5, 6, 7, 8)

Jan. 5	Sold $24,000 of merchandise to Zwingle Company, terms n/15.
20	Accepted Zwingle Company's $24,000, 3-month, 9% note for balance due.
Feb. 18	Sold $8,000 of merchandise to Gerard Company and accepted Gerard's $8,000, 6-month, 8% note for the amount due.
Apr. 20	Collected Zwingle Company note in full.
30	Received payment in full from Kaye Noonan Company on the amount due.
May 25	Accepted Isabella Inc.'s $4,000, 3-month, 7% note in settlement of a past-due balance on account.
Aug. 18	Received payment in full from Gerard Company on note due.
25	The Isabella Inc. note was dishonored. Isabella Inc. is not bankrupt; future payment is anticipated.
Sept. 1	Sold $12,000 of merchandise to Fernando Company and accepted a $12,000, 6-month, 10% note for the amount due.

Instructions

Journalize the transactions.

PROBLEMS: SET B

P8-1B At December 31, 2013, Globe Trotter Imports reported the following information on its balance sheet.

Prepare journal entries related to bad debt expense.

(LO 2, 3, 9)

Accounts receivable	$220,000
Less: Allowance for doubtful accounts	15,000

During 2014, the company had the following transactions related to receivables.

1. Sales on account	$2,400,000
2. Sales returns and allowances	45,000
3. Collections of accounts receivable	2,250,000
4. Write-offs of accounts receivable deemed uncollectible	13,000
5. Recovery of bad debts previously written off as uncollectible	2,000

Instructions

(a) Prepare the journal entries to record each of these five transactions. Assume that no cash discounts were taken on the collections of accounts receivable.

(b) Enter the January 1, 2014, balances in Accounts Receivable and Allowance for Doubtful Accounts. Post the entries to the two accounts (use T-accounts), and determine the balances.

(c) Prepare the journal entry to record bad debt expense for 2014, assuming that an aging of accounts receivable indicates that estimated bad debts are $22,000.

(d) Compute the accounts receivable turnover ratio for the year 2014.

(b) Accounts receivable $312,000
ADA $4,000

(c) Bad debt expense $18,000

P8-2B Information related to Shin Company for 2014 is summarized below.

Compute bad debt amounts.

(LO 3)

Total credit sales	$920,000
Accounts receivable at December 31	369,000
Bad debts written off	23,400

Instructions

(a) What amount of bad debt expense will Shin Company report if it uses the direct write-off method of accounting for bad debts?

(b) Assume that Shin Company decides to estimate its bad debt expense to be 3% of credit sales. What amount of bad debt expense will Shin record if Allowance for Doubtful Accounts has a credit balance of $3,000?

(c) Assume that Shin Company decides to estimate its bad debt expense based on 7% of accounts receivable. What amount of bad debt expense will Shin Company record if Allowance for Doubtful Accounts has a credit balance of $4,000?
(d) Assume the same facts as in (c), except that there is a $2,000 debit balance in Allowance for Doubtful Accounts. What amount of bad debt expense will Shin record?
(e) What is the weakness of the direct write-off method of reporting bad debt expense?

Journalize entries to record transactions related to bad debts.

(LO 2, 3)

P8-3B Presented below is an aging schedule for Garry Owen Company.

Worksheet.xls

	A	B	C	D	E	F	G
1				Number of Days Past Due			
2			Not				
3	Customer	Total	Yet Due	1–30	31–60	61–90	Over 90
4	Alma	$ 26,000		$11,500	$14,500		
5	Browne	45,000	$ 45,000				
6	Conlon	75,000	22,500	7,500		$45,000	
7	Dalton	57,000					$57,000
8	Others	189,000	138,000	22,500	19,500		9,000
9		$392,000	$205,500	$41,500	$34,000	$45,000	$66,000
10	Estimated percentage uncollectible		2%	6%	10%	25%	50%
11	Total estimated bad debts	$ 54,250	$ 4,110	$ 2,490	$ 3,400	$11,250	$33,000
12							

At December 31, 2014, the unadjusted balance in Allowance for Doubtful Accounts is a credit of $14,000.

Instructions

(a) Journalize and post the adjusting entry for bad debts at December 31, 2014.

(a) Bad debt expense $40,250

(b) Journalize and post to the allowance account the following events and transactions in the year 2015.
   (1) March 1, a $1,900 customer balance originating in 2014 is judged uncollectible.
   (2) May 1, a check for $1,900 is received from the customer whose account was written off as uncollectible on March 1.

(c) Journalize the adjusting entry for bad debts on December 31, 2015. Assume that the unadjusted balance in Allowance for Doubtful Accounts is a debit of $3,400, and the aging schedule indicates that total estimated bad debts will be $42,300.

(c) Bad debt expense $45,700

Journalize transactions related to bad debts.

(LO 2, 3)

P8-4B The following represents selected information taken from a company's aging schedule to estimate uncollectible accounts receivable at year-end.

Worksheet.xls

	A	B	C	D	E	F	G
1			Number of Days Outstanding				
2							
3		Total	0–30	31–60	61–90	91–120	Over 120
4	Accounts receivable	$383,000	$220,000	$90,000	$40,000	$18,000	$15,000
5	% uncollectible		1%	3%	5%	8%	10%
6	Estimated bad debts						
7							

Instructions

(a) Calculate the total estimated bad debts based on the above information.

(b) Prepare the year-end adjusting journal entry to record the bad debts using the allowance method and the aged uncollectible accounts receivable determined in (a). Assume the current balance in Allowance for Doubtful Accounts is a $1,600 credit.

(c) Of the above accounts, $1,100 is determined to be specifically uncollectible. Prepare the journal entry to write off the uncollectible accounts.

(d) The company subsequently collects $700 on a specific account that had previously been determined to be uncollectible in (c). Prepare the journal entry(ies) necessary to restore the account and record the cash collection.

(e) Explain how establishing an allowance account satisfies the expense recognition principle.

(a) Tot. est. bad debts $9,840

P8-5B At December 31, 2014, the trial balance of Mariette Company contained the following amounts before adjustment.

Journalize entries to record transactions related to bad debts.

(LO 3)

	Debits	Credits
Accounts Receivable	$250,000	
Allowance for Doubtful Accounts		$ 1,400
Sales Revenue		600,000

Instructions

(a) Prepare the adjusting entry at December 31, 2014, to record bad debt expense under each of the following independent assumptions.

(1) An aging schedule indicates that $13,800 of accounts receivable will be uncollectible.

(2) The company estimates that 2% of sales will be uncollectible.

(a) (2) $12,000

(b) Repeat part (a) assuming that instead of a credit balance, there is a $1,400 debit balance in Allowance for Doubtful Accounts.

(c) During the next month, January 2015, a $3,200 account receivable is written off as uncollectible. Prepare the journal entry to record the write-off.

(d) Repeat part (c) assuming that Mariette Company uses the direct write-off method instead of the allowance method in accounting for uncollectible accounts receivable.

(e) What are the advantages of using the allowance method in accounting for uncollectible accounts as compared to the direct write-off method?

P8-6B Gehrig Co. closes its books monthly. On June 30, selected ledger account balances are:

Prepare entries for various notes receivable transactions.

(LO 2, 4, 5, 8, 9)

Notes Receivable	$60,000
Interest Receivable	435

Notes Receivable include the following.

Date	Maker	Face	Term	Interest
May 16	Fulton Inc.	$12,000	60 days	9%
May 25	Ascot Co.	30,000	60 days	10%
June 30	Trayer Corp.	18,000	6 months	12%

During July, the following transactions were completed.

July 5 Made sales of $7,200 on Gehrig Co. credit cards.

14 Made sales of $1,300 on Visa credit cards. The credit card service charge is 3%.

14 Added $510 to Gehrig Co. credit card customer balances for finance charges on unpaid balances.

15 Received payment in full from Fulton Inc. on the amount due.

24 Received notice that the Ascot Co. note has been dishonored. (Assume that Ascot Co. is expected to pay in the future.)

Instructions

(a) Journalize the July transactions and the July 31 adjusting entry for accrued interest receivable. (Interest is computed using 360 days.)

(b) Enter the balances at July 1 in the receivable accounts. Post the entries to all of the receivable accounts.

(b) Accounts receivable $38,210

(c) Show the balance sheet presentation of the receivable accounts at July 31.

(c) Total receivables $56,390

Prepare entries for various receivable transactions.

(LO 2, 4, 5, 6, 7, 8)

P8-7B On January 1, 2014, Valdez Company had Accounts Receivable $91,000 and Allowance for Doubtful Accounts $8,100. Valdez Company prepares financial statements annually. During the year, the following selected transactions occurred.

Jan.	5	Sold $8,400 of merchandise to Patrick Company, terms n/30.
Feb.	2	Accepted a $8,400, 4-month, 10% promissory note from Patrick Company for the balance due.
	12	Sold $13,500 of merchandise to Marguerite Company and accepted Marguerite's $13,500, 2-month, 10% note for the balance due.
	26	Sold $7,000 of merchandise to Felton Co., terms n/10.
Apr.	5	Accepted a $7,000, 3-month, 8% note from Felton Co. for the balance due.
	12	Collected Marguerite Company note in full.
June	2	Collected Patrick Company note in full.
July	5	Felton Co. dishonors its note of April 5. It is expected that Felton will eventually pay the amount owed.
	15	Sold $14,000 of merchandise to Planke Co. and accepted Planke's $14,000, 3-month, 12% note for the amount due.
Oct.	15	Planke Co.'s note was dishonored. Planke Co. is bankrupt, and there is no hope of future settlement.

Instructions

Journalize the transactions.

PROBLEMS: SET C

Visit the book's companion website, at **www.wiley.com/college/weygandt**, and choose the Student Companion site to access Problem Set C.

COMPREHENSIVE PROBLEM

CP8 Victoria Company's balance sheet at December 31, 2013, is presented below.

Victoria Company
Balance Sheet
December 31, 2013

Cash	$13,100	Accounts payable	$ 8,750
Accounts receivable	19,780	Common stock	20,000
Allowance for doubtful accounts	(800)	Retained earnings	12,730
Inventory	9,400		$41,480
	$41,480		

During January 2014, the following transactions occurred. Victoria uses the perpetual inventory method.

Jan.	1	Victoria accepted a 4-month, 8% note from Leon Company in payment of Leon's $1,500 account.
	3	Victoria wrote off as uncollectible the accounts of Barker Corporation ($450) and Elmo Company ($330).
	8	Victoria purchased $17,200 of inventory on account.
	11	Victoria sold for $25,000 on account inventory that cost $17,500.
	15	Victoria sold inventory that cost $780 to Joe Haribo for $1,200. Haribo charged this amount on his Visa First Bank card. The service fee charged Victoria by First Bank is 3%.
	17	Victoria collected $22,900 from customers on account.
	21	Victoria paid $16,300 on accounts payable.

24 Victoria received payment in full ($330) from Elmo Company on the account written off on January 3.
27 Victoria purchased advertising supplies for $1,400 cash.
31 Victoria paid other operating expenses, $3,218.

Adjustment data:

1. Interest is recorded for the month on the note from January 1.
2. Bad debts are expected to be 5% of the January 31, 2014, accounts receivable.
3. A count of advertising supplies on January 31, 2014, reveals that $470 remains unused.

Instructions

(You may want to set up T-accounts to determine ending balances.)

(a) Prepare journal entries for the transactions listed above and adjusting entries. (Include entries for cost of goods sold using the perpetual system.)
(b) Prepare an adjusted trial balance at January 31, 2014.
(c) Prepare an income statement and a retained earnings statement for the month ending January 31, 2014, and a classified balance sheet as of January 31, 2014.

CONTINUING COOKIE CHRONICLE

(*Note:* This is a continuation of the Cookie Chronicle from Chapters 1–7.)

CCC8 One of Natalie's friends, Curtis Lesperance, runs a coffee shop where he sells specialty coffees and prepares and sells muffins and cookies. He is eager to buy one of Natalie's fine European mixers, which would enable him to make larger batches of muffins and cookies. However, Curtis cannot afford to pay for the mixer for at least 30 days. He asks Natalie if she would be willing to sell him the mixer on credit. Natalie comes to you for advice.

Go to the book's companion website, www.wiley.com/college/weygandt, to see the completion of this problem.

Broadening Your PERSPECTIVE

Financial Reporting and Analysis

Financial Reporting Problem: CAF Company

BYP8-1 CAF Company sells office equipment and supplies to many organizations in the city and surrounding area on contract terms of 2/10, n/30. In the past, over 75% of the credit customers have taken advantage of the discount by paying within 10 days of the invoice date.

The number of customers taking the full 30 days to pay has increased within the last year. Current indications are that less than 60% of the customers are now taking the discount. Bad debts as a percentage of gross credit sales have risen from the 2.5% provided in past years to about 4.5% in the current year.

The company's Finance Committee has requested more information on the collections of accounts receivable. The controller responded to this request with the report reproduced below.

CAF Company
Accounts Receivable Collections
May 31, 2014

The fact that some credit accounts will prove uncollectible is normal. Annual bad debt write-offs have been 2.5% of gross credit sales over the past 5 years. During the last fiscal year, this percentage increased to slightly less than 4.5%. The current Accounts Receivable balance is $1,400,000. The condition of this balance in terms of age and probability of collection is as follows.

Proportion of Total	Age Categories	Probability of Collection
60%	not yet due	98%
22%	less than 30 days past due	96%
9%	30 to 60 days past due	94%
5%	61 to 120 days past due	91%
$2\frac{1}{2}$%	121 to 180 days past due	75%
$1\frac{1}{2}$%	over 180 days past due	30%

Allowance for Doubtful Accounts had a credit balance of $29,500 on June 1, 2013. CAF has provided for a monthly bad debt expense accrual during the current fiscal year based on the assumption that 4.5% of gross credit sales will be uncollectible. Total gross credit sales for the 2013–2014 fiscal year amounted to $2,800,000. Write-offs of bad accounts during the year totaled $102,000.

Instructions

(a) Prepare an accounts receivable aging schedule for CAF Company using the age categories identified in the controller's report to the Finance Committee showing the following.
(1) The amount of accounts receivable outstanding for each age category and in total.
(2) The estimated amount that is uncollectible for each category and in total.

(b) Compute the amount of the year-end adjustment necessary to bring Allowance for Doubtful Accounts to the balance indicated by the age analysis. Then prepare the necessary journal entry to adjust the accounting records.

(c) In a recessionary environment with tight credit and high interest rates:
(1) Identify steps CAF Company might consider to improve the accounts receivable situation.
(2) Then evaluate each step identified in terms of the risks and costs involved.

Comparative Analysis Problem: PepsiCo, Inc. vs. The Coca-Cola Company

BYP8-2 PepsiCo, Inc.'s financial statements are presented in Appendix A. Financial statements of The Coca-Cola Company are presented in Appendix B.

Instructions

(a) Based on the information in these financial statements, compute the following 2010 ratios for each company. (Assume all sales are credit sales and that PepsiCo's receivables on its balance sheet are all trade receivables.)
(1) Accounts receivable turnover ratio.
(2) Average collection period for receivables.

(b) What conclusions about managing accounts receivable can you draw from these data?

Real-World Focus

BYP8-3 ***Purpose:*** To learn more about factoring from websites that provide factoring services.

Address: **www.ccapital.net**, or go to **www.wiley.com/college/weygandt**

Steps: Go to the website, click on **invoice Factoring**, and answer the following questions.

(a) What are some of the benefits of factoring?
(b) What is the range of the percentages of the typical discount rate?
(c) If a company factors its receivables, what percentage of the value of the receivables can it expect to receive from the factor in the form of cash, and how quickly will it receive the cash?

Critical Thinking

Decision-Making Across the Organization

BYP8-4 Hilda and Tim Piwek own Campus Fashions. From its inception, Campus Fashions has sold merchandise on either a cash or credit basis, but no credit cards have been accepted. During the past several months, the Piweks have begun to question their sales policies. First, they have lost

some sales because of refusing to accept credit cards. Second, representatives of two metropolitan banks have been persuasive in almost convincing them to accept their national credit cards. One bank, City National Bank, has stated that its credit card fee is 4%.

The Piweks decide that they should determine the cost of carrying their own credit sales. From the accounting records of the past 3 years, they accumulate the following data.

	2014	2013	2012
Net credit sales	$500,000	$650,000	$400,000
Collection agency fees for slow-paying customers	2,450	2,500	2,300
Salary of part-time accounts receivable clerk	4,100	4,100	4,100

Credit and collection expenses as a percentage of net credit sales are uncollectible accounts 1.6%, billing and mailing costs 0.5%, and credit investigation fee on new customers 0.15%.

Hilda and Tim also determine that the average accounts receivable balance outstanding during the year is 5% of net credit sales. The Piweks estimate that they could earn an average of 8% annually on cash invested in other business opportunities.

Instructions

With the class divided into groups, answer the following.

(a) Prepare a table showing, for each year, total credit and collection expenses in dollars and as a percentage of net credit sales.

(b) Determine the net credit and collection expense in dollars and as a percentage of sales after considering the revenue not earned from other investment opportunities.

(c) Discuss both the financial and nonfinancial factors that are relevant to the decision.

Communication Activity

BYP8-5 Lily Pao, a friend of yours, overheard a discussion at work about changes her employer wants to make in accounting for uncollectible accounts. Lily knows little about accounting, and she asks you to help make sense of what she heard. Specifically, she asks you to explain the differences between the percentage-of-sales, percentage-of-receivables, and the direct write-off methods for uncollectible accounts.

Instructions

In a letter of one page (or less), explain to Lily the three methods of accounting for uncollectibles. Be sure to discuss differences among these methods.

Ethics Case

BYP8-6 The controller of Vestin Co. believes that the yearly allowance for doubtful accounts for Vestin Co. should be 2% of net credit sales. The president of Vestin Co., nervous that the stockholders might expect the company to sustain its 10% growth rate, suggests that the controller increase the allowance for doubtful accounts to 4%. The president thinks that the lower net income, which reflects a 6% growth rate, will be a more sustainable rate for Vestin Co.

Instructions

(a) Who are the stakeholders in this case?

(b) Does the president's request pose an ethical dilemma for the controller?

(c) Should the controller be concerned with Vestin Co.'s growth rate? Explain your answer.

All About You

BYP8-7 Credit card usage in the United States is substantial. Many startup companies use credit cards as a way to help meet short-term financial needs. The most common forms of debt for startups are use of credit cards and loans from relatives.

Suppose that you start up Brothers Sandwich Shop. You invested your savings of $20,000 and borrowed $70,000 from your relatives. Although sales in the first few months are good, you see that you may not have sufficient cash to pay expenses and maintain your inventory at acceptable levels, at least in the short term. You decide you may need to use one or more credit cards to fund the possible cash shortfall.

Instructions

(a) Go to the Internet and find two sources that provide insight into how to compare credit card terms.
(b) Develop a list, in descending order of importance, as to what features are most important to you in selecting a credit card for your business.
(c) Examine the features of your present credit card. (If you do not have a credit card, select a likely one online for this exercise.) Given your analysis above, what are the three major disadvantages of your present credit card?

BYP8-8 Individuals need to evaluate their personal credit positions using the same thought processes used by business people. Some of you might consider the idea of not having a credit card a ridiculous proposition. But the reality is that the misuse of credit cards brings financial hardship to millions of Americans each year. Credit card companies aggressively market their cards with images of glamour and happiness. But, there isn't much glamour in paying an 18% to 21% interest rate, and there is very little happiness to be found in filing for personal bankruptcy.

Should you cut up your credit card(s)?

YES: Americans are carrying huge personal debt burdens. Credit cards encourage unnecessary, spontaneous expenditures. The interest rates on credit cards are extremely high, which causes debt problems to escalate exponentially.

NO: Credit cards are a necessity for transactions in today's economy. In fact, many transactions are difficult or impossible to carry out without a credit card. People should learn to use credit cards responsibly.

Instructions

Write a response indicating your position regarding the situation. Provide support for your view.

FASB Codification Activity

BYP8-9 If your school has a subscription to the FASB Codification, go to *http://aaahq.org/ascLogin.cfm* to log in and prepare responses to the following.

(a) How are receivables defined in the Codification?
(b) What are the conditions under which losses from uncollectible receivables (Bad Debt Expense) should be reported?

Answers to Chapter Questions

Answers to Insight and Accounting Across the Organization Questions

p. 390 How Does a Credit Card Work? Q: Assume that Nordstrom prepares a bank reconciliation at the end of each month. If some credit card sales have not been processed by the bank, how should Nordstrom treat these transactions on its bank reconciliation? **A:** Nordstrom would treat the credit card receipts as deposits in transit. It has already recorded the receipts as cash. Its bank will increase Nordstrom's cash account when it receives the receipts.

p. 394 Can Fair Value Be Unfair? Q: What are the arguments in favor of and against fair value accounting for loans and receivables? **A:** Arguments in favor of fair value accounting for loans and receivables are that fair value would provide a more accurate view of a company's financial position. This might provide a useful early warning of when a bank or other financial institution was in trouble because its loans were of poor quality. But, banks argue that estimating fair values is very difficult to do accurately. They are also concerned that volatile fair values could cause large swings in a bank's reported net income.

p. 396 Bad Information Can Lead to Bad Loans Q: What steps should the banks have taken to ensure the accuracy of financial information provided on loan applications? **A:** At a minimum, the bank should have requested copies of recent income tax forms and contacted the supposed employer to verify income. To verify ownership and value of assets, it should have examined bank statements, investment statements, and title documents and should have employed appraisers.

Answers to Self-Test Questions

1. d **2.** c ($1,000 − $300) × (100% − 2%) **3.** a **4.** b ($60,000 − $5,000) **5.** d ($60,000 + $5,000) **6.** b ($800,000 × 1.5%) + $15,000 **7.** b ($750,000 × 3%) + ($18,000 − $30,000) **8.** d ($800,000 − $65,000) **9.** c **10.** c **11.** a **12.** b **13.** d $10,000 + ($10,000 × 120/360 × 9%) **14.** a **15.** c $800,000 ÷ [($100,000 + $150,000) ÷ 2]

A Look at IFRS

The basic accounting and reporting issues related to recognition and measurement of receivables, such as the use of allowance accounts, how to record discounts, use of the allowance method to account for bad debts, and factoring, are essentially the same between IFRS and GAAP.

Key Points

- IFRS requires that loans and receivables be accounted for at amortized cost, adjusted for allowances for doubtful accounts. IFRS sometimes refers to these allowances as *provisions*. The entry to record the allowance would be:

Bad Debt Expense	xxxxxx	
Allowance for Doubtful Accounts		xxxxxx

- Although IFRS implies that receivables with different characteristics should be reported separately, there is no standard that mandates this segregation.
- The FASB and IASB have worked to implement fair value measurement (the amount they currently could be sold for) for financial instruments. Both Boards have faced bitter opposition from various factions. As a consequence, the Boards have adopted a piecemeal approach; the first step is disclosure of fair value information in the notes. The second step is the fair value option, which permits, but does not require, companies to record some types of financial instruments at fair values in the financial statements.
- IFRS requires a two-tiered approach to test whether the value of loans and receivables are impaired. First, a company should look at specific loans and receivables to determine whether they are impaired. Then, the loans and receivables as a group should be evaluated for impairment. GAAP does not prescribe a similar two-tiered approach.
- IFRS and GAAP differ in the criteria used to determine how to record a factoring transaction. IFRS is a combination of an approach focused on risks and rewards and loss of control. GAAP uses loss of control as the primary criterion. In addition, IFRS permits partial derecognition of receivables; GAAP does not.

Looking to the Future

It appears likely that the question of recording fair values for financial instruments will continue to be an important issue to resolve as the Boards work toward convergence. Both the IASB and the FASB have indicated that they believe that financial statements would be more transparent and understandable if companies recorded and reported all financial instruments at fair value.

That said, in *IFRS 9*, which was issued in 2009, the IASB created a split model, where some financial instruments are recorded at fair value, but other financial assets, such as loans and receivables, can be accounted for at amortized cost if certain criteria are met. Critics say that this can result in two companies with identical securities accounting for those securities in different ways. A proposal by the FASB would require that nearly all financial instruments, including loans and receivables, be accounted for at fair value. It has been suggested that *IFRS 9* will likely be changed or replaced as the FASB and IASB continue to deliberate the best treatment for financial instruments. In fact, one past member of the IASB said that companies should ignore *IFRS 9* and continue to report under the old standard, because in his opinion, it was extremely likely that it would be changed before the mandatory adoption date of the standard arrived in 2013.

IFRS Practice

IFRS Self-Test Questions

1. Under IFRS, loans and receivables are to be reported on the balance sheet at:
   (a) amortized cost.
   (b) amortized cost adjusted for estimated loss provisions.
   (c) historical cost.
   (d) replacement cost.
2. Which of the following statements is *false*?
   (a) Loans and receivables include equity securities purchased by the company.
   (b) Loans and receivables include credit card receivables.
   (c) Loans and receivables include amounts owed by employees as a result of company loans to employees.
   (d) Loans and receivables include amounts resulting from transactions with customers.
3. In recording a factoring transaction:
   (a) IFRS focuses on loss of control.
   (b) GAAP focuses on loss of control and risks and rewards.
   (c) IFRS and GAAP allow partial derecognition.
   (d) IFRS allows partial derecognition
4. Under IFRS:
   (a) the entry to record estimated uncollected accounts is the same as GAAP.
   (b) loans and receivables should only be tested for impairment as a group.
   (c) it is always acceptable to use the direct write-off method.
   (d) all financial instruments are recorded at fair value.
5. Which of the following statements is *true*?
   (a) The fair value option requires that some types of financial instruments be recorded at fair value.
   (b) The fair value option allows, but does not require, that some types of financial instruments be recorded at amortized cost.
   (c) The fair value option allows, but does not require, that some types of financial instruments be recorded at fair value.
   (d) The FASB and IASB would like to reduce the reliance on fair value accounting for financial instruments in the future.

IFRS Exercise

IFRS8-1 What are some steps taken by both the FASB and IASB to move to fair value measurement for financial instruments? In what ways have some of the approaches differed?

International Financial Reporting Problem: Zetar plc

IFRS8-2 The financial statements of **Zetar plc** are presented in Appendix C. The company's complete annual report, including the notes to its financial statements, is available at *www.zetarplc.com*.

Instructions

Use the company's annual report to answer the following questions.

(a) According to the Operational Review of Financial Performance, what was one reason why the balance in receivables increased relative to the previous year?

(b) According to the notes to the financial statements, how are loans and receivables defined?

(c) In the notes to the financial statements, the company reports a "one off item" related to receivables. Explain what this item was.

(d) Using information in the notes to the financial statements, determine what percentage the provision for impairment of receivables was as a percentage of total trade receivables for 2010 and 2009. How did the ratio change from 2009 to 2010, and what does this suggest about the company's receivables?

Answers to IFRS Self-Test Questions

1. b **2.** a **3.** d **4.** a **5.** c

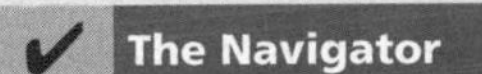

✔ Remember to go back to The Navigator box on the chapter opening page and check off your completed work.

Chapter 9

Plant Assets, Natural Resources, and Intangible Assets

Feature Story

How Much for a Ride to the Beach?

It's spring break. Your plane has landed, you've finally found your bags, and you're dying to hit the beach—but first you need a "vehicular unit" to get you there. As you turn away from baggage claim, you see a long row of rental agency booths. Many are names you are familiar with—Hertz, Avis, and Budget. But a booth at the far end catches your eye—Rent-A-Wreck. Now there's a company making a clear statement!

Any company that relies on equipment to generate revenues must make decisions about what kind of equipment to buy, how long to keep it, and how vigorously to maintain it. Rent-A-Wreck has decided to rent used rather than new cars and trucks. It rents these vehicles across the United States, Europe, and Asia. While the big-name agencies push vehicles with that "new car smell," Rent-A-Wreck competes on price.

Rent-A-Wreck's message is simple: Rent a used car and save some cash. It's not a message that appeals to everyone. If you're a marketing

The Navigator

- Scan Learning Objectives
- Read Feature Story
- Read Preview
- Read text and answer **DO IT!** p. 427, p. 433, p. 435, p. 438, p. 444
- Work Comprehensive **DO IT!** **1** p. 446, **2** p. 447
- Review Summary of Learning Objectives
- Answer Self-Test Questions
- Complete Assignments
- Go to **WileyPLUS** for practice and tutorials
-  Read A Look at IFRS p. 470

Learning Objectives

After studying this chapter, you should be able to:

1. Describe how the cost principle applies to plant assets.
2. Explain the concept of depreciation and how to compute it.
3. Distinguish between revenue and capital expenditures, and explain the entries for each.
4. Explain how to account for the disposal of a plant asset.
5. Compute periodic depletion of natural resources.
6. Explain the basic issues related to accounting for intangible assets.
7. Indicate how plant assets, natural resources, and intangible assets are reported.

 **The Navigator**

executive wanting to impress a big client, you probably don't want to pull up in a Rent-A-Wreck car. But if you want to get from point A to point B for the minimum cash per mile, then Rent-A-Wreck is playing your tune. The company's message seems to be getting across to the right clientele. Revenues have increased significantly.

When you rent a car from Rent-A-Wreck, you are renting from an independent business person. This owner has paid a "franchise fee" for the right to use the Rent-A-Wreck name. In order to gain a franchise, he or she must meet financial and other criteria, and must agree to run the rental agency according to rules prescribed by Rent-A-Wreck. Some of these rules require that each franchise maintain its cars in a reasonable fashion. This ensures that, though you won't be cruising down Daytona Beach's Atlantic Avenue in a Mercedes convertible, you can be reasonably assured that you won't be calling a towtruck.

Preview of Chapter 9

The accounting for long-term assets has important implications for a company's reported results. In this chapter, we explain the application of the cost principle of accounting to property, plant, and equipment, such as Rent-A-Wreck vehicles, as well as to natural resources and intangible assets, such as the "Rent-A-Wreck" trademark. We also describe the methods that companies may use to allocate an asset's cost over its useful life. In addition, we discuss the accounting for expenditures incurred during the useful life of assets, such as the cost of replacing tires and brake pads on rental cars.

The content and organization of Chapter 9 are as follows.

PLANT ASSETS, NATURAL RESOURCES, AND INTANGIBLE ASSETS

Plant Assets	Natural Resources	Intangible Assets	Statement Presentation and Analysis
• Determining the cost of plant assets • Depreciation • Expenditures during useful life • Plant asset disposals	• Depletion	• Accounting for intangibles • Research and development costs	• Presentation • Analysis

✔ The Navigator

Plant Assets

Plant assets are resources that have three characteristics. They have a physical substance (a definite size and shape), are used in the operations of a business, and are not intended for sale to customers. They are also called **property, plant, and equipment; plant and equipment**; and **fixed assets**. These assets are expected to provide services to the company for a number of years. Except for land, plant assets decline in service potential over their useful lives.

Because plant assets play a key role in ongoing operations, companies keep plant assets in good operating condition. They also replace worn-out or outdated plant assets, and expand productive resources as needed. Many companies have substantial investments in plant assets. Illustration 9-1 shows the percentages of plant assets in relation to total assets of companies in a number of industries.

Illustration 9-1
Percentages of plant assets in relation to total assets

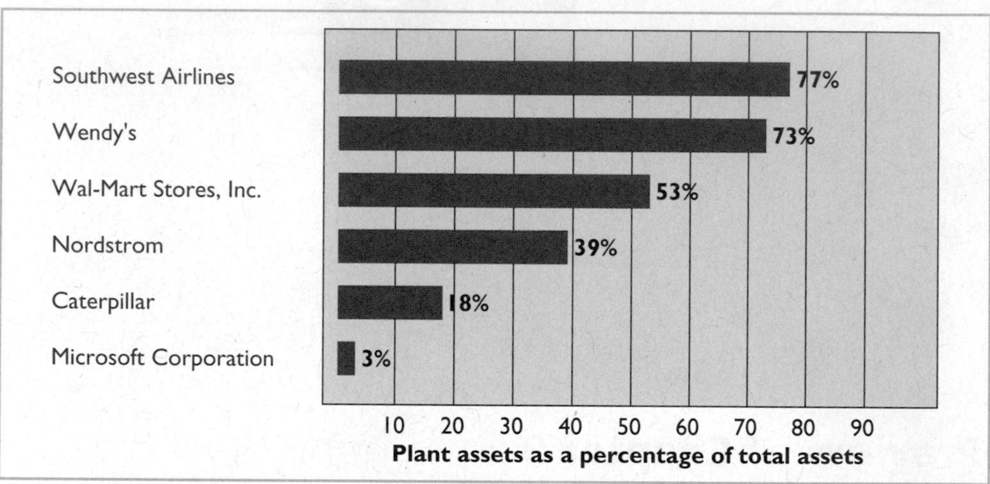

Determining the Cost of Plant Assets

LEARNING OBJECTIVE 1

Describe how the cost principle applies to plant assets.

The cost principle requires that companies record plant assets at cost. Thus, Rent-A-Wreck records its vehicles at cost. **Cost consists of all expenditures necessary to acquire the asset and make it ready for its intended use.** For example, the cost of factory machinery includes the purchase price, freight costs paid by the purchaser, and installation costs. Once cost is established, the company uses that amount as the basis of accounting for the plant asset over its useful life.

In the following sections, we explain the application of the cost principle to each of the major classes of plant assets.

LAND

Companies often use **land** as a building site for a manufacturing plant or office site. The cost of land includes (1) the cash purchase price, (2) closing costs such as title and attorney's fees, (3) real estate brokers' commissions, and (4) accrued property taxes and other liens assumed by the purchaser. For example, if the cash price is $50,000 and the purchaser agrees to pay accrued taxes of $5,000, the cost of the land is $55,000.

Helpful Hint
Management's intended use is important in applying the cost principle.

Companies record as debits (increases) to the Land account all necessary costs incurred to make land **ready for its intended use**. When a company acquires vacant land, these costs include expenditures for clearing, draining, filling, and grading. Sometimes, the land has a building on it that must be removed before construction of a new building. In this case, the company debits to the

Land account all demolition and removal costs, less any proceeds from salvaged materials.

To illustrate, assume that Hayes Company acquires real estate at a cash cost of $100,000. The property contains an old warehouse that is razed at a net cost of $6,000 ($7,500 in costs less $1,500 proceeds from salvaged materials). Additional expenditures are the attorney's fee, $1,000, and the real estate broker's commission, $8,000. The cost of the land is $115,000, computed as shown in Illustration 9-2.

Illustration 9-2
Computation of cost of land

Land	
Cash price of property	$ 100,000
Net removal cost of warehouse	6,000
Attorney's fee	1,000
Real estate broker's commission	8,000
Cost of land	**$115,000**

When Hayes records the acquisition, it debits Land for $115,000 and credits Cash for $115,000.

LAND IMPROVEMENTS

Land improvements are structural additions made to land. Examples are driveways, parking lots, fences, landscaping, and underground sprinklers. The cost of land improvements includes all expenditures necessary to make the improvements ready for their intended use. For example, the cost of a new parking lot for Home Depot includes the amount paid for paving, fencing, and lighting. Thus, Home Depot debits to Land Improvements the total of all of these costs.

Land improvements have limited useful lives, and their maintenance and replacement are the responsibility of the company. As a result, companies expense (depreciate) the cost of land improvements over their useful lives.

BUILDINGS

Buildings are facilities used in operations, such as stores, offices, factories, warehouses, and airplane hangars. Companies debit to the Buildings account all necessary expenditures related to the purchase or construction of a building. When a building is **purchased**, such costs include the purchase price, closing costs (attorney's fees, title insurance, etc.) and real estate broker's commission. Costs to make the building ready for its intended use include expenditures for remodeling and replacing or repairing the roof, floors, electrical wiring, and plumbing. When a new building is **constructed**, cost consists of the contract price plus payments for architects' fees, building permits, and excavation costs.

In addition, companies charge certain interest costs to the Buildings account. Interest costs incurred to finance the project are included in the cost of the building when a significant period of time is required to get the building ready for use. In these circumstances, interest costs are considered as necessary as materials and labor. However, the inclusion of interest costs in the cost of a constructed building is **limited to the construction period**. When construction has been completed, the company records subsequent interest payments on funds borrowed to finance the construction as debits (increases) to Interest Expense.

EQUIPMENT

Equipment includes assets used in operations, such as store check-out counters, office furniture, factory machinery, delivery trucks, and airplanes. The cost of equipment, such as Rent-A-Wreck vehicles, consists of the cash purchase price, sales taxes, freight charges, and insurance during transit paid by the purchaser. It also includes expenditures required in assembling, installing, and testing the unit. However, Rent-A-Wreck does not include motor vehicle licenses and accident insurance on company vehicles in the cost of equipment. These costs represent annual recurring expenditures and do not benefit future periods. Thus, they are treated as expenses as they are incurred.

To illustrate, assume Merten Company purchases factory machinery at a cash price of $50,000. Related expenditures are for sales taxes $3,000, insurance during shipping $500, and installation and testing $1,000. The cost of the factory machinery is $54,500, computed in Illustration 9-3.

Illustration 9-3
Computation of cost of factory machinery

Factory Machinery	
Cash price	$ 50,000
Sales taxes	3,000
Insurance during shipping	500
Installation and testing	1,000
Cost of factory machinery	**$54,500**

Merten makes the following summary entry to record the purchase and related expenditures.

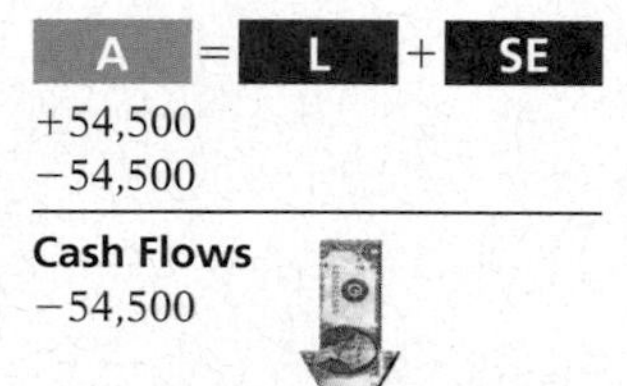

Equipment	54,500	
Cash		54,500
(To record purchase of factory machine)		

For another example, assume that Lenard Company purchases a delivery truck at a cash price of $22,000. Related expenditures consist of sales taxes $1,320, painting and lettering $500, motor vehicle license $80, and a three-year accident insurance policy $1,600. The cost of the delivery truck is $23,820, computed as follows.

Illustration 9-4
Computation of cost of delivery truck

Delivery Truck	
Cash price	$ 22,000
Sales taxes	1,320
Painting and lettering	500
Cost of delivery truck	**$23,820**

Lenard treats the cost of the motor vehicle license as an expense, and the cost of the insurance policy as a prepaid asset. Thus, Lenard makes the following entry to record the purchase of the truck and related expenditures:

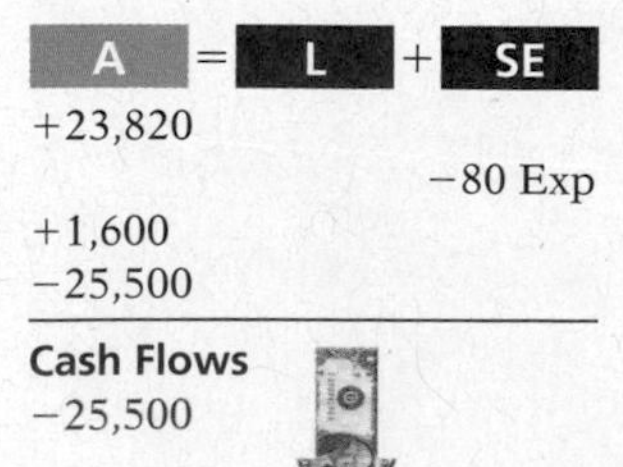

Equipment	23,820	
License Expense	80	
Prepaid Insurance	1,600	
Cash		25,500
(To record purchase of delivery truck and related expenditures)		

ACCOUNTING ACROSS THE ORGANIZATION

Many U.S. Firms Use Leases

Leasing is big business for U.S. companies. For example, business investment in equipment in a recent year totaled $709 billion. Leasing accounted for about 31% of all business investment ($218 billion).

Who does the most leasing? Interestingly, major banks such as Continental Bank, J.P. Morgan Leasing, and US Bancorp Equipment Finance are the major lessors. Also, many companies have established separate leasing companies, such as Boeing Capital Corporation, Dell Financial Services, and John Deere Capital Corporation. And, as an excellent example of the magnitude of leasing, leased planes account for nearly 40% of the U.S. fleet of commercial airlines. In addition, leasing is becoming increasingly common in the hotel industry. Marriott, Hilton, and InterContinental are increasingly choosing to lease hotels that are owned by someone else.

? Why might airline managers choose to lease rather than purchase their planes? (See page 469.)

> DO IT!

Cost of Plant Assets

Assume that Drummond Heating and Cooling Co. purchases a delivery truck for $15,000 cash, plus sales taxes of $900 and delivery costs of $500. The buyer also pays $200 for painting and lettering, $600 for an annual insurance policy, and $80 for a motor vehicle license. Explain how each of these costs would be accounted for.

Action Plan

✔ Identify expenditures made in order to get delivery equipment ready for its intended use.

✔ Treat operating costs as expenses.

Solution

The first four payments ($15,000, $900, $500, and $200) are expenditures necessary to make the truck ready for its intended use. Thus, the cost of the truck is $16,600. The payments for insurance and the license are operating costs and therefore are expensed.

Related exercise material: **BE9-1, BE9-2, E9-1, E9-2, E9-3, and**  **9-1.**

✔ **The Navigator**

Depreciation

LEARNING OBJECTIVE 2

Explain the concept of depreciation and how to compute it.

As explained in Chapter 3, **depreciation is the process of allocating to expense the cost of a plant asset over its useful (service) life in a rational and systematic manner**. Cost allocation enables companies to properly match expenses with revenues in accordance with the expense recognition principle (see Illustration 9-5).

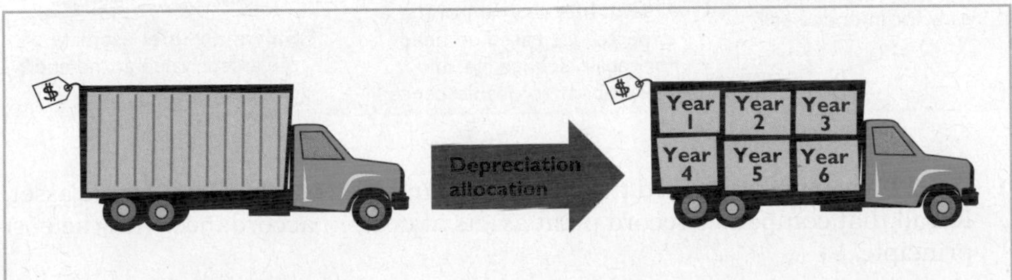

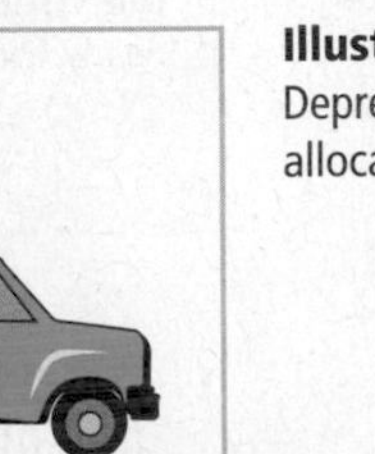

Illustration 9-5
Depreciation as a cost allocation concept

It is important to understand that **depreciation is a process of cost allocation. It is not a process of asset valuation.** No attempt is made to measure the change in an asset's fair value during ownership. So, the **book value** (cost less accumulated depreciation) of a plant asset may be quite different from its fair value. In fact, if an asset is fully depreciated, it can have a zero book value but still have a significant fair value.

Ethics Note

When a business is acquired, proper allocation of the purchase price to various asset classes is important since different depreciation treatments can materially affect income. For example, buildings are depreciated, but land is not.

Depreciation applies to three classes of plant assets: land improvements, buildings, and equipment. Each asset in these classes is considered to be a **depreciable asset**. Why? Because the usefulness to the company and revenue-producing ability of each asset will decline over the asset's useful life. Depreciation **does not apply to land** because its usefulness and revenue-producing ability generally remain intact over time. In fact, in many cases, the usefulness of land is greater over time because of the scarcity of good land sites. Thus, **land is not a depreciable asset**.

During a depreciable asset's useful life, its revenue-producing ability declines because of **wear and tear**. A delivery truck that has been driven 100,000 miles will be less useful to a company than one driven only 800 miles.

Revenue-producing ability may also decline because of obsolescence. **Obsolescence** is the process of becoming out of date before the asset physically wears out. For example, major airlines moved from Chicago's Midway Airport to Chicago-O'Hare International Airport because Midway's runways were too short for jumbo jets. Similarly, many companies replace their computers long before they originally planned to do so because improvements in new computing technology make the old computers obsolete.

Recognizing depreciation on an asset does not result in an accumulation of cash for replacement of the asset. The balance in Accumulated Depreciation represents the total amount of the asset's cost that the company has charged to expense. It is not a cash fund.

Note that the concept of depreciation is consistent with the going-concern assumption. The **going-concern assumption** states that the company will continue in operation for the foreseeable future. If a company does not use a going-concern assumption, then plant assets should be stated at their fair value. In that case, depreciation of these assets is not needed.

FACTORS IN COMPUTING DEPRECIATION

Three factors affect the computation of depreciation, as shown in Illustration 9-6.

Illustration 9-6
Three factors in computing depreciation

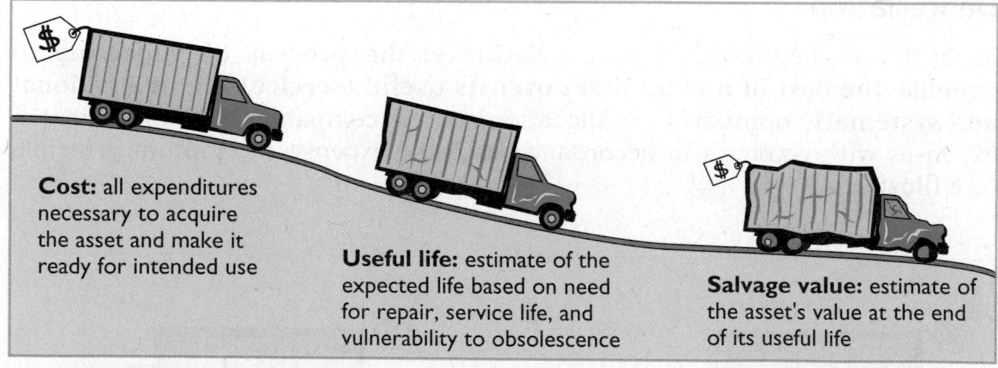

$
Cost: all expenditures necessary to acquire the asset and make it ready for intended use
Useful life: estimate of the expected life based on need for repair, service life, and vulnerability to obsolescence
$
Salvage value: estimate of the asset's value at the end of its useful life

Helpful Hint
Depreciation expense is reported on the income statement. Accumulated depreciation is reported on the balance sheet as a deduction from plant assets.

1. **Cost.** Earlier, we explained the issues affecting the cost of a depreciable asset. Recall that companies record plant assets at cost, in accordance with the cost principle.

2. **Useful life. Useful life** is an estimate of the expected *productive life*, also called *service life*, of the asset for its owner. Useful life may be expressed in terms of time, units of activity (such as machine hours), or units of output. Useful life is an estimate. In making the estimate, management considers such factors as the intended use of the asset, its expected repair and maintenance, and its vulnerability to obsolescence. Past experience with similar assets is often helpful in deciding on expected useful life. We might reasonably expect Rent-A-Wreck and Avis to use different estimated useful lives for their vehicles.
3. **Salvage value. Salvage value** is an estimate of the asset's value at the end of its useful life. This value may be based on the asset's worth as scrap or on its expected trade-in value. Like useful life, salvage value is an estimate. In making the estimate, management considers how it plans to dispose of the asset and its experience with similar assets.

Alternative Terminology
Another term sometimes used for salvage value is *residual value*.

DEPRECIATION METHODS

Depreciation is generally computed using one of the following methods:

1. Straight-line
2. Units-of-activity
3. Declining-balance

Each method is acceptable under generally accepted accounting principles. Management selects the method(s) it believes to be appropriate. The objective is to select the method that best measures an asset's contribution to revenue over its useful life. Once a company chooses a method, it should apply it consistently over the useful life of the asset. Consistency enhances the comparability of financial statements. Depreciation affects the balance sheet through accumulated depreciation and the income statement through depreciation expense.

We will compare the three depreciation methods using the following data for a small delivery truck purchased by Barb's Florists on January 1, 2014.

Illustration 9-7
Delivery truck data

Cost	$ 13,000
Expected salvage value	$ 1,000
Estimated useful life in years	5
Estimated useful life in miles	100,000

Illustration 9-8 (in the margin) shows the use of the primary depreciation methods in 600 of the largest companies in the United States.

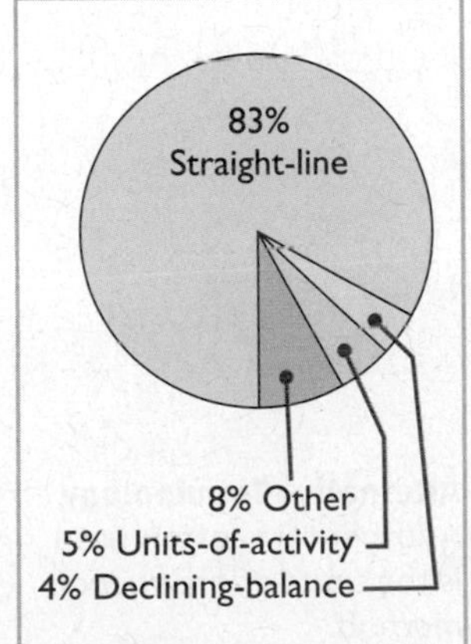

Illustration 9-8
Use of depreciation methods in 600 large U.S. companies

STRAIGHT-LINE Under the **straight-line method**, companies expense the same amount of depreciation for each year of the asset's useful life. It is measured solely by the passage of time.

To compute depreciation expense under the straight-line method, companies need to determine depreciable cost. **Depreciable cost** is the cost of the asset less its salvage value. It represents the total amount subject to depreciation. Under the straight-line method, to determine annual depreciation expense, we divide depreciable cost by the asset's useful life. Illustration 9-9 (page 430) shows the computation of the first year's depreciation expense for Barb's Florists.

Illustration 9-9
Formula for straight-line method

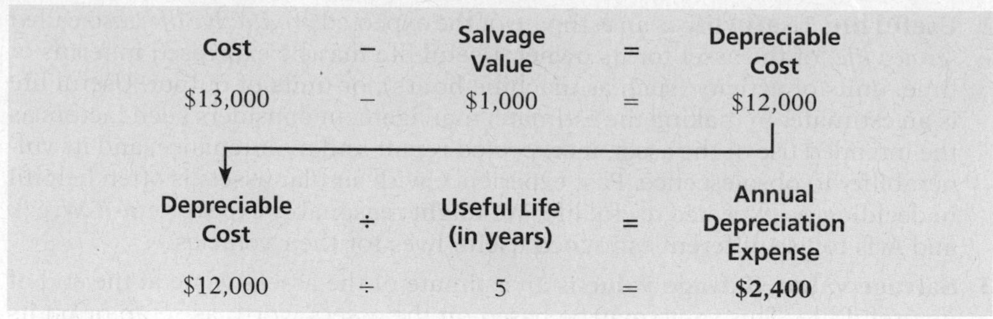

Cost − Salvage Value = Depreciable Cost
$13,000 − $1,000 = $12,000
Depreciable Cost ÷ Useful Life (in years) = Annual Depreciation Expense
$12,000 ÷ 5 = $2,400

Alternatively, we also can compute an annual **rate** of depreciation. In this case, the rate is 20% (100% ÷ 5 years). When a company uses an annual straight-line rate, it applies the percentage rate to the depreciable cost of the asset. Illustration 9-10 shows a **depreciation schedule** using an annual rate.

Illustration 9-10
Straight-line depreciation schedule

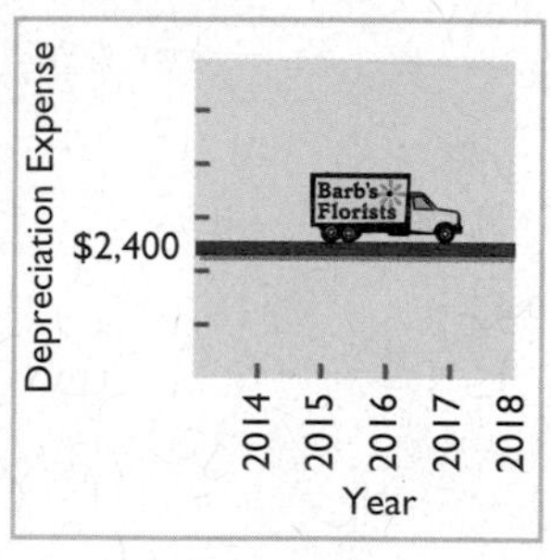

Barb's Florists

	Computation			Annual	End of Year	
Year	Depreciable Cost	× Depreciation Rate	=	Depreciation Expense	Accumulated Depreciation	Book Value
2014	$12,000	20%		**$2,400**	$ 2,400	$10,600*
2015	12,000	20		**2,400**	4,800	8,200
2016	12,000	20		**2,400**	7,200	5,800
2017	12,000	20		**2,400**	9,600	3,400
2018	12,000	20		**2,400**	12,000	**1,000**

*Book value = Cost − Accumulated depreciation = ($13,000 − $2,400).

Note that the depreciation expense of $2,400 is the same each year. The book value (computed as cost minus accumulated depreciation) at the end of the useful life is equal to the expected $1,000 salvage value.

What happens to these computations for an asset purchased **during** the year, rather than on January 1? In that case, it is necessary to **prorate the annual depreciation** on a time basis. If Barb's Florists had purchased the delivery truck on April 1, 2014, the company would own the truck for nine months of the first year (April–December). Thus, depreciation for 2014 would be $1,800 ($12,000 × 20% × 9/12 of a year).

The straight-line method predominates in practice. Such large companies as Campbell Soup, Marriott, and General Mills use the straight-line method. It is simple to apply, and it matches expenses with revenues when the use of the asset is reasonably uniform throughout the service life.

Alternative Terminology
Another term often used is the *units-of-production method.*

UNITS-OF-ACTIVITY Under the **units-of-activity method**, useful life is expressed in terms of the total units of production or use expected from the asset, rather than as a time period. The units-of-activity method is ideally suited to factory machinery. Manufacturing companies can measure production in units of output or in machine hours. This method can also be used for such assets as delivery equipment (miles driven) and airplanes (hours in use). The units-of-activity method is generally not suitable for buildings or furniture because depreciation for these assets is more a function of time than of use.

To use this method, companies estimate the total units of activity for the entire useful life, and then divide these units into depreciable cost. The resulting number represents the depreciable cost per unit. The depreciable cost per unit is then applied to the units of activity during the year to determine the annual depreciation expense.

Helpful Hint
Under any method, depreciation stops when the asset's book value equals expected salvage value.

To illustrate, assume that Barb's Florists drives its delivery truck 15,000 miles in the first year. Illustration 9-11 shows the units-of-activity formula and the computation of the first year's depreciation expense.

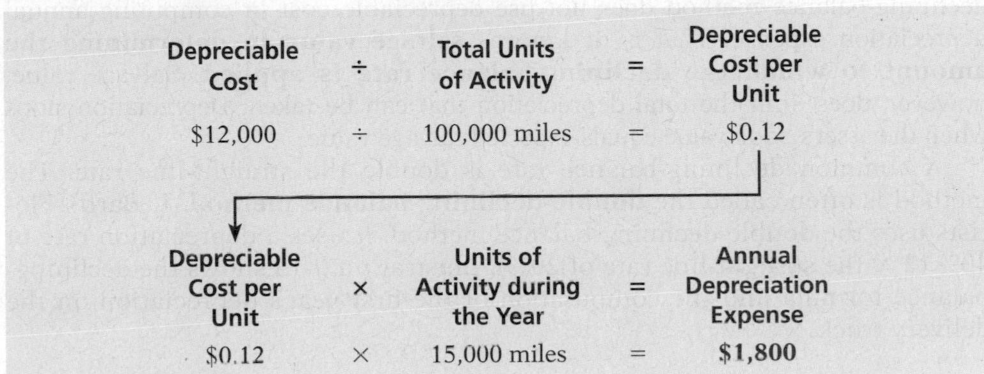

Depreciable Cost ÷ Total Units of Activity = Depreciable Cost per Unit
$12,000 ÷ 100,000 miles = $0.12
Depreciable Cost per Unit × Units of Activity during the Year = Annual Depreciation Expense
$0.12 × 15,000 miles = $1,800

Illustration 9-11
Formula for units-of-activity method

The units-of-activity depreciation schedule, using assumed mileage, is as follows.

Barb's Florists

	Computation				End of Year	
Year	Units of Activity	× Depreciation Cost/Unit	=	Annual Depreciation Expense	Accumulated Depreciation	Book Value
2014	15,000	$0.12		**$1,800**	$ 1,800	$11,200*
2015	30,000	0.12		**3,600**	5,400	7,600
2016	20,000	0.12		**2,400**	7,800	5,200
2017	25,000	0.12		**3,000**	10,800	2,200
2018	10,000	0.12		**1,200**	12,000	**1,000**

*($13,000 − $1,800).

Illustration 9-12
Units-of-activity depreciation schedule

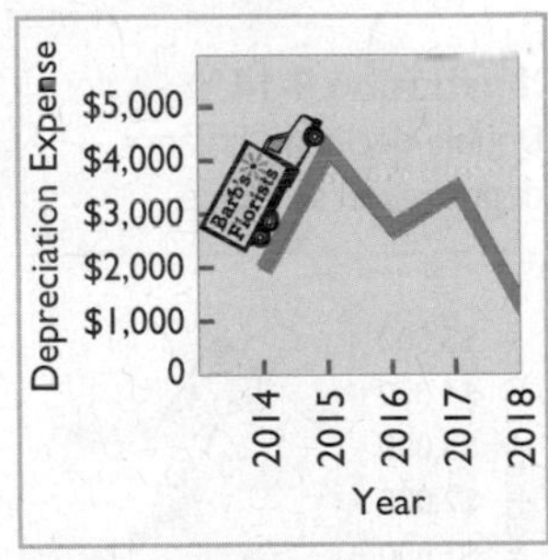

This method is easy to apply for assets purchased mid-year. In such a case, the company computes the depreciation using the productivity of the asset for the partial year.

The units-of-activity method is not nearly as popular as the straight-line method (see Illustration 9-8, page 429), primarily because it is often difficult for companies to reasonably estimate total activity. However, some very large companies, such as Chevron and Boise Cascade (a forestry company), do use this method. When the productivity of an asset varies significantly from one period to another, the units-of-activity method results in the best matching of expenses with revenues.

DECLINING-BALANCE The **declining-balance method** produces a decreasing annual depreciation expense over the asset's useful life. The method is so named because the periodic depreciation is based on a **declining book value** (cost less accumulated depreciation) of the asset. With this method, companies compute annual depreciation expense by multiplying the book value at the beginning of the year by the declining-balance depreciation rate. **The depreciation rate remains constant from year to year, but the book value to which the rate is applied declines each year.**

At the beginning of the first year, book value is the cost of the asset. This is because the balance in accumulated depreciation at the beginning of the asset's useful life is zero. In subsequent years, book value is the difference between cost and accumulated depreciation to date. Unlike the other depreciation methods, the declining-balance method does not use depreciable cost in computing annual depreciation expense. That is, **it ignores salvage value in determining the amount to which the declining-balance rate is applied**. Salvage value, however, does limit the total depreciation that can be taken. Depreciation stops when the asset's book value equals expected salvage value.

A common declining-balance rate is double the straight-line rate. The method is often called the **double-declining-balance method**. If Barb's Florists uses the double-declining-balance method, it uses a depreciation rate of 40% (2 × the straight-line rate of 20%). Illustration 9-13 shows the declining-balance formula and the computation of the first year's depreciation on the delivery truck.

Illustration 9-13
Formula for declining-balance method

Book Value at Beginning of Year	×	Declining-Balance Rate	=	Annual Depreciation Expense
$13,000	×	40%	=	**$5,200**

The depreciation schedule under this method is as follows.

Illustration 9-14
Double-declining-balance depreciation schedule

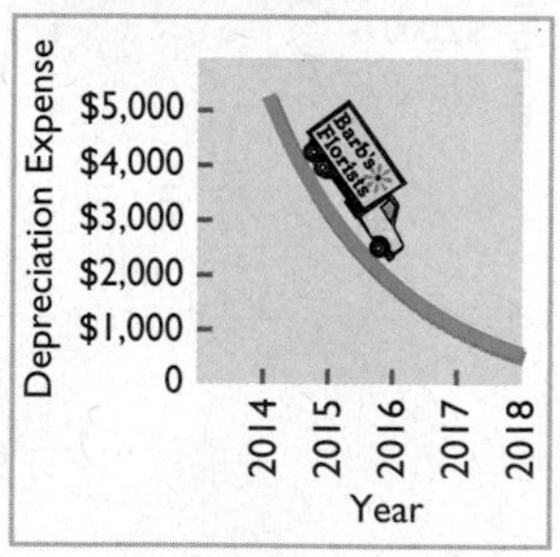

Barb's Florists

	Computation				Annual	End of Year	
Year	**Book Value Beginning of Year**	×	**Depreciation Rate**	=	**Depreciation Expense**	**Accumulated Depreciation**	**Book Value**
2014	$13,000		40%		**$5,200**	$ 5,200	$7,800
2015	7,800		40		**3,120**	8,320	4,680
2016	4,680		40		**1,872**	10,192	2,808
2017	2,808		40		**1,123**	11,315	1,685
2018	1,685		40		**685***	12,000	**1,000**

*Computation of $674 ($1,685 × 40%) is adjusted to $685 in order for book value to equal salvage value.

Helpful Hint
The method recommended for an asset that is expected to be significantly more productive in the first half of its useful life is the declining-balance method.

The delivery equipment is 69% depreciated ($8,320 ÷ $12,000) at the end of the second year. Under the straight-line method, the truck would be depreciated 40% ($4,800 ÷ $12,000) at that time. Because the declining-balance method produces higher depreciation expense in the early years than in the later years, it is considered an **accelerated-depreciation method**. The declining-balance method is compatible with the expense recognition principle. It matches the higher depreciation expense in early years with the higher benefits received in these years. It also recognizes lower depreciation expense in later years, when the asset's contribution to revenue is less. Some assets lose usefulness rapidly because of obsolescence. In these cases, the declining-balance method provides the most appropriate depreciation amount.

When a company purchases an asset during the year, it must prorate the first year's declining-balance depreciation on a time basis. For example, if Barb's Florists had purchased the truck on April 1, 2014, depreciation for 2014 would become $3,900 ($13,000 × 40% × 9/12). The book value at the beginning of 2015 is then $9,100 ($13,000 − $3,900), and the 2015 depreciation is $3,640 ($9,100 × 40%). Subsequent computations would follow from those amounts.

Straight-Line Depreciation

On January 1, 2014, Iron Mountain Ski Corporation purchased a new snow-grooming machine for $50,000. The machine is estimated to have a 10-year life with a $2,000 salvage value. What journal entry would Iron Mountain Ski Corporation make at December 31, 2014, if it uses the straight-line method of depreciation?

Action Plan

- ✔ Calculate depreciable cost (Cost − Salvage value).
- ✔ Divide the depreciable cost by the asset's estimated useful life.

Solution

$$\text{Depreciation expense} = \frac{\text{Cost} - \text{Salvage value}}{\text{Useful life}} = \frac{\$50{,}000 - \$2{,}000}{10} = \$4{,}800$$

The entry to record the first year's depreciation would be:

Dec. 31	Depreciation Expense	4,800	
	Accumulated Depreciation—Equipment		4,800
	(To record annual depreciation on snow-grooming machine)		

Related exercise material: **BE9-3, BE9-4, and DO IT! 9-2.**

✔ The Navigator

COMPARISON OF METHODS Illustration 9-15 compares annual and total depreciation expense under each of the three methods for Barb's Florists.

Illustration 9-15 Comparison of depreciation methods

Year	Straight-Line	Units-of-Activity	Declining-Balance
2014	$ 2,400	$ 1,800	$ 5,200
2015	2,400	3,600	3,120
2016	2,400	2,400	1,872
2017	2,400	3,000	1,123
2018	2,400	1,200	685
	$12,000	**$12,000**	**$12,000**

Annual depreciation varies considerably among the methods, but **total depreciation is the same for the five-year period** under all three methods. Each method is acceptable in accounting because each recognizes in a rational and systematic manner the decline in service potential of the asset. Illustration 9-16 (page 434) graphs the depreciation expense pattern under each method.

Illustration 9-16
Patterns of depreciation

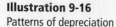

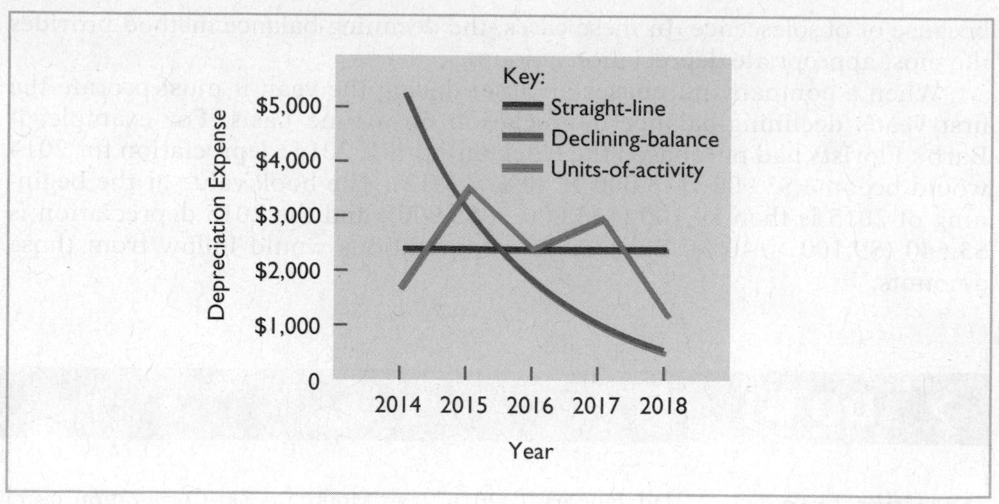

DEPRECIATION AND INCOME TAXES

The Internal Revenue Service (IRS) allows taxpayers to deduct depreciation expense when they compute taxable income. However, the IRS does not require taxpayers to use the same depreciation method on the tax return that is used in preparing financial statements.

Many corporations use straight-line in their financial statements to maximize net income. At the same time, they use a special accelerated-depreciation method on their tax returns to minimize their income taxes. Taxpayers must use on their tax returns either the straight-line method or a special accelerated-depreciation method called the **Modified Accelerated Cost Recovery System** (MACRS).

REVISING PERIODIC DEPRECIATION

Depreciation is one example of the use of estimation in the accounting process. Management should periodically review annual depreciation expense. If wear and tear or obsolescence indicate that annual depreciation estimates are inadequate or excessive, the company should change the amount of depreciation expense.

When a change in an estimate is required, the company makes the change in **current and future years. It does not change depreciation in prior periods.** The rationale is that continual restatement of prior periods would adversely affect confidence in financial statements.

Helpful Hint
Use a step-by-step approach: (1) determine new depreciable cost; (2) divide by remaining useful life.

To determine the new annual depreciation expense, the company first computes the asset's depreciable cost at the time of the revision. It then allocates the revised depreciable cost to the remaining useful life.

To illustrate, assume that Barb's Florists decides on January 1, 2017, to extend the useful life of the truck one year (a total life of six years) and increase its salvage value to $2,200. The company has used the straight-line method to depreciate the asset to date. Depreciation per year was $2,400 [($13,000 − $1,000) ÷ 5]. Accumulated depreciation after three years (2014–2016) is $7,200 ($2,400 × 3), and book value is $5,800 ($13,000 − $7,200). The new annual depreciation is $1,200, computed as follows.

Illustration 9-17
Revised depreciation computation

Book value, 1/1/17	$ 5,800	
Less: Salvage value	2,200	
Depreciable cost	$ 3,600	
Remaining useful life	3 years	(2017–2019)
Revised annual depreciation ($3,600 ÷ 3)	**$ 1,200**	

Barb's Florists makes no entry for the change in estimate. On December 31, 2017, during the preparation of adjusting entries, it records depreciation expense of $1,200. Companies must describe in the financial statements significant changes in estimates.

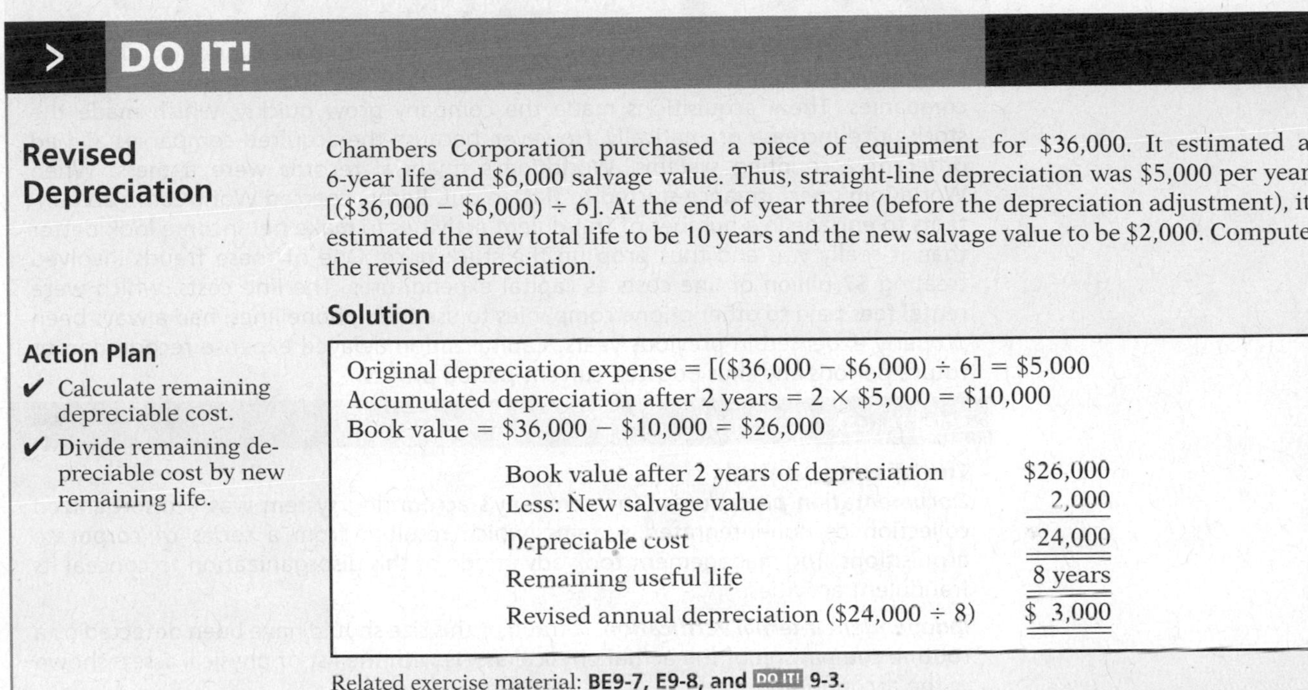

> DO IT!

Revised Depreciation

Chambers Corporation purchased a piece of equipment for $36,000. It estimated a 6-year life and $6,000 salvage value. Thus, straight-line depreciation was $5,000 per year [($36,000 − $6,000) ÷ 6]. At the end of year three (before the depreciation adjustment), it estimated the new total life to be 10 years and the new salvage value to be $2,000. Compute the revised depreciation.

Action Plan

- ✔ Calculate remaining depreciable cost.
- ✔ Divide remaining depreciable cost by new remaining life.

Solution

Original depreciation expense = [($36,000 − $6,000) ÷ 6] = $5,000
Accumulated depreciation after 2 years = 2 × $5,000 = $10,000
Book value = $36,000 − $10,000 = $26,000

Book value after 2 years of depreciation	$26,000
Less: New salvage value	2,000
Depreciable cost	24,000
Remaining useful life	8 years
Revised annual depreciation ($24,000 ÷ 8)	$ 3,000

Related exercise material: **BE9-7, E9-8, and DO IT! 9-3.**

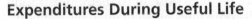

✔ The Navigator

Expenditures During Useful Life

LEARNING OBJECTIVE 3

Distinguish between revenue and capital expenditures, and explain the entries for each.

During the useful life of a plant asset, a company may incur costs for ordinary repairs, additions, or improvements. **Ordinary repairs** are expenditures to **maintain** the operating efficiency and productive life of the unit. They usually are fairly small amounts that occur frequently. Examples are motor tune-ups and oil changes, the painting of buildings, and the replacing of worn-out gears on machinery. Companies record such repairs as debits to Maintenance and Repairs Expense as they are incurred. Because they are immediately charged as an expense against revenues, these costs are often referred to as **revenue expenditures**.

In contrast, **additions and improvements** are costs incurred to **increase** the operating efficiency, productive capacity, or useful life of a plant asset. They are usually material in amount and occur infrequently. Additions and improvements increase the company's investment in productive facilities. Companies generally debit these amounts to the plant asset affected. They are often referred to as **capital expenditures**.

Companies must use good judgment in deciding between a revenue expenditure and capital expenditure. For example, assume that Rodriguez Co. purchases a number of wastepaper baskets. Although the proper accounting would appear to be to capitalize and then depreciate these wastepaper baskets over their useful life, it would be more usual for Rodriguez to expense them immediately. This practice is justified on the basis of **materiality**. Materiality refers to the impact of an item's size on a company's financial operations. The **materiality concept** states that if an item would not make a difference in decision-making, the company does not have to follow GAAP in reporting that item.

ANATOMY OF A FRAUD

Bernie Ebbers was the founder and CEO of the phone company WorldCom. The company engaged in a series of increasingly large, debt-financed acquisitions of other companies. These acquisitions made the company grow quickly, which made the stock price increase dramatically. However, because the acquired companies all had different accounting systems, WorldCom's financial records were a mess. When WorldCom's performance started to flatten out, Bernie coerced WorldCom's accountants to engage in a number of fraudulent activities to make net income look better than it really was and thus prop up the stock price. One of these frauds involved treating $7 billion of line costs as capital expenditures. The line costs, which were rental fees paid to other phone companies to use their phone lines, had always been properly expensed in previous years. Capitalization delayed expense recognition to future periods and thus boosted current-period profits.

Total take: $7 billion

The Missing Controls

Documentation procedures. The company's accounting system was a disorganized collection of non-integrated systems, which resulted from a series of corporate acquisitions. Top management took advantage of this disorganization to conceal its fraudulent activities.

Independent internal verification. A fraud of this size should have been detected by a routine comparison of the actual physical assets with the list of physical assets shown in the accounting records.

Plant Asset Disposals

LEARNING OBJECTIVE 4

Explain how to account for the disposal of a plant asset.

Companies dispose of plant assets that are no longer useful to them. Illustration 9-18 below shows the three ways in which companies make plant asset disposals.

Whatever the disposal method, the company must determine the book value of the plant asset at the disposal date to determine the gain or loss. Recall that the book value is the difference between the cost of the plant asset and the accumulated depreciation to date. If the disposal occurs at any time during the year, the company must record depreciation for the fraction of the year to the date of disposal. The company then eliminates the book value by reducing (debiting) Accumulated Depreciation for the total depreciation associated with that asset to the date of disposal and reducing (crediting) the asset account for the cost of the asset.

Illustration 9-18
Methods of plant asset disposal

Piper Co.
$
Lowy Co.
Sale
Equipment is sold to another party.
Joe's
Retirement
Equipment is scrapped or discarded.
Piper Co.
+ $
Lowy Co.
Exchange
Existing equipment is traded for new equipment.

In this chapter, we examine the accounting for the retirement and sale of plant assets. In the appendix to the chapter, we discuss and illustrate the accounting for exchanges of plant assets.

RETIREMENT OF PLANT ASSETS

To illustrate the retirement of plant assets, assume that Hobart Enterprises retires its computer printers, which cost $32,000. The accumulated depreciation on these printers is $32,000. The equipment, therefore, is fully depreciated (zero book value). The entry to record this retirement is as follows.

Accumulated Depreciation—Equipment	32,000	
Equipment		32,000
(To record retirement of fully depreciated equipment)		

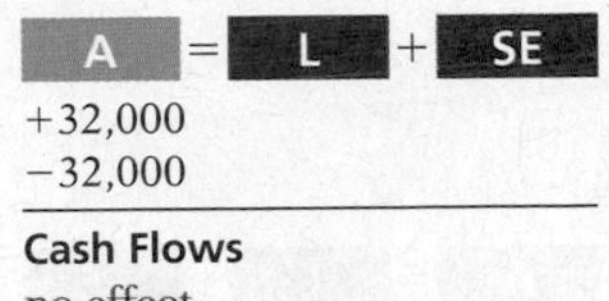

Cash Flows
no effect

Helpful Hint
When a company disposes of a plant asset, the company must remove from the accounts all amounts related to the asset. This includes the original cost in the asset account and the total depreciation to date in the accumulated depreciation account.

What happens if a fully depreciated plant asset is still useful to the company? In this case, the asset and its accumulated depreciation continue to be reported on the balance sheet, without further depreciation adjustment, until the company retires the asset. Reporting the asset and related accumulated depreciation on the balance sheet informs the financial statement reader that the asset is still in use. Once fully depreciated, no additional depreciation should be taken, even if an asset is still being used. In no situation can the accumulated depreciation on a plant asset exceed its cost.

If a company retires a plant asset before it is fully depreciated, and no cash is received for scrap or salvage value, a loss on disposal occurs. For example, assume that Sunset Company discards delivery equipment that cost $18,000 and has accumulated depreciation of $14,000. The entry is as follows.

Accumulated Depreciation—Equipment	14,000	
Loss on Disposal of Plant Assets	4,000	
Equipment		18,000
(To record retirement of delivery equipment at a loss)		

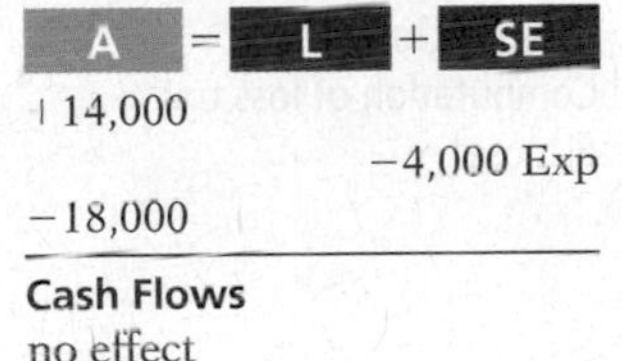

Cash Flows
no effect

Companies report a loss on disposal of plant assets in the "Other expenses and losses" section of the income statement.

SALE OF PLANT ASSETS

In a disposal by sale, the company compares the book value of the asset with the proceeds received from the sale. If the proceeds of the sale **exceed** the book value of the plant asset, **a gain on disposal occurs.** If the proceeds of the sale **are less than** the book value of the plant asset sold, **a loss on disposal occurs.**

Only by coincidence will the book value and the fair value of the asset be the same when the asset is sold. Gains and losses on sales of plant assets are therefore quite common. For example, Delta Airlines reported a $94,343,000 gain on the sale of five Boeing B727-200 aircraft and five Lockheed L-1011-1 aircraft.

GAIN ON SALE To illustrate a gain on sale of plant assets, assume that on July 1, 2014, Wright Company sells office furniture for $16,000 cash. The office furniture originally cost $60,000. As of January 1, 2014, it had accumulated depreciation of $41,000. Depreciation for the first six months of 2014 is $8,000. Wright records depreciation expense and updates accumulated depreciation to July 1 with the following entry.

July 1	Depreciation Expense	8,000	
	Accumulated Depreciation—Equipment		8,000
	(To record depreciation expense for the first 6 months of 2014)		

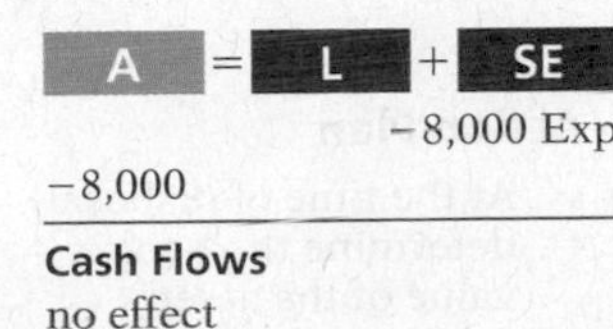

Cash Flows
no effect

After the accumulated depreciation balance is updated, the company computes the gain or loss. The gain or loss is the difference between the proceeds from the sale and the book value at the date of disposal. Illustration 9-19 (page 438) shows this computation for Wright Company, which has a gain on disposal of $5,000.

Illustration 9-19
Computation of gain on disposal

Cost of office furniture	$60,000
Less: Accumulated depreciation ($41,000 + $8,000)	49,000
Book value at date of disposal	11,000
Proceeds from sale	16,000
Gain on disposal of plant asset	**$ 5,000**

A = L + SE
+16,000
+49,000
−60,000
+5,000 Rev
Cash Flows
+16,000

Wright records the sale and the gain on disposal of the plant asset as follows.

July 1	Cash	16,000	
	Accumulated Depreciation—Equipment	49,000	
	Equipment		60,000
	Gain on Disposal of Plant Assets		5,000
	(To record sale of office furniture at a gain)		

Companies report a gain on disposal of plant assets in the "Other revenues and gains" section of the income statement.

LOSS ON SALE Assume that instead of selling the office furniture for $16,000, Wright sells it for $9,000. In this case, Wright computes a loss of $2,000 as follows.

Illustration 9-20
Computation of loss on disposal

Cost of office furniture	$60,000
Less: Accumulated depreciation	49,000
Book value at date of disposal	11,000
Proceeds from sale	9,000
Loss on disposal of plant asset	**$ 2,000**

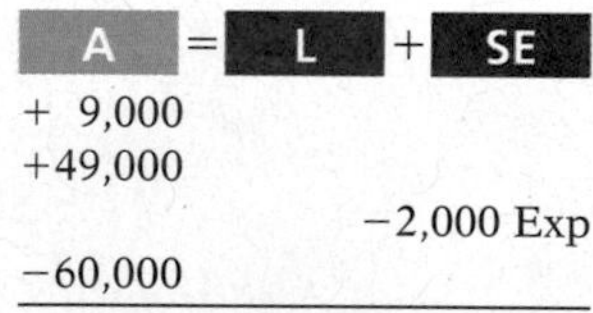
A = L + SE
+ 9,000
+49,000
−2,000 Exp
−60,000
Cash Flows
+9,000

Wright records the sale and the loss on disposal of the plant asset as follows.

July 1	Cash	9,000	
	Accumulated Depreciation—Equipment	49,000	
	Loss on Disposal of Plant Assets	2,000	
	Equipment		60,000
	(To record sale of office furniture at a loss)		

Companies report a loss on disposal of plant assets in the "Other expenses and losses" section of the income statement.

> DO IT!

Plant Asset Disposal

Overland Trucking has an old truck that cost $30,000, and it has accumulated depreciation of $16,000 on this truck. Overland has decided to sell the truck. (a) What entry would Overland Trucking make to record the sale of the truck for $17,000 cash? (b) What entry would Overland Trucking make to record the sale of the truck for $10,000 cash?

Action Plan
- ✔ At the time of disposal, determine the book value of the asset.
- ✔ Compare the asset's book value with the proceeds received to determine whether a gain or loss has occurred.

Solution

(a) Sale of truck for cash at a gain:

Cash	17,000	
Accumulated Depreciation—Equipment	16,000	
Equipment		30,000
Gain on Disposal of Plant Assets [$17,000 – ($30,000 – $16,000)]		3,000
(To record sale of truck at a gain)		

(b) Sale of truck for cash at a loss:

Cash	10,000	
Accumulated Depreciation—Equipment	16,000	
Loss on Disposal of Plant Assets [$10,000 − ($30,000 − $16,000)]	4,000	
Equipment		30,000
(To record sale of truck at a loss)		

Related exercise material: **BE9-9, BE9-10, E9-9, E9-10, and DO IT! 9-4.**

✔ The Navigator

Natural Resources

LEARNING OBJECTIVE 5

Compute periodic depletion of natural resources.

Natural resources consist of standing timber and underground deposits of oil, gas, and minerals. These long-lived productive assets have two distinguishing characteristics: (1) They are physically extracted in operations (such as mining, cutting, or pumping). (2) They are replaceable only by an act of nature.

The acquisition cost of a natural resource is the price needed to acquire the resource **and** prepare it for its intended use. For an already-discovered resource, such as an existing coal mine, cost is the price paid for the property.

The allocation of the cost of natural resources to expense in a rational and systematic manner over the resource's useful life is called **depletion**. (That is, *depletion* is to natural resources as *depreciation* is to plant assets.) **Companies generally use the units-of-activity method** (learned earlier in the chapter) **to compute depletion**. The reason is that **depletion generally is a function of the units extracted during the year**.

Helpful Hint
On a balance sheet, natural resources may be described more specifically as *timberlands, mineral deposits, oil reserves,* and so on.

Under the units-of-activity method, companies divide the total cost of the natural resource minus salvage value by the number of units estimated to be in the resource. The result is a **depletion cost per unit of product**. They then multiply the depletion cost per unit by the number of units extracted and sold. The result is the **annual depletion expense**. Illustration 9-21 shows the formula to compute depletion expense.

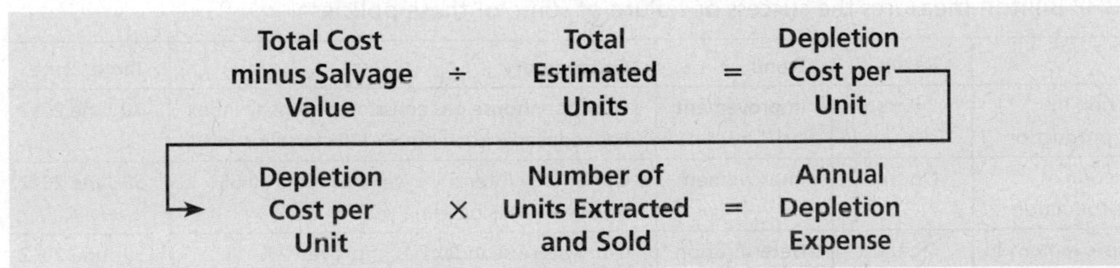

Illustration 9-21
Formula to compute depletion expense

To illustrate, assume that Lane Coal Company invests $5 million in a mine estimated to have 10 million tons of coal and no salvage value. In the first year, Lane extracts and sells 800,000 tons of coal. Using the formulas above, Lane computes the depletion expense as follows.

$5,000,000 ÷ 10,000,000 = $0.50 depletion cost per ton

$0.50 × 800,000 = $400,000 annual depletion expense

Ethics Note 

Investors were stunned at news that Royal Dutch/Shell Group had significantly overstated its reported oil reserves—and perhaps had done so intentionally.

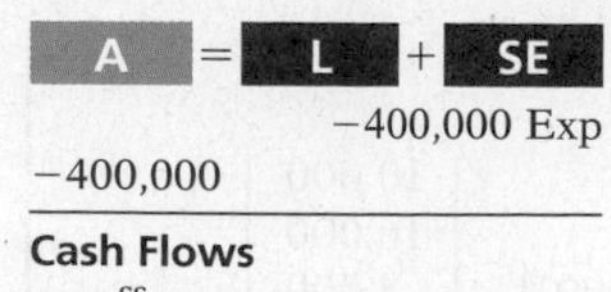

Lane records depletion expense for the first year of operation as follows.

Dec. 31	Depletion Expense	400,000	
	Accumulated Depletion		400,000
	(To record depletion expense on coal deposits)		

The company reports the account Depletion Expense as a part of the cost of producing the product. Accumulated Depletion is a contra-asset account, similar to accumulated depreciation. It is deducted from the cost of the natural resource in the balance sheet, as Illustration 9-22 shows.

Illustration 9-22
Statement presentation of accumulated depletion

Lane Coal Company
Balance Sheet (partial)

Coal mine	$5,000,000	
Less: Accumulated depletion	**400,000**	$4,600,000

Many companies do not use an Accumulated Depletion account. In such cases, the company credits the amount of depletion directly to the natural resources account.

Sometimes, a company will extract natural resources in one accounting period but not sell them until a later period. In this case, the company does not expense the depletion until it sells the resource. It reports the amount not sold as inventory in the current assets section.

PEOPLE, PLANET, AND PROFIT INSIGHT

Sustainability Report Please

Sustainability reports identify how the company is meeting its corporate social responsibilities. Many companies, both large and small, are now issuing these reports. For example, companies such as Disney, Best Buy, Microsoft, Ford, and ConocoPhilips issue these reports. Presented below is an adapted section of BHP Billiton's (a global mining, oil, and gas company) sustainability report on its environmental policies. These policies are to (1) take action to address the challenges of climate change, (2) set and achieve targets that reduce pollution, and (3) enhance biodiversity by assessing and considering ecological values and land-use aspects. Here is how BHP Billiton measures the success or failure of some of these policies:

Environment	Result	Trend	Commentary	Target Date
Aggregate Group target of 6% reduction in greenhouse gas emissions per unit of production	On track	Improvement	Our greenhouse gas emissions intensity index has reduced 7% on our FY2006 baseline year	30 June 2012
Aggregate Group target of 13% reduction in carbon-based energy use per unit of production	On track	Improvement	Our energy intensity index has reduced 6% on our FY2006 baseline year	30 June 2012
Aggregate Group target of a 10% improvement in the ratio of water recycled/reused to high-quality water consumed	On track	Deterioration	Our water use index has improved 7% on our FY2007 baseline year	30 June 2012

In addition to the environment, BHP Billiton has sections in its sustainability report which discuss people, safety, health, and community.

Source: BHP Billiton, *2010 Sustainability Report.*

Why do you believe companies issue sustainability reports? (See page 469.)

Intangible Assets

Intangible assets are rights, privileges, and competitive advantages that result from the ownership of long-lived assets that do not possess physical substance. Evidence of intangibles may exist in the form of contracts or licenses. Intangibles may arise from the following sources:

LEARNING OBJECTIVE 6

Explain the basic issues related to accounting for intangible assets.

1. Government grants, such as patents, copyrights, licenses, trademarks, and trade names.
2. Acquisition of another business, in which the purchase price includes a payment for *goodwill*.
3. Private monopolistic arrangements arising from contractual agreements, such as franchises and leases.

Some widely known intangibles are Microsoft's patents, McDonald's franchises, Apple's trade name iPod, J.K. Rowlings' copyrights on the *Harry Potter* books, and the trademark Rent-A-Wreck in the Feature Story.

Accounting for Intangible Assets

Companies record intangible assets at cost. Intangibles are categorized as having either a limited life or an indefinite life. If an intangible has a **limited life**, the company allocates its cost over the asset's useful life using a process similar to depreciation. The process of allocating the cost of intangibles is referred to as **amortization**. The cost of intangible assets with **indefinite lives should not be amortized.**

Helpful Hint
Amortization is to intangibles what *depreciation* is to plant assets and *depletion* is to natural resources.

To record amortization of an intangible asset, a company increases (debits) Amortization Expense and decreases (credits) the specific intangible asset. (Unlike depreciation, no contra account, such as Accumulated Amortization, is usually used.)

Intangible assets are typically amortized on a straight-line basis. For example, the legal life of a patent is 20 years. Companies **amortize the cost of a patent over its 20-year life or its useful life, whichever is shorter**. To illustrate the computation of patent amortization, assume that National Labs purchases a patent at a cost of $60,000. If National estimates the useful life of the patent to be eight years, the annual amortization expense is $7,500 ($60,000 ÷ 8). National records the annual amortization as follows.

Dec. 31	Amortization Expense	7,500	
	Patents		7,500
	(To record patent amortization)		

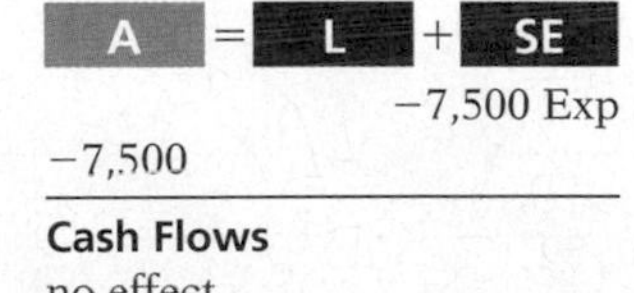

Companies classify Amortization Expense as an operating expense in the income statement.

There is a difference between intangible assets and plant assets in determining cost. For plant assets, cost includes both the purchase price of the asset and the costs incurred in designing and constructing the asset. In contrast, cost for an intangible asset includes **only the purchase price**. Companies expense any costs incurred in developing an intangible asset.

PATENTS

A **patent** is an exclusive right issued by the U.S. Patent Office that enables the recipient to manufacture, sell, or otherwise control an invention for a period of 20 years from the date of the grant. A patent is nonrenewable. But, companies can extend the legal life of a patent by obtaining new patents for improvements or other changes in the basic design. **The initial cost of a patent is the cash or cash equivalent price paid to acquire the patent.**

The saying, "A patent is only as good as the money you're prepared to spend defending it," is very true. Most patents are subject to litigation by competitors. Any legal costs an owner incurs in successfully defending a patent in an infringement suit are considered necessary to establish the patent's validity. **The owner adds those costs to the Patents account and amortizes them over the remaining life of the patent.**

The patent holder amortizes the cost of a patent over its 20-year legal life or its useful life, whichever is shorter. Companies consider obsolescence and inadequacy in determining useful life. These factors may cause a patent to become economically ineffective before the end of its legal life.

COPYRIGHTS

The federal government grants **copyrights**, which give the owner the exclusive right to reproduce and sell an artistic or published work. Copyrights extend for the life of the creator plus 70 years. The cost of a copyright is the **cost of acquiring and defending it**. The cost may be only the small fee paid to the U.S. Copyright Office. Or, it may amount to much more if an infringement suit is involved.

The useful life of a copyright generally is significantly shorter than its legal life. Therefore, copyrights usually are amortized over a relatively short period of time.

TRADEMARKS AND TRADE NAMES

A **trademark** or **trade name** is a word, phrase, jingle, or symbol that identifies a particular enterprise or product. Trade names like Wheaties, Monopoly, Big Mac, Kleenex, Coca-Cola, and Jeep create immediate product identification. They also generally enhance the sale of the product. The creator or original user may obtain exclusive legal right to the trademark or trade name by registering it with the U.S. Patent Office. Such registration provides 20 years of protection. The registration may be renewed indefinitely as long as the trademark or trade name is in use.

If a company purchases the trademark or trade name, its cost is the purchase price. If a company develops and maintains the trademark or trade name, any costs related to these activities are expensed as incurred. Because trademarks and trade names have indefinite lives, they are not amortized.

FRANCHISES AND LICENSES

When you fill up your tank at the corner Shell station, eat lunch at Subway, or rent a car from Rent-A-Wreck, you are dealing with franchises. A **franchise** is a contractual arrangement between a franchisor and a franchisee. The franchisor grants the franchisee the right to sell certain products, provide specific services, or use certain trademarks or trade names, usually within a designated geographic area.

Another type of franchise is that entered into between a governmental body (commonly municipalities) and a company. This franchise permits the company to use public property in performing its services. Examples are the use of city streets for a bus line or taxi service, use of public land for telephone and electric lines, and the use of airwaves for radio or TV broadcasting. Such operating rights are referred to as **licenses**. Franchises and licenses may by granted for a definite period of time, an indefinite period, or perpetually.

When a company can identify costs with the purchase of a franchise or license, it should recognize an intangible asset. Companies should amortize the cost of a limited-life franchise (or license) over its useful life. If the life is indefinite, the cost is not amortized. Annual payments made under a franchise agreement are recorded as **operating expenses** in the period in which they are incurred.

GOODWILL

Usually, the largest intangible asset that appears on a company's balance sheet is goodwill. **Goodwill** represents the value of all favorable attributes that relate to a company that are not attributable to any other specific asset. These include exceptional management, desirable location, good customer relations, skilled employees, high-quality products, and harmonious relations with labor unions. Goodwill is unique: Unlike assets such as investments and plant assets, which can be sold *individually* in the marketplace, goodwill can be identified only with the business as a whole.

If goodwill can be identified only with the business as a whole, how can its amount be determined? One could try to put a dollar value on the factors listed above (exceptional management, desirable location, and so on). But, the results would be very subjective, and such subjective valuations would not contribute to the reliability of financial statements. **Therefore, companies record goodwill only when an entire business is purchased. In that case, goodwill is the excess of cost over the fair value of the net assets (assets less liabilities) acquired.**

In recording the purchase of a business, the company debits (increases) the identifiable acquired assets, credits liabilities at their fair values, credits cash for the purchase price, and records the difference as goodwill. **Goodwill is not amortized** because it is considered to have an indefinite life. Companies report goodwill in the balance sheet under intangible assets.

INTERNATIONAL INSIGHT

Should Companies Write Up Goodwill?

Softbank Corp. is Japan's biggest Internet company. At one time, it boosted the profit margin of its mobile-phone unit from 3.2% to 11.2% through what appeared to some as accounting tricks. What did it do? It wrote down the value of its mobile-phone-unit assets by half. This would normally result in a huge loss. But rather than take a loss, the company wrote up goodwill by the same amount. How did this move increase earnings? The assets were being depreciated over 10 years, but the company amortizes goodwill over 20 years. (Amortization of goodwill was allowed under the accounting standards it followed at that time.) While the new treatment did not break any rules, the company was criticized by investors for not providing sufficient justification or a detailed explanation for the sudden shift in policy.

Source: Andrew Morse and Yukari Iwatani Kane, "Softbank's Accounting Shift Raises Eyebrows," *Wall Street Journal* (August 28, 2007), p. C1.

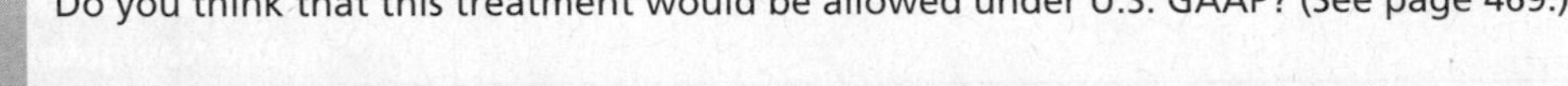

Do you think that this treatment would be allowed under U.S. GAAP? (See page 469.)

Research and Development Costs

Research and development costs are expenditures that may lead to patents, copyrights, new processes, and new products. Many companies spend considerable sums of money on research and development (R&D). For example, in a recent year, IBM spent over $5.1 billion on R&D.

Helpful Hint
Research and development (R&D) costs are not intangible assets. But because they may lead to patents and copyrights, we discuss them in this section.

Research and development costs present accounting problems. For one thing, it is sometimes difficult to assign the costs to specific projects. Also, there are uncertainties in identifying the extent and timing of future benefits. As a result, companies usually record R&D costs **as an expense when incurred**, whether the research and development is successful or not.

To illustrate, assume that Laser Scanner Company spent $3 million on R&D that resulted in two highly successful patents. It spent $20,000 on legal fees for the patents. The company would add the lawyers' fees to the patent account. The R&D costs, however, cannot be included in the cost of the patent. Instead, the company would record the R&D costs as an expense when incurred.

Many disagree with this accounting approach. They argue that expensing R&D costs leads to understated assets and net income. Others, however, argue that capitalizing these costs will lead to highly speculative assets on the balance sheet. Who is right is difficult to determine.

> DO IT!

Classification Concepts

Match the statement with the term most directly associated with it.

Copyrights	Depletion
Intangible assets	Franchises
Research and development costs	

1. ______ The allocation of the cost of a natural resource to expense in a rational and systematic manner.
2. ______ Rights, privileges, and competitive advantages that result from the ownership of long-lived assets that do not possess physical substance.
3. ______ An exclusive right granted by the federal government to reproduce and sell an artistic or published work.
4. ______ A right to sell certain products or services or to use certain trademarks or trade names within a designated geographic area.
5. ______ Costs incurred by a company that often lead to patents or new products. These costs must be expensed as incurred.

Action Plan

✔ Know that the accounting for intangibles often depends on whether the item has a finite or indefinite life.

✔ Recognize the many similarities and differences between the accounting for natural resources, plant assets, and intangible assets.

Solution

1. Depletion
2. Intangible assets
3. Copyrights
4. Franchises
5. Research and development costs

Related exercise material: **BE9-11, BE9-12, E9-11, E9-12, E9-13, and**  **9-5.**

✔ **The Navigator**

Statement Presentation and Analysis

LEARNING OBJECTIVE 7

Indicate how plant assets, natural resources, and intangible assets are reported.

Presentation

Usually, companies combine plant assets and natural resources under "Property, plant, and equipment" in the balance sheet. They show intangibles separately. Companies disclose either in the balance sheet or the notes the balances of the major classes of assets, such as land, buildings, and equipment, and accumulated depreciation by major classes or in total. In addition, they should describe the depreciation and amortization methods that were used, as well as disclose the amount of depreciation and amortization expense for the period.

Illustration 9-23 shows a typical financial statement presentation of property, plant, and equipment and intangibles for The Procter & Gamble Company (P&G) in its 2010 balance sheet. The notes to P&G's financial statements present greater details about the accounting for its long-term tangible and intangible assets.

Illustration 9-23
P&G's presentation of property, plant, and equipment, and intangible assets

The Procter & Gamble Company
Balance Sheet (partial)
(in millions)

	June 30	
	2010	**2009**
Property, plant, and equipment		
Buildings	$ 6,868	$ 6,724
Machinery and equipment	29,294	29,042
Land	850	885
	37,012	36,651
Accumulated depreciation	(17,768)	(17,189)
Net property, plant, and equipment	19,244	19,462
Goodwill and other intangible assets		
Goodwill	54,012	56,512
Trademarks and other intangible assets, net	31,636	32,606
Net goodwill and other intangible assets	$85,648	$89,118

Illustration 9-24 shows another comprehensive presentation of property, plant, and equipment from the balance sheet of Owens-Illinois, Inc. The notes to the financial statements of Owens-Illinois identify the major classes of property, plant, and equipment. They also indicate that depreciation and amortization are by the straight-line method, and depletion is by the units-of-activity method.

Illustration 9-24
Owens-Illinois' presentation of property, plant, and equipment, and intangible assets

Owens-Illinois, Inc.
Balance Sheet (partial)
(in millions)

Property, plant, and equipment			
Timberlands, at cost, less accumulated depletion		$ 95.4	
Buildings and equipment, at cost	$2,207.1		
Less: Accumulated depreciation	1,229.0	978.1	
Total property, plant, and equipment			$1,073.5
Intangibles			
Patents			410.0
Total			$1,483.5

Analysis

Using ratios, we can analyze how efficiently a company uses its assets to generate sales. The **asset turnover ratio** analyzes the productivity of a company's assets. It tells us how many dollars of sales a company generates for each dollar invested in assets. This ratio is computed by dividing net sales by average total assets for the period. The formula in Illustration 9-25 shows the computation of the asset turnover ratio for The Procter & Gamble Company. P&G's net sales for 2010 were $78,938 million. Its total ending assets were $128,172 million, and beginning assets were $134,833 million.

Illustration 9-25
Asset turnover formula and computation

Net Sales	÷	Average Total Assets	=	Asset Turnover Ratio
$78,938	÷	$\frac{\$128,172 + \$134,833}{2}$	=	**.60 times**

Thus, each dollar invested in assets produced $0.60 in sales for P&G. If a company is using its assets efficiently, each dollar of assets will create a high amount of sales. This ratio varies greatly among different industries—from those that are asset-intensive (utilities) to those that are not (services).

> Comprehensive DO IT! 1

DuPage Company purchases a factory machine at a cost of $18,000 on January 1, 2014. DuPage expects the machine to have a salvage value of $2,000 at the end of its 4-year useful life.

During its useful life, the machine is expected to be used 160,000 hours. Actual annual hourly use was 2014, 40,000; 2015, 60,000; 2016, 35,000; and 2017, 25,000.

Instructions

Prepare depreciation schedules for the following methods: (a) straight-line, (b) units-of-activity, and (c) declining-balance using double the straight-line rate.

Solution to Comprehensive DO IT! 1

Action Plan

- ✔ Under the straight-line method, apply the depreciation rate to depreciable cost.
- ✔ Under the units-of-activity method, compute the depreciable cost per unit by dividing depreciable cost by total units of activity.
- ✔ Under the declining-balance method, apply the depreciation rate to **book value** at the beginning of the year.

(a)

Straight-Line Method

	Computation					End of Year	
Year	Depreciable Cost*	×	Depreciation Rate	=	Annual Depreciation Expense	Accumulated Depreciation	Book Value
2014	$16,000		25%		$4,000	$ 4,000	$14,000**
2015	16,000		25%		4,000	8,000	10,000
2016	16,000		25%		4,000	12,000	6,000
2017	16,000		25%		4,000	16,000	2,000

*$18,000 − $2,000.
**$18,000 − $4,000.

(b)

Units-of-Activity Method

	Computation					End of Year	
Year	Units of Activity	×	Depreciable Cost/Unit	=	Annual Depreciation Expense	Accumulated Depreciation	Book Value
2014	40,000		$0.10*		$4,000	$ 4,000	$14,000
2015	60,000		0.10		6,000	10,000	8,000
2016	35,000		0.10		3,500	13,500	4,500
2017	25,000		0.10		2,500	16,000	2,000

*($18,000 − $2,000) ÷ 160,000.

(c)

Declining-Balance Method

	Computation					End of Year	
Year	Book Value Beginning of Year	×	Depreciation Rate*	=	Annual Depreciation Expense	Accumulated Depreciation	Book Value
2014	$18,000		50%		$9,000	$ 9,000	$9,000
2015	9,000		50%		4,500	13,500	4,500
2016	4,500		50%		2,250	15,750	2,250
2017	2,250		50%		250**	16,000	2,000

*¼ × 2.

**Adjusted to $250 because ending book value should not be less than expected salvage value.

 The Navigator

Comprehensive DO IT! 2

On January 1, 2014, Skyline Limousine Co. purchased a limo at an acquisition cost of $28,000. The vehicle has been depreciated by the straight-line method using a 4-year service life and a $4,000 salvage value. The company's fiscal year ends on December 31.

Instructions

Prepare the journal entry or entries to record the disposal of the limousine assuming that it was:

(a) Retired and scrapped with no salvage value on January 1, 2018.

(b) Sold for $5,000 on July 1, 2017.

Solution to Comprehensive DO IT! 2

Action Plan

✔ At the time of disposal, determine the book value of the asset.

✔ Recognize any gain or loss from disposal of the asset.

✔ Remove the book value of the asset from the records by debiting Accumulated Depreciation for the total depreciation to date of disposal and crediting the asset account for the cost of the asset.

		Debit	Credit
(a) 1/1/18	Accumulated Depreciation—Equipment	24,000	
	Loss on Disposal of Plant Assets	4,000	
	Equipment		28,000
	(To record retirement of limousine)		
(b) 7/1/17	Depreciation Expense	3,000	
	Accumulated Depreciation—Equipment		3,000
	(To record depreciation to date of disposal)		
	Cash	5,000	
	Accumulated Depreciation—Equipment	21,000	
	Loss on Disposal of Plant Assets	2,000	
	Equipment		28,000
	(To record sale of limousine)		

 The Navigator

SUMMARY OF LEARNING OBJECTIVES

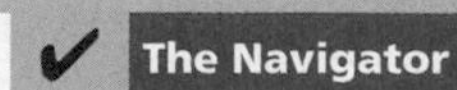

1 **Describe how the cost principle applies to plant assets.** The cost of plant assets includes all expenditures necessary to acquire the asset and make it ready for its intended use. Once cost is established, a company uses that amount as the basis of accounting for the plant asset over its useful life.

2 **Explain the concept of depreciation and how to compute it.** Depreciation is the allocation of the cost of a plant asset to expense over its useful (service) life in a rational and systematic manner. Depreciation is not a process of valuation, nor is it a process that results in an accumulation of cash.

Three depreciation methods are:

Method	Effect on Annual Depreciation	Formula
Straight-line	Constant amount	Depreciable cost ÷ Useful life (in years)
Units-of-activity	Varying amount	Depreciable cost per unit × Units of activity during the year
Declining-balance	Decreasing amount	Book value at beginning of year × Declining-balance rate

Companies make revisions of periodic depreciation in present and future periods, not retroactively. They determine the new annual depreciation by dividing the depreciable cost at the time of the revision by the remaining useful life.

3 **Distinguish between revenue and capital expenditures, and explain the entries for each.** Companies incur revenue expenditures to maintain the operating efficiency and productive life of an asset. They debit these expenditures to Maintenance and Repairs Expense as incurred. Capital expenditures increase the operating efficiency, productive capacity, or expected useful life of the asset. Companies generally debit these expenditures to the plant asset affected.

4 **Explain how to account for the disposal of a plant asset.** The accounting for disposal of a plant asset through retirement or sale is as follows.

(a) Eliminate the book value of the plant asset at the date of disposal.
(b) Record cash proceeds, if any.
(c) Account for the difference between the book value and the cash proceeds as a gain or loss on disposal.

5 **Compute periodic depletion of natural resources.** Companies compute depletion cost per unit by dividing the total cost of the natural resource minus salvage value by the number of units estimated to be in the resource. They then multiply the depletion cost per unit by the number of units extracted and sold.

6 **Explain the basic issues related to accounting for intangible assets.** The process of allocating the cost of an intangible asset is referred to as amortization. The cost of intangible assets with indefinite lives are not amortized. Companies normally use the straight-line method for amortizing intangible assets.

7 **Indicate how plant assets, natural resources, and intangible assets are reported.** Companies usually combine plant assets and natural resources under property, plant, and equipment; they show intangibles separately under intangible assets. Either within the balance sheet or in the notes, companies should disclose the balances of the major classes of assets, such as land, buildings, and equipment, and accumulated depreciation by major classes or in total. They also should describe the depreciation and amortization methods used, and should disclose the amount of depreciation and amortization expense for the period. The asset turnover ratio measures the productivity of a company's assets in generating sales.

GLOSSARY

Accelerated-depreciation method Depreciation method that produces higher depreciation expense in the early years than in the later years. (p. 432).

Additions and improvements Costs incurred to increase the operating efficiency, productive capacity, or useful life of a plant asset. (p. 435).

Amortization The allocation of the cost of an intangible asset to expense over its useful life in a systematic and rational manner. (p. 441).

Asset turnover ratio A measure of how efficiently a company uses its assets to generate sales; calculated as net sales divided by average total assets. (p. 445).

Capital expenditures Expenditures that increase the company's investment in productive facilities. (p. 435).

Copyrights Exclusive grant from the federal government that allows the owner to reproduce and sell an artistic or published work. (p. 442).

Declining-balance method Depreciation method that applies a constant rate to the declining book value of the asset and produces a decreasing annual depreciation expense over the useful life of the asset. (p. 431).

Depletion The allocation of the cost of a natural resource to expense in a rational and systematic manner over the resource's useful life. (p. 439).

Depreciation The process of allocating to expense the cost of a plant asset over its useful (service) life in a rational and systematic manner. (p. 427).

Depreciable cost The cost of a plant asset less its salvage value. (p. 429).

Franchise (license) A contractual arrangement under which the franchisor grants the franchisee the right to sell certain products, provide specific services, or use certain trademarks or trade names, usually within a designated geographic area. (p. 442).

Going-concern assumption States that the company will continue in operation for the foreseeable future. (p. 428).

Goodwill The value of all favorable attributes that relate to a company that is not attributable to any other specific asset. (p. 443).

Intangible assets Rights, privileges, and competitive advantages that result from the ownership of long-lived assets that do not possess physical substance. (p. 441).

Licenses Operating rights to use public property, granted to a business by a governmental agency. (p. 442).

Materiality concept If an item would not make a difference in decision-making, a company does not have to follow GAAP in reporting it. (p. 435).

Natural resources Assets that consist of standing timber and underground deposits of oil, gas, or minerals. (p. 439).

Ordinary repairs Expenditures to maintain the operating efficiency and productive life of the plant asset. (p. 435).

Patent An exclusive right issued by the U.S. Patent Office that enables the recipient to manufacture, sell, or otherwise control an invention for a period of 20 years from the date of the grant. (p. 441).

Plant assets Tangible resources that are used in the operations of the business and are not intended for sale to customers. (p. 424).

Research and development (R&D) costs Expenditures that may lead to patents, copyrights, new processes, or new products. (p. 443).

Revenue expenditures Expenditures that are immediately charged against revenues as an expense. (p. 435).

Salvage value An estimate of an asset's value at the end of its useful life. (p. 429).

Straight-line method Depreciation method in which periodic depreciation is the same for each year of the asset's useful life. (p. 429).

Trademark (trade name) A word, phrase, jingle, or symbol that identifies a particular enterprise or product. (p. 442).

Units-of-activity method Depreciation method in which useful life is expressed in terms of the total units of production or use expected from an asset. (p. 430).

Useful life An estimate of the expected productive life, also called service life, of an asset. (p. 429).

APPENDIX 9A EXCHANGE OF PLANT ASSETS

LEARNING OBJECTIVE 8

Explain how to account for the exchange of plant assets.

Ordinarily, companies record a gain or loss on the exchange of plant assets. The rationale for recognizing a gain or loss is that most exchanges have **commercial substance**. An exchange has commercial substance if the future cash flows change as a result of the exchange.

To illustrate, Ramos Co. exchanges some of its equipment for land held by Brodhead Inc. It is likely that the timing and amount of the cash flows arising from the land will differ significantly from the cash flows arising from the equipment. As a result, both Ramos and Brodhead are in different economic positions. Therefore, **the exchange has commercial substance**, and the companies recognize a gain or loss in the exchange. Because most exchanges have commercial substance (even when similar assets are exchanged), we illustrate only this type of situation, for both a loss and a gain.

Loss Treatment

To illustrate an exchange that results in a loss, assume that Roland Company exchanged a set of used trucks plus cash for a new semi-truck. The used trucks have a combined book value of $42,000 (cost $64,000 less $22,000 accumulated depreciation). Roland's purchasing agent, experienced in the second-hand market, indicates that the used trucks have a fair value of $26,000. In addition to the trucks, Roland must pay $17,000 for the semi-truck. Roland computes the cost of the semi-truck as follows.

Illustration 9A-1
Cost of semi-truck

Fair value of used trucks	$26,000
Cash paid	17,000
Cost of semi-truck	$43,000

Roland incurs a loss on disposal of plant assets of $16,000 on this exchange. The reason is that the book value of the used trucks is greater than the fair value of these trucks. The computation is as follows.

Illustration 9A-2
Computation of loss on disposal

Book value of used trucks ($64,000 − $22,000)	$ 42,000
Fair value of used trucks	26,000
Loss on disposal of plant assets	**$16,000**

In recording an exchange at a loss, three steps are required: (1) eliminate the book value of the asset given up, (2) record the cost of the asset acquired, and (3) recognize the loss on disposal of plant assets. Roland Company thus records the exchange on the loss as follows.

A	= L +	SE		Debit	Credit
+43,000			Equipment (new)	43,000	
+22,000			Accumulated Depreciation—Equipment	22,000	
		−16,000 Exp	Loss on Disposal of Plant Assets	16,000	
−64,000			Equipment (old)		64,000
−17,000			Cash		17,000
			(To record exchange of used trucks for semi-truck)		

Cash Flows
−17,000

Gain Treatment

To illustrate a gain situation, assume that Mark Express Delivery decides to exchange its old delivery equipment plus cash of $3,000 for new delivery equipment. The book value of the old delivery equipment is $12,000 (cost $40,000 less accumulated depreciation $28,000). The fair value of the old delivery equipment is $19,000.

The cost of the new asset is the fair value of the old asset exchanged plus any cash paid (or other consideration given up). The cost of the new delivery equipment is $22,000, computed as follows.

Illustration 9A-3
Cost of new delivery equipment

Fair value of old delivery equipment	$ 19,000
Cash paid	3,000
Cost of new delivery equipment	**$22,000**

A gain results when the fair value of the old delivery equipment is greater than its book value. For Mark Express, there is a gain of $7,000 on disposal of plant assets, computed as follows.

Illustration 9A-4
Computation of gain on disposal

Fair value of old delivery equipment	$19,000
Book value of old delivery equipment ($40,000 − $28,000)	12,000
Gain on disposal of plant assets	**$ 7,000**

Mark Express Delivery records the exchange as follows.

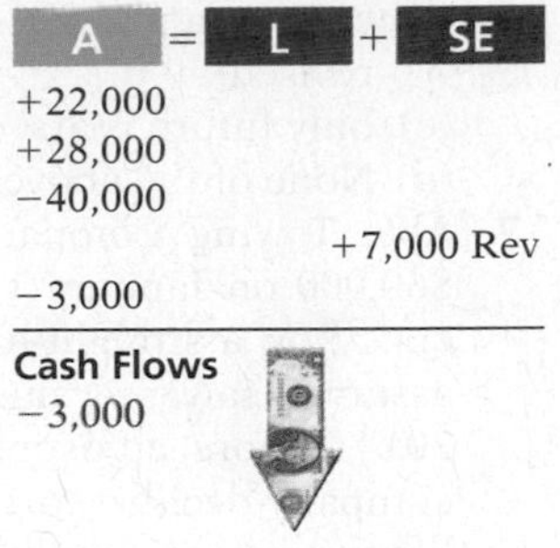

Account	Debit	Credit
Equipment (new)	22,000	
Accumulated Depreciation—Equipment (old)	28,000	
Equipment (old)		40,000
Gain on Disposal of Plant Assets		7,000
Cash		3,000
(To record exchange of old delivery equipment for new delivery equipment)		

In recording an exchange at a gain, the following three steps are involved: (1) eliminate the book value of the asset given up, (2) record the cost of the asset acquired, and (3) recognize the gain on disposal of plant assets. Accounting for exchanges of plant assets becomes more complex if the transaction does not have commercial substance. This issue is discussed in more advanced accounting classes.

SUMMARY OF LEARNING OBJECTIVE FOR APPENDIX 9A

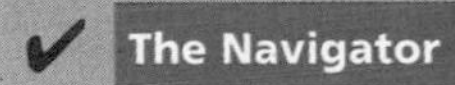

8 Explain how to account for the exchange of plant assets. Ordinarily, companies record a gain or loss on the exchange of plant assets. The rationale for recognizing a gain or loss is that most exchanges have commercial substance. An exchange has commercial substance if the future cash flows change as a result of the exchange.

Self-Test, Brief Exercises, Exercises, Problem Set A, and many more components are available for practice in WileyPLUS.

**Note:* All asterisked Questions, Exercises, and Problems relate to material in the appendix to the chapter.

SELF-TEST QUESTIONS

Answers are on page 469.

(LO 1) **1.** Erin Danielle Company purchased equipment and incurred the following costs.

Cash price	$24,000
Sales taxes	1,200
Insurance during transit	200
Installation and testing	400
Total costs	$25,800

What amount should be recorded as the cost of the equipment?

(a) $24,000. (c) $25,400.
(b) $25,200. (d) $25,800.

(LO 2) **2.** Depreciation is a process of:

(a) valuation. (c) cash accumulation.
(b) cost allocation. (d) appraisal.

(LO 2) **3.** Micah Bartlett Company purchased equipment on January 1, 2013, at a total invoice cost of $400,000. The equipment has an estimated salvage value of $10,000 and an estimated useful life of 5 years. The amount of accumulated depreciation at December 31, 2014, if the straight-line method of depreciation is used, is:

(a) $80,000. (c) $78,000.
(b) $160,000. (d) $156,000.

4. Ann Torbert purchased a truck for $11,000 on January 1, 2013. The truck will have an estimated salvage value of $1,000 at the end of 5 years. Using the units-of-activity method, the balance in accumulated depreciation at December 31, 2014, can be computed by the following formula: (LO 2)

(a) ($11,000 ÷ Total estimated activity) × Units of activity for 2014.
(b) ($10,000 ÷ Total estimated activity) × Units of activity for 2014.
(c) ($11,000 ÷ Total estimated activity) × Units of activity for 2013 and 2014.
(d) ($10,000 ÷ Total estimated activity) × Units of activity for 2013 and 2014.

5. Jefferson Company purchased a piece of equipment on January 1, 2014. The equipment cost $60,000 and has an estimated life of 8 years and a salvage value of $8,000. What was the depreciation expense for the asset for 2015 under the double-declining-balance method? (LO 2)

(a) $6,500. (c) $15,000.
(b) $11,250. (d) $6,562.

6. When there is a change in estimated depreciation: (LO 2)

(a) previous depreciation should be corrected.

(b) current and future years' depreciation should be revised.
(c) only future years' depreciation should be revised.
(d) None of the above.

(LO 2) **7.** Able Towing Company purchased a tow truck for $60,000 on January 1, 2012. It was originally depreciated on a straight-line basis over 10 years with an assumed salvage value of $12,000. On December 31, 2014, before adjusting entries had been made, the company decided to change the remaining estimated life to 4 years (including 2014) and the salvage value to $2,000. What was the depreciation expense for 2014?
(a) $6,000. (c) $15,000.
(b) $4,800. (d) $12,100.

(LO 3) **8.** Additions to plant assets are:
(a) revenue expenditures.
(b) debited to the Maintenance and Repairs Expense account.
(c) debited to the Purchases account.
(d) capital expenditures.

(LO 4) **9.** Bennie Razor Company has decided to sell one of its old manufacturing machines on June 30, 2014. The machine was purchased for $80,000 on January 1, 2010, and was depreciated on a straight-line basis for 10 years assuming no salvage value. If the machine was sold for $26,000, what was the amount of the gain or loss recorded at the time of the sale?
(a) $18,000. (c) $22,000.
(b) $54,000. (d) $46,000.

(LO 5) **10.** Maggie Sharrer Company expects to extract 20 million tons of coal from a mine that cost $12 million. If no salvage value is expected and 2 million tons are mined and sold in the first year, the entry to record depletion will include a:
(a) debit to Accumulated Depletion of $2,000,000.
(b) credit to Depletion Expense of $1,200,000.
(c) debit to Depletion Expense of $1,200,000.
(d) credit to Accumulated Depletion of $2,000,000.

(LO 6) **11.** Which of the following statements is *false*?
(a) If an intangible asset has a finite life, it should be amortized.
(b) The amortization period of an intangible asset can exceed 20 years.
(c) Goodwill is recorded only when a business is purchased.
(d) Research and development costs are expensed when incurred, except when the research and development expenditures result in a successful patent.

12. Martha Beyerlein Company incurred $150,000 of research and development costs in its laboratory to develop a patent granted on January 2, 2014. On July 31, 2014, Beyerlein paid $35,000 for legal fees in a successful defense of the patent. The total amount debited to Patents through July 31, 2014, should be: (LO 6)
(a) $150,000. (c) $185,000.
(b) $35,000. (d) $170,000.

13. Indicate which of the following statements is true. (LO 7)
(a) Since intangible assets lack physical substance, they need be disclosed only in the notes to the financial statements.
(b) Goodwill should be reported as a contra-account in the stockholders' equity section.
(c) Totals of major classes of assets can be shown in the balance sheet, with asset details disclosed in the notes to the financial statements.
(d) Intangible assets are typically combined with plant assets and natural resources and shown in the property, plant, and equipment section.

14. Lake Coffee Company reported net sales of $180,000, net income of $54,000, beginning total assets of $200,000, and ending total assets of $300,000. What was the company's asset turnover ratio? (LO 7)
(a) 0.90 (c) 0.72
(b) 0.20 (d) 1.39

***15.** Schopenhauer Company exchanged an old machine, with a book value of $39,000 and a fair value of $35,000, and paid $10,000 cash for a similar new machine. The transaction has commercial substance. At what amount should the machine acquired in the exchange be recorded on Schopenhauer's books? (LO 8)
(a) $45,000. (c) $49,000.
(b) $46,000. (d) $50,000.

***16.** In exchanges of assets in which the exchange has commercial substance: (LO 8)
(a) neither gains nor losses are recognized immediately.
(b) gains, but not losses, are recognized immediately.
(c) losses, but not gains, are recognized immediately.
(d) both gains and losses are recognized immediately.

Go to the book's companion website, www.wiley.com/college/weygandt, for additional Self-Test Questions.

✔ **The Navigator**

QUESTIONS

1. Rick Baden is uncertain about the applicability of the cost principle to plant assets. Explain the principle to Rick.
2. What are some examples of land improvements?
3. Lexa Company acquires the land and building owned by Malta Company. What types of costs may be incurred to make the asset ready for its intended use if Lexa Company wants to use (a) only the land, and (b) both the land and the building?
4. In a recent newspaper release, the president of Wanzo Company asserted that something has to be done about depreciation. The president said, "Depreciation